FAMILY PROBLEM SOLVING

FAMILY
PROBLEM
SOLVING

A Symposium on Theoretical, Methodological, and Substantive Concerns

---

EDITORS:

Joan Aldous, *University of Minnesota*
Thomas Condon, *University of Minnesota*
Reuben Hill, *University of Minnesota*
Murray Straus, *University of New Hampshire*
Irving Tallman, *University of Minnesota*

The Dryden Press Inc.
Hinsdale, Illinois

"Some Principles for the Design of Clarifying Educational Environments" by O. K. Moore and A. R. Anderson in David Goslin, ed. *Handbook of Socialization Theory and Research*, pages 751–610, © by Rand-McNally, Skokie, Illinois. Reprinted by permission of the publisher.

Preface

This book is about a beginning and a process. It represents the initial efforts of a group of social scientists to isolate and define central issues pertaining to research on the family as a problem solving group. Our purpose in this volume is two-fold: (1) to present to the reader the carefully measured and precisely formulated thinking of several distinguished scholars pertaining to the general question of family problem solving behavior, and (2) to involve the reader in the process of problem solving itself, that is, in the not always logical, not always precise attempts to grapple with the many-sided aspects of a problem. In short we hope not only to present an end product but also to provide some insight into the processes by which these end products are reached. Our goal is to combine the benefits of a crisp, logical, well-formulated position with the richness of the multidimensional and multifaceted considerations that go into formulating such positions.

We have adapted this somewhat self-conscious stance because, like many other students of human behavior, we are all too aware that our usual published formulations represent a kind of reconstructed logic in which we select from a conglomerate of myriad meanings those which we consider most salient. We do not say this apologetically nor do we feel that this process does not make important contributions; rather we believe that, at our present stage of scientific development, there are many meanings and many approaches and only by an examination of the process by which conclusions are reached can we approximate an understanding of the issues involved. In this sense we invite the reader neither to accept nor reject what follows but rather to join us in the process of thinking through the critical issues. The issues include such questions as: Do families have problems that are researchable? Are families small groups like other small groups? Can experimental research be undertaken using families? Can any aspects of social theory be tested in natural groups such as the family? Still more basically, the question is asked as to how the blinders worn by the researcher modify, distort, or determine his findings. Finally, perhaps the most critical question is what, if anything, can we learn from each other given the state of imprecision in our methods of communication? Are we able to grow and build on each other's work, or are we so bogged down in labyrinths of vague language and unrelated concepts that we are unable to make use of cumulative effects?

We said this volume is a beginning and as such the reader cannot hope to find the closure we all wish for. No neatly packaged theoretical statement will be used to summarize what appears in the following pages; in fact, no summary is warranted. Yet, those of us who sat in on the discussions which are to be reported feel strongly that we underwent not only a personally rewarding and enriching experience, but that our attempts to grapple with some of the difficult issues raised have had a profound effect upon our thinking and the research we will conduct. It is our hope that in reporting the content of those discussions, we can indicate some of the pleasure of discovery and understanding that we experienced.

What follows then is a report of a symposium held over three days, January 24, 25, and 26, 1969, on the campus of the University of California in Riverside. We have organized this report in a way that we think will best recapitulate for the reader the flavor of our experiences over those three days. We shall, therefore, present the formal papers of the participants in the order in which they were given and, for reasons of space, a greatly edited version of the discussions which followed as well as commentary on those discussions.

The participants in the symposium were invited not only because of eminence as scholars but also because they represented a variety of theoretical and methodological perspectives. In terms of formal disciplines, the group included sociologists, psychologists, and an anthropologist, but perhaps more important, the perspectives ranged from those advocating the development and testing of formal theory in the classic scientific mode to a dependence on the perceptiveness of the observer in understanding the multifaceted meanings of events. But even this global description is too facile. Our participants were less members of "schools" than they were serious, sometimes troubled and always thoughtful, students of human behavior. Each out of his own experience and training illuminated some perspectives and obscured others.

The range of perspectives with which we would have to grapple became clear in the first day. Karl Weick's imaginative and penetrating paper raised critical questions about the applicability of general theories of problem solving to family behavior. Implicit in Weick's paper and the discussion which followed is the perpetually annoying question of how much our own orientations and perspectives allow us to reify concepts by modifying the perceptions of the events we observe. Weick suggests a number of ways in which the family may be a unique group. He also highlights the difficulties resulting from investigators' perspectives being channeled along predetermined lines. His paper seems to call for special theories and special methods.

Zelditch, on the other hand provides a rather clear paradigm: Given a theory of human behavior which stipulates certain relationships between variables, the only effective way of testing such theory is by means of experimental research in *ad hoc* small groups. The knowledge thus gained can be applied in incremental fashion to natural groups such as the family. As we are able to deal with more complicated theories in experimental settings we will be better able to account adequately for complicated structures such as the family.

It would appear, at first glance, as if the two papers represented irreconcilable positions. Yet throughout the discussion and particularly through the comments of Robert Leik, Weick's ideas were fitted into an experimental mold.

The second day brought a somewhat altered and more specific focus on the processes by which we learn and go about the business of problem solving. O. K. Moore's presentation provided an unusual melding of theoretical sophistication with applied research. The dialogue between Moore and Hamblin was a debate between kindred souls. Theirs is not a dispassionate objectivity but rather a commitment to use research and service in combination. They make the rather convincing argument that the two not only can occur simultaneously but that each aspect tends to benefit the other. Although the discussion involves such issues as the relative importance of intrinsic as opposed to extrinsic motivation, it seemed that the critical issue was "payoff." That is, could their techniques effect sizable benefits in children's learning? This discussion was so vital and in some ways so frustratingly incomplete that we invited Professor Hamblin to present his views in a formal paper for publication in this volume. (See Part II)

The Gumperz presentation and Inkeles response makes it clear that the difficulties in language analysis extend (as Gumperz points out) to communications between scholars who ostensibly share the same universe of discourse. The problem extends beyond the ability to communicate research findings or describe methodologies—it is imbedded in different notions about the nature of research and knowledge. Since the purposes differ, methods that are appropriate for one set of purposes may not be appropriate for another set. It would appear that where Inkeles is seeking some systematic method of analysis, Gumperz is more concerned with understanding the particular coding used by given individuals. Whereas Inkeles, in the classic mode of science, is willing to impose *his* model on the situation and observe how closely the data fit, Gumperz appears intent on avoiding such an imposition and attempts to determine the meanings of events to the actors being observed.

Helen Bee's contribution is significant in two principal ways. First, it provided the participants with a clear and precisely designed research product with available empirical findings. And second, it dealt with many of the variables that had been discussed in previous sessions. Thus language, problem solving, affection, structure, and communication all become operationalized and, in the process, specified, so that in the tearing away of vague notions there is also a loss of specific meanings that were dear to some of the discussants. Bee's paper reminds us that we are concerned with empirical questions and the conclusions are limited to what we are able to test. Her results are clear enough—mothers who provide direction but allow for a degree of self-generating activity on the part of the child have better problem solving children (within the limits of how problem solving is defined in her study). But as she herself points out, the causal sequences of this relationship are not determinable from her research. The research is significant because it adds additional knowledge supporting previous research on the effects of independence on problem solving and competence (Inkeles). It is also significant because it raises important questions as to how language is used in socializing children to problem solving behavior, and suggests that perhaps language is not always critical. Such research, therefore, contributes increments, albeit at times small, to knowledge and theory—in the long run these bits and pieces of verifiable and reliable information supporting established propositions may prove the most profitable if least glamorous route to the development of powerful social theory.

The emphasis in this introductory section on the self-conscious look at ourselves as researchers comes primarily from two sources. The first is the initial paper by Karl Weick. Professor Weick's paper in a very real sense keynoted this symposium by raising the question of the effects of the "metaphor" used by investigators, by suggesting not only that family problems may not be amenable to research, but even more basically, that family problem solving is not or need not be a central theoretical issue for understanding family behavior.

The second sensitizing influence came from the work of Tom Condon who edited the tapes and has written the narrative which summarizes, describes, and analyzes the discussions. In addition he has contributed commentaries which are intended as a kind of third level reading. Condon sees the first level, composed of the prepared papers, as highly structured and formal. The contrasting second level, the edited transcript of the symposium discussion is casual, contradictory, and contentious. Most of the editorial decisions, whereby he cut the transcript to approximately one sixth of its original size, were made with the interplay of these two levels in mind. Consequently, the third level is an attempt to highlight some of the themes and directions which appeared during the editing, and from the dialetic between discussion and formal presentations indicating possible productive syntheses.

Condon emphasizes that if we are adequately to understand the product of our research we must first understand ourselves and the processes we use in developing these products. His work forcibly reminds us that the search for truth is often a passionate and driving phenomenon with the process in the social sciences being more apparent than the products. Thus this book contains few "last words," but many beginnings for those concerned with examining problem solving in the family or among highly verbal, intellectually keen social scientists. We would like to think it is a sign of the increasing maturity of the social sciences that we can acknowledge our confusion in the symposium papers and examine ourselves in a somewhat playful fashion handling this confusion in the discussions. In the process detailed in the book the problem solving becomes more clearly defined and its linkage to micro variables and macro issues illuminated. We are pleased to think others beyond the symposium circle can share our many questionings as well as our conviction that problem solving is worth studying.

ACKNOWLEDGMENTS

The editors had fewer problems to solve in organizing the Family Problem Solving Symposium because of Janice Porter, administrative assistant for the Department of Sociology at the University of California (Riverside). Graduate students Joe Floyd, Kathy Shaw, and Barbara Ambrose who set up and ran the recording equipment ensured that no word would be lost from the record. Transcribing and typing the finished manuscript was the responsibility of Schelly Braden, Jane Erickson, Margaret Johnson, and Janice Linden. The editors hope that seeing their name in print, a cold medium, will indicate something of the gratitude, a warm medium we feel for our Symposium aides. The index was prepared by Vera Cerny of the Minnesota Family Study Center and the Inventory of Published Research in Marriage and Family Behavior. The editors wish to express their appreciation to Mrs. Cerny for her creative and careful preparation.

Finally, the Symposium was made possible by the National Institute of Mental Health Grant, 5 RO1 MH 15521.

Minneapolis   The Editors
May 1971

SYMPOSIUM PARTICIPANTS

Joan Aldous, Family Study Center, University of Minnesota

Helen Bee, Department of Psychology, University of Washington

Thomas F. Condon, Department of Sociology, University of Minnesota

John Gumperz, Department of Anthropology, University of California

Robert Hamblin, Department of Sociology, Washington University

Reuben Hill, Family Study Center, University of Minnesota

Alex Inkeles, College of Education, Stanford University

Robert Leik, Department of Sociology, University of Washington

Gary J. Miller, Department of Sociology, Indiana University

Omar K. Moore, Department of Sociology, University of Pittsburgh

Paul J. Reynolds, Department of Sociology, University of Minnesota

Murray A. Straus, Department of Sociology, University of New Hampshire

Irving Tallman, Department of Sociology, University of Minnesota

Karl E. Weick, Jr., Department of Psychology, University of Minnesota

Morris Zelditch, Jr., Department of Sociology, Stanford University

Contents

Part II   APPLICATIONS AND IMPLICATIONS

Introduction

APPENDIXES

Part One

THE SYMPOSIUM

This section preserves the written record of the Symposium on Family Problem Solving. Herein are the formal papers which provided the basis for specific prepared critiques followed by general discussion. The latter have been sharpened in their focus through judicious excising of redundancies, irrelevancies, and verbal elaborations. There is also a final comment on each paper following its critique and discussion. Thus, if one thinks of the formal papers as intellectual problems presented to the group, it is clear that a great deal of effort went into their resolution. The relation the papers held to existing knowledge as well as their implications for new perspectives were both of interest to Symposium participants.

Because of the variety of disciplines and interests represented in the papers, the reader has a range of subjects from which to choose. It is our belief, however, that the discussions and commentaries are sufficiently interrelated that he will be enticed into exploring the printed Symposium in its entirety.

Group Processes, Family Processes, and Problem Solving*

KARL E. WEICK

T wo quotations are relevant to what this paper attempts to do. One is George Herbert Mead's (1956) characterization of the scientific method: "The scientific method is, after all, only the evolutionary process grown self-conscious" (p. 23). The second is McGrath and Altman's (1966) portrait of the current state of group research: "The modern small group researcher has set his intellectual sights quite low. He often selects a limited range of variables, methods, and instruments, and then runs them into the ground. He is not, emotionally, on the trail of something big. . . . Associated with this lack of zeal (though not lack of vigor) is an absence of intellectual controversy. . . . [This absence] seems to arise because research in the small group field is so segmented—in the form of idiosyncratic variables, tasks, and measures peculiar to individual investigators—that no one has a common base from which to argue" (p. 80). The last quotation makes one wary over what he can say about group processes to those who study family problem solving. But the first quotation is more optimistic since it suggests a way in which one might be able to contribute more to this discussion. The McGrath and Altman quotation makes it clear that the number of "conceptual mutations" in group research available for selection is small, homogeneous, and of questionable significance. This suggests that one means to contribute information about group process would be to increase the number of variations available from which people interested in groups might select. These variations will obviously have to be speculative since the data relevant to many of them have yet to be collected. However,

---

* Preparation of this paper was supported in part by the National Science Foundation through Grant GS-1927. The author is indebted to Robert Leik, Joseph McGrath, O. K. Moore, and Harold B. Pepinsky for their helpful comments on an earlier draft of this chapter.

some of the points I will raise do seem to have a certain plausability, and if some of them were pursued they might enrich both group theory and our understanding of family problem solving. However, one must also be mindful of the fact that in any thriving evolutionary sequence the majority of mutations go unselected and die a quiet death. I fully accept that as the possible fate of the majority of what I will say. The point is, if group research is to become more robust then some new things have to be tried.

NEGLECTED PROPERTIES OF THE FAMILY PROBLEM SOLVING GROUP

My job would be made much easier if I could glibly assert that families are just like any other group that solves problems, and then simply strike the work "college sophomore" from many group process studies and insert the word "family member." Fortunately I can't do that. I say fortunately because in many ways family problem solving is unlike most other kinds of problem solving that have been studied so far. This is a decided benefit because many of the variables which surface when one thinks about families turn out to be variables that seem important for understanding groups in general.

To illustrate this point I will discuss 11 properties of family problem solving which suggest that families fall on different portions of dimensions relevant to problem solving than do nonfamily groups. Each of the properties to be discussed should be treated as a dimension along which various kinds of groups may sort themselves. And it should be said for the sake of complete-ness, that any family potentially could assume any one of the various points along the dimension. However, each point to be raised implies that families typically reside in a specific portion of each dimension, that the portion in which they reside is not often found to be characteristic of nonfamily groups, and in this latter sense, this list of properties can also be read as suggesting something of the uniqueness of the family as a problem solving group. Thus the list is intended to discuss some properties of all groups that have not been given much attention, and to make the further point that families seem to assume a particular region on dimensions associated with these properties.

Energy Level

It is probably safe to assume that a sizable portion of family problem solving occurs when members have low energy levels. This derives from the point that the family as a unit is together usually either at the beginning of the day (members are concerned with the major task of simply getting their bodies in motion) or at the end of the day when a full schedule of activities and demands on energy has already occurred. If one then asks, how do people solve problems when they are tired versus when they are fresh, the answer has to be we simply don't know. Assume the situation that in the laboratory we manipulated the variable of exhaustion. Subjects report for a group experi-ment and have to climb either 1, 5, or 10 flights of stairs; or subjects participate in a group experiment at 10 a.m., 2 p.m., or 6 p.m. I would argue that whatever happens in the ten flights or the 6 p.m. groups resembles more closely what happens in family problem solving than is true of the one flight or 10 a.m. group.

Intentional Masking of Expert Power

In ad hoc problem solving groups, the five common bases of power, legitimacy, reward, coercive, expert, and referent, (French and Raven, 1959) are all to some extent salient and it is typical for expert power to supersede the other four when the group is task oriented. The discriminations that people make of one another with regard to expertness for the problem at hand, typically correlate positively with attributed and perceived power. Control over the decision drifts toward those who seem to have the expertise to make the decision. However, in families with well-defined role structures and differentiation of these roles in terms of legitimate power, decision making may occur in such a way that it is delegated by those with greater expertness to those with lesser expertness in the interest of validating and reaffirming legitimate power. This would occur, for example, when the mother presents the father with a family problem which, in the father's view, the mother "obviously" knows more about. This may well be true. But in the mother's view, the problem may be one in which she regards expertness to be less important than reaffirmation of legitimacy.

Some dynamics associated with this masking of expertness in the service of legitimacy can now be suggested. One point is that the expert who uses this tactic may encounter hostility from the person to whom it is directed because he "erroneously" uses expertness as the sole criterion for judging who should retain power over a particular issue. If this occurs, it is not the issue that creates a family problem, it is the fact that the members make differing assumptions about the basis of power on which the matter should be resolved and refuse to resolve it. The likelihood of such dilemmas should decline if legitimacy has been clearly established. Such insignificant family events as who drives the car, answers the phone, serves the meal, and so forth, could be handled so that a clear picture of legitimate power results. Legitimacy is then not a question and if it is frequently reaffirmed, then expertness might be the more prominent basis on which family decisions are made.

Rather than view masking of expertness from the viewpoint of the expert who delegates in order to validate legitimacy, the same events could be viewed as efforts to usurp decision making from experts to reaffirm uncertain legitimacy. It is not that the expert delegates to the nonexpert, rather that the nonexpert takes decisions from the expert. In either case, validation and demonstration of legitimacy is responsible for this shift in decision making; the difference is which person (expert versus nonexpert) senses the need to reaffirm legitimacy and takes the initiative to do so.

The point here is that problem solving in families faces the delicate

problem of balancing legitimacy with expertness in problem solving procedures. To the extent that the mother spends more time with children and is
seen as the expert in matters dealing with them, the legitimate power associated with family role structures could be jeopardized if family problems
concern the activities of children, and if members use expertness as their sole
criterion for determining who will influence whom. Reliance on expertness
could create uncertainties around issues of legitimate power, and to the degree
that reaffirming legitimate power is crucial for the stability of a family, some
masking of expertness is crucial. Notice that this analysis begins with the
assumption that time spent with children determines the degree to which an
adult family member is judged to be an expert. As children become older,
and as the adult members spend increasingly equivalent amounts of time with
the children, then it would be expected that both adults would view themselves and each other as equivalent experts and that masking would not occur.
As a consequence, it might be predicted either that legitimacy will be the
more salient power base for family decision making, or that one of the other
three bases will be more salient. This latter possibility is probably more likely
since as children grow older they may raise more questions as to whether
legitimacy is the sole warranted basis for power in the family, and the relevant
bases may shift to some combination of reward, coercive, and referent power.

The implication of this for research on nonfamily groups is that unless
participants in these groups are presented with the legitimacy versus expertness
dilemma, and unless there is some uncertainty as regards legitimacy, then the
resulting problem solving interaction may tell us less about what occurs in
families.

Unequal Access to Primary Data

It is commonplace in laboratory and task-oriented groups for members
to have relatively equal access to information concerning the problem, its
precipitating events, its contingencies, its consequences, and its potential importance. This may be a slight exaggeration, but it is typical in most task
groups for at least two people to have overlapping, shared, partially redundant
information about the problem. However, it is likely that the primary data
concerning many family problems resides in the hands of a single member.
The only way in which other family members can gain access to these data is
by reports of the person with greatest access, and the person with the greatest
access to the information may also be the person with the most investment in
the outcome.

One implication of this can be discussed in terms of Maier's (1963) characterization of the two dimensions of a solution, quality and acceptance.
Quality refers to objective features of the decision and acceptance refers to the
degree to which the group that must execute the decision accepts it. Hoffman
(1965) makes the following comment on this distinction: "The theoretical
usefulness of this distinction lies in the fact that the quality of a decision reflects
the group's ability to produce and utilize information effectively, while accept-

ance reflects the members' feelings about the solution and about the way it was reached. This is a helpful distinction since effective real life decisions require both high quality and high acceptance, else they fail from lack of attention to the facts or from members' unwillingness to carry out the decision" (p. 121). In the case of unequal access to data, the family confronts a unique situation. The member who must implement the decision and is most concerned with acceptance, is also the person who controls the "facts" that supposedly are essential to a high quality solution. The further complication is that the noninformed members may be more concerned with the quality of the solution and the informed member more concerned with acceptability. Given the mixed quality of the salient criteria by which the solution will be judged (some use quality and some use acceptance) and given the fact that the person who is the major resource person for quality is also the person less concerned with this dimension, then it can be seen that the background in which family problem solving unfolds resembles less those laboratory settings where acceptance is not salient. Furthermore, families resemble more closely groups where those members most able to invest the solution with quality because of their detachment, are dependent for their data on the member most involved and concerned with acceptance, and where pressures for acceptance can be directed at the uninformed members through the medium of the *selectively* transmitted data with which they must work.

Noncontingent Behavior

A disconcerting puzzle in day-to-day family life for children and adults alike is how it can be that, despite some of the most unruly actions, members still retain the affection of other members. The family member sometimes confronts the fact that he is loved for no apparent reason. The love is not conditional, it's there regardless of what happens. This noncontingent overlay of affection suggests that the actions of members during problem solving may be less susceptible to shaping via contingent reinforcements in the form of positive sentiments than is the case in other problem settings (see Joslyn and Banta, 1966). Since a rather substantial portion of the group process literature is conceptualized in terms of the flow of reinforcements during interaction and the effects of this flow on the outcome, one can question whether this research has that much to say about family problem solving. A more precise way to state this point is that the more noncontingent affection that is expressed and perceived in a family, the less their problem solving will be under the sole control of reinforcement contingencies or be able to be shaped by manipulation of such contingencies.

Problem Solving as Expressive Behavior

Typically we view problem solving as instrumental activity pointed toward generating solutions to problems. Within families, however, there is the interesting behavior seldom found in other groups which we can label *problem hitchhiking.* This is the phenomenon in which the member states a problem, appears to have completed his statement of the problem only to say "and furthermore," after which an entirely different problem—often somewhat more remote in time—is enunciated. This can cause any problem solving discussion to amplify in intensity and in number of issues raised. This same cascading, even the direct usage of the phrase "and furthermore" is relatively rare in nonfamily groups. Why? One possibility is that problems are singled out by family members, not so much because they need to be solved or even can be solved, but rather, because they are a means to express strong sentiments to other members in a manner which may have more impact than will direct verbal expression of the sentiment. One need only think of the rather common-place situation in which one member says to another in a fit of anger, "I hate you," a comment which the other often shrugs off as he says to himself "not really." If the anger persists, it is entirely possible that if the enraged member can single out problems which the *target* person apparently causes, then expression of anger will be more successful, and a feeling of justice will finally prevail. The point is that the problem statements are incidental. Notice, this implies that if the target person *does* treat the expressive outburst at the manifest level as an actual set of problems to be taken seriously and solved (he treats the problem as an instrumental issue), then the anger of the enraged person should remain the same or intensify. The statement of problems has not deprecated the recipient. Instead he emerges as a rather exemplary person whose biggest shortcoming is that he wants to get on with solving the problems that have been mentioned.

Voluntary Membership Muddle

It is conventional practice in the group process literature (Thibaut and Kelley, 1959) to distinguish groups in which membership is voluntary or involuntary and to explain important differences in process in terms of this distinction. There is an interesting sense in which the family problem solving group straddles this distinction; it is an involuntary voluntary unit. It is involuntary in the sense that you're a blood member of the group, you remain a blood member, you're dependent on other members for satisfaction of certain needs that cannot be met elsewhere, and legally, while a husband can divorce a wife, there is no parallel by which a child can divorce a parent. But this unit has a voluntary property if one begins to talk about the psychological invest-ment in this group versus other groups such as peers, colleagues, or neighbors. At any moment in the life of the family group, the member could regard his psychological membership as voluntary, capable of being withdrawn at any moment, available as a potential threat to other members, and a basic source of vulnerability should others decide to withdraw. The point of this is that unless we examine group processes wherein membership retains this mixed quality, we may be misled as to some of the more prominent processes that operate in families or other problem solving groups.

Embedded Problem Solving

There is a sense in which one gets highly discomforted by the phrase, "family problem solving." The discomfort arises because the phrase carries the *connotation* of a relatively discrete, separable, distinctive set of activities which are somehow set apart from things like family fun having, family snow shoveling, or family aggression making. The phrase, *family problem solving*, has somewhat the aura of the family *meeting*, convened at the fireside by the benevolent father, at which everyone takes turns airing the gripes that have accumulated since the last meeting. This caricature is not meant to be cynical; instead, the point is that the phenomenon in which we are interested is probably difficult to isolate. It is part of an ongoing stream of behavior when members interact with each other, and many problems undoubtedly get stated and solved without the outside observer even knowing that something was amiss or being worked on.

This point has several implications. For example, any laboratory group that is given a ready-made, distinct problem and the task of solving it probably bypasses many of the crucial dynamics in family problems. They bypass such questions as how one comes to know that a problem exists, what it does to solution adequacy to be working on several different things *concurrently* with problem solving, what it's like to go about solving a felt, intuited problem rather than an explicitly stated consensually validated problem which was made visible to all members at a specific point in time. The importance of this point cannot be stressed too much.

For example, suppose it were true that the greater the severity of a problem, the more tense the members are, and the less adequate are their solutions. It is conceivable that many apparently severe family problems are solved more adequately than we might expect, due to the simple fact that members are doing several things concurrent with what the observer defines as problem solving. Since their attention is focused on *several* different projects, the importance, significance, and severity of any one of them is diminished; thus solution quality and acceptance increases. Not very much is known about problem solving amidst distractions, competing sources of attention, or a diffusion of activity, and the argument is that to the degree that we are uninformed about the effect of these variables, we are uninformed about family problem solving.

Embedded problem solving may also have a decidedly retrospective quality to it (Garfinkel, 1967; Schutz, 1967; Weick, 1969). Having only the vague sense that a problem exists, it is entirely possible that only when the family stumbles on a solution, does it discover retrospectively that a problem ever existed. Solutions single out problems that the members were not even aware of, and this is likely to be an important process in problem solving as will be seen later.

Encapsulated Problem Solving Units

The fact that studies of group process frequently focus on interaction among relative strangers has several twists for family problem solving. There is a sense in which problem solving processes in families are sealed off from the external environment more so than may be true of almost any other kind of group. The problems faced by the family obviously involve the external world, it is the *process* that is sealed off. To understand this, one should think of experimental situations in which other members are unknown commodities, they have problem solving styles that are different, they produce unexpected behaviors and ideas, newcomers occasionally are added, and in general there is some means whereby the processes used to solve problems are scrambled and some of the changes are incorporated while some previous modes are deleted. To use an evolutionary metaphor, the pool of possible problem solving behaviors available to nonfamily groups is both larger and replenished more frequently than is the case for family problem solving units. This may seem to be nothing but a restatement of the fact that family problem solving is characterized by a high degree of familiarity among members and a high degree of habituation. That conclusion misses the nuance I wish to preserve. Both problem definition and solution adequacy in family problem solving, as these are affected by process, should exhibit less variance than is true of other groups simply because the process itself is relatively immune from revision. At best, the range of revisions which this process will undergo should be significantly less than is true of other groups. Stated in a different way, families will be handicapped in the solving of problems to the degree that different classes of problems are best solved by *different* processes of solution. For example, there may exist problems that can be solved by thinking only, by doing only, by doing then thinking, or by thinking and then doing. If a family confronts problems that fall into each of these four categories, yet they use only one means of problem solving for all problems, then only a very small portion of their problems will be solved adequately.

What Is Normal, Natural Trouble

One of the unique features of family problems is that a significant number of them contain a developmental confound. The nature of this confound is that members can never be certain whether a problem that is singled out is better left alone since it is growth related or whether intervention is required since it may be situationally induced.

The thrust of family life may well be in the direction of underestimating this developmental confound and attributing an excessive amount of blame to situational conditions. The reasoning here is built on the assumption that the greater the amount of familiarity one has with another person, the less able he is to recognize changes in the other person. A subtle property of familiarity is that one assumes he knows most of what the other person is like, there is little the other can do that is surprising, changed behavior tends to be assimilated to previous behavior rather than recognized as new behavior, and there is the overall assumption that each member is a constant. The implication of this is that a problem which may be finite in duration and is occasioned by one member changing in some way and being in the midst of this change may be attributed to some other element due to the assumption of constancy. The solution which then occurs should serve only to disrupt some other portion of the situation which previously had been functioning smoothly.

Problems considered by nonfamily groups seem to contain fewer of the developmental confounds, this factor does not have to be weighted heavily either in problem location or solution development. An additional implication of this is that nonfamily groups seldom have to consider the solution alternative, let it pass (Garfinkel, 1967). Instead, problems in nonfamily groups seem to require some solution, members feel compelled to come up with a solution, and there is at least a consensus that some solution must be arrived at even if members differ as to what the solution should be. What nonfamily groups do *not* have to consider during their deliberations is whether there *is* a problem or whether it's "just a phase," and whether the "let it pass" solution should be invoked. The argument here is that when the solution alternative "let it pass" is introduced into a problem solving sequence, and when there exists the distinct possibility that the problem on which members are working is more apparent than real, then the nature of that sequence and its outcomes will differ considerably from processes in which these two considerations are not salient for members.

As a final point, it should be noted that within families, members may have different views as to the number of currently active problems that signify a state of well being, a state of normal natural trouble. Some members may think all is going well, others may conclude that there is trouble, but the reason for this diversity may not lie so much in the fact that members try to evade or overlook problems, rather it may lie in the fact that they have different baselines as to the number and kind of problems that constitute normal trouble.

The Predominance of Unfinished Business

It is probable that at any moment in time, the family as a group contains more unsolved problems than is true of other nonfamily groups. Whenever any one problem is handled in a family, there is likely to be a backlog of problems that were discussed earlier but which were never brought to a successful resolution. Families are ripe for Ziegarnik effects. There are several reasons why this may occur. Members differ considerably in their criteria as to what constitutes an adequate solution, the consequences of any solution typically are less concrete and occur with more gradualness than is typical in the nonfamily group, the consequences of the solutions do not have equal impact on all members, and by the time the consequences have occurred and are reported to other members, these consequences may have been filtered and modified in content due to their differential impact.

This point expands the earlier comment about problem hitchhiking. A cascading presentation of problems could evidence expressive behavior, but it also could represent the circumstance in which one member's presumed solution simply compounded the problems of another member, and this unfinished business intrudes into subsequent discussions.

Unfinished business can also arise because of very different locations of a given problem. For example, suppose we assume that having a baby is a family problem. The question is where is this problem located: preconception, first indication of pregnancy, explaining the imminent child to other children, consideration of where to house him, birth, bringing the baby home, disruption of house routine, and so forth. The person who defines the problem of having a baby at a late stage in the sequence mentioned above will have more unfinished business for a longer period of time than will a member who locates the problem at an earlier step. The wife may simply want to become pregnant whereas the husband wants to preserve normal, uncluttered house routine. His unfinished business is available for intrusion into family problem solving much longer than hers is.

Problem Solving Amidst Pub Art

Lesley Conger (1968) whimsically describes the interior decoration of her home, the chief motif of which is that it is littered with books, magazines, newspapers, virtually every form that is *pub*lished (hence Pub art). "Whatever you call it, it doesn't much matter what the upholstery looks like if it is hidden with a slipcover of newspapers all day long, or how the dining room table has been indented with a Babylonian cuneiform by years of homework done in a pressing rage if it is stacked, between meals, with everything from Playboy to Scientific American plus school books, library books, and stray volumes of the encyclopedia" (p. 8). Much as we may resonate to this portrait as family members, there is also reason to resonate to it as scientists.

The ecology of family problem solving differs drastically from that found in many other groups. To the extent that ecology affects group process, this variable must be taken seriously (see Craik, 1968 and Sommer, 1967 for discussions of this point). For example, how often do family members solve problems when they are seated on identical straightback chairs, looking into each other's faces, notepads at hand, no visual distractions, an absence of interruptions from a ringing telephone, and with a definite time at which the discussion is to conclude? The gestural, facial, and bodily cues available for members to use in trying to decide how to take someone else's remarks are undoubtedly affected to a considerable degree by such things as slouched postures, overstuffed chairs that mask considerable movement, and with the backsides of members being as much in view as frontsides.

The growing body of work on multichannel communication (Scheflen, 1968) makes it clear that nonverbal indices contribute a sizable number of amendments to verbal statements, yet the ecology of the family setting should have a considerable effect on the availability of these cues. What we need to study, in order to learn more about the process of family problem solving, are groups in which the environment is disorderly and gestural, and bodily cues are cryptic if they are even available. When a parent complains to a child, "you're not paying attention to me," he may be saying something much more profound than we realize. Inattention means the missing of nonverbal cues plus possible overreliance on tonal inflections to interpret the words that are uttered.

WHAT IS THE APPROPRIATE METAPHOR?

Because of the complexity of group processes, investigators in this field often resort to metaphors to maintain some control over their phenomenon. This usage is more often implicit than explicit, yet it has a significant effect on the portions of that phenomenon that are emphasized and suppressed. The potency of metaphors is well-illustrated in the following comment by Colin Turbayne: "The chess metaphor, for example, used to illustrate war, emphasizes the game-of-skill features while it suppresses the grimmer ones. A good metaphor produces thereby shifts in attitude. The attitude-shifts produced by an effective metaphor point to a later stage in its life. A story often told—like advertising and propaganda—comes to be believed more seriously. Those details stressed tend to stay stressed while those suppressed tend to stay suppressed until another effective metaphor restores them. . . . The tomato reallocated to the fruit class changes its taste history. A dry martini health drink loses its flavor." (1962, pp. 21–22.)

The argument I wish to develop in this section is the following. The ways in which we will study family problem solving are influenced by the metaphor which we think is most accurate in characterizing this activity. Furthermore, it is virtually impossible to divest oneself fully of metaphorical thinking. The author John Fowles (1968) has stated this perhaps most pointedly: "One cannot describe reality: only give metaphors that indicate it. All human modes of description (photographic, mathematical, and the rest, as well as literary) are metaphorical. Even the most precise scientific description of an object or movement is a tissue of metaphors" (p. 89). Now, there are several metaphors implicit in the literature on group problem solving. It is likely that these same metaphors may be smuggled into the study of family problem solving without warrant, and thereby misdirect investigations in this area. So, my purpose is to examine briefly two group metaphors that are available, and two general nongroup metaphors which could have a considerable effect on the way inquiry is structured.

The Scientist

Perhaps the most pervasive metaphor in group problem solving is the individual problem solver (see Bales, 1950). Individuals go through certain steps in solving a problem, hence one can expect to see analogous steps in a group that solves problems. The strengths and weaknesses of this metaphor are detailed, complex, and would fill an entire paper by themselves. Rather than detail these issues I would like to take a broader cut at this metaphor.

When one reads closely the steps in problem solving that are attributed to the individual, the individual being portrayed rather subtly gets transformed from Everyman to Scientist-Everyman. The steps that are imported into the group process turn out to be the way the scientist goes about his work, not the way the man in the street does. But this being the case, the more important point for family problem solving is that a very particular scientist has been used in this portrait and he may be the *least* appropriate kind of scientist to be used as a metaphorical referent when one thinks about family problem solving.

The distinction that I have in mind here can be illustrated by a recent review of *The Double Helix* by Eugene Rabinowitch (1968). In assessing the work of Watson and his associates in unraveling the molecular structure of the DNA molecule, Rabinowitch makes a rather telling comment about this discovery and how it is qualitatively different from the work of men like Einstein and Planck. He uses the metaphor of the detective story to illustrate the distinction. "The problem solved by these four young investigators, however important, was not a deep one: its solution required ingenuity and persistence, not inspiration and genius . . . [However] such breakthroughs (as Einstein's theory of relativity) cannot be narrated as detective stories, because they are not solutions of clearly recognizable problems, to which a correct solution *had* to exist—as a murderer has to exist if a murder is committed—thinkers (such as Einstein) were confronted with apparent confusion, contradiction, and lack of logic in natural phenomena, rather than a clear-cut question; they made order out of disorder by creative thought, not by detective skill. . . . The reader of *The Double Helix* must know that any similarity between the fascinating story presented by Watson and the true story of a great scientific discovery is mostly superficial, and that the difference is greater, the deeper and more revolutionary the discovery" (p. 28). To flesh out this distinction, the scientist as detective metaphor is elaborated in such sources as Platt (1964), Homans (1967), and Mach (1953) and the scientist as creator metaphor is elaborated in Hein (1967), Polanyi (1968), and Garfinkel (1967).

To bring this distinction closer to the area of family problem solving, we can use Maruyama's distinction between goalless and goal-oriented dissatisfaction (1967). Goalless dissatisfaction is dissatisfaction "which negates the present but which has no alternative yet to propose" (p. 170). This condition exists when the person has a desire not to be what he is or a desire not to be in the situation he is in. Goal-oriented dissatisfaction "has a goal to propose, and is caused by the negated ideal" (p. 170). This situation would occur when the person has a desire to be something which he is not or a desire to be in a situation he is not in. Goal-oriented dissatisfaction is akin to the detective story; it is clear that there is something definite and tangible to be discovered. The question is how to get there. However, goalless dissatisfaction is more akin to the question, "something is amiss, what is it." Obviously, families confront both kinds of problems. But the point is that a different scientist metaphor is appropriate to each of these general classes; and in all likelihood, the detective metaphor is invoked more often than is warranted.

Earlier I mentioned that many family problems are embedded and often originate from a background of general confusion, contradiction, unlabeled unease, and that much time is consumed in problem location. The family's problem is often more akin to "is there a victim" than to "who was the murderer." The importance of the distinction between these two types of scientific activity is that they imply different modes of problem solving. The emphasis in the detective metaphor is on planning, step by step covering of possibilities, sizable use of deduction, deliberateness, and systematic explora- tion. The creator metaphor emphasizes the indeterminancy of proper proce- dure and the phenomenon to be apprehended, relies more heavily on action rather than deliberation, places greater emphasis on unsystematic, quasirandom exploration as the means to discover problems and solutions, and contains a more prominent emphasis on retrospective thinking. The investigator who uses a scientist metaphor to construct his model of group problem solving would be well advised to construct two models—is there a victim, and who is the murderer—if he intends to comprehend significant portions of family problem solving. Recalling an earlier distinction, the problem solving sequence, think then do, implies the murderer metaphor; the sequence, do then think, implies the victim metaphor. Both modes may be used in families, and in all likelihood the dissatisfactions to which these modes will be applied are both goalless and goal-oriented.

The Same Old Faces

While it is straining a bit to label this a metaphor, an important distinc- tion between types of group studies needs to be re-examined in the light of previous points made about family groups. The metaphor which is most likely to be invoked for thinking about family problem solving is a closed system, a stable set of persons, high in familiarity with one another, who interact frequently, and whose interactions spread over a number of years. This suggests that one should preserve stability of membership and high familiarity in laboratory studies of problem solving. The metaphor requires the same group of subjects who come to the laboratory for several hours, several days a week, for several years, and solve problems.

In fact, I think that this metaphor and its implied laboratory procedures may be of limited value in capturing the processes found in family problem solving. Instead, I would propose that laboratory studies involving several generations of *different* subjects (Jacobs and Campbell, 1961) may be the more appropriate metaphor and medium for research. The salient property of these studies is that a small group of *founders* participate in some task. After time has elapsed one member is removed and a stranger is added; the trio of two veterans and a stranger continue to solve the problems, then another veteran is removed and another stranger inserted, and so forth. Of interest in these studies is the rapidity with which strategies, norms, and standards, embedded in the initial generation, decay as a function of the number of generations observed and the nature of the item embedded.

At least two features of family life seem to argue for the relevance of a generation metaphor. First, family members do undergo developmental change. Although these changes are gradual they may be sufficient at any point in time to render the apparent old-timer in actuality a newcomer. Second, as the age of members increases, more time is spent away from home doing a greater variety of things and having a more unique set of experiences. Relative to the person they were in the family problem solving group before, members return to that group as something of a stranger, a person unlike the previous participant in that group. In other words, the more rapid the developmental changes characteristic of family members and the less frequent the interaction of the participants, due to participation in activities outside the family, the more likely are family problem solving processes to resemble those in groups where members are replaced than in groups where the membership is closed.

But the importance of this point resides also in the fact that, at all stages in the flow of generations, there is always a majority of persons who have had prior experience in that setting and who have developed some habitual ways of problem solving. The tug one finds in any generational study is that between the older members trying to socialize the newcomer in the ways that have worked for them in the past, and the newcomer being either insensitive or resistant to these efforts. If a superior problem solving strategy is intentionally planted with the newcomer, the effort required for him to socialize the old-timers frequently exceeds the apparent advantages of the newer strategy and the newcomer eventually capitulates and adopts the older solution. While there are limited data on the precise activities that occur between newer and older members when personnel is reshuffled, the argument is that observing process under these conditions would shed additional light on mechanisms operative in family problem solving.

The point being made here sounds to be in direct contradiction to the argument developed in the section on the encapsulated unit. There the argument was made that family problem solving processes were essentially sealed off from any significant revisions in the way they unfold. Here, we are asserting that in fact there is a potential for revision due to development and mobility. However, these potential revisions encounter the dynamics operative in groups where members participate under varying degrees of strangeness. And it is not at all apparent that the acceptability of superior problem solving strategies under these conditions is identical to that in groups where membership and expertise is more constant.

Competition Against the World

In this metaphor, assumptions about family life begin to merge with assumptions about the basic problem solving processes found in families. The nature of this metaphor is preserved in the phrase, "the fittest survive," and is exemplified in the following rather chilling set of lines written by John Updike (1965, p. 98).

Xyster
"An instrument for scraping bones"
Defines the knife.
The word is rarely used—but why?
What else is life?

This metaphor emphasizes the relation of the group to its external environment, underplays intrafamily competition, leads one toward game-theoretic concepts and methodologies, portrays the family as basically a reactive unit, implies that the environment is malevolent and that contact with it must be assertive rather than passive, implies that vigilance is crucial in order to detect significant changes to which adaptation is required, and suggests that suspicion or a measure of doubt be entertained toward nonfamily participants in this environment.

Lest we get carried away with nuances of this metaphor, an important implication should be noted if it is used. Evidence indicates that when there is intergroup competition (we can insert group-environment competition here just as easily), one major consequence of this competition is that it solidifies relationships among the members who share an interest in gaining competitive advantage, that cohesion is high, that evaluation of other members is less intense and frequent, that stereotypes of the *competitor* are stated with greater intensity and contain increasingly negative content, and that any member who deviates from the position in which the group is becoming entrenched is confronted by prompt and powerful sanctions. Notice, that if one invokes the competition metaphor, there is a rather detailed way in which he will presume families go about problem solving, and the particular features of this problem solving, so highlighted, are rather different from other models used.

Playing With the Capricious Environment

A sizable number of writers portray life more as comic, absurd, and not to be taken all so seriously, and the problems that one comes up against are to be thought of annoyances rather than wars. This view is exemplified by

G. K. Chesterton's (1960) remark that, "An adventure is only an inconvenience rightly considered. An inconvenience is only an adventure wrongly considered" (p. 315).

Now suppose one used surviving in an absurd world as his metaphor for family problem solving. What might be the consequences? In the first place he would probably place greater emphasis on the role of social-emotional features of group process, in particular the shrewd placement of jokes, tension release, laughter, and so forth. The argument would be that since there is a certain amount of absurdity in the world with which the family copes, to the degree that the absurd view intrudes into their process in the form of levity, their process is more appropriate for the kinds of problems they confront. In contrary manner, as the process reflected more task orientation, a greater incidence of taking things seriously, and less sensitivity to some humorous aspects of the problem, the family's problem solving would be less adequate.

One must be careful in using this metaphor to note that it does not imply that problems are unimportant, that solutions are a waste of time, and that the family is a little bit foolish to spend all its time fretting about problems. Instead, it emphasizes that implementing any solution and the eventual outcome of this implementing are under relatively little control by those doing the implementing. (Note, in this regard Gumperson's Law: "The contradictory of a welcome probability will assert itself whenever such an eventuality is likely to be most frustrating": The Editor, 1968, p. 5.) The absurdity metaphor further emphasizes that laughter is not antithetical to importance, that within humor lies considerable creativity necessary to define and solve problems (Koestler, 1964), that problems may arise accidentally without any intent by the perpetrator, that some situations simply elude analysis—they are pure and simple nonsensical and no attempt at sense making can remove this quality— and that solutions have a relatively short life span.

Other group process considerations that follow from the usage of the absurdity metaphor might include the following. Group process would be viewed more as expressive behavior in which members are venting some of their frustrations at the absurdities, but are not actually presenting items requiring a solution. One might also take a second look at those problem solving groups in the laboratory in which subjects sometimes show an exasperating unwillingness to take the exercise as seriously as the experimenter intends. All of us have found ourselves in the position of running subjects who "just can't seem to understand that this experiment is serious business and not a joking matter." Yet, if we could relax our omniscience for a moment and watch how they go about solving group problems anyway, it might be that the process by which they reach solutions would be more like families than is true for our obedient subjects.

If one invoked this metaphor he would also be more concerned about the conditions under which it is possible for members to step aside from the role they are playing during group discussions and see their performance for what it is—both its comic and serious aspects. To the degree that members are unable to do this or are too threatened to do so for themselves and others, then one might predict that the problem solving will be less productive.

In What Sense Is the Family Really a Group?

Implicit in everything written in this section has been the use of the group metaphor to talk about families. While we have looked at a few metaphors for conceptualizing groups, it also seems appropriate to examine the relevance of the group metaphor for the family. Obviously this can become an issue or not, simply as a function of how one defines groups. However, I wish to make three points that should be kept in mind when we assume that family problem solving is group problem solving. And these three points have relevance to the notion of a group and how to think about it.

First, if one takes seriously the argument that a substantial portion of meaning is retrospective—we know what we are doing only after we have done it—then the group as a problem solving entity takes on a rather different appearance. It is conceivable that we often act and problem solve in a concerted fashion without realizing that this is what is occurring. It is only when the action has reached some terminus that it is possible to say as we look backward at what occurred, we solved that problem as a group. The perception, "we are a group," may well occur quite late in the history of a set of people acting collectively; and if this is so, then this perception has little real consequence for the process since many of the crucial events have already taken place.

It seems to me that the notion of the group as a unit which is constituted retrospectively must be taken seriously if there is any merit to the argument that a sizable portion of family problem solving is embedded activity. If the retrospective argument is pursued, it implies that some members at the conclusion of concerted activity may single out prior events that compel the explanation, this was *individual* problem solving. This disparity of interpretation should be especially likely when group problem solving occurs concurrently with other activities, and as we have argued, this may well be the case for much of family problem solving.

A second point that must be considered when we think about the group metaphor is that it is entirely possible that persons have considerable ambivalence regarding the benefits of group membership. To understand family problem solving may be to understand that members wish to keep their sociability to a workable minimum and that, as ties exceed this minimum, there will be effort toward disengagement. This argument turns on the conditions under which it is possible for an individual to establish a sense of identity and uniqueness. There is a major thread in the group literature which argues that a person learns who he is largely on the basis of comparison with others. But to compare oneself with others requires that one observe, interact with, and at times work interdependently with these other persons. To the extent that the outcomes of interdependent activity cannot be separated into the individual contributions made by each person, the person's desire to know who he is may be thwarted. In other words, it could be argued that identity can be defined only relative to that portion of the individual's self that is *not* included in any group. Only this portion constitutes what he himself can be certain of. Thus, if a family member wishes to get some sense of his identity and uniqueness—and this is a problem which should be frequent in families—then it is possible that to gain clarity on this issue the member will reduce the number of his ties until they constitute a small, sociable minimum. By doing this he maximizes his chances to learn more about himself as an individual.

The importance of this discussion is not so much that some ideas about identity are being developed, but rather that the family may become less group-like and behave less like nonfamily groups in their problem solving if members are concerned with the issue of identity and if they perceive that feedback from interdependent activity is confounded feedback and of little value in clarifying this issue.

As the third point regarding the group metaphor, we mentioned earlier that problems in families are less often consensually defined and more often consist of problems that are presented by a subset of members, this subset having the most stake in the outcome. We also stated that this probably would lead the more involved member to press harder for solutions and to insert tentative solutions into his statement of the problem. If this is the case then it seems more appropriate to think of the group activity as social influence rather than problem solving. But if this makes sense, it becomes less certain whether we need to talk about this as any form of group activity. The reason for this is that if I am successful in influencing other people to accept my position, then these other people emerge from the interaction thinking more like me than they did before. In essence what I have done is multiplied myself and some of my assumptions. On the issue that was just discussed, the other people who were influenced can now act as standins for me on that particular issue. We came together dissimilar, we parted more similar. Now the question is, what do we add by calling this group activity? Instead of family problem solving, what we have witnessed is family acceptance of a member solution. The solution spread from one person to more than one, but that seems to be the bulk of what occurred. If we subsume this under the label of a group process, nothing very important seems to be added.

THE PROCESS OF FAMILY PROBLEM SOLVING

So far we have examined some unique properties of family problem solving and some metaphors within which such activity can be viewed. The purpose of this section is to state, in more detail, some specific problem solving processes that should be prominent in families but about which we know very little. The four issues that I wish to explore are attention span, problem solving templates, problem severity, and means interdependence.

Attention Span

One of the properties of family problem solving is that members have dissimilar skills and abilities to perform this activity. This heterogeneity could have profound effects on the ways in which problems are solved. One of the more crucial variables should be attention span, how long it is possible for various members to remain attentive to the problem that is being discussed. The reason this variable may be important is that it could influence whether members are more concerned with immediate or deferred gratification. To develop a deferred gratification solution, members will have to consider more issues, construct a more detailed plan, and spend more time anticipating contingencies. All of this activity takes time, and if the mean attention span is relatively short, the discussion should be terminated before the necessary work for a deferred gratification solution can be completed.

Also, one might hypothesize that the attention span of the problem solving group will drift toward the attention span of the member with the shortest span. This is so because the discussion can continue with everyone contributing only so long as the member with the shortest span continues. Once he starts to become inattentive, the likelihood that further discussion will be productive decreases. It is also likely that the shorter the attention span in the group, the more it will be solution rather than problem centered. The argument would be that the less time that is available before members become inattentive, the more pressure there will be to generate and evaluate solutions.

But there is another feature of attention span which seems important. If you take seriously the argument that a considerable portion of meaning in family problem solving is derived retrospectively, then you look at attention span in a slightly different way. Rather than say that attention span determines how long members will stay attuned to present activities, one might argue that attention span determines how frequently the member will look back over what *has occurred* in order to determine the meaning of what is occurring. Notice that if members vary in the frequency of their retrospective glances and the points in time when they make them, then they will undoubtedly arrive at different conclusions as to what is going on and very possibly will arrive at different conclusions as to what the problem is with which they are concerned.

There is one final point about attention spans which affords a bridge to the next section. One of the more useful propositions regarding problem solving is that as ambiguity and stress increase, there is a greater likelihood that people will resort to more primitive modes of problem solving. Faced with uncertainty, members tend to respond with their most habituated problem solving strategies, and these typically consist of rather elementary, highly evaluative ways of responding. For the moment, the point I wish to raise is that as the uncertainty of a family problem arises (whether this uncertainty be produced by ambiguous role structures, instability of procedures, unclear solutions, or whatever), there is a higher probability that members will regress to their most habitual attention spans. Adults and children alike should show this regressive effect, and the net result should be that the already limited attention spans available in the family problem solving group would become even shorter. Thus, there would be even more pressure toward getting a solution and a greater likelihood that a relatively "poor" solution would be adopted.

Problem Solving Templates

The proposition stating that as ambiguity increases there is a regression toward more primitive styles of problem solving can be extended into group processes in several interesting ways. To illustrate this point, we can examine two hierarchies of problem solving processes, one proposed by William James (1960) and one by Campbell (1966).

James, in an essay on the "Energies of Men," proposes that it takes more energy to sustain increasingly "higher qualitative levels of life" but as one expends this greater energy at these higher levels, his control of the environment also increases. The particular hierarchy he proposes is the following: "Writing is higher than walking, thinking higher than writing, deciding higher than thinking, deciding 'no' higher than deciding 'yes'—at least the man who passes from one of these activities to another will usually say that each later one involves a greater element of *inner work* than the earlier ones. . . . Just how to conceive this inner work physiologically is as yet impossible, but psychologically we all know what the word means. We need a particular spur or effort to start us upon inner work; it tires us to sustain it; and when long sustained, we know how easily we lapse" (p. 296). There are several interesting implications in this excerpt (it should be read in light of the earlier discussion that families solve problems under low energy levels), but we will avoid the temptation to pursue them in order to focus on the regression proposition.

Campbell (1966) has proposed that there is a hierarchy of knowledge processes, and this includes the following levels ranging from least to most complex.

1. Non-neumoic problem solving: random locomotor activity in search of nutritive or non-noxious environments.
2. Vicarious locomotor devices: distance receptors (such as the eye) perform the random trial and error locomotion in lieu of locomotor exploration.
3. Habit
4. Instinct
5. Visually supported thought: insightful problem solving in animals which depends on the presence of a visually represented environment. Having seen the environment, presumably there is random trial and error locomotions in thought.
6. Mnemonically-supported thought: This stage consists entirely of vicari-

ous processes, the environment is reproduced from memory, "thought" trials are used to generate alternatives, and a representation of the external state of affairs is used to select among these alternatives.

7. Socially vicarious exploration: observation of the trial and error exploration of another member substitutes for similar actions by the observer.

8. Language: trial and error actions and the environment are not represented visually or vicariously, they are reproduced by linguistic symbolism.

9. Cultural accumulation: vicarious selection processes operating on social trial and error processes (such as borrowing from other cultures).

If we examine both James' and Campbell's hierarchies, we can argue that groups develop increasingly complex ways of knowing. These ways of knowing and problem solving can be viewed as templates that are overlaid on the environment. At any given moment a group has potentially available to it all the templates it has evolved up to that point. Presumably when faced with a problem, they will use the most recently evolved template since it is the least imperfect and most accurate of those templates currently available. Viewing group processes in this way it is possible for us to talk about the fixation of group problem solving processes. Fixation means being stalled at some point in the process of evolving templates, the template currently available cannot generate the next more complex template, and all the group can know for certain about the environment is whatever their currently available template will generate.

Notice some additional things that the usage of hierarchies permits us to do. Templates afford a means to talk about group development and dissolution. The argument would be that as a group develops, it moves from lower to higher templates, as it dissolves, it moves from higher to lower templates. The assumption we are making here is that evolutionary processes and products are reversible.

But the particular usage we wish to make of the hierarchy notion concerns the relationship between ambiguity and regression. The general proposition would read, the greater the amount of ambiguity a group confronts during problem solving, the greater the likelihood that it will return to its earliest modes of acquiring knowledge. This proposition is interesting for several reasons. The most regressive mode of acquiring knowledge is "moving around." And this is precisely what one sees when groups with high ambiguity are observed (for example, milling, wandering, disorderly gestural patterns, and so forth). There is also the implication that if a group attains a level of knowing that is high in the hierarchy (socially vicarious exploration, level 7); and if the group confronts ambiguity or experiences considerable stress, they still can know about the environment in several ways since they can try six other ways of knowing before the problem will defy solution. The proposition also should be joined to the earlier discussion of members trying to hold their group ties to a sociable minimum in order to establish identity. This juxtaposition would suggest that in a minimal group, one should see rather primitive knowledge-gathering processes in operation (for example, resort to vicarious locomotor devices, habit, instinct). It is important to note that we are talking about group modes of acquiring knowledge. This qualification is crucial because it is entirely possible that individuals within this minimal group could still, *as individuals*, be capable of using complex problem solving templates.

So far we have talked about the situation in which the group normally uses one template to engage in knowledge acquisition. However, for completeness we need to discuss what happens when more than one template is used. It will be noted that each of the templates is imperfect, but each is imperfect in a different way. The errors that filter through one template are caught by another one. Thus, if a group confronts an equivocal environment that must be rendered more certain, then there is a greater likelihood that certainty will occur, the greater the number of templates that are used against that environment. This point is crucial. So far it might appear we are making the general assumption that the higher the level of template evolved, the more adequately will the group solve the problems it confronts. But, the more complete argument would be that it is *both* the level in the hierarchy to which the group has evolved, plus the *number* of levels the group applies to an equivocal environment, which determines how certain that group will be that it "knows what it knows." This could be rephrased in terms of a proposition about knowledge certainty in group problem solving: The higher the knowledge level evolved and the more templates applied to an equivocal datum, the more certain the group will be that its "version" of reality is *the* version.

Severity

The point here is simple, but potentially important. Suppose that members of a family perceive that a problem exists, but each member judges the problem to be at a different level of severity. Which level of severity controls the level of severity at which members will consensually judge the problem to be and work on it? This is a difficult question on which to make any a priori predictions. One could predict that there will be a simple regression to the mean if discussion is drawn out over time, a prediction which implies that the majority of family problems will turn out to be quite similar in their assumed severity. One could argue that the final level of severity will drift toward the level of least severity, under the assumption that people wish to avoid unpleasantness or the assumption that the member who judges the problem to be least severe will have the shortest attention span for that problem and that the group will accommodate to his limited span and severity level. On the other hand, it is plausible that the consensual level of severity will drift toward the most severe level. The person who defines the problem as of the greatest severity presumably is the most discomforted, is most desirous of having a solution, and will be most active during the problem solving interaction.

The point of this is simply that severity could have a considerable effect on group processes. And given that severity levels undoubtedly are different among family members relative to any given problem, it becomes crucial to know what the fate of these disparate judgments is when they are pooled and problem solving is undertaken.

Means Interdependence

A salient characteristic of many families is that members have diverse goals and as a consequence goal interdependence may be substantially lower than is true for many ad hoc groups. To understand family problem solving processes may require that we pay more attention to means-interdependence (see Raven and Eachus, 1963). The implication of this is that we need to examine more closely problem solving when there is means-interdependence amidst goal diversity, and also we must accord the phenomenon of agreement on means a more central place in our notions about the developmental stages that groups go through.

One way in which the role of means convergence in problem solving can be discussed is in terms of the following model of group development. This model will be discussed at some length since it summarizes in fairly economical form many of the points that have been made earlier.

A developmental model of group problem solving assumes that interlocking of behaviors among participants goes through predictable stages. In later stages, interlocked behaviors are executed differently than in earlier stages. Knowing the stage at which a group is, it is possible to specify precedents that have accumulated in the form of solutions to prior problems, content of present activities, resources that are of value, and what the group may be troubled by next. Furthermore, one can discuss the possibility that a group becomes fixated at a stage or that it skirts the stage through an inadequate solution which increases subsequent problems. Knowing the problems that a group will encounter and the sequence in which they will occur, it is possible to examine the individual resources available within the group and predict the adequacy and acceptability of solutions to these problems.

The formation, continuation, and dissolution of any group can be assumed to follow four steps. These steps are diagrammed in Figure 1. Examination of

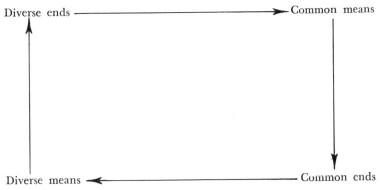

Figure 1. A Model of Group Development.

this figure will show that the traditional assertion that groups form around common goals has been replaced by the assertion that groups form around common means. The rationale for this reversal will be elaborated later.

We assume initially that all groups form among people who are pursuing *diverse ends*. It is commonplace to assert that individual differences exist, but the full implication of this assertion often gets lost in theories of group behavior. In any potential collectivity, members have different interests, capabilities, preferences, and so forth. They want to accomplish different things. However, to achieve some of these diverse ends, concerted, interdependent actions are required.

As a group forms, members converge first on common means, *not* on common goals. In the early stages of group formation, it is not essential to agree on ends in order to implement interdependence. Instead the more basic agreement involves interdependence as a means to pursue ends which need not be similar. It should be recalled that a basic property of reciprocal actions is that a member emits some behavior, *any behavior*, which is valuable to the other person in return for which he receives a behavior that is valuable. There is no immediate requirement for a shared goal. Rather, there is a commitment to pursue diverse ends through the common means of collectively structured behavior.

Perhaps the most important consequence of treating the developmental sequence as starting with diverse ends⟶ common means is that it preserves the crucial point that people *create* social structure. Considerable group theorizing assumes that social structure influences people and makes them what they are. The problem once again is that we do not know where the structure came from, what it looks like, or precisely who does the influencing. A reversal of sequence and the postulation that diverse ends are *followed* by common means avoids this problem.

Existing data demonstrate that people constrain structure, that diverse ends control common means. For example, Tuckman (1964) has shown that triads composed of persons who possess varying degrees of abstractness-concreteness in their cognitive structures organize themselves differently and process different kinds of information to "beat" a simulated stock market. Once the members converge on interlocked behaviors as the means to pursue diverse ends, there occurs a subtle shift away from diverse to *common ends*. The diverse ends remain, but they become subordinated to an emerging set of shared ends. This shift is one of the most striking that occurs in group life and it is exceedingly complex.

One of the initial ends shared in common is that of preserving and perpetuating the collective structure. Evidence of this convergence is found in the articulation and enforcement of norms, categorization of members and actions, increased regularity in frequency and form of interpersonal communication, and explication of boundaries.

But, there is a more subtle sense in which common ends follow rather than precede common means. An important insight which occurs in a variety of sources (see Garfinkel, 1967; Schutz, 1967) is that meaning is often retrospective, not prospective. Actions occur for any of several reasons and only when the actions are completed is it possible for a person to review them and know what decision he made or what he intended to do. Furthermore, it is impossible for behaviors to be reinforced and for their probability to increase until they have been emitted at least once. The point being made is simple, but crucial. The assertion that groups form around a common goal, often hinders an understanding of group behavior and the reinforcers that control these behaviors. There tends to be avoidance of the crucial issue, precisely how *does* intent affect action. Consider the problems that an investigator has when he is committed to the framework that group behavior is instrumental to some prior common goal. Whatever behaviors occur somehow must be related to the original goal. Thus the investigator concentrates on trying to work out some elegant statement about how that behavior could be instrumental to goal attainment. If he tries hard enough he probably will be able to show how it relates to a shared goal. But he has not added anything very important to our understanding of groups. We do not understand the particular behavior any more now that we have some plausible statement regarding how it *might* be furthering goal attainment.

It makes more sense to look at the behaviors themselves, lay aside concern for the way in which the behaviors are instrumental to attaining some prior goal, and take seriously the idea that the control and meaning of behavior often are clearest once the behavior has been produced. By positing that common means precede common ends, and by restricting the concept of common ends mostly to events that preserve a collective structure in which diverse ends can be pursued, then it is possible to look more closely at group behaviors and make sense of them in their own right. We are also in a better position to understand capricious, self-oriented acts that are common in the early stages of a group. Given the present model, it is clear that some behaviors may be oriented to an incipient common goal but most are not. *And yet*, when a person retrospectively sorts out the meaning of a group for himself and becomes more or less involved in it, *all* of the events that occurred earlier may affect his reconstruction. It will *not* be just the "goal-oriented" behaviors that he notices, other behaviors also will be noticed. Thus, it is not surprising that diversity is prominent in any aggregate of persons, and that people may leave before the common goal is attained. Diverse ends remain salient because persons have coalesced around means and not ends, and because the ends which they do eventually share in common are tied to the actual behaviors which have taken place in this group (for example, the perceived ends make sense of immediately prior behavior generated within the group), and the ends that are shared concern mostly the preservation of a collective structure.

The next stage in the developmental sequence assumes that common ends are followed by *diverse means*. There are several reasons why this shift may occur. First, when some convergence on common ends has occurred, it is typical to find that groups implement a division of labor to aid task performance.

They exploit with greater intensity the *unique* resources that are available. Thus, members are valued more for what they do *not* share with others than for what they do share. And, as Merton (1940) has argued, when tasks are specialized, persons tend to become more attentive to their component task and less concerned with the larger assignment of which it is a part. They become less concerned with how their contribution will fit with the contributions of others.

But there are two additional reasons why means should diversify. One concerns stabilization of attribution (Kelley, 1967), the other concerns increased pressures toward individuated action. First, means may diversify because a durable collective structure does impose stability and order. But if some portion of the continually changing world becomes orderly, other portions in comparison could seem even more disorderly, unpredictable, and ambiguous than they did originally. Precisely because some portion of the world makes sense, other portions make even less sense. The basic dynamic operating here is a "contrast effect." Under conditions of increased ambiguity, one should observe a higher incidence of ideosyncratic behavior, persons should act in more dissimilar ways. It has been demonstrated in several studies (such as Sherif and Harvey, 1952) that as the environment becomes more ambiguous, persons act in more individual ways. This proposition has figured prominently in the work of Sherif and Sherif (1956) and in Lazarus's research on psychological stress (1966). Stated formally, the contention is that "ambiguity permits maximum latitude for idiosyncratic interpretations of situations, based on the individual's psychological structure" (Lazarus, 1966, p. 118). In the absence of an external anchor for actions, the person uses the only remaining anchor, namely himself. Thus, it is suggested that when a collective structure forms and serves to stabilize some portion of the world, other portions that are less orderly become noticed and because of the operation of a contrast effect, they appear even more ambiguous than they may be. This ambiguity fosters diversity of action (diverse means).

But there is a second reason why diverse means may follow common ends. The complete model proposed here argues that there are diverse ends, followed by common means, followed by common ends. Notice that there are two adjacent steps that involve commonality and sharing. There are two stages where accommodation, convergence, concessions, and compromise have been required for the group to remain intact. As noted earlier, several compromises in the interest of concerted action can produce frustration and obscure a sense of self-identity. Thus, it seems reasonable to argue that a second dynamic which pushes toward diverse means is that of increased pressure to reestablish and assert uniqueness, to demonstrate dissimilarity from the associates with whom one has become interdependent. Interdependence does entail costs and these costs become most apparent at later stages in a group.

The model completes itself because as means diversify, as persons act in more idiosyncratic ways, they begin to pursue different ends. Having acted in an increasingly dissimilar manner from their associates, dissimilar ends become defined, preferences and desires diverge; thus the group once again consists of members with *diverse ends.*

The model covers both the history of a group from its formation to dissolution and repeated events within the same group among the same members. In short, it traces the fate of a set of reciprocal behaviors over time. If a group consists of only a single set of reciprocal behaviors that become disengaged when the task is completed, then the model traces the entire history of the group. If the group stays together, and reciprocities change over time, then *each* set of interlocked behaviors should follow the proposed sequence.

Although the model is unique, it is also consistent with existing theories and research on group development. For example, Tuckman (1965) analyzed several existing theories of group development and concluded that groups seem to pass through four stages which he labels forming, storming, norming, performing. There are several parallels between his stages and those proposed here.

Forming consists of hesitant participation during which people search for points of similarity, but also try to "bend" the imminent interaction toward their own ends. Similar behaviors are associated with the transition from diverse ends to common means. *Storming* occurs when questions of leadership, position in status hierarchies and control emerge and when most members are in competition for these relatively scarce resources. As Tuckman describes it, "The second point in the sequence is characterized by conflict and polarization around interpersonal issues, with concomitant emotional responding in the task sphere" (p. 396). The present formulation has less to say about the intensity and direction of affect at this stage. However, there are similarities because the phrase "common means" describes convergence around the mechanics, means, and procedures by which the group will function. Common means involve the recognition that interdependent action is necessary if ends are to be attained and efforts are made to implement such action. The concern at this stage is not with ends but rather with ways to implement what all members acknowledge as being important, namely, interdependency.

The third stage in Tuckman's model, *norming*, parallels closely the stage of *common ends.* In both models there is the explicit recognition that once the mechanics of interdependency have been worked out, there is shared concern to preserve these mechanisms and insulate them from disruption. The mechanisms must be made reliable and dependable, and it is the function of norms to produce these stabilities.

Tuckman's final stage, *performing*, is the point at which the emphasis in the two formulations is most dissimilar. Tuckman's model implies that *unless* the group solves the problems at each prior stage, it cannot work effectively (p. 396). The same implication is not found in the present model, partly because means convergence occurs earlier and is an antecedent of group formation. For this reason, effective work appears earlier in our sequence and occurs during more stages. Our model is based on the assumption that convergence precedes group formation, while Tuckman assumes the reverse sequence, an assumption that is reflected in his characterization of stage 4 as performing. The present model does parallel Tuckman's ideas when it is argued that diverse means are fostered in part by task specialization. However, the present model is more comprehensive because it includes two additional dynamics in the fourth stage, contrast effect between orderly and disorderly events, and increased pressures toward individuation. By adding these two dynamics to the fourth stage, it is easier to argue that developmental sequences will be repeated. This cycling is more difficult to see in Tuckman's model, because once the group starts "performing," it is not apparent how or why they would shift from "performing" to "forming" (aside from the obvious dynamic of new personnel). It is more difficult in Tuckman's scheme to argue that a stable group would repeatedly go through the four stages. Once groups begin to perform, they are destined to terminate. The present model does not imply that termination is inevitable. As means diversify, ends do too, thus the group starts a new sequence *without* any necessary external pressure (for example, new task or personnel). All of the dynamics that produce development in the present model are contained *within* the members themselves. Thus it is more logical to argue that the group will repeatedly move through the hypothesized cycle of events.

CONCLUSION

Given the assortment of ideas presented in the preceding pages, the reader may be wondering precisely what kind of person or way of thinking is being criticized. The answer to this question is provided by Robert Canzoneri's (1968, p. 67) elegant poem entitled, "Man with an Axiom to Grind":

> He took a bath twice a day
> And washed his body oils away,
> Which bared him to the fact that, oddly,
> Though cleanly, true, was next to godly,
> Yet cleanly was as cleanly did.
> And what he knew he cleanly hid.
>
> A stitch in time caused his surmise
> The cream it was that didn't rise.
> Horse sense, he swears spurred him to think,
> Led him from water and made him drink.
> Now he believes with both his eyes
> Each tub on its bottom lies.
>
> Every dogmatic has his day,
> The saying goes, and who's to say
> He won't draw wealth as well as flies
> Oily to bed, oily to rise?

If the ideas presented here lessen the impact of those with axioms to grind and enrich the pool of conceptual mutations available to scholars of family problem solving, they have served their purpose.

To make this point clearer, the preceding discussion does not contain explicit definitions as to what constitutes a family problem or when a family is a group and when it is not. Without such definitions the phenomenon we have been discussing is admittedly elusive. However, I do not regard this absence of definitional clarity to be a serious drawback at this stage of inquiry. The absence does create a vacuum, but my interest is more in expanding the data, concepts, and methodology that may eventually fill this vacuum than in filling it immediately with arbitrary distinctions that select against more promising ways to think and talk about families.

REFERENCES

Bales, R. F., *Interaction Process Analysis*. Cambridge: Addison-Wesley, 1950.

Campbell, D. T., "Evolutionary Epistemology," in P. A. Schilpp, ed., *The Philosophy of Karl R. Popper*. Lasalle, Ill.: Open Court Publishing Co., 1966.

Canzoneri, R., *Watch Us Pass*. Columbus: Ohio State University, 1968.

Chesterton, G. K., "On Running After One's Hat," in H. Preston, ed., *Great Essays*. New York: Washington Square Press, 1960. Pp. 312–315.

Conger, Lesley, "Interior Decoration and Pub Art." *The Writer* (October, 1968), 8–10.

Craik, K. H., "The Comprehension of the Everyday Physical Environment." *AIP Journal* (January, 1968), 28–37.

Editor, "Short Takes." *Scholarly Books in America* (January 1968), 5–6.

Fowles, J., "Notes on Writing a Novel." *Harpers Magazine* (July, 1968), 88–97.

French, J. R. P., Jr. and Raven, B. H., "The Bases of Social Power," in D. Cartwright, ed., *Studies in Social Power*. Ann Arbor: University of Michigan, 1959. Pp. 118–149.

Garfinkel, H., *Studies in Ethnomethodology*. Englewood Cliffs, N. J.: Prentice-Hall, Inc., 1967.

Hein, P., "On Order and Disorder, Science and Art, and the Solving of Problems." *Architectural Forum*, Vol. 127 (1967), 64–65.

Hoffman, L. R., "Group Problem Solving," in L. Berkowitz, ed., *Advances in Experimental Social Psychology*, Vol. 2. New York: Academic Press, 1965. Pp. 99–132.

Homans, G. C., *The Nature of Social Science*. New York: Harcourt, Brace, and World, 1967.

Jacobs, R. C. and Campbell, D. T., "The Perpetuation of an Arbitrary Tradition Through Several Generations of a Laboratory Microculture." *Journal of Abnormal and Social Psychology*, Vol. 62 (1961), 649–658.

James, W., "The Energies of Men," in H. Preston, ed., *Great Essays*. New York: Washington Square Press, 1960. Pp. 294–310.

Joslyn, W. D. and Banta, T. J., "Modifying Speed of Group Decision Making Without Awareness of Group Members." *Psychomonic Science*, Vol. 6 (1966), 297–298.

Kelley, H. H., "Attribution Theory in Social Psychology." *Nebraska Symposium on Motivation.* Lincoln, Nebraska: University Press, 1967. Pp. 192–238.

Koestler, A., *The Act of Creation.* New York: The Macmillan Co., 1964.

Lazarus, R. S., *Psychological Stress and the Coping Process.* New York: McGraw-Hill, Inc., 1966.

Mach, E., "The Economy of Science," in P. P. Wiener, ed., *Readings in Philosophy of Science.* New York: Charles Scribner's Sons, 1953. Pp. 446–452.

Maier, N. R. F., *Problem-Solving Discussions and Conferences: Leadership Methods and Skills.* New York: McGraw-Hill, Inc., 1963.

Maruyama, M., "Goal-Generating Dissatisfaction, Directive Disequilibrium and Progress." *Sociologia Internationalis* (1967), 169–188.

McGrath, J. and Altman, I., *Small Group Research.* New York: Holt, Rinehart and Winston, Inc., 1966.

Mead, G. H., *Social Psychology* (ed. by A. Strauss). Chicago: University of Chicago, 1956.

Merton, R. K., "Bureaucratic Structure and Personality." *Social Forces,* Vol. 18 (1940), 560–568.

Platt, J. R., "Strong Inference." *Science,* Vol. 146 (1964), 347–353.

Polanyi, M., "Logic and Psychology." *American Psychologist,* Vol. 23 (1968), 27–43.

Rabinowitch, E., "Review of The Double Helix." *Bulletin of the Atomic Scientists,* Vol. 24, No. 10 (1968), 27–28.

Raven, B. H. and Eachus, H. T., "Cooperation and Competition in Means-Interdependent Triads. *Journal of Abnormal and Social Psychology,* Vol. 67 (1963), 307–316.

Scheflen, A. E., "Human Communication: Behavioral Programs and Their Integration in Interaction." *Behavioral Science,* Vol. 13 (1968), 44–55.

Schutz, A., *The Phenomenology of the Social World.* Evanston: Northwestern University, 1967.

Sherif, M. and Harvey, O. J., "A Study in Ego Functioning: Elimination of Stable Anchorages in Individual and Group Situations." *Sociometry,* Vol. 15 (1952), 272–305.

Sherif, M. and Sherif, Carolyn W., *An Outline of Social Psychology.* New York: Harper and Row, 1956.

Sommer, R., "Small Group Ecology." *Psychological Bulletin,* Vol. 67 (1967), 145–152.

Thibaut, J. W. and Kelley, H. H., *The Social Psychology of Groups.* New York: John Wiley & Sons, Inc., 1959.

Tuckman, B. W., "Personality Structure, Group Composition, and Group Functioning." *Sociometry,* Vol. 27 (1964), 469–487.

Tuckman, B. W., "Developmental Sequence in Groups." *Psychological Bulletin,* Vol. 63 (1965), 384–399.

Turbayne, C., *The Myth of Metaphor.* New Haven: Yale University, 1962.

Updike, J., *Verse.* New York: Crest, 1965.

Weick, K. E., "Retrospect in Tasks," in B. M. Bass, J. Haas, and R. Cooper, eds., *Managing for Task Accomplishment.* In press.

CRITIQUE AND DISCUSSION————————

The initial portion develops an argument about some unique properties of family groups and the implied comparison here is with laboratory groups. The point being that, if you pay attention to some of these unique properties, you find that certain variables relevant to group processes have not been looked at thoroughly. There are a number of propositions advanced in that particular section as to how some of these variables might affect process.

The second section asks the question, "What might be the appropriate metaphor for us to use in thinking about family problem solving or group problem solving?" Four different kinds of metaphors are explored in terms of how you would think about group processes. The implication of that being: if you accept one of those metaphors, you're going to look at the family in a particular kind of way and look at particular portions of its processes——so one ought to be alert in advance to which one of these metaphors he's using.

In the next section there is simply a more concentrated focus on certain aspects of the process: if attention span is heterogeneous among members, what might the effects of this be in terms of how long the problem solving discussion continues? There is the notion of "hierarchies of knowledge processes" from more primitive to more complex, more complicated forms. The argument here is that groups evolve increasingly more complex templates, or ways of knowing. Several questions are raised in terms

of "what might happen to a family or a problem solving group which is under stress" in terms of regression to earlier, more primitive templates. The second question being posed is: "Is it more important to know the highest level of template that a group has evolved, or is it more important to know how many of different kinds of templates are applied to a problem situation at one time in order to best characterize the group?"

There is a discussion—a very short one—on the issue of problem severity. The main question is, suppose, in a group, you had members who had defined a problem at different levels of severity. Which level of severity is most apt to control the final or consensual definition of how severe that problem is and how that particular problem would be approached?

There are several major conceptual themes that run throughout the paper. The paper is decidedly biased toward or emphasizes the role of retrospect in gathering meaning or understanding the actions of participants ——Oftentimes you'll solve something before you even realize that you had a problem, so that the solution retrospectively singles out, if you will, some initial problem situations, and one of the conceptual threads that runs throughout is a considerable emphasis on this retrospective quality.

Another major thread would be concerned with the fact of embedded problem solving that goes on within families. The more I think about it, the more that strikes me as one of the more significant variables. This is rather quickly handled in the section entitled "embedded problem solving." But the major thing that seems to be of concern is that if we look at problem solving in laboratory groups and even in conventional short-term groups, problems seem to come in more discreet, specifiable, bounded fashion than may be true in the family problem solving situation. As a result with the family you get much more concerned with "how do people locate problems in an ordinary on-going flow of activities?" Furthermore, you find yourself much more interested in "what happens to people who are trying to solve problems when they're working with other kinds of activities concurrently?" This factor of embedded problem solving also alerts you much more to this retrospective quality of understanding.

I guess the major conclusion I arrived at was that there was much more of interest in groups than I ever realized was there, and some of the variables that I first thought were unique to families would, if you relax your constraints a little bit, exhibit these same kinds of processes even if in a slightly different form.

When we look at a family, such variables as high amount of familiarity, high amount of interaction frequency, stability of membership, and so forth, arise as immediately-salient characteristics. One would then think that that should set the model for what kinds of groups we want to have in the laboratory. Here the suggestion is made that, instead, a more appropriate laboratory technology is, for want of a better term, the generational kind of study. For a period of as many

as maybe ten to fifteen generations you simply watch the fate of several problem solving strategies embedded in the first generation.

Now, the argument here is that that might be a useful laboratory technology to address issues of family problem solving for two reasons: One is the fact that in family groups you do have developmental change, even though these changes are gradual. If a considerable amount of developmental changes are going on through certain periods in the family, essentially what you have are relative groups of strangers coming together in order to work on problems. In a sense, some of the members get reintroduced into the family setting essentially as newcomers or strangers. That is, the greater amount of time members spend away from home doing a variety of things and having outside demands imposed on them, once they re-enter the family group they are a different kind of commodity from what they were in an earlier kind of session. Therefore, the argument would go that they are more akin to a newcomer or a stranger in these generation studies than a stable member about whom one is highly informed.

Another kind of dynamic in these generational studies is the fact that there usually are two or three people who remain in the group and they have a tendency to perpetuate the traditions. They are most closely linked with those initial strategies that were embedded. What happens is you typically run into coalition situations in which newcomers have different ideas and different strategies or are

not nearly as bound to former problem solving styles; therefore, they find
themselves in a tug of war with the
veterans who favor these more established styles.

LEIK'S DISCUSSION

In general, Weick's paper raises two fundamental questions. First, in what way should theory in family problem solving be viewed? Second, how should we go about our task?

Now, more specifically, I want to begin by discussing the 11 discrepancies between family and laboratory groups in four clusters. In the first set, I would include "low energy levels," "embedded problem solving," and "problem solving amidst pub art." These three form a set, it seems to me, or a kind of cluster, having related implications. One of the implications is that there would be incomplete and confused solutions to problems, if you get solutions at all. People aren't going to be very patient——they are not going to be entirely sure what's being resolved. They're not going to be entirely clear about what other people have contributed.

Secondly, it seems to me these conditions will imply dissatisfaction with the solution process. One of the nice variables in laboratory work which has to do with satisfaction is the end result. There may not even be an end result if these conditions are held in the extreme, and to the extent that there was one, there is likely to be less satisfaction with it. Certainly, the conditions would imply little contribution to solidarity of the group.

A third implication, I think, would be annoyance with having to be bothered with any kind of "group problem solving" process. Consequently, it seems that one could predict aversion to family problem solving in general and to any kind of "group orientation" implied in family problem solving, to the extent that these things are true.

A second cluster of differences are "unequal access to primary data," "variable energy level" of the participants, and "voluntary membership muddle." These imply differential participation on the part of the members and differential involvement on the part of the members over time and over problems. Given that there's an unequal access to data; you would expect that on a particular problem to which a person has major access, he would be an active participant. On another problem to which he has minor access to data, he would be a minor participant. If this happens to be a time when he's full of energy and rested, he would much more likely be a major participant. To the extent that these conditions hold, you can expect variation in the patterns of directiveness, dominance, contributions of ideas, supportiveness, and a number of other kinds of interpersonal and group aspects.

Hence, you would expect instability over time of family role structures with respect to problem solving. If you don't have essentially constant contributions, you can hardly have a particularly stable role structure. The consequence of this, it seems to me, would be uncertainty, hesitancy, and apprehension generated by the recognition of the problem regardless whether the problem itself poses these difficulties. That is, if your structure is uncertain and if you have variability of participation on the parts of others, you're not entirely sure of what's going to happen. This sounds to me like classical conditions for withdrawal from any kind of a context that might be problematic.

A third set of comparisons made had to do with an "absence . . . of models" for problem solving, "noncontingency of behavior," and "encapsulation of problem solving units." Now, the matter here is that the family is just not connected with sources of feedback outside itself. The implication of these would be a limited set of possible solutions or approaches to solutions for any particular problem, minimal feedback from within the group, and minimal feedback from outside the group. To the extent that these conditions hold, you can expect low probability of either self-correcting or externally-correcting processes, and consequently, essentially no learning. From this consequence you can predict a sort of autistic approach to problems with relatively frequent failure.

Finally, the last set of related traits or related discrepancies concern "problem solving as expressive behavior," "the indeterminant character of normal, natural trouble," and the "predominance of unfinished business." It seems to me these imply confusion over problems versus self-terminating sequences and confusion over boundaries. To the extent that these conditions hold, I think you can expect indecision of the members over what to focus on as "a problem," an inability to attend to a single problem, a tendency to wander and be sidetracked, and a preference for hoping that if left alone the problems will disappear. Consequently, I think you could predict a general lassitude, fatalism, and a feeling of defeat with regard to family problem solving.

Now, these comments are rather extreme, but they suggest that, to the extent that all of these properties obtain, families will be segmented, withdrawn, ineffectual, and fatalistic about their ability to solve problems. Surely this is a strong contrast to typical laboratory groups, or is it? [Ed. note: Professor Leik then proceeded to mention several experiences in his labs where subjects refused to talk to each other, and a family "attacked" the experimenter by turning off the lights.]

Now let's turn to the metaphor problem and come back to this point in a few moments. The "what is an appropriate metaphor for the family" question is really asking how do we want to look at this thing, or how do we want to conceive of the family for predictive purposes? The suggestion in that section would seem to be that the appropriate metaphor is a collection of separate entities involved in minimal accommodation to circumstances and to each other.

I would argue that——first of all, this metaphor might well be applied to all groups, not necessarily just family groups. I don't know whether a metaphor quite that strong was intended but let's stick with it for a moment. The processes and regularities of accommodation are really our area of inquiry, if, in fact, we have a number of individuals who are concerned with accommodating to each other and to environmental problems. And to the extent that the sets of conditions discussed earlier obtain, these processes will tend toward random behaviors, and regularities will be of the simplest, individualistic sort. However, to the extent that these sets of conditions do not obtain, processes will be selective, innovative where needed, and integrated in consequences. Regularities will occur which will satisfy what we've usually meant by such terms as "effective group structure."

Now regarding one of the main questions raised by the paper, I believe it would be appropriate to conclude that families are indeed part of the spectrum labeled "the group," that—dependent upon many factors—families may vary across that spectrum from much like what you'd expect in the lab to grossly different. To the extent that we study variabilities due to those factors, we can learn about family groups whether or not we are studying family groups.

Now, finally, I want to turn to the model proposed at the end——briefly it was suggested that there are four stages in this group process. There are some questions I want to raise here. First of all a distinct cycling process, which is testable, should emerge. That is if you have, in fact, a model you should be able to observe a cycling process which concurs with that model. However, there are some problems with cycling processes. Most such processes either converge or explode, for example, the cobweb model in economics. If explosion occurs, we're saying that the group dissolves. This would suggest a study of critical boundary conditions to the convergence process, probably more ethical in lab simulation then with real family groups. Nevertheless, it seems to me that this would be suggested by the cyclic conceptualization.

Secondly, note the emphasis on a given set of interlocked behaviors. To what extent could such sets be expected to encompass all members? Some of the issues raised in the paper suggest, perhaps, that they would not. To be temporally separable, can you tell when one of these sets of interlocked behaviors terminates and another set initiates, or to be separable from related or tangential sets of interlocked behavior. I think there might be a real conceptual quagmire here.

In short, might the model imply that all portions of the cycle might be observable at any given time because you've got so many different cycles going on, and if so, is the model really testable? If we're not concerned with testing the model, then the question becomes does it have heuristic value, and what is that value?

Let me then briefly suggest a parallel model—not to try to do away with Professor Weick's model—which is another way of saying essentially the same kind of thing, but one that may highlight certain features of the suggested model. It seems to me that we can assume that individuals attend to their own problems; problem solving is in fact, if we take a symbolic interaction approach, mental activity or vice versa, and where problems are sufficiently recurrent that we can do so, we work out habit structures to handle the standardized solutions to these problems. To the extent that we have adequately worked out habit structures, we stop paying attention to the particular characteristics of the problem and we sort of recognize problem X, habit structure X, and away we go. That is to say, then, that we ignore new data when we have adequately structured our behaviors to handle particular problems.

Now habits become disrupted when gross negative feedback occurs resulting in reattention to the problem area. In terms of interpersonal behaviors, this produces a kind of cyclic process of an initial adaptation which involves attention to the other people, the other individuals or whatever, to the point where we have learned enough about that person that we can form appropriate habits for dealing with the individual. We learn what's meant by a raised eyebrow or a cough or a choke or a gasp or whatever else. We learn how to respond routinely to these kind of things with a "Yes, dear," over the paper at breakfast or something like that. This is a kind of initial point. There's a similarity here to the common means–divergent ends part of the Weick model.

Then, it seems to me, progressively, as the consequence of inattention— because we now have the habit structure operative—we diverge from adequate response to the others in the group. People are in fact dynamic, they're not static, but habits are static and so there is gradual divergence, a decreasing appropriateness of our responses. Individuals seem to have a strong desire to have their behavior validated, to have their self validated in the behaviors of others with whom they're interacting. To the extent that the others' responses are inappropriate, it's because their habits have become inappropriate and we are no longer being validated in the circumstances in which we're involved. We're likely to explode. As a consequence of such a blowup, reassessment of the problem and reattention to detail and perhaps a reformation of habit might occur, leading to a distinct cycling process.

This suggests conceiving of individuals as solving a complex equation for reaching their own ends. As many variables are included in this equation as would be necessary and as few variables are included as possible because a person does have other demands on his time and he doesn't want to spend all his time solving this one equation if he has other concerns. How many variables are necessary depends on how much can be treated as constants in the system. If your own ends are met with few variables being considered, then there will be little concern with others in the system. If you can treat everybody else as a constant, then you've got a simple equation; if you have to treat everybody else as a variable, you've got a complex equation. If your own ends are dependent upon others, then you're going to have to incorporate more "other" data, more data pertaining to others, more variables in your equation.

Now the adequacy of a simultaneous solution, that is a group solution, of your equations depends upon whether enough common terms appear in those equations. All the factors which were discussed earlier that may reduce motivation, energy, perceptual clarity, awareness of alternatives and consequences, and so on, will reduce the number of "other" terms in the equation that people are trying to solve. To the extent that common terms vary widely from time to time and person to person, solutions will be chaotic and frequently unsuccessful; of course there will be times when there will be good solutions. To the extent that common terms are too few, group problem solving is inadequate or impossible. To the extent that common terms are too many, individuals will prefer to forego the ends that they were seeking by the equation rather than to struggle with such a messy equation.

The problem, under whatever conceptualization, becomes determining sufficient commonality without exhaustion of the individuals or loss of their own ends in the process. Interestingly, this problem becomes a preamble to the adequate solution of other problems of a more routine sort. To me the Weick paper has raised a series of questions regarding the conditions of and the conceptualization of interpersonal accommodations, which are logically prior to the more typically studied questions of family problem solving.

GENERAL DISCUSSION

WEICK: One point that I really did resonate to and hadn't really thought seriously about, until Bob (Leik) raised it, was the one raised very early in his critique . . . when he was talking about the possibility that several of the points that clustered suggested a certain amount of dissatisfaction with the solution process. And, that in the particular groups he was talking about, the solutions may contribute very little to group solidarity. I simply wanted to underscore that I think it's a very trenchant observation that I really hadn't thought too much about. Conventionally when we look at the outcomes of groups, we really see the favorable consequences of the solutions having quite an important impact on how much validity occurs subsequent to that kind of an occasion. . . . It may well be that solutions simply are much less powerful for their solidifying or cohesive effects than we might ordinarily think.

One point of different emphasis was when Bob was talking about the uncertainty of family problem solving. For him, the major consequence of uncertainty is the prediction that you'll find withdrawal behavior. I guess the thrust in my paper is more that you'll find regressive behavior toward earlier or more primitive forms of problem solving rather than withdrawal.

I'll admit your point about the different cycles for each set of interlocked behaviors, or several interlocking behaviors, that each set may be at different stages . . . it's going to be a very difficult research problem. We are tooling up right now to test the cycling process and, as you intuited, that's turning out to be much more difficult to get a hold on than we had thought.

TALLMAN: I'd like to ask Karl a question regarding the 11 elements or variables that you argue contribute to the uniqueness of family problem solving. I wondered if you really make the argument for uniqueness as much as "these are variables that ought to be taken into consideration in family problem solving?" You allow for the family as being different from other groups and maybe less effective than a lot of other groups. But still, these are important variables that when you look at them as varying within families, they may account for individual differences in family problem solving?

WEICK: Yes. In our lab groups most of those 11 are there in some form or another.

I guess the argument would be that families may load higher on those variables than our conventional lab groups. And that being the case, one would expect that if we look at those variables, they would account for more of the variance in family problem solving than we might expect them to in the laboratory. In my reading of the group process literature, I haven't run into a lot of studies where those are manipulated so that we can see them take on a variety of values. Nor do we know concretely what effect they have on process even though one can intuit that they don't have a whale of an effect on it.

HAMBLIN: I wonder if you'd tell us a little bit more about the distinction of "problem-oriented versus solution-oriented" groups. [Ed. note: The distinction appeared in the preliminary draft, but was dropped in the revised paper. However, because the distinction caught on and sustained a considerable amount of the ensuing dialogue, we have retained it.]

WEICK: That distinction grows mostly out of Norm Maier's research. One of the properties of it would be that in the solution-oriented group, whenever a solution is proposed, it is immediately evaluated as either something to be discarded or something to be adopted at that moment . . . The solution gets evaluated right away as opposed to our wondering why anybody should even bring up the issue . . . for example, is there something in the group that's disturbing the one making the suggestion. It is characterized by immediate evaluation of solution, minimal discussion of the problem, or any attempt to amplify on it at all. The typical finding is that if you get problem-oriented groups, the kind of solution that they come up with tends to be more elegant or of a higher quality than is true of solution-oriented groups.

Now, the point I wanted to raise is that if you look at Maier's kind of groups, there are several kinds of problems that they face other than just the presented problem which take time to work out so that you can then get to the manifest problem. The argument would be that in the families, some of these kinds of surplus issues (like people trying to present a certain kind of impression or trying to gain control of the agenda) may be short-circuited or not that prominent, which means that the family doesn't have to spend so much time elaborating the problem because they don't have those instrumental issues to deal with.

HILL: Now, to what extent, as you talk about problems, is the source of a [group] problem an individual who can't get his individual problem solved by himself, but has to have the help of others? And to what extent is it all analogous to the problem set for a group like an academic department that has a set of tasks and their own unfinished business which is not entirely individual but is partly departmental? It seems to me that the vast majority of family problems are somehow——the problems of individuals to which others will have to make certain accommodations.

LEIK: That is the implication of my talking about each person as solving his own equation. And he needs to accommodate others by including them in his variables.

WEICK: Yes, and I think that's the reason why there's a lot of emphasis in the paper on goal heterogeneity and the idea that you're probably at best going to find convergence around means or instrumental kinds of activity. Furthermore, because of the strikingly different nature of problems, it's very tough to get consensus on just what group goals are. Families can be seen as an instrument through which a person can get some kind of a solution, while others, at the same time, don't necessarily share his ends.

HILL: In our research on preplanned actions it is interesting that the actions would again and again occur before a plan had been articulated. The subjects described an inchoate or an inexplicit plan as having been back there. They just couldn't tell us at the time we came in for our first interviews that it was on the agenda for action at all.

WEICK: This is one of the reasons why I think the attention span variable has been paid so much attention in terms of a retrospective model. If you have several people working on a problem but each of them tunes out at different stages because they simply can only handle so much information, they then kind of sweep back to see what's happening up to this point. If they sweep back at different points in that discussion, they are going to come up with different ideas about what's going on and may even come up with different conclusions as to what the problem is that they're working on or how well they're progressing.

BEE: I would think we need some clarification as to the functions of various family properties, depending on the problem faced. I understood Karl Weick to say, when you were talking earlier, that you thought perhaps the solution-orientation on the part of the family wasn't so bad because they didn't have so many surplus problems to cope with. Then a little later, I understood you to describe a whole series of such surplus problems that the family has to cope with—the fact that it has a lot of individuals—each with his own individual problems that he's trying to get solved and each with his own pet means of solution—converging together and having power struggles, concern about whose problem is going to get solved first and so forth which may be precisely the kind of situation in which the solution orientation rather than the problem orientation is less adequate. (See Weick's reply later.)

HILL: The children disproportionately are the source of problems without providing any reasonable quantum of solutions, and in conceiving the family as a problem solving group you have the asymmetry of adults with inadequate information attempting to cope with problems, the full definition of which . . . is never satisfactorily arrived at because of communication problems and because their children are not admitted to full communication in stating what's bothering them or hurting them.

ALDOUS: Another thing that I have noticed in the discussion is that we've been talking mostly about individual problem solving. Nowhere does the family as a group come in. Can you even say that the family is a problem solving group, or is it a collection of individuals who present alternatives like a closed type of test where others assent to certain solutions?

LEIK: I wonder if it might help to talk about an entirely different kind of group structure. When I think of our faculty meetings, it occurs to me that for years we've been promising ourselves—and now and then we approach this——that we're going to get down to the basic policy questions——curriculum revision, relationships between faculty and students, and so on and so forth, all manner of these basic questions that ought to be resolved. Well, we never do resolve them; what we do is we take a whole series of actions. If you look over the minutes of our faculty meetings, you see all kinds of little patch work. Something has to be decided here. Something has to be decided there. You have to get an action, you have to get a motion made and passed out of the way so that you can get on to other more individual things. I'm suggesting that this is going to be true in any complex organizational structure; a large corporation does not give extensive continual concern to the basic problems of "why are we here in the business world" and "what are our contributions to society" and that sort of issue, but rather all manner of little points that have to be cleared off. Now this is an analogue to the family. We have, in fact, tended to treat the family as if it were a group discussing policy matters. And I would think it appropriate, and clearly suggested in Karl's paper, that the family tends more often to be like a complex organizational structure in which the members occasionally meet to deal with these crummy little details so they can get them swept out of the way and get on with their own individual living.

MOORE: I was wondering if it would be worthwhile to make a distinction . . . between problems that arise "*within* the family setting" from "problems *of* the family"—for example, a seductive secretary at the husband's office? In other words, there would be sets of problems that would——be problems of the family which, if not solved, the price would be you wouldn't have a family. Now, it might be that a long term group is solving its "problems of the family" very well by keeping their energy levels fairly low and non-involved. That might be one indication that they don't even have a problem, or not a very serious one. The fact that they just sort of get up in the morning and they're not prepared for emergencies may be an indication that the problems of the group staying together and undertaking its major institutionally prescribed tasks are being handled relatively successfully. Now, when we turn to laboratory groups we almost never assign them the task of sticking together over any given period of time. Implicitly they're supposed to stay in the place while you run your experiment——but, until we define a task extending over time I don't think we'll have comparability along that task dimension, and that would be an important difference. One can imagine the difficulty in trying to get experimental groups to stay together—you know, indefinitely.

WEICK: May I comment on Helen's earlier comment because——it was a good one. It was the issue that in the early part of the paper family solution orientation doesn't look so bad——last part of the paper picks up more of these surplus problems families have and that——you know, that is jarring——I guess the reason I get into that position is because I assumed a lot of the family problem solving goes on concurrently with other kinds of activity so that there *are* surplus kinds of issues but somehow they don't stand out quite the same way as in the laboratory problem solving group.

ZELDITCH: I would like to reinforce the comments of both Bee and Moore. I think that the word "problem" is so ambiguous that the whole discussion became obscured. For example, if I followed the argument, it was something like: the traditions of the family were sufficiently established that a lot of questions about the social structure of the family really are worked out, while in problem solving groups that are ad hoc, you have a large number of these questions that have to be resolved as part of the hidden agenda. I really question that these "structural issues" in the family are really so unproblematic. Every time our family starts to discuss a problem, the latent content of the discussion is really: "What are my rights?" "What kind of a person am I?" "What do you feel about me?"——Nobody cares what the "presented" problem is that's being discussed.

BEE: It seems to me that the real relevance of this point is that the nature of problem solving in a family, where family means including children, is going to vary enormously depending on how old the children are. Problem solving—the surplus issues—in the family with very young children will, I suspect, be quite different than a description of problem solving in a family including adolescents.

LEIK: I'm trying to straighten out my thoughts on the issue of problem types. In particular I've been bothered by the extent to which we may have confused simple problems—where parameters are clearly specified and you go through a big accounting operation—with the crummy little problems that tend to encumber families, which tend to raise all sorts of surplus problems. This baggage implies the need for a heavy orientation to solutions of the trivial problems——the daily existence, but the "not basic to group structure" kinds of problems. These are the real questions of family relationship, and of interpersonal accommodation. These are the ones that, perhaps, ought to receive our attention. But they are usually such a quagmire that you can't get hold of the necessary conditions to go into them and nobody really has time for that. These are a kind of unapproached problem and they, therefore, form a continual battleground.

HILL: I hear a recommendation to family researchers that we need a careful mapping of the tremendous trivia that encumber families. I think I also heard, by inference, that this task of description would be difficult to move ahead with in the laboratory-instigated type of setting.

LEIK: Only on that latter point would I disagree. That is, we have, I think, ample opportunity to create laboratory situations which will get at what we are talking about. We may not have, but we certainly could.

GUMPERZ: Yes, I wonder if I could make comment on this problem of adequacy of our description of both day to day problems and long term structural issues. I recall a Thurber story where these trivial issues are talked about on the surface as temporary problems but actually they revolve about the possible break up of the husband and wife team. Somehow it seems to me that these distinctions are all right on a conceptual level, but when you look at actual conversations, they deal with both these underlying status, rights and duties levels, and serve us at the same time. So I wonder if our data is adequately recorded. Do we have adequate descriptions? Is there a way of getting at both levels through analysis, depending on what factors we as analysts pick out?

ZELDITCH: I just want to underline Professor Gumperz's point . . . it was a good point that the distinctions Moore made earlier between "problems in the family" and "problems of the family" are essentially analytic.

LEIK: I was just thinking about a way of structuring an experiment in a laboratory situation that might help distinguish the kinds of levels of problems we've been discussing. Suppose you were to put a set of people—family or not—in a situation in which some kind of essentially routine production task is necessary, in fairly high volume. For example, their pay for their activity depends upon how much they turn out and this requires some individuated behavior and some coordinated behavior but it requires a fair degree of attention to this.

However, you have a lot of other little things that are occurring. For example, maybe you haven't enough space for them all to be in the same area so they have to be distributed to different rooms. You don't necessarily have the materials that they require in logically-coordinated series——You don't impose any structure on them and they have no structure when they come into the situation. Since the task is continually demanding, they don't have time to develop logically, in a coordinated manner, the structure they need in order to do what they're trying to do.

I'm just trying to suggest a situation in which procedural things, interpersonal relational things, aren't resolved at the outset, but don't really have time to be resolved in an analytical manner because there are so many other little things pressing continually. It would be a way of structuring a lot of things that we have been talking about.

BEE: I'm beginning to be bothered by this distinction that seems to be coming out of our discussion. It seems to me that to some extent we're saying that we ought to be studying what the family ought to be solving; that the family should somehow be solving these deeper problems instead of coping continuously with these day to day things; and that what we ought to study is what the family ought to solve. But if it's true that the family does not deal with these, then, if we're studying the family as a problem solving unit, maybe we should study the kinds of problems the family actually solves, rather than concerning ourselves with the problems that the family doesn't solve.

HAMBLIN: I would like to respond to that. If I'm sick with a raging temperature and I've come to the conclusion that I can't solve it. I don't want to go to a doctor who says he can't solve it either; I want to find somebody who'll help me solve it. I think that's the task of the social scientist . . . helping families who are having these underlying problems they can't solve.

BEE: Alright, I agree. I'm playing devil's advocate for the moment. But if that's what we're talking about, then perhaps we need to redefine the topic in some way because when you say you're discussing the family as a problem solving unit, it sounds as if you're focusing on the kinds of daily problems that the family actually does cope with, and it might indeed be very difficult to study a family solving the kind of problems which we think they need to solve because they rarely do so. So it may be very hard to find out how this is done since it just isn't done very often.

ZELDITCH: Well, there's a relationship between the energies devoted to these two things . . . If they aren't solving these problems that we think they ought to solve, it really effects how they solve trivia.

ALDOUS: I was just thinking that since we are concerned with the trivial problems that families have difficulty with, rather than neat, crisp ones, that it might very well be that this would be the place where your generational type lab experiment would be very valuable, where we would not necessarily have to use families. The point at issue would be to confront them with some very fundamental problem such as the maintenance of cohesion, which is probably one of the central issues the family has to face.

WEICK: I'd like to mention one supplementary comment with respect to the generational study. The generational studies we are working on trace the fate of a problem solving strategy over fifteen generations rather than the fate of the judgmental norms which has been the conventional treatment. In other words, if you start out the first generation making rather bizarre judgments of the autokinetic effect, you typically see a decay of those kinds of things and that's interesting but it's not all that surprising.

What we're interested in is: If we've embedded in the first generation different strategies for solving the common target game task and some of which are both arbitrary and rather unworkable, would a very unworkable problem solving strategy decay in quite the same way the judgmental norms do (there is no verbal communication). Surprisingly what we find is that by the fifteenth generation the groups that start out with the very clumsy and very unworkable, not particularly obvious solutions, are holding on to them when it's fairly apparent if you just put naive subjects in that they will come up with a much easier kind of strategy.

LEIK: The question that I would raise here, in opposition to the generational thing, is that with school age children you have, in fact, a good deal of contact with outside sources of problem solving templates or whatever else you might want to call them. You would have the possibility of external input, therefore, because there is this increasing contact with members outside. And yet the very fact that there is increasing contact outside means that there is decreasing contact within and probably decreasing validation of the member's participation in problem solving procedure. It would be desirable, therefore, to structure an entire range all the way from the virtually disjoint generational possibilities to the totally fixed kind of structure. How about considering experimental circumstances under which you provide either the requirement or at least the opportunity—We don't ever do this—of the subjects wandering in and out of the group process. You could have things that you allow them to do elsewhere, for personal interest gain, perhaps you allow them to participate freely in a half a dozen things simultaneously. They can wander in and out if they wish and there's reason for individuals to be attracted to different groups. We could determine to what extent there is a variation in the validation of their participation in this group and to what extent there is an input of variability from outside rather than a maintenance of not even very good structure that causes it over generation after generation.

(QUESTION: I was just wondering about why these wrong strategies persist?)

WEICK: They're not wrong. They will get you the solution, but they're extraordinarily complicated to calculate.

(QUESTION: Do they persist because newcomers assume the veterans are experts?)

WEICK: Yes, that's a good hypothesis. We've got data which will tell us that, because there are some items in post-questionnaires which will ask what assumptions they make going in.

HILL: I wonder if I could raise a question, which goes back to the issue of types of problems with which families are primarily concerned, to add the question of the priority of the problems. Take, for example, the preoccupation that the family has with socialization. Now, what is problematic about the socialization issue at one stage as against another of the life cycle might point to the types of problems that have highest priority at any particular stage. Bob Leik, for instance, was struggling with the issue of the adolescent's coming and going. A certain number of families are concerned with the problem of releasing their members into new groups outside, into jobs and marriage, so that the generational metaphor that you use would see the family as not focusing upon the correct solution to internal problems of organization but with the releasing phenomenon at the very point where they might want to make use of the member as a newcomer moving in and out. We have ahead of us some discussion of socialization for problem solving and that very way of phrasing it makes the family less of a problem solving group than a socializing group to solve problems.

WEICK: Yes, and the thrust of most of our discussion has been not so much that the family does socialization as much as it has to make some peace with the debris that's left by whatever kind of socializing goes on inadvertently. This is the sense in which I think Bob Leik is concerned with the trivial issues in a family, and his recommendation that maybe the solution-orientation is vital, is very functional. I think it really makes some sense. It may not be the deliberate socialization as much as handling those kind of things that go along with it, and that's partly what I was trying to bring out in my talk about "normal, natural trouble" in families. Some of the time, it's just best to stay out of it, which is one of the things Omar Moore was mentioning also.

COMMENTARY

AN INTRODUCTORY NOTE

The commentaries which are interspersed throughout this section of the book are intended as a kind of third level reading. The main characteristic of this sense of levels is that it attempts to look at the symposium processes from somewhat unaccustomed angles. The first level, composed of the prepared papers, is very formal, guarded and well constituted. The second level, the edited transcript of the symposium itself, is, on the contrary, casual, sometimes contradictory and synergistic. Most of the editorial decisions, whereby the transcript was cut to approximately one-sixth its original size, were made with the interplay of these two levels in mind. Consequently, the third level is an attempt to highlight some of the shapes and directions which appeared during the editing.

Karl Weick's paper had a very pervasive influence on the symposium, pointing our attention in two directions. First, there is a route which leads to the consideration of a number of relatively new properties ". . . which have not been looked at thoroughly." They provide a partial, but very provocative, solution to the small-bore, uninspired quality of research. These properties have that quality of something new, yet something that we'd been looking for all along. As a result they expand and occupy a great deal of the symposium's attentional energy.

The second direction—more of an orientation than a trail—is toward a self-conscious, reflexive look at research as an evolving, self-conscious social system. Since, perhaps following some natural law of academic decorum, the first route was the more favored, the commentaries are intended as a crude balance—a kind of third order look—reflecting insights back on the research process itself. One image that I have, having gone along both routes, is that the directions are not all that separate. They constitute, in effect, two intertwined spirals, and the prospects for research development would seem to imply attention to both. There are several grounds for this view of the products of the symposium. First, there is the curious sense in which the research paradigms which guide inquiry are the last to benefit from any resulting insights. The attentional boundaries implied by the work of problem solving inhibits any consideration of "how the researcher is solving the problem of how the subject is solving the problem." Furthermore, if the research produces any new insights into problem solving, for instance, it does so without the benefit of that insight, in any antecedent sense, or does it? One of the central themes of the symposium is that there is a kind of "silent dimension" to research (and the very fact of sensing it makes it somewhat less silent) which renders that question a bit more problematic than it first appears.

The second basis for the image is a bit harder to indicate, except by using examples from the transcript. In a word, the point is that there's a lot more "in the air" these days than our well-tailored coding schemes are prepared to accept, but some assimilation does occur, assuring continued development. This can be appreciated, for example, in Karl Weick's paper, if you skip over *what* he says and look at *how* he says it. In his opening statements, Weick reveals his thematic structure, a dialectic between the themes: "Science is the evolutionary process grown self-conscious," and, the characterization of modern small group research as limited, uninspired, and idiosyncratic.

These two themes have a "signal to static" kind of relationship. The signal is the self-conscious promotion of the evolution of our mastery of our environment, considered extensively and intensively. Modern social research—our current state of evolution—is marked by an irritatingly high degree of noise. Consequently, it is very hard to reach any kind of object language for a consistent and adequate decoding of the signal. Several impli-

cations for the conduct of social science flow from this:

1. In the absence of any sure baseline standard, one survival strategy calls for a high tolerance for alternative selections.

2. Despite the law of attentional energy, one cannot take a single course too seriously, since the particular choice may not have survival value.

3. Since social science involves a "new" kind of subject matter (one that is essentially reflexive, reactive, and at this stage in the scheme of things, primarily retrospective), the modes of inquiry derived from earlier established sciences may not be appropriate.

4. Finally, there is a subjective tendency to "identify with the noise," to emphasize acceptance over quality —much like the process of identifying with the aggressor—which calls for some measures to assure a balance in our perspective. That is, we may need to build up structural supports to counterbalance system constraints on both high quality and high acceptance of research modes.

At any rate, the spirit which arises from this image of the enterprise is: "Let the hundred flowers bloom, let the hundred schools contend."

The second part of the "how" Weick presented has the distinctive flavor of a dialectic: The collision of some new properties with conventional rhetoric. Weick did his homework well for, while the gap between rhetorics is enormous, the new terminology was sufficiently seductive, referential, and manageable to sustain a good deal of the dialogue. In other words, there was a sufficient blend of the familiar and the problematic to assure that some process would develop. The essence, incidentally, of the dialectic is between a modern reference scheme which is highly dependent on agreeable, mappable, sensible "objects" and one which is complex, shifting, and shadowy.

The third element is concerned with the appropriate setting for getting the process going. Weick uses such phraseology as "relax your constraints," or "I'll know when I get there" (referring to his belief in a retrospective model). These provide a clue for the implied setting, which links up with O. K. Moore's "autotelic principle" (which appears in the Session III), excursions into new areas are best done under conditions which are relatively free from external constraints. For a strong taste of how this setting works, compare Weick's "metaphor" with Zelditch's "theory" (appearing in the Session II). In a sense the two terms are centered on the same sociological task of symbolically representing the social world. But the boundaries of inclusion are quite different, the former being much broader and permeable than the latter.

The extensive and variegated effect of these three elements established the conceptual boundaries of the symposium. One consequence of this is that participants had a lot of difficulty gathering in and sustaining all of what was going on. One way of visualizing the problem might go something like this: Weick introduced a new and exotic rhetoric for representing group processes which was picked up and elaborated by others. A lot of what is

in these terms is "unconscious" and/or "imperceptible." Because ten or fifteen years ago the dominant thinkers in social science discarded the "unconscious" as somewhat unmanageable and intractable (and "quagmirish"), interest shifted to a more cognitive rhetoric, a more logically elegant model, of social life. As the shift in focus took root, the unconscious element was squeezed out to the periphery of our standard, scientific speech. By reintroducing these underlying dimensions, Weick placed an unaccustomed burden on the shared-symbol system of the seminar members. Consequently the pattern of exchange between participants occasionally drifts toward what might be called a "collective monologue."

A second and related consequence, and despite the problem of individual difficulty, is that there is a distinctly synergistic quality to the symposium. An obvious example will be seen in the series of comparisons and contrasts between Morris Zelditch and Robert Hamblin in Session II. Somewhat less obvious, but just as fertile, are some of the *possible* comparisons the reader can make between, for example, Gumperz and Leik, or between Moore and Bee. A rather impressive array of potential mutants can be generated by such comparisons by employing variable reading strategies. For instance, by choosing one character (for example, Bob Leik, the synthesizer) and ignoring the rest, one can, by reading across all of his comments, develop a broader context for reading what he has to say. As this is done with each of the major participants, you begin to realize that the best of what an individual had in mind very rarely made it through the media to some significant other.

In sum, the Weick paper—in work and spirit—set an ambitious and provocative pace for the symposium. The pace made for haste so that much of what was said was lost while much of what was recorded was unguarded. Consequently, there are two levels, much of the time, to what transpired and these can be labelled as the "focal" and the "tacit" dimensions. The spirit (for example, relaxed constraints) complements the effects of the pace, protecting the individual from his unguarded productions. On the positive side, recognition of this spirit does two things: it allows for much more to occur than we thought could, and, at the same time, allows us to recognize what is going on a bit better.

IMPACTS OF THE WEICK PRESENTATION

Each section of the Weick paper, which he quickly reviews in his oral presentation, holds as much promise for illuminating the *system of research* as it does the system that is *being researched*. For example, in one of his remarks as discussant, Leik indicates that the effects of the eleven properties "had been there in his lab" studies all along, but had been treated as nuisances or noise—things to be avoided, stripped away, or simplified. There is, incidentally, a kind of "solution orientation" written into Leik's comment. With little fuss and a lot of skill he assimilates the expansive impact of the eleven properties into his preferred research scheme, the lab. But nowhere is there a comment that would indicate any curiosity as to *why* this lab scheme had previously ignored these properties.

The point is, then, that this kind of orientation signals a curious flow in some of our operating boundaries. It indicates that the more elegant a research membrane is, the less permeable it is. Moreover, there is—by some natural law—a tendency to favor elegant research systems—those prepared to handle well defined, easily managed signals. At several points in the transcription this tendency surfaced. For example, Moore's somewhat inconsistent comment to Hamblin, in a later session in effect stated, "if you can't map your 'game' mathematically, you are not doing 'science,' because you can't tell us what it is that produces your effect" (however robust that may be). Rephrasing this in Weick's terms, the operating schemes of social research appear fixated at an advanced, but highly vulnerable, level or "template." Part of the explanation for this fixation is the greater promise for earlier and better *career* payoff (W. O. Hagstrom's study). Unfortunately, career payoff and social scientific payoff are not inevitably linked.

A number of instances, illustrating Weick's theme of self-consciousness, appear throughout the transcription. Later in the symposium, Moore picks up on the "developmental" model of research in his description of his team's 20-year clarifying environments project. Gumperz will also offer an interesting content to the property, "unequal access to data."

He begins by stating that we have no adequate ethnographic data bank for America. He then suggested that of those few attempts which do exist, social scientists are given access only to highly suspect reconstructions of the data (see page 219). There are some very general and provocative questions contained in this series of comments:

1. How much of the "raw" data of research—the total data domain—is accessible to the scientific public?
2. How much of the "raw" (or tacit) domain is under scientific scrutiny—for example, epistemological assumptions? Could more of these dimensions be incorporated into our operating schemes?
3. What kind and amount of distortion is introduced by a heavy, almost singular, reliance on written media for gathering, storing, analyzing, and reporting data? Can multimethod logic be extended to our use of such media? Since media provide both informational and status functions, might over-reliance on one media by overly restrictive as to what and who gets professional recognition?

Another interesting reflection on the research enterprise is produced by the section on "hierarchy of knowledge processes." First, if you order

academic disciplines in the general terms of the appropriate blend of "thinking" and "doing," where would sociology fit on this scale? The distinction of internal-external valitity suggests, for example, that sociology should be heavier on the "doing" side of the scale, than, say, physics, and even more so than math. Second, if you throw the notion of "embedded problems" into the hopper, then the question "is it more important to know the highest template evolved, or the number of them applied to a particular problem?" takes on a new significance. That is, a focal issue and a corresponding "template" may appear quite adequate until some of the less perceptible, embedded problems waft into view.

On the other hand, it has been suggested that there is a tendency—Benbow Ritchie calls it the "law of affect"—to be not too surprised by such disruptions and to make minor adjustments in the template or in attentional focus—in other words, ignore the new data. This latter would be a stronger tendency the more focussed, serious, and sacred the process. In other words, the "law of affect" suggests that just so much "uncertainty" can be absorbed before an "antibody system" gets triggered which neutralizes excessive uncertainty.

ROBERT LEIK'S CONTRIBUTIONS

Reading across all of the sessions, Leik's contribution appears as a series of syntheses between troublesome issues and the possibilities of the laboratory as a means for solving them. (It would indeed be unfortunate if the clarity of his syntheses inhibited the

exploration of other approaches, such as one as far out as socio-linguistics.) For instance, he seems to be very clear on an appropriate definition of "problems," one which builds on the issues raised in the Weick paper. The day to day, rather trivial, encumbering type of problems, which typically are very difficult to describe or approach, are the key class of problems. This class is distinct from both the long term, basic-to-group-structure type or the well-bounded, trivial, accounting type of problems frequently explored in lab research. Now, since members of this key class are such a quagmire (for both sides) they tend to remain outside of consideration and consequently become the basis for continual battles (such as embedded problems). In several of his remarks, spread throughout the transcription, Leik suggests some strategies for approaching these in the lab. He furthermore assumes that it would not be necessary to include actual families as the unit of study, although the payoff would have application for them. (This last point proved to be a bit controversial).

A second type of synthesis has to do with the source and not the type of problem. Other members identified several competing views of the source: individual versus group, or problems *of* versus problems *within* the family. Leik synthesizes the issue through his definition of "accommodation." He then goes on to describe how hang-ups in accommodation might be studied through the use of powerful contingencies. Such a strategy could again be employed without the use of families, and would seem to hold some promise for both individuals (they can get their own needs met) and for the group (more viable group structures). This stance at the interface between individual and group systems has a great deal of appeal. It could help clarify the ground between individual and social psychology. It might resolve the debate over emergent or compositional effects of individuals in a group. There is a check on the tendency toward "realism" in discussing family sociology. The related idea of "habit structures," which carries implications for the quality of group effectiveness, provides a link between cognitive and affective variables.

Leik's treatment of "habit structures," as sets of variable equations has an agreeable ring to it. If you allow these structures to carry the embedded meanings implied in the notion of a tacit dimension and then turn them around to reflect on the researcher, they are very suggestive. Our working tools are structures which develop as standard solutions to research problems—with variable degrees of appropriateness. Since, as habits, they tend to be static, there is the prospect that they may be increasingly inappropriate with changes (for example, our perception) in the external systems. It would then require "gross negative feedback" to alert us to this. Now applying this to research habit structures, the question is, "how likely is it that we will receive feedback from our subjects?" To the degree that we are more profession-centered than client-centered we will have built a barrier to the reception of such feedback. Both Weick and Leik allude to this when they diagnose the trivial quality of much lab research. This leads to two related implications. On the side of professional relations we perhaps ought to occasionally relax the "serious" constraints a bit, tolerating a more playful attitude toward the enterprise—allowing for the assimilation of new materials. With respect to the subject side, our need for more immediate feedback—how is our "science" going over—perhaps indicates the need for an earlier investment in programmatic involvement. The body of the text is replete with examples of this, which might be captured as the following: a programmatic involvement is a "strategic perspective" which links the virtuosity of the social scientist with that of his public. For instance, the social scientist brings his knowledge of the formal principles of accommodation, and some particular public brings the knowledge of its local culture. For some exciting instances of this linkage look at John Gumperz' or Hamblin's suggested research strategies appearing in later sessions.

Overall, this introductory session served the purpose of alerting us to some of the potential hangups in the conduct of social inquiry. The insights that we derive from the strategies employed by our subjects in the course of problem solving have an applicability to research-as-problem-solving as well. But in a sense the subjects may be in a better position to benefit from new knowledge. The assumption of our expertise, the seriousness of inquiry, the link between recognition and professionally meaningful performance, the cognitive traps of metaphors and thought modes are all habit structures which, while inevitable to some degree, constitute impediments to the evolutionary process.

COMMENTS ON THE GENERAL DISCUSSION

Weick, as a kind of master weaver, built a frame that was a bit larger than anyone had anticipated. Consequently much of this general discussion was spent knotting our separate threads together. The result is an instructively crude mesh. The warp and woof, respectively, are attempts to define a "problem" and discussion of the best methods to handle problem solving. The result is surprisingly porous. Hill, for instance, very late in the discussion, is struggling to set down a definition which would capture a host of family-type problems and arrives at a sense of the family as less of a problem solving group than one concerned with "socialization for problem solving." But as Weick's response suggests, it may be the debris, which is left by whatever inadvertently occurs, that is the more central concern. This way of phrasing the focus

has two related implications. The ratio between conscious, purposeful roots of behavior and those which are not, is probably much smaller than we ordinarily imagine. This would hold *on both sides* of the research relation. Consequently, and in view of the dimensions of the unchartered terrain, the extent of our expertise is likewise very small. So the second implication, to paraphrase Weick, is that sometimes a solution orientation may be very functional—we can't expect too much from our puny tools, taxing our attentional energies too much by disturbing our survival habits. Some of the flavor of these implications are captured in one of Moore's statements, that families with very low levels of energy may be "solving" their problems quite well by not bothering with them.

Attempts to define a "problem"

stirred up a number of distinctions: "presented" versus surplus; trivial versus basic to group structure; neat, discrete types versus unapproached ones; problems *of* versus problems *within* the family; problems actually solved versus problems that should be solved. As the discussion darted in, out, and around these distinctions, several key issues began to solidify: (a) there may be a connection between little problems and big ones; (b) there may be a symptomatic connection between problems being faced *by* a family and problems *of* the family; (c) it may not always be the case that research should simply reflect the world as it is, rather it may be that research has a creative, exploration-of-the-possible, effect-producing role to play; (d) there may be logical or instrumental priorities (such as accommodational) when considering the "relations" between existing social structure, individuals, and small groups; and (e) finally, when viewed over time the relation between an individual and his family may be a very complex network of variables (for example, subjective degrees of familiarity, developmental shifts).

On the methods or "how should we go about it" side, the context of the responses suggests a diversity of opinion and perhaps, thus, a sense of the essential multiplicity required for the task. In a word, the central question is, how to build a system that comprehends and utilizes a variety of strategies without curdling? More specifically the issues are something like the following. First, how to focus our best effort on a problem without foregoing some ability to register ambiquity—how to square productive intelligence with receptive intelligence? Second, should prime weight be given to theory testing or to producing some effects—or is it possible to know how to produce an effect without a conceptually well developed representation of the process?

Third, how to establish a link between the best expertise of the researcher and that of the varieties of subject classes—finding the appropriate blend of formal principles and particular cultural contents. Fourth, how to get at the link between little problems and big problems—can it be done in the lab or would it require a larger "field involvement"? Finally, there is a suggested model for representing *developmental* processes. The model holds a good deal of promise for family researchers in that it can be used to register a lot of "more or less qualities"—such as degrees of membership, participation. It also provides a matrix for linking individual and external system processes.

REFERENCES

Cattell, Raymond B., *Handbook of Multivariate Experimental Psychology*. Skokie, Ill.: Rand-McNally & Co., 1966.

Chomsky, Noam, *Aspects of the Theory of Syntax*. Cambridge: MIT Press, 1965.

Furth, Hans, *Piaget and Knowledge*. Englewood Cliffs, N.J.: Prentice-Hall, Inc., 1969.

Hagstrom, Warren O., *The Scientific Community*. New York: Basic Books, Inc., 1965.

Heider, Fritz, *The Psychology of Interpersonal Relations*. New York: John Wiley & Sons, Inc., 1958.

John, Vera, "The Basil Bernstein Fad"

Miller, Daniel R. and Swanson, Guy E., *The Changing American Parent*. New York: John Wiley & Sons, 1958.

O'Rourke, John F., "Field and Laboratory: The Decision Making Behavior of Family Groups in Two Experimental Conditions." *Sociometry*, Vol. 26:4 (1963), pp. 422–435.

Ritchie, Benbow, "An Essential Unpredictability in Human Behavior," in Benjamin Wolman and Ernest Nagel, ed. *Scientific Psychology: Principles and Approaches*. New York: Basic Books, Inc., 1965.

Scott, John Finley (A critique of lab research cited by Bob Leik)

Simon, Herbert, "The Logic of Heuristic Decision Making," in Nicholas Rescher, ed. *The Logic of Decision and Action*. Pittsburgh: University of Pittsburgh Press, 1967.

Tumin, Melvin, "On Inequality." *Am. Soc. Rev.* (February 1963).

Winch, R. F. and Campbell, D. T., "Proof? No! Evidence? Yes! The Significance of Significance Tests." *Am. Soc.* Vol. 4:2 (May 1969), pp. 140–143.

Experimental Family Sociology

MORRIS ZELDITCH, JR.

For many sociologists the idea of an experimental family sociology is justified by two assumptions: One is that the nuclear family is a small face-to-face group and small face-to-face groups are what experimental sociology properly studies. From this assumption one concludes that it is more natural to equate what takes place in laboratory groups with families than it is with armies, factories, or universities. The other is that the natural family is sufficiently small that it may be brought directly into the laboratory in a way that a factory, or an army, or a university cannot. From this assumption one concludes that laboratory families are natural groups that may be equated with families in natural settings.

I think both assumptions are wrong. Furthermore, they miss the point of what takes place in the laboratory. From this fact I would not draw the conclusion that no experimental family sociology is possible, but rather that it must be put on a different basis. It is the purpose of the present paper to explore just what this different basis ought to be.

THE SOCIAL STRUCTURE OF LABORATORY GROUPS

The typical laboratory group is a small, ad hoc, face-to-face group, the interaction of which is of short duration, the task of which is minimally involving, the social structure of which is simple. The members depend on each other for very little, they have neither a past nor a future together, and their interaction is neither very intimate nor very deep. Mills' three-person groups are a good illustration; good in part because, as we will see, it has occurred to someone to see if the results are generalizable to families.

144 student volunteers were recruited through the Harvard Student Employment Service to participate in 48 three-person discussion sessions. Subjects (S's) had not previously interacted with one another and there were no obvious visible status

55

differences between them. Each group performed for two sessions, each lasting 30 minutes, a task in which they were asked to create a single dramatic story about 3 TAT cards. All the groups were observed from behind a one-way mirror and their interaction recorded according to Bales Interaction Process Analysis (IPA). Their interaction scores showed, first, who initiated an action and to whom it was directed; second, it indicated the relevance of the act either to the solution of the group task or to the state of integration of the group; and third, it was able to show how many unit-acts each person contributed. (Mills, 1953.)

It was thought at first that the results of such observations could be directly equated with what takes place in families. This assumption was soon found to be wrong. Strodtbeck, for example, replicated Mills' research with families but did not find the same regularities in the distribution of power and support that Mills had found. Nor has Leik (1963), more recently, found it possible to replicate the results of Bales research on role differentiation (Bales and Slater, 1955; Zelditch, 1955), results based on very similar sorts of laboratory groups.

It is possible to argue that the reason why we are unable to equate the results of laboratory groups with results obtained in families is that the structure of the family is so different. Families have stable structures, with both a past and a future. They are organized around differences in age and sex. Their interaction is intimate, involving. Their activities, concerning, as they do, sex, status, and economy, are meaningful, important, and the members of the family are dependent on them for the satisfaction of deeply felt needs. In all these ways families are very different from the typical laboratory group. But if we push this argument far enough, we will end by wondering just what the purpose of the laboratory group can be. For the truth is that laboratory groups differ not only from families, but from *all* natural social groups. Are Mills' groups more like college peer groups than they are like families? They are not. Peer groups are no more ad hoc, traditionless, short in duration, neutral in interaction, set down in meaningless settings to perform silly tasks than families.

Laboratory groups, we will find if we compare enough examples, are not like *any* natural social group whatever. But if they are not like any social group whatever, just what *are* they? We will find that their principal purpose is simplicity: *Hence laboratory groups are groups that reproduce social process in simplified forms.* I do not mean by this that the social structure of laboratory groups is necessarily simple in a sociological sense. Laboratory groups can, if desired, be made very complex in the sense that they can be given many levels of authority, many social strata, or many subunits of organization (Hopkins and Zelditch, 1961; Zelditch and Evan, 1962; Zelditch, 1968). Rather, what simplicity means in the present context is simplicity of the *process* reproduced in the laboratory; or more exactly, simplicity in the number of *aspects* of a social situation produced in the laboratory. Compared to any natural social situation, what the laboratory reproduces is only selected aspects of the real world. In particular it produces just those aspects relevant to some particular theoretical formulation. What we will want to see, therefore, is just why laboratory groups should be simplifications; and how, if they are, such simplifications can be made to say anything about more complicated natural settings.

WHY EXPERIMENTS SIMPLIFY

I suppose that most people's notion of an experiment is roughly this: There are two groups, an experimental group and a control group, that are alike in all relevant respects save one; the only difference is in something that the experimenter (E) has done to the experimental group. If what E has done has any effect on the experimental group that is not also found in the control group, the effect must be attributed to E's manipulation since in no other way do the two groups differ. The whole purpose of the design is to rule out what are otherwise plausible rival hypotheses that might account for the effect found in the experimental group, by showing that no similar effect has occurred in the control group.

I do not claim that this notion of an experiment is wrong, but there are many experiments which it does not adequately describe. For example, notice how control is obtained in the following experiment:

> A number of S's are exposed to two video tapes, one of which shows the behavior of an 18-month old girl, the other of which shows the behavior of an 18-month old boy. S's are required to describe the behavior of the two children in terms of a semantic differential using such adjectives as "aggressive," "soft," and so on. Careful pretesting has shown that without instruction S's are about as likely to call the first tape a boy and the second a girl as they are to identify the sexes correctly; for the two tapes are not readily differentiated by sex. It is possible, therefore, for E to instruct half the S's that the first tape is a boy and the second a girl, and half the S's that the first tape is a girl and the second a boy. (Meyer and Sobieszek, 1969.)

The purpose of this experiment is obviously to eliminate actual sex differences as an explanation of any differences that are found in how S's describe the behavior of the two children. I do not know which group you will want to call the control group; but in any case, this would be beside the point. What is really going on is that the experimenters have *simplified* the situation by comparison with the natural setting in which sex-typing is observed. By *simplification* here, I mean that something that typically takes place in a natural setting is prevented from taking place in the experiment; the experimenters do not allow *all* the factors that operate in the natural setting to operate in the experiment. We may say that what takes place in the experiment is something *artificial*, something that does not normally take place; and all the objections to artificiality in experiments are justified in claiming that what happens in experiments is not what happens in natural situations, for that is precisely why experiments are designed. They do not *intend* that what occurs should be natural.

The aim of simplification in the Meyer-Sobieszek experiment is to exercise control over the several possible interpretations that might be made of it. But there are other reasons for simplification. The first is that, given some process, say ϕ, our theory of this process may involve a fairly complicated causal system, such as:

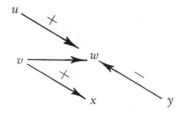

Given a causal system this complicated in structure, we will usually want to vary one or only a few circumstances at a time in order to answer such questions as: (1) Is there, in fact, any regularity in the behavior of w if the obscuring effect of y is removed? (2) If there is, is there any real effect of x on w, or is their observed correlation due only to the fact that both x and w are independently associated with v? (3) If it is v, and not x, that is associated with w, to what degree does u also have an effect on w, independent of the effect of v?

What does it mean to vary one circumstance at a time? It means that to answer the second question, for example, I would hold constant the effects of y, v, and u, allowing only x to vary. To accomplish this, incidentally, I would not need an experiment if there were a sufficient variety of natural settings and the variables had sufficiently slight correlations; but very often the variety is insufficient, or the correlations sufficiently high, that an experiment is required to fully achieve the necessary control and simplicity. The simplicity here lies in the fact that only one of the circumstances is varied at a time, whereas in natural settings the entire system is free to vary at will.

Though the causal system ϕ is complicated enough, it is not nearly as complicated as even the simplest natural setting. Most of the phenomena we actually observe in the "real world" are complex products of several different processes that join, in a particular setting, to produce a complex effect. To establish vocabulary, I will say that if ϕ alone is observed, the process is *unitary*; whereas if ϕ combines with θ, . . . , the process is *complex*. Now the main difficulty with complex processes, as opposed to unitary ones, is that they are not regular. Or perhaps more exactly, their regularity is very narrowly circumscribed, so that they are not in *general* regular. The combination of two or more processes produces an effect that, if sought in other situations, is sometimes found, sometimes not. Often the behavior of one of the processes is such as to markedly obscure the behavior of the other, so that when we think we are looking at ϕ in another setting what we see is so different as to confuse, cloud, and contradict all we thought we knew about it.

A good illustration is the problem of role-differentiation. In groups such as we mentioned on page 55, which are essentially the same as those used by Bales, it is found that members tend to specialize in either task or social-emotional roles (Bales and Slater, 1955). This finding depends on the observation that the task leader is usually not the best-liked man in the group, although he is the person who contributes most, is thought to have the best ideas, does most to guide the group, and is talked to by others the most. When other investigators generalize the results of this laboratory investigation, they look for the same sort of pattern, for example, in families (compare Zelditch, 1955). But the process of role differentiation is not at all a regular one; in part, of course, because the conditions necessary to produce it vary in different kinds of natural settings, but also because there are actually two processes going on at the same time in Bales' groups. One is a process by which expectations about relative competence are formed and come to determine the distribution of participation, the evaluations made of particular contributions to the task, and the distribution of influence. This is the process, I believe, that Bales thought he was studying. The other is a process of resistance, strain, and status struggle (Heinecke and Bales, 1953) that is caused by the fact that initially the participants are alike in status, creating an expectation that they should be alike in competence, which, as differentiation begins to take place, makes for an imbalance between initial expectations and the internal structure actually emerging in the group. The hostility to the leader that Bales used as a mark of differentiation is actually produced not by the expectation process but by the imbalance process. Hence it is not always found when the expectation process is studied; for example, it is not found by Hurwitz, Zander, and Hymovitch:

> Discussion groups are formed of mental health specialists who, although they are strangers to each other, do know how much expert knowledge they expect to be associated with doctors as distinct from nurses and social workers, and who know the personal reputations of some of the "experts" who participate. The usual results are found with respect to who becomes task leader, and how this affects the distribution of participation and influence. But the task leader is also found to be best-liked man. (Hurwitz, Zander, and Hymovitch, 1953.)

In these groups, expectations are determined by pre-existing status differences, and what occurs in the discussion groups, is in balance with prior expectations. Hence no status struggle is found.

Thus, Bales and Slater (and Zelditch) sent everyone off after a red herring. Or, if you prefer more dignified language, the process they described will not replicate with any very high degree of generality. It will occur very regularly under just those circumstances in which balance and expectation processes combine in the same way as they did in Bales' laboratory; but these are rather special circumstances, and they do not regularly recur. To investigate a process that *is* general, it is necessary to isolate a *unitary* process, for at least in a unitary process the *same* factors are operating all the time. But to isolate a unitary process typically requires a high degree of simplification by comparison with any natural setting.

The desire to investigate unitary processes is the second reason for simplicity in experiment, though it is evident, from my choice of example, that even experiments may fail to be sufficiently simple. I am not claiming that all experiments are simple, for they are not; I am claiming, rather, that they *aim* at simplicity, and that experiments offer the *possibility* of simplicity where natural settings typically do not. Another experiment that did not in fact achieve simplicity is the Lippitt-White experiments on authoritarian leadership—again an experiment that has had a good deal of impact on thinking about such things as authority and permissiveness in the family. From the Lippitt experiments one might draw the conclusion that "authoritarian" leadership disrupts both groups and individuals. What authoritarian leadership meant was directiveness, aloofness, capricious reward, and circumscribed knowledge of future plans (Lippitt, 1939). Thus, it was not one variable but four. I think many people supposed that the results were produced by, and authoritarianism equivalent to, directiveness. But in fact the results could equally well have been produced by capriciousness of reward, and whatever effect might have been due to directiveness would have been obscured by the peculiar reward process of the experiment. Only if the same particular conjunction of processes is repeated will there be the same effects; and I, for one, do not believe that the particular circumstances of the Lippitt experiment are very general.

Thus, the regularity, generality, and explanatory power of some theory T will be less if it is formulated to explain a complex process $\phi + \theta$ than if it is formulated to describe ϕ or θ alone. Therefore it is the aim of an investigator who wants power, generality, and regularity to simplify complex processes, which in turn requires that his experiments simplify what takes place in natural settings. What he finds will clearly not be like the behavior of ϕ in *any* natural setting; but he will have a more general knowledge of ϕ than he would find by any other method.

GENERALIZATION FROM EXPERIMENT

If simplicity is the aim of experiments and no laboratory group is like any natural group, how can the results of experiment be used? How is the gap between experiment and natural setting to be bridged? I think most sociologists believe that what one does is to "generalize" from experiments to those natural situations which appear to be similar. But one does not generalize in this way, and in any case what sociologists generalize from experiments is usually the wrong result. For example, Strodtbeck designed a careful and inventive experiment to determine whether Mills' findings on power in three-person, ad hoc groups would generalize to families. His purpose is clear enough, for he says that:

". . . our results should contribute to the understanding of the extent to which propositions concerning ad hoc three-person groups may be extended to family groups. . . ." (Strodtbeck, 1953, 23–4.)

He found that they did not. But no experiment can be generalized in this particular sense. What he is saying is that he wishes to test the truth of an expression having the form:

(1)   "If *F* is a family, then *y* will be true."

And this expression is not and can never be the result of any experiment, or for that matter of any other scientific investigation. I do not say that sociologists, and perhaps others, do not often make claims of this sort. How often do we hear that the result of Sherif's autokinetic experiment is that "people tend to form norms"; or that Asch found that "people conform to majorities." But the fact that it is often heard does not justify an elementary logical fallacy.

What is wrong with (1) is that the antecedent contains, not a variable or a set of variables, but a concrete entity. But generalizations are not made in terms of concrete entities. Generalization of any kind has two important properties. First, it is conditional; that is, it is based on expressions such as

(2)   Given *u, v, w*: if *x*, then *y*.

Second, the terms *u, v, w,* . . . that appear in expressions such as (2) are *all* variables. One cannot generalize to *entities*, hospitals, armies, or families, but only to variables or *aspects* of concrete things, influence, differentiation, or participation. We may suppose that when we say "family" we mean some list of properties possessed by families, but no such list is agreed on; and furthermore it is, it must in the nature of the case be, an infinite list. And no logical deductions are possible either to or from infinite lists.

The fact that generalization is both conditional and abstract sometimes makes strange bedfellows. For example, Leik has performed an experiment in some ways like Strodtbeck's, and with much the same purpose.

> Nine 3-person families are brought into an observation room much like Bales' laboratory, given a decision-making task, and observed from behind a one-way mirror using Bales' IPA. Each family consists of a father, mother, and teenage daughter. The 27 S's are arranged not only in family groups, but also in two other kinds of group: They are reconstituted in ad hoc, homogeneous groups (e.g. 3 mothers or 3 fathers or 3 daughters) and in ad hoc, differentiated groups (e.g. a father from one family, a mother from a second, a daughter from a third would form each of the groups). (Leik, 1963.)

Leik compared his results with those of Bales, and concluded that sex role differentiation was *least* likely to occur in families. From this, in turn, he concluded, or strongly implied, that results of small groups research are not generalizable to "families." But in fact I propose to compare them to findings of groups even more different than Bales'; for the Leik experiment is in my view both clever and informative, but not about Bales.

The experiment I want to "equate" with Leik's is the following experiment by Moore:

> Two junior college girls are seated on either side of an opaque partition, each under the impression that the other is from a four-year college of higher status that is in the same neighborhood as their own college. Projected on a screen in front of them is a consecutive series of 38 large rectangles, each composed of 100 smaller black and white rectangles in varying arrangements. Every rectangle contains about the same number of black and white rectangles, but the girls are to decide, for each slide, whether it has more black or more white rectangles.

Each S makes an initial decision, exchanges opinions with the other, and then makes a final decision at each repetition of the stimulus. The exchange of opinions is controlled by the experimenter: in front of each S there is a console of switches and lights that permits one S to operate a switch on his own console that flashes a light indicating S's choice on the console of the other S. The circuit passes through a master control panel, permitting E to arrange any desired pattern of agreement or disagreement between S's. If the two are made to disagree, each S must then either change his initial opinion or stay with it in his final decision. Whether S changes or not is the measure of influence in the experiment. The S's, instead of being led to believe that the other is from the four year college may be led to believe that the other is from a local high school. (Moore, 1968.)

The purpose of Moore's experiment is to show how status characteristics determine expectations of relative competence that, in turn, determine influence in interaction. For what is found is that the S's defer to their partner when they believe the partner to be of higher status, but ignore the opinion of the partner when they believe the partner to be of lower status. This effect will only occur if the status characteristic used is associated with stereotypes and evaluations that are diffuse, if there is no other knowledge of the partner, and if S's are intent on making the right decision (compare Berger and others, 1966). To equate Leik's experiment with Moore's, what we look for is a similarity in variables, not entities. We find that the relevant variables are present in Leik's experiment, for there are status characteristics (age and sex), there is a measure of influence, there is a decision-making task, and where the initial conditions are the same as in the ad hoc-differentiated condition, the results are the same. What is particularly informative is that where one of the conditions is relaxed, that is, where the S's do have a good deal of prior personal knowledge of each other as in families, the effect disappears.

Thus, generalization from one instance to another, whether from an experiment or not involves, first showing that the variables in the second instance are the same variables as found in the first, and second showing that the initial conditions in the two instances are the same. If these two requirements are satisfied, a proposition true in the first instance is true in the second. But now we must face the fact that the very purpose of experiments often leads us to establish conditions that are seldom found in natural situations. Our view of generalization, consequently, appears to put us in the position of confessing that there is no possibility of generalizing from experiment.

In one sense, this is precisely what I mean to say: Very seldom do we generalize *directly* from a particular experiment to some particular event in a natural setting. The fact is that experiments are typically performed to be informative about some theoretical formulation, say T. They deform the world, simplify it, manipulate it for the purpose of discovering how some variable in T behaves. Usually at any particular time it is only *part* of T that is being investigated, one variable is studied while others are held constant. It therefore requires not one, but a whole program of experiments to establish T, to understand the process T is designed to explain. To what any single experiment is relevant, therefore, is some proposition in a theoretical formulation such as T. It is the *theory* that is relevant to natural settings. The purpose of the theory is to embody a system of principles that will explain what happens when applied to particular kinds of events. If an experiment serves its purpose, therefore, it is no objection to it that the conditions found in the experiment are not found in many natural settings, *providing* it is informative for a theory *and* the theory itself is of some use. For what generalization comes down to is this: If the theory T is applicable in natural setting S, it will tell us what ought to happen given the kinds of conditions found in S. Therefore, the bridge over the gap between experiments and natural setting is theory; and if we do not and cannot very often generalize *directly* from an experiment to a natural setting, we can do so *indirectly* by making an experiment informative for T and making T sufficiently powerful to explain what is taking place in some natural setting.

LABORATORY FAMILIES

Even if families are not small groups, even if small groups are in any case not what experiments are about, could we not base our confidence in an experimental family sociology on the fact that the family is one of the few social institutions that can be brought intact into the laboratory? And if we can, the realism of the laboratory family is very appealing, for surely here is one case where we *can* directly generalize what takes place in the laboratory to "families" outside it.

But the laboratory family is not the family in its natural state. It is unnatural partly because any experiment involves structures and events that are never found in natural families and partly because even the laboratory family is a simplification compared to the family in its natural setting.

The capacity to experiment depends on a particular kind of social structure, usually on the professor-student relation, sometimes on the doctor-patient relationship, but always on some sort of authority structure in which the "scientist" has power over the subject. This social structure produces effects that are not found in "natural settings." (Compare Orne, 1962.) Furthermore, the setting of any experiment is bound in many ways to appear strange. The task, the measurement procedures, the whole apparatus is almost always sufficiently peculiar that one must suppose any experiment to include a process of conjecture, hypothesis testing, and fantasy about what is taking place that would not occur in a more natural setting. Any laboratory, therefore, is a *reactive* setting in Campbell's sense of that term (compare Webb and others, 1966), and what occurs in it cannot be supposed to be natural, no matter how "natural" the social group *in* it may be.

But the laboratory is not only reactive, it is also a simplification of the family's more natural setting. For a "home" is a system of symbolic "place" cues that define the appropriate occasions for various sorts of social relations. The "place" cues of a laboratory are almost always different, and the culture of the family in the laboratory cannot, therefore, be thought of as complete and whole. Some part of its culture is left at "home."

From the fact that the laboratory is not natural, and the laboratory family a simplification, it follows that we are in the same position with the laboratory family as with experiments generally. To generalize from the laboratory family we must think of it as a simplified system; we must think carefully about the conditions under which its interaction has taken place; we must generalize not to entities, such as families, but to variables such as influence and participation. And above all, there is no avoiding the fact that, even though we have the right sort of "entities" in the laboratory, generalization from them requires some sort of bridge; and that bridge is still some abstract and general theoretical formulation. Thus, generalization is no less conditional and abstract, the social arrangements of the laboratory are no less unnatural, and we are no less dependent on theory to give meaning to what takes place in the laboratory than we were before.

Furthermore, the laboratory family encourages weaknesses of design and research strategy that are not encouraged by the experiment generally. These are of three kinds: First, with the laboratory family we very often measure rather than manipulate the independent variable of the experiment. If we are interested in rigidity of structure, we do not manipulate rigidity in the laboratory, we bring in some rigid and some nonrigid families and compare them. This has some advantages from the point of view of our capacity to study rigidity, for it permits a precision of measurement and control over conditions that should assure greater regularity of replications, if anything is there to be regular, than if the same variable were studied outside the laboratory. Still, there is no getting away from the fact that this is not a fully experimental design. Instead we have what Campbell and Stanley correctly call a "quasi-experiment." (See Campbell and Stanley, 1963.) A fully experimental design requires the random allocation of treatments to subjects. Randomization assures that relevant but unknown variables normally confounded with the experiment's independent variable will, in repeated experiments of the same sort, have an expected covariance with the independent variable of zero. But quasi-experiments do not permit the random allocation of treatments to subjects, for what we have done is to take advantage of the value of the independent variable the family naturally possesses. Nor is it a simple matter to repair the damage done, for example, by matching experimental and control groups on relevant, known variables. Not only is there still the problem of relevant but *unknown* variables; there is also the fact that matching often produces regression artifacts that cloud the interpretation of the experiment (Thorndike, 1942; Campbell and Stanley, 1963). You will be aware of the fact that if a group is tested twice with respect to some variable, on the second test some individuals will be found to "regress toward the mean." What is important is that they regress towards their *own* population mean. If all S's are drawn from one population, this presents no problem; but if they are not, matching will not succeed in equating experimental and control group. For example, in the Moore experiment on status and influence, a different, and at first sight more natural, design would be to use junior college and four-year college S's in pairs. This would eliminate the deception required to persuade S that her partner was of higher or lower status, thus eliminating, among other things, the partitions and a rather elaborate reception process. Of course, there may be intelligence differences in the two populations, so it would be necessary to match pairs by IQ. If in fact there were IQ differences between the two populations, this would mean matching some of the lower IQ's of the four-year college with some of the higher IQ's of the junior college. After the experiment there would be a noticeable effect; but it could as well have been brought about by regression as by the experimental variables, for the four-year college S's would regress towards a *higher* mean IQ while the junior college S's would regress towards a *lower* mean IQ, and intelligence might well be a plausible rival hypothesis to account for the differences in the Moore experiment. As a matter of fact, I have some doubts that the two colleges are actually that different in IQ; nevertheless, it might be hard to convince anyone disposed to doubt the results of the experiment.

Second, even though the laboratory family is simplified by comparison with any natural family, it is still complex compared to a pure laboratory group. The family brings with it into the laboratory a history, a culture, a social structure that is not under the experimenter's control. Not only does this encourage a weakness in experimental design in the technical sense, it also means too many things are going on about which the experimenter is ignorant; and some of these things may be relevant to his investigation. From the point of view of sheer realism, for example, the best possible family experiment is one like Strodtbeck's (1954) study of three-person families, in which every family was visited in its own home. I have remarked already on his interest in Mills' results with three-person ad hoc groups, but Strodtbeck had another interest as well, he was interested in talent (see Strodtbeck, 1958). He therefore used a very elaborate counterbalanced design in which Jewish families were compared to Italian families. At the same time, SES and achievement of the son were controlled with 48 families being distributed in the following manner:

	Jewish families		Italian families	
	Over-achieving sons	Under-achieving sons	Over-achieving sons	Under-achieving sons
High SES	4	4	4	4
Medium SES	4	4	4	4
Low SES	4	4	4	4

(SOURCE: Strodtbeck, 1958, p. 160)

This is not an experimental design, since there is no possibility of allocating S's to an appropriate cell by any random process; but what is more important, this is, from the point of view of simplicity, no better than we would have been able to do in a survey. Its real advantage, and it is an advantage that I would not at all like to belittle, is from the point of view of the measurement of the dependent variable. Strodtbeck is able to look at actual behavior—he can do so in a very precise manner—and the conditions of measurement are under fairly secure control. Nevertheless, he cannot eliminate any of the many possible processes that might affect the process in which he is mainly interested. They will all operate simultaneously to produce whatever effect he observes, and he therefore is observing a very complex process. The elaborate counter-balancing does nothing to simplify what takes place, and the result can only be of very limited generality from the point of view of our understanding of talent and its use.

Finally, in those cases where the process of interest *is* in fact general (for example, decision-making) the desire to study it through laboratory families will often lead to *lateral* accumulation of results rather than real accumulation of knowledge. By *lateral accumulation* I mean the repetition of a finding in various kinds of entities or concrete situations, as opposed to finding out something new about how the variables involved are related to each other. If there is a general body of studies about decision-making, for example, there is very little point in embarking on a large program of research designed to discover all over again the same things for families. Of course, the objective might be more sophisticated, it might be to show that something about families brings about a difference in the way decisions are made; but it is still not a matter of studying "how families decide" as opposed to other concrete entities. What will matter is just *what* it is about families that produces a difference; and unless it is completely impossible as a practical matter, the optimum research strategy is still to try to produce the relevant abstract variable in a pure laboratory group rather than studying laboratory families for themselves. What matters, again, are the variables not the entities, and how they are related to each other. It does little or no good to discover that somehow or other families behave differently if we have no idea *why* they do.

Given such weaknesses, the use of the laboratory family would seem to be a costly strategy. Whether or not one used them would seem to depend on whether or not there were some compensating gains. Whether or not there are compensating gains, in turn, depends a good deal on the attitude one takes to the subject matter of "family sociology." Two views are possible about this subject. One is that "the family" is a concrete entity, like shoes, automobiles, or airplanes. It labels a long list of properties, many of which are organizable into systems of variables to some degree independent of each other (as the theory of motion that describes a suicide jumping off the Golden Gate Bridge is independent of the theory of motivation that explains why he did it). The other view is that the family can be expressed as an *abstract* entity, like an electromagnetic field or an adiabatic gas. It is therefore the subject of a particular system of abstract variables attributed to this class of systems and not to others. It would therefore be the subject of a unique theoretical formu-lation. Put a little oversimply, the question is: Is "the family" an automobile or a system of mechanics? My own view is that the family is a concrete entity, a domain of application of many fairly distinct, more general theories—such as a theory of power, a theory of socialization, a theory of solidarity, and so on endlessly. If I am right about this—and I readily admit there are grounds to dispute it—the costs of the laboratory family are not compensated by much in the way of gains.

Nevertheless, the issue is not wholly decided by one's attitude towards the existence of a body of specifically family theory, for there are at least three occasions for the use of laboratory families even if there is no such theory. The first is that even where the variables themselves are general, the family may in some cases constitute a unique combination of circumstances not found in other social situations. This is not the same as saying there is a unique class of abstract systems called "families" requiring a special theoretical formulation true only of such systems. The variables themselves are all general, true of other kinds of social relations and situations, and even the relations among the variables are true in any sort of social situation. But it is still possible that the combinations of states that interests us occurs only in families. The Bateson double-bind situation is a rather good illustration. Notice that the variables are rather general: multiple levels of communication, contradictions between levels, dependency, constraints on leaving the field, constraints on talking about the contradiction. But in the family these combine in a peculiar way. Perhaps only in the family is the person to whom the communication is directed capable of being so dependent, the guilts associated with contradictions in message so great that it is unbearably threatening to point out the discrepancy; or is it so difficult for the person caught in the bind to leave the situation. The study of this situation would therefore seem to require laboratory families, if it is to be studied experimentally at all.

Second, though considerably more trivial, there may be occasions where we doubt that some theory is applicable to families; that is, theory T may be well-formulated and quite general, but it may be doubtful that families are the kind of social system to which T applies. Are families really the sort of system in which resources are distributed, in which power strategies are used, in which people are made (because of their needs) to do things they don't want to do? Had there never been a theory specifically of *family* power we might regard it as a demonstration of the applicability of a power theory to show by experiment that there are power processes in families. For this purpose we would require laboratory families.

Third, there is no point in pretending that theories are always well-formulated, definite, and complete, or their variables always clearly general *ab initio*. And if they are not, the way in which the variables ought to be formulated, and just which ones we ought to omit, hold constant, or isolate in simplifying concrete situations are often unclear. When this is the case, we often must rely on quite concrete entities and study quite complex processes, hoping gradually to simplify them. In the meantime, because of our choice of a particularly strategic concrete entity we hope that nothing very important is being left out. Thus, in the early phases of formulation of a theory of vicarious learning, of identification with models and learning from them, we would probably choose to study this process in a family setting. The importance of power in socializing agents, the relative unimportance of nurturance, the way in which cross-sex identification operates, the role of attention to the same versus the opposite sex, and other such variables would be comparatively unclear, though it would be fairly plausible that whatever they are they are bound to be true of families, and families bound to be an instance of the process. (See Bandura and Huston, 1960; Bandura, Ross, and Ross, 1963; Bandura and Walters, 1963.) Families might therefore be good groups in which to begin exploring such problems, and it should not be supposed that exploratory research is always observational while verification is always experimental. The replication of a process under constant conditions, assured only in laboratories, is useful in discovering regularities and even in defining phenomena that need to be explained, even where processes may not be unitary and variables unclear or confounded.

WOULDN'T REALISM BE AN ADVANTAGE?

The previous section argued that we were in no better position using laboratory families than using ad hoc laboratory groups in constructing an experimental family sociology because even the laboratory family is to some degree unreal and simplified. Hence we cannot directly equate results obtained from laboratory families with the properties of nonlaboratory families. Furthermore, though laboratory families are simple and unreal they are not simple and unreal *enough*, so that their use often commits us to technical weaknesses of design and makes more difficult the isolation of unitary processes. Hence they are strategically optimal only in special circumstances, though such circumstances do arise in practice.

This argument, which is an argument about the virtues and costs of realism in family experiments, depends on an important assumption: Not *all* the properties of a family are relevant to the theory T that it is the purpose of our experiments to investigate. List L of variables true of any entity has two fundamental properties: One is that L is infinite. Given any list L there is at least one property that can be added to the list, no matter how long L is. The demonstration is simple if one keeps in mind that even the properties that the entity does not possess count as properties of the entity; for example, that a family is not a community is a property of a family. The other important property of list L is that some of its variables are independent of the others. For example, from the point of view of the process ϕ the list is divisible into two parts: properties relevant to ϕ and properties not relevant to ϕ. The two parts are independent, for if any property *were* relevant to ϕ it would be in the first class. And in general the second class is nonempty. Thus, to power in family decision-making it may make a difference that the husband in the

Smith family is a lawyer, that his wife is a clerical worker, that the husband contributes $20,000 to the family income while the wife contributes $8,000, that the couple has two children who are 13 and 16 years old, that the wife has a weak ego requiring a good deal of support and that the husband is capable of giving such support, that the wife's family is wealthy while the husband's is not, but the husband's family had rather cultivated tastes while the wife's family was rather vulgar, and perhaps many more. But there are some facts that are irrelevant. The wife's mother is deaf, the husband's cousins are all quite tall, the husband and wife were both born in the same town in which they now live, the husband has twice as many cousins as the wife, they have a large circle of friends, their baby sitter, when they had one, lived a block away, . . .

If not all properties of families are relevant to the process that our experiment is designed to investigate, there is no reason to argue that the realism of laboratory families is an advantage to experimental family sociology. What matters is that experiments be able to reproduce the variables in theory T, not that it be able to reproduce the variables in list L. Thus the entities in experiments may be quite unlike families in appearance and still be relevant to family sociology.

It will sometimes be objected that families and only families possess some condition c, and c is relevant to T. There is no rebuttal to such an objection, except to note that what matters is not so much that only families possess c, but that c is relevant to T. For the objection that families and only families possess condition c is no objection to the use of unreal entities in laboratories if c is irrelevant. Of course, the objection can be turned on end to show that in certain circumstances we *must* use laboratory families: If c is relevant to T and is found only in families, then as a practical matter, realism is required by any laboratory investigation of T.

But the objection that c is found only in families should be regarded with some suspicion; for often the objection is a consequence of confusing a general variable with its particular instances. Thus, families may be regarded from the point of view of husband's or wife's occupation, income, age, and so on, and these variables may be difficult to reproduce in laboratory groups though they are evidently relevant to family decision-making. It does not follow that either we use laboratory families or we give up studies of family decision-making in the laboratory. The reason why income, occupation, age, and so forth, are relevant to family decision-making, so far as we now understand the process, is that they affect the distribution of resources in the family and determine the expectations its members have about relative abilities. If income, occupation, and age differences are difficult to reproduce in the laboratory, resources and expectations are not. By manipulating them in the laboratory, the *instances* of the variables may differ, but the same process may be made to occur. Obviously it is the way the process works that interests us, not the behavior of the particular instances of the variables.

Thus, it may be argued that as a practical matter some variables can be produced only by using laboratory families; but *in general*, realism in the laboratory is no virtue.

WHAT BASIS IS THERE FOR AN EXPERIMENTAL FAMILY SOCIOLOGY?

My main argument is that one cannot directly equate what takes place in laboratory groups with what takes place in natural families. What the laboratory does is to isolate and simplify some phenomenon for study. What it is relevant to is some theoretical formulation of that phenomenon. Its purpose is to confirm, disconfirm, modify, elaborate, or in some manner provide information about that formulation, and this is the most that it can be made to do. The argument is the same whether the laboratory group is an actual family or not. In either case, if the experiment is to say something about families it does so only indirectly; it is the theory, not the experiment, that says whatever it is necessary to say.

The basis of an experimental family sociology, therefore, is neither that the family is a small group, small groups being what experiments are about, nor that families are small enough to be brought into the laboratory in their natural state. Families are not small groups, small groups are not what experiments are about, and laboratory families are not in their natural state. With all three assumptions the basic difficulty lies in thinking in terms of *entities* (such as families, peer groups, army platoons, air crews) rather than *variables* (such as participation, resources, rigidity, or dependency). The basis of an experimental family sociology can be made unassailable only if states of the *variables* relevant to some theory, T, can be produced in the laboratory; if producing them there provides us with better evidence about T than we can obtain by other methods, and if T is applicable, among other things, to families. This foundation will support an experimental family sociology even though no laboratory group, even a laboratory family, is like the family in its natural state. The logic makes the experiment relevant to families, not directly but indirectly; the experiment is relevant to some theory, the theory is relevant to families, and because of the logical link provided by the theory, the experiment is relevant to families.

If we build on this foundation, we appear also to solve an important question of strategy: Is it better to use laboratory families or not? The argument claims that there is no logical reason to prefer the laboratory family. This is reassuring in the face of the technical weaknesses of the family in the laboratory, most important of which is its complexity. But there are two circumstances where the argument fails to hold. First, it may be that some value of one or more variables in T are producible only in families, so that only families satisfy the requirements of a relevant experiment. Second, it may be that some variable is known to be relevant, but what values of it are relevant or how it is relevant, is not known; all that is known is that, whatever the variable, it is possessed by families. Laboratory families will, in such instances, assure us of not overlooking something of importance. In both circumstances I think it fair to say that the difficulties are practical in nature, and do not touch the basic logical issue, which is that laboratories do not exist to reproduce the world as it naturally is but to simplify it.

REFERENCES

Bales, R. F. and Slater, P., "Role Differentiation in Small, Decision-Making Groups," in T. Parsons and R. F. Bales, ed., *Family, Socialization and Interaction Process.* New York: The Free Press, 1955. Pp. 259–306.

Bandura, A. and Huston, A., "Identification As a Process of Incidental Learning." *Journal of Abnormal and Social Psychology*, Vol. 24:1–8 (1960).

Bandura, A., et al., "Vicarious Reinforcement and Imitative Learning." *Journal of Abnormal and Social Psychology*, Vol. 67:601–7 (1963).

Bandura, A., et al., *Social Learning and Personality Development.* New York: Holt, Rinehart and Winston, Inc., 1963.

Berger, J., et al., "Status Characteristics and Expectation States," in J. Berger, et al., ed., *Sociological Theories in Progress*, Vol. 1. Boston: Houghton Mifflin, 1966. Pp. 29–46.

Campbell, D. and Stanley, J., "Experimental and Quasi-Experimental Designs for Research," in N. Gage, ed., *Handbook of Research or Teaching.* Skokie, Ill.: Rand McNally & Co., 1963. Pp. 171–246.

Heinecke, C. and Bales, R. F., "Developmental Trends in the Structure of Small Groups," *Sociometry*, Vol. 16:7–38 (1953).

Hopkins, T. and Zelditch, M., "Experiments With Organizations," in A. Etzioni, ed., *Complex Organizations: A Sociological Reader*, 1st ed. New York: Holt, Rinehart and Winston, Inc., 1961. Pp. 465–478.

Hurwitz, J., et al., "Some Effects of Power on the Relations Among Group Members," in D. Cartwright and A. Zander, ed., *Group Dynamics.* Evanston, Ill.: Row, Peterson, 1953. Pp. 483–492.

Leik, R., "Instrumentality and Emotionality in Family Interaction," *Sociometry*, Vol. 26:131–145 (1963).

Lippitt, R., "Field Theory and Experiment in Social Psychology: Autocratic and Democratic Group Atmospheres," *American Journal of Sociology*, Vol. 45:26–49 (1939).

Meyer, J. and Sobieszek, B., Unpublished investigation in process, Stanford, Laboratory for Social Research, 1969.

Mills, T., "Power Relations in Three-Person Groups," *American Sociological Review*, Vol. 18:351–357 (1953).

Moore, J., "Status and Influence in Small Group Interactions," *Sociometry*, Vol. 31:47–63 (1968).

Orne, M., "On the Social Psychology of the Psychological Experiment: With Particular Reference to Demand Characteristics and Their Implications," *American Psychologist*, Vol. 17:776–783 (1962).

Strodtbeck, F., "Family Interaction, Values, and Achievement," in D. McClelland et al., ed., *Talent and Society.* Princeton, N.J.: D. Van Nostrand Co., Inc., 1958. Pp. 135–194.

Strodtbeck, F., "The Family As a Three-Person Group," *American Sociological Review*, Vol. 19:23–29 (1954).

Thorndike, R. L., "Regression Fallacies in the Matched Groups Experiment," *Psychometrika*, Vol. 7:85–102 (1942).

Webb, E., et al., *Unobtrusive Measures: Nonreactive Research in the Social Sciences.* Skokie, Ill.: Rand McNally & Co., 1966.

Zelditch, M., "Can You Really Study an Army in the Laboratory?" in A. Etzioni, ed., *Complex Organizations: A Sociological Reader,* 2d Ed. New York: Holt, Rinehart and Winston, Inc., 1968. Pp. 528–539.

Zelditch, M., "Role Differentiation in the Nuclear Family: A Comparative Study," in T. Parsons and R. F. Bales, ed., *Family, Socialization and Interaction Process.* New York: The Free Press, 1955. Pp. 307–352.

Zelditch, M. and Evan, W., "Simulated Bureaucracies: A Methodological Analysis," in H. Guetzkow, ed., *Simulation in Social Science.* Englewood Cliffs, N.J.: Prentice-Hall, Inc., 1962. Pp. 48–60.

CRITIQUE AND DISCUSSION

I assumed, when the invitation to write this paper was made, that I was expected to write a paper that would try to persuade sociologists who are suspicious about laboratory experiments that you can do sociologically interesting things in the laboratory; that we aren't confined to doing what is always known as "small groups research." I would like to go back and review a little bit the progressive development of this particular argument before I explain how it is that I got around to writing a somewhat different paper than I had intended.

To begin with, I became involved in doing organizational experiments largely as a consequence of a late luncheon argument one day. I couldn't see any reason at all why the idea of an experiment had to be confined to five or six subjects solving a problem, sitting around a table, talking directly to each other, and so forth, which was a conventional kind of decision-making experiment. Indeed, I felt that you could construct not only face-to-face groups, but something like an orga-nizational structure (for instance, an army) in the laboratory.

The problem that such experiments faced from the outset had to do with realism in experiments—how much should the thing you do in the laboratory look in all its detail like the behavior, the phenomenon, the organization, that you are trying to represent? I decided that it wasn't necessary to produce in a laboratory something which concretely looked in all its respects like an organization. All that was required was to produce those properties which, in some theory about the organizations, were regarded as relevant——things like the very large size of the organization didn't seem to enter——in significant ways ——into theories about organization. What people were concerned about was the complexity of structure. And I certainly could produce complexity of structure in the laboratory even if I didn't use 10,000 or 5,000 or even 200 people to do so.

So, insofar as it was complexity and not large size which was relevant,

I argued that I could produce it. The problem immediately arose——once you agree that it was only necessary to produce, in the laboratory, those variables which are relevant to a theory and that you don't need to produce every concrete feature of the organization that's being represented ——the problem arose, how do you go from what's in the experiment to what's in the natural setting. It became clear to me that the relationship between what goes on in the experiment and what goes on in natural settings is not a diadic or direct relationship where you go straight from the experiment to a natural setting, but it's a triadic relationship where the experiment is really relevant to your theoretical process, and your problem is to apply the theory that you have somehow verified or modified or created with this experiment in some natural setting.

But the problem is a little different when you think about the family. First, it struck me that people are much less suspicious about doing experiments with the family than they are about hospitals or armies. A lot of people think, you know, that it's really much simpler. Why? Well, first of all, the family is small enough to bring into the laboratory. Secondly, a family is a small discussion group in many of its aspects, so you should (many people feel) be able to equate what goes on in the lab groups with what goes on in the family.

That looked nice until I thought about it for a while and I decided that really those two justifications are wrong, or at least they are inconsistent with my previous thinking about the nature of experiments and their rela-

tionship to natural settings, especially with respect to the problem of simplification. As I got involved in more and more experiments, I became convinced that what was important about the experimental process was not control, which is what everybody talks about as the important thing in experiments, but the fact that you are simplifying the processes you are studying. You strip away more and more of the irrelevancies and the complications and the obscuring processes and get at the theoretical process that you are really concerned with studying.

So the problem, as I see it, is to find some rationale for the use of experimental methods in family sociology which does not depend on assuming that——if you bring a family into the lab, it is a real natural group and you can simply say what goes on there is what goes on in the real world; or, alternatively, that what goes on in small group labs is what goes on in families. The problem is not really that the family is not like a small group. Laboratory groups aren't like small groups either. The question of what is a small group is really irrelevant. The purpose of experiments is, in part, to simplify, somehow, a theoretical process and abstract it from other processes so that it can be produced in the laboratory. You don't generalize from experiments, rather you use experiments to be informative about theories and then your problem is to apply the theories to natural settings.

The problem then becomes the degree to which our theories about decision making in the family are unique to the family. My first reaction is that there is not, somehow, a unique theory of family decision making. There is a theory of decision making which, it seems to me, applies to the family—but it's not a theory of family decision making, which is somehow different. The only thing really characteristic of the family is the peculiar combination or configuration of all these properties together, as was mentioned this morning, which is very hard to reproduce in any group except in the family.

Well, isn't that a solution to the problem? The family is a natural group—an intact institution—so that you want to study it in the lab and analyze these configurations. Well, I don't believe you can say that, even though the group is a natural group, what you're producing in the lab is natural behavior. Nor is it true to say that you have brought the family intact into the laboratory, because actually you have simplified the situation. When we bring the family into the lab there are things left behind. There is a private culture of the family which I couldn't find words for, so I used the expression "place cues." These cues exist not only in certain social situations, but they're attributed to physical settings. When you are in a certain part of the house, like the living room, you know a certain kind of social relationship is supposed to be taking place. The home is, among other things, a symbolic structure of all of these socially-defined meaningful situations, all of which is left at home when you bring the family into a laboratory, so that in many ways you have simplified the culture of the family by bringing it into the laboratory.

But the real difficulty, I think, is the danger, created when you bring families into the laboratory, of starting to think concretely about the family. I think a statement which says "families do so and so" is really an inadequate expression, scientifically, of what we want to say. The family is a concrete entity—it has an enormous number of properties. We can talk about variables but we don't go around talking about "families," which are essentially concrete entities. We have to specify what it is about families that is theoretically relevant to the particular behavior that we are talking about. Furthermore, the use of laboratory families has weaknesses in design not shared by other kinds of experiments. With the family in the laboratory, we don't ordinarily, as we do in the classic experiment, allocate a treatment, or some kind of structural state, to the families randomly.

Now from a different angle, the thing that bothers me more is that ——even though I argue the laboratory family is simplified in comparison with the natural family——it's not simple enough. It's very difficult to separate out any particular process in which we might be interested. Too much is going on with families that we don't know about when we bring them into the lab. Nevertheless, in the paper, I have developed several occasions where we might want to use families in the lab.

Finally, underlying the whole argument is an issue which has nothing to do with the problem of laboratory research, but has to do rather with the question of: "What is the field of family sociology? What is the subject matter?" Is it an abstract theoretical discipline with a unique theory of its own, or is it simply a concrete domain to which you apply large numbers of theories which are more general? And, I guess the attitude you take toward that question has a lot to do with how you feel about the use of families in the laboratory.

HAMBLIN DISCUSSION

Having had something of history myself, both in family and in small group research as well as laboratory organizational research, I can appreciate very deeply the concerns to which Morris addressed himself. I would agree substantially with most of what he said except I agree with it less now than I did seven or eight years ago; and in part, because I have in that time gone through a change in thinking about experiments and about theory and about the field of social science. This change in thinking has made me something of a radical——But I'm radical for a reason and so I want to respond to this paper today in a number of ways. I want to make a couple of alternative suggestions—alternative ways of looking at the problem of experimentation and at the problem, in effect, of applied sociology.

I, for many years, did the kind of work that's been talked about thus far on this program; and in the last few years, I've become more and more applied in my orientation and I'd like to talk a little bit about some of the reasons for that. There was an indication of this in the exchange that I had with Dr. Bee earlier this morning over what we "ought to be studying." We were essentially talking about the problems of expertise. I think it's to the problem of expertise that we, as social scientists have a big responsibility. Somehow we have to come up with solutions to these problems.

There are two or three approaches to the study of man. One that seems to be predominant is that you study man as he is in his present environment. You come to your conclusions about him and his behavior and his problems and the behavior of the groups that he participates in by not disturbing the situation. You can learn a great deal about man this way: This morning Karl talked about a detective approach. I think the normal science approach is kind of a detective approach; but there's an alternative to the detective approach which is that of the inventor. What you do with this approach is create new systems. You create new conditions under which to put man and by pushing him into the unknown, you find out something about his operating characteristics that you didn't know before. Now as I see it, the value of an experiment is, in effect, to arm the social scientist with a series of cause and effect relationships so that he knows what to do to produce a particular effect, and that experiments of proper design test the causal assumptions in the theory. [Ed. note: At this point Professor Hamblin reviewed a number of experiments on academic achievement, representing 23 theories in all, none of which produced even "moderately" strong confirmation of the theory.]

Well, the point I wanted to make out of all of this is that here is field experimentation that's been done for almost fifty years in the field of education, adding up to almost no overall results, and the reason why is that there wasn't an inventive social scientist to tell the teachers what to do to produce an effect. The causal assumptions in all those theories were incorrect or extremely weak so that they didn't have any practical result——I've asked myself why, in those many comparisons, do you get those weak results? One reason is because the theories are weak.

The second reason may be because the experimental designs that they used were weak. Now, in most cases they used the typical laboratory design of an experiment with a control group, control by randomization. Elsewhere I've criticized this method as being a method which really violates good experimental procedure.

It violates the canons of constancy. In effect, you give up or surrender when you use this method. Since you can't equate, you can't hold constant, you do the next best thing and randomize differences. But in doing that, even if you have a powerful theory, the best you can come out with is about 15% or 20% explained variance, except in rare cases.

Now, my criticism of the theories that we ran over quickly is that all of them ignore the operating characteristics, at least as they're reflected in behavioral change and maintenance, of the learning mechanisms with which the human body is outfitted.

To give you an example of both of these things, I want to put one more slide on the screen and we'll focus first on the method and then on the results. These are the results of an experiment using what I consider to be one of the more radical designs—the A-B-A-B design—and this particular one uses what is called the "multiple base-line technique." Now, these designs are specifically to be used with an on-going group, one advantage is that you don't have to construct a group, you don't have to have fifty groups, you can do your study with one group. You can test the causal assumptions which is one of your purposes, and at the same time you can solve a problem. [Ed. note: the project introduced a "game" into a problem classroom during the "B" phases of the design, during both reading and math periods, with rather robust results.]

Now, with changes like that, you know that by putting in your game and taking it out again, you in effect produce these changes in behavior. Nothing else has changed——everything else has been constant. You don't have a Hawthorne effect because——remember in the Hawthorne studies when they did the reversal?——they took the thing out again but it didn't go back to what it was before, here it did. So that's behaved nicely the way it should. But to double-check, you use what is known as the multiple base-line approach. Behavior changes during the math period are similar to those during the reading periods.

This approach allows you to test your causal assumptions and to produce substantial effects. What you've got, in effect, is a teacher with a terrible problem, you've come in and analyzed the situation and recommended to her to behave in a certain way, and she solves her problem. But not only have you helped her solve her practical problem, you've also tested your theory at the same time, and that's the power in this kind of approach.

Now, what kind of a game? This comes from an experiment by some acquaintances of mine from Kansas City. What they did was to try to devise a game that was cheap. The game is essentially: that points are marked on a blackboard each time a member of one of two teams talked or was out of his seat without permission. The team with fewer points is excused for recess three minutes early and is given a half hour free study period at the end of the day. If both teams earn less than five points, both teams win.

It's a special case of a more general theory. If you want to change behavior, it's very easy to do so by structuring what I call a "positive exchange." The teacher gives the children something they want and they can earn it as often as they want and as frequently as they want if they, in turn, do something that she wants. It . . . has to be something that's worthwhile to them, and having a half hour free study period and going out to recess three minutes earlier apparently was enough.

Now, the last point I want to make——concerns the problem of generalization that Morris talked about. I'm a lot less sanguine about it than he is. I've come to a very hard-nosed point of view, as a matter of fact, and that is that it's really improper to generalize any experimental results without performing the same experiment the second time and demonstrating it will hold the second time. What it means is that you might have a theoretical proposition that has been demonstrated in one situation. It might work in some new situation, but that is always problematic, so you have to test it out with the same rigor there as elsewhere.

So to summarize, these more powerful types of design allow you to test your theory, while at the same time providing expert solutions to the problems that ongoing groups have. This general strategy should work about as well with the family as it does with the laboratory group. In fact—I don't use laboratory groups anymore. My general strategy now is to find natural groups with a problem, take baseline measures, study what the problem is, and then run an experiment to try to modify the situation.

GENERAL DISCUSSION

MOORE: One question that occurs to me right away to ask, due to the theoretical issue, is how do you recognize a game as a game? For instance, if you show me an experiment where a game reduced ill-mannered behavior in the class by so much, I could show you a game with the same mathematical structure that would not work. It might be a dull game that the kids hate. Then we can't say it's just the game that did this, there may be certain properties of this situation that are confounding the result. So isn't there a level of abstractness in theory construction that you are just going to have to have?

HAMBLIN: I have learned a technique from the ethologists. In their observations of animal behavior, they have come to the conclusion that for every internal state there is an external reflexive response which mirrors it in magnitude. So what you can do is simply watch the ongoing interaction patterns and you begin to figure out what the interactors are, what the external responses are that signal pleasure——The point is you just watch——you observe them to find out the things that they enjoy and you substitute the things that they enjoy in the game.

ZELDITCH: It's really a serious methodological problem. I don't basically disagree with what you're trying to say, but obviously the whole experiment is a tautology in the sense that if you were to find that it didn't work—it's not to say that the principle was wrong—you would say, "I didn't find the right game," or "I didn't establish the right magnitude of reward and I'll look for something else"—— You just keep trying over and over again until you find the game that works. But to test the hypothesis, you're in the position of not knowing what went wrong; is the game wrong or are the principles wrong?

HAMBLIN: It is a serious problem, and that's why it's important beforehand to have the independent baseline measures for testing the value of the output that you wish to exchange. If you have that independent means, then it isn't a tautology.

ZELDITCH: Right. You've got to have independent means. But I would also like to point out a second implication regarding your remark about applications. That is, essentially, you never want to assume that your principles will apply in a setting without an experiment designed to show that the principles behave as you expect them to behave. Those are the properties, after all, of particular natural settings. So, if those things are always in doubt, then you are always required, as you suggest, to test the applications.

WEICK: I have a couple of questions for Morris. The first one concerns the "place cues" argument that you were talking about. In the study you did at Columbia, you seemed to be pretty successful in getting trappings that were highly convincing, and it seemed to generalize across business situations; but here you seem to be making the argument that family "place cues" are really family specific. I wonder if you don't see the possibility of maybe relaxing that assumption a little bit in the way that you may have in the Columbia situation.

The second question concerns your use of the phrase "natural behavior." You said, "there's too much going on in families" to really get a handle on it. This statement is laid alongside the statement that "you simply can't reconstruct natural situations for the families in the laboratory." My argument would be that I don't think you can get anything but natural behavior of the family in a laboratory.

In other words, if my family and I are being watched, I would bet that our typical style—whether it be exhibitionism, or paranoia, or whatever—would probably be played out in that setting so that you might have to shift the research question a little bit, but I don't think you'd argue we're acting unnatural.

ZELDITCH: Let me answer your first question. The place cues argument, as you recall, is that when you bring a family into a laboratory setting, a part of their culture is really left at home—each physical entity and object they interact with is not only a physical object but part of the symbolic structure that tells people when certain kinds of social relations are to be activated and when they are not. Decision making in the home, which I assume is where it often takes place, is triggered in part by these cues which look like they're physical but are not, they're really part of the symbol system. You bring them into the laboratory and there's a whole new set of cues. Now these cues all have meanings—I'm not arguing that—they look at the mike, they look at the mirror, they look at the experimenter, everything, and they construct new meanings around them. But this is not part of the decision making situation of home.

MOORE: Can't we have sofas, stoves, clutter, magazines, junk in the lab rooms?

ZELDITCH: Well, that's tricky. The question is, how specific are these things to particular families? I don't know. One obvious answer really is to go into the home.

INKELES: The function of the critic, of course, is to show the flaws in experimental design and we couldn't live successfully unless we did that. On the other hand, we have to consider that this is a game which if played too vigorously can lead to paralysis, total discouragement. It seems to me that merely to point to variations in situations and to suggest that these variations might produce results, although it's a nice game for a critic to play, doesn't advance science.

One should make such observations only if one has a relatively specific theory which leads one to believe that in the particular case, it would produce a very substantial effect. Take Dr. Bee's research, for example. In light of a theory that I have, I would ask that possibly the experiment might be rerun with a change in the instructions, because I think there was an unconscious element in the research design which would have a powerful effect (anxiety) on lower class mothers.

Now, this sounds very nice and very reasonable. In a way it probably isn't because, if we were to go around the table, everyone might have what he considered was a reasonable objection to the design based on theory, it might complicate the experiment endlessly. But I think there is some kind of a middle ground, and the critical thing is not whether one is reproducing a situation, but whether one understands the situation that one is producing, because there's always bound to be an enormous amount of variability that you don't have under control even when you think you have.

ZELDITCH: I completely agree both with the philosophy and the specific comment. Let me remind everyone that I am only criticizing the assumption that what you do is to produce a precisely natural situation when you bring a family into the lab. I claim that under no conditions is that what you do. You are producing an abstractly simplified situation which should be relevant to your theoretical ideas, so that essentially we're in agreement.

BEE: Well, there's a general point involved in this: suppose there are 15 variables, all of which are in your theory supposedly interacting in some way and you isolate them one or two at a time in experiments. You're always stuck with the question of whether to have all 15 going at once, whether they would add up in quite the same way as they would when there's only one or two. Whereas, in an intact family, even in an artificial situation, you are getting a larger chunk of all of these things. I do grant that when you're talking about place cues, when you take the family out of their home situation, things are different. But they're less different than they would be if you created a completely arbitrary kind of group.

ZELDITCH: Don't misunderstand what my argument about the place cues was. All I am arguing is that when you experiment with families, you're in a position no different than when you experiment with anything else. You still have a simplified situation. You still require theoretical formulation to tell you what's going on and how to generalize it.

INKELES: Morris, don't you have to introduce into that same conception——some kind of a continuum of natural situations as you imagine them? It isn't just a matter of natural and unnatural—that is, it's not a dichotomy—it's a continuum and you can classify experiments in terms of the amount or irrelevant variability you're probably introducing, the amount of puzzlement and reaction to the situation rather than to the experimental control feature itself. I think this is accessible if you know the culture. It's also accessible for interviewing.

ZELDITCH: I agree. But there are two sources of irrelevant variability and they work at cross purposes. On the one hand, you bring a family into the laboratory setting and you create "irrelevant variability" by the strange apparatus. The apparatus raises all sorts of fantasies in the minds of the family members. But as you get closer and closer to the natural end of the continuum, you have the other kind of problem. Now you don't have artificiality anymore, now you've got too damn much going on.

You are always compromising between these two extremes and what happens is essentially you get better and better theoretical understanding of what is taking place and get closer and closer to understanding what is going on. Incidentally the idea that one experiment will produce for you all the results you want is one of those myths that psychologists and sociologists have.

GUMPERZ: The whole notion of place cues, processing of place cues, is something that has been of concern to anthropological linguists for something like ten years. For example, we lived for two years in an Indian village under conditions where we constructed our own environment, but where the environment after a year or so became home for both us and the members of these traditional Indian villages. We found that very soon their behavior in our environment became very predictable. For example, they had images about Western types of buildings as being associated with electricity. There was no electricity but we had a gasoline pump and showers. Now, invariably, everytime a villager would come in he'd look at our showers and he'd reach up to turn on the electricity and he'd get wet under the shower. The point isn't that they treated our place cues differently from theirs but that they did so predictably. Similarly, as I think back over the visual experiences I had, they treated our space, certain portions of our space, in the same way they treat their own space.

LEIK: The comment I was going to make is closely allied to what's just been said only with perhaps a little different emphasis. There was a very nice study about 1963 or 1964 by O'Rourke. The purpose was not so much to say: "Is the home behavior the same as the laboratory behavior?" so much as it was to say: "Does the theory of family structure predict changes from home to the lab?" The problem is, therefore, not one of saying "here is artificiality," "there is reality." Rather, since a family like any other unit is so organized, in patterns of individual behavior we could expect the individual to adapt differentially to circumstances that are very familiar or partially familiar or totally unfamiliar.

MOORE: It seems to me that one of the troubles with our labs——getting the meaning of the laboratory experience defined for our subjects——is that the laboratory is a relatively new phenomenon in terms of conceptual categories in any society, including our own. People in all societies are used to "artificial situations." But when we created our sociological and psychological laboratories we posed a real problem for our subjects to know which of their available categories for interpreting these things would be relevant categories to apply. Here's where I think Hamblin's point begins to come in about therapy. One of our tasks is going to have to be to define what we want laboratories to mean to people. When some "lower class" people come into a laboratory, I would guess they think it's something like going to a doctor's office in which they should be quite proper——they would put it in that category——while some very sophisticated middle-class kids whose parents have explained a lot about studies and experiments know it's a kind of lark. If they say they're going to give you an electric shock up to a point where it might really hurt, they're not going to. They're not going to hurt you, and you know they're not going to hurt you.

ZELDITCH: ——Or you sue them.

MOORE: Right. So right now, historically speaking, we're faced with the problem of not just deciding what laboratory experiences mean or don't mean, but partly a strategic question as investigators as to what kinds of definitions we should give our laboratories. And Hamblin's suggestion, as I was listening to him, is that . . . they should be a kind of preserve where you are free from terribly serious consequences but that you might very well emerge helped or better off or understand things a little better and not be exploited.

Now with respect to the place cues idea, the issue is "what part of a household might we want to mock up in our laboratory?"——making the distinctions that they make. It's partly a perspective question, "How can we, and what sorts of laboratories could we, define?" Then we must make it clear to people where they are——without these definitions people get confused, possibly hostile, frightened, producing lots of error variance all over the place because of differences in understanding.

HILL: Now with respect to families and family research, are we at the point where there is any consensus about what would be the optimum definition of a research center?——To what extent have we as experimenters by our very demeanor communicated that we think it is——a grim business and a terribly serious business? The sacredness of the data we're trying to get is so obvious that it isn't playful to us as to what they engage in. It has to be——their behavior really has to conform to certain structures or else we've lost precious data.

LEIK: I have a series of impressions and maybe a suggestion or two that kind of wander around what we've been talking about today. One issue that's been mentioned—that Bob mentioned—has to do with the very undesirable kind of results we get from most of our research. This morning Karl raised the issue of contingency in family interaction. John Finley Scott, among others, has written a nice critique of laboratory work saying that it is pretty "blah" because we have no powerful contingencies operating. We get fair-to-middling results because we don't use contingencies like "You will get fired if you don't do this well," or "I'll get a divorce if you don't do this well," or something of that sort.

What might be said in reference to the data that Bob Hamblin pointed to earlier is, that if you look at pieces of research that have specifically set out to apply a powerful contingency to a particular behavior, you can get some beautiful results. I've seen other of Bob's work that shows that. We don't typically do this sort of thing in laboratory work. We don't typically have this sort of situation in the family.

The point then would be whether we are working on current kinds of procedures, whether we are working in labs, or whether we are observing the natural unit of the family, we're still going to end up in a muddle. That is, the data will not be clean no matter how we structure it under current approaches. Therefore it might be reasonable to say, rather than try, at this point, to watch families, to see what's going on, maybe try to experiment a little bit with families in the usual way of experimenting, or rather than trying to operate at a theoretical level——saying this causes, that causes——perhaps what we ought to do is to look at some specific behaviors that we think are key parts of the total puzzle we would like to resolve and ask, "Can we find contingencies that will manipulate these behaviors?" As we start getting such regularities of that sort, can we then mold the contingencies into some sort of systematic process, getting at what Morris is trying to do with the process that Bob was talking about.

GUMPERZ: I don't know if I'm saying something in agreement with what you're saying, but I'm reminded of some time that we spent during this last year trying to review the results of language teaching in the classroom. The one thing that we came away with—that we were convinced of—is that if you want to study language in the classroom, you'd better not confine yourself to the classroom even at the initial stages, because you cannot know what's going on in the classroom without knowing what people bring to the classroom. Now, it seems to me that there's strictly too much assumption that you can select samples of families without knowing a great deal about their backgrounds. In other words, you've got to have some kind of an initial theory that has to specify how you think families vary which will be useful as you start selecting your initial sample. Otherwise, no matter how good your observations the final theory that you're going to arrive at—after the end of five years—is still going to be limited, because your initial population was limited in some unknown way.

HAMBLIN: I'd like to go back to the issues of whether or not there is a theory of family problem solving——You said, "I can't imagine that there's a theory about problem solving that is peculiar to the family."——But there are problems that are peculiar to the family and these may or may not have a general solution.

ZELDITCH: Well, you see . . . I feel somehow that the problems are of a more general nature. I could be wrong about that and I'm not going to fight about it. But the attitude you take towards this, I think, depends crucially on whether you feel that problem solving is a general process which goes on in families but also goes on in other kinds of groups and what you want to understand is problem solving; or, whether you believe that what happens in families is fairly unique or at least quite different, and that the places you have to look for what's going on is in families and only in families.

Actually, I hadn't thought about it before, but one of the interesting properties that came out this morning are the structural problems of families shifting through time. The fact that a child goes from four years old to sixteen years old fundamentally changes the kinds of social structures you have to evolve and there's a continual evolutional structure built into the family. I cannot think of another system which has that property.

INKELES: I think the advice you are giving has quite serious implications for researchers concerning whether or not, if you're interested in problem solving behavior in the family, it would be a good idea to invest more energy in understanding problem solving in the abstract, to use your words, or to concentrate in the family. Because I believe that when you talk about something like problem solving in the abstract, any statements you were to make of that order clearly would have to be a summation of experience over a very wide number of different situations. In other words, it would not be highly situation specific.

Now, from everything we know about human behavior with certain very rare exceptions, our ability to explain or predict behavior depends upon our control over a large number of the relevant variables. In the experiment that Dr. Hamblin was suggesting, although they weren't built into the experiment, there were a great many elements of that situation——a large apperceptive mass—which he knows about which were taken into account.

I believe that, even if we were able to state any general—what you called abstract—principles of problem solving and applied them in any particular situation, the part of the total variance that we could explain would be very, very modest because we would have abstracted across a very large number of situations. If eventually we want to make a statement in abstract terms of what are the general principles of problem solving, that should be a summation of what we have learned about problem solving in a variety of different problem solving situations.

If you, in looking for experimental situations other than families, try to maintain the general structure of conditions that are satisfied by a family relationship, I think they would be very hard to create without the family.

As a matter of fact these properties of the family are so interesting that if I were an experimenter and the family didn't exist I would want to create it, because it seems to me that this set of relationships that exist in the family is, from the social science point of view, generically really interesting, even if we didn't have families.

ZELDITCH: I think that Alex comes close to thinking in the way I believe experimenters ought to think, when he said that if the family didn't exist then we'd have to create it. That is, we are interested in constructing states of affairs in order to see how they affect the phenomena we are particularly interested in. It's often necessary, in order to produce an understanding—a sufficient understanding—of how things are related to each other, to create situations which just don't commonly occur, which is one of the original justifications that most people have for experimenting. It may be that sometimes to understand problem solving as it occurs in the family, you may actually want to use nonfamily groups, precisely to understand how in their whole range certain variables are related to each other, which typically in the family have very narrow ranges of variation.

I think again the mistake is to think concretely of families all the time. What you want to know is, what is it about the family which is related to some particular kind of behavior that you are interested in. This is equally true incidentally of "situations." What bothers me about the business of suggesting that we should always be looking at a variety of situations is that it encourages the sociologist to think very concretely about situations instead of describing situational classes in terms of the variables which are important in them.

COMMENTARY

With Morris Zelditch at the helm, the symposium took a rather radical turn from its initial course. Where Karl Weick began his presentation with the assumption that something is wrong with modern small group research, Zelditch's argument begins with a firm belief in the central importance of laboratory experiments. Drawing upon his own developing perspective, Zelditch provides a finely tuned, sometimes original, sometimes standard, position on the relations between theory, experiment, and substantive focus. One effect of this position, in addition to its intrinsic merits, is to provide a series of contrasts with other thematic perspectives. First, there is a contrast with the mood and pace established by the Weick presentation. Second, the Zelditch session leads to a kind of open competition over the priorities in the sociological enterprise. For instance, Hamblin raises the question, should our attention be allocated to "testing a theory" or to "producing an effect."

Several additional contrasts appear, intermittently, throughout the remainder of the text. Both the "place cues" argument and the question of "what is the field of family sociology" are sufficiently controversial to raise a number of provocative alternatives. The final contrasts occur within what might be called the "levels" of the Zelditch position. For example, in the formal paper Zelditch takes issue with the status of *"experimental* family sociology," while in the oral presentation he shifts to the question of the proper place of "family sociology." Lastly, in some of his more casual remarks, Zelditch alludes to the importance of the family—hidden agendas, double-bind—and admits to the dearth of reconstructed theory for specifying these kinds of researchable "properties."

The shifts which occur across these three levels suggests that the phenomena of "code switching" which John Gumperz raises in his paper might be fruitfully applied to the languages of research.

The counterpoint between the Weick and Zelditch presentations suggests variations in the two distinct and essential layers of a sociological inquiry: substantive and methodological. Furthermore, the contrast in how they approach the issue of family problem solving illustrates two separate stages of inquiry. Weick's paper, while not questioning the value of the experimental method, attempts to restore the depleted substantive or conceptual stock. Consequently his process is one of *divergent* thinking: relaxed, exploratory, responsive, and descriptive.

The main thrust of Zelditch's position, on the other hand, is to equate science with method. He attempts to establish a position of strength where some "theory" specifies relevant properties, and where the experimental "method" can test the adequacy of the theory. Consequently, his process is one of *convergent* thinking: serious, focussed, analytic and prescriptive. In other words, he assumes a theory, ab initio, and then proceeds to describe the most powerful means for testing it. As it turns out, Zelditch's position appears to be vulnerable on several counts. First, by his own admission, "there is no point in pretending that theories are always well-formulated, definite, and complete." Second, if you plug in a concern for "policy" as Inkeles does, or a concern for producing effects as Moore and Hamblin do, then the validation of some simplified process is only half of the task. That is, there yet remains the complementary task of generalizing the theory to a natural setting.

Another source of vulnerability in the Zelditch position is the context within which it occurs. Weick's opening remarks, read at a tacit level, produced an open, elaborative context. As a consequence, constraints were down and participants were prepared to expect shifting perspectives, to playfully entertain new data. In this context, Zelditch's paper appears to reach methodological closure prematurely and thus to cut off discussion of substance. The result is a chorus of protests against some of Zelditch's more controversial arguments, such as place cues and natural behavior.

Notwithstanding this contextual response, the Zelditch contribution firmly establishes a number of key issues with which the problem solving issue must cope. The problem of realism and concreteness, applied both to properties and situations, alerts us to one of the cognitive "threats" to the validity of social research. The insistence upon public, reconstructed theory—as opposed to private intuitions—and its place in the enterprise converges nicely with Weick's premise that science is developmentally self-conscious.

The discussion over "natural" versus "artificial" research settings generates several provocative themes. First, it alerts us to the issue of research continuity, for, as Zelditch remarks, we are always compromising between these two, and our hope is that we can get better and better understanding. Furthermore, this problem of the symbolic meaning of a research setting—the subjective significance for both researchers and researched—produces a number of fruitful exchanges, such as where to do research, the problem of strategically producing a mutually acceptable set of definitions for our labs, the science versus service controversy, and the appropriate research unit for registering social processes.

CONTRASTING VIEWS OF THE SOCIOLOGICAL ENTERPRISE

The evolutionary process could not have been more beneficent when it produced the remarkable contrasts between Zelditch and Hamblin. The range of differences across a number of topics provides a full-color dialectic. Where Zelditch's virtuosity shows up in his verbal skills, Hamblin is a slightly inaudible system designer.

Zelditch leans on logic, while Hamblin depends, in a large part, upon his intuitive appreciation of natural systems. Zelditch is more tuned to the permissible, while Hamblin is tuned to the possible. Taken together they vitalize a number of subjects:

1. Type of metaphor: detective or inventor.

2. Logic of samples: probability or natural constancy.

3. Expectation of effects: test a theory or produce an effect.

4. Preferable designs: experimental or A-B-A-B.

5. Appropriate setting: artificial or natural.

6. External applications: generalization or replication.

7. Types of insight: deductive or intuitive.

8. Salient instigator: professional or "client."

9. Salient audience: professional or "client."

Now, the point of these contrasts is *not* to choose up sides, but to indicate the range of design problems (for instance, between our actions as researchers and states of the social universe).

Zelditch's position can be represented as follows. Research is concerned with theory construction. It begins by testing some property relations specified by some existing theory. Research is a means of stripping away interference of irrelevant properties in order to estimate the fit among relevant ones. These results can then be used to modify the theory which can then be projected to property configurations not included in the manipulated range. There is a considerable investment in either probability theory or situational manipulation to rule out the extraneous influences. As a portrayal of the formally elegant side of social science this approach holds a lot of appeal. But as a practical guide to the conduct of empirical research, it sometimes appears to be a case of equivocation.

Hamblin's position could be described in this way. He invests about ten percent of his coin in rather simple but refined principles (such as social exchange) and about ninety percent in a kind of intuitive apprehension. The initiating stimulus is a system in trouble and the goal is to produce some better system of exchange or shared expectations. The use of natural groups and natural problems obviates the possibility of generalizing beyond the level of formal principles, except that the hope is that the 10-90 ratio will gradually shift to 15-85 and so forth. Meanwhile, and despite the meager explanatory power, the sociologist employs whatever expertise he has in the service of clients. His check against the seeming arbitrariness of this procedure is the design employed: A-B-A-B with multiple baselines.

Cross-ruffing between these two hands, one picks up a number of variations on some of the major themes of the symposium. Both have a sense of a formal, reconstructed theory, but in Zelditch's case it occupies a major, dominant role while in Hamblin's work this type of theory has a very limited, yet developing

place. This contrast in theoretical usage has several parallels in other parts of the symposium. In Session III, for instance, O. K. Moore distinguishes between what he calls guiding principles and formal models, and allocates attention to both on the assumption of some future convergence. In Session IV, Gumperz indicates that Chomsky's theory can serve as an *example* of how to construct a theory of usage. But his emphasis on *example* implies that there is a difficulty in the transfer from a theory of grammar to a theory of language usage. In other words both Moore and Gumperz show an appreciation for the elegance of formal theory, yet recognize that there are different developmental schedules for theory, depending on the nature of the content—such as grammar before usage. So the image which emerges from this sense of different schedules of theoretic development is that, perhaps for some time to come, hunches and intuition may play a dominant but decreasing role in the enterprise.

Hamblin is prepared for this eventuality with what he calls an "observation phase." During such a phase he attempts to intuit what goes with what, what kind of game is being played, what kinds of payoff are expected. One obvious difficulty with this kind of tacit appreciation, of course, is that a lot of the phase is private—in other words, not communicable. Zelditch, on the other hand does not give explicit attention to informal theory, but several of his remarks suggest that it has a place in his system, albeit implicit. First, he described a process whereby he arrived at his present position, for which the stimulus was a "late luncheon argument." Second, he stated that we are always compromising between artificiality and complexity, with the *hope* that we'll get better and better understanding of what's going on.

DIFFERENT MODELS OF SOCIAL RESEARCH

Perhaps the most dramatic difference in the two perspectives is captured in what Hamblin called the "approaches to the study of man." The different modes or approaches are given more and more amplification in subsequent sessions. Briefly stated, the distinction revolves around two issues: whether or not the task of social science ends with "testing" a theory or "applying" it to some system in need, and whether or not it's possible to provide expert solutions with only partial theories. Zelditch, in remarks made in this and later sessions, seems to favor an approach which is consonant with traditional definitions of "pure" science. Hamblin, on the other hand, prefers a mode which includes both testing and amelioration simultaneously. It is this difference which gives life to the nine contrasts listed earlier.

The issue of generalization, for example, pinpoints contrasting strengths and weaknesses in both approaches. Zelditch views research as a process of simplification in order to test causal connections between properties specified by some developing theory. One reason for using labs is that naturally occurring events are enormously complicated. However, as Inkeles was quick to point out, simplification and generalization lie in opposite directions. To the degree that one simplifies, he will be able to explain less and less variance, unless of course he has gone through a whole series of tests and emerged with a very complex theory.

The systems which Hamblin creates suffer from a different ill. He produces very robust results, controls a lot of the variance, but he is not always in a position to explain what it is that produces the effect. The foundations of his expertise tend to be private, and thus not immediately generalizable *across* researchers.

Moore alludes to this problem when he notes that Hamblin can't distinguish mathematically between successful and unsuccessful games. He might be able to do so privately, or intuitively, but not in any testable way. Moore's comment on the problem, incidentally, suggests a dual or balanced approach, which attends to both levels. In describing his own project later, Moore suggests a type of long term enterprise that might do the job: building theories and effects *simultaneously*, and learning to live with the resulting ambiguity, while at the same time gradually constructing a bridge between. Leik also attempts a synthesis which would employ the powerful logic of a laboratory setting on problems which do not logically settle down very neatly via his focus on accommodation, and powerful contingencies.

In short, theory construction tied to research is a varied task, nesting at least two levels, each of which has its own subjective, temporal, and empirical dimensions.

So the question seems to be, not what is *the* appropriate attitude to take, but what array of attitudes need to be coordinated to what properties of the world out there.

THE "PLACE CUES" CONTROVERSY

The issue of "place cues" which entered the symposium at this point, and reappeared at several later points, is one of the juicier issues which never gets completely clarified. If there was some way of doing a reflexive rerun—for example, using some of Moore's principles, enunciated in Session III—I would choose this as a prime candidate for such an experience.

The controversy can be broken down into several more manageable issues:

1. What is the appropriate setting for doing research?

2. Can we predict what kinds of reactivity research situations will produce?

3. What degree of mutual definition of social research is necessary between researcher and researched to assure meaningful outputs from research?

4. What strategy or strategies might be employed to offer optimum solutions to the dilemma of choosing between theoretical clarity and the solution of pressing social problems.

Weick, and then Moore, question Zelditch about the issue of natural behavior and thus the appropriate setting for research. In his response, Zelditch says a rather funny thing. He states, "one obvious answer really is to go into the home." What is curious about this remark is that while the solution may reduce the unwanted reactivity of the family, for the researcher it raises the problem of knowing where he is—in other words, his puzzlement. Furthermore, the response is inconsistent with Zelditch's primary concern with simplification.

Other comments by Zelditch, however, furnish what may be a key to the inconsistency. He established a context for choosing artificial/natural strategies when he suggests that we are always compromising between these two contrary sources of irrelevant variability. Furthermore, he chooses not to use families—although he admits several cases where they might be used. In this context, the strength behind the simplification argument is more a matter of personal preference than optimum prescription. When he grants Weick's assumptions and accepts the family as a subject unit, he then makes his choice in favor of reducing the subject-reactivity problem. The point seems to be that, in the short run, there is going to be lots of noise in the research system regardless. So the choice between simplified and natural settings may be simply a matter of preference.

The issue of predicting types of subject-situation reactivity produced several interesting responses. Inkeles, for instance, suggested that we need to "know the culture." Leik's comment indicated how we might go about this. Citing some of O'Rourke's research, Leik suggested that as we get to know something about organized patterns of behavior we can predict reactions to new circumstances which vary in their degree of familiarity. Gumperz tuned in to the matter with several interesting comments. First, he indicated that we need to do some careful field work to determine how unfamiliar circumstances might be interpreted. In line with this comment he also suggested that we may be handicapping ourselves when we allow sampling procedures to rest on probability theory without attention to variations in background differences. That is, from a cultural perspective, do our definitions of a population seem reasonable.

Moore in the third session of the symposium gives an extended treatment to the question of defining social research. His comments in the present session can be taken as introductory, but suggest an underlying theme to his overall perspective: a developmental view of symbolic interaction. He is arguing, in effect, that there are stages in the ability of one person (such as the researcher) to take the role of the other. Two of these stages are of particular interest: agent and strategist, with the former developmentally—in the Meadian sense— more primitive. The models of research which we have adopted from natural science tend to emphasize the more primitive stage, partly because natural science could treat its subject matter quite adequately with this orientation, and partly because the strategic perspective evolved as a scientific possibility *after* the tacit dimensions of natural science had been institutionalized. So Moore is suggesting that the shift in subject matter, and the accumulated products of science, require a leap to a more reciprocal model of researcher-researched relations. Actually, there are several things to be considered in shifting models: (1) broadcasting some acceptable definition of social science to our many publics; (2) considering a more equitable researcher-researched exchange —for example, would researchers want to hold still for the kind of payoffs they presently provide their subjects? (3) building some self-conscious feedback mechanisms into the process of research—such as routing new information about human systems back into the research paradigm.

Robert Leik addressed the issue of a strategy for producing both theoretical clarity and providing a service. His synthesis attempts to combine the strengths of both Zelditch's and Hamblin's approach. That is, by beginning with simplified conditions, can we find powerful contingencies which facilitate interpersonal accommodation. As we discover these, can we then mold them into more complex systems (such as working with families) without them losing their effectiveness. While this suggestion suffers the difficulty of generalization noted earlier, it does serve to indicate that participants were seriously grappling with the issue. A number of additional suggestions occur in subsequent discussions.

Some Principles for the Design of Clarifying Educational Environments*

OMAR KHAYYAM MOORE

ALAN ROSS ANDERSON

W hen the ordinary typewriter was an exciting novelty, Mark Twain, who was an early typewriter buff, called it a "curiosity-breeding little joker"—and so it was, then. The *talking typewriter*, invented by Moore and Kobler [Moore and Kobler (1963), Kobler and Moore (1966)], is a contemporary novelty which also elicits a good deal of curiosity. There have been numerous popular articles about it, and most of those who have played with it find it fascinating. Unfortunately, the interest generated by this machine does not carry over, necessarily, to the theoretical ideas which lie behind it. We say "unfortunately" for good reason. The machine itself is less important than the principles which guided its construction. The talking typewriter is merely one of a large number of possible inventions which can be made, we think, using this same theoretical context as a guide.

Our main purpose in this paper is to explain and to illustrate a set of principles, four in number, for designing learning environments within which even very young children can acquire complex symbolic skills with relative ease. We intend to show, as we go along, that these principles for designing *clarifying* educational environments [where by a "clarifying educational environment" we mean an educational environment aimed to make the student

---

* Most of the theoretical work reported here was supported by the Office of Naval Research, Group Psychology Branch, Contract #SAR/Nonr-609 (16). With respect to applications, the major source of support has been the Carnegie Corporation of New York. The cost of developing the "talking typewriter" (Edison Responsive Environment) was borne exclusively by the McGraw-Edison Company of Elgin, Illinois.

(subject? victim?) *clear* about what he is doing, and more generally, what is going on] are systematically related to both a theoretical analysis of human culture and an interpretation of the socialization process, for example, that process whereby a human infant, beginning life as a biological *individual*, becomes a *person*—and whose infantile *behavior* is gradually transformed into adult *conduct*.

In order to understand the "design principles" alluded to above, we must first explain the theoretical system out of which they emerged. We will then go on to a statement of the principles themselves, and finally we will consider, in some detail, an illustrative application of these principles to the problem of designing an actual learning environment. At this point, we will have come full circle—the talking typewriter will appear in a meaningful context as one part of a learning environment.

It will also be obvious that the talking typewriter is itself fundamentally a "social science invention." Because it *is* a social science invention, it is difficult to use it or similar devices intelligently without an appreciation of the social scientific ideas on which it is based.

Finally, before turning to our first task, that of sketching out the theoretical system upon which the set of principles is founded, we wish to acknowledge the contributions to our thinking of George Herbert Mead (1932, 1934, 1936, 1938),[1] the father of the symbolic interactionist position in social psychology, and Georg Simmel (English translation, 1959), the originator of the school of formal sociology. We regard these men as central figures in the creation of the kind of sociology which can yield applications both at the level of mechanical inventions and social inventions. It may seem strange to some that we believe that Mead and Simmel have ideas which lend themselves to applications. Mead and his followers often have been criticized for spawning ideas which lacked testable consequences—to say nothing of applications; and to the best of our knowledge we are the only ones who have seriously entertained the thought that Simmel was within a light year of a practical application. We hope to show here that leading ideas taken from these two men can be reshaped into working principles for designing educational environments.

THEORETICAL BACKGROUND[2]

Folk Models

We think that it is a mistake to regard the ordinary human being as an *a*theoretical or a *non*theoretical or even an *anti*theoretical creature. Some con-

---

[1] From time to time we will try to acknowledge our indebtedness to various authors, but a complete list of those authors to whom we feel indebted would be impossible for either of us to make out.

[2] Since this section is mainly a summary of our own ideas, some worked out jointly, some separately, we have felt free to paraphrase our own papers without specific references. However, anyone who wishes to go more deeply into these ideas should read (A. R. Anderson, Moore, 1959, 1962, 1966; Moore, 1957, 1958, 1961, 1964, 1965, 1968; Moore, A. R. Anderson, 1960a, 1960b, 1960c, 1962a, 1962b, 1968).

temporary behavioral scientists seem to assume that the ordinary man, a citizen in good standing in whatever community he lives, is woefully lacking in intellectual resources to guide him in managing his affairs. He is credited only with some folk sayings and proverbs, some practical knowledge, some skill at rule-of-thumb reasoning, some tradition-based explanations—and that is about it.

In a contrary vein, we suggest a different view of "man." We think that early in human history, probably at about the time men developed natural languages, they also created models of the most important features of their relations with the environment.[3] These were relatively abstract models which collectively covered relations holding between (1) man and nature, insofar as nature is not random, (2) man and the random or chancy elements in experience, (3) man in his interactional relations with others like himself, and (4) man and the normative aspects of group living. Cultural structures falling within these four classes of models were created in early history by many unsung Edisons and Einsteins. (Perhaps it would be more appropriate to say that they were created by the unsung Meads and Simmels of prehistory.) Consequently, there does not exist a society however "primitive" that does not have cultural objects falling within these four categories of models. It is convenient to have a name for all four classes of models, a name that suggests their origin early in human history. We call them "folk models."

Every society, as far back as we have any evidence, has *puzzles* which, we suggest, stand in an abstract way for nonaleatory man-nature relations. Every society has some *games of chance*. According to our view of the matter, games of chance are abstract models of the aleatory aspects of existence. Every society has *games of strategy* in the sense of von Neumann (1947). These games capture some of the peculiar features of interactional relations among men, relations in which no party to an encounter controls all of the relevant variables upon which the final outcome depends, though each controls some of these variables and each participant must take some account of the potential actions of others involved in the situation if he is to behave intelligently. Every society has *aesthetic entities*, such as art forms which we claim give people the opportunity to make normative judgments about and evaluations of their experience. All societies make use of these folk models in the socialization of the young and for the re-creation, or recreational enjoyment, of those who are older. Simple forms of these models are internalized in childhood and more complex versions of them sustain us in adulthood.

It should be pointed out that until mathematicians had made formal analyses of the structure of some of these folk models, their depth and subtlety were not appreciated fully. Of the four classes of folk models distinguished

---

[3] In common with many contemporary philosophers, we acquire a certain sick feeling when hearing talk about "man," or even worse, "Man." When one reads translations of Aristotle, and finds that "Man is a rational animal," one has the idea that something deep is going on, but obvious parallels ("Whale is a large animal," "Mouse is a small animal") make the locution seem as ludicrous as it is. We nevertheless defer to a tradition, with the understanding that when we use the term "man" we are referring to human beings, and that, in consequence, all the appropriate verbs should be in the plural.

above, two have received adequate formal treatment, specifically, the various mathematical theories of probability have all games of chance as models, and the various mathematical theories of games of strategy have all games of strategy as models. The formal analysis of puzzles is not in as satisfactory a state as are games of chance and games of strategy; however, we have suggested that the methods of natural deduction may help clarify the structure of puzzles.[4] When it comes to aesthetic entities, everyone is at sea and it is not known whether mathematical analyses of aesthetic objects, should such analyses prove possible, would result in *only one* or *more than one* distinct class of models. It is well to remember that until the work of von Neumann no one was in a position to make a mathematically rigorous distinction even between games of chance and games of strategy, so we should be careful about making the assumption that aesthetic objects would yield to but one overall formal theory. Regardless of this, the mathematical research into the structure of folk models has made it perfectly obvious to us that early man was not a simple-minded clod. It required inventors of genius to create these intricate objects, but even a child can begin to play with most of them. Not much in the way of technical expertise was needed to fashion the equipment used in connection with folk models—bits of wood, or stone, would do for the "pieces" used in most board games; a primitive technology was no bar to the creation of conceptually complex cultural entities.

Historically speaking, man not only invented and developed these fascinating folk models, he also devised suitable techniques for seeing to it that they were mastered by the ordinary citizen. If we think of these models as constituting the basic theoretical arm of a society's culture, then it is quite important that everyone, or virtually everyone, learns them. To put it another way, if folk models are abstract schemata which help orient us toward a wide variety of problems, then we should get them down pat. With respect to their inculcation, observe that, in general, they are learned but not taught. What is taught are the "rules of the game," and once the rules are understood, each participant is largely on his own, except when the models are perverted by professionalism.

In every society there are social norms which distinguish between serious matters on the one hand, and fun and games on the other. Usually, specific times and places are set aside for the enjoyment of folk models. Also, the stakes for winning or losing are kept at some nominal value insofar as profit and loss enter. In addition, there are norms which regulate expressions of feeling and emotion with reference to using folk models. During the course of playing with a model, one is permitted to experience a fairly wide range of

---

[4] A good simple treatment of natural deduction is contained in Fitch's text in symbolic logic (1952). Experimentation on human higher-order problem solving which takes into consideration natural deduction is rare. However, some of our colleagues have attempted to take this into consideration. (See Carpenter et al, 1961.) The preparation for an approach to natural deduction in terms of experimental techniques was worked out largely by Scarvia B. Anderson and Moore in a series of studies beginning in 1952 (S. B. Anderson, 1955, 1956, 1957; Moore and S. B. Anderson, 1954a, 1954b, 1954c).

feelings and emotions, but extremes are excluded. These models serve, as it were, as a school for emotional expression—this is a kind of "school" in which boredom is unlikely and uncontrolled emotional frenzy is forbidden. All in all, the set of norms governing the use of folk models, and the models themselves, have proved so successful that people have to be prohibited from playing with them too much, despite the conceptual depth of the materials with which they deal. If we think of the models as teaching devices, then they are instructional with respect to relatively universal features of man's environment; they are abstract symbolic maps of human experience. We also can see that they "teach" in ways that satisfy the following conditions:

1. They are "cut off" in some suitable sense from the more serious sides of the society's activity; that is to say, they are cut off from immediate problems of welfare and survival. For example, if a child is learning the intricacies of social interaction, the activity in which he is experiencing or practicing the interaction must allow him to make many mistakes without endangering the lives or future of those around him, to say nothing of his own safety. Similarly, such rewards as he receives from the activity must not be too expensive to those around him; or again, the activity would have just those serious consequences which these models, as teaching devices, must avoid.

2. But in spite of the fact that the teaching devices must avoid serious consequences, some motivation must be built into them, or else the learner may lose interest. If we rely on the distinction between activities that are intrinsically rewarding, and those that are rewarding only as a means, or extrinsically rewarding, we may say that the rewards in the learner's activities must be intrinsic or inherent in the activity itself. We call such activities "autotelic"; they contain their own goals and sources of motivation.

3. And finally, these teaching devices, if they are to be theoretically relevant to the problems which are likely to be encountered outside the context of an autotelic environment, indeed must be models of serious activities.

Thus far we envisage a situation like this: Every society makes up abstract symbolic models of its most serious recurrent problems. Despite the complex structure of these models, everywhere they are learned with pleasure by ordinary people. Every society has social norms governing the use of its folk models and these norms have the effect of making the models autotelic, so even though the models are models of serious matters, they must be treated playfully.

The notion that materials, in the sense of the contents of everyday life are somehow abstracted from the stream of living and reappear as the play forms of sociability, is a distinctively Simmelian idea—we borrowed it from him. It is he who argues that:

> Actual forces, needs, impulses of life produce the forms of our behavior that are suitable for play. These forms, however, become independent contents and stimuli within play itself or, rather, *as* play. There are, for instance, the hunt; the gain by ruse; the proving of physical and intellectual strength; competition; and the dependence on chance and on the favor or powers that cannot be influenced. (Simmel, 1959, p. 42.)

And he goes on to say that:

> To the person who really enjoys it [play], its attraction rather lies in the dynamics
> and hazards of the sociologically significant forms of activity themselves. The
> more profound, double sense of "social game" is that not only the game is played
> in a society (as its external medium) but that, with its help, people actually
> "play" "society." (Simmel, 1959, p. 50.)

What Simmel did not do was to carry through a mathematical analysis of
his cherished "play forms" of human association. He did see the need for such
a formal analysis; in fact, he called for the creation of a kind of "social
geometry" which would be up to characterizing the structure of play forms.
He did not see that probability theory does the trick for games of chance,
and, of course, the work of von Neumann on games of strategy did not come
along until ten years after Simmel's death. And we all are still waiting for an
intellectual giant the size of von Neumann to do a satisfactory mathematical
analysis of aesthetic play forms. Nonetheless, the basic program for formal
sociology, as envisaged by Simmel, is being carried out and we like to think of
ourselves as helping a little.

It should be remarked that the possibilities for developing an appropriate
"social geometry" are not limited to analyzing folk models. For example,
normative systems are of obvious importance in interpreting human interaction. Prior to the past decade, very little had been done toward developing
a mathematical analysis of such systems. It was partly in response to our sense
of the need for a program of formal sociology in this area that we undertook
studies in what is now called "deontic logic." This topic has been treated by
a vast number of investigators since von Wright's seminal essay of 1951, and
the improvement in our own understanding of the basic ideas involved can
be seen by comparing the analysis we offered in 1957 (Anderson and Moore,
1957) with a 1967 version (Anderson, 1967).[5]

Another problem area which has significance for formal sociology is the
mathematical treatment of the notion of relevance. Human affairs are conducted within universes of discourse in which some standards of relevance are
presupposed, but the study of "relevant implication" was a neglected area in
mathematical logic, so efforts were made to create the required formal machinery.[6] Interestingly enough, the improvement in our understanding of
problems in deontic logic came about mainly because of this apparently unrelated work on the logic of relevance. This was one of those "unexpected"
bonuses which we come to "expect" from what seems, on the surface, to be
merely remote abstract considerations.

---

[5] Though the interest in deontic logic is our common concern, most of the relevant
work under this project has been done by A. R. Anderson (1956a, 1956b, 1958a, 1958b, 1959,
1962). For a reference to von Wright's essay, and a reasonably complete bibliography as of
1966, see the reprinted version of A. R. Anderson (1956a).

[6] Again, the logic of relevant inference and entailment is of common concern. In this
case the work has been done by Anderson and Belnap (Anderson, 1957, 1960, 1963; Anderson
and Belnap, 1958, 1959a, 1959b, 1959c, 1961a, 1961b, 1961c, 1963; Anderson, Belnap and
Wallace, 1960; Belnap, 1959a, 1959b, 1960a, 1960b, 1960c, 1960d, 1967; Belnap and Wallace,
1961), building their work on an important paper of Ackerman (1956).

Another area of investigation should be mentioned which also fits into the program of formal sociology. It turned out that there were almost no mathematical analyses of the logical structure of questions and answers. Yet surely here, if anywhere, is a distinctively human preoccupation, namely the asking and answering of questions. The form treatment of questions and answers is called "erotetic logic," a term introduced in 1955 by Mary and Arthur Prior (1955). It is being pursued by our colleague, Nuel D. Belnap, Jr. (among others), whose *An Analysis of Questions* (1963) provides a substantial treatment of this topic with bibliographic references.

Personality

Turning now from folk models *qua* cultural objects to some of their implications for personality, there is another possibility with reference to them that Simmel did not pursue. If our folk models and his play forms have the theoretical importance we attribute to them, then they should be of help in analyzing the structure of human personality. We have given some thought to this matter and our considerations have led us in the direction of the work of George Herbert Mead. As a heuristic gamble, we were willing to assume that the major functional components of human personality, and the organization of these components, reflect the structure of the folk models. By taking this view of human personality, we were led to ask whether each of the four kinds of folk models corresponds to a characteristic attitude or perspective that a person might take toward his world. It is our thesis that each class of models does so correspond, and that the models build upon one another in a particular order.

In capsule form, our position is:

1. Puzzles emphasize a sense of agency. We call this the "agent perspective." This is the outlook that perhaps Cooley (1902) had in mind when he spoke of "the joy of being a cause."

2. Games of chance emphasize a sense of patienthood, that is, being the recipient of consequences over which we have virtually no control. We call this the "patient perspective."

3. Games of strategy presuppose an agent-patient perspective, but emphasize what we call the "reciprocal perspective." In Meadean terminology, this would seem to be the perspective of a "significant other." For example, in playing bridge there is room for meaningful acts of agency and we are sometimes patient to all manner of outrageous happenings, some due to chance, some due to our opponent, some due to our partner, and even a few of our own doing. But the heart of the game (as von Neumann showed with beautiful precision) lies in the possible interrelations between the two opposing teams, each of which must take the other into account. This means that a genuine game of strategy, such as bridge, does not reduce mathematically into either the form of a puzzle or the form of a game of chance. This means, also, that a person who is looking at the world from the standpoint of the reciprocal perspective does not see another human being as merely puzzling or unpredictable, but rather he sees him as someone who is capable of looking at him as he looks at the other.

4. Aesthetic entities emphasize a sense of assessing, evaluating or judging. This perspective presupposes *significant others* in interaction; that is, it presupposes entities that behave in terms of the other three perspectives. We call this judgmental stance the "referee's perspective." The point of view of a judge in a bridge tournament (or any given player when he looks at his own play or the play of others as if he were the judge) is not that of any player *qua* player, nor is it some sort of average or consensus of the players' viewpoints. The referee's concern ranges over the whole game—his viewpoint presupposes that there are players with their reciprocal perspectives. With reference to Mead's analysis of personality, we think that the concept of the referee's perspective is a plausible explication of his concept of the "generalized other."

We made this point in connection with the reciprocal perspective that it did not collapse, logically speaking, into either of the two perspectives upon which it builds, namely, the agent and the patient perspectives. The reason we said this is that the mathematical structure of games of strategy is not reducible to either puzzles or games of chance. We want to make a similar argument now about the referee's perspective—it does not reduce to or collapse into any or all of the other three perspectives. Our reason for being confident about this is that the mathematics of the referee's perspective, insofar as it is deontic or normative, does not reduce to ordinary extensional logic, nor to the logic of possibility, nor to the logic of probability. The referee's perspective is a logically distinct realm. We realize that not everyone would find this line of reasoning convincing—and perhaps it should not be relied on too heavily— but we remember that not long ago there were those who thought it very unlikely that deontic logic could be set up on a solid footing, namely, on a basis which would not immediately collapse into the standard extensional systems.

A human being who has been socialized in the sense of Mead, an individual who has acquired a social self, should be able to take any of the four perspectives mentioned above. What is more, he should be able to handle them one by one, in pairs, in triples, and in one superordinate quadruple—depending, of course, on the nature of the problem with which he is confronted. We say that his social self is constituted, in part, by the organization of these perspectives. A social self is neither something that anyone is born with, nor does it come about automatically through the processes of physiological maturation; rather, it is an achievement in learning which we think is guided in part by autotelic folk models.

We agree with the general Meadian analysis about how the social self, as an organization of perspectives, emerges out of a matrix of social processes—

and how it, in turn, may affect these same processes. We appreciate particularly the suggestions Mead makes concerning the process whereby the interplay among human beings begins with a "conversation of gestures" and leads on to symbolic interaction. This interaction takes place through the use of "significant symbols"—these symbols being defined in terms of a common universe of discourse. This universe of discourse, in turn, gains its relevance by virtue of its systematic relations to the set of social processes out of which the social interaction arises. For us, among the most significant of what Mead calls "significant symbols" are the symbolic complexes which we have dubbed "folk models." Of course, natural languages as systems of significant symbols are of prime importance, too. We agree completely with Mead about this.

Mead was well aware of the importance of play and of games as part of the process whereby a social self is acquired. In fact, he made a distinction between playing and taking part in a game to drive home his point that the development of the human personality takes place in a series of interrelated phases. A young child may *play* in the sense of taking the role of a series of significant others, but until he grasps the structure of the rules which make a game a game—that is, until he can govern his on-going conduct in the light of what we call the referee's perspective, or in Mead's terminology, the "generalized other"—the child is only *playing* and not *gaming*. And, to the extent that he is not up to handling games, he is only partially socialized. Clearly, it is compatible with the Meadean position to assume that conduct which flows from a mature social self would involve the use of each of the perspectives in the solution of challenging problems. It is convenient to think of each perspective as a part of the social self. As has been made clear above, we think that there are at least four such parts of a socialized human being: agent, patient, reciprocator, and referee.

Information Processing

Any problem worthy of the full talents of an adult human being requires that he carry out a great deal of information processing with respect to it. Obviously, this information processing is subject to some kind of control. The question is "what kind?" In terms of an engineering analysis, there are two major kinds of control systems that we can consider: those of the *open-loop* variety and those of the *closed-loop* variety.

An open-loop control system is one which exercises its control in a way that is independent of the output of the system. Open-loop systems, generally speaking, are not bothered by problems of instability.

A closed-loop control system is one in which the control is somehow dependent upon the system's output (or some symbolic representation of that output).

Closed-loop systems tend to suffer from various forms of instability. As was remarked before, human beings must have some sort of a control system to govern their information processing. Judging from the tendency of human beings to become unstable, we guess that the human control system is of the closed-loop variety. As a matter of fact, we assume a great deal more than that—we posit that the four perspectives constitute a subsystem which functions as part of an overall control system governing information processing.

It may seem to some that our brief discussion above about control systems is very remote from a Meadian analysis. We do not think that this is the case at all. Mead attempted to formulate a number of ideas which, in retrospect, can be recognized as brilliant anticipations of concepts which later received explicit treatment along the lines that he suggested. The Meadian notion of an attitude or perspective is a case in point. Let us listen to Mead a bit as he tried to tell his students and colleagues what he meant by an attitude.

> Present results, however, suggest the organization of the act in terms of attitudes. There is an organization of the various parts of the nervous system that are going to be responsible for acts, an organization which represents not only that which is immediately taking place, but also the later stages that are to take place. If one approaches a distant object he approaches it with reference to what he is going to do when he arrives there. If one is approaching a hammer he is muscularly all ready to seize the handle of the hammer. The later stages of the act are present in the early stages—not simply in the sense that they are all ready to go off, but in the sense that they serve to control the process itself. They determine how we are going to approach the object, and the steps in our early manipulation of it. We can recognize, then, that the innervation of certain groups of cells in the central nervous system can already initiate in advance the later stages of the act. The act as a whole can be there determining the process. (Mead, 1934, p. 11.)

When Mead advanced this analysis of an attitude, his remarks were interpreted by many to be sheer teleological nonsense. Now we understand these ideas much better—he is saying that ongoing human activity is subject to a closed-loop control system. No contemporary engineer would regard this as metaphysics (in the *ba-a-ad* sense).[7]

Information Processing for Human Beings

We posit a control system which governs information processing that is sufficiently reflexive to allow a human being to stand back from himself in order to view himself as an object. What is more, this control system must allow him to see himself from the standpoint of any of the perspectives while he is planning or executing actions. This hypothetical control system must make provision for the fact that we can and do soliloquize. It must both permit and control internal dialogues such as: "I would like to do X, but I am not

---

[7] We are well aware that "metaphysics" has an honorific sense, stemming from Aristotle's attempt to figure out how the universe ticks, and a pejorative sense, stemming from the logical empiricist rejection of theology and its sister-disciplines (such as Mariology). A good bit of what we are trying to convey in this article is probably metaphysics, in what we *hope* is a "good" sense.

sure that it would make me happy. My father approves, but he doesn't understand. My mother doesn't approve and she does understand. It's illegal, but my friends say it is good." We all go round and round like this, looking at the world in terms of what we can do, what might happen to us, what our friends and enemies think, and what the referee might say. Sometimes these considerations get out of hand and we become bogged down in repetitious and viciously circular chains of reasoning. Sometimes we fail to consider a problem from some important perspective.

The upshot is: we *assume* that a fully socialized human being, in a state of good emotional health, would have a control system which permits him to consider himself in a reflexive way from the standpoints which are represented abstractly in cultural terms by the four autotelic folk models.

Order of Mastering Perspectives

If the social self consists in part, at least, of an organization of perspectives, and if these perspectives are learned, then the question can be raised as to whether they are acquired in some particular order. Is the socialization process some sort of ordered sequence? We believe so and our analysis of human developmental phases follows our interpretation of Mead quite closely. We assume that the agent and patient perspectives are the first to develop—they are "twin born" to use Mead's expression. The notion of an agent is linked to that of a patient—but it may take an infant some time to discover that this is so; there are indeed studies which indicate that it takes a while for new-born infants to begin to understand the difference between their own bodies and their environment. But even if the agent-patient pair are twin-born, we still think of this pair as one term in a relation with the reciprocal perspective. Finally, the complete development of personality involves the pair-wise combination of the complex term agent-patient-reciprocal with the referee perspective. As was remarked earlier, the building up of this system into its most complex form does not mean that all parts need be involved in the solution of all problems; the system is sufficiently flexible, if its development goes well, so that the "parts" can be used one at a time, or in various combinations. As one can see, this is a fairly complex system even without further complications; there are some, on which we would now like to comment.

Complications Concerning Kind-Heartedness

Up to the present point, this summary of our position about human personality has made only passing reference to feeling and emotion. Are we to imagine that human beings are engaged mainly in the processing of information *sans* an involvement with affect? This would be an odd view of human nature, though the Meadian system tends to be odd in just this way. Mead had little to say about feeling and emotion. At the very least, we believe that it is essential to posit a *system* of feeling and emotion, and to make some assumptions about this system. This obviously is a complex topic. Here we will mention only a few of our assumptions—some which will help us later in the task of formulating principles for designing educational environments.

1. Each perspective is directly connected to the system of feeling and emotion so that the control system gets a "reading" from the system of feeling and emotion about reactions to plans and the execution of plans, or, more generally, about ongoing activity. This means that we can have, but need not have, "mixed feelings and emotions." For example, a mountaineer, in thinking about rappelling down a cliff, may feel elation as an agent, anxiety as a patient, shame of the possibility of showing fear, and guilt for rappelling at all since he is a family man and knows he should not take such risks—his own (kind-hearted) referee perspective says he is out of bounds.

2. The system of feeling and emotion is so organized that, under some circumstances, at least, it is possible to change the scale of feeling and emotion without necessarily altering its relative proportions. For example, in playing a game of chess, we can run through a wide gamut of emotions in, as it were, "attenuated" form—we can experience token amounts of anxiety, fear, and so forth, without literally panicking. Of course, the system of feeling and emotion may get out of control as in some kinds of mental illness—the scale of intensity may be shifted in the direction of gross exaggeration on the one hand, or flatness of affect on the other.

3. We not only have feelings and emotions, but each individual, in a reflexive way, can learn about his own reactions. The possibility of gaining some reasonable self-control with respect to affect, depends upon learning to recognize, differentiate, and generalize about this vital aspect of ourselves; in other words, feeling and emotion can be schooled—and the use of autotelic folk models is normally part of this educational process.

INTERLUDE

Someone who has followed the heuristic ideas presented above about human culture and the socialization process might be tempted to ask the following question: "If you regard these autotelic folk models so highly as guides to action, if they, indeed, represent abstractly so many salient features of human existence, and if they provide a basis for the structure of human personality, then do we need scientific models as opposed to folk models?" Our answer is that we do need scientific models. Folk models have served man well during most of his history, but there is something radically wrong with them with respect to their present theoretical relevance—something has happened which has rendered them worse than obsolete.

So long as the ordinary man lived out his life within the context of a static social framework, these models matched his world; the models themselves are essentially static entities. For instance, in any play of the game of chess, the rules—that is, the boundary conditions—remain constant. There may be plenty of lively action going on within this stable frame of reference and the participants may feel a wide range of emotions, but the rules are both fixed and inviolable in a normative sense. If you are working a puzzle, say a jigsaw puzzle, the picture to be completed does not change as you work on the puzzle, and the pieces preserve constancy of size and shape. If you go to see a play two nights in a row, it remains the same play with trivial variations; the actors do not change their lines because you have seen it before, though you may appreciate it more thoroughly on seeing it the second time. The basic point we are attempting to make is that folk models mirror the static quality of unchanging or imperceptibly changing societies. The folk models in this respect are like the Newtonian conceptions of space and time—both presuppose a frame of reference which is invariant with respect to all that goes on within it.

Today we live in a new world, a world in acceleration, a dynamic fluid world. In the 1940's the major industrial societies underwent a massive acceleration in technological development. This increase in the rate of technological change was so large, as far as its social consequences were concerned, as to amount to a difference in kind rather than one of degree.[8] Because of this, we, along with many others, have come to divide technological history into two main periods—the primitive, from the dawn of human history to the 1940's, and the modern, from the 1940's on. In order to make this case we draw graphs of technological functions, plotting, on a time scale of 10,000 years, such things as the speed of travel, the force of explosives, the size of objects which can be manipulated with precision, and the number of people who can be included simultaneously within one communication network. The curves for these and many other technological functions bend sharply upward at about this time and they are now heading off the graph. Of course, there are some who are unhappy with the notion of pinpointing this acceleration in the decade of the 40's. They prefer to think in terms of a series of accelerations, each jolt larger than its predecessor. The time span for this series is taken to be the first half of the 20th century. In any case we agree with those who see a radical change.

Many aspects of this radical change in technological capability have become matters of grave concern. For example, most reasonably well-informed people understand that because the first fission device multiplied the explosive force of previous weapons a thousandfold, and a few years later a fusion device multiplied explosive force a million times, mankind now is in a position to do

---

[8] We yield to none in insisting on our inability to make the difference between "kind" and "degree" clear, and this is not the place to try to go into the matter. But it does seem apparent that the difference between two chicken eggs of a slightly different size is a difference of degree, whereas the differences between either of the two eggs or a behemoth is of rather more startling proportions; the latter we think of as a difference in kind.

something it could never do before—to wit, it can commit suicide. All of this boggles the mind, but the aspect of the matter to which we want to draw attention here is the significance of the new technology for the socialization process.

We think that one important result of this technological leap is that we are in transition from what we have called a "performance" society to a "learning" society. In a performance society it is reasonable to assume that in adulthood one will practice skills which were acquired in youth. That, of course, has been the traditional educational pattern for human beings, and it is reflected in our linguistic conventions. We say that a medical student, for instance, learns medicine and the doctor *practices* it. There is also the *practice* of law, and, in general, adults have been the *practitioners* of the skills which they learned as apprentices. In contrast, in a learning society, it is not reasonable to assume that one will practice in adulthood the skills which were acquired as a youth. Instead, we can expect to have several distinct careers within the course of one lifetime. Or, if we stay within one occupational field, it can be taken for granted that it will be fundamentally transformed several times. In a learning society, education is a continuing process—learning must go on and on and on. Anyone who either stops or is somehow prevented from further learning is reduced thereby to the status of an impotent bystander.

We assume that the shift from a *performance* to a *learning* society calls for a thoroughgoing transformation of our educational institutions—their administration, their curricula, and their methods of instruction. Education must give priority to the acquisition of a flexible set of highly abstract conceptual tools. An appropriate theoretical apparatus would range not only over the physical and biological sciences, but over the subject matter of the behavioral and social sciences as well. What is required is the inculcation of a deep, dynamic, conceptual grasp of fundamental matters—mere technical virtuosity within a fixed frame of reference is not only insufficient, but it can be a positive barrier to growth. Only symbolic skills of the highest abstractness, the greatest generality, are of utility in coping with radical change. This brings us back to the folk models which are inculcated in childhood. If they "teach" a conception of the world which is incompatible with a civilization in acceleration, then we have the challenge of creating new models appropriate for these changed and changing circumstances—we need models that are fundamentally dynamic.

In the next section of this paper we will present some very general principles for designing educational environments. It will be apparent at once that we have tried to learn some lessons from the thousands of years of human experience with autotelic folk models, but as was indicated above, we do not think that it is wise to be bound to them in any exclusive sense. The usual kinds of autotelic folk models could get along very nicely with sticks and stones on their physical side; however, dynamic models for a learning society seem to require the imaginative use of a much more subtle technology.

PRINCIPLES FOR DESIGNING CLARIFYING ENVIRONMENTS[9]

Our task now is to state and explain a set of four principles for designing educational environments. Any environment which satisfies all four of these principles will be said to be a "clarifying environment."

It will be seen that the first three principles to be treated are directly related to the notion of a folk model. The fourth principle seeks to make provision for the fact that we live in a world undergoing dynamic change.

1. *Perspectives Principle.* One environment is more conducive to learning than another if it both permits and facilitates the taking of more perspectives toward whatever is to be learned.

2. *Autotelic Principle.* One environment is more conducive to learning than another if the activities carried on within it are more autotelic.

3. *Productive Principle.* One environment is more conducive to learning than another if what is to be learned within it is more productive.

4. *Personalization Principle.* One environment is more conducive to learning than another if it: (a) is more responsive to the learner's activities, and (b) permits and facilitates the learner's taking a more reflexive view of himself as a learner.

The statement of the foregoing four[10] principles is sufficiently cryptic to make even a phrenologist happy. In spite of this fact, we believe they make some sense; and we forthwith proceed to try to explain the sense we think they make.

Perspectives Principle

The perspectives to which this principle refer are, of course, the four discussed in the previous section, namely, agent, patient, reciprocator, and referee. This principle assumes, *ceteris paribus*, that learning is more rapid and deeper if the learner can approach whatever is to be learned: (a) from all four of the perspectives rather than from just three, from three rather than from just two, and from two rather than from only one, and (b) in all combinations of these perspectives—hence, an environment that permits and facilitates fewer combinations is weaker from a learning standpoint than one that makes provision for more combination.

Another aspect of environmental flexibility with respect to the assumption

---

[9] It should be made clear that though this paper is in a certain sense a joint venture, the experimental and sociological part of the work belongs entirely to Moore. There is no particular point in trying to disentangle our contributions to what goes on here, beyond noting that the present paper represents the results, some of which have been reported elsewhere, of about ten years of collaboration. Formulation and application of the principles to follow are the results of Moore's work.

[10] C. S. Peirce observed somewhere that he had a "certain partiality for the number *three* in philosophy." From what follows, the reader will observe that *we* have a partiality to its successor. On the other hand, even Peirce occasionally gave way to *four* (1868).

of perspectives has to do with the attitude the learner brings to the environment each time he enters it. Imagine a learner who, one day, if filled with a sense of agency—he is in no mood, for instance, to be patient to anything or anybody. An environment will be more powerful from a learning standpoint if it lets him start off with whatever perspective he bring to it, and then allows him to shift at will.

As a parenthetical remark about shifting from one perspective to another, we think that young children do not have what is sometimes called a short "attention span," but they do have a relatively short and unstable "perspective span." This is one reason why there is little use in trying to deliver a lecture to a young child—he is not up to assuming the stance of a patient for very long at a time. But he can stay with the same topic or subject matter if he is permitted to run through a rather wide range of perspectives in whatever order he pleases.

When experts in education maintain that formal schooling is unsuitable for the very young child, the use of the word "formal" denotes the typical classroom situation in which most acts of agency are allocated to the teacher, the referee's role is also assigned primarily to the teacher, and the assumption of the reciprocal perspective in the form of interacting with peer-group members is forbidden through rules which are against note passing and which impose silence. About all that is left to the child is to be patient to the acts of agency of the teacher. This undoubtedly is an unsuitable learning situation for most young children—and the perspectives principle says that it is not as conducive to learning as a wide variety of alternative arrangements.

Another way to get the flavor of the perspectives principle is to pose the question as to why amusement parks amuse the young, but pall so rapidly. Think about the merry-go-round, the roller coaster, the fun-house with its surprises, and so forth—it is apparent that what all of these "amusements" have in common is the rapid, involuntary shift in viewpoint within the context of one basic perspective; specifically, each exploits some facet of patienthood. Any environment which tends to confine people to one basic perspective is apt to become boring rather quickly. Of course, the symbolic level of amusement-park entertainment is relatively low, too, although it is high in its appeal to simple feelings and emotions. Consequently, a few trips to an amusement park go a long way.

Clearly, the theater is a more subtle form of entertainment; with it the shifts in perspectives are largely symbolic in character, rather than grossly physical. However, like the amusement park, the theater shares a weakness. Both force us to be spectators—patient to what goes on. An amusement park ride hauls us through a predetermined course without any opportunity for changes due to our own acts of agency; similarly, plays run their predetermined courses. Though the patient perspective is salient at the amusement park and the theater, the referee's stance comes into the picture, too, as we assess and evaluate what goes on. There is also the vicarious opportunity to place ourselves in the roles of others, as, for instance, when we witness the screams and squirmings of others on a roller-coaster ride.

It should be noted that these and related forms of amusement are changing. Recent innovations in motion pictures permit the audience to vote from time to time on how they want things to come out. This is a step, though a crude one, in allowing for the agent perspective in entertainment. Some new amusement park rides gives a few controls to the passengers. Also, turning our attention for the moment to "cultural" entertainment, the traditional museum seems to be on its way out—more and more displays are subject to some sort of control by the visitor. So, we see the amusement park, the theater (at least motion pictures), and the museum moving away from the boredom inherent in a confining perspective. They are coming closer to satisfying the perspectives principle, which (to repeat) says that "one environment is more conducive to learning than another if it both permits and facilitates the taking of more perspectives toward whatever is to be learned."

Autotelic Principle

For an environment to be autotelic it must protect its denizens against serious consequences so that the goings on within it can be enjoyed for their own sake. The most obvious form of protection is physical. There are sports which come perilously close to violating their own autotelic norms because of physical risks—mountaineering is one. When a mountaineer is asked why he climbs, the fact that this question arose indicates something is amiss. People do not go about asking bowlers, chess players, and tennis players, to take one mixed bag of players, for deep reasons to justify their activities. Mountaineers, like racing-car drivers, are always trying to prove that their sport only appears to be dangerous—they argue that it is not hazardous for those who are properly trained.

When it comes to designing educational environments, especially those concerned with the acquisition of intellectual skills, almost everyone is pretty well agreed to keep physical risk out. True, there are some advocates of corporal punishment; and we should remember that there is the occasional fanatic, such as a teacher we once knew who thought that the only way to do mathematics was in an ice cold room. He began each class by throwing open the windows, even on bitterly cold days, which gave a kind of chilly introduction to algebra.

It is relatively easy to keep physical risks out of educational environments though there may always be the school-yard bully who punishes the scholar for his scholarship, and today, big-city schools increasingly require policemen to maintain order. Even so, it is more difficult to keep psychological and social risks out of an educational environment. If a student feels, while taking an exam, that he may disgrace himself and blight his future by failing to make a mark high enough to get into some special program, or if he feels that learning is simply a means of staying on a gravy train with stops only for prizes, honors, and scholarships on the way to success, then the whole learning environment is shot through with high psychological and social risks. For a learning environment to be autotelic, it must be cut off from just such risks.

Granted the nature of our present public and private school systems, and their relation to the broader society, it is doubtful that, at this time, more than a small fraction of the school day could be made autotelic. As a matter of fact, it is very difficult to arrange matters so that even a preschool child can have as much as thirty minutes a day that is really his, in the sense that none of the significant adults in his life is in a position to manipulate him, and where the things to be learned in the environment have a chance to speak persuasively to him in their own tongue.

Most contemporary education is nonautotelic; in fact, it prides itself on its nonautotelic status—school counselors carefully explain the financial and social rewards of further schooling. Through public service announcements, officials plead with dropouts to come back, and again, the basic argument given for returning to school is for rewards—financial and social. We never have heard a public service announcement which said something like, "Come back to school. Algebra is better than ever!"

The school day is so crammed full of activities that are planned to lead directly to the goal of at least one college degree, that a student seldom has the leisure to follow out the implications of an interesting problem, should he have the social misfortune of becoming intrigued by something truly puzzling. If a highly competent student works very hard, he may win a little extra time in which he can entertain a few ideas without having to cash them in at a science fair or some other parody of independent thinking.

Not only is the educational system largely nonautotelic in character, but the traditional folk models are in danger of being swept away. Little-league baseball replaces vacant-lot baseball. Amateur athletics in general seem to be turning into quasi-professional activities. On the more intellectual side our puzzles have been incorporated into the structure of tests—all current tests of ability are really a series of short puzzles.

Regardless of all of this, the autotelic principle states that the best way to learn really difficult things is to be placed in an environment in which you can try things out, make a fool of yourself, guess outrageously, or play it close to the vest—all without serious consequences. The autotelic principle does not say that once the difficult task of acquiring a complex symbolic skill is well underway, it is then not appropriate to test yourself in a wide variety of serious competitions. It is a common misunderstanding of the notion of an autotelic environment to assume that *all* activities should be made autotelic. Not so. The whole distinction requires a *difference* between a time for playfulness and a time for earnest efforts with real risks.

Productive Principle

Our statement of the productive principle is enigmatic at this point because we have not yet clarified the term "productive" though we have made implicit use of the concept of "productivity," in our prior discussion of folk models. So let us be explicit now.

We will say that one cultural object (a cultural object is something that is socially transmissible through learning) is more productive than another cultural object if it has properties which permit the learner either to *deduce* things about it, granted a partial presentation of it in the first instance, or *make probable inferences* (Peirce anthology, 1955) about it, again assuming only a partial exposure to it.

Some examples may help. A perfect instance of a productive cultural object is a mathematical system. We can give the learner some axioms, some formation and transformation rules, and then he is at liberty to deduce theorems on his own. The logical structure of the system is what makes it productive. However, we are not always in a position to deal with such beautifully articulated structures. A case in point is the periodic table of elements. Its structure is productive on the basis of *probable inference* as opposed to *deductive inference*. Our evidence for productivity in this case is that empty cells in the table have been filled in with elements having the predicted properties. But compare the periodic table with an alphabetical arrangement of the same elements. The latter is less productive than the former by a country mile. In order to be more precise about all of this we would need a general theory of "probable inference" as well as a theory of "deducibility." We hope that a crude characterization of productiveness will be sufficient for our present purposes.

Turning back to the principle itself, it says, again *ceteris paribus*, that of two versions of something to be learned, we should choose the one which is most productive; this frees the learner to reason things out for himself and it also frees him from depending upon authority.[11]

Folk models, taken collectively, are good examples of productive cultural objects. To illustrate, once the simple rules for playing chess are mastered, it is not necessary to consult anyone in order to go on playing chess. It is true that one may be playing badly, but the structure of the rules for playing are sufficiently productive to guarantee that it is bad chess and not bad checkers that is being played.

Now that we have cleared things up a bit, someone might wonder why anyone would bother to state the productive principle as a principle for de-

---

[11] Though we do not know exactly how to characterize "productivity," we can give at least one clear example. The "natural deduction" methods of Gentzen, Jaskowski, Fitch (see Fitch, 1952, for references), and others are "productive" in that they help the student figure out what is going on. By contrast Nicod's single axiom for the propositional calculus prompted Irving Copi to quote Dr. Johnson's alleged remark about a woman preaching: it is ". . . like a dog's walking on his hind legs. It is not done well; but you are surprised to find it done at all."

signing educational enviornments. Surely, people would not select the less productive of two versions of something to be learned. Yes, they would! The example above concerning the periodic table did not just pop into our heads. We observed, not long ago, a science teacher who had his students learn the atomic numbers and the atomic weights of the elements in *alphabetic order*. This is a tough task, and only a few of the children could manage it. Doubtless, you say, this is a rare aberration. Again, we beg to disagree. Let us take, as our case in point, the teaching of reading in the United States.

As everyone knows, or is supposed to know, there are two contrasting kinds of orthographic systems. On the one hand, there is the ideographic sort in which knowing some "words" gives almost no clues as to how to handle the next written word. The Chinese system of writing is of this kind; it is barely productive at all.[12] On the other hand, there are many systems of writing which are alphabetic. Once the learner has cracked the code which relates the written and spoken versions of the language to each other, he can write anything he can say, or he can read anything that has been written. (The only things sacrificed by not referring to authority are the niceties of spelling and punctuation, but the phonetics carry the meaning.) Such alphabetic systems of writing are productive cultural objects, even, we should point out, in the case of a child of our acquaintance who spelled the word for eyes as "is." Given our usual spelling habits, this looks at best like an imaginative leap at an attempt to spell "eyes," but as Moore has pointed out elsewhere (1963), English orthography has more coherence than it is given credit for. However, many of the standard textbooks for teaching beginning reading used in our country today treat written English as if it were Chinese.

Personalization Principle

This principle, unlike the others, has two distinct parts: the idea is that the environment must be both (1) responsive to the learner's activities and (2) helpful in letting him learn to take a reflexive view of himself. The explanation comes in two pieces.

The Responsive Condition. The notion of a responsive environment is a complex one, but the intuitive idea is straightforward enough. It is the antithesis of an environment that answers a question that was never asked,[13] or, positively stated, it is an environment that encourages the learner first to find

---

[12] There is some *slight* productivity in the fact that such characters as those for *tree, grove,* and *forest* have a reasonable connection: a tree looks like 木, a grove like 林, and a forest like 森. Similarly the character 口 means (among other things) *mouth, entrance, opening, hole.* But whoever would have guessed that 龜 meant "turtle"?

[13] We are all familiar with situations where we are given information we did not want to have. Our earlier discussion indicates our belief that many school children are in this situation (as we both were), and we suppose that the adult analogue is wading through all that dreary stuff about soap, while waiting for the eleven o'clock news on TV.

a question, then find an answer. The requirements imposed upon an environment in order to qualify it as "responsive" are:

1. It permits the learner to explore freely, thus giving him a chance to discover a problem.

2. It informs the learner immediately about the consequences of his actions. (How immediate is immediate will be discussed later.)

3. It is self-pacing, for example, events happen within the environment at a rate largely determined by the learner. (The notion that the rate is *largely* determined by the learner and not wholly determined by him is important. For example, some hyperactive children rush at their problems so much that the consequences of their actions are blurred—there must be provision for slowing down the learner under some circumstances; also, there are occasions when he should be speeded up. Nonetheless, it is basically self-pacing.)

4. It permits the learner to make full use of his capacity for discovering relations of various kinds. (No one knows what anyone's full capacity for making discoveries is, but if we hand the learner a solution we certainly know we are not drawing upon his capacity.)

5. It is so structured that the learner is likely to make a series of interconnected discoveries about the physical, cultural, or social world. (What this amounts to depends, of course, upon what kinds of relations are being "taught" within the environment.)

The conditions for responsiveness taken together define a situation in which a premium is placed on the making of fresh deductions and inductions, as opposed to having things explained didactically. It encourages the learner to ask questions, and the environment will respond in relevant ways; but these ways may not always be simple or predictable. For a learner to make discoveries, there must be some gaps or discontinuities in his experience that he feels he must bridge. One way that such discontinuities can be built into a responsive environment is to make provision for changing the "rules of the game" without the learner knowing, at first, that they have been changed. However, it will not do to change the rules quixotically—the new set of rules should build upon the old, displacing them only in part. Such changes allow the learner to discover that something has gone wrong—old solutions will no longer do—he must change in order to cope with change. In other words, if you want a learner to make a series of interconnected discoveries, you will have to see to it that he encounters difficulties that are problematic for *him*. When he reaches a solution, at least part of that solution should be transferable to the solution of the next perplexity.

Finally, though a responsive environment does respond, its response has an integrity of its own. It is incorrect to think of a responsive environment as one which simply yields to whatever the learner wants to do—there are constraints. To take a trivial example, if the question is how to spell the word "cat," the environment permits the learner to attempt to spell it K-A-T— there is no rule against trying this, but he will not succeed that way, where by "succeeding," we mean *both* getting a satisfactory response from the environment, *and* learning the sort of thing the environment was devised to help him learn. Without the latter condition the environment would not be informative.

The Reflexive Condition. One environment is more reflexive than another if it makes it easier for the learner to see himself as a social object. We previously made the point, the Meadian point, that the acquisition of the social self is an achievement in learning. Unfortunately, some of us are underachievers. One reason, we think, for our ineptitude in fashioning ourselves is that it is hard to see what we are doing—we lack an appropriate mirror. The reflexiveness which is characteristic of maturity is sometimes so late in coming that we are unable to make major alterations in ourselves. The "reflexive condition" is fairly heavy terminology; all we mean is that if an environment is so structured that the learner not only can learn whatever is to be learned, but also can learn about himself *qua* learner, he will be in a better position to undertake whatever task comes next. It facilitates future learning to see our own learning career both retrospectively and prospectively. It is a normal thing for human beings to make up hypotheses about themselves, and it is important that these hypotheses do not harden into dogma on the basis of grossly inadequate information.

We find it not at all surprising that athletic coaches have made more use of reflexive devices in instruction than have classroom teachers. This does not surprise us because of our confidence in play forms. It is in the realm of sports that motion pictures of learning and practice have come into wide usage. Coaches go over games with their players, spotting weaknesses, strengths, and so forth—they do not forget their opponents, either. Of course, motion pictures used reflexively have limitations, but surely coaches have taken a step in the right direction.

　　　　　*　　　　　*　　　　　*

The four principles presented above, perspectives, autotelic, productive and personalization, are offered as heuristic guides[14] for constructing educational environments. Undoubtedly, they are vague and ambiguous; the critical question is whether they are so deficient as to be useless. We do not think that they are totally without merit. In the next section we offer an application of the principles to show what can be made of them.

AN APPLICATION OF THE FOUR PRINCIPLES

Imagine that for some unaccountable reason you were given the problem of designing an educational environment for preschool children. Imagine also

---

[14] Some people might prefer that we convert the principles into empirical propositions and then proceed to test their truth. We would caution that they would require a much more rigorous formulation if they were to be treated as anything more than heuristic guidelines. The difficulty in such reformulations is that the principles make use of a number of concepts which are not very well understood mathematically. So, for the moment, let us take them as guides, and *only* as such.

that this environment is to be one in which the children learn to read their natural language. What would you do?

One of us has taken upon himself the task of building several such environments, beginning with the very simple, and gradually working up to larger, more complex ones. This evolution of environments was marked by a gradual increase in the sophistication of the technology which went into them. The four principles we have discussed were used in designing both the overall structure of these environments and the technology used within them. We would like to make it clear, incidentally, as a methodological point, that the ideas came first and the applications (both in logic and behavioral science) came afterwards. However, our understanding of the principles and the clarity with which we saw their relevance increased with the experience of actually constructing learning environments.

Let us go over each principle to see what it "tells" us to do.

Perspectives Principle—Application

If the children who come to the environment are to learn to read, we should ask what sort of an activity reading is. In the simplest terms, reading involves the decoding of a message which was previously encoded.[15] Leaving aside the special case where the reader decodes his own material, as a reader we are patient to the symbolic consequences of someone else's activity. We read what the writer wrote. This is banal, all right, but it does point to a one-sided emphasis in reading that the principle seeks to avoid. Is there some way to allow the learner to stand in the relation of agent as well as patient to reading material?

First, the perspectives principle urges that we think about this. An answer comes readily. Reading should be treated as part of a correlative process. Specifically, the decoding and encoding of messages, that is, reading and writing, should be developed together. Reading emphasizes patienthood and writing emphasizes agency. Once one begins to look around for correlative processes which give the learner an opportunity to take more perspectives toward his task, other combinations come easily to mind. For instance, what about listening and speaking? Obviously, listening stands to reading as writing stands to speaking. The first pair, reading and listening, is on the side of patienthood, the other is on the side of agency.

Thus we are being led by the perspectives principle to widen our definition of the learner's task. Originally, we thought of him as learning to read, now we see him as learning to handle a four-fold set of linguistic processes: reading, writing, listening, speaking. With regard to this set, the learner's redefined task is to communicate more effectively rather than simply to read.

---

[15] Here we are simply going to bypass the usual hornet's nest of questions about the logical and ontological status of "information" about "type-token" distinctions and the like. We will also fail to discuss the question as to whether speech is encoded writing, or writing is encoded speech. Not that these are unimportant issues, but this is not the place to discuss them.

Up to this point we have drawn on only two of the four basic perspectives, agent and patient, but the reciprocal perspective suggests something else. As will be recalled, to take the reciprocal perspective is to look at our own behavior from the standpoint of someone else. What implications does this have for reading?

If we are reading something, we may want to know who wrote it. We may wish to understand the context out of which the message comes. It would seem that we should begin to learn very early to distinguish among various sources of messages if we are to put ourselves in the frame of reference of the sender. Some messages come from ourselves; that is, we are decoding what we have previously encoded. Some messages come from persons whom we know, and some messages come from strangers. This, of course, is looking at the sources of messages from the standpoint of the pair of perspectives, patient-reciprocal. If we think of writing, or more broadly, of preparing a message, again we need to know whether the message is being done for our own later use, for the use of others whom we know (and whose peculiarities we may wish to take into account) or for strangers. From this standpoint the perspectives pair which is involved is agent-reciprocal.

In designing our educational environment according to the reciprocal perspective, the learner should be led to distinguish among the various possible targets for his messages, and he should be led to discriminate among the various possible sources of messages which come to him. If, for instance, all of the reading material in the educational environment is prepared by anonymous outside experts, then how will the learner have any chance to make the discriminations about which we have been talking? It will not do, either, for all the material to come from the learner himself or from those he knows. Perhaps an illustration may make our meaning plain. In one of our laboratories some of the children were taking dictation at three and four years of age. The children had a chance to learn to distinguish between themselves and others as "dictators." One little boy, who took dictation quite well, his own and others, would at first refuse to recognize himself if he had botched his recording. One moment he would say, "That little boy doesn't speak right," and in the next breath he would take credit for something well done.

Taking the reciprocal perspective seriously encourages us to design the environment so that the learner can come to make clearer distinctions between himself and other people, both in the encoding and decoding of messages. Concretely, this means that the environment must make explicit provision in terms of time, place, and equipment for the learner to produce material (a) for his own exclusive use, (b) for those he knows, and (c) for general consumption, as well as to receive information (a) from himself, (b) from those he knows, and (c) from total strangers, such as Mark Twain.

It should be remembered, in terms of either the Meadian or our own theoretical position, that to say the learner should come to make clearer distinctions between himself and other people does not presuppose that his "self" is a preformed finished product. Quite to the contrary, learning to make such distinctions is part of the process whereby the learner develops a sense of self-identity or, in general, a more adequate self.

This account helps us take care of agents, patients, and reciprocators, or so we believe; now how about referees? Clearly, encoding and decoding messages has to be done in accordance with some set of rules, otherwise the messages would be meaningless or garbled. The rules of a natural language and its written counterpart are so difficult to formulate that linguistics has not yet succeeded in adequately characterizing the formal structure of any natural language. Therefore, it is impossible for us to teach the learner the rules of the game in an explicit didactic way.

How are we to handle this? How are we to encourage the learner to view his own acts of communication and those of others from the standpoint of a set of common ground rules? We could, of course, bring in a teacher who would tell the student such things as "Read more clearly," or "That is an improperly constructed sentence." To have a teacher behave in this fashion would provide a referee, a very authoritative referee, but the perspectives principle says that the learner is to be encouraged to take the referee's perspective *himself* in evaluating his own and other's ongoing activities. In order to get him to assume this stance, what seems to be required is to have breaches of the common rules of communication become problems for the learner. The example above of the little boy who took dictation is to the point. When this boy originally either told a story or read a story (which was being recorded) there was always a strong tendency to criticize him for speaking unclearly, garbling words, and so on. However, his inadequacies became problems *to him* when he attempted to decipher his own speech. Since the environment was arranged so that he easily could re-do sections of his own recordings, and compare his messages with messages from others, he had the opportunity of assessing and evaluating the adequacy and appropriateness of his own communication.

The idea of making rule violations a genuine problem to the learner as a step toward getting him to take the referee's perspective seems sound enough, but it does not go to the heart of the problem—it might result only in the learner's taking a rule oriented view of what just happened to become problematic to him. He needs to be placed in a position where he can oversee the whole communication process as it goes on within the environment. To put it another way, he needs to be put in a position that is *super*ordinate to the component processes of communication: reading, writing, listening, and speaking (all of which are being carried out in terms of an appropriate variety of message sources and targets).

The referee's perspective suggests, then, that we create a superordinate task which will use the subordinate communications skills as means to accomplish it. The overall task which was set up in several environments was that of publishing a newspaper. (It will be made clear below, when we treat the autotelic principles, that the publishing of a newspaper goes on in what is called a "transfer room," rather than in the autotelic environment *per se*.

Newspaper publishing is not treated as a purely autotelic matter in this transfer room.) This is a task in which the participants not only can use their communication skills, but they have to establish standards for what is published. If the children are permitted to work out their own criteria for interest, relevance, and clarity for the intended audience, they must oversee the whole operation as an umpire would.

To get the newspaper started, two highly competent children, who had been in this special educational environment for three years and who could read, write, type, and take dictation, were selected as editors. When they were five years old they began to publish their own newspaper with some initial assistance from adults. By the time they were seven, another group of five-year olds was ready to start its newspaper. So, instead of having adults help in establishing another newspaper, the two senior editors were asked to select two editors for the paper-to-be, and then to explain to them what the job of editor amounted to. The experienced editors were none too sanguine about the feasibility of explaining anything to children so young, but they agreed to try. They had the satisfaction of knowing that the children with whom they would be dealing were of their own choosing.

A convenient way to get some feel for how the children behave in terms of the referee's perspective is to follow one of their discussions. Given below is a transcript of part of an editors' conference. The cast consists of a seven-year-old girl, Venn, co-editor of the first newspaper; a seven-year-old boy, Jeffrey, co-editor of the first newspaper; Pam, newly appointed five-year-old girl, co-editor of the newspaper; Larry, four-year-old boy, co-editor of the new newspaper. The extent to which four able children can deal meaningfully with the problems of deciding what is "fit to print" (apologies to the New York Times) is indicated in an extended quotation below. But first, a parenthetical remark.

Four children are serving as editors. Explicit provision must be made in the environment for rotating this role, otherwise the opportunity to see what goes on from the editor's desk would be a restricted one. Plainly enough, some children are prepared to be editors at first and others will come along later. Some may not be up to the job at all, in which case they should be given a chance to rise as high as they can. Also it is important for former editors to serve as contributors who have to put up with editors. One practical way to rotate the role of editor is to have different editors for different issues. We shall now "listen in" on a conversation the children had on the subject.

Editors' Conference

VENN: Jeffrey and I have chosen you two to be the editors of the first-grade newspaper.
   My first question is, Would you like to be the editors of the first-grade newspaper?
LARRY AND PAM (in unison): Yessssssssssss!!!!
VENN: Well——one of——the editor is the boss of the newspaper and you are going to be the boss, so, one of the ways to get an article is, you can tell a child——
LARRY: What's a child?

VENN: You can tell a child, give a child an idea——

LARRY: But what's a child?

VENN: You're a child——

LARRY: Oh——

VENN: give a child an idea and he can think about it for a while, or a child can think up his own ideas. He'll type that once he gets it, and then he will give it to you. If there are too many errors, give it back. If it's OK—its OK. But if there's a few errors, correct them. But if there's too many errors——you can't just——

LARRY: Correct them?

VENN: correct them or it would be more——

LARRY: Could Pam help me, then, correct them?

VENN: Yes——if there's too many you shouldn't correct them because if you did correct them, you might be correcting too many and it would be more of your article than theirs. Once you get a lot of this material, like riddles, poems, jokes, cartoons and——

JEFFREY: And comics——

VENN: and comics, you can choose the ones that——you can both decide the ones that are most interesting and the ones that aren't you leave out, then you type them on stencils—and then when you get all the stencils you run them off on the mimeograph machine. Now, a mimeograph machine is this thing right there.

LARRY: How do you work it?

VENN: You'll find out. After you mimeograph it, you collate it. And then you staple it, and then it is ready to give out. And—Pam? Do you have any questions? Pam——

PAM: Well, what if all of them are not too good—what do you do, really?

LARRY: (at the same time Jeffrey is talking): You correct all of them——

JEFFREY: You give them back and make them start all over again on a different one.

VENN: As you would if they were wrong, you would send them back——

PAM: Ahhh——

VENN: Before, if they were wrong as we told you——

LARRY: All of them?

PAM: Why?

VENN: Because——

LARRY: If we get tired then we couldn't be the editors if we got too tired, right?

VENN: Editors——if you are going to be an editor, editors don't get tired!

LARRY: But erasing all those things, right? they will——

JEFFREY: On stencils you don't erase—special kind of correcting fluid——

VENN: Stencils are made out of wax.

LARRY: I think I've used them before——

VENN: No, Larry——

LARRY: But I think I've seen them run once.

PAM: I think he has seen them once, but I'm not quite sure cause I haven't seen them once.

God may allow himself the luxury of resting on the seventh day, but this privilege evidently is not for editors—"Editors don't get tired!" It isn't too often that we have a chance to listen to young children discuss a difficult problem. We find their viewpoints fascinating, leaving aside the little exchange about "What's a child?" the rest is really quite subtle. By the way, the recording of the conference indicates that Venn slurred the word "child" when she first used it—it sounded like "chile." Larry misunderstood her. Also, he may have been surprised by a child using the word "child" because adults generally are the ones who use this term.

It is interesting to contrast the views of the experienced children with the inexperienced youngsters. For little Larry, the main problem he saw in correcting errors was the time and effort it might take—he wanted to be certain he had Pam's help in this. Venn and Jeffrey knew that the sheer physical act of correcting errors, for instance on a stencil, was trivial. As experienced editors, their point was the delicate one having to do with human relations and the integrity of other people's work. Venn said it quite well: "If there's too many [errors] you shouldn't correct them because if you did correct them, you might be correcting too many, and it would be *more of your article than theirs.*" Evidently, Venn and Jeffrey feel that at some point an editor would become the contributor if he "corrected" the article too much. The same sort of point was brought up by Pam when she said, "Well, what if all of them are not too good—what do you do, really?" Venn replies that it is the same problem as correcting too many errors. Jeffrey and Venn agree, give it back and have them start over.

It seems to us that all of the editors, especially the experienced ones, are too confident of the "rightness" of their judgments. There is still an absolutistic streak in their attitude toward what it means to be the referee. None of them, at that time, ever had had to put up with an unreasonable editor.[16] It would be intriguing to know whether they would evolve some mechanism whereby contributors who felt they had been unfairly or improperly judged would have some court of appeal. (We did not get to find out because the grant under which we were working ran out the next year.) In any case, the perspectives principle urges us to create opportunities for the learners to get an overview of their environment and to learn to make assessments and evaluations of a normative kind.

Autotelic Principle—Applications

The most obvious application of this principle is to the physical safety of the children. Since they are permitted to explore the environment freely and much of what they do is self-determined, it is imperative to examine every aspect of the environment for hazards. Naturally enough, the safety of the children is of first importance, but the environment needs some protection, too. We use the somewhat awkward expression "child-proofing the environment" to cover both aspects of this relation—we want the children to be safe,

---

[16] It may come as a surprise to the reader, as it did to us, that the concept of an "unreasonable editor" can be made mathematically precise. As Dana Scott pointed out in a discussion in Ann Arbor in 1955, this fact follows from his work on "A Short Recursively Unsolvable Problem," an abstract of which was published in (1956).

but we do *not* want to ruin the environment. This is much easier said than done. It has taken as much as three months of engineering time to work out solutions for some seemingly simple problems. For example, the automatic carriage return on the ordinary electric typewriter is dangerous because a tiny child could have his fingers hurt if he is unlucky enough to have them in the wrong place when the carriage snaps back. We designed a clear plastic shield to prevent this from happening. This sounds easy to do, but it takes a good deal of thought to come up with a practical shield which the operator can remove quickly but the child cannot. Most educational environments are not troubled by the safety factor because the children are not given sufficient freedom to get into serious difficulties and the environments are relatively bare.

An autotelic environment must afford the learner more than physical safety—he must be free from various kinds of social pressures. At the very least, this means privacy *vis-à-vis* the authority figures in his life. We can remember very well explaining the autotelic principle to an architect who was to design an autotelic environment for a public school. He seemed to understand what was wanted and in about two weeks he came back with beautiful colored drawings showing an open park-like area which was sprinkled with clear plastic bubbles, each bubble slightly larger than a phone booth, and each bubble containing a child who could see everything around him, and who could be seen by anyone who chanced by. This is not quite the idea.

As most of us can recall from our own childhood, play means *both* not having to do something *and* not having to do it in the presence of authorities. The demand for privacy during playtime seems to require children to disappear into cracks between buildings, or cellars, caves, tree houses, and other uncomfortable places. They seem to care little about comfort if its sacrifice will purchase some freedom. So the idea is to make a place into which children can disappear during (autotelic) playtime—a place where they cannot be followed by those whom they may be trying to avoid.

There is an indefinitely large number of architectural arrangements which would do for this purpose so long as whatever structure is used is protected by norms which prevent a bossy older sister, a domineering mother, an anxious father, or a meddling grandparent from coming in. Sometimes we have used air-conditioned, windowless, prefabricated buildings as the shell for such environments. Inside there is compartmentalization—there are sound-proofed booths for individuals and larger rooms for groups. Sometimes, rather than constructing a separate building for the environment, we have used space within an existing structure. In either case, the heart of the matter is to delineate clearly the protective boundary of the environment so that even a two-year old will be led to recognize the distinction between being in it and being out of it. This distinction can be conveyed physically in many ways and we try to use as many *differences* as we can, partly because some children, mentally retarded ones, for example, need all the help they can get to make this distinction. We have used differences in color, texture, temperature, and so on, very freely to define the environmental boundary.

Even if the architecture of the environment spells privacy for the learner, the social norms which define the environment as autotelic must be made clear to him. We have found that most children are more likely to believe what other children say than they are to believe adults when it comes to the question of freedom. Therefore, we rely on children to explain the rules of the environment to newcomers. The rules are simple enough—the problem is to make them credible. The first rule is, you do not have to come here at all. The second rule is, you may leave when you wish. The third rule is, you do not need to explain your comings and goings. These are the basic explicit rules. There are some implicit rules which bind the staff and which may or may not be of direct concern to the learner. The prime implicit rule is that the behavior of the learner in the environment is a private matter for the staff. The learner himself may talk about it in any way he pleases and to whom he pleases. What all this means is that parents, for example, are not allowed to watch their own children, nor do they get reports which would enable them to follow their child's progress in the environment. The children are not graded. Of course, if the staff sees a serious medical, educational, or social problem developing, this is promptly brought to the parent's attention. The point is *not* to neglect measles, or hysteria; it is rather to give the tykes a little time off every day, when they can enjoy learning something without being under the nose of Mommy, or Daddy, or Big Brother.

After a child has been coming to a well-run autotelic environment for some time, he will have learned some things which he may wish to practice. In several of our educational ventures we have designed a kind of half-way station between the world outside the autotelic environment and the autotelic environment *per se*. We call this a "transfer room" (a concept to which we referred earlier). It is physically and normatively distinct from the basic autotelic environment. It is in the transfer room, for example, that the children publish a newspaper. They begin such activities only after they have learned how to read, type, and so forth. In the transfer room they practice these skills within the context of some superordinate task. The normative rules for the transfer room might best be described as permissive rather than autotelic. For instance, several groups of youngsters not only published a newspaper but they sold it. The newspaper itself with its signed articles gave parents and others a pretty good idea of what their children were doing and thinking. By definition, a newspaper is not private, but public. The children used the newspaper to gain and to express criticism. In brief, there are many kinds of extrinsic rewards and punishments associated with this activity. We think that the transfer room is a valuable adjunct to an autotelic environment if there is any reason to believe that the world outside that environment does not provide adequate opportunities for the learners to apply their skills. An appropriately designed transfer room and suitable transfer-room activities allow for the "transfer" of what is learned within an autotelic environment to problems outside its boundary.

Sometimes the question is asked as to why the children should trust the adults in the autotelic environment to be autotelic toward them if children are assumed to be somewhat distrustful of adults in general. We, of course, do not assume that all children are distrustful of adults. We do assume, however, that most children two years of age and older have discovered that questions such as "Would you like to wash your hands?" are best translated as the imperative "Wash your hands!" We find that children only gradually come to trust the adult staff who manage the environment. It helps to create this trust if the staff avoids taking nonautotelic roles with the children outside the environment. An instructive mistake will show what is to be avoided. In one educational experiment the director reported to us that his children did not behave at all as he would have expected—they did not seem to explore very much, they frequently refused to come to the laboratory, they stayed for relatively short periods of time—evidently something had gone wrong. It turned out that this project director used his laboratory staff in two conflicting roles. Some of them served as part-time bus monitors. As bus monitors they had to discipline the children in a variety of ways to assure the safe operation of the bus. Then these same people would appear in the laboratory as staff members who are carefully instructed not to reward or punish the children. Quite understandably these preschool children were confused. Older, more sophisticated children might have been willing to accept the thesis that one person can wear two hats, but it was asking too much of this particular group. When this was pointed out, the director changed his job assignments appropriately and within a few weeks the behavior of the children became more relaxed, refusal rates went down, and length of stays increased.

It seems to us that the autotelic principle gives some general guidance in constructing the physical side of an educational environment and in formulating its rules and procedures. When we first began to experiment with autotelic environments we held our breath lest the children really would not come back unless they were given candy, gold stars, or some such, on the one hand, and threats and punishments, on the other. These environments were not built for a day, a week, or even a month—we hoped the children would find them fascinating for years! We now know that such attractive environments can be built and that the children will come to them for an indefinitely long period of time. If suitable transfer rooms and transfer-room activities are provided, the children can develop exceedingly high levels of skill and they take considerable pride in their accomplishments. An article by a teenager written for a high school newspaper conveys some sense of the way the children felt about their experience in one laboratory. This piece was written by Nancy Jordan, an assistant editor of her paper.

Reading Lab Produces Paper

The first grade in connection with the reading lab puts out its own newspaper. We felt it might be to our advantage to interview the Staff. We walked in a little apprehensively wondering just what to ask and how to approach our competitors. They seemed to regard us with awe and a little hesitation as to our true intentions. But they were a rather talkative group and it didn't take very long for each to willingly expositate on his contributions and prove an individual superiority.

Everyone Contributes

The paper is compiled solely by the children and they seem to regard any assistance as an infringement upon their skill. Everyone in the class is a contributing reporter who types up his own story and then several others type up the sheets for the newspaper itself and run them off on the thermo-fax machine, an instrument whose complexities are clearer to the first-grade than they are to us. We were also proudly told by one interested, lively little girl, "I could type when I was two years old!"

A boy standing nearby not to be outdone added "I learned to type four years ago." Since they are both only six and we are sixteen and hardly able to pluck out a few lines with one finger, we began to feel slightly inferior.

Satisfies Literary Needs

The stories are typed in the lab and one of the editors assured me that everybody in the class "liked" to participate in this sort of literary self-expression. Some of the others appeared more dubious but all were extremely fond of typing and genuinely enjoyed this program.

The development of the paper was adequately expressed in a rather concise sentence by the editors, "Well one day Mrs. Coogan told us a surprise and we were the editors."

Mrs. Coogan helps to correct the articles and when questioned how they knew the spelling of such a variety of words, the response was naturally that they were fully acquainted with the use of the dictionary. They all seemed to think reading and correcting articles was fun or anyway the finding of other people's mistakes. We complimented them on their paper and someone quickly apologized "I saw a little mistake but we decided to skip it."

Sacred Document

By accident a copy of their paper was dropped, a hush fell over the room. Two or three children quickly retrieved the journal with stricken faces for they had an intense pride in their achievement and were not ready to see a product of such hard effort mutilated or destroyed in any way.

We asked for any final comments; first we received a blank stare but then someone kindly volunteered "Well I was thinking if you wanted to use my riddle . . ." Another boy with a rather dream-like expression said, "I have something to say . . . I was at the beach and . . ." As we left we overheard one boy say to a friend, "We were having a meeting!" and with the aptness of childhood logic the other's reply was "Who cares, that's stupid?"

Productive Principle—Application

The guidance which this principle gives us with respect to reading is quite straightforward. It invites us to consider very carefully the structure of what is to be learned. If children are to read, they must break the code that relates the spoken language to the written language (the spoken part having been learned already in an autotelic way; mothers do not send their babies to the Sorbonne for lectures—the babies learn to speak because *they* find it fun to communicate in some more sophisticated way than crying). For present purposes we will confine ourselves to the English language as an example, but the reader will see that many of our considerations would carry over to any language with a similar orthography, for example, a system of symbols designed to mirror speech. Among such we mention Greek, Hebrew, Russian, Arabic, German, Latin—all of which have had, at one time or another, distinctive *alphabets*: conventional squiggles on paper intended to indicate the sounds made in the course of talking (a writing system quite different from that of the Chinese, mentioned above).

If we ask ourselves whether our present English alphabet is better than some alternative versions of it, we can see at once that it leaves a good deal to be desired. Too few symbols are trying to do too much work. This produces unnecessary ambiguity, which in turn produces confusion for the learner.

Sir James Pitman (1965), the grandson of Sir Isaac Pitman, inventor of the system of shorthand which bears his name, developed an alphabet consisting of 44 symbols, more than enough to represent the 40 phonemes of English. This system is intended to be used as an initial teaching alphabet (i.t.a.) after which the learner is expected to switch over to the conventional alphabet. There is no question about it, Pitman's system is more productive than the conventional alphabet. It is being used on an experimental basis in our country now. We have not used it largely because the typewriters employed in our work have the standard keyboard. Now some typewriter companies are offering the Pitman symbols.

Besides the question of productivity, there are some other issues which arise with respect to Pitman's system. What happens if some children do not switch easily to the conventional system? Might not some people welcome a group of second-class readers (those who never switched) as targets for exploitation? There are many other issues of this kind which come up when the question is one of adopting or not adopting an innovation on a mass basis. Here, all that we wish to note is that the productivity principle alerts us to alternatives, some of which are clearly superior to the conventional system.

Personalization Principle—Application

Responsive Condition. In applying the responsive condition to the learning of basic communication skills, we will concentrate here on the design of responsive environment equipment. Equipment is not the whole story, but it will be recalled that one of the requirements imposed on an environment in order to qualify it as responsive is that it should permit the learner to explore. We mean that he should be able to explore the entire environment, not just the equipment it may contain.

Suppose we wish to design a machine which will help a child learn to "read." Following our prior application of the perspectives principle, we place reading within the context of the four-fold set of linguistic skills: speaking/listening; writing/reading. We have mentioned five conditions for responsiveness, and we will now attempt to design our machine so that it will satisfy these conditions.

1. *It permits the learner to explore.* . . . It seems simple enough to say that the learner should be free to explore and presumably what he is free to explore is our hypothetical machine. Does this mean that he should be free to take the machine apart? Leaving aside the complication that he might hurt himself—a contingency forbidden by our prior application of the autotelic principle—the idea is not to explore the machine as such. Rather, what we want him to do is to explore something else using the machine as a tool or means for exploration. True, he will have to learn something about the machine in order to use it as a tool, but most of the machine's characteristics *qua* machine are irrelevant to the task of enhancing communication skills.

What in the world is it, then, that the learner is to explore? We have agreed to confine ourselves to English, for present purposes. The English orthographic system, as we all know, consists of more than the upper and lower case alphabets—it also has various punctuation marks. What is more, all of these symbols must be used in accordance with certain conventions, such as proceeding from left to right, from top to bottom, and with various kinds of juxtaposition. It is this complex system of English orthography that we want to open up for exploration.

The learner should find it easy to produce any part of it at will; it should be convenient to expose him to it; and whatever is done with it should exemplify its various conventions. Our task, then, as clarified by the responsive condition, is to design a machine which the learner can use to explore this system. When the matter is looked at in this light, it is quite apparent that clever inventors have anticipated us, in part. There already exists an inexpensive, reliable orthographic machine—it is called a "typewriter." It has both the upper and lower case alphabets, standard punctuation, and its mode of operation exemplifies the basic orthographic conventions—its carriage goes from right to left so that the writing proceeds in the approved left to right fashion (of course some typewriters go "backwards," such as Arabic typewriters, which are just right for Arabs), the carriage return and the line feed give us the required top to bottom movement, and the appropriate combined use of the space bar, tab, margin settings and carriage return provides for the many conventions pertaining to juxtaposition.

The typewriter is patently the kind of machine that we want but it is inadequate in certain respects. As long as we stay with reading and writing it does well enough, but it makes no provision for speaking and listening. If we are to tie our four linguistic processes together then the capabilities of the typewriter must be extended. It needs a voice so that the learner can begin his exploration of the complex relations holding between the spoken and written forms of English. It also needs some of the attributes of dictation equipment, that is, it needs a recording-reproducing component. It needs all of these capabilities if the system to be explored is not just English orthography, but English orthography combined with spoken English. The "talking type-writer," which we promised to place in perspective, represents a first step toward the construction of an adequate responsive machine to be used as a part of an overall *clarifying* environment in which the learners have the opportunity to acquire basic communication skills.

Returning for the moment to the topic of English orthography, let us think a little bit about the keyboard of our "orthographic machine." The responsive condition urges that we use a full keyboard so that the learner can explore freely the alphabets and punctuation.

Although we know that there are conflicting views about exposing the full standard keyboard to the learner, we still believe that this is a useful way of introducing children to the kind of thing they find in books. We have, indeed, had encounters with prominent and highly respected authorities who object strenuously to this idea. We recall vividly long discussions with them about exceptional children, their feeling being that a retarded child would be overwhelmed by a full keyboard. They wanted to cover the keyboard, except for perhaps two or three letters at first, and when their "subjects" had learned these letters, they could move on to others. Finally, after the alphabet was mastered, they conceded that it might be advisable to teach a few punctuation marks.

Their argument has a plausible ring to it—also, it surely is an empirical matter to determine how much of a system a learner should be exposed to initially. Nevertheless, the responsive condition suggests that we allow free exploration. Why? The basic answer is that we presuppose that *the what* of what is to be learned constitutes a system and not a random or miscellaneous collection of things. This is certainly true of language both in its written and spoken forms and their interrelations. Language is a system. If language is presented in such a way that its systemic properties are hidden or obscured, the learner may fail to master it. The more stupid the learner, the more essential it is to make these systemic properties evident. With respect to orthography the punctuation marks are the basic "traffic" signs which govern the flow of the symbols of the linguistic code, for example, stop, go, caution. The distinction between upper and lower case letters is also part of this system of traffic signs. We asked these authorities whether they thought these symbolic traffic signs were most needed by the gifted or the retarded. They thought that the gifted had less need for explicit well-marked symbolic highways. Agreed! But it was precisely the retarded who were to be deprived of the opportunity to come in close contact with periods, commas, question marks, exlamation points, and other aids!

In designing the keyboard for the talking typewriter, provision was made for an overlay to cover the keys so that they can be exposed selectively. We made this provision because we knew that for some research purposes, the total keyboard would be too much or somehow irrelevant. Nevertheless, free exploration means *free exploration of a system*. On the negative side, it can serve as a warning that restricted exploration entails the risk of the learner not coming to grips with whatever it is he is to master.

2. *It informs the learner immediately about the consequences of his actions.* . . . This condition, like the one above, is related to the notion of a system. We really do not mean that the learner is to be informed about *all* the consequences of his actions—this would be an impossible requirement. What we mean is that the consequences of the learner's actions which are *directly relevant* to the linguistic system which he is learning are to be reported back to him. For example, it is relevant to the relation holding between English orthography and English speech that the written C-A-T is pronounced as we generally say it. Hence, if the learner writes C-A-T he should hear it as well as see it. This connection should be as close as possible—we can easily obtain a verbal response from the machine in a little less than 1/10th of a second, and for many purposes this is fast enough.

There is a deeper point here, though, than the one having to do merely with the machine's speed of response, namely, it has to do with making it manifest to the learner that the pronunciation of the word *cat* is a consequence of his having typed C-A-T. After hitting the final "T" he might strike another key. How does he know that the verbal consequence had nothing to do with his final action? He cannot be certain unless the machine is designed so that for varying periods of time we can block or stop all machine actions except those that are consequential *vis-à-vis* certain actions of the learner. In our simple-minded illustration here, we need to provide for the blocking of the keyboard until the pronunciation of "cat" is complete, otherwise the learner will find it very difficult to trace the consequences of his own actions. The selective blocking of various machine functions at certain times, depending, of course, on what the learner has done, will help make it evident to him that some things are system-relevant consequences of his actions, and certain other things are not. From an engineering standpoint, this blocking of machine functions is again one of those things which is much easier said than done. This condition which we place upon a responsive environment may simplify things for the learner but it leads to nightmarish engineering problems if the system handled by the equipment is at all complex.

The talking typewriter as a responsive environment device has within it explicit provision for the blocking of machine functions so that the learner can find out more easily what follows from what.

3. *It is self-pacing.* . . . Many instructional systems are not at all self-pacing, for example, educational TV. Self-pacing devices must have controls for the learner himself. The concept of self-pacing should go beyond the mere slowing down or speeding up of a process. It should include controls suitable for bringing about both the repetition of sequences and scanning ahead. The controls for office dictation equipment are a good example of what is wanted—

with a touch of a finger the operator can stop, repeat, go forward normally, and speed forward or backward. It is this kind of flexibility that gives practical reality to the notion of self-pacing. We will want to include appropriate self-pacing controls in our machine—they should be at least as flexible as those built into standard dictation equipment.

4. *It permits the learner to make full use of his capacity for discovering relations.* . . . It is easier to say what this condition does not mean than to state its positive attributes. The trouble is, we know so little about human capacities. However, we can be reasonably certain that our machine is not drawing upon these capacities if the learner is told what to do, how to do it, and what to think about what he has done.

The notion of discovery carries the connotation of obtaining the sight or knowledge of something for the first time. Many present-day machines falling under the general educational classification of "computer-aided instruction" are quite frankly for drill, not discovery. Drill undoubtedly has its place in education; no one could possibly learn to spell or play a musical instrument without it, but drill is not what we are talking about when it comes to the notion of a responsive environment.

It is very hard to decide how far one can go in making things clear to the learner without spoiling his chance of making a discovery. Let us return to the keyboard of our hypothetical machine. Imagine that we place a light under each key. Now, suppose that whatever key should be struck next, say for the spelling of *Mississippi*, lights up. The subject probably would notice this very quickly—a small discovery in itself. The trouble with this discovery, at least as far as spelling is concerned, is that it eliminates the need for any further discoveries. A pigeon could learn to peck only the lighted key and he could get along just fine without learning anything about English orthography. We have placed three fringe lights on the keyboard of the talking typewriter: one for upper case, one for lower case, and one for space bar. These lights (which can be turned off or made to blink) are not there to tell the learner what to do next, as was true in the case of the pigeon example, but to signal the major states of the system for which there are virtually no visual clues provided otherwise by the system.

There are many other clues which we can build into our keyboard without eliminating the need for further discoveries. For example, since the learner will eventually be able to type and it is convenient to use standard typing conventions, we can color code his fingers to match a color coding of the keys. This means that by striking the right keys with the right fingers he will be learning "correct fingering." To give him a clue about the proper domain of keys for each hand a noticeable pressure difference can be made between the left- and right-hand keys. This clue can help him orient his hands.

Notice that the clues that we have mentioned, namely, the left hand-right hand pressure difference, the matched color coding of keys and fingers, and the fringe lights, serve to help the learner to master the machine. They neither give away secrets about the mysteries of orthography nor do they obviate the need to make discoveries about them.

5. *It is so structured that the learner is likely to make a series of inter-connected discoveries.* . . . What is emphasized in this condition is the idea of interconnectedness among discoveries. We want the learner to be put in a position where he can use the results of one discovery for making the next, and so on. In effect, if you think of him as playing a kind of game with the machine, then it must be possible to change at least some of the rules quickly, and turn the situation into a new game.

This condition suggests that the machine's supervisor, as opposed to the user of the machine, must have a set of remote controls. Let us imagine that some learner is playing happily with the individual characters of the ortho-graphic system. However, suppose also that there are signs that he has just about mastered these characters in the sense that he can accurately match the visual to the auditory, and vice versa. Before long he will tire of this. If the supervisor must stop the learner while he changes the machine, then this is a clumsy interruption—it tells the learner to expect something. If, instead, the supervisor can throw some switches at a remote station, the learner will suddenly find himself confronted with a new problem. It will be up to him to notice that something has gone wrong and to work out a new pattern of play. If the new game bears no relation to the old, then the results of learning will not be cumulative, so we have to decide what of the old should be carried over into the new situation.

In the case of English orthography, it is a straightforward matter to use letters to make words, words to make sentences, sentences to make paragraphs, and from there to many different kinds of higher-order entities. Games can be played at each level and the transition from level to level can be turned into a new opportunity for discovery. So our machine must be flexible enough to handle a series of interconnected language games.

As we remarked before, it is best if the transition from game to game can be controlled from a remote station. In the talking typewriter, provision has been made for just such a series of remote control transitions. At the simplest level the mechanical system can handle games with individual char-acters of the orthography up to games at the level of paragraphs and stories.

From what has been said about the application of the responsive condition it should be perfectly evident that there are an indefinitely large number of different machines which could satisfy the various requirements for "respon-siveness." It should be equally clear that the human personality can serve as a "responsive instrument," too.

There is one danger to which we would like to call your attention con-cerning all of this, namely, there is the risk of assuming that since a particular machine *can* be used as part of a responsive environment that it necessarily *will* be so used. The talking typewriter is a case in point. It can be a useful part of a responsive environment if it is properly programmed. However, it can be programmed so that it negates each and every condition for responsiveness. It can (a) limit exploration, (b) mislead the learner about the consequences of his actions, (c) force someone else's gait on the learner, (d) make it unnecessary for the learner to make discoveries, and (e) make it difficult for the learner to build upon his insights.

Reflexive Condition. There is a good deal being said these days about individualized instruction. There are those who maintain that one of the principal contributions which advanced technology can make to education is through the exploitation of the capacities of computers to treat each learner as a class of one. Each learner can be branched off in ways that are appropriate for him —there is to be an educational "prescription" written for each student. In principle, no two students need have the same prescription.

We are very much in favor of such individualization, but there are further distinctions to be made. Let us suggest, in terms of the reflexive condition, that what is wanted is a personalized, as opposed to a merely individualized, instructional milieu. According to the reflexive condition, the educational environment should be so constructed that it is convenient for the learner to acquire a historical knowledge of himself as he develops over time. He should come to see himself as having a career as a learner. The various perspectives which he can assume as agent, patient, reciprocal other, and referee should come to be seen as parts of a personality system, namely, his own personality.

Concretely, how are we to go about designing reflexiveness into our environment so that the learner will come to see himself developmentally? One of the first things that comes to mind, because of its use in sports, is to exploit the resources of sound-color motion picture photography. The same films which the investigator may want as part of his documentation of laboratory procedures and results can be shared with the learners. In one laboratory, for instance, we constructed a learning booth with an automatic photographic system for the making of high-quality 16 mm sound-color motion pictures. Learners were then shown films of themselves in various phases of their learning experiences. Their interest, as you might expect, was extremely high. There is no question in our minds that this was an enlightening experience for them. But this is only one step in the right direction. Are we simply to try for complete photographic coverage? Are we to show learners everything that they do? Clearly, this would be both uneconomic and *self*-defeating. This would lead toward vicious circularity with learners watching themselves, and so on. Of course, the high cost of film making would keep this reflexive process from becoming absurd. However, on the positive side, we need some direction with respect to the appropriate use of reflexive techniques.

Let us remind ourselves of our goal as it is defined by the reflexive condition. We want the learner to see himself develop over time, to see his own personality as a whole. This means that he needs to see himself in perspective. You will recall that in our previous discussion of the perspectives principles, we stipulated that the learner should find it convenient to engage in acts of agency, to be patient to events, to see himself through the eyes of others, and to evaluate his conduct from the standpoint of a referee. Now, in terms of the reflexive condition, he should be encouraged to see himself learning to do these same things. Therefore, if we are, for instance, using photographic techniques, we need to sample his behavior as an agent, as a patient, and so forth.

To be specific about this, imagine that we have 1000 feet of sound-color motion pictures of a learner. Assume that in accordance with the reflexive condition we want to help him develop a sense of history about himself. So, let us place the learner in the position of a film editor. Let us ask him to select 250 out of the 1000 feet for his own film library. Next, let us have the laboratory staff select 250 feet from this same 1000. Next, let some significant person in the learner's life select 250 feet from the 1000. (We have to be careful here so as not to violate the autotelic principle.) Let all of these selections be made independently—each "editor" is to act without knowledge of the others. Further, let both the filming and the editorial work continue over some reasonably long period of time so that the learner has had an opportunity to develop and increase his degree of skill and sophistication. Let us make one further assumption—we shall stipulate that each editor who selected from the basic film stock operated under the instruction to produce a film that is characteristic of the learner. We have now reached the point for the learner and the other editors to be patient to the consequences of the others' acts of agency. The learner will have the opportunity to see himself as others see him. We then can make it possible for him to make a new set of selections, that is, to make a new film, one that takes into account what others noticed about him. He may want to go back to the original footage and look for aspects of himself which everyone has neglected.

All of the foregoing may sound hopelessly expensive and time consuming but with the advent of video tape and convenient editing devices this is not so impractical. In any case, in discussing the reflexive condition, as in the discussion of each of the other principles, the basic idea has been to illuminate possibilities. A clearer understanding of what is possible and desirable will undoubtedly have an effect on the development of appropriate technology.

CONCLUSION

Now that the reader has been hauled through this essay, probably kicking and screaming for all we know, what is it that he is supposed to have gotten from this panoramic view of our position, besides intellectual indigestion? For one thing, we hope that we have made good on our promise to show the talking typewriter for what it is, namely, a social science invention. We hope the reader agrees that there is scientific continuity holding between the contributions of Mead and Simmel and our own efforts. Our most important aim, however, has been to make plausible the contention that it is our general theoretical or heuristic orientation which led to the formulation of principles for the design of *clarifying* environments, and to the illustrative applications of these principles. If we have accomplished this, then our main goal has been reached.

We yield to no one (for the second time in this paper) in feeling dissatisfied with the lack of formal rigor which pervades our whole enterprise. But, being perennial optimists, despite all the common-sensical grounds for pessimism, we trust that we will become more sure-footed as we proceed.

REFERENCES

Ackermann, W., "Begrundung einer strengen Implikation." *J. Symbolic Logic*, 1956, 21: 113–128.

Anderson, Alan Ross, *The Formal Analysis of Normative Systems.* Technical report #2, Office of Naval Research, Group Psychology Branch, Contract SAR/Nonr609(16), New Haven, 1956a. [Also in: *Logic of Action and Decision*, Nicholas Reschner, ed. Pittsburgh: University of Pittsburgh Press, 1967.]

——— "Review of Prior and Feys." *J. Symbolic Logic*, 1956b, 21: 21, 379.

——— "Review of Wilhelm Ackermann, Begrundung einer strengen Implikation." *J. Symbolic Logic*, 1957, 22: 327–328.

——— "A Reduction of Deontic Logic to Alethic Modal Logic." *Mind*, 1958a, 67n.s.: 100–103.

——— "The Logic of Norms." *Logique et analyse*, 1958b, ln.s.: 84–91.

——— "On the Logic of Commitment." *Philosophical Studies*, 1959, 10: 23–27.

——— "*Completeness Theorems for the Systems E of Entailment and EQ of Entailment with Quantification.* Technical report #6, Contract SAR/Nonr-609(16), Office of Naval Research, Group Psychology Branch, New Haven, 1960. [Also in: *Zeitschrift fur mathematische Logik und Grundlagen der Mathematic*, 1960, 6: 210–216.]

——— "Reply to Mr. Rescher." *Philosophical Studies*, 1962, 13: 6–8.

——— "Some Open Problems Concerning the System E of Entailment." *Acta Philosophica Fennica*. Helsinki: fasc. 16, 1963.

——— "Some Nasty Problems in the Formal Logic of Ethics." *Nous*, 1967, 6: 345–360.

Anderson, Alan Ross and Belnap, Nuel D., Jr., "A Modification of Ackermann's Rigorous Implication." [Abstract] *J. Symbolic Logic*, 1958, 23: 457–458.

——— "A Simple Proof of Gödel's Completeness Theorem." [Abstract] *J. Symbolic Logic*, 1959a, 24: 320–321.

——— "Modalities in Ackermann's 'Rigorous Implication'." *J. Symbolic Logic*, 1959b, 24: 107–111.

——— "A Simple Treatment of Truth Functions." *J. Symbolic Logic*, 1959c, 24: 301–302.

——— "Enthymemes." *J. of Philosophy*, 1961a, 58: 713–723.

——— "The Pure Calculus of Entailment." *J. Symbolic Logic*, 1961b, 27: 19–52.

——— "Tautological Entailments." *Philosophical Studies*, 1961c, 13: 9–24.

——— *First Degree Entailments.* Technical report #10, Contract SAR/Nonr-609(16), Office of Naval Research, Group Psychology Branch, New Haven, 1963. [Also in: *Mathematische Annalen*, 1963, 149: 302–319.]

Anderson, Alan Ross, Belnap, Nuel D., Jr., and Wallace, John R., "Independent Axiom Schemata for the Pure Theory of Entailment." *Zeitschrift fur mathematische Logik und Grundlagen der Mathematik*, 1960, 6: 93–95.

Anderson, Alan Ross, and Moore, Omar Khayyam, "The Formal Analysis of Normative Concepts." *Amer. Sociological Rev.*, 1957, 22: 1–17. [Also in: *Social role: Readings in Theory and Applications*, B. J. Biddle and E. Thomas, ed. New York: John Wiley and Sons, 1966.]

———— *Autotelic Folk Models*. Technical report #8, Contract SAR/Nonr-609 (16), Office of Naval Research, Group Psychology Branch, New Haven, 1959. [Also in: *Sociological Quarterly*, 1960, 1: 203–216.]

———— "Toward a Formal Analysis of Cultural Objects." *Synthese*, 1962, 14: 144–170. [Also in: *Boston Studies in the Philosophy of Science*, 1961/1962, M. W. Wartofsky, ed. Dordrecht, Holland: D. Reidel, 1963.]

———— "Models and Explanations in the Behavioral Sciences." *Concepts, Theory, and Explanation in the Behavioral Sciences*, G. J. DiRenzo, ed. New York: Random House, 1966.

Anderson, Scarvia B., "Shift in Problem Solving." *Naval Research Memorandum, Report #458*, Washington, D.C., 1955.

———— "Analysis of Responses in a Task Drawn from the Calculus of Propositions." *Naval Research Laboratory Memorandum, Report #608*, Washington, D.C., 1956.

———— "Problem Solving in Multiple-Goal Situations." *J. Exp. Psychology*, 1957, 54: 297–303.

Belnap, Nuel D., Jr., "Pure rigorous implication as a *Sequenzenkalkul*." [Abstract] *J. Symbolic Logic*, 1959a, 24: 282–283.

———— "Tautological Entailments." [Abstract] *J. Symbolic Logic*, 1959b, 24: 316.

———— *A Formal Analysis of Entailment*. Technical report #7, Contract SAR/Nonr-609(16), Office of Naval Research, Group Psychology Branch, New Haven, 1960a.

———— "Entailment and Relevance." *J. Symbolic Logic*, 1960b, 25: 144–146.

———— "First Degree Formulas." [Abstract] *J. Symbolic Logic*, 1960c, 25: 388–389.

———— "EQ and the First Order Functional Calculus." *Zeitschrift fur mathematische Logik und Grundlagen der Mathematik.*, 1960d, 6: 217–218.

———— *An Analysis of Questions: Preliminary Report*. Santa Monica: Systems Development Corporation, 1963.

———— "Intensional Models for First Degree Formulas." *J. of Symbolic Logic*, 1967, 32: 1–11.

Belnap, Nuel D., Jr. and Wallace, John R., *A Decision Procedure for the System L₁ of Entailment with Negation*. Technical report #11, Contract Sar/Nonr-609(16), Office of Naval Research, Group Psychology Branch, New Haven, 1961.

Carpenter, John A., Moore, Omar Khayyam, Snyder, Charles R., and Lisansky, Edith S., "Alcohol and Higher-Order Problem Solving." *Quarterly J. of Studies on Alcohol*, 1961, 22: 183–222.

Cooley, Charles Horton, *Human Nature and the Social Order*. New York: Charles Scribner's Sons, 1902 [1922, 1930], 217.

Fitch, Fredric B., *Symbolic logic*. New York: Ronald, 1952.

Kobler, Richard and Moore, Omar Khayyam, *Educational System and Apparatus*. U. S. Patent #3,281,959, 27 figures, 51 claims granted, 12 references. Also granted in many foreign countries, 1966.

Mead, George Herbert, *The Philosophy of the Present*. La Salle, Illinois: The Open Court, 1932.

———— *Mind, Self and Society*. Chicago: University of Chicago Press, 1934.

———— *Movements of Thought in the Nineteenth Century*. Chicago: University of Chicago Press, 1936.

———— *The Philosophy of the Act*. Chicago: University of Chicago Press, 1938.

Moore, Omar Khayyam, "Divination—a new perspective." *American anthropolo-*

gist, 1957, 59: 69–74. [Also in: *Reader in Comparative Religion: an Anthropological Approach,* W. A. Lessa and E. Z. Vogt, ed. New York: Harper & Row, 2d ed., 1965, 377–381. Also in: *Ecology: an Anthropological Reader,* A. P. Vayda, ed. (One of a series called American Museum Source books in Anthropology, ed. P. Bohannan). New York: Natural History Press.]

———— "Problem Solving and the Perception of Persons." *Person Perception and Interpersonal Behavior,* R. Tagiuri, and L. Petrullo, ed. Palo Alto: Stanford University Press, 1958, 131–150.

————"Orthographic Symbols and the Preschool Child—a New Approach." *Creativity: 1960 Proceeding of the Third Conference on Gifted Children,* E. P. Torrence, ed., University of Minnesota, Center for Continuation Study, 1961, 91–101.

———— *Autotelic Responsive Environments and Exceptional Children.* Report issued by The Responsive Environments Foundation, Inc. Hamden, Conn., 1963. [Also in: *The Special Child in Century 21,* J. Hellmuth, ed. Seattle: Special Child Publications of the Sequin School, Inc., 1964. Also in: *Experience, Structure and Adaptability,* O. J. Harvey, ed. New York: Springer, 1966.]

———— "Technology and Behavior." *Proceedings of the 1964 Invitational Conference on Testing Problems.* Princeton: Educational Testing Service, 1964, 58–68.

———— "From Tools to Interactional Machines." *New Approaches to Individualizing Instruction.* A report of a conference on May 11, 1965a, to mark the dedication of Ben D. Wood Hall. Princeton: Educational Testing Service. [Also in: *Instructional Technology: Readings,* J. W. Childs, ed. New York: Holt, Rinehart and Winston, Inc. 1968, forthcoming.]

———— "Autotelic Responsive Environments and the Deaf." *Amer. Annals for the Deaf,* 1965b, 110: 604–614.

———— "On Responsive Environments." *Proceedings of the Abington Conference '67 "New Directions in Individualizing Instruction."* Abington, Pa.: The Abington Conference, 1968.

Moore, Omar Khayyam and Anderson, Alan Ross, *Early Reading and Writing, Part 1: Skills:* 16 mm sound-color motion pictures, Basic Education Inc., Pittsburgh, Pa. 1960a.

———— *Early Reading and Writing, Part 2: Teaching Methods.* 16 mm sound-color motion picture, Basic Education, Inc., Pittsburgh, Pa. 1960b.

———— *Early Reading and Writing, Part 3: Development.* 16 mm sound-color motion picture, Ba ic Education, Inc., Pittsburgh, Pa. 1960c.

———— "Some Puzzling Aspects of Social Interaction." *Rev. of Metaphysics,* 1962a, 15: 409–433. [Also in: *Mathematical Methods in Small Group Processes,* J. H. Criswell, H. Solomon, and P. Suppes, ed. Stanford: Stanford University Press, 1962a, 232–249.]

———— "The Structure of Personality." *Rev. of Metaphysics,* 1962b, 16: 212–236. [Also in: Motivation and Social Interaction, O. J. Harvey, ed. New York: Ronald Press, 1963.]

———— "The Responsive Environments Project." *Early Education,* R. D. Hess and R. M. Bear, ed. Chicago: Aldine Press, 1968.

Moore, Omar Khayyam and Anderson, Scarvia B., "Modern Logic and Tasks for

Experiments on Problem Solving Behavior." *J. of Psychology*, 1954a, 38: 151–160.

—— "Search Behavior in Individual and Group Problem Solving." *Amer. Sociological Rev.*, 1954b, 19: 702–714.

—— "Experimental Study of Problem Solving." *Report of NRL progress.* 1954c, August, 15–22.

Moore, Omar Khayyam and Kobler, Richard, *Educational Apparatus for Children.* U. S. Patent #3,112,569, 6 figures, 13 claims granted, 6 references. Also granted in many foreign countries, 1963.

Peirce, C. S., "Some Consequences of Four Incapacities." *J. Speculative Philosophy,* 1868.

Pitman, Sir James, "Man—the Communicating Animal, Par (Verbal) Excellence," *New Approaches to Individualizing Instruction,* A. C. Eurick, ed. Princeton: Educational Testing Service, 1965, 49–60.

Scott, D., "A Short Recursively Unsolvable Problem." *J. Symbolic Logic,* 1956, 21: 111–112.

Prior, Mary and Prior, Arthur, "Erotetic Logic." *Philosophical Rev.,* 1955, 64: 43–59.

Simmel, G., *Georg Simmel, 1858–1918.* A collection of essays, with translations and a bibliography, K. H. Wolff, ed. Columbus: The Ohio State University Press, 1959.

von Neumann, John, "Zur Theorie der Gesellschaftsspiele," *Mathematische Annalen,* 1928, 100: 295–320.

von Neumann, John and Morgenstern, Oskar, *Theory of Games and Economic Behavior.* Princeton: Princeton University Press, 1947.

CRITIQUE AND DISCUSSION————————

In the paper you will find that I have stated a set of four principles—four heuristic principles for designing clarifying environments. The point of my paper is to take these four principles and to apply them to the analysis of the family. In there I also want to introduce the concept I call a "failsafe family." I want to introduce that as a technical concept.

When I was asked to be part of this conference, I regarded it as an opportunity, because in our own work, particularly in my project which is called the "Clarifying Environments Project," we had just reached the point in which we wanted to say some things about the family. This project is approximately ten years old and—— this is a team effort——we think of ourselves as being about halfway through a projected 20-year program. The program itself has four major parts. I want to just briefly describe them for you.

The first section we call the formal section. Over ten years ago we decided that there were fundamental deficiencies in the social and behavioral sciences in terms of the conceptual tools which would be needed. In our opinion anyway, most systems of mathematics were devised with the interests of physicists or hard, natural scientists in mind and very little of the mathematics was pointed in the direction of the social or behavioral sciences.

We haven't been served very well by mathematics mainly because we aren't part of its socialization process; we haven't been historically speaking. So we tried to guess what new fields of mathematics would be required. So this first section of our project has to do with the development of new branches of mathematical logic (Deontic, Erotetic, and Entailment) that we think will provide tools for the social or behavioral science.

Another fourth of our energy goes into the development of new technology. Because of the other parts of our project, it became apparent to us that 10 years ago modern technology had reached the point where it would be possible to create very subtle environments through the use of computers and automation. These would allow you a lot more latitude experimentally than was possible prior to technology becoming that competent. And so we began to try to design principles for constructing environments and that meant trying to construct some and trying to create new instrumentation to serve our research and applied purposes.

Unfortunately, this one aspect of our project has overshadowed all others and has produced a severe distortion in the perception of what we're up to. One device, namely our Talking Typewriter, immediately captured everybody's attention. It's a fun device and the sort of thing if you're with it you like to play with it and it's photographable, it's tangible. So

for too many people, including social and behavioral scientists, our project is the talking typewriter.

Incidentally, there's a whole family of instruments we call responsive instruments that we have been working on. The guiding ideas behind these are not those of efficiency, which is the usual engineering concern, but with what I call efficacy. We're not interested in things that are efficient, but efficacious in changing the state of mind, or attitude, or position, or something, of human beings; and that is a different criterion.

Now, a third area of concern is to try to come up with theoretical structures covering our efforts—to develop a general theory of human problem solving and social interaction. We do not have anything that we're willing to call a theory that meets the standards of rigor for theoretical construction. Instead, our efforts have been largely in the direction of coming up with guiding principles to help direct our efforts. It's harder than one might think to try to state a principle to guide you in the design of an environment.

Now, our last area of work, to which we give the remaining fourth of our time, is to empirical studies which range from quick and dirty studies, in order to familiarize ourselves——whether it's trying out a prototype to see whether children like it at all, or whatever——to controlled experiments. We're just now moving into the phase of controlled experiments. Until recently it took a resident engineer to keep the talking typewriter, for example—as one piece of equipment—going. When you have that much unreliability there is just no use fielding a beautiful looking experiment in which the noise, due to unreliability, is throwing the whole thing off.

In the first five years we had so little done in each quadrant that we really looked sick. The equipment didn't work, our math was weak——— at the 10-year point, we had done enough in each that people began to see what it was we were trying to do. We pay a heavy price to not concentrate fully on the math or technology to try to get a balanced program. It is a very punishing thing to do because in the early phases we seemed to be superficial and inadequate with respect to everything. But the overall sense of balance is terribly important to avoid letting the technology run away with everything, or the math, or the empirical studies, or something.

Now let's turn to the four principles—four heuristic principles— which are currently helping us design our environments. First, we try to design environments in which we put the children under conditions that are autotelic, and by autotelic we mean activities that are carried out for their own sake and their own intrinsic interest. Now we want to maintain that an autotelic environment is the best sort for learning complex material——very, very difficult materials ——because among other things anxiety levels don't reach such a high degree that the subject is immobilized. With respect to the family, I am suggesting that we take a look at them and ask ourselves to what extent do various families make provision within their own structure for their youngsters to have autotelic experiences. If

you find that a youngster has no place——no way to make a fool of himself especially outside the censorship, including rewards, from significant adults (for example, little league baseball)——on the theoretical grounds we argue for here, we would say that this would interfere with his acquisition of complex symbolic maps that he is going to need.

Our second principle, personalization, divides into two parts—responsiveness and reflexiveness. The responsive principle involves a set of complex conditions. We say an environment is responsive, a piece of equipment is responsive if it meets the following conditions: It permits the learner to explore freely. It informs the learner about the consequences of his actions. It's self-pacing, that is, the pace is not determined by an adult or someone else. It gives the learner a chance to use his capacity for discovering relations as opposed to having the solutions explained to him very didactically. It is set up so that a series of interconnected discoveries can be made.

The reflexive condition, which is the other half of this personalization principle, depends upon whether the environment is such that a person can see himself as a learner. For example, in our transfer room we use a video tape camera. In the family, the question is what are the reflexive devices —albums, motion pictures, and so forth? Can you come to see yourself, in that family, as having a history. Now our thesis is, with the other things being equal, the more reflexive provisions are made, the stronger, the more happily the socialization process will proceed.

Turning to the productive principle, this refers to the "cultural content" of the family. We maintain that, other things being equal, one situation is more conducive to the acquisition of complex and difficult material—symbolic material—if the cultural objects that the people internalize are more productive. We define a productive cultural object as one from which given part of it, you can deduce or induce the rest of the structure; for example, compare an alphabetic with a nonalphabetic language. What we're saying is that if you look at the cultural objects that are internalized in the family, if one family has internalized relatively nonproductive cultural objects, then it's bound to be the case that the learner is going to be more dependent on those around him every step of the way.

In any case, we think that families differ in terms of productivity of the cultural objects they internalize. Incidentally, so do academic disciplines —for example, compare math with social science——We are stuck with fields in which just getting acquainted with what's there is a long process with minimal deductive consequences from whatever we do learn which gets pretty old before we even get the hang of it.

The final principle we call the perspective principle which says that one environment, and this would involve the family environment, is more conducive to learning than another if it both permits and facilitates the taking of more perspectives towards whatever is to be learned. In this circumstance we define four major perspectives: patient, agent, reciprocal or significant other, and referee or generalized other.

In a game of chance—if you are not cheating—you are patient to the consequences and have no control over it. No active agency of yours is relevant to the conclusion. Puzzles, on the other hand, illustrate that the agency in which the variables that are required to be handled to solve the problem are under your control.

Games of strategy conceptually allow you to take the role of reciprocal other or what Mead called the significant other. You can't play a game of strategy without putting yourself into the position of another player. He is not a pattern of dead variables. Complex or not, he's an active player over there who has control over some variables on which the outcome depends. You've also got some control and the ultimate result is the interrelation between these two sets, neither of which lie uniquely in the hands of either player. While chess ultimately reduces to a kind of puzzle——bridge does not, it is a game of strategy. The last perspective — *referee* — revolves around the rules which are to be applied independently of the wishes of particular players.

Now we're saying that the learning situation or the family environment that allows you, in tackling a problem, to move from agent to patient to significant other to referee, and various combinations, is more conducive to solving problems than one that holds you, say, in the role of patienthood, which is somewhat chronic in the lower classes.

HAMBLIN'S INTERVIEW OF MOORE

HAMBLIN: I would simply like to start and, in effect, interview Omar for a while to bring out some features of his social science work that I don't think have been communicated. Now, first, what is a talking typewriter?

MOORE: It's a responsive device——it consists of a computer circuitry and is an automated control display which can be played with by a learner without any instruction on the part of the person in charge of the area. So it's a "free-standing portable responsive device."

HAMBLIN: OK. Suppose you have some children in these learning booths with a talking typewriter and the child does get hooked onto the machine and starts exploring it. How long does he ordinarily stay there?

MOORE: Well we set an upper limit——generally when they're first starting about fifteen minutes. Later that's extended to thirty minutes. But we don't want them ——we have children who, I think, would stay all day but we figure that there are a lot of other things for their days.

HAMBLIN: How long does it take a child to learn his alphabet and to start typing—and to start reading?

MOORE: The fastest child we ever had learned the whole upper and lower case keyboard in five half-hour sessions. We've had mentally retarded youngsters in the IQ range of the 50's who have taken nine months to learn that——and not as well either. So you get that kind of variation, from a week to nine months range.

HAMBLIN: OK. What is a transfer room?

MOORE: A transfer room is——remember what we've been describing thus far—an individual, learning, and working in individual booths. We have, adjacent to these booths, an area for group learning in which we are trying to allow for group structures to form——a small group to develop which will undertake, eventually, superordinate tasks that use the skills that are learned individually. For instance, one of the tasks we've used the most is turning out a newspaper. The transfer room is for group activity so that a leadership pattern develops among the kids. The leadership is directed toward using the symbol systems they are acquiring in constructive ways. What this really means is that the gifted youngsters, the most gifted, become leaders, but they're not just leaders who take off on their own and learn things and leave other people behind. We had a group that included a girl that had an IQ of 180 in one program, and in that same group there was a boy with an IQ of about 60 and he was still part of the newspaper. He ran the mimeograph machine and they assigned him group relevant tasks that he could do.

HAMBLIN: Now regarding your emphasis on these four kinds of folk models—let me ask you a few questions about those. What if a child simply doesn't have experience in learning how to play games of chance? How is that likely to show up in his behavior?

MOORE: Well, in general, we would claim that to omit a major class of models would conceptually handicap people severely. And to forbid them several classes of models would produce intellectual indigestion. Now, societies differ in terms of the distribution of these models and their utilization. This would be a difference in culture or a difference in . . .

HAMBLIN: Sure, but what if somebody had a deficit so that he really didn't know about games of chance and how to approach the world using that model, how would this probably show up in his behavior?

MOORE: In decision-making processes under conditions of uncertainty and high risk, he might be too anxious to act, find it hard to make decisions. Now turning the question around, if you look in the slums, for example, games of chance are heavily used. Most of the folk models that the very poor use are related to, and help symbolize, the fact that they are mainly passive. They are patient to events in the world, and the folk models they use the most help put them in that position. On the other hand, I would say that a youngster who was raised in the middle class would put a heavy emphasis on puzzles and agency control—— wouldn't utilize games of chance much. Most of our tests of adequate functioning are puzzles. All IQ tests, for example, consist of series of puzzles and do not deal with chanciness or aesthetic objects or games of strategy. In other words, if you have kids who are oriented around the puzzle model, which is the dominant successful white middle class model, and you put them in a situation in which that model isn't being used they would have very little preparation for assuming other perspectives.

HAMBLIN: What about somebody who's been slighted on games of strategy. Or say, given a heavy dose of it. How does that affect their perspectives?

MOORE: Well, say for example, if he were a behavioral scientist——but his favorite models did not include games of strategy, he would have a hard time conceptualizing—understanding—the whole Meadian scheme of "significant others." He would tend to look at the world, say, as a detective putting together pieces. Subjects would not be treated as fellow interactors. He would see them as part of a very complex puzzle for which he was seeking the answer. You see, in games of strategy, you must recognize other interactors who are not merely puzzling. I would say the whole orientation, historically, of behavioral science has been ——has used what is appropriate in the natural sciences, and in the natural sciences atoms are not out to get people. They have passive subject matter that you can handle as a puzzle, but in the behavioral sciences we've tried to carry over directly the ethos of a puzzle orientation into the study of people, only to find that they won't stay put for us. They want to know why they're being studied and they want to read the reports and they want to disagree. Our usual "out there separateness" isn't going down any too well with them.

HAMBLIN: OK.——So, as I understand what you're trying to do then in your school is to give people an opportunity to learn how to work from——to use these four models in orienting to the world. You are developing their language skills from the four perspectives; and do you have this all integrated so that their problem solving is guided by the four models and this allows them then a level of competence that people ordinarily don't achieve if they don't have this experience or if they have a deficit in it?

MOORE: Yes, that's what we maintain but I wouldn't say it's proved. One other thing. We think there's something radically wrong with the historical folk models. They have served man from the earliest time until now, but there is something wrong with them. They all presuppose a static frame of reference. Historically speaking, social change was not so rapid that during the course of a lifetime——the rules of the game would be changed in fundamental ways. All folk models have this implicit stability, even though they can have lots of excitement and a lot of possibility for drama and overturned surprise. But we don't live in that sort of society anymore. The rate of social change has reached the point at which you cannot assume that the game will remain constant while you play. And so we are trying to build dynamic models——with a heavy emphasis on technology.

(*Ed. note*: From here Hamblin went through a number of questions concerned with how well the children performed. In general, Moore's responses indicated very robust effects.)

HAMBLIN: What kind of style or personality does a child develop as he goes through this system that you have designed? How does he respond emotionally or tend to develop in his emotional response?

MOORE: Let's say as a group they tend to scare teachers——not because they're bad—— our lead group drove three teachers out of the classroom, not by bad behavior, they did not break anything——They're quite intellectual, and have a lot of fun, and a little noisy. They scared the wits out of the parents of the third, fourth, fifth, sixth, seventh, eighth graders, so much so that they got the head-master fired.

HAMBLIN: I have two final questions. What happens without the transfer room— two words?

MOORE: Doesn't work.

HAMBLIN: What happens if you put in a kid who's six years old and not four years old?

MOORE: He doesn't learn very well, he's too frozen.

HAMBLIN: Thank you Omar. Now I think——social scientists, generally, have taken one of several modes. One of these is the mode of demonstration—of truth. You have a theory and you test it, and this is the kind of mode I think that Morris Zelditch represented yesterday in his presentation. There is, however, another mode of scientific work and that's invention. There is almost nobody in the social sciences that is inventing. I think Omar is an inventor. In his social science work at the present time, he is running a lot of informal experiments. They're not formal ones——but out of all this, he's developed a number of principles. He's not willing to call them a theory, but I would call them a theory. He hasn't tested them individually. What he has done is an engineering thing in which he, in effect, has designed these things and clarified what he was doing. And he's got a big glob there that produces, as you've seen, extremely robust results.

And I knew from our own research, that if you do this with young children you're going to get tremendous IQ changes, at least with some of them. In our project we have been there also. We've got an IQ change of 75: 57 to 132. And I think it's a valid one. All of the other indicators point to the change—— Anyway he's got very robust results and I want to say something about the theory that's developed out of this. It's a theory that, as far as I can see, is culture-free. And it doesn't——it has a very formal quality and a quality that I think social scientists are unaccustomed to. I would characterize it as——he's beginning to discover—along with others of us who attempt to design systems to produce effects with human beings——what the operating characteristics of the human organism are.

GENERAL DISCUSSION

(QUESTION:) I was just wondering which of the aspects of your program is going to be critical? You've put your finger on a number of operating principles, but then your next problem is how you are going to deal them out.

HAMBLIN: Let me try and respond to that. If you want to understand behavior, you have to look at the interaction, interaction in a technical sense, between the social system properties of the environment and the operating characteristics of the individual. The behavior that emerges is an interaction of these two. Omar has been able to get the big effect that he has because he has designed structural systems that capitalize on the operating characteristics of the human organism. It's a theory of interaction, and in an interaction, the relationship doesn't obtain unless both factors are just right.

(QUESTION:) I guess I didn't make myself clear. I was simply asking—will you experiment with different combinations of these principles? Is that where, theoretically, you are heading?

MOORE: Let me give you an example. We could have, for example, fooled with the differences in keyboard design or exposure time or things of that sort. But we're more likely to be worried about something much less specific. Up until very recently we didn't have anything, technologically, to handle the reflexive side of things in a very adequate way. So you can find whole areas in which the principles aren't being carried out very well. Rather than worry about such issues as the different dosage levels, or what might be considered minor variations, we made a lot of arbitrary decisions. Hundreds. If you build a whole new environment you're going to just make a lot of decisions each of which could be a doctoral dissertation, and which collectively could change the quality of the thing too. I don't want to say that those are trivial details, collectively they can add up.

HILL: I am wondering whether there are not sources of negative consequences as the child leaves this constructive environment with respect to the teachers that are frightened, the parents that are puzzled, the peers in the neighborhood who are outdistanced, or what have you——If there isn't something here with which you have to cope.

MOORE: This has been one of the dilemmas of innovations. Innovations that don't work are more likely to succeed because they don't produce problems. But if innovations really succeed in the sense of changes, hopefully in the direction say of competence, you're bound to upset the system. Now five years ago it finally got through to me that the middle class really does not want change. They already have a monopoly on learning that's working pretty well—and they really don't want change. So that's when we shifted to the ghettos. We moved to the ghettos when we realized that we had to work with people who would put up with the inconvenience, (we hope—we still do not know this)——who are so far behind and want to catch up, so to speak, so much so that they will put up with the inconvenience of real change. So we shifted our whole operation directly to the ghettos because we feel that otherwise you're carrying coals to Newcastle.

GUMPERZ: A lot of people present things that they claim are culture-free. I looked at this and just rapidly ran through my ethnographic experiences and I'm afraid I can't find——I mean, it is fascinating. In some respects it does appear to be. For example, when you talked about looking for people who really want education, I'm thinking of a lot of case histories documenting the transitions from pre-industrialism to industrialism where people walk through dark forests for days, weeks in order to take a school examination.

But I also have some reservations. You said that your system doesn't work well——it works better with four-year olds then with six-year olds. Does this mean that in some way you're unable to deal with the cultural baggage that either children acquire or people acquire as they get socialized into a social system?

You are, I take it, unable to deal with this. Do you have any explanations as to why this might be?

MOORE: Well, I think that by age six, children in our society are very likely to, for example, want to be told or expect to be told what to do and want to be told that they're right. They expect little stars. Now, if you set up a system such that free exploration is part of the learning process and already people are sitting around saying "What is it I'm really supposed to do?", you've got an enemy of free exploration. Now, I can imagine cultural circumstances——I don't think that's sixness——of being six years old, per se.

GUMPERZ: As you acquire the rules of a society, one of the rules is that you're not alone and that you need reinforcement of some kind.

MOORE: And you would like to know what it is you're supposed to do so that you're not failing.

GUMPERZ: Exactly.

MOORE: And the little ones are not that set yet. These expectations are not that developed.

HAMBLIN: They've just been through the experience also of working out the language all by themselves so that they have a feel for syntax and . . .

MOORE: Yes, it's just going right on with what they're doing.

HAMBLIN: Right. They've done that independently and all by themselves and been terribly reinforced for it and they're ready to move on to new learning experiences of the same order.

INKELES: Well, I have a series of questions here, just an effort to elicit information. First, would you say something about the method whereby you select the children for participation in the program, and in particular, the proportion of the children who had difficulty with the system and what you did with them. Second, you have often substituted a person for the talking typewriter. I'd be interested in your telling us something about those results; and going beyond that, if you'd give us some hints about the extent to which one might possibly go still further and not merely substitute a person for the machine but to substitute another environment in the technological, material, or physical sense—one which still met the principles that you are talking about. Finally, you say it is a culture-free system and that's great in a way, and in a way it's a funny thing to say because it's a system so pegged to electronics and to the electronic era that it's an enormously culture-bound system.

HAMBLIN: His system is culture-bound but his theory is culture-free.

MOORE: With respect to the question of selectivity, the answer, in general, is no. There have been a small amount of dropouts where parents have moved from the city. But we never drop a subject. We would drop a child under some circumstances, but we haven't. What we generally try to do because of the transfer room situation is——we want whole natural groups intact. In our recent start in Pittsburgh we looked for the worst ghetto school. They had a class unit of twenty and we took them all. They said "all right, but don't you want to screen them or something?" "No, we want them all because it's a naturally occurring unit of the kind we're interested in working with." Our N is really with twenty kids in a class as one. Our N is not the individual child, because we're working with group structure. Now, there's a point where they fan out as individuals; but if they're to turn out, say a newspaper, they do that as a group, so our N is terribly low when you look at it that way.

If you look at how the system works, half of the process concerns the interactional patterns that these youngsters, as a group, build using the skills they acquire in the learning booths. We can lose them, but it's very hard to gain them. That's a real problem. Once, they have group structure and role allocation——all the things that human groups do over time——a newcomer coming in finds it very hard. We do not get classes that look good by dropping our losers. In fact, this is very good on the dull or losing type child because he's got group support.

On Alex's substitution, let me say one thing. I think that all the technology we currently have should be regarded as primitive, and will be totally displaced over time. It would be utterly amazing if it weren't.

INKELES: But do you think it is free of machine technology . . . ?

MOORE: No, not if they are to be dynamic models. I see no way to get around advanced technology for dynamic models. Dynamic models are ones in which the rules can be changed in very complex ways.

GUMPERZ: In a sense, isn't that what we do when we put——the ghetto kids in middle class schools, we change the rules. We may be able to design experiments with natural groups that would transfer people from one group to another which would not require technology.

MOORE: But when you actually bring the groups in, you have serious consequences. We want to be able to do this in terms of models you can play with. If you're going to really move a group into a new situation with new rules, it would be very handy for them to be playing with models of moves like that, at an abstract level.

LEIK: We haven't, it seems to me, said much about the relevance for family problem solving. One thing that I think is pertinent that might answer some of the other questions raised is that the kinds of problems that we were talking about yesterday, with respect to family difficulties, are not, for example, knowing an alphabet or some of the things that are fairly easily conceived of as being machine type things or things which are at a fairly early level of learning.

Now it seems to me that shifts in the games, when you are talking about interpersonal accommodation have to do with rules pertaining to social structure, pertaining to role relationship, pertaining to power, status, and so forth. It's entirely conceivable that some of the same conceptual operations which you've been going through could be transposed to a kind of game which is concerned with interpersonal process rather than with learning in the sense that your project must be considering. I don't know that it is even necessary to worry about machinery in a case like this; the changes in the game rules have to do with just arbitrary shifts in family role relationships, status problems, power, this, that, and the next thing——these kinds of variable which foul up the works.

MOORE: Alright, but most of those things are serious problems, whereas our whole lab is meant to be autotelic—which means it's not a model of life with respect to serious matters. We're not suggesting turning families into autotelic enterprises. They have serious business. What I'm really saying about the family is——I'm asking questions like this——thinking about a number of families, do they differ in significant ways between whether they provide—make some provision for autotelic experiences for their members? Or do they define life in such a way that it's almost impossible to have any? There are some children, for example, who come from very highly motivated young families, academically motivated. But the children have virtually no play time. Now I'm saying that we are part of their socialization but we're only a part of it. There is a serious side of this thing in the family and there's no way to turn that into a game—in fact, it shouldn't be a game. It is serious.

TALLMAN: The thing I'm not clear about is——granting the rapid social change, and granting, perhaps, the ineffectiveness of these traditional folk models for handling this——are you proposing another model, or are you suggesting that right now we're in a state of "cultural lag" in so far as the kinds of orientation that we do have——that families do develop.

MOORE: At the very least I'm saying that each of the examples——instances of each of the four kinds need to be shifted to dynamic forms. By the way, you will notice that artists are starting on that——where you can enter into their aesthetic object. You don't just go to a museum and look at something that'll stay on the wall and stay put. They're creating plays in which you, as part of the audience, can change the ending——get it to branch——participate in the formulation of what happens. There are aesthetic objects you walk into and respond differently depending on what you do. This is just a beginning.

HAMBLIN: I just want to respond to that. Omar has been saying in various ways that we need the machines. Now I've been designing quite different systems using some of the same principles. I haven't got results quite as good as O. K. Moore's in some direction——in others I've done better. But we have almost no technology whatsoever—it's all on the basis of the social system.

STRAUS: In your opening remarks you mentioned a fail-safe family. What is the fail-safe family?

MOORE: That's a family in which, if the child has a failure in school for example, there is a built-in correction process. Say that the child does have a failure in algebra——not only would the child know how to take the problem home, but the correction process puts him one step ahead, and furthermore, gets the family involved in what is going on at school. In other words, instead of a failure cycling into further failures, it would have very beneficial effects. In a sense we would argue that a child needs a few bad teachers every once in a while, so that the family can come in and take a hand in the process of straightening out the curriculum and keeping it relevant to the child. A failure would, for certain families, set some corrective procedures in motion——the kid takes it home, the family discusses it, they go to work on it. So that, by the time the kid goes back to school he is ahead of where he was. But had he simply passed, the family wouldn't know where he was in the system.

In other words, a failure in the school system triggers a remedial loop which corrects the failure and allows the system to move ahead. Whereas, if there is no such family process, a failure may really ruin a kid. Now, roughly speaking, the blacks don't have such remedial loops. They don't have an uncle or sister or aunt or anybody. They don't know anybody who can work algebra problems.

HAMBLIN: Well, this last comment sort of contradicts what you said earlier. That is, how are you ever going to help the lower class if they don't have this kind of fail-safe method? You said earlier that you can't do it in the schools.

MOORE: Yes. That means we need to create some additional institutions. And it means having educational procedures powerful enough to carry the child into these additional resources beyond the family such as libraries, planetariums, black culture groups, and so forth. In other words, we need to create a fail-safe institution, or sets of them, to augment some of these areas where they are deficient.

COMMENTARY_____

THE PROBLEMS OF "BALANCE": RESEARCH AND ITS ENVIRONMENT

In sketching out the profile of his project, Moore touches on a number of the major themes of the conference. His presentation, much like that of Karl Weick, provides a set of criteria for reading the research enterprise in either of two directions: as a set of principles for treating a substantive interest, and as a self-conscious orientation to the silent language of sociology.

He begins by stating that the Clarifying Environments Project is a long-term, cross-discipline, team effort. The team has been working simultaneously in four major areas, which can be divided equally into *thinking* (math models and guiding principles) and *doing* (technology and "quick and dirty" studies) domains. While in the early stages the team "seemed to be superficial and inadequate with respect to everything——the overall *balance* is terribly important." As a commentary on the "sociology of sociology," this description of "balance" is very elusive but highly suggestive.

For instance, either domain can be further subdivided into focal, logical subdomains (math and technology) and into tacit, intuitive subdomains (principles and "quick and dirty" studies). So the notion of "balance" is a complex and dynamic dialectic between surface and deep structures, on the one hand, and between thought and experience, on the other.

Secondly, there are very definite *developmental properties* to be considered in this balance issue. One property would be level of task: from individual to superordinate. A second property would be a longitudinal perspective: from agent-patient (one-sided) to strategic (reciprocal) to referee, which is the most advanced and least perceptible.

A third ingredient to the issue of balance was introduced by Weick as a "regressive" tendency. In this context, regression—for example, due to limits on energy or attentional resources—is a tendency toward surface structures and primitive perspectives. So the concept of balance implies some attention to both these tendencies in order to produce a dialectic process between regressive habits and the requirements of new data, and between a one-sided outlook and the discovery of a symbolic mode of interaction between researcher and researched. When this notion of balance is plugged into the shadowy substance of sociology, a number of *threats* to *balance* can be suggested. First, it is easier to "think" than to "do" sociology. Second, it is easier to test surface structures than deep ones. Third, it is easier to handle problems scaled down for individual researchers than to construct a research team scaled up to the nature of an environmental issue. Fourth, it is easier to treat subjects as patients than to develop a relationship which takes them into active account.

Moore alerts us to one kind of threat to balance in one of his opening remarks. The talking typewriter is an

Table 1

Problems of Balance:

Degrees of Ease in Scientific Performance

Thinking $>$ Doing
Focal $>$ Tacit

	Thinking $>$	Doing
Focal $\vee$ **Tacit**	Math models	Technology
	Heuristics— guiding principles	Quick and dirty studies

apparently self-contained device which can be purchased by consumer-like school boards (to the tune of $40,000 apiece) and plugged in as some kind of special program. Unfortunately, without the "whole package," such as the symbolic transfer room, "it doesn't work."

This problem of "distortion" is somewhat akin to the problem of "realism" which Zelditch raised. Now this tendency to perceive tangible aspects more easily than the intangibles seems rather obvious. But a remark in the general discussion by Moore suggests that there is some kind of underlying developmental process to it. He indicates that the appropriate social science perspective is one of "strategy" and not "puzzle solving." This latter, in Meadian terms, is developmentally more primitive than the former. He further maintains that the dominant perspective in (social)

science is, historically, one of puzzle-solving.

In other words, he maintains that we are currently at the stage of development where we tend to take an active, but one-sided sense of a relationship. Now, with the talking typewriter (as opposed to its human prototype), Moore has created the one-sided relationship *par excellence*. In the automated booth the child can play either agent or patient with a device that is inexhaustible. But, presumably, the rationale behind purifying these twin-born perspectives can only be understood in terms of the transfer room where the two highest perspectives (strategist and referee) are encouraged. So the problem of perceiving Moore's project solely in terms of the technology is one of fixation at a primitive perspective.

The position Moore takes on the requisite technology is itself an example of this tendency. Viewed from below, each of the major branches of his project involves the distinctions of doing and thinking. For instance, the talking typewriter, as a responsive device, is an engineering thing which *reconstructed* processes that originally involved humans on both sides of the relation—for example, his initial, non-automated booths. The technology was developed *after* he had learned how to produce an effect, using human subjects *and* human "responders."

So in a sense, Moore, in his insistence on the fundamental requirement of technology, falls victim himself to the threats of imbalance. It is, furthermore, instructive to see in how many ways others perceived his imbalance, for example where his project was vulnerable on the side of omissions:

1. context—unable to handle cultural baggage (Gumperz); or unable to deal with other systems, such as peers, siblings (Hill);

2. instrumentation—not essential to employ electronic equipment (Inkeles);

3. subjects—linked essentially to the very young (Gumperz);

4. substantive focus—overly concerned with machine-type stuff, such as grammar, and not social science type stuff (Leik).

Moore's comment that social sciences are "stuck" with relatively nonproductive fields also touches on this issue of balance in the social system of research. One could take from that remark that he had better find something more productive than the gooey quagmire of social interaction. Or one might conclude that the system needs a less restrictive timetable, a greater tolerance for ambiguity, more support and protection for development. In a way the problem is similar to that of "how do we react to the 'discovery' of experimenter effects?" We could try to build blinds into the labs, to divest them of human variation, or we could begin to incorporate such effects into a larger purview of science, finding some new sense of purchase in such effects. The dilemma is quite similar to the one raised earlier by Zelditch: A programmatic sense of research, where we are always compromising between theoretical clarity and natural complexity.

For me, a lot of themes of the conference coalesce to tease the imagination in this session. The main issue which emerges is "what kind of *social system* is essential to the sociological enterprise?" "What kinds of constraints and supports does it need, what type of timetable?" Another way of asking the question is "what kinds of structures do we need on the research side, in order to map the subject side?" And then, "to what extent does our own cultural baggage inhibit the appropriate development?" "What kinds of strategic monitoring and reflexive feedback loops are needed to achieve a *relative balance*?"

Comparisons of the Moore–Hamblin Approaches

Hamblin's interview of Moore was a very creative endeavor revealing, first, a great deal of sympathy between the two, and second, the possibility of building appreciative bridges between two very different approaches, at least different on the surface. Let's review these projects through what I call in the summary the several "data domains."

Moore sets his theoretical anchor with George Herbert Mead and Georg Simmel, while Hamblin's theoretical debt is to, let's say, the behaviorist tradition. While these are widely discrepant at the focal level, the amount of tacit investment in both projects is a basis for much commonality—for example, both are keyed to producing effects. The point is, that reading the published reports, one does not get a picture of this underlying similarity.

As researchers, both have chosen a mode which is less concerned with "doing science" than it is with producing an effect. While there are differences in the mode, invent new environments versus manage natural ones, both seem to operate within the "strategic perspective" in contrast to the more characteristic "scientist as detective."

On the "subject" side, both approaches emphasize the virtuosity of the subjects. There is a similarity in the way the subjects are sampled. First, they use a "nested" or stacked sense of the subject unit, where individuals *and* their natural groups are the units. There is not the usual random sample (N = 1, from the "group" point of view). Moore explains, in a somewhat facetious vein, that his control group consists of all who are not part of the program. This nested sense of the subject unit combines with a technical notion of "interaction" which Hamblin later discusses. Simply stated, this means that

behavior is the product of interaction between the "operating characteristics" of the subject unit and the external environment (which includes both human and nonhuman aspects).

There are differences in the type of setting selected. Moore is attempting to *create* an environment for learning, while Hamblin works with *natural* environments. The creative aspect tends to produce a lot of problems—such as getting the headmaster fired—which, the other one solves—reducing social system tensions. The social structures which emerge in Moore's lab are, in some ways, at odds with those which develop in the schools. Hamblin, on the other hand, appears to be working within the school's value system, but you get the sense that this may be less true than it appears. For example, see his description in Part II of the teacher who uses the ratan whip. Hamblin's social systems may very well be considered (disruptive) inventions also, at least for teaching systems which place a heavy emphasis on repressive control.

The "underlying structures" were treated as different by Moore, when he stated that he was developing "competence" and Hamblin was improving "performance." Focally that may hold up, but not if we start searching about in the "deep structure" dimension. A big jump in performance beyond what we would expect on the basis of standard conditions would certainly sound like it is tapping what the term competence is taken to indicate: operating potentials. Moore attempts to get free of existing cultural constraints and maximize learning potentials, but in a sense so does Hamblin. The latter's program produces some whopping leaps in IQ—that is, some impressive changes in, at least, one kind of performance.

Moore seems to restrict his project to linguistic stimuli, while Hamblin's "multiple base-line" approach employs, for example, both math and language. So the focal stimuli are different, but at the deeper level the similarities may outweigh the differences. The thrust of Chomsky's sense of "deep structure" might suggest that the differences are at the level of content and the social meaning of the content, and not different in any formal sense. (See Helen Bee's discussion of this problem of language and thought.)

The idea that their research projects select from several data domains, is cross cut with the idea that there is a deep structure, as well as a surface structure. Where appearances might indicate differences between Moore and Hamblin, an attempt to reach into the deeper recesses may reveal a lot of similarities—for example, with respect to some of the themes of this conference. This same picture can be applied to the following session where Gumperz and Inkeles *appear* to take radically different turns (and actually *do*, in some cases,) but closer examination suggests a great deal of convergence.

Miscellaneous Remarks on the Social System of Research

The first question raised in the general discussion of Moore's paper, and the remarks which follow, serves to highlight the distinction of the modes of conducting social science. The question "suffers," if you will, from a desire to be too specific, theoretically, and thus requires a level of detail that Moore (and Hamblin) are not prepared to offer. The direction that the project takes is partially planned and partially retrospective. Furthermore, the level of composition of the project makes a number of discreet, tangible issues subject to intuitive decision. That is, issues which sometimes constitute the upper reaches of research are quickly dealt with and put aside, even though "they could make a difference."

In his response to the question, Hamblin's reference to *interaction* holds some interesting implications for our view of the system of research.

Organizational studies have recently begun to pick up on this sense of interaction, suggesting that variations in the environment (such as uncertainty) call forth variable organization structures. Furthermore, across similar environments, organizational effectiveness varies depending on internal conditions. Now what is significant about this sense of interaction is that it represents, developmentally, an advance in perspective. For example, Fritz Heider once suggested that the individual—when involved in a social attribution situation—tends to attribute "causality" to either the individual *or* the environment. So a sense of interaction between research systems and their environment raises some interesting questions: How certain is the environment of social science and with how much certainty do we treat it? How appropriate is the fit between the environment and the structure of research, and how might the structure be improved? For every adjustment to uncertainty, such as specialization, is there an appropriate counter balance, such as reintegration?

Other comments, in the remainder of the general discussion, indicate just how important this concept of interaction is. Hill, for instance, points to an aspect of the environment with which the Moore project is unable to cope: the larger web of affiliations that may be affected negatively by the constructive consequences on a child. This dilemma of innovation suggests just how complex is the environment with which we contend.

Moore's remark concerning the security of the middle class with the status quo alludes to a distinction that Leik raises later: policy measures as "relevant but unacceptable" versus measures that are "acceptable but not relevant." This suggests a problem, not only of having an effective package, but of providing for its acceptability by some target population.

The other questions raised about the relation between Moore's program and its environment pinpoint other difficulties. Gumperz, for example, notes that the program can't handle the vast majority of older children whose advanced socialization acts as an "enemy of free exploration." Inkeles wondered if it wasn't possible to create other environments which would not be so dependent upon the complex technology that the project employs. In this same vein, Leik suggests that, if we switch the task to interpersonal accommodation, we could produce a dynamic condition which is not pegged to electronics.

Sociolinguistics and Problem Solving in Small Groups

JOHN J. GUMPERZ

Since family problem solving is a form of interaction, it is largely dependent on verbal communication. It is hardly possible to analyze the processes involved without some reliance on verbal evidence. Language is relevant to the study of problem solving in two ways. On the one hand, it serves as a medium for the exchange of ideas and interaction among group members whose conversations can be recorded and analyzed by social scientists observing their behavior. On the other hand, the social scientist wishing to study group processes indirectly (through nonobservational methods like interviews, projective tests, and so forth) must also rely on language for much of his information. In either case, it is necessary for the success of the research that all concerned, participants and researchers, control the same code.

But unfortunately, communality of code has been more frequently assumed than demonstrated empirically. To the extent that they have explicitly dealt with language, social scientists have treated it largely as a reflection of individual psychology. They have focused on the content of what is communicated, assuming that as long as everyone concerned "speaks the same language," form presents no problem. Choice of expression, words or speech style, is regarded primarily as a matter of individual intent, a reflection of a person's attitude or psychic state. Yet, these very choices also convey important information. Members of any speech community ordinarily have little difficulty in distinguishing informal from formal or familiar from deferential speech. They can tell whether people are engaged in a serious discussion, or just chatting, without knowing exactly what is being talked about. Similarly, one can learn much about a speaker's social background, educational achievements, and sometimes also his regional origin just from the way he speaks. Since it conveys important social information, language usage is not, and cannot be, merely a matter of individual choice. It must be rule-governed. This paper will review some recent research on the relationship of group processes and cultural milieux to choice of linguistic form, for its implications for problem solving in small groups.

LINGUISTICS AND SOCIOLINGUISTICS

Linguistics is best known as the formal study of grammatical systems. Social scientists in recent years have been particularly interested in Chomsky's (1965) notion of linguistic competence—that is, the study of the speaker-hearer's knowledge of his language, defined as his control of the rules by which meanings are encoded into sounds. The linguist's remarkably explicit models of these processes have come to serve as examples of scientific rigor to investigators in related fields of psychology and anthropology.

One of the most significant features of the notion of competence is the fact that it deals with underlying constraints upon behavior rather than with actual performance. It refers to ability to act, rather than to what is done in particular instances. The goal of a linguistic analysis of competence is not to classify forms appearing in a particular body of data, but rather to explain occurring patterns in terms of deeper, more abstract regularities. It has been possible to show, for example, that although the number of sentences in a particular language is infinitely varied, they can in fact be generated from a finite body of rules. Generative grammar, as it is called, thus captures the creativity which is inherent in human language processes and which distinguishes them from nonhuman sign systems (Lenneberg, 1967).

The processes by which speakers code meanings into sound are largely automatic and hence only partially subject to conscious control. Regardless of individual intent, the form of one's speech always depends on the grammatical system of his language, and his interpretation of what he hears. There is no such thing as impartial observation or measurement of verbal behavior; measurement is always affected by distortions. To some extent these distortions can be overcome by analytical techniques, however, and the study of linguistic forms provides tools to deal with a level of subconscious behavior which, when compared with an individual's actual behavior on the one hand and his expressed opinions about his behavior on the other, can offer entirely novel insights into social processes.

The findings of generative grammar and its general orientation to the study of human action have had a profound effect on psychology and anthropological study of cognition (Chomsky, 1959; Smith and Miller, 1966). Attempts to establish direct relationships between grammatical rules and broader social processes, however, suffer from the fact that until quite recently, formal grammatical analysis dealt only with relatively limited aspects of verbal messages. In their search for methodological rigor, linguists tended to confine themselves to the internal linguistic patterning of linguistic forms within isolated sentences, ruling out consideration of the broader conversational context or the social settings in which such sentences are embedded. The resulting grammars account for what can be said in a particular language, but they make no attempt to specify what constitutes appropriate behavior in particular social circumstances.

In an effort to extend some of the general principles of formal grammatical analysis to the study of speech as a form of social interaction, sociolinguists have advanced the concept of communicative competence (Hymes, 1967). Whereas linguistic competence covers the speaker's ability to produce grammatically correct sentences, communicative competence describes his ability to select, from the totality of grammatically correct expressions available to him, forms which appropriately reflect the social norms governing behavior in specific encounters. The following examples of communication failures will illustrate the contrast between the two approaches to language.

1. From William Francis Allen, Charles Pickard Ware, & Lucy McKim Garrison, *Slave Songs of the United States* (New York, 1867, p. xxvii) quoted by Stewart (1968): A report by a white teacher of a century ago on an interchange with southern Negro boys:

> I asked a group of boys one day the color of the sky. Nobody could tell me. Presently the father of one of them came by, and I told him their ignorance, repeating my question with the same result as before. He grinned: "Tom, how sky stan'?" "Blue," promptly shouted Tom.

The difficulties in communication here are linguistic. We assume that since Negro boys did not understand the teacher's question, it was no more grammatically correct in their dialect than "How sky stan'?" is in English. The boys speak only Gullah, a plantation Creole of the Carolina coast current at the time; the teacher speaks only standard English. Their languages have different grammatical systems and therefore speaker and addressee are unable to exchange factual information.

2. From a report of a Congressional hearing in the New York Times, March 9, 1968, p. 28C:

> Studies of the Detroit riot show that Negroes are more interested in human dignity than in jobs, housing, and education, George Romney said.
>
> He quoted a survey showing that 80 percent of the Negroes of Detroit complain of the way they are treated by whites. They particularly object to being patronized, as when a white policeman addresses a Negro man as "boy," he said.
>
> Mr. (John L.) McClellan broke his silence. In his section of the country, he said, it was an old custom for whites to call Negroes "boy," and no offense was intended.
>
> "I sometimes use it, as a custom, a habit," he said. "But I mean no disrespect."
>
> "I try to avoid it, but sometimes I say, 'Boy, this, or boy, that.'"
>
> Negroes are too sensitive about that, he said. It makes no sense to start a riot over such a matter as being called "boy," he said.
>
> "People have to rise above these little things," he added.
>
> It was the Governor's turn to sit silent. Then he stammered, "Well, it's a hard thing—"

Mr. McClellan interrupted, "Yes," he said sternly, "and if it comes to it, we can deal with it in a hard way."

As in the first example, the two speakers do not seem to be communicating. Yet in this case both have the same grammar. They may differ in pronunciation but this is not relevant. What is important here is that they differ in the social norms governing the appropriate use of the address form "boy."

A third example illustrates how such divergence in sociolinguistic norms can be used to the communicative advantage of one party to an exchange, and the disadvantage of another.

3. From an experience of a Negro psychiatrist on a streetcorner in the southern United States in 1967, quoted by Ervin-Tripp (1969):

"What's your name, boy?" the policeman asked. . . .
"Dr. Poussaint. I'm a physician. . . ."
"What's your first name, boy? . . ."
"Alvin."
   'As my heart palpitated, I muttered in profound humiliation. . . .
For the moment, my manhood had been ripped from me. . . . No amount
of self-love could have salvaged my pride or preserved my integrity.'

Here the two speakers understand each other perfectly; the policeman means to insult, and he achieves this by an inappropriate demand for the victim's first name and by addressing a physician with a term reserved for a servant.

All three examples show rule-governed behavior. But only in the first case would the relevant rules be covered in the linguist's analysis. The alternants involved in the second and third examples—"Alvin," "Dr. Poussaint," and "boy"—are all equally grammatical and have the same basic function in the sentence. They are terms of address which may refer to the same individual. Use of one term or another does not change the nature of the message as a form of address; but it does determine how the person addressed is to be treated, and to what social category he is to be assigned. Selection among such grammatically equivalent alternants thus serves social rather than linguistic purposes. The study of sociolinguistic categorization processes provides a method of relating verbal behavior to social processes, adding an important dimension to the linguist's grammatical analysis.

Although our evidence is somewhat scanty, there is some reason to believe that sociolinguistic selection, like the coding of meanings into sounds, constitutes automatic behavior. The following example from recent fieldwork in a small Norwegian community (Gumperz 1964) shows that the discrepancies between actual speech behavior and the speaker's opinions about his actual behavior may be surprisingly large. Residents of this community speak both a local dialect and standard Norwegian (Bokmål) and read the latter. Their feelings about the appropriate times and places in which to use these two varieties are very strong. The standard language is used primarily in formal situations: teaching, business negotiations, and church services. On all other occasions, but above all in casual meetings, only the dialect is considered appropriate. To test the relationship of these attitudes about language usage to actual speech practice, we organized a series of informal gatherings for three local groups of differing social characteristics. In each group, various topics of conversation were introduced and the conversations recorded. In two of the three groups, speech practice was found to conform closely to locally-held stereotypes about language usage. Since the gathering was considered an informal one, even such topics as community affairs and the economic development of the region were discussed in the dialect. The third group, however, differed, in that "serious" topics like economic development and politics usually elicited a shift from the dialect into standard Norwegian, even though the members of the group were friends and the gathering informal. The majority of this group were university students spending about six months of the year in various university centers far distant from the community. Their residence in the city, however, had not changed their attitudes to the dialect. So strong was their allegiance to local values regarding speech behavior that they claimed, with perfect sincerity, that their entire conversation had been in the dialect. When the recorded conversation was played back to them, they were appalled and vowed not to repeat such slips of the tongue again. Yet the same phenomenon was observed during a subsequent meeting of this group! The cause of this group's difference in speech behavior is complex and does not concern us here. What is important for us is the evidence this example provides for the existence of compelling patterns of speech behavior which may not be realized by the speaker at all.

Research in sociolinguistics has dealt with socially determined selection in a variety of societies and at a variety of levels of analysis. What aspects of language are subject to this kind of variation? The problem is one which has never been completely neglected, and social variations in speech have been observed in many different kinds of societies around the world (Hymes, 1964). Until quite recently, however, such social variations have tended to be described only when they were clearly reflected in the data gathered by linguists as part of their ordinary linguistic field work procedures. What has tended to be studied are phenomena which, like the choice between "tu" and "vous" in French, are reflected in the grammatical system itself. This has created the impression that social distinctions are revealed only in some languages but not in others.

But this is not the case. Although members of all societies categorize each other through speech, groups differ in the linguistic means by which such categorization is accomplished. What some groups accomplish by alternating between familiar and respectful personal pronouns, such as "tu" and "vous," others achieve by shifting between Mr. Smith and John. Still others may achieve similar ends by simply switching from a local dialect to a standard language.

The major reason that such social variation in speech has not been studied systematically in all societies lies not in the speech behavior of the populations concerned, but rather in the way in which their speech has been recorded. The almost exclusive concern of linguistic elicitation procedures with reference (in the sense in which that term was used above) has led to the recording of the most commonly used equivalent for particular objects or ideas. The very artificiality of settings where linguists interview a single informant, and where speech samples must be produced in isolation from the customary circle of friends and family is hardly likely to bring forth the subtleties in selection of speech forms, shifts in formality and informality, which characterize every-day interaction.

The reproduction of natural conversation is difficult even for a highly skilled writer. It is certainly more than could be expected from the ordinary person. At best the linguist-informant interview yields samples of a single speech style, usually a relatively formal one. Suitable data for the analysis of communication processes has therefore simply not been available. The systematic study of communicative competence requires special elicitation techniques capable of capturing the speaker's skill in responding appropriately to significantly different social stimuli. Complete records of actual conversations must replace the recording of single sentences. Furthermore, comparison of the same speaker's verbal responses in at least two different settings should be emphasized.

SOCIOLINGUISTIC ELICITATION TECHNIQUES

How can such data be collected, and what information do we need to interpret it? One of the most obvious elicitation methods is the recording of naturalistic speech in unobserved settings. In a pioneering study of this type Soskin and John (1963) secured the assistance of a married college student couple for this task. The subjects were given two week's free vacation at a holiday resort. After their arrival they were each equipped with small microphones disguised as part of their clothing. They had the option of turning off the microphones when privacy was desired, but they were asked to keep the microphones on during much of their day, especially to record their meetings with other vacationers at the resort. Their speech was recorded through a transmitter station located a few miles from the locale of their activities. Similar naturalistic techniques of observation have been used in studying the behavior of nursery and kindergarten play groups. In one such study (Sher and Harner, 1968) all children were equipped with microphone pins of which all but one or two were dummies. Recordings were then made by experimenters seated behind a one-way mirror. This type of situation offers the advantage of allowing the investigator to make visual observations of the group while they were talking.

Methods of this type have produced some of our first extensive recordings of natural speech, providing much material potentially useful for sociolinguistic analysis. But the analysis of such conversation presents some serious problems. At the outset, masses of recorded data are necessary if a sufficiently large range of stylistic variation is to be obtained. This presents serious transcription problems, since even a roughly accurate transcription of one hour of recorded natural speech requires ten to twelve hours of transcription time. More faithful transcription involves a much heavier investment of time. Even after the material has been recorded, it is sometimes impossible to evaluate its social significance in the absence of ethnographic knowledge about social norms governing linguistic choice in the situation recorded.

Consider the account of the Congressional hearing cited above. In order to understand what is going on, we must be aware of the difference between Senator McClellan's traditional Southern speech norms and Governor Romney's egalitarian Northern values. The policeman in the Poussaint incident effectively degrades Dr. Poussaint because both speakers share a common set of values about the social meaning of the alternants employed. One problem with so-called naturalistic observation is that the experimenter sometimes cannot "understand" what he hears because of his unfamiliarity with the norms of the group he is observing. It is one of the striking characteristics of our society, and for that matter of any society undergoing rapid change, that values about speech behavior may differ from small group to small group and sometimes from generation to generation. Failure to recognize these sources of variation in value systems makes it difficult for us to understand such phenomena as hippie speech or black power rhetoric. Naturalistic observation and random sampling of speech must therefore be preceded by "ethnographies of communication" (Hymes, 1964a)—that is, by unstructured observation not tied down to any rigid experimental design.

The Norwegian experiment mentioned in the beginning of this paper was based on such fieldwork. The discussion sessions reported above took less than a week to stage, but this phase of the project was preceded by more than two months of intensive ethnographic study by two anthropologists, including an examination of local demographic records, study of economic life, local class stratification and its relation to friendship patterns, formal interviews about speech, and above all, participant observation. One of the investigators was a native Norwegian with several years of ethnographic experience in village Norway. Elaborate preparatory fieldwork of this kind provided the basis for selection of conversational groups whose speech behavior could be predicted by our knowledge of the local social organization.

Several kinds of group elicitation techniques were employed in Labov's (1968a) study of six adolescent and pre-adolescent peer groups in Harlem. Here is Labov's description of his procedures:

> "The paradigm for investigating the language of these peer groups may be summarized as follows:
>
> (1) The group was located by the field worker—in most cases a participant-observer living in the area.
>
> (2) Several individuals, including the leaders of the group, were interviewed in face-to-face situations.
>
> (3) Our staff met with the group on several outings and trips to various parts of the Metropolitan area. The field worker maintained daily contact with the group, and made notes on group membership and activities.

(4) In several group sessions, multi-track recordings were made of the group in spontaneous interaction; in these sessions, the dominant factors controlling speech are the same as those which operate in everyday conversation.

(5) All of the remaining individuals were interviewed in face-to-face interaction, and in addition, a large number of isolated individuals in the neighborhood ("lames") were interviewed."

In a recent study of London school children, Bernstein succeeded in generating stylistic variation by exposing children to different communication tasks as part of a half hour, structured interview session (Robinson, 1968). To initiate proceedings the child brought a painting or model to the interview room and talked about it. The child then constructed a model room with furniture and family figures supplied by the interviewer and answered several questions about these. The other tasks comprised the narration of stories about three sets of pictures, the description of objects and events in three postcard-size reproductions of paintings by Trotin, an open-ended story about what a child did in a free day, an explanation of how to play one of three games, and the description and explanation of the behavior of a toy elephant.

In interviews where the investigator brings a portable tape recorder to interview a small group of individuals (as in a family), it has sometimes been found useful for the investigator to leave the room or to step aside for a time, leaving the tape recorder running while participants talk among themselves. This technique proved productive during a recent interview with black West Indian high school children in Birmingham, England. We had asked the principal of a local school to get together a group of students to talk to us. The students met us in a small seminar room seated around a table. All of them were native speakers of Jamaican Creole who use a very Creolized form of English among themselves and in family settings, although most of them can also employ normal Birmingham English in the classroom. When we entered the room, we questioned them about their background, their schoolwork, and their interests. They answered in fairly formal English. During the course of the conversation it appeared that the students frequently performed skits in the classroom dealing with everyday life. When they volunteered to put on a skit for us, we offered to step out of the room to give them an opportunity to plan their performance. We left the tape recorder running during our absence, and when we listened to the tape later, we found remarkable shifts both in style and fluency. Students who seemed to have difficulty in talking when we were present suddenly became very fluent when the style of the language shifted to Creole.

While the elicitation procedures reported here differ greatly, they all depend to a large extent on the investigator's knowledge of the cultural norms and behavior patterns of the group concerned. Given such background knowledge, investigation need not be confined to a few small groups randomly selected. There is no reason why systematic and structured interview methods cannot be designed which can accommodate samples of relatively large size. Bernstein's group, for example, sampled a total of 350 children and their mothers in London. It is crucial, however, that procedures are followed which are meaningful to both interviewer and interviewee. The right questions must be asked in exactly the right way. This is especially important in working with small friendship or family groups where communication, as Sapir and Bossard have pointed out, relies heavily on shared knowledge. As Labov, a highly skilled sociolinguistic investigator, remarks: "If you want a child to tell you about baseball, questions such as 'Tell us the rules of baseball' are unlikely to elicit responses." To obtain a natural answer, the investigator must display his own knowledge of the game by questions like "How do you know when to steal third base?" Labov's recently completed study of peer group speech in the New York ghetto is perhaps the best examples of this approach (Labov, 1968b).

STRUCTURAL ASPECTS OF SPEECH BEHAVIOR

To suggest that the structure of longer conversational passages bears significant resemblances to the structure of sentences is to say that these passages must be patterned along two dimensions: the sequential or syntagmatic, and the paradigmatic. By paradigmatic structure, we refer to the fact that in any one speech event, speakers always select from a limited repertoire of alternates. Take, for example, the sentence, "We —————— out to dinner last night." In filling the slot here, we select one of a number of possible forms of the verb "go": go, goes, went. Note that selection is determined by the grammatical environment; only the last of the three forms fits, because of the adverbial phrase "last night." Since grammatical rules are automatic, all but beginning learners of English as a second language are unaware of the possibility of selection in this case. When we decide how to address someone who enters our office, similar selection among alternates takes place. But here social factors, rather than grammatical rules, are operative. Thus we may say "Come in and sit down, John," "Come in, Mr. Smith," or "Won't you come in, Sir?" Our choices in these matters are never quite free. We select a form of address on the basis of what we know about our interlocutor and what the behavioral norms allow. The difference between grammatical and sociolinguistic selection rules is one of degree, not one of kind.

By syntagmatic or sequential structuring, we refer to the fact that longer stretches of speech can be divided into distinct elements which are ordered in relation to each other. Just as sentences consist of clauses and phrases, conversations subdivide into episodes (Watson and Potter, 1962) or discourse stages, as Frake (1964) has termed them in his highly detailed and suggestive analysis of drinking encounters among the Subanum tribe in the Phillipines. These drinking encounters are culturally important as dispute settling mechanisms. Yet, the introduction of information about interpersonal conflicts is strictly constrained by the order of discourse stages. Encounters begin with long, ritualized introductions, in which wording is relatively predetermined. They end with similarly ritualized codas. Only a skillful speaker knows how to introduce new information in the transitions between these ritualized sequences.

A dramatic example of the importance of order in conversations is provided by Schegloff (1969) in an analysis of opening gambits in telephone conversations. Schegloff shows among other things that the person who answers a ringing telephone is always the first speaker, and that the caller speaks next. Thus the conversation has a defined order, like the order of words in a sentence. So strong are our expectations about the order in which the conversation will proceed, Schegloff has discovered, that it is possible to foil obscene telephone calls by simply picking up the ringing telephone but refusing to say "Hello." Schegloff further shows how purposeful distortions in sequential ordering can seriously affect the intelligibility of the message.

> A phone rings in Jim's home:
> JIM: Hello.
> GEORGE: Hi, how are you?
> JIM: O.K., but listen. I'm in a phone booth and this is my last dime. Barbara's phone is busy and I won't be able to meet her at seven. Could you keep trying to get her for me and tell her?
> GEORGE: What the hell are you talking about?

The key linguistic concept for the analysis of paradigmatic aspects of language behavior has been the notion of sociolinguistic variables as developed by Labov (1966) and others. Alternate terms of address and formal-informal word pairs such as "buy-purchase," "munch-eat-dine," can all be regarded as instances of such variables. A striking discovery based on contextual realistic linguistic fieldwork has been that social variation is by no means confined to lexical features and address terms. It affects all aspects of grammar including phonology and syntax. This is true for both monolingual societies like the United States and for bidialectal or multilingual societies.

In a pioneering study of verbal behavior in New York City, Labov (1966) noted that variations in the pronunciation of certain words were so extensive as to cut across the articulatory range of what structural dialectologists using traditional field techniques had analyzed as distinct phonemes. The vowel in *bad* for example could be homophonous with the "i" in *beard*, the "e" in *bed*, or the "ae" in *bat*. Three distinct phonemes thus seem to collapse into a single articulatory range. Since there is no phonetic basis for isolating distinct articulation peaks within this range, Labov argues that any attempt to deal with such shifts by postulating alternation between distinct systems is without empirical foundation. They must be treated as variables within a single system. He goes on to suggest that the discreteness of phonemic systems is an artifact of the linguist's field practice of abstracting rules from the speech of one or at most a few informants and of de-emphasizing variation. Intensive study of speech behavior should, in any one speech community, reveal both phonemes and variables. While phonemes are characterized by pronunciations clustering around definable articulation peaks, variables are defined by a starting point and a scale of values varying in a certain direction. The values along such scales are conditioned by social factors in a manner analogous to that in which phonological environments condition the phonetic realizations of allophones.

Not all grammatical or lexical alternates in a language can automatically be regarded as sociolinguistic variables, however. Since the same language may be spoken in a number of socially distinct societies, it must be demonstrated that selection among alternates carries social significance for some group of speakers. Furthermore since social meaning is always embedded in reference, it is useful to speak of sociolinguistic variables only when alternates are referentially equivalent, such as when they signify the same thing in some socially realistic speech event. Items with the same or similar dictionary meanings may not be substitutable in actual conversation and, per contra, some variables are semantically equivalent only in specific contexts. An example will illustrate the problem. Few would ordinarily claim that the words "wife" and "lady" are homonyms in English. Yet they are used as such in the following extracts from an invitation to an army social quoted in a recent issue of the San Francisco Examiner: "Officers with their ladies, enlisted men with their wives." Referential equivalence here underlines social differences.

There is evidence to show that selection of sociolinguistic variables is rarely completely free. Variables tend to be selected in co-occurrent clusters. In other words, the speaker's selection of a particular value of a variable is always constrained by previous selections of variables. Thus, if a speaker varies between [i·], [e·], and [æ] in *bad*, and, in addition, has alternates *ain't, is not, going*, and *goin'*, he is most likely to say "This ain't gonna be [bi·d]" in some situations and "This is not going to be [bæd]" in others. It would be unusual for him to say "This is not going to be [bi·d]." It is important to note that sociolinguistic selection constraints which generate such co-occurrences cut across the normal components of grammar. Their study, therefore, extends the application of linguistic analysis to data not ordinarily considered a part of grammar.

So far, our discussion of linguistic variables has dealt only with features of phonology and grammar. During the last few years, some of the methodological principles employed in the study of grammar have also begun to be applied to the sociological analysis of communication content. Content, however, is not studied for its own sake. The goal here is the empirical investigation of the manner in which contents is manipulated as part of communicative strategies. Stereotyped opening gambits such as "What's new?" suggest that the selection of conversational topics often serves social ends other than the transmission of factual information. Here, the speaker identifies himself as a friend and signals his readiness for further talk. Ervin-Tripp (1969) points out similarly that when a wife greets her husband by announcing that her visitors are discussing nursery schools, she may be suggesting that he absent himself, since in our culture husbands are not potential members of nursery school mothers' groups. In both cases, the important information in the conversation is contained in inferences hearers are expected to draw from their knowledge of the social relationships underlying the ostensible topic. Choice of content, therefore, is part of the code; like choice of grammatical form, it is a means to an end, not an end in itself.

To say that selection of topic communicates information about social relationships is to imply that these relationships, or for that matter, social structures in general, cannot simply be regarded as fixed, jural rules having an existence of their own apart from human action. They must themselves be part of the communicative process, and thus presumably subject to change or reinforcement as the cumulative result of everyday communicative acts. The view that social structures are assigned through interaction is most clearly documented in the writings of Erving Goffman (1963). Through his study of interaction in various special settings, such as games, hospitals, work groups, and the like, he provides dramatic evidence for the fact that a single role or relationship may be realized through different types of behavior in different situations.

Building upon similar theoretical premises, Harold Garfinkel (1967) concentrates somewhat more directly on the cognitive rules by which members of a society assess the significance of actions in everyday life. In essence, Garfinkel's view is that a person's previous experience and his knowledge of the institutions and practices of the world around him act to constrain his interpretations of what he sees and hears, in somewhat the same way that grammatical rules constrain his perception of sound sequences. He uses the term "background expectation" to characterize the outside knowledge that an individual employs in the interpretation of events.

In a study of the function of such "background expectations" in everyday communication, Garfinkel (1969) asked a group of students to report a conversation in which they had participated in the following fashion: they were to write on the left-hand side of a piece of paper what was actually said, and on the right-hand side they were to explain in detail what they understood the conversation to mean. Here is a sample of the record obtained in this way:

Speaker	Verbatim Transcript	Detailed Explanation
HUSBAND:	Dana succeeded in putting a penny in a parking meter today without being picked up.	This afternoon as I was bringing Dana, our four-year-old son, home from the nursery school, he succeeded in reaching high enough to put a penny in a parking meter when we parked in a meter zone, whereas before he had always had to be picked up to reach that high.
WIFE:	Did you take him to the record store?	Since he put a penny in a meter that means that you stopped while he was with you. I know that you stopped at the record store either on the way to get him or on the way back.

The interchange in the verbatim transcript would be inexplicable without an assumption of shared background expectations.

Garfinkel then went on to demonstrate the function of background expectations by asking his students to substitute detailed explanations of the kind shown in the right-hand column in the example above for the usual expressions employed in ordinary family discourse. The results were instructive: when they did, they were accused of "acting like strangers." One wife asked her husband, "Don't you love me any more?" Thus, the students' relatives perceived detailed explanatory language as a rejection of family values. Reliance on background expectations thus seems to serve an important purpose in distinguishing small group or family conversations from interaction with nonmembers.

Where Garfinkel points out the importance of background expectations in communication, Harvey Sacks (1967) proceeds to specify how the speaker's implicit use of these expectancies generates conversation exchanges. Among the most important of these are the "social categories" or social relations implied by speech content. Sacks' basic data is derived from natural conversations. In analyzing the following sentence sequence taken from a verbatim transcript of a child's story, "The baby cried. The mommy picked it up," he notes that members of our society will automatically recognize the "mommy" in sentence 2 as the mother of the infant in sentence 1. Yet, there is nothing in the overt linguistic structure of either sentence which provides for this identification. Pronouns such as "his" or "her" which ordinarily express such relationships are lacking.

What perceptual or cognitive mechanisms, Sacks asks, must we postulate in order to explain the hearer's understanding of the mother-child relationship in the absence of linguistic clues? Sacks observes that forms like "mommy" and "baby" can be regarded as "membership categorization devices" which assign actors to certain social categories and invest them with the rights and duties implied therein. It is not possible, however, to determine the social category implied by a term by considering that term in isolation. The isolated term "baby," for example, could be part of the collection baby-child-adult, or of the collection mommy-daddy-baby. In the example given above, we identify it as part of the latter collection by examining both sentences. The cognitive process is somewhat as follows: (1) We perceive a semantic tie between baby and the activity of crying, which is more reminiscent of family relationships (mommy-daddy-baby) than of age grading (baby-child-adult); (2) This hypothesis is confirmed by the fact that the mommy in sentence 2 forms part of the collectivity (mommy-daddy-baby) but not of the collectivity (baby-child-adult).

The concept of membership categorization device has some similarity to the symbolic interactionists' concept of role. Both Sacks and Garfinkel, however, seem to avoid this conventional terminology in order to circumvent the association of roles with separately existing jural rules which has been built up by much earlier writing on role. As Cicourel (1968) has pointed out, they see social structure as constraining behavior in somewhat the same way that syntax constrains the encoding of sounds. The goal is to devise empirical methods by which to discover social categories directly through conversational data. Despite the newness of these insights, a recent study of Moerman's (1969) shows that Sacks' concepts can be used, with the aid of an informant, to analyze the cultural basis of everyday behavior in groups whose culture is strange to the observer. These techniques should also be applicable to the analysis of subcultural differences in family groups in American society, and seem to me to hold considerable potential value for a range of applications from group therapy for families to social psychological and anthropological analysis of small groups.

Although Sacks limits his analysis to communication content, sociolinguistic variables of the types discussed above can also be regarded as membership categorization devices. In the following joke told to my colleague Alan Dundes by a black student, the social label "Negro" is conveyed by the syntactically and phonologically marked utterance "Who dat?":

> Governor W. died and went to heaven. When he knocked on the door, a voice answered: "Who dat?" He said, "Never mind, I'll go to the other place."

The notion of categorization devices thus extends to both linguistic form and linguistic content. Although I know of no serious study of the use of linguistic form as a categorization device, it would seem that both types of evidence should be utilized in the study of interpersonal relations in small groups.

HOW DO DIFFERENT GROUPS DEVELOP DIFFERENT LINGUISTIC CODES?

This question is but one aspect of the broader problem of social differentiation in speech: of how a person's social origin affects his ability to communicate with others. Basil Bernstein's (1969) theories of restricted and elaborated codes represent the first systematic attempt to deal with this question in cross-culturally valid or universal terms. In the United States, Bernstein's earlier work has frequently been taken to assert that there is a direct or causal relationship between middle and working class status and elaborated and restricted codes, respectively. His recent writings present a considerably different picture (Bernstein, 1969). The basic assumption underlying Bernstein's empirical research is that the network of social relationships in which the individual interacts, and the communicative tasks which these relationships entail, ultimately shape his linguistic potential. Following Elizabeth Bott (1957), he makes a scalar distinction in family role systems between closed or positional systems, and open or person-oriented systems. The former polar type emphasizes communal values at the expense of freedom of individual expression and initiative. Such emphasis tends to limit the introduction of new information through verbal means, stressing social propriety in speech and leading to a predominance of ritualized exchanges. Hence the term "restricted code" to describe a way of using language which is largely formulaic, and more suited for reinforcing pre-existing social relationships than for the transmission of new factual information. Person-oriented role systems, on the other hand, emphasize individual freedom and adaptability. They tend to generate "elaborated codes," capable of expressing information about the physical and social environment and emphasizing the ability to use speech creatively, for the transmission of such information.

While all speakers show some control of both types of speech code, there are important social differences in the extent to which elaborated speech is used. Individuals socialized in open role systems, while they may use restricted codes in their own family or small-group settings, are trained to speak in and respond to elaborated codes in serious discussion, in school, and in public life. Persons socialized in closed role systems are less flexible. The socialization process they have undergone has generated certain attitudes to speech as a vehicle for the transmission of new information. These attitudes create conflicts when children are faced with the kind of verbal learning tasks usually required in school. Bernstein suggests that it is the schools' inability to bridge the communication gap with restricted code speakers which accounts for the fact that so many children are slow to learn verbal skills. He rejects the notion of cultural or linguistic deprivation; the problem is one of differing socialization methods, and the difficulty lies in devising a strategy for communicating with children unaccustomed to the types of social relations required in school.

The value of Bernstein's theory for sociolinguistics lies in the fact that it postulates a direct relationship between socialization practices and the individual's ability to express social relationships through speech. The relationship thus postulated is subject to empirical verification both through interview methods and the study of natural conversations of mothers and children. Recently published studies conducted by Bernstein's group (Robinson, 1968) have in fact produced some impressive evidence of the connection between mothers' socialization practices and the way their children perform on communicative tasks of the type mentioned in the discussion of field methods given above. There is no doubt that, at least in Britain, children of various groups differ significantly in their ability to take the role of the other, and that this difference is measurable through the study of the childrens' language.

Recent sociolinguistic research in the United States, however, raises some doubt about the generalizability of the concepts of restriction and elaboration in their present form. William Labov (1969) using elicitation techniques which relied heavily on natural conversation, found that the very children who in school or in interviews with strangers speak only in short and highly formulaic utterances, usually characterized as "restricted codes," show themselves to be highly creative and effective communicators when they are interviewed in a setting which they perceive culturally realistic, or when their natural interaction with peers is recorded. Similarly, Herbert Kohl's (1968) stimulating account of his classroom experiences in ghetto schools shows that children who place low on conventional linguistic achievement tests are capable of highly creative and effective writing under the right conditions.

Labov's and Kohl's observations are confirmed by preliminary results from cross-cultural research on language socialization by a group of anthropologists from the University of California at Berkeley, who lived as participant observers with the groups they studied and were thus able to compare psycholinguistic test results with their own observations and tape recorded natural conversations (C. Kernan, 1969, K. Kernan, 1969, Blount, 1969, Stross, 1969). Findings, some of which are summarized by Ervin-Tripp (1969a), point to the importance of peer group socialization in verbal development in the non-Western cultures and in lower class Western groups. Whereas parent-child interaction tends to be quite restricted, peer group interaction shows a great deal of verbal communication. Black teen-age groups in American ghettos place unusual value on such verbal skills as story telling, word games, verbal dueling, and so forth (Labov, 1966). If they seem uncommunicative in formal interviews or if they perform badly on tests, this may be in large part due to the unfamiliarity of the setting or to their attitude to the test.

The present state of our knowledge therefore provides little justification for associating absolute differences in verbal skills with class or ethnic background. It would be more useful to assume that different social groups use different verbal devices for the transmission of social meaning. "Lexical elaboration," to paraphrase Bernstein's term for the code which relies most heavily on the expression of nonreferential meaning through words, is only one of these devices but by no means the only one. Similar information can be conveyed through style shifting, intonation, special "in-group" vocabulary, topical selection, and like devices. The sense of 'who dat' in the joke cited above could for instance also have been conveyed by the phrase "A heavily accented negro voice answered: Who is that?" The social significance would have been the same, but the joke less effective.

Differences in communicative devices have important social consequences. Communication through style shifting, special intonation, special in-group terminologies, topical selection basically relies on metaphor and is heavily dependent on shared background knowledge. Only individuals who are aware of the cultural stereotype which associates the pronunciation "who dat" with the Negro race can understand the joke cited above. On the other hand, the greater the verbal explicitness, the less the reliance on shared commonality of background. At the extreme end of the explicitness scale an individual needs to know little more than the rules of grammar and the relevant vocabulary. Wherever education is public and open to all, these matters can be learned by everyone regardless of family background. The cultural knowledge necessary for the understanding of metaphors is not that easily accessible. Ability to understand and communicate effectively here depends, above all, on informal learning through regular interaction. Frequency of interaction alone moreover is not enough. The context in which the communication occurs and the social relationships relevant to it are also important. Whites in our society may regularly interact with blacks, but in most cases such interaction is relatively impersonal. Communication in intimate family contexts of the kind which is characterized by free, unguarded give and take, is still quite rare. It is therefore not to be expected that whites have the cultural basis for judging the quality of interaction in black family groups.

SOME APPLICATIONS FOR PROBLEM SOLVING IN FAMILY GROUPS

The fact that family communication relies heavily on shared background expectations, which so far have received relatively little formal study has some serious consequences for the investigator working with family groups. Small group studies depend on the observer's or coder's ability to evaluate communication content. Bales' (1950) well known twelve categories for interaction analysis, for example, require that the observer make relative fine judgments as to the degree of solidarity or tensions expressed in an utterance, or that he distinguish between suggestions or expressions of opinions, and so forth. It is exactly this type of judgment of speech function which is most radically affected by subcultural variation and is likely to cause difficulties for investigators working with populations of social class and ethnic background different from their own. The difficulties are compounded by the fact that speakers think of themselves as speaking the same language. It is assumed that as long as speakers share a grammar and vocabulary they can always make sense of each others statements. But the investigator's interpretation of what is meant by a particular utterance may be radically different from that of his subjects.

An example from my own recent field work experience will illustrate the problem. In the course of a discussion session with a group of black teenagers in a ghetto neighborhood in which my assistant and I were the only whites present I felt myself repeatedly the target of remarks such as the following: "You are racist." "You wouldn't give a black man a chance." A series of these and similar remarks made me feel increasingly under attack. I responded, "You know nothing about me. How do you know that I discriminate?" The reply was, "You means the system not *you*. We are not blaming you personally."

Communication difficulties are not confined to evaluation of behavior in small groups. A family therapist attempting intervention techniques may similarly find that his instructions are misunderstood or that his comments unaccountably cause resentment. The white middle class school teacher's experience with ghetto children provides many examples for this type of failure. How can such communication gaps be overcome? Should the investigator learn to speak his subjects' language? This would be difficult and not necessarily effective. An outsider using "in-group speech" may give the impression of talking down or intruding on others' private affairs. It is more important to concentrate on methods for diagnosing the relevant differences in language usage. In the examples cited above for instance, the problem lies in the ambiguity between the personal and impersonal meaning of "you." In middle class English usage the impersonal "you" tends to be marked linguistically either by occurring in constructions such as "you people" or in stereotyped expressions like "you never know" or by appearing in the same sentence with an abstract impersonal noun. In lower class English, as well as in lower class black speech the interpretation of "you" as personal or impersonal is more frequently ambiguous and its interpretation depends on the nonlinguistic context. My reaction was due to my failure to see this possible ambiguity. The speaker took advantage of this failure on my part to show me up.

In the absence of detailed ethnographic data, intensive analysis and exposure to natural conversation of culturally different groups is one of the best ways of acquiring the cultural background necessary to interpret their speech. It would be useful here to adapt a practice which is becoming more and more common in minority schools (Labov, 1968b): to employ as an assistant a local resident—not necessarily someone with a proper degree, but a person who through leadership in local groups has shown himself to be a good communicator. Such an individual would act as an intermediary between the researcher and his subjects, to make sure that instructions are given in the right manner and that explanations are properly understood. He would tutor the investigator in the usage rules and politeness formulas of the group, teach him such matters as how best to open a conversation, when to interrupt, when not to speak his mind, and also provide tapes of natural conversation in relevant settings for analysis.

The natural unit for such conversational analysis is the interactional exchange or sequence of two or more utterances, not an isolated utterance. Two questions are relevant in the analysis: (1) What is meant by the exchange? What does it reflect about the speaker's state of mind and his relationship to the group? Comparison of the assistant's judgment in these matters with those of the investigator should be useful to reveal relevant subcultural differences. (2) By what verbal devices are the relevant effects obtained? Are there any special features of style, such as pronunciation of special vocabulary, which are significant? It is here that the work of Sacks (1967) and Schegloff (1969) and Moerman (1969) should be useful.

With relatively little additional research, an investigator with some training in sociolinguistics could develop indices for the study of interaction patterns in family solving groups, to be used in addition to conventional communication indices such as those now employed by Straus (1968) and others. The method here would be to follow the sociolinguist's practice in studying the same individual's reaction under varying social stimuli. A subject's performance on similar problem solving tasks could be measured first in a family group and then in a peer group setting. Techniques for the study of variable selection devised by Labov (1966) as well as the recent linguistic work by Bernstein's group (Mohan and Turner, 1968, Henderson, 1968) on measures of elaboration and restriction could be adapted here.

Throughout our discussion we have given primary attention to sociolinguistic analysis as a diagnostic or ethnographic tool for the study of small group interaction. Little if any attempt has been made to make direct predictions, such as the effect of particular types of speech behavior on problem solving ability. In part this is due to the newness of sociolinguistics.

Although we have made considerable advances in basic theory we are faced with a great paucity of reliable descriptive data. More direct application would require more detailed research on family problem solving by skilled sociolinguists. In the absence of such work it would seem that the basic understanding we have achieved can aid the student of problem solving primarily by giving him an insight into basic communication processes and thus improve the validity of his own field work both cross-culturally and within his own society.

REFERENCES

Bales, Robert F., *Interaction Process Analysis*. Reading, Mass.: Addison Wesley Publishing Co., 1950.

Bernstein, Basil, "A Sociolinguistic Approach to Social Learning." *Social Science Survey*. Baltimore: Penguin Books, Inc., 1965.

——— "A Sociolinguistic Approach to Socialization." *Directions in Sociolinguistics*. John Gumperz and Dell Hymes, ed. New York: Holt, Rinehart and Winston, Inc., 1969.

Blount, Ben G. Dissertation in preparation, University of California, Berkeley, 1969.

Bott, Elizabeth, *Family and Social Network*. London: Tavistock Publications, 1957.

Chomsky, Noam, Review of B. F. Skinner's "Verbal Behavior." *Language* 35:1 (1959), 26–28.

——— *Aspects of the Theory of Syntax*. Cambridge, Mass.: MIT Press, 1965.

Cicourel, Aaron, "The Acquisition of Social Structure: Towards a Developmental Sociology of Language and Meaning." Harold Garfinkel and Harvey Sacks, ed. *Contributions to Ethnomethodology*. Bloomington: Indiana University Press, 1968.

Ervin-Tripp, Susan, "Sociolinguistics." L. Berkowitz, ed. *Advances in Experimental Social Psychology*, Vol. 4, Academic Press, 1969a.

——— "Sociolinguistics Summer Training." *Items* (1969).

Frake, Charles O., "How to Ask For a Drink in Subanum." John Gumperz and Dell Hymes, ed. "The Ethnography of Communication," *American Anthropologist*, 66:6, II (1964), 127–132.

Garfinkel, Harold, *Studies in Ethnomethodology*. Englewood Cliffs, N.J.: Prentice Hall, Inc., 1967.

——— "Remarks on Ethnomethodology." John Gumperz and Dell Hymes *Directions in Sociolinguistics*. New York: Holt, Rinehart and Winston, Inc., in press.

Goffman, Erving, *Behavior in Public Places*. New York: The Free Press, 1963.

Gumperz, John J., "Linguistic and Social Interaction in Two Communities." John Gumperz and Dell Hymes, ed. "The Ethnography of Communication," *American Anthropologist*, 66:6, II (1964), 137–153.

Henderson, Dorothy, "Social Class Differences in Form-Class Usage and Form-Class Switching Among 5-Year-Old Children." W. Brandis and Dorothy Henderson, ed. *Social Class, Language and Communication*. London: I. Routledge and Kegan Paul, 1968.

Hymes, Dell, "Toward Ethnographies of Communication," John Gumperz and Dell Hymes, ed. "The Ethnography of Communication," *American Anthropologist* 66:6 II (1964b), 1–34.

—— "Models of the Interaction of Language and Social Setting," John Macnamara, ed. "Problems of Bilingualism," *Journal of Social Issues* 23:2 (1967).

Kernan, Claudia, Dissertation in preparation, University of California, Berkeley, 1969.

Kernan, Keith, Dissertation in preparation, University of California, Berkeley, 1969.

Kohl, Herbert, *Thirty-Six Children*. New York: New American Library, 1967.

Labov, William, *The Social Stratification of English in New York City*. Washington, D.C.: Center for Applied Linguistics, 1966.

—— "Contraction, Deletion and Inherent Variability of the English Copula." (Typescript), 1968a.

—— *A Study of the Non-Standard English of Negro and Puerto Rican Speakers in New York City*. Mimeographed. Columbia University, 1968b.

Lenneberg, Eric, *Biological Foundations of Language*. New York: John Wiley & Sons, 1967.

Moerman, Michael, *Analysis of Lue Conversation*. Working paper No. 12. Language-Behavior Laboratory, University of California, Berkeley, 1969.

Mohan, B., and Turner, G. J., "Grammatical Analysis, Its Computer Program, and Application," Basil Bernstein, ed. *Social Class and the Speech of 5-Year-Old Children*. London: I Routledge and Kegan Paul, 1968.

Robinson, W. P., *Social Factors and Language Development in Primary School Children*. (Typescript), 1968.

Sacks, Harvey, Typescript of classroom lectures. Division of Social Sciences, University of California, Irvine, 1967.

Schegloff, Emanuel, "Sequencing in Conversational Openings." *American Anthropologist* 70:6 (1969), 1075–1095.

Smith, Frank, and Miller, George A., *The Genesis of Language*. Cambridge, Mass.: MIT Press, 1966.

Soskin, William, and John, Vera, "The Study of Spontaneous Talk," R. G. Barker, ed. *The Stream of Behavior*. New York: Appleton-Century-Crofts, 1963, 228–281.

Stewart, William A., *Continuity and Change in American Negro Dialects*. (Typescript), 1968.

Straus, Murray A., "Communication, Creativity, and Problems Solving Ability of Middle and Working Class Families in Three Societies." *American Journal of Sociology* 73:4 (1968).

Stross, Brian, Dissertation, University of California, Berkeley, 1969.

Watson, Gene, and Potter, R. J., An Analytic Unit for the Study of Interaction. *Human Relations* 15:245–263 (1962).

CRITIQUE AND DISCUSSION_____

Let me just say I think most of the basic theory that has been presented thus far doesn't in general reflect the kind of work on language that some of us in sociolinguistics are doing.

I will start by describing in what sense linguists deal with social phenomenon and their goals. The goals of linguistic analysis deal with the strategies of behavior and not with the consequences of behavior. We're not immediately concerned with evaluating whether a certain kind of behavior is functional or disfunctional. In other words, those are conclusions that can be reached after the analysis is done. They are subject to empirical verification.

Now language, when used in the broadest sense, is symbolic behavior and the emphasis is on the strategy rather than on the consequences. Nevertheless, by the analysis of strategy, I think one could notice things such as tiredness, fatigue, things of the sort that were mentioned yesterday. And there are other kinds of things that you can determine purely by linguistic studies. If you have a group talking, you can determine the degree of centrality to the group of particular individuals. Some of my students have been working with conversations from "hippie" groups. They are studying the use of terms identified with hippie subculture and one of the findings that regularly comes out is that there is an inverse correlation between the frequency of use of these terms and centrality in the group.

Now, I think that linguistic data can be used in a number of ways by social scientists. Language can be used as an example of how to construct theories about behavior. This is what psycholinguists, working on generative grammars, have done. They're interested in——they're using language as a way of getting at competence. However, while they can tell us what grammars look like they cannot tell us what speech behavior looks like because they make the assumptions, "We are dealing with an ideal speaker in an ideal speech community who's not subject to tiredness effects and to making mistakes." They deal with single speakers and are really concerned with language as universal, as it mirrors some universal properties of the human mind. As an example of theory construction, I think it's important because this theory is a universal one. We can study a system in this manner as long as we artificially make it relatively simple. We can't study role switching with this conceptual apparatus. We can study language codes, but not code switching. We're just beginning to be able to study code switching. (Compare Zelditch's remarks regarding theory as simplification and the "place cues" argument, plus Inkeles' comment.)

Now, the issue is both of these—grammar and speech—are rule governed. So, the question is what's being communicated? How do we describe this? How does a speaker select from a repeatoire of possible linguistic behaviors in relation to various kinds of social factors. And I think the best kind of theory, the best kind of social theory that I know of for this is the kind of interaction theory that is beginning to be developed by people like Goffman. The basic image is the communicating individual operating under certain constraints and as I see sociolinguistics, it is a way of describing these constraints.

These are communicative restraints: the environment, the place cues that Zelditch talked about, as well as the clues from social structure, your knowledge of possible sanctions deriving from social factors; the fact that you can't be too inventive, because if you were the rest of your family or peers would come down on you. All of these can be handled as constraints at the same abstract level as long as you realize that these constraints and the physical clues by which you learn about them is not a one-to-one relationship.

Now, another aspect of this image is that when you look at these rules or constraints, every individual has different sets of rules. The total community rules cannot be stated in terms of an overall metasystem of some sort. There is individual selection with this metasystem, so you have to take account of individual variation.

I do have a section in the paper that deals with field methods. How do you collect data on behavior? There are three things that have to be built into any kind of data collection techniques. One is you have to be prepared to find variations in value systems. To define individuals who can handle several value codes——code switch or role switch. In other words, people handling language usage rules are like bridge players in a way and

you have to know what convention they're in. (Compare Moore's definition of a strategic perspective.)

The second thing is the problem of boundaries. Now, anthropologists are still thought of as dealing with cultures. I don't think any serious linguistic anthropologist would say that it is possible to describe a culture. There is no such thing——we can describe domains in cultures. We can describe kinship behavior, we can describe disease terminology, we can describe dress, but we cannot describe cultures as units. We are beginning to think that there are no such units except as abstractions and this raises the problem of boundaries. In other words, you have to keep your boundaries, community boundaries, flexible. When we began our study of Puerto Ricans, we started out by talking about the Puerto Rican speech community. But we found that the big distinctions were within what we were studying rather than without.

The third principle of experimentation is varying the environment in such a way as to generate not only different kinds of behavior but predictably different kinds of behavior. We were talking this morning about manipulating groups. Now, we carried out an experiment of this kind in northern Norway, manipulating groups. We had studied speech behavior in this community and we had described the local dialect and standard Norwegian but we knew very little about usage patterns. So we also did an ethnography. We did an analysis of friendship patterns, we did a great deal of participant observations, we collected the usual demographic information, educational data. On the basis of this we were able to know ethnographically what an individual's position in the community was, who his friends were, basically, how central he was. Using this information we then set out to construct two kinds of groups, open and closed network groups that would vary significantly in linguistic behavior. And it turned out to be very simple. In other words, we were able to construct groups that conformed to our independently arrived at predictions about linguistic behavior.

Now, let me just say one or two other things about technique. One thing that we've found about group discussion is that it's not true that you can't tape record unobtrusively. In other words, you can have your tape recorder right in the middle where everybody sees it and you can still get natural speech, because if you have a natural group the members mutual obligation to each other soon takes over. With respect to recording technology, the one that I would use is a technique that William Labov in New York employs. You usually want to work with relatively small groups of five or six people. You use six relatively cheap tape recorders with the level of each mike adjusted to a member. Then a single powerful tape recorder is mounted in the middle. You then get separate track recordings from each person and you compare

each person's track with the master track. He has found some fantastic things.

Finally, I would like to talk about the two kinds of analyses that you can use with this kind of material. This relates to what was said yesterday about interaction always occurring at two levels: a sort of status seeking and an overt level. Linguistic analysis gets at the overt level in many ways. But you could also take the same conversation that you're analyzing and you could analyze it for content. You could do a content analysis at the same time and on the same kind of material that you're doing the overt analysis. And you have two relatively independent measures. Linguistically you could do something that is more sophisticated than the content analysis. This would be the kind of method that Harvey Sacks is developing now, basing himself primarily on Harold Garfinkel's work. This is an analysis of how speakers react to each other through speech. Now, basically Sacks does this at what a linguist would call a semantic level or a pragmatic level, and he's beginning to find a way of making pragmatics an experimental science. What you do, to put it simply, is look at the speech context for clues——for example, see how a speaker's choice of topics relates to all previous choices across a whole conversation.

INKELES DISCUSSION

I'd like to take this opportunity to point us back in the direction of our consideration of families. I'll stick to Professor Gumperz' focus of attention mainly by trying to talk about language. I'll focus on something that he didn't take up because he rather explicitly emphasized that he doesn't want to deal with function. So I want to concentrate on that as a supplement to what he said. Around language, I believe, there are a whole series of problematic issues——they're problematic in the sense that the outcomes are by no means guaranteed. Nevertheless, the resolution of the issues involved are enormously important in judging the extent to which the family is or is not fulfilling one of it's functions, namely, the socialization of children.

One of the peculiar things about language in the family is that you are dealing with a phenomenon which is simultaneously two very different things. To an exceptional degree, language is the central vehicle through which socialization is carried on . . . but it's not merely an instrument of socialization. It's one of the things that socialization wishes to produce. It's not just a vehicle. The vehicle and the object are both the same thing. So I'd like to indicate a number of tasks which the family faces and say something about the implications for language work in the family with regard to these tasks.

As I went about this, what I found increasingly is that I got rather discouraged, if you consider families which have or don't have a lot of what we think families should have. It turns out that to think of ways in which the deficiencies which families may have——to compensate for these deficiencies within the framework of the family system if it already begins with a low level of capacity—is going to be very, very difficult. So that, with respect to these tasks, in most instances what I'm arguing for is supplementation with regard to what's in the deficient family. That is, the fulfillment of these tasks seems to rely on external resources rather than resources internal to the family itself. Because some of these changes would require adult resocialization, which is something we know very little about and which we know is enormously difficult. Furthermore, it may seem relatively inefficient if you want to help the children. So the social policy implications might, in fact be, terrible as it might sound, to write off the parental generations and attempt to correct these deficiencies by more direct action with the children, or perhaps not.

The most obvious point, on the task side, is that what must be acquired by the child are language skills which are adequate to learning and expression with regard to still higher skills. That is, there is an aspect of language which is enormously productive. A great many other things become possible once you have mastered language. So, in the language of industry, this is a "tool-making tool" or a "tool for tooling up." When these tools are lacking in the family, external enrichment may be absolutely indispensible.

Now, just as a side light on the kind of things you often encounter, I've been beaten many, many times with the response, "Well, it's a mistaken assumption. The language of the people you're talking about isn't more impoverished, it's just different." I don't believe it's just different. I believe, on certain measures which are quite definite and standard, that it is in fact more impoverished. But it is also true that in certain respects it is different. This confusion is a very serious mistake from which I think you are saved when you concentrate on the task aspect and see the task in a larger context.

For example, it's pointed out to me again and again that lower class people in Spanish cultures have an ability to produce elaborate——flowery, metaphorical——forms of expression. There seems to be a richness in the vocabulary and in the ability to describe emotions and feelings. As a matter of fact, one might argue that many of the Spanish speaking or Latin peoples are able to produce more elaborate forms of expression than many of the more relatively well-educated but verbally constipated people in our own Anglo-Saxon culture. But the point is that this kind of skill is not terribly useful in a culture which gives prime emphasis on precision in expression and on the use of language that most approximates something mathematical or instrumental.

The second point involves the importance, in the socialization process, of giving the child a sturdy ego. Here, the way I point to language is to ask to what extent is the language rich in forms, and how is the culture or the modes of use of language likely to produce a disposition to use certain forms rather than others which would have consequences for the sense of self that each individual carries.

Now, a third theme has to do with language as a skill in interpersonal relations. Part of the socialization process, obviously, is that you come out with a repertoire of skills, a capacity, if you like, for dealing with interpersonal relations of different types and also of producing different effects. The effects, incidently, may not be those that you intended.

Some languages are very, very good at providing you with tools for beating up on people, for outsmarting them, for playing dumb, and for being tangential. While this kind of a language skill is very useful for survival, it is not well suited to an environment which requires, instead, maximization of skills of negotiation. I have in mind here such things as knowing what to do about the schools, the town, the tax office, the police, even the guard at the gate you want to go into, or a parking lot attendant.

Now, there's a lot of research, I think, that increasingly bears on this subject and which suggests that here you can maybe bring about very substantial changes which, although they don't originate in the family, at least will be mediated through the family. These seem to be particular derivatives from the kinds of occupational experiences people have. So you can bring about changes in the milieu which the child experiences with regard to these dimensions by changing the occupational experience of the father. I think Perlin's research shows this quite clearly. So this is a kind of external leverage, and may be very effective in transforming what happens to the child.

Now, a fifth theme, which I have already touched on, has to do with language and emotional expression, and especially language as against physical expression. I think when you consider the disadvantaged families, that what you would find to be exceptionally true about them (this is partly because of their impoverishment and partly it is their preferred style) is that acting out, that is the physical expression rather than verbal expression, becomes the standard, the normative, and indeed in some ways the preferred mode. Now, I would argue that to some extent, perhaps to a very substantial extent, this is not just the preferred mode, but in fact is a consequence or an exemplification of an inability to work out these very same issues verbally and it has all kinds of implications. One of these is limited access to therapy. In the long haul, it seems to me that it would be very valuable to think about the possibilities of training laboratories in which we could teach people new expressive modes—more verbal ones—which might have some possibility for transfer into the home situation. Again, perhaps a very difficult task, but I think one well worth while. Some of the techniques with instantaneous television that O. K. Moore is working on that make people confront more what they're actually doing might in fact be a way of doing that, because, I think for example, that these mothers are not aware of the impact they are having on the child.

Now, in summary, I don't think the great problem is motivation. I think the problem is learning the appropriate and relevant techniques of accomplishing what people have in mind and, for social scientists, this has all kinds of policy implications.

GENERAL DISCUSSION

GUMPERZ: I just want to emphasize that these are two different papers. They are from two completely different traditions of what the problem is. The emphasis in sociolinguistics is that linguistics is an analytic tool, one that we are only now beginning to master. So the other question, how we can use linguistics as a tool for intervention, is highly dependent on our ability to establish this analytic baseline.

This distinction comes from a long tradition of dissatisfaction with the . . . kind of things that have been done in social science. It's a dissatisfaction exactly of the kind that Professor Hamblin talked about: people working on experiments, getting part systems——part theories——and trying them out with very elaborate techniques, but they find that nothing happens and they can't figure out why things don't work. I think we're beginning to know why things don't work. There are a number of things that Professor Inkeles talked about that have been tried. This whole business about correction, vocabulary enrichment, that's the usual method that is used in schools. It doesn't work. It is too grammatical ("Professor Henry Higgins" model). You see, minority groups speak a language which we don't understand. The problem is that we are too caught up in the need for action to look—to take a careful look—below the surface of language usage. Vera John, for example, wrote an article entitled "The Basil Bernstein Fad" in which her thesis is that people have taken Basil Bernstein as doing something that's far from what he's really doing. People have set up so-called intervention programs that have had disasterous results on students.

So the main theme of my paper is that if we are going to learn what to do with such groups, we've got to look at what they are doing. We should observe everyday behavior, study their everyday behavior. Let me give an example from a successful correction technique. One of our students this summer ran an OEO program for 15–16 year old Mexican-Americans who were being trained for jobs on the Berkeley campus. She found from the beginning that the kids said "We don't want to hear about grammar, we don't want to hear that we speak different." She spent half the summer trying to structure the situation in such a way as to want to make these people want to learn. Deciding on something they really wanted to do was the major task. Apparently the thing that got them was something that didn't seem reasonable at all, like, "How do you go into a store and make a salesman show you everything in the shop and then walk out and not buy?" They tried doing this and then they wanted to learn more about language. This was very imaginative but not something we would have predicted.

BEE: I have a comment that refers to both of these papers. I don't want to say that language isn't important . . . in precisely the ways that you describe. I think it would be a mistake for us to see language as the major, or the crucial, or the only vehicle through which some of these processes of socialization or problem solving, for example, take place. There are a lot of kinds of communication systems other than oral language which are frightfully important in exactly the same areas that you mentioned; the fact, for example, that lower class families not only have impoverished language but they also are very authoritarian toward their children, not just with their language but in other ways. Those two things go together and it's awfully hard to tease out whether the result in the child is a function just of the impoverished language or these other communication things.

HILL: Can I raise a question that a family sociologist might be pardoned for raising? What would sociolinguistic concepts and methods do for a concern which marriage educators have for training engaged couples in being able to communicate across the gender line, where not infrequently you find two individuals marrying who had no sibs of the other gender, and therefore, a deficit in the more casual training that might have occurred in a multiple sex-sib family?

And similarly, what would such a discipline have to offer to parents for understanding the language of their children as these children shifted from infants into the mastery of increasingly complex skills? In both cases we have parties who are desperately interested in communication yet singularly free of explicit training to understand what they are hearing and seeing.

GUMPERZ: Well, let me give you two kinds of things. One of them I hinted at in the last part of the paper and is applicable to the question of how do husbands and wives communicate. One of the interesting findings of recent research in psycholinguistics is the effect that language has on perception, especially in the relation between language and content. If there is a conflicting message, if you say something that has favorable content but you say it in a whining voice or other negative paralinguistics cues, you will flub your semantic intent, because people respond to the whining rather than to the content of the message. This is true not only of some of these extreme things. It is also true of conflicting accents. I hear Californians I know from Berkeley complain about their neighbors from New York. They tell me that their neighbors are always quarreling. They perceive these people as snarling when they really are having a good time talking normally, and vice versa. I think this happens quite frequently. Especially when you think of a girl being socialized largely by other women and a man being socialized largely by male company. They employ different usage rules and different speech conventions.

Now, what I think a sociolinguist would do in this case—is he'd take two measures, the girl with other women and then with her husband, the man with other men, and with his wife. Then he'd compare, and I think this would be a fascinating diagnostic idea.

You could show them that really, in fact, they're not responding to each other. You can do this by tape recording. Show her that he is not responding to the content of what she is saying——You could show him that the whining is simply accent, and we know that she can't help it because this is the way she was raised. But maybe she'd better work at it a little bit. So once they are aware of this they could invest some time in correcting it. You can't correct it right away. You always lapse into it again, but it's a matter of a little bit of learning. I think you can overcome it, you can diagnose the problem, and you can help people to work it out.

BEE: This was the point I was trying to make earlier. Can people be made aware of the discrepancy between what they think they're saying and think they have said and what the other person thinks they said, the cues they think they're giving off and the cues the other person is responding to? So that, if you can get to the point where it's the same cues that are being responded to in both directions, then communication is facilitated.

ZELDITCH: Occasionally, during the afternoon we've confused, I think, the problem of language with the problem of the thing that language is used to express. Some of these issues are problems not of language but of therapy. For example, the "double-bind" situation.

But that's not a problem as far as I can see in dealing with language. That's a problem of dealing with a basic therapeutic situation and that's to be distinguished from the kind of thing Reuben raised where the accent or the training you came from expresses things quite different to the other person than you intended.

GUMPERZ: Well, I think what you are saying is exactly problematic. Most of the kind of sociolinguists that I have been talking about assume that it's rather useless to make a dichotomy between language and social system. On the one hand you can regard these levels of communication as fused or interdependent. On the other hand, these levels differ in their mutability and their accessibility to consciousness. I recall one of my students last summer who wrote a paper. She was a psychologist and her first sentence was "Until I began to think about sociolinguistics, I never realized that the Rosenthal effect was communicated."

The relationship between these levels is most obvious when there is discontinuity between them. Assume that there is a teacher face to face with a black student who responds in hostile ways. Now the first time the teacher faces this, she says, "Well he doesn't really mean it, he speaks different, he's culturely different." A teacher may do this for ten days in a row but after awhile she says, "Now goddamn it, I've been patient enough. I can't, I just can't stand this any more"———or the very typical things that happen to an anthropologist after he's alone for a while, he experiences a kind of *culture shock*, never seeing a human being in the sense of the Yiddish "mench."

WEICK: I wanted to ask John if he had any comments on Alex's point concerning the possible substitutability of language expressiveness versus physical expressiveness. Have you any data or any thoughts about the fact, that, if you could train people in expressing things linguistically you would find the physical expressiveness extinguishing?

GUMPERZ: The problem with this is that in most cases it's not that these people are less expressive linguistically, but they differ in the ways they use language. Their use of language tends to be metaphoric rather than elaborate. They use—their language is restricted in many ways and they use language for different purposes. Now, the problem here in the retraining is as before. Before you can do any kind of linguistic retraining you have to know what their linguistic baseline is, what to build on and we don't know enough about this except that we are saying that black people are more violent. We say they have less language, therefore, we've got to give them language training. We can't give them language training without knowing the way in which they use language. A diagnostic program should precede it——describing ways you can build on the metaphoric abilities that they already have and extend those. Show them that the same forms of communication that they're using for other purposes can be used in conflict situations with slight modifications.

WEICK: Is it easier to build on a metaphoric baseline than it would be on a non-metaphoric baseline?

GUMPERZ: No, metaphors are as difficult to understand as jokes. They imply a shared culture.

INKELES: There are two things that I think were misunderstandings——that I'd like to comment on. I believe that as a rule the direct didactic approach fails. My own practical suggestion would be for much more indirect approaches, which, I take it, you also had in mind, especially those which capture on existing motivation. I think this is what O. K. Moore and Robert Hamblin are also doing.

The example (compare Gumperz example of Mexican-Americans) which sticks most in my mind is that of a young lady I know who is a very gifted teacher in a Harlem school. This is a school from which all the older, more experienced teachers have long since fled. But this girl is still in there fighting it out and as near as I can tell from observing her classroom and talking with her she is very effective. What she did in reading, for example——she very quickly discovered that the things that the board of education told her to read to the kids in New York were totally without meaning to them. So she just ignored what the board of education said, and she began to read these kids Mickey Spillane. Their response to this was tremendous and it confirmed them in the belief that there are really important things in something called books which are very intimately connected with your life, which are enormously important, and which they wanted to have more access to. And then they were after her to help them to master the reading skills that would enable them to go with more Mickey Spillane.

Now secondly, you seem to question some of the spill-over effects, at least I have a feeling that you did. That is, for example, that by increasing the vocabulary of either the child or the mother that you could make a really substantial difference. I don't know what the evidence for that is, I just can't believe it could be true because my observation is that every increase in the effective capacity of individuals does have diffuse effects in other parts of the personality.

GUMPERZ: I was not questioning that you could produce some kind of effect. I was saying that you would not if you merely touched the surface of language without taking into account some of its underlying meaning.

INKELES: Okay. I'm with you there. As a matter of fact, I haven't talked about my research on modernization, but one of the things that's astounding to me is the change in the verbal capacity of the men we're dealing with as a result of their working in factories. Now, nobody's teaching them words there, but in fact, on tests of antonyms and on a variety of other tests of that type which we've given them, we've found these men are increasing their score year by year over a period of fourteen years in direct association with the amount of time they spend in industrial establishments.

(QUESTION:) Well, how about the other way around——if you increase their vocabulary would they be better workmen?

INKELES: I greatly doubt it——I'm not sure we want them to be better workmen in that sense. What we find is the most modern workman is least liked by his foreman because he's a trouble maker. He asks too many questions, has too many ideas, and wants to do things in too many innovative ways. Now, finally I would like to comment on this issue of language and emotional expression versus physical acting out. I would think that if we could increase this ability to find satisfactory and effective modes of verbal expression of very intense emotions we could reduce the amount of acting out of those emotions. I think in some of the work Hamblin's doing, there's a possibility of doing that. His research suggests he's observed that because he says that he's getting much less disruptive behavior as he changes the behavior of the kids in certain ways. These are, in good part, verbal aren't they?

HAMBLIN: Yes, but I look at it from a slightly different perspective. The way emotions are used by people—their habitual uses of them—are often instrumental uses to get a particular effect in other people, for example, aggression, violence, and various types of disruption. You're getting specific effects and what I generally try to do in my systems is substitute verbal or some other instrumental type of behavior that gets a comparable effect, thus short circuiting the need for more violent, more disruptive modes of expression and behavior.

COMMENTARY————————————————

TAKING A STEP BEYOND PROFESSOR HENRY HIGGINS

If one were looking for some neat solutions to some tidy problems, it would be very easy to underestimate the contribution of John Gumperz. For instance, one commentator stated: "Well, I guess we'll just have to wait until sociolinguistics develops a bit more before it will be of any use. . . ." One explanation for this reception could be the point in the symposium process where his ideas were presented. Participants' capacities to ingest had been taxed rather heavily by this time, so that new views were not being solicited. But another trouble (which applies to the following session as well) is what might be called the "mind-motor-mouth-mass" matrix.* Gumperz is not one of the verbose generation. Rather there seems to be a well-managed fit between his theoretic aspirations and his subject matter—a perspective which is essentially "field induced."

In this sense, there is a resemblance between Gumperz, Moore, and Hamblin. These three seem to have struck a balance between field exploration and the tendency toward theoretical prolixity. Moore, for example, has differentiated the more-productive from the less-productive scientific contents (such as models from orientations) and set his aspirations for each

* (Editor's Note: The four dimensional matrix is a ludic take-off on the idea of "hierarchies of knowledge." Mind refers to the qualities of our representational schemas—the degree of equilibrium between an "object" and our representation of it. Motor refers to the degree of exploration of a phenomenon; mouth refers to the degree one can express his representational schema when he is broadcasting; and mass refers to the amount of expertise—social density—attributed to the broadcaster. The point is that depending upon the type of object being addressed and the type of audience, a particular location within the matrix is more or less appropriate.)

on different schedules. Hamblin balances theory and apperception on the fulcrum of his "robust" effects.

Gumperz' orientation to theory displays a remarkable balance between reserve and ambition on the one hand, and a lot of flexibility up and down the hierarchies of knowledge on the other. He opens his session by providing several perspectives on theory in sociolinguistics. There, theory is concerned with the *strategies* and not the *consequences* of speech. This remark carries the suggestion that previous views had been concerned with consequences—and had generated negative results. Such feedback jarred the orientation enough to recognize that language usage has several levels, and even within any "speech community," a great deal of variation. Apparently Gumperz is prepared to assume, as did Weick, that "there is a lot more going on in groups than you think," but you have to "relax your constraints" to appreciate this.

Another perspective, one that resembles Zelditch's approach to theory, is contained in the statement that linguistics can be used as an "example of how to construct theory." The basis for this comment is the appeal, for instance, of Noam Chomsky's theory of generative grammar. But the theory *stresses* what might be called productive contents, and thus *suppresses* much of the richness and variety of social life. In other words, the seductive appeal of this type of theory depends, for its success, on a set of *simplifying* assumptions which abstract across all of the basic data domains (for example, grammar, not symbolic usage patterns; an ideal speaker in an ideal situation, speaking an ideal language, not subject to fatigue, distractions, and so forth).

By contrast, the theoretical orientation which seems to be more appropriate to *usage patterns* is only beginning to emerge as something recognizable. As it begins to unfold, initial impressions suggest that it looks like "the communicating individual (is) operating under certain constraints." Since much of what is called "constraint" is imperceptible or tacit, this orientation has rejected the "Prof. Henry Higgins" model of intervention. In place of that model is a "strategic" sense of language usage, where the speakers are like bridge players trying to establish (and sometimes mask) their conventions. In other words, this image of the present stage of sociolinguistics relies on a heavy investment in field work, *accommodating* to the field, rather than attempting to *assimilate* (simplify) it to scientific structures.

Consequently, this mode of research is prepared to expect variations depending on situations, speakers, and the levels of meaning. Put a bit differently, it is prepared to find problems and solutions wherever they may fall. For example, in terms of the "hierarchy of knowledge" process, this perspective is rooted in sensory-motor exploration, but is also able to avail itself of higher templates such as Chomsky's theory. The concept of "competence," for instance, which is defined in Chomsky's terms as a universal, biologically-given, information-processing device, is employed as a guard against leaping to functional consequences. It provides just enough leverage—in a usage context—to make one wonder if any speech community can be evaluated, except on its own terms.

One output of this flexibility is a balance for the feeling of "being *stuck* with an unproductive field." That is, as a view of the "craft of social science," this perspective has a more flexible time table. It can be comfortable with both the exploratory, and with the well-made, powerful design. Field work can range from ethnographic to manipulative. It can employ paper and pencil tests or utilize mobile labs. Gumperz' description of the project in northern Norway, for instance, suggests a kind of developing verticality to the notion of multitrait, multimethod—that is, stacking more rigorous methods on top of more exploratory ones.

Finally, this perspective provides another look at the idea of "interaction"—between an action-unit and its environment. External contents, both physical and symbolic, interact with a speaker's competence and his internalized cultural set. This systemic sense of interaction leads to a very flexible range of system boundaries. The flavor of this range of natural boundaries is illustrated in his comment to Zelditch that you can tape record—or use other scientific paraphenalia—*unobtrusively*, depending on how much the subject pool shares a common culture.

In short, the view or views of doing science conveyed by Gumperz is a model of balance. But it is, on the other hand, one that can be easily overlooked. One reason for this is that it is, as yet, short on the content side. But as a medium (and thus a *message*) of research themes, it certainly captures the best parts of what is contained in the symposium. It strikes a balanced, "strategic" relation with the subjects. It is hard-headed in method, but highly responsive to the situation. It holds promise for both theory and effects, and, as a central concern, it takes notice of some of the ·silent dimensions of behavior.

A CONTRASTING VIEW OF LANGUAGE: FUNCTIONAL CONSEQUENCES

There is, in the Inkeles discussion, the distinct tone of an energetic and steadfast commitment to the alleviation of consequences. In this way it contrasts sharply with the Gumperz paper, and perhaps illustrates just how big the trap of "consequences" is. Read at another level, however, the tone is rather harmonic with that of Gumperz'. His closing remark, about motivation, indicates Inkeles' reluctance to buy into the Professor Henry Higgins model also. That is, intervention is plausible only on the grounds that there are deep (motivational) commonalities among the haves and have-nots. Therefore, the task is really one of adjusting surface structures (such as expressive skills) and building on these common deep-structures.

Where Gumperz' perspective derived from field experience, the keystone to Inkeles' seems to be a functional view, tied to a heavy concern for policy and intervention. The major difficulty with this view is that it presupposes that some "functional" criteria—for example, the path to modernity—of the social system are somehow the ultimate or constant *standard* for assessing performance. No such assumption is made in Gumperz' approach.

Inkeles indicates a "sense of discouragement" when considering ways for improving the lot of families which begin with profound deficiencies. He concludes that it will require external enrichment, and particularly of the "youth environment." Now, this is a curious way to state the problem, because all families in our society depend upon an "enormous investment in external enrichment," such as the education system. So that, in a sense, the criteria of deficiency and the proposed solution are one and the same, that is, take middle class conditions as their standard.

The sense of urgency contained in his message is communicated in his decision to overleap, or write off the parental generation. He states that we know very little about adult socialization or resocialization, but what we do know is that it is very difficult and relatively inefficient. But, a counter-argument (strategies as opposed to consequences) might maintain that it is precisely the efficiency of infant-socialization, which makes some children "good little white noodniks," that is especially appalling to those who don't buy middle-class efficiency—for example, Moore is after efficacy, and had to leave the middle class. If one assumes that the analysis of the cultural baggage of both successful and deficient families holds the key to deciding, to put it crassly, whether assimilation or pluralism makes the most sense, then his argument avoids a crucial encounter.

In explaining why he believes they are not merely different but are in fact deficient, Inkeles appeals to the use of "quite *standard* measures." To illustrate he cites the deficiencies of Spanish expression "which lacks the precision of a language which approximates something mathematical or instrumental." Now, the trouble with a comment like that is, I think, due to this sense of urgency—a strong bent toward solutions of ill-defined problems. In that sense it carries much the same evaluative load as Moore's statement that social science is "stuck" with unproductive cultural content.

The flaw in the functional approach is that it fails to distinguish the individual from the social elements in an interactive sense. "Flowery Spanish expression is not useful in an instrumental society," is a statement which can be taken in a number of ways. The *individual* user may be deficient, but Inkeles does not mean that. There may be *no* social use for it, but he does not intend that either. According to some established set of social standards, such as achievement values, whose human value is not itself assessed, the flowery mode is "functionally" deficient. This seems to be what is left.

Another way of assessing the assumptions is to ask the questions which Moore's position raises: "Who holds the referee perspective?" "Is there a strategic or reciprocal sense of middle-lower class relations?" These questions can be plugged into the issues of "developing a sturdy ego" or skill in "interpersonal relations." There is something of a consonant ring to the idea that children from "deficient families" may lack a sturdy ego, or that members of such families may not possess sharply honed verbal skills for negotiations with their environment. That is, to the extent that they have identified with the oppressor, they may indeed internalize his definition of themselves. Now the point is not that Inkeles' position is wrong—and the "newer rhetoric" is correct—it is that the pressure for modernity may be an impediment to a balanced view of the "possible" (or of the silent) dimension. For instance, if you take a reading of Inkele's background position you find that his causal analysis reduces again and again to "milieu (immutable) effects" and, more specifically, to the effects of occupational experiences. Thus there is relatively little room for the *possible* —for example, "we don't want workmen to be too troublesome."

The context of this remark about troublesome workmen produces, in a more positive vein, some provocative suggestions. In response to a question Inkeles' suggests that there is some kind of intimate link between what might be called the "locus of use" and the "locus of learning." That is, he hints at some kind of multilevel correspondence between learning and performance situations and thus argues against the Henry Higgins model of direct surface treatment. There are two kinds of kernals contained in this position. First, there is, for as yet unknown reasons, some kind of intimate configurational link between the setting and content of learning and the future appropriateness of communication skills thus learned, for example, negotiation in variable settings. Second, it is dangerous to introduce a discrepancy between the cultural package of learning and the cultural package of use. For example, working class children who aren't conditioned for the first 17 years of their lives to tolerate long hours of monotony probably won't stand for nine-hour diets of daily monotony during their adult lives, and that is a dangerous prospect, indeed.

His treatment of language and mental ability, is on the surface, an allusion to the two levels of behavior. However, it lacks some of the neutrality of passion communicated by Gumperz sense of individual competency. His sense of language as a skill seems to carry a great deal more than the sense of an individual skill. It tends to stress the collective and social-valuational side of the skill. By so doing, it runs into the same kind of definitional problem which Leik attempts to sort out periodically, such as accommodation as a logically prior question to relational issues. This difficulty can be illustrated with the issue of language and emotional expression. If you say that the lower class lacks appropriate expressive skills, what do you mean? Do they have the internal goods to, at least potentially, express themselves? Yes! Then, is the deficiency due to external circumstances? Maybe! Are they lacking in socially meaningful modes? No! They are fantastically good at metaphors. Then do you mean that others in society (referees) define their modes and a lot else about them as deficient? Yes! And while they can be very expressive within their own groups without resort to meaningless violence, with respect to the larger system's referees or agents they are very angry and they act this out.

EXPLORATION OF THE HIDDEN DIMENSION

There are in the general discussion two very interesting examples of the relation between background and focal dimensions of research. Both Gumperz and Inkeles' mention a teaching technique which is not "merely" grammatical. Both suggest that the success of the technique depended upon finding a strategic perspective between teacher and student (how to negotiate with salesmen or finding some common denominators between books and experience). Gumperz indicates that the success of the technique is beyond the pale of "what we would have predicted." Now the point that I would glean from this is that in a strategic view of social science, theory, techniques and so forth, have a place or role, but only a partial one. The subjects (now no longer in a vertical sense) also have some kind of virtuosity, and this will probably lie on the side of "knowing (or expressing) the culture." Then the point is, that this perspective argues for the necessity of incorporating this into the research relationship.

In response to one of Hill's questions, Gumperz produces a truly exciting illustration of this for handling communication hang-ups. He suggests a technique for assisting engaged couples (or parents) in understanding the manifold messages which they are sending and receiving. Furthermore, the technique employs a multisituational approach which would provide the couples, for example, with a contrasting receiving-sending situation. Now as a research suggestion, this ranks at least as high as any other in the symposium, plus it meets the issue of strategically defining research as, at worst, "playful, and maybe a place where you can be helped."

As a variation of the themes of the symposium, Gumperz' response is really right in the groove. With some modest principles and a bit of technology, it is possible to enter the field and render more and more of the underlying dimensions explicit. The researcher can use his subjects' behavior, and commentary on same, as a way of mapping the unknowns or noise in his modest theoretical system. The successes thus gained might help to generate a sense of trust between researcher and subject. The researcher could begin selecting among the data-domains to flesh out more and more of the general patterns, or he might employ techniques to get at background information, or employ methods which come closer to rigorous tests. In other words this illustration provides an example of how a modest sense of virtuosity, a sense of openness, and of a strategic relation with subjects could be most effective in building lateral and vertical paradigms.

Several of Gumperz' comments call attention to the "mind-motor-mouth-mass" matrix. First, he suggests that minority groups might be speaking a language that we don't *understand*. While the languages, for example, may be identical on the surface, they may be widely discrepant in their background informational content. The point is that remedial programs have frequently neglected a "motor" exploration of this content. Secondly, and in a parallel vein, the notion of a

Basil Bernstein fad suggests that some researchers don't *understand* other researchers. That is, they respond to a research report in terms of its surface meaning or in terms of some strong subjective disposition. Perhaps the appropriation of another disciplinarian's theory or research requires an appreciation for some of the tacit distinctions between research and research reports, between the media of field work and the reconstructed written (or oral) media for publishing the results.

A final example—of mind-mouth ratio—occurs where Gumperz gets caught in a verbal bind. He haltingly states that "I don't think . . . we have the technology. . . ." Now I don't think, reading across all of his commentary, that he meant *technology* at all. What he was arguing for was some relaxation of the push for remedies. We can't always *predict* what cultural contents would turn deficient subjects on. Furthermore, if you do find a key for turning them on, then you'd better have a substantial program for follow through. Anyway, the point is, that it's possible to divorce the media of speech from the context of meaning.

Socialization for Problem Solving*

HELEN L. BEE

The invitation to present a paper on the topic of socialization for problem solving came at an opportune moment for me, since my colleagues, Dr. Ann Pytkowicz Streissguth, Dr. Lawrence Van Egeren, and Dr. Barry Nyman, and I have just completed a large study including assessment of mother-child interaction and its relationship to problem solving (Bee, Nyman, Pytkowicz, Sarason and Van Egeren, 1968; Bee, Van Egeren, Streissguth, Nyman, and Leckie, in press). This Symposium provides me with an opportunity to present and discuss our latest findings, as well as some thoughts about the theoretical and methodological implications of our work and the work of others in this area. To put our work into perspective, however, let me begin with a brief look at the earlier research in the area.

The problem of the impact of environment on cognitive functioning, of which this topic is a part, has had a rather checkered history within psychology, with at least two distinct phases. During the early years of the development of intelligence tests, there was a substantial series of studies designed to show, contrary to the then prevailing view, that variations in environment did indeed affect the test scores. The work of Skeels, Wellman, and Skodak at Iowa (compare Skeels, Updegraf, Wellman, and Williams, 1938; Wellman, 1940; Skeels and Dye, 1939) illustrates one facet of this research. In a series of studies, they attempted to show that providing nursery school experience to children from deprived backgrounds could raise the IQ. (See Hunt, 1961, pp. 10–34, for a general review of this literature.) At about the same time, a substantial number of studies of institutionalized children, although designed to test hypotheses derived from Freudian theory, also focused attention on the fact that institutional environments resulted in what appeared to be severe intellectual impairment (compare Spitz, 1945; Goldfarb,

---

* The research described was supported by the Office of Economic Opportunity, Contract #1375, as part of the Social Change Evaluation Project, University of Washington.

1945, 1955). (See Casler, 1961, and Yarrow, 1961, for reviews of this literature.) Although both series of studies have been justly criticized on methodological grounds, they nonetheless represent important antecedents of the current research on the role of environment in intellectual development. They helped to lead to the now-accepted assumption that intellectual functioning is jointly influenced by environment and heredity.

The current Head Start program may be seen as a logical outgrowth of these early studies. It is based on the assumption that the experiences of a young child from a poverty environment can be augmented in ways which will improve his intellectual functioning, and more specifically, improve his school performance. Evidence to date (compare Gray and Klaus, 1968; Long, 1966; Weikert, 1967) indicates that increases in the IQ are indeed found after a period of Head Start experience, although the long range impact of such enrichment programs is still very much in doubt.

In the early studies, and to some extent in the Head Start program as well, the nature of relevant environmental variation was not clearly specified. The focus, in general, was on the amount of stimulation available to the child; the number of toys, the amount of contact with adults, the number of varied environments experienced. A separate line of research, becoming dominant more recently, has focused on a somewhat different sort of environmental variable, namely the nature of the interaction of the child with the adults in his environment. Witkin and his associates, for example, (Witkin, Dyk, Faterson, Goodenough, and Karp, 1962; Dyk and Witkin, 1965) have examined the relationship between the child's functioning on the cognitive style dimension of field independence versus field dependence and the extent to which the mother's training techniques "foster differentiation" in the child. Mother-child interactions of children with differential patterns of cognitive ability have also been studied (Bing, 1963), as have the parent-child interactions of distractible and nondistractible children (Bee, 1967). In all of these studies, it appeared to be the quality rather than the quantity of interaction which differentiated the parents of the various groups of children. Perhaps the most important of the studies in this general vein, at least from the point of view of our own current research, is the work of Bernstein (1961, 1962a, 1962b), and that of Hess and Shipman (1965, 1967, 1968).

Basil Bernstein, in a series of both theoretical and empirical papers, has proposed that certain formal features of the language habitually spoken by an individual affect the type of problem solving of which he will be capable. More specifically, Bernstein postulated the existence of two distinct "linguistic codes," used for communication and organization of experience. The "public" or "restricted" code is characterized by very rigid and restricted use of grammatical possibilities. The sentences are short, contain few clauses, and are dominated by verbs rather than modifiers. Such a linguistic style cannot be used easily to deal with fine distinctions among experiences and restricts the form of conceptualization of the speaker. In contrast, the "formal" or "elaborated" code is one in which language is used more flexibly, exploiting its structural possibilities for richer and more varied communication. Typically, only the "public" code is used by individuals from lower class backgrounds, while both the public and the formal codes are available to the middle class speaker. Bernstein suggested that a lower class child, exposed primarily to the more restricted language usage, would be deprived of a tool which is useful, if not essential, in complex problem solving.

Hess and Shipman's work was designed, in part, as a verification of Bernstein's hypothesis, but more generally as a test of the general assertion that "early social experience shapes cognition, that the most significant figure in the organization of this experience is the child's mother or mother surrogate, and that the effects of her interaction with the child induce enduring forms of information processing in him." (Hess and Shipman, 1967, p. 57.) With a sample varying in social class level in order to insure variability along the interactional dimensions of interest, Hess and Shipman examined maternal language as well as teaching strategies, along with the child's cognitive functioning on a number of general tests. They found, as did Bernstein, that the social class groups differed in linguistic style, with the more "restricted" mode characteristic of the lower class groups. More importantly for our purposes, they also found a relationship between social class, language usage, and the adequacy of the teaching strategy used by mothers in problem solving situations with their child. Mothers who used the more restricted linguistic style were not skillful in giving clear directions to their child in a problem situation, and were not effective in guiding the child toward a solution to the problem. The children of such mothers were also not as effective individual problem solvers as were the children of mothers using more efficient teaching strategies, and their overall intellectual functioning, as assessed by an IQ test, was lower.

Our own work is, in some respects, a replication of Hess and Shipman, although we have assessed mother-child interaction in several new ways, and we have a much more extensive assessment of the child's cognitive functioning than is the case in earlier studies. Like Hess and Shipman, we have assumed that the characteristics of the mother's teaching strategies, and her general interactions with the child, have a marked impact on the child's cognitive functioning, and that a full understanding of individual differences in children's intellectual skills will require a full analysis of those interactions.

DESCRIPTION OF THE PROJECT

The data to be described are part of a large scale evaluation of a particular Head Start program in Seattle, Washington. The traditional evaluation of Head Start, or of any comparable early intervention program, involves a comparison of change in children enrolled in the program versus children from equivalent backgrounds not enrolled in the program, with some general scores, such as IQ, used as the dependent variable. This strategy, while sound in a number of respects, seemed insufficient to us in several ways. First, we wished to know much more explicitly the nature of the "deficits" characteristic of

Head Start eligible children. We know they are low in IQ, but what specific cognitive skills do they have, and which are they lacking? We know that Head Start programs have succeeded in raising the IQ, but what more precisely is it that is altered in the child as a result of the "enrichment"? The answers to these questions required a more extensive battery of tests to be administered to the children, and more importantly, required the inclusion of an additional group of subjects. To determine the areas of "deficit," it was essential to have a group of subjects with whom to compare the Head Start eligible children. In order to get the maximum amount of divergence between the groups, we selected, for our comparison group, children with the greatest probability of success in school, namely middle class children from an academic community. Thus, in determining "deficits," we are comparing a group of children with a very low probability of school success (Head Start eligible children) with a group of children with a very high probability of school success (middle class children).

A second area of concern, which took our study beyond the typical evaluation of Head Start, was the nature of the child's interaction with the mother. We assumed, as I have already indicated, that the mother's typical interaction with the child may set limits on or enhance his cognitive functioning in specific ways. An examination of mother-child interaction was thus included not only so that social class comparisons on maternal behavioral dimensions could be made, but also so that the relationships between the maternal teaching strategies and the child's cognitive functioning could be examined.

The full design included three groups of mothers and children; two lower class groups, one involved in the Head Start program, and the other not, and a middle class comparison group, with 38 mother-child pairs in each group. The first round of testing in the Fall of 1967 included all three groups, and involved the following:

1. Waiting room: unstructured mother-child interaction session
2. Mother interview: 1 hour semi-structured interview
3. Child tests: 13 individual tests, assessing the following areas of behavior:
   a. Curiosity and exploratory behavior (2 tests)
   b. Imitation (2 tests)
   c. Problem solving (1 test)
   d. Impulse control (2 tests)
   e. Delay of gratification (1 test)
   f. Level of aspiration (1 test)
   g. Distractibility (1 test)
   h. Persistence (1 test)
   i. Color knowledge (1 test)
   j. Spontaneous verbalization (assessed throughout the testing session)
4. Problem solving interaction: structured mother-child interaction

The two groups of Head Start eligible children and their mothers were reassessed after six months of the Head Start program had elapsed. The second round of testing included retesting of the child on all individual child tests, and a brief interview with the mother. The mother-child interaction sessions were not included in the second series, and the middle class comparison group was not retested. Since the concern in the present paper is with the mother-child interaction patterns and their relationship to the child's cognitive functioning, only data from the first round of testing will be presented. And since at that time the two lower class groups were alike in that neither group of children had entered Head Start, these two groups will be combined for all analyses.

Description of the Sample

All of the children in the sample were between ages 4 and 5½. Thirty-seven boys and 39 girls were included in the lower class sample, with 22 boys and 14 girls in the middle class sample. All middle class families were white, while the lower class group included 49 blacks and 27 whites. The samples also differed in the number of fathers present in the homes, in mean income, parents' education, and in the total number of siblings or other children in the home.

Lower class subjects were selected primarily from among those who had applied for Head Start in the fall of 1967. Some additional subjects in this group were obtained from among families living in public housing who had children of the appropriate age, but who had not applied to Head Start. Middle class families were all volunteers who responded to a letter sent to all graduate students at the University of Washington.

Mother-child Interaction Sessions, Procedure and Results

The two mother-child interaction situations differed in their degree of structure. The first, which occurred at the very beginning of the experimental session, we called the "waiting room." Mother and child were brought into a room which contained comfortable chairs, magazines, and a large variety of toys for the child. They were told that we weren't quite ready for them, and asked to wait until someone came to get them. Their behavior during a 10-minute period was then observed through a one-way mirror. In a relatively unstructured situation of this kind, in which the range of potential behavior from both mother and child is large, a really exhaustive scoring system is difficult to devise. In this situation, we had to be content with a procedure focusing on verbal interactions between mother and child, as well as global ratings, made every 15 seconds, of the mother's degree of attention to the child. The mother's verbalizations were scored as questions, suggestions, information statements, control statements, approval, and disapproval. For the child, questions, information statements, acceptance and rejection of maternal verbalizations, and movements about the room and from one toy to another, were scored.

The second mother-child interaction situation, since it specifically involved problem solving, is perhaps of greater interest here. At the very end of the testing session, after the mother had been interviewed and the child tested individually, the two were brought together in a small room with an Experimenter. Mother and child were seated next to each other at a table, with *E* sitting opposite. *E* then presented to the child a model of a block house approximately 6 in. high, 8 in. long, and 4 in. deep, constructed out of 17 blocks of seven different shapes and four different colors. The house was complex, with two windows, a door, and a pitched roof. The child was given an identical set of blocks, and asked to make a house out of them which looked just like the model. The child was told that he could ask his mother for help if he wished, and the mother was told: "Mrs. ————, you can give ———— as much or as little help as you like, whatever you think will help him to do his best." The entire session was tape recorded and transcribed.

In this problem-solving situation, with a task which was purposely too difficult for the child to perform alone, the range of possible behaviors is much smaller, and a finer-grained analysis is more feasible. The focus here was primarily on four dimensions of the mother's behavior:

1. The form in which suggestions were given, whether declarative or interrogative. For example, the mother could say, "Start with the front of the house," or "Should we start at the front of the house or at the back?" These suggestions both deal with the same general problem, but the interrogative form requires some decision from the child, a decision hopefully based on an analysis of the problem, while the imperative or declarative form requires only action.

2. The specificity of the suggestions. A mother's task-oriented statements could, in theory, range from very general, orienting suggestions, such as "Look at the lady's house," or "Is your house just the same as hers?" to highly specific suggestions in which the entire solution was given, such as "Put this piece here," or "The red one goes next to the yellow one." The less specific suggestions, like those phrased as questions, require more from the child. If a mother says, "Start at the front of the house," the child must still decide which blocks go at the front; a more specific suggestion reduces the range of remaining decisions to be made by the child.

3. The nature of the feedback given after some action by the child. When the child makes some sort of move, the mother may wish to indicate whether he was correct or not. More generally, she may wish to inform him whether he is on the right general track or not. Some of both positive and negative feedback would seem to be necessary in this situation, but of interest was the relative weight given to the two. A mother who emphasizes negative feedback may give the child information about what *not* to do, but she is not reinforcing the more positive strategies, and she may effectively reduce the child's incentive to continue with the task. A mother who emphasizes positive feedback not only reinforces specific responses and strategies, but maintains the child's level of involvement in the task.

4. The extent to which the mother became physically involved herself in the task. The task was presented initially as one for the child to do, but the mother was instructed that she could give as much or as little help as she wished. To what extent did a mother get involved to the point of building part or all of the house herself? To the extent that she does so, she further restricts the degree of the child's independent action.

Specific measures relevant to these four dimensions were obtained by scoring each suggestion made by the mother first as a question or an imperative statement, and secondly for the degree of specificity on a three-point scale. Each feedback statement was scored as positive or negative, and the number of "non-verbal intrusions" by the mother was counted by the experimenter at the time of the actual interaction. Interrater reliabilities for these categories, and for those derived from the waiting room situation, ranged from 75% to 91% agreement.

The results of the comparison of middle class and lower class mothers in the waiting room situation are given in Table 1, with only those variables presented which are of particular theoretical interest, or on which significant differences were obtained. The data are presented as rate-per-minute scores for each category.

Table 1 Comparison of Middle and Lower Class Mothers on Selected Variables From the Waiting Room

Variable	Lower Class Mean (N = 76)	Middle Class Mean (N = 38)	±
Mother's rate per minute of control statements ("Stop that!")	0.565	0.258	4.47[2]
Mother's rate of approval ("That's good.")	0.753	0.987	1.92
Mother's rate of disapproval ("That's not a very pretty picture.")	0.234	0.139	2.49[1]
Mother's rate of information statements ("It's a miniature piano.")	1.582	2.107	2.00[1]
Mother's rate of attention			
Level 0 (no attention)	1.567	1.195	1.65
Level 1 (some attention)	0.961	0.700	2.29[1]
Level 2 (moderate attention)	1.346	1.839	2.36[1]
Level 3 (total attention)	0.541	0.639	.73

[1] $p < .05$
[2] $p < .001$

Significant social class differences were obtained in four areas. First, control statements (those in imperative form, involving a demand that the child cease or begin some activity, such as "be quiet!" or "come here") were more than twice as common among lower class mothers as among middle class mothers. Second, the relative weight of approval and disapproval differed between the two social class groups. Lower class mothers showed significantly more disapproval and less approval than did the middle class mothers. Third, information statements (those providing some specific information to the child about the room, some specific toy or object, and so forth) were significantly less common among lower class mothers. Finally, there were differences in the amount of attention paid by the mother to the child. Each 15 seconds the mother was scored for one of four levels of attention ranging from no attention to full involvement. For any one minute of interaction, then, the possible score at any attention level would be 4. The scores in Table 1 represent the mean number of scores given per minute for each attention level. The data indicate that lower class mothers were typically less attentive to the child than were middle class mothers.

The picture that emerges is one of two quite distinct patterns of maternal behavior. The lower class mother was more frequently inattentive, and when she did attend to the child, it was more often to tell him to stop doing something, or to disapprove some action. The middle class mother was more frequently verbally involved with the child, and her interaction with him was more frequently discussion rather than discipline. That these are indeed somewhat coherent patterns is substantiated by the set of correlations shown in Table 2. Mothers who were attentive to their children were more approving and gave more information statements, while mothers who were high in control statements were more disapproving. There is also some indication of a verbal/nonverbal distinction, since attentive mothers tended to be higher on all types of verbal behavior, but that finding does not override the two rather distinct patterns which emerge.

Table 2 Intercorrelations Among Selected Maternal Behaviors From the Waiting Room (N = 114)

Variable	Variable Number	2	3	4	5	6	7	8
Control statements	1	.07	.43[3]	.13	−.30[2]	.06	.09	.31[2]
Approval	2	—	.19	.58[3]	−.60[3]	−.20[1]	.57[3]	.26[2]
Disapproval	3		—	.32[3]	−.36[3]	.00	.22[1]	.25[2]
Information statements	4			—	−.58[3]	−.28[2]	.46[3]	.49[3]
Attention level 0	5				—	.08	−.76[3]	−.51[3]
Attention level 1	6					—	−.47[3]	−.26[2]
Attention level 2	7						—	.08
Attention level 3	8							—

[1] $p < .05$
[2] $p < .01$
[3] $p < .001$

It is also of considerable interest that mothers who used high rates of information statements, high levels of attention, and high rates of approval were the mothers whose children also showed high rates of information statements. The correlation between approval from the mother and information statements from the child was +.65 ($p < .001$), between information statements from the mother and information statements from the child was +.57 ($p < .001$), and between the mother's *modal* attention level and the child's information statements +.42 ($p < .001$). Thus at least conversation between mother and child, if not problem solving, was fostered by attentiveness, approval, and informative comments from the mother.

More direct evidence on the socialization of problem solving comes from the analysis of mother-child interaction during the house building task. The main results, comparing middle class and lower class mothers on the four dimensions outlined above are given in Table 3. Again the data are presented as rate-per-minute scores for each category.

Table 3   Comparison of Middle and Lower Class Mothers and Children on Selected Variables From the House Building Task

Variable	Lower Class Mean (N = 76)	Middle Class Mean (N = 38)	±
Mother's rate per minute of suggestions phrased as questions	2.254	3.120	2.84[2]
Mother's rate per minute of suggestions phrased as statements	6.568	5.778	1.34
Mother's rate of suggestions at specificity level 1 ("Look at the lady's house")	2.591	3.816	4.50[3]
Mother's rate of suggestions at specificity level 2 ("Where's the blue one?")	4.027	3.332	1.83
Mother's rate of suggestions at specificity level 3 ("Put this one there.")	2.385	1.886	1.52
Mother's rate of nonverbal intrusions (placing a block herself)	2.373	0.695	4.78[3]
Mother's rate of positive feedback	2.067	3.073	3.18[2]
Mother's rate of negative feedback	1.855	1.018	4.50[3]

[1] $p < .05$
[2] $p < .01$
[3] $p < .001$

It is clear that there were marked social class differences on all four dimensions identified. Lower class mothers less often phrased their suggestions in interrogative form, and less often gave suggestions at the lowest level of specificity. They gave more negative and less positive feedback, and their rate of nonverbal intrusiveness into the problem solving task was markedly higher than for the middle class mothers.

Again here, as in the waiting room, we have evidence of two rather distinct styles of interaction. The style typical of the middle class mother included the use of questions, general, orienting suggestions, and positive feedback, while the contrasting style included much more concrete, directed suggestions, high rates of negative feedback, and a great deal of physical help. The first of these styles seems optimally designed not only to teach the child strategies that may generalize to other situations, but also to maintain the maximum scope of independent action for the child. The middle class mother guided the child's action with a kind of "Socratic" questioning; she was active, but not intrusive; she participated in the problem, but encouraged the child to do the task himself insofar as possible. In contrast, the style most typical of the lower class mother markedly reduced the scope of independent action available to the child, and did not focus his attention on the basic features of the problem. In Hess and Shipman's terms (1967), the interaction lacks an emphasis on "patterns." It is difficult to imagine that the child exposed to this more controlled and restricting style of problem solving learns much that could be generalized to other problem situations. Further, the dominance of negative reinforcement, in relationship to the amount of positive, does not place emphasis on correct solutions, but on incorrect ones, and may in the long run affect the child's feelings of confidence and mastery in problem-solving situations. (See Allen, 1966, and Stevenson and Snyder, 1960, for some experimental corroboration of this effect.)

To illustrate these styles of maternal behavior, let me quote from the transcripts of several mothers and children in the house-building situation. First, a lower class mother:

M: Oh no. You don't do it like that. You're doing it wrong already. You build it right here. Put the blocks right here, standing up.

C: Standing up?

M: Come on. Pick this one up. These two. Get these two here. Where's this go? O.K. Leave them there.

C: O.K.

M: Wait, William Junior. Like this. Put this one right here. And now these two.

*   *   *

M: Come on. You want to help me? Watch. Watch. Wait, don't push it down. Oh, brother. No, I quit now. William Junior, we got to start all over. Let's try and do it like this. Okay. No, William. William Junior. Oh, we can't make this one. Oh, come on. Let's turn it around again so we can see the front and start all over. Come on. Wait. Turn it like this so Mommy can see it. No.

This mother was one of the most physically intrusive mothers in the sample, and she clearly conveys little useful task information verbally. The child is merely instructed to watch while the mother solves the problem for him. Contrast this with the following excerpt from a middle class mother.

c: How do we do this, Mommy?

m: O.K. Why don't you turn it and look at the back? Look at the back of it. O.K. Can you find a block that looks like these?

c: Now what do you do, Mommy?

m: Well, that's the roof. You have to start and build the bottom part first.

c: How do you do it?

m: Can you find one that looks like this?

c: Um, humm.

m: Well, set it down there. Now find one that looks like the one next to it. What about on this side? But you've got to leave space for the window. See how it is? There you go. O.K. Now you have the back of it, don't you? Shall we turn it to look at the side? O.K.

The child, in this example, is unusually dependent, but the mother's responses were quite consistently in the form of questions, or general suggestions. She directed the child's problem solving activity, but did not solve the problem for the child.

While it is difficult to convey the quality of an interaction from a transcript, these excerpts do illustrate some of the differences in both tone and content, and in addition, they indicate that individual mothers did not necessarily show all of the qualities of the two alternate styles. The extent to which the various indices of maternal behavior tended to occur together, both within and across social class groups, can be seen from the intercorrelations shown in Table 4.

Table 4   Intercorrelations Among Selected Maternal Behavior Variables From the House Building Task (N = 114)

Variable	Variable Number	2	3	4	5	6	7	8
Suggestions phrased as questions	1	02	46[3]	51[3]	−01	−30[2]	44[3]	08
Suggestions phrased as statements	2	—	20[1]	69[3]	78[3]	−10	53[3]	48[3]
Suggestions at specificity level 1	3		—	10	−20[1]	−27[2]	29[2]	16
Suggestions at specificity level 2	4			—	46[3]	−16	52[3]	34[3]
Suggestions at specificity level 3	5				—	−01	48[3]	38[3]
Nonverbal intrusions	6					—	−22[1]	03
Positive feedback	7						—	21[1]
Negative feedback	8							—

[1] $p < .05$
[2] $p < .01$
[3] $p < .001$

The clearest relationships are with the rate of suggestions phrased as questions. Mothers who used a large number of questions also used positive feedback, low specificity suggestions, and did *not* intrude as much into the child's problem solving. In contrast, mothers who used high rates of suggestions phrased in imperative form gave primarily suggestions at the highest levels of specificity, and high rates of negative feedback as well as positive feedback. Since the same general pattern of intercorrelations was obtained when the data were analyzed separately for each social class level, we have some indication that there is consistency for any given mother, regardless of her social class level; social class comparisons are thus only a very gross way of contrasting the two styles of interaction.

Maternal Linguistic Codes

A third source of data concerning the mothers' teaching behavior is the mother interview. At the beginning of the interview, the mother was asked several very open-ended questions; she was asked to describe her child, to indicate the "best" things about him, the things which were of most concern to her, the things she thought she could give to or do for her child, and what she tried to teach him. The mothers' answers to these questions were transcribed and scored for a number of variables relating to Bernstein's two linguistic codes. Specifically, the quantity of speech, the mean sentence length, the number of adjectives relative to the number of verbs, the number of clauses per sentence, and the percent of personal pronouns were scored. Significant social class differences were obtained on all five variables, with middle class mothers using longer sentences, relatively more adjectives, more complex sentences, and fewer personal referents. These are all speech characteristics associated with the "elaborated" linguistic code identified by Bernstein (1961), while the shorter sentences, high relative rate of verbs, high rate of personal pronouns, and simple sentences used by the lower class mother are all identifying characteristics of the public or restricted linguistic code.

Thus, not only did lower class mothers use what appear to be less efficient teaching strategies with their child in a problem solving situation and emphasized control and disapproval in a free situation, they used a form of language which may further restrict the type of problem solving skills developed by the child. Bernstein says of the public code, it "provides a speech form that discourages the speaker from verbally elaborating subjective intent, and progressively orients him to descriptive rather than analytic concepts. It limits the type of stimuli to which the speaker learns to respond" (1961, p. 961). Thus the habitual use of the more restricted form of language in the presence of the child may not only limit the form of stimuli to which the child attends, but perhaps more importantly, insofar as language serves as a mediator in complex problem solving, it *may* restrict the type of mediational concepts available to the child.

Children's Cognitive Functioning, and its Relationship to Maternal Behavior

The existence of marked social class differences in maternal teaching behavior and linguistic style have been rather extensively documented here. But what of the children of these mothers? The styles of socialization seem to be different in the two social class groups; but how is this reflected in the child's cognitive functioning?

First, at the very least there should be equivalent social class differences in the children's performance on the tests of their cognitive functioning. Such differences were found. Significant social class differences in the performance of the children were obtained on tests of persistence, impulse control, imitation, and problem solving; lower class children were less persistent, more impulsive, less likely to imitate, and less skillful in learning a problem solving strategy. But no social class differences were obtained on measures of curiosity or exploratory behavior. That is, in our testing situation, children from poverty environments were just as talkative, just as curious and exploratory when freely examining materials in a relatively unstructured situation. But when they were required to perform some specific action, they were less able to focus their behavior in the required way.

The social class differences on the "problem solving" task are of particular interest. This task, devised by Dr. Streissguth and by one of our graduate students, Mr. Larry Seide, requires the child to copy patterns on a peg board. The child is initially given a peg board containing 24 holes and shown how to place pegs in them. He is given time to explore this, and to practice placing pegs. *E* then shows the child another board which contains pegs already placed in a pattern, asks him to look at it carefully, and then, from memory, to try to make one just like it. Should the child fail on this task (and most 4-year-olds do), on the second trial the experimenter again shows the pattern board, but this time *E* points out the pattern using gestures as well as words. The child is then given another chance to copy from memory. Finally, all children are given a generalization trial in which a second pattern is shown and a copy attempted.

In essence, this task examines the extent to which the child can learn a new problem solving strategy from instruction, and then generalize that strategy to a similar problem. The social class differences on this task were enormous. On the first trial, before any attention was called to the pattern by *E*, there were very few children from either social class group who managed a perfect copy. (The difference favored the middle class group but was not statistically reliable.) On the second trial, after the pattern had been emphasized by *E*, 32 of 38 middle class children copied the pattern perfectly, while only 17 of 76 lower class children did so. The results for the generalization trial were similar. The middle class child, even though he was essentially as unskilled at the task initially as was the lower class child, was able to profit from the instruction provided, whereas the lower class child was not. This difference is not surprising, particularly in view of the fact that the type of instruction offered to the child in this task—in other words, focusing on the basic features of the task—is precisely the type of instruction typically offered by the middle class mother to her child in the house building situation.

The more specific interconnections between the children's cognitive functioning and the mother's behavior in interaction situations are difficult to document in a brief presentation, in part because the analysis itself was extremely complex. But one further aspect of our findings may be reported. As a first step, separate factor analyses were performed on (a) the variables from the two mother-child interaction situations, (b) the variables from the tests of the children's functioning, and (c) the variables derived from the mother interview. A total of 55 factors were extracted from these three separate analyses, and factor scores on each factor were computed for each family. These 55 factor scores, instead of the original 170 variables, may be used to represent the behavior of the mother and child in the three types of situations, and they may be treated statistically in the same manner as one would treat raw scores. Finally, a second-order factor analysis was performed using the 55 factor scores as the basic data for each family, and yielded 24 new factors illustrating the relationships among behaviors assessed in the three situations. The first second-order factor so extracted is of considerable interest, since loading on it were factors from all three sources. The factor table for this second-order factor is given in Table 5.

Table 5   Second Order Factor 1

Loading	Description of Variable
.87	Social class
.68	Successful cognitive performance and color knowledge (child-test factor)
.51	Positive versus negative maternal feedback (problem solving interaction factor)
.49	Personal-emotional child orientation (mother interview factor)
.44	Nonspecific maternal question suggestions versus specific non-question suggestions (problem solving factor)
.42	Highly verbal, intellectually stimulating mother (mother interview factor)
.35	Cognitive control (child test factor)
.34	Objective, descriptive speech (mother interview factor)
.33	Child-paced problem solving (mother-child interaction factor)
.30	Attentive, noncontrolling, encouraging mother (waiting room factor)
.29	Frustration relieved by instructions versus physical help (mother interview factor)
.25	Persistence (child test factor)

The factor labeled "successful cognitive performance and color knowledge" was the most general factor obtained from the analysis of the child test scores; it included performance on the peg-board task, impulse control, and persistance as well as color knowledge. This general factor loads together with several important factors from the mother-child interaction, including one representing maternal emphasis on positive versus negative feedback and another involving maternal emphasis on teaching by questions rather than statements. In addition, two major factors from the maternal interview, "objective-descriptive speech," and "highly verbal intellectually stimulating mother," which included scores from the analysis of language style, also loaded on this first second-order factor. When all the factors from either the mother-child interaction session or the mother interview which loaded on this second-order factor were used to predict the child's score on the general factor of "successful cognitive performance and color knowledge" a multiple r of .50 was obtained. Thus, knowing only the maternal behavior on these factors enables us to predict approximately 25% of the child's test performance on the most general factor from the child-test factor analysis. When only the scores from the factors of "negative versus positive feedback," and "specific maternal nonquestion suggestions versus nonspecific maternal question suggestions" were used to predict the child's performance, a multiple r of .35 was obtained.

Overall, then, there is evidence that lower class and middle class children differ in their performance on tests of cognitive and motivational behavior in much the same way that their mothers differ in teaching behavior. Further, there is evidence that *specific* aspects of the mother's teaching behavior, as well as her language style, predict aspects of the child's functioning on the cognitive tests.

Theoretical Implications

Beginning at the purely empirical level, it is clear even with the rather gross and artificial procedures used in the present research, and in previous work on the same problem, that there is some relationship between the child's cognitive functioning (his problem-solving ability if you will) and the nature of the mother's interactions with him. This is clear both from the social class comparisons, in which we find that potentially successful and potentially unsuccessful children differ in the interactions experienced with their mothers, and from the second-order factor analysis, which shows factors defining maternal behavior and factors defining problem-solving ability in the child loading together on a single general factor. Mothers who, in the problem-solving situation, emphasized teaching the child *how* to solve problems, rather than solving the problem for him, who guided the child's activities rather than telling him each move, had children who were more successful in independent problem solving.

On the basis of these findings, and those of others, we would suggest that the observed differences in children's cognitive functioning are in large part *caused* by the differences in the nature of the interpersonal interactions experienced by the child in his home environment. Those mothers, regardless of social class, who use the more general (and generalizable) teaching strategies will have children who are more skillful in a variety of intellectual tasks. The often observed social class differences in children's cognitive skills and school performance is merely a special case of this general phenomenon, arising from the fact that there are differences between the two social class groups in their typical mode of interaction with the child. Middle class mothers, for any one of several possible reasons, are simply more apt to use the more optimal teaching strategies and the more complex language.

But this is a very easy kind of theoretical statement to make. What is more difficult is to specify precisely why this might be so. What is the mechanism through which the mother's type of language, or her form of teaching strategy, translates into a type of cognitive functioning in the child? And can we be sure that it is not the child who is the primary causal agent?

Although it is perfectly clear that definitive answers to these questions cannot now be given, let us nonetheless take up each of these questions in turn. First, then, in what way could the mother's linguistic style or teaching strategy be causally related to the child's cognitive functioning? In answer to this question, Hess and Shipman propose the following:

> "It is our view that the structures of the social system and of the family shape communication and language and that language shapes thought and cognitive styles of problem solving. In the context of the deprived family, this means that the control system which relates parent to child restricts the number and kind of actions and thoughts that are possible; such construction precludes a tendency for the child to reflect, to consider and choose among alternatives for speech and action. Constriction develops modes for dealing with stimuli and problems that are impulsive rather than reflective, that deal with the immediate rather than the future, and that are disconnected rather than sequential." (1967, p. 58.)

According to this type of view, language is the dominant causal factor in the child's developing cognitive skills. If the language which he hears is restricted, focusing on specific solutions rather than general ones or alternatives, on a specific instance rather than comparison of instances, on concrete rather than superordinate concepts, then the child's thinking will be restricted as well. To go beyond Hess and Shipman's formulation somewhat, it may be that in a nonrestricted linguistic environment, the child acquires, through imitation or direct shaping, a series of what may be called "analytic" linguistic responses. He learns to say "this is bigger than that," or "this is different from that," and such responses, once internalized, may form an essential basis for problem solving. Because of the language, the child has learned skills which will make it possible for him to select among alternatives, to make decisions, and to focus his attention on the general, in addition to the specific features of a particular problem. By the time the child is four, the mother may use questions or nonspecific suggestions to elicit such analytic responses from the child, which she then reinforces through the use of positive feedback, thus further strengthening the necessary analytic behavior.

While this formulation does not represent a rigorous theory of the socialization of problem solving, it is nonetheless persuasive in many respects. The major problem with this view, however, is its most fundamental assumption, namely that language dominates thought, and that without an elaborated language, complex problem solving is not possible. While the general issue of the relationship between language and thought in the developing child is by no means settled, there is impressive evidence against the assertion that language in any direct way determines the form of thought, or conversely, that having a particular linguistic form means that the equivalent "thought" is necessarily present. For example, Furth (1966) and Lenneberg (1967), as well as others, have found that young, congenitally deaf children, when tested with nonverbal procedures, show no general deficiency in cognitive skills. Lenneberg reported that young deaf children performed no differently from young hearing children on the Leiter scale, which is a largely language-free concept formation test; Furth has shown that deaf children do not differ appreciably from normals on such tasks as conservation of quantity. Furth (1966), in summarizing his own and others' data on this question, asserts:

> "The major significance of the reported findings for theories of thinking is the demonstration that logical, intelligent thinking does not need the support of a symbolic *system*, as it exists in the living language of society. Thinking is undoubtedly an internal system, a hierarchical ordering within the person of his interaction with the world. The symbol system of language mirrors and in a certain way expresses that internal organization. However, the internal organization of intelligence is not dependent on the language system; on the contrary, comprehension and use of the ready-made language is dependent on the structure of intelligence." (P. 228.)

While Furth's conclusion represents an extreme view on the other end of the theoretical spectrum, the fact that young deaf children perform on various cognitive tasks much as do hearing children creates some problems for the type of explanation of socialization for problem solving which Hess and Shipman have suggested, and which has been elaborated above. In addition, Lenneberg (1967) has offered a convincing argument for the proposition that the form of language (syntax) develops in much the same way in all children, regardless of environment, and Bruner, Olver, and Greenfield (1966) have also argued convincingly that the form of language includes complexities and abstract features long before such features are present in the child's thought. All of these lines of argument suggest that thought, on which problem solving is presumably based, develops separately from at least the form of the child's language. This is not to say that language is not a *useful* tool in problem solving, nor that the content of language (the vocabulary, if you will) may not affect the child's ability to solve a particular problem. But it does suggest that the degree of complexity in the form of language spoken around the child is probably an insufficient basis on which to explain individual differences in the child's cognitive functioning.

Where does this leave us in attempting to explain the relationship between maternal behavior and the child's cognitive functioning? What is needed, I feel, is a formulation which does not rely so heavily on the mother's language, one which would allow for the encouragement of cognitive development in extralinguistic ways. The one feature of the mother's behavior in our problem solving situation which has this characteristic is the extent to which she allows the child some independent scope of action on the task. The "ideal mother" may be the one who (a) guides the child sufficiently so that his attention is focused on relevant portions of the problem, or on important strategy decisions, but then (b) leaves the decisions and the action to him.[1] In the house building situation, questions and low specificity suggestions serve these dual functions well, but the same goal *could* be accomplished in nonlinguistic ways.

The notion that it is the child's independent action which is crucial is not altogether far fetched. Certainly, Piaget has emphasized the importance of the child's action in the development of cognition, and there is some relevant experimental evidence as well. Sonstroem (1966) has shown that training in the conservation of quantity with solid objects (balls of clay) was facilitated when the child performed the transformations himself. Language still played a role, however, since the effect of the child's manipulation of the clay was clearest when the manipulation was accompanied by labeling by the experimenter. Labeling *alone*, unaccompanied by manipulation by the child, did not have a significant effect. Held and his associates (Held, 1965) have also shown the importance of physical action for an organism's adaptation to prisms which displace the visual field. Held reported that "visual experience" alone was not sufficient to lead to adaptation; motor experience was also necessary.

But I am suggesting something more than just the necessity for independent action on the part of the child. If independent action were sufficient, a neglected child might show maximal cognitive development, and this is clearly not the case. What is needed, in addition to independence of action, is some structuring provided by the mother or others in the environment. The mother focuses the child's attention on some relevant feature of a task, and structures the task in such a way that the most useful kinds of comparisons, decisions, and analyses are highlighted. Such structuring *can* be done without language, but it is clearly easiest to do this linguistically, through such devices as question and low specificity suggestions. The mother's language is thus important, but not for the reasons initially suggested by Hess and Shipman.

One attractive feature of this alternative formulation is that it is, at least

---

[1] There are, of course, many other ways in which to conceptualize the "ideal" mother which rely to widely varying degrees on language. John and Goldstein (1964), for example, have focused on the dialogue aspect of language, rather than on specific usage. They say, for example, "It is our contention . . . that the crucial difference between middle-class and lower-class individuals is not in the quality of language, but in its use." (p. 461.) This formulation is not altogether inconsistent with what has been said above, since it emphasizes the importance of interaction, rather than mere exposure.

Quite a different framework is that suggested in the Moore and Anderson paper which appears in this volume. Many of the specific maternal behaviors assessed in our own interaction situations may be seen in terms of the degree to which they encourage the adoption of different perspectives, or provide opportunities for autotelic experience, or create a responsive environment. The dimensions of environment suggested by the Moore and Anderson analysis deserve careful attention, especially as they suggest new kinds of variables in the assessment of socialization for problem solving.

in gross ways, amenable to experimental test. Suppose, for example, we begin with a large group of children who are all equally unskilled at some specific type of problem solving task. For one group of children we provide training which involves a combination of questions and low specificity suggestions, but after each question and suggestion, we allow the child to make the decision or the next move in the problem. For another group, the experimenter makes the same verbal statements, but answers his own questions and solves the problem for the child; the child is merely a spectator. For yet another group, the experimenter solves the problem without verbalization, and for the final group, the child solves the problem without verbalization from the experimenter. The children are then retested on a similar problem to determine the degree of improvement in their problem solving skills. If it is the language alone which makes a difference, then the first two groups of children should be equivalent. If it is the child's action alone which is crucial, then the first and last groups should be similar, while if it is a combination of structuring (in this case, verbal) and independent action by the child, then the first group should differ from all the remaining groups.

Obviously, this alternative formulation, like Hess and Shipman's, is not a fully developed theory. But it offers a way around the reliance on verbalization as the sole vehicle for fostering intellectual development, and it may focus our attention on a somewhat different set of dimensions of maternal behavior.

But can we be sure, at all, that the direction of causality runs from the environment to the child? May it not be the child's characteristics which affect the mother's behavior? One possibility of this kind, which seems unlikely, is that the mothers may be responding to inborn differences in the child. If most children from lower class homes have innately less capacity, the mothers may have discovered that it is easier to give explicit directions than to try to teach general problem solving. We cannot, of course, prove that this is not the case, but it seems far too simple an explanation to account for the complexities of maternal behavior observed in the interaction situations. A second possibility, which seems more tenable, is that there may be some circular type of causal relationship. A child who at age two or three is a less skillful problem solver because the mother has previously used inefficient teaching strategies with him presents a different stimulus to the mother than a child who is a skillful problem solver. The child's lack of skill may make it even more difficult for the mother to use more general teaching strategies; she may continue with the specifics because they at least produce immediate results. Thus, poor teaching on the part of the mother results in poor problem solving in the child, which perpetuates the poor teaching in the mother, and so forth.

We cannot make firm decisions concerning the direction of causality with the data available from our study, or from similar research. What is needed is experimental research in which the mother's behavior is systematically altered in ways which we might consider relevant, such as the use of questions, nonspecific suggestions, and so forth. If the child's behavior, as well as the mother's, is assessed both before and after training is provided for the mother, and some change in the child's cognitive functioning can be demonstrated following a change in the mother's teaching strategy, then we have some support for the contention that it is the mother's behavior which is most crucial. Alternatively, we may attempt to train the child in specific ways and see if the mother's teaching strategy has changed.

Some research of the first type, in which training for mothers was used, has already been reported. Karnes, Studley, Wright, and Hodgins (1968) worked with the mothers of 13 preschool age children, with 13 matched controls who received no training. The mothers in the experimental group attended eleven two-hour sessions in which specific educational materials were constructed, and the mothers trained to use those materials with the child in the home. Language and vocabulary development were specifically emphasized. IQ scores, obtained on the children both before and after the training given to the mothers, showed a mean increase of 7.46 points for the experimental group, and .07 points for the controls; the difference in the amount of change in the two groups was statistically reliable. In addition, the experimental group children improved significantly more than did the controls on several subtests of the Illinois Test of Psycholinguistic Abilities. While neither the specific behaviors emphasized during training, nor the measures of the child's cognitive functioning are ideal, the findings from this study are at least consistent with the contention that changes in the child's general cognitive functioning may be obtained by changing the mother's behavior toward the child.

Other research suggests that more specific changes in maternal behavior may be obtained through training. Risley (1968), for example, has been successful in training lower class mothers to use higher rates of positive reinforcement during problem solving interactions with a child. More recently, Carole Menig, an undergraduate student working in our laboratory, carried out a small pilot mother-training study with six mothers. Training included the presentation of a tape recording of excerpts of other mothers working with their children in the house building situations with the excerpts selected so as to illustrate "good" and "bad" maternal teaching on each of three main dimensions of verbal behavior: questions versus statements, low versus high specificity suggestions, and positive versus negative feedback. After training, we observed significant increases in the rate of suggestions, a decrease in negative feedback, and a decrease in physical instrusiveness. These results suggest, at the least, that it may well be feasible to modify maternal behavior in important ways, although it remains to be seen whether modifications of this sort will result in changes in the child's problem solving abilities.

Methodological Considerations

There are two questions I wish to discuss here. The first deals with the adequacy or appropriateness of the measures of maternal behavior thus far used in analyses of problem solving interactions; the second has to do with the problem of measurement in a laboratory situation versus a more naturalistic setting.

Lacking a clear-cut theory which would specify the precise ways in which maternal behavior should affect the child's developing problem-solving skills, it has been difficult to develop a comprehensive set of measures of maternal behavior. The selection of variables for study in the research I have already described was based in part on earlier theoretical statements, and in part on prior observation of such interaction sessions. With respect to three types of measures, questions versus statements, specificity of suggestions, and degree of maternal physical involvement in the problem solving, the focus was on the degree to which the mother's action encouraged and left room for independent action on the part of the child. The interest in positive versus negative feedback was based on the assumption that the generalization of problem solving strategies acquired in one situation would be affected by the degree to which the mother rewarded or punished the child's specific efforts, or encouraged or discouraged him in his general strategy. The measurement of linguistic style from the interview was obviously influenced by Bernstein's theoretical statements.

Although we did find social class differences on all of these variables, and all seem worthy of further exploration, our current thinking would suggest that the dimensions of questions, specificity, and physical involvement may be the most crucial. In addition, the theoretical analysis presented above would argue for at least three changes in, or additions to, the list of potentially relevant variables.

First, the measurement of specificity of suggestions, while already undertaken, requires some additional modification. Initially, we began with four levels of specificity, but found that we could obtain good reliability with only three. Nonetheless, it was the impression of those who scored the protocols that there were many finer shadings in the suggestions given by the mothers, and that eventually we would need a scoring system which took this into account. For example, some mothers used rhetorical questions at a very high level of specificity, for example, "This one goes here, doesn't it?" We did not score this as a question, but as an imperative statement at the highest level of specificity. But is this qualitatively different from simply saying, "This one goes here"? Perhaps the use of the rhetorical question, even with a very specific suggestion, keeps the child more involved in the task, since it provides at least an aura of participation for the child. Or, as another example, are impulse control suggestions such as, "Let's go slow now, so we won't knock the house down" substantively different from a suggestion such as, "Look at the lady's house"? We scored both of these at the lowest level of specificity because they were both strategy suggestions in some sense, but one deals with physical control in addition to dealing with the task itself. There are many other examples of this kind which point to the need for a finer grained analysis of the mother's task-relevant messages to the child.

Second, the mother's timing in providing task information would appear to be an important neglected variable. Does the mother give a suggestion to the child when he is already working on something else, or does she wait until the child is stuck, or until he has completed the action specified in her last suggestion? A mother may give low specificity suggestions, or ask questions, but give her statements so close together in time that the child does not have time to respond to the first before the second arrives. Timing may be particularly crucial in the case of questions, since the child must be given time to reply, either in words or in actions.

In an earlier study involving an assessment of parent-child interaction (Bee, 1967), I attempted to measure this variable by scoring each suggestion given by either parent during a similar set of problem solving situations as either an interrupting or a noninterrupting suggestion. Unfortunately, the interrater reliability for this distinction remained distressingly low (about 50%) despite extensive consultation and additional observation. The difficulties in making judgments of this sort while an interaction is going on are obvious; such judgments require, at the least, that the observer be able to watch the interaction continuously, and that is not possible if scoring is done simultaneously. In addition, the inferences on which the scoring is based are complex. How does one decide if a child is "ready" for another suggestion? If he is silent, it may well be that he is planning his next move. If the child is in the process of complying with the prior suggestion from the parent when the next suggestion is given, is this necessarily an interruption? It seems clear on the basis of these considerations that assessment of timing of the parent's teaching behavior will require a film or videotape of the interaction; such a film would make continuous observation possible, and would provide the data on which decisions concerning inferences could be made.

A third new relevant variable, dealing with the sequencing of suggestions from the mother to the child, is also needed. We need some measure which describes the order in which the mother gives task messages, as well as the nature of the messages. Does she begin with a very general strategy suggestion or a question? Does she follow this with a more specific suggestion if the child did not understand the first suggestion, or does she rephrase the more general suggestion? There is no immediately obvious means of approaching questions of this kind in a continuous interaction situation. For assessing this particular facet of the mother's behavior, a series of very short problem situations would be more useful, since then one could examine the mother's sequence of task messages for each task without having to be concerned about determining the beginning and end of each task, or subtask unit.

A second major methodological issue is the question of laboratory versus naturalistic observation of parent-child interaction. It is perfectly obvious that in a laboratory setting, when a mother knows she is being watched and tape recorded, her behavior will be altered in at least some ways. She may attempt to behave in ways which she sees as most socially desirable, and different mothers may well interpret task instructions differently. But these same difficulties, in some form or another, are present in more naturalistic settings as well. If an observer goes into a home to observe the mother interacting with the child, again the mother knows she is being watched, and this will presumably affect her behavior in much the same way as would a laboratory setting. On this basis alone, it is difficult to make a clear argument for either procedure.

A more serious objection to laboratory assessement is its artificiality. It can be argued that the situations in which the mother and child are observed are unlike those encountered in the home; measuring the mother's behavior in such abnormal situations may tell us little about her habitual behavior with the child. Lacking observations on the same group of mothers in the laboratory and in the home, we cannot answer this objection directly. But there are several sorts of indirect evidence which can be used to support at least the initial use of laboratory measurement.

First, in the procedure we used, we included assessment of mother-child interaction in two situations which varied in their structure and perhaps in their artificiality. The waiting room situation is not unlike many situations previously encountered by mother and child, and is not totally unlike a home situation. Yet as we have shown, the dimensions of behavior which differentiated middle and lower class mothers in this situation were very similar to the dimensions which differentiated them in the more artificial house building task. Second, the house building task itself is not altogether artificial. Mothers do work with children on problems of various sorts, from teaching the child how to tie his shoes, to helping him build with blocks. The concentrated, continuous involvement of the mother with the child over a ten to fifteen minute period may well be rare, but the task demands themselves are not completely novel. Third, there is some evidence, albeit unsystematic, from a study by Hertzig, Birch, Thomas, and Mendez (1968) that unstructured home observation would reveal variables of very much the same sort as those seen in the laboratory. In visiting the homes of children of several social class and ethnic groups, these researchers noted environmental variations not only along physical dimensions (for example, number of toys or books, number of rooms, and so forth), but also on interpersonal dimensions such as the extent of demand for independent activity and the use of language for task orientation versus social and affective communication. While we cannot be sure that the mothers who use language in a task-directed way with their children in the home would be the same mothers who would use the more efficient teaching strategies in the laboratory, at least there is some evidence that the dimensions of behavior noted in the laboratory are also noted in the home.

All of these arguments in support of laboratory assessment do not constitute arguments against home observation. Ultimately, it will be essential to do both, and to determine the relationship between measures obtained in the two situations. For the moment, however, laboratory assessment has the distinct advantage of being more efficient, since it is possible to construct situations designed to elicit certain types of behavior, and in this way obtain measures in minutes which might take hours or days in a more naturalistic setting.

SUMMARY

To summarize, we have observed very clear social class differences in the style of maternal interactions in problem-solving interactions. One of the contrasting styles, used most commonly by middle class mothers, includes the use of questions rather than statements, low specificity suggestions, positive feedback, and little physical involvement. Such a strategy is correlated with more adequate independent problem solving on the part of the child. I have suggested that the individual differences in the children's cognitive functioning may be conceived of as having been caused, in large part, by the typical style of interaction with the mother, and further, that the most crucial feature of the mother's interactional style is the extent to which she arranges the task so as to increase the probability of relevant independent action on the part of the child.

REFERENCES

Allen, S., "The Effects of Verbal Reinforcement on Children's Performance As a Function of Type of Task." *Journal of Experimental Child Psychology* (1966), *3*, 57–73.

Bee, H. L., "Parent-child Interaction and Distractibility in 9-year-old Children." *Merrill-Palmer Quarterly* (1967), *13*, 175–190.

Bee, Helen L., Nyman, Barry A., Pytkowicz, Ann Roth, Sarason, Irwin G., and Van Egeren, Lawrence F., *A Study of Cognitive and Motivational Variables in Lower and Middle Class Preschool Children: An Approach to the Evaluation of the Impact of Head Start*, Volumes I and II. Research Report Number 8, Social Change Evaluation Project, University of Washington, Office of Economic Opportunity Contract 1375, 1968.

Bee, Helen L., Van Egeren, Lawrence F., Streissguth, Ann Pytkowicz, Nyman, Barry A., and Leckie, Maxine S., "Social Class Differences in Maternal Teaching Strategies and Speech Patterns." *Developmental Psychology*, in press.

Bernstein, B., "Social Class and Linguistic Development: A Theory of Social Learning." In A. H. Halsey, J. Floud and C. A. Anderson, eds. *Education, Economy and Society*. New York: The Free Press, 1961. Pp. 288–314.

——— "Linguistic Codes, Hesitation Phenomena, and Intelligence." *Language and Speech* (1962), *5*, 31–46 (a).

——— "Social Class, Linguistic Codes, and Grammatical Elements." *Language and Speech* (1962), *5*, 221–240 (b).

Bing, E., "Effect of Child Rearing Practices on Development of Differential Cognitive Abilities." *Child Development* (1963), *34*, 631–648.

Bruner, J. S., Olver, R. R., Greenfield, P. M., *Studies in Cognitive Growth*. New York: John Wiley & Sons, 1966.

Casler, L., "Maternal Deprivation: A Critical Review of the Literature." *Society for Research in Child Development Monographs* (1961), No. 26.

Dyk, R. B., and Witkin, H. A., "Family Experiences Related to the Development of Differentiation in Children." *Child Development* (1965), *36,* 21–55.

Furth, H. G., *Thinking Without Language.* New York: The Free Press, 1966.

Goldfarb, W., "Effects of Psychological Deprivation in Infancy and Subsequent Stimulation." *American Journal of Psychiatry* (1945), *102,* 18–33.

——— "Emotional and Intellectual Consequences of Psychologic Deprivation in Infancy; a Re-evaluation." In P. Hock and J. Zubin, eds. *Psychopathology of Childhood.* New York: Grune & Stratton, Inc., 1955. Pp. 105–119.

Held, R., "Plasticity in Sensory-Motor Systems." *Scientific American* (1965), *213,* No. 5, 84–94.

Hertzig, M. E., Birch, H. G., Thomas, A., and Mendez, O. A., "Class and Ethnic Differences in the Responsiveness of Preschool Children to Cognitive Demands." *Society for Research in Child Development Monographs* (1968), *33,* #1.

Hess, R. D., and Shipman, V., "Early Experience and the Socialization of Cognitive Modes in Children." *Child Development* (1965), *34,* 869–886.

——— "Cognitive Elements in Maternal Behavior." *Minnesota Symposium on Child Psychology, Vol. 1.* Minneapolis: University of Minnesota Press, 1967. Pp. 57–81.

——— "Maternal Influences Upon Early Learning: The Cognitive Environments of Urban Pre-school Children." In R. D. Hess and R. M. Bear, eds. *Early education.* Chicago: Aldine, 1968. Pp. 91–103.

Hunt, J. McV., *Intelligence and Experience.* New York: Ronald Press, 1961.

John, Vera P., and Goldstein, L. S., "The Social Context of Language Acquisition." *Merrill-Palmer Quarterly* (1964), *10,* 265–275.

Karnes, M. B., Studley, W. M., Wright, W. R., and Hodgins, A. S., "An Approach for Working with Mothers of Disadvantaged Preschool Children." *Merrill-Palmer Quarterly* (1968), *14,* 174–184.

Klaus, R. A., and Gray, Susan, "The Early Training Project for Disadvantaged Children: A Report After Five Years." *Society for Research in Child Development Monographs* (1968), *33,* #4.

Lenneberg, E. H., *Biological Foundations of Language.* New York: John Wiley and Sons, 1967.

Long, E. R., "The Effect of Programmed Instruction in Special Skills During the Preschool Period on Later Ability Patterns and Academic Achievement." Cooperative Research Project No. 1521, Bureau No. 5-0654. University of North Carolina, Chapel Hill, North Carolina, 1966.

Risley, T., "Jenny Lee: Learning and Lollipops." *Psychology Today* (January, 1968), 28–31 and 62–65.

Skeels, H. M., Updegraff, R., Wellman, B. L., and Williams, H. M., "A Study of Environmental Stimulation: An Orphanage Preschool Project." *University of Iowa Studies in Child Welfare* (1938), *15,* No. 4.

Skeels, H. M., and Dye, H. B., "A Study of the Effects of Differential Stimulation on Mentally Retarded Children." *Proceedings of the American Association in Mental Deficiency* (1939), *44,* 114–136.

Sonstroem, A. M., "On the Conservation of Solids," J. S. Bruner, R. R. Olver and P. M. Greenfield, ed. *Studies in Cognitive Growth.* New York: John Wiley and Sons, 1966. Pp. 208–224.

Spitz, R. A., "Hospitalism: An Inquiry into the Genesis of Psychiatric Conditions in Early Childhood." *Psychoanalytic Studies of the Child* (1945), *1*, 53–74.

Stevenson, H. W., and Snyder, L. C., "Performance as a Function of Interaction of Incentive Conditions." *Journal of Personality* (1960), *28*, 1–11.

Weikert, D. P., "Preliminary Results From a Longitudinal Study of Disadvantaged Preschool Children." Paper presented at the 1967 convention of the Council for Exceptional Children, St. Louis, Missouri.

Wellman, B., "Iowa Studies on the Effects of Schooling." *Yearbook of National Society for the Study of Education* (1940), *39*, 377–399.

Witkin, H. A., Dyk, R. B., Faterson, H. F., Goodenough, D. R., and Karp, S. A. *Psychological Differentiation.* New York: John Wiley & Sons, 1962.

Yarrow, L. J., "Maternal Deprivation: Toward an Empirical and Conceptual Re-evaluation." *Psychological Bulletin* (1961), *58*, 450–490.

CRITIQUE AND DISCUSSION

I would like to spend a few minutes reviewing the nature of the findings of our research and then use the remaining time to tie in with some of the other things that have already gone on in the last two days.

We did not start out to study problem solving in families. We started out to evaluate the Head Start program. We were asked to do this and felt that if we were going to evaluate Head Start we wanted to build in as many other things as we could into the research strategy. So, instead of just assessing Head Start and non-Head Start lower class children, we also looked at a group of middle class children. We looked at the mothers interacting with children of all of our families on the assumption that the way a mother interacted with the child might tell us a great deal about the differences which exist between poverty children and non-poverty children in terms of their intellectual functions. We also hoped that it might be possible to predict which children would change the most as a result of Head Start from

knowing something about the family patterns. That, incidentally, turned out to be impossible for a number of reasons.

Now, just to summarize the results very briefly. We find that we get very large social class differences on four dimensions. Middle class mothers ask more questions. When they say something to the child about the task, it's much more likely to be stated in interrogatives. I think that's important for a number of reasons. Lower class mothers as a group tend to phrase things very often in imperative form or in some sort of declarative sentence. They do do a lot of "Put this here, put that there."

This relates to the second dimension which has to do with how specific the information is that they're giving. Lower class mothers are very specific. A very high proportion of the task messages that they give are really solution messages. They're telling the child precisely how to do some specific thing. The remaining options for the child are really very limited. Middle class mothers, on a whole, use a great deal more of a less specific kind of suggestion, something which we came to call "strategy suggestions" or "focusing suggestions."

The third dimension on which they differ has to do with the nature of the feedback that they give. Middle class mothers give about three positive feedback messages for every negative one. Lower class mothers give about the same number of each, and that relative difference is such that the tone of the interaction of lower class families is very different. It has a negative quality and the tone of the mother's voice is more querulous and demanding.

The fourth dimension on which they differed was the extent to which the mother actually did the task for the child. The problem of the mother's intrusiveness is a tough one because you can't tell the extent to which this is a response to the specific task situation. I suspect that lower class mothers may have felt some need to involve themselves more physically because of the demands of the situation itself. One can't be sure about this without testing in other situations. In any case, these four dimensions of difference create two quite distinct patterns of interaction. Presumably this reflects differences in the way they solve problems at home. (I might add, incidentally, that in general these differences are not racial differences.)

For the middle class mothers the strategy seems to be, and this is a step beyond the data, one of teaching the child how to solve problems. She approaches this specific problem as a vehicle for instruction. The lower class mother is getting the job done, the task is being accomplished, but she's very specific-solution oriented. The middle class mother is very much more oriented to the child and to the child's need to learn something from the situation.

I've been struggling to come up with some sort of theoretical orientation that will make some sense out of these two groups rather than just describing them. There's a correlational relationship, but what's the nature of the causal connection? As you know, I suggested in the paper that I didn't think it was just the language. The language is a vehicle for something else. At the time that I wrote that paper I thought the patterns had a good deal to do with what other people have called "independence training." You structure the situation so that the child is paying attention to the right things but then you let him do it himself. It's not complete freedom for the child. There are guidelines laid down and the child is aimed in the right direction so that you maximize the useful learning that he will obtain from this situation.

Now this way of looking at it ties in with the kinds of dimensions that O. K. Moore has provided. For example, what we see as the less optimal strategy on the part of the mother is one in which the child has only one perspective. He is always in the patient perspective—never allowed to take the dominant role. There's very little reciprocal action and he is given little opportunity to serve as the referee. There were some middle class mothers who really allowed the child in some ways to take the more dominant perspective. The mother would say, "Gee, Mommy isn't very good at this, is she?" "What do you think we ought to do next?" which almost reversed the roles entirely.

To be sure, in our situation the possibilities for examining changes in "perspective" or other of these dimensions were not as good as they might be. Nevertheless I did want to indicate how our results might tie in with O. K. Moore's dimensions.

In conclusion, assuming that what the mother did in our situation tells us something about her habitual patterns of interaction, I think that we're beginning to get some clues about why these kids have so much difficulty coping with the school environment. Also why these families have so much difficulty coping with other kinds of family problems. Precisely which of all of these dimensions is the crucial one, or which combination is the thing that creates the differences in the children, we simply can't say at this point. We just don't have those kind of data, and I don't think we have a theory yet that is going to permit us to be very precise about it.

One of the things we're trying to do now is to follow up our findings by trying to train mothers. If what the mother does is causally connected to the child's difficulties, then you ought to be able to improve the child by changing the mother. That's a large undertaking, and it may not be successful but this is one way of finding out what the crucial factor is.

INKELES DISCUSSION

The main lines of the findings I think most of us are probably prepared to accept. They seem highly congruent with the great deal of information that we've been acquiring over the last two or three decades. Nevertheless I think it is extremely useful to have the effort that is made here—to reduce to much more precise components—the things that make the differences, because we're all quite clear that there is a big difference in how middle class mothers raise their children as against how working class mothers raise their children. Incidentally, I'm not sure that your dimensions really need to be reduced to another scheme. The bridge between the study and mother-child relations is quite clear-cut. We can easily see how what the mother does becomes an analogue of the child's own later problem solving efforts. She also provides the child with certain opportunties that are critical to developing the capacity for generalized solutions for problem solving capacity as against something which is highly specific.

I do have several methodological issues to raise——I think that in this case the situation that we're dealing with is an appropriate example of problem solving behavior——It seems to me that there is a surface or face validity in the choice of the problem with reference to the phenomenon to which it is being generalized, because all through life we're always going to be putting together objects. In this age almost everything comes knocked down. You might say that one of those fundamental requirements for success in the present world, at least the physical part of the world, is the ability to put together things which have been knocked down by Sears Roebuck and Co.——

But——On the methodological side several things did occur to me. The nature of the instructions given may or may not have played a very substantial role in the outcome. The mothers were told that they are to try to help their child do as well as possible. This was defined as a test situation and therefore whatever are the class-typed response propensities with regard to situations of that kind will come out. Now, I believe that in lower class mothers, in the kind of setting you were talking about, this induces a lot of anxiety. But the middle class mothers, perhaps just because they've gotten more experience with it, are able to bring on a somewhat different strategy. So you might want to check in a different setting.

Closely related to this is the problem of time orientation. You did not set any time limits for this performance apparently. You left it completely open, and you might argue that the lower class were anxious knowing that they had unlimited time——but just what would happen if you changed the time definition I don't know. Perhaps the middle class have a different calculus about the payoffs that are involved in the situations they're engaged in. They take the view that they have lots of time now, and they probably have. That is, they are subject to fewer pressures in terms of the resources they have available to meet the situations of daily life; whereas a large part of lower class behavior is an effort to somehow put a stop to the possibility of chaos because of the influx of all kinds of demands. The middle class mother, I think, in the normal situation, is really taking the position that she can in a sense have less candy now——she can accept the notion that the thing doesn't get built more rapidly and well and so on because it's a long term investment. She is not caught in this one situation, but she recognizes it as part of a general pattern in which she is trying to help the child to solve problems on his own because, in time, that means that she'll have much less pressure.

I have a question that goes a bit further, have you attempted to rework these correlations with class controls? Because it seems to me you have the possibility of very substantial contamination in the sense that some of these patterns may have become so widely diffused in the middle class and maybe so relatively rare in the lower class groups that the seeming difference in the pattern is in fact not effective or operative. It's only the global class factors, and therefore what you seem to be explaining, you are not in fact explaining. This has a lot to do with the possibilities about changes in these conditions. Clearly there are a lot of other factors here that are not controlled. They are part of the middle class or working class milieu which you will not be able to transform by the retraining programs.

Now, I'm taking advantage of having the floor to go just one bit further, to urge the extension, the elaboration of the dimensions that are touched on here by Dr. Bee so that we develop a somewhat more elaborate battery of what it is that characterizes these different kinds of homes on some set of reasonably standard dimensions. I started to play around with some of the things that we have been talking about thus far——as an illustration, the time dimension seems to enter in here very much——so here I came up with a distinction of whether in a programmatic sense, you were "long-term" or "short-term" and, within that, whether you were "part-time" or "full-time."

In my own research on the factory as an environment, one of the reasons it has this tremendous impact is that it has, along with the school environment, a very distinctive structural character. Both of them are long-term. That is, once you get into the factories, it is a life-time operation. The school also is very long-term and a critical part of your life, just as the family in certain ways is very long-term.

Moore's operation, as he described it is relatively long-term but the engagement is decidedly part-time which is one of the very interesting things about it. The question is, then, do we really have to make the kind of investment that we ordinarily assume we have to make. That is not only long-term, but full-time——In some ways I thought that what Hamblin was doing is even more interesting because it's short-term as well as part-time, at least on certain of his projects.

Now a second theme that I have concerns the type of rewards being used. For instance, the issue of "intrinsic" versus "extrinsic" or "delayed" verus "immediate" rewards. These two get confused somewhat in the factory. Everyone says the factory uses extrinsic rewards, but they are also relatively delayed. Very few people have tried giving bonuses or pay every hour. That might enhance productivity——.

GUMPERZ: Isn't that one of the main problems in underdeveloped countries——that people aren't used to this delayed sort of thing? As a result you get a great deal of absenteeism.

Well, there's a myth to that effect. It's not true. Labor discipline is as good or better in most underdeveloped countries, for exactly the same plant, as it is in developed countries. When there are departures from this system there are usually quite good and rational reasons for this being the case. For example, in cases where wage labor is introduced in an environment where you can't do anything with wages people stop working much earlier, but that's because the rest of the package hasn't been provided.

It may be that these rewards aren't what are producing the effects, that it's the intrinsic aspects which are producing the effects——what I call the efficacy inducing qualities of industrial labor.

A subtheme under rewards is distribution——whether they are mainly individual or group. In the factory the distribution is according to presumed technical competence and personal output, but it's a situation which is very heavily dependent on the structure and effectiveness of a larger system. All the productivity studies, for example, show this. It really doesn't matter how hard the worker tries; the real thing that determines his productivity is the ratio of capital to labor. Once you've settled that then there's a little bit of room left to play, so that creates a little different kind of situation.

Now, the distribution system in the family, we are told over and over again, is unique from all of this. It depends not on productivity but, in fact, it depends on a conception of need and some socio-culturally defined rules of responsibility. I believe this is a myth. I don't believe families work that way. So the point is that closer study of what goes on in families would suggest that there are, in fact, very, very carefully worked out and precisely toned relationships which link with things like relative productivity.

GENERAL DISCUSSION

MOORE: Just by way of clarification, I think you can get confused when talking about the effects of rewards on behavior between "performance" criteria and the notion of "competence." Hamblin is dealing with performance theory and his systems have to do with increasing the probability that a response will occur after it has been learned——increasing its intensity, or power if you like. Unfortunately most learning theory is not about learning, but about performance. Your factory examples are typically concerned with this same outcome, and that's fine.

Now, on the other hand, our project is concerned with the initial learning or acquisition of complex symbolic materials. We are looking at a very small phase of this issue of outcomes. It is this issue of the optimal circumstances for real learning that is the context for our discussing intrinsic rewards. This is our primary focus.

Now, with reference to Helen Bee's paper. I'm so appreciative of how much she has already done that it is gratuitous to say "please go out and do some more," but I think——The middle class mother had two built in advantages here which probably shows, still and all, one of her strengths. First, the task was one that was very congenial to the controlling middle class which is heavily puzzle-oriented. The intelligence tests which her kids are going to take are little puzzles. The standards for admission to school are puzzles, not games of strategy, and not aesthetics.

Secondly, probably she knew more about settings for labs so that her definition of the situation came closer to being—maybe it was somewhat threatening but—at least quasi-autotelic. Whereas for the lower class mother it is an open question as to where she was and what she thought could be gained or lost. We don't know how much she thought this was a safe enclave for her and her children, as opposed to being a world of severe evaluations where she might lose an option for her kids. What we would suggest is that a task, out of games of chance or of strategic games, might give you a better sense of what these mothers are up to.

Another thing is the crucial question of definition—social definition—of our laboratories. If we are getting into a period of heavy involvement in family research, in experimentation, then the nature of the definition of it—whether it's simply a place where you're researched and studied as if you were a bug or whether it's a research and helping place—is going to be a crucial issue of definition. We have a chance to shape the professions' definition and gradually the publics' definition of what we're doing. We're going to have to start saying what these laboratories are because if people come to them and don't know——

have no social category, especially the blacks and the disadvantaged who don't know where they are——In so far as their definitions of the situation vary all over the place, you have error variance of unknown proportions.

ZELDITCH: Well, there are two suggestions and I think they must be kept separate. Both are important. One is you can't just not define the situation. The second suggestion is how you should define it. I gather O.K. wants to define it as a helping as well as an investigative kind of a structure.

MOORE: It's at this point, I think, that some of Hamblin's suggestions are very much to the point. Namely that the process of investigation is perhaps best done under circumstances of making changes.

HILL: There is a related question and that is the appropriate laboratory setting—— How to locate a place in which all groups that would come in would feel equally at home. The suggestion's been made two or three times that we come closest to that in their own homes because this has all of the place cue settings with which they are familiar.

MOORE: This is where mobile units come in—at least in our own work—now that we're shifting in the direction of taking the family into account. This is especially true for the disadvantaged mother——even to take the kids to a central place half a block away to be picked up by bus can cause a great deal of confusion and difficulty for her.

Let me get several other issues on the record. Consider the issue of "deficit" versus "difference" in performance. I would want to begin with the question of defining. Let me put in a plug for some of our stuff. Part of our logic of norms includes an analysis of these types of concepts. We need to be a little more careful initially in our definitions, producing not one type of "performance" but families of meanings of performance. So you can select and say, for example, that it appears that this group has a normative system, including their ideas about performance, like type "A1" as opposed to another, type "A2".

Secondly, it's a mistake to take a one institutional approach to the family. I think it's very important to take two at least. For example, in building a curriculum or procedures for schools, the builders should look at the relevant family structures and try to see that the tasks that the family groups must solve as their youngsters grow up and the curriculum they're taking are meshed. There is a very complicated interrelation between these two sets of parallel institutions, each long-term, each self-terminating at some point, each having to do with socialization and education in various mixes. I think the school people have been planning in isolation and the family mainly adjusts to things happening in institutions outside the control of the family. I would say that from our observation of children so far there's such an intimate relationship between school processes and family processes that it's very hard to consider the health of families without taking both into consideration.

GUMPERZ: Omar, you mentioned black culture groups. The same children who can't do algebra do fantastically well at memorizing baseball scores, or if you tested them on their knowledge of Muslim ritual would know an amazing number of facts. In other words, they have their own fail-safe institutions, they just learn the wrong thing, maybe.

MOORE: Well, it's the wrong level of abstractness to live in our kind of civilization. In other words, a long list of baseball scores isn't at the level of abstractness which allows you to meet the problems of a dynamic, evolving society.

HAMBLIN: This is all very interesting, but I have a comment and I hope you will excuse me and try to get the point in what I'm saying. It seems to me that, in terms of engineering, a solution of the ghetto problems——that a much simpler and direct solution is to provide the motivation and the learning experiences in school. In general, the way this works out is we design a system which should work for the vast majority of the students. There will be some students for whom it doesn't work, and for those students there is a method whereby they are picked up and another program is devised for them which is adequate to the job of handling their problem. We try to devise an alternative learning system that is appropriate for these other children, and often you can bring them right out of it.

HILL: I suspect we have a great deal of exploring to do. I took Dr. Moore's suggestion as opening up for us the way to conceptualize, if you will——the phenomenon of problem solving in such a way that you will see it not only as an internal problem but as a transactional one. What isn't clear to me yet is how you would translate a number of these things into experimental tasks that were appropriate, into experimental settings that were appropriate, into experimental designs that didn't have confounding influences at work. This is certainly a large task that remains ahead, although I think we have sharpened up some of these issues.

BEE: Well, one of the things that we are planning to do which gets at some of the difficulties of confounded definitions is to do the training, if we can possibly manage this, in the type of neighborhood houses that are fairly well integrated institutions within the poverty community. These are places where these mothers are accustomed to going for various kinds of services or assistance of one kind or another.

With respect to tasks, I would argue for the type of strategy in which you try to vary, as systematically as you can (although we don't know all the dimensions yet on which this variation should take place), the nature of the situations in which the families are placed, so that you can see not only what kinds of individual variations you get in these situations, but also for any given family, how they change their strategies, if they do, when confronted with tasks of various kinds.

HAMBLIN: I think you have a good point there and the notion of giving them two or three different tasks would follow up on the kind of thing that Omar was saying in terms of the different types of "performance." Let's see how they perform on several members of the "class." My guess is that you'd find the same type of interaction patterns developing regardless of the type of task.

HILL: Didn't Miller and Swanson in the *Changing American Parent* suggest that the entrepreneurial family was differently oriented than the bureaucratic family, addressing itself to the issue of interpersonal relations——possibly to Moore's "games of strategy." If you introduced the game of strategy into your repertory of experimental tasks you may, within the so-called middle class, show up still another category of families.

GUMPERZ: There is an ethnographic point that I want to make. We're dealing with a wide variety of different systems, but since we are all middle class we tend to make assumptions. I have here a paper that I received just before I left by Dan Slobin of our group. He put together some of the data that we got from six ethnographic studies of socialization—language-socialization—done by six psychologically trained anthropologists. Five of these were done in nonmiddle class families in India, in Mexico, one in the Oakland ghetto, one in Samoa, and one in Africa. Then we had one done in Albany, California. The findings universally are—regarding mothers' input to children—that after the age of three the association between the mother and child begins to drop off and the major source of learning, source of socialization, is the older sibling, or a peer two or three years older. This is true for Oakland ghetto families as well as for all the other non-Western, non-American families. This supports some of the things that anthropologists have been saying, that "the nuclear family is an invention of the American middle class."

Secondly I wanted to point out that one of the things that Bernstein has found is that this "elaborated" kind of training by the middle class tends to produce disorientation in people. As a matter of fact, he says that it is likely to produce psychosis, or something like the middle class neurotic personality. In other words, it tends to take away security. In any case, the point that I would draw from either of these problems is that we really need some meticulous ethnographic studies. Almost no ethnographic work, worth the name, has been done in American cities so far. Oscar Lewis has given us some very interesting reports but his findings are——not available to other ethnographers——I don't know what their value is but they've been questioned. Lewis is an ethnographer and he has to say how he arrived at his——fascinating accounts. The book does not meet the requirements of what a professional ethnographer would want. Rather, he has to tell us "Now here are my tapes, and here is what I've come up with"——in other words what we need is ten volumes somewhere, in some library, on microfilm that are accessible so somebody can go back to them.

ZELDITCH: I'd like to ask a question about this sibling as socializer, about the structure of the family in which it occurs. That is, in a lot of these families there is no father and the mother is operating in many instrumental activities so that the "mother role" devolves on someone else.

GUMPERZ: The structures of families vary—these are quite different kinship systems. Nevertheless in many cases the father is present.

ZELDITCH: I had a comment concerning Helen Bee's paper. One of the things that differentiates your situation between the middle class and the working class mother is——the perception of it as a learning situation. It would be fairly easy, then, to introduce a condition where you get lower class mothers and inform them that you want to see them help the child learn how to do this. I suspect you will get the same results. That is, their methods of socializing will be like their general response in the situation but you want to know that and you can do that.

DR. HILL: Alex raised the issue of whether or not you had controlled for social class and suggested how there might be rather different policy implications, depending on the outcome of that.

BEE: Social class seems to be a useful, very gross place to start looking at this but it is the real cluster of correlated behavioral variables which is the independent variable, not social class. If we are going to do anything further with this, it will have to be done on the basis of where the families stand on a continuum of strategies rather than on a class basis because there is within-class variation.

ZELDITCH: Yes, but from the technical point of view, the real problem is——Are the intercorrelations so high that you can't easily select any ways to separate them out, and that's not an easy problem. I'm not offering you some easy thing to go out and do, but that I think is a serious issue. That's more important, for example, than trying to find a variety of tasks, although that's also important. The task you've got, at least, has a great virtue of portability, it is so flexible. You can take a house trailer into neighborhoods with this task on it and get families to come to your lab. It certainly offers you enormous flexibility which most of us don't have in our work.

GUMPERZ: I want to make one comment on Helen Bee's notion of "specificity." I think one of the examples that you gave is the use of "you." Now the danger here is, I think, something that is related to the amount of information that is conveyed by speech versus the amount of information that is implied by what Harold Garfinkel called "background knowledge." "You" may mean either you in particular or you in general. That is, it might be classified as either a "position-oriented" or a "person-oriented" appeal. This suggests that whole conversations be looked at for patterns and for degree of reliance on shared culture.

LEIK: My comment moves in somewhat the same direction. I have the feeling that somehow——we're creating kind of an ideal situation which I think would be far from ideal under many circumstances.

The lower the economic level of the family, the less likely it is that you can have all kinds of things done for you. The more likely it is that you, therefore, don't have any time to be patient, and leading, and so on. You don't have time to wait for the kid to figure it out in the real world. This implies that we need to do something about the circumstances of these families. Otherwise, the techniques or training program that we set up are going to be acceptable but not relevant to the people with sufficient leisure, and unacceptable though relevant to the people without sufficient leisure because it's obviously a leisure-oriented approach.

STRAUS: I would like to comment on that. The environmental difficulty still leaves us with the fact that these things which are appropriate adaptations to the immediate environmental situation of the family have long-term negative consequences for the children.

LEIK: Okay, but if part of what's going on here is oriented to finding ways of attacking the problem, that attack, perhaps, does not belong in the family—it may belong elsewhere.

COMMENTARY

POLES OF THE RESEARCH SYSTEM: INSTIGATORS AND PUBLICATION MEDIA

Since, as Inkeles' suggests, "most of us are prepared to accept the main lines" of her findings, I just want to comment on some of the background issues raised in the Helen Bee paper. Bee introduces us to her project by stating that the staff had been *invited* to do an evaluation of Head Start. In itself, this is not an earth-shaking statement, but it does call our attention to the question of the initial instigator of social research. Insofar as we are concerned with the system of research, then we should be concerned with the process whereby research questions, and research processes get initiated. For instance, if sociology is defined as an exploration of the "possible," then the "imported meaning"—as a threat to our exploration—would vary greatly, depending upon the ideological commitments of the researcher and those of the instigator.

A second point of interest is the way Bee reports her results. The report contains very little about the silent dimensions of her research. For instance, I once heard Virginia Shipman give an oral report, in a very informal atmosphere, of a project that was very similar to the Bee project. Shipman spent the hour or so alloted her describing some of the extraordinary measures taken to get the *lower* class mothers into the lab. These efforts indicated an enormous investment of time and money, including everything from the hiring of taxis and babysitters to repeated "desensitizing" visits to the sample subject's home. The pitch of the presentation was the researcher's lesson in what it takes to make a "strategic" perspective. In other words it was a far cry from a factor analysis of focal dimensions.

Now just to tie this in with the thematic character of the symposium, several points are raised by this Shipman–Bee comparison. The first is concerned with the media itself. Since most of the published accounts of the Shipman project are similar to Helen Bee's we might argue for a *multi*-(both formal and informal) *media balance* in reporting. The second issue is concerned with the context. A published account of research is not merely more formally informational, it also carries heavy career weight. Perhaps this mixture of information and status is one of the strongest

guarantees against "scientific revolutions." In an easy, informal atmosphere (loosened constraints) more of the data became admissable. Consequently, in the Shipman example the kind of data reported was clearly an addition to what was contained in the published reports (those under the weight of "serious" evaluative scrutiny).

At any rate, the point would be that, in order to increase the information entering the channels and in order to deepen the public reaches into the data domains, we need to consider variable media, crossed with variable degrees of scrutiny. This carries implications for Leik's characterization of research as "blah." If one is up-tight about how he is going to broadcast his findings—and this occurs from the very beginning of the research project—then this is going to influence what one sees all the way through, for example, concern for the "acceptable." Secondly, the media of the written word is one of the more difficult in which to work—in other words, full of constraints in itself. So an over-reliance on written communication is almost going to guarantee the exchange of well reconstructed but trivial issues.

The third point of interest is the operating assumption of the Bee project: mother-child interaction is a key to why lower class kids have so much difficulty. But it is interesting to pick out the number of competing assumptions. Gumperz, for instance, suggests that maybe the mother is not the primary socializing agent in a lot of different settings (that is, besides the middle class). Weick noted earlier that it may not be "primary" socialization that goes on within the family (*if* the family does do it), but only the residue. Moore, in his recommendation for a two-institutional approach, argues that at least some of the problem may lie with the school, and not the child or his relation with mother. Now that's a farout comment. It seems unlikely that, given an invitation from OEO, someone would set out to find out what's wrong with the school system (Hamblin and Moore types excepted). That is, school systems are much less likely to be suspected. Lastly, Inkeles' assumptions about the problem are even further removed from the mother-child relation. At best, the family is seen as some kind of mediator between the child and the power and pervasiveness of the *milieu*.

Tying these background issues together, the Bee report, in addition to its own intrinsic merits, directs our attention to a number of points of interest in the social system of research. There is the subtle selection factor imported into the science by such things as the initiating stimulus —the opportunity structure. There is distortion introduced by such constraints as an over-reliance on written media and a too heavy emphasis on acceptability of results. The dilemma of evaluation is obvious: the need to assure competence in research coupled with the requisite environment (such as autotelic) to assure some modicum of new materials. The seriousness of the dilemma is evidenced by one of Leik's early comments where he admits that many of the properties that Weick alerted us to had been there *in* his labs, but had been treated as noise. This raises a series of questions: Is there a major discrepancy between what is admissable into our communication networks and the total package of data perceivable by an investigator? Or, have research reports become so structured that there is a discrepancy between what an investigator sees and what he could see? Does the close tie between career and inquiry produce a heavy emphasis on protecting the private reaches (what Benbow Ritchie calls the "Law of Affect") of one's data, while at the same time reconstructing (distorting) it so as to make it acceptable (that is, orderly, logical)?

I guess that the underlying point is can more and more of the inquiry process be made publicly accessible for social science development? Is it true that the bulk of the unchartered landscape of social science is artificial and subjective, both deep and extensive in structure. The problems posed by "external validity" suggest that we need a much heavier investment in replications across the data domains. That is, the heavier dependence in social science on a mind-motor coordination indicates the need for a much heavier investment in field work and in depth analysis. As an initial step—one that reinforces Gumperz point—I would like to suggest a national or regional social science archive prepared to receive and reproduce a lot of the raw data sitting around in private offices or in storage basements, to be made accessible to others to rework or replicate. Perhaps, as a condition for publication, each study would file a "background report," a set of raw data, and coding forms in some such archive.

LOCUS OF THE SOCIALIZATION PROBLEM: INTERPERSONAL OR MILIEU

In his remarks, Inkeles delicately balances courtesy and criticism, beginning with the statement that "most of us are probably prepared to accept" Bee's results because they fit with a great deal of information that has been accumulating. But then he subtly shifts to building an alternative perspective which states that child-parent interaction is not all that critical and that the problem is mainly attributable to *milieu differences*. Sandwiched in between are a number of suggestions about task and setting which would be remarkable only if this factor of milieu differences did not loom so important. He concludes by suggesting that if, in fact, there are "class-typed response propensities" then the conclusions for *policy* that one might draw from that would be radically different from those drawn from Bee's research.

In his effort to extend the dimensions which characterize the milieu Inkeles does several things. IIc attempts a synthesis between a number of themes presented thus far, for example, types of investment in intervention: long versus short term or part versus full time. Secondly, he integrates some of the work of Moore and Hamblin into a sketch of the types of programs which might address some of these problems. Finally, he attempts to flesh out what he means by milieu (or social structural) effects. He begins by remarking that there is probably nothing wrong with labor discipline in underdeveloped countries. That what supports the evidence for this "myth" is that the

total package has not been provided. One thought that immediately pops out is what kind of "perspective" to take toward the provision of the total package. Can a policy maker provide the rest of the package—independent of any consideration for the receiving population? Does Hamblin's sense of expertise—such as depending on appreciation of the tacit dimension—offer an appropriate model? In other words, while one might dispute whether or not the sociologist's role in the processes of modernity is to encourage wage-labor, the point at issue is that things like absenteeism are probably traceable to the subjective significance of the larger system. Furthermore, these structural effects are the source of a lot of the negative characteristics which are attributed to individuals' deficiencies. Finally, Inkeles' last package of dimensions indicate a few of the ways we might want to evaluate the milieu: efficacy, individualizing, distributively just.

In looking at the general discussion of the Bee–Inkeles dialogue, it's rather curious how the issues of the focal paper more or less get lost. Part of the reason is that most of the discussion zeroes in on background issues and the Bee paper is rather specific (something akin to Zelditch's). A second reason is that each participant, having injected a lot of his own perspective into the text, is at this point preoccupied with tending to his own conceptual patch. Nevertheless, a synergistic ferment is still in evidence. For instance, Moore and Zelditch get into a minor squab-

ble over the issue of the social definitions of our labs. Zelditch remarks
that there are really two issues: (a)
you cannot not define—that is, you
cannot not communicate; and (b) how
should we define. Now this difference
recalls an earlier Hamblin–Zelditch
exchange on the modes for doing
social science. There the points at issue were a puzzle-solving, scientist-as-
experimenter mode versus a mode
which gave equal play to expertise
and theory construction.

It might be useful to reconstruct
some of the bases for each individual's
position. Zelditch, for instance, wears
two distinct hats and the boundary
between the proper occasion for the
two is well drawn. For instance, as a
scientist, he is oriented to *manipulation, simplification, portability,* and so
forth. Meanwhile, under his other hat,
he is aware of the hidden agenda of
family life, the double-bind (silent
language) of schizogenesis, and so
forth. So, in the role of scientist, we
can understand why it is that Zelditch
does not have much sympathy for the
Moore–Hamblin style of defining the
labs: a safe preserve—where you might
be helped. We can also see why in
more relaxed occasions he can play
comfortably in that idiom.

Now, alongside this portrait, let's
lay Gumperz statement that there are,
in fact, at least two levels of communication: overt and background.
Furthermore, the latter is a much
larger and more substantial layer of
meaning, so that, if you send one kind
of overt message but contradict that
with background cues, "you will flub
your scientific intent."

With this in hand, we now have
four issues—that is, adding two layers

to the two issues that Moore–Zelditch
isolated. When you say that you "cannot not define a lab" you mean, for example, that some definition occurs at
both levels. But that poses a problem, very much like the double-bind
of being consistent on both levels of
meaning, so that if you think you are
accountable for only the overt (scientific) layer—detective mode—the
probability of producing some kind of
bind in the subject is much more
likely to occur.

Perhaps this way of phrasing the
problem will bring us a bit closer to
what Moore seems to have in mind
when he talks about a *strategic* perspective and a *balanced* perspective.
The strategic perspective *does not*
simply mean that a researcher should
have the best interests of his subject
in mind—that might still be a puzzle
orientation—while he goes about his
professional business. A strategic perspective means that at the very least
the subject has some sense of agency
—some say in the research relationship—and that does not look like the
established cultural mold for pro-
fessional-client relations. Somewhere
above this minimum, a strategic relationship suggests that: (a) the researcher must be willing, as he enters
this field, to make adjustments in
some of his basic arrangements, to reflect the subjects' degree of control—
for example, what kind of setting,
rules, pace; (b) that as analysis piles
up some general principles, that the
implications of these—for both sides
of the relationship—be incorporated
into the relationship; and (c) that the
model of the relationship be a complementary linkage between different
kinds of virtuosity. That is, each is in

partial control and in a state of partial dependence.

In a series of miscellaneous observations, Moore introduces or reiterates a number of his very provocative themes in this session. These include: a bundle of issues surrounding the problem of defining the labs, how the social classes might differ in their response to Bee's lab, the lower class fear of losing some options, the problem with a puzzle-solving orientation to research, treating subjects like they were "bugs"; the use of mobile labs as a compromise in the "place cues" controversy, the use of modal logic for classifying "families of meaning" of a concept, for example "different" or "deficient"; a rationale for the use of a two-institutional approach to the family; and finally, the creation of additional institutions for the disadvantaged to provide remedial loops when failures occur in existing institutions.

Gumperz dropped two bombs on the gathering, but their delayed fuses allowed much of the discussion to escape unscathed. First, he introduced some evidence which throws a shadow of suspicion on the universal importance of parent-child relations in socialization. (His point combined with that of Weick (the family makes peace with socialization debris) and Zelditch (we don't need families to study family-like processes) would be some of the issues which I would submit as candidates for further, reflexive and autotelic, discussion.) Second, he suggested that intervention, especially training in elaborated codes, a kind of surface-grammatic training, could have very undesirable side-effects. An additional comment by Gumperz regarding the public reaches into the (ethnographic) data domains has been one of the main themes of the present discussion.

Some Final Thoughts

INTRODUCTION

In the course of cutting and splicing the transcript we occasionally found ourselves in a bit of a dilemma; some sections of the tape seemed to have a great deal of intrinsic worth, but they did not fit in with the flow of ideas under considerations. Consequently, these tangents or digressions were deleted, and then several were selected for a kind of closing medley. Since they appear out of context, some background information is in order.

The first selection is a highly condensed slice of the transcript which recorded the closing moments of the symposium. One reason for its inclusion is that it reflexively illustrates several of Karl Weick's eleven properties and the effects they can have on interaction. During the final hours of discussion, the participants were physically and psychologically drained. Attention spans, for example, were short with the result that the encounter heats up, drifts, and disengages as members vacillate between their private data recesses and some rather unguarded contentiousness.

Beginning with the issue of contingent rewards, a whole series of problems cascade into view: sibling rivalry, masked conflict, the tattling phenomena, and divorce. Finally, two members got into a hassle around the issue of sibling rivalry (solidarity). The question under discussion was "are siblings less and less competitive or simply better and better at masking it?" From a retrospective angle, one reason the engagement doesn't quite come off is that there are very different assumptions embedded in the two positions.

Since the effect produces some distortion of a speaker's overt meanings, I have left most of the sources anonymous. Nevertheless, there does appear to be a kind of validity to the result—one which captures some covert properties in the communication process.

The second selection in the medley is addressed to the issue of "problem

226

solving under stress." Again, the issue was enjoined very late in the meetings, and, consequently, has the quality of unfinished business. Reuben Hill initiates the discussion by attempting to conceptualize stress as an external factor which taxes a family's coping strategies, and, at the same time, may strengthen its crisis capacity. In a curious way the process underlying the ensuing discussion mirrored the topic of concern (stress). The group found it quite difficult to sustain a collective representation of the problem. The result of this was a regression to more individualized perspectives.

Part Three is a collection of specific research strategies that were cropped from the main text because they detracted from the engagement of the moment. Nevertheless, each one has some general operational value, and, since they are pretty much self-contained, they are presented in this miscellaneous section.

The first suggestion was presented by Robert Leik as a way of getting at the process whereby groups managed some of the external factors which encumber or intrude on their mutual accommodation. The suggestion appeared, originally, in the general discussion of Karl Weick's paper where the issue of problem solving had exploded into a rather unwieldly mixture of factors. Leik attempts to pull some of these factors back together in a research framework.

Robert Hamblin's description of his research project was addressed to the problem of noncontingent rewards and their effect. At several points in the main discussion, someone would question the merits of the "democratic family ideal," but the issue was always dropped. It can, however, be revitalized by reading Hamblin's remarks in the context of several others: O. K. Moore's comment that older children (six as opposed to four) are already conditioned to expect little stars; and Leik's discussion of artificial shortage which appears as the last part of this collection of strategies.

The concluding research suggestions, by Robert Leik, can be read as a sequel to Part I—the monologue on contingent rewards. In this extended commentary, Leik starts by discussing the issue of "competition," and then proceeds to pull together a number of seemingly disparate threads: artificial shortage, properties that encumber family groups, an autotelic environment, and the use of Moore's reflexive principle which can be used to show members of a group how certain strategies for problem solving are self-defeating.

PART I—A COLLECTIVE MONOLOGUE FOCUSING ON CONTINGENT REWARDS

A: I was struck by Bob Leik's comment that affection was regarded as one of the things in the family which wasn't scarce. The Freudian theory of sibling rivalry suggests that affection is something which is scarce. Scarce precisely because its source is a mother or father and they're scarce. Their time is scarce.

B: Yes. Particularly where the stance is conditional love to get certain results. Karl Weick suggested that there was a minimum of such contingent behavior but now you've really joined the issue by suggesting that some families, at least, and maybe more than we think, use conditional love as the means of shaping their children's behaviors.

A: Well, I actually didn't intend that. That's probably also so, but——the point is that one of the most important kinds of relational elements in a family is affection——it's a fairly scarce commodity. As a result there is competition among children which, incidentally, doesn't stop when they cease to be members of the household.

C: Right. Later on it's the inheritance.

A: Exactly.

D: Could I comment on that? I really couldn't agree with you more. I think there is a question here about the removal of affection and different levels of affection. That is, while I agree that it may be optimal——that certain kinds of authoritarian procedures in families on certain issues and in certain decision processes may be optimal. Still, it is an entirely different question as to what goes on, what value systems prevail in given families and how these value systems control the distribution of rewards.

LEIK: Regarding the question of affection in the family, the way I made the point earlier was there need *not* be a limitation on the affection available for distribution. Although, in fact, there may be plenty of limitations, I would not challenge that in the slightest. There may be a limitation on time available and that might be a coin by which affection is measured. There's certainly nothing wrong with that.

Now it might well be in the case where affection is a problematic circumstance (that is, not sufficient affection) that you get a kind of competitiveness under which the assumption is made that the better you do the more affection you ought to get. Some kind of a merit system operating. But where there is no real problem level of affection——there would no longer be any feeling that there is any relevance to a differential distribution.

C: I have a couple comments. Suddenly I thought they were very interesting. One is, I think you often get the push for equality and away from the proportional rewards according to merit whenever a merit system gets stiff or the socialization gets so botched up that people can't really move up that merit system. Sometimes it's a case of extreme competition and can lead to a kind of atomization phenomenon. For instance, the "tattling system" among Korean POW's or among drug addicts.

I think the same phenomena happens in the family when the parents attend tattling and punish the one who is tattled on. It can become a real vicious system that turns siblings not into rivals but into bitter enemies in many instances.

B: There has been insufficient attention given to sibling solidarity. It's quite possible that for two generations coexisting within the family their cohesion as a family is a partial function of their cohesion as cohorts and that this tattling phenomenon actually tends to break up the sibling solidarity that enables them to achieve equity in treatment for one another.

C: What you are suggesting is that this isn't so bad then?

B: The tattling? No, I'd be very much interested in seeing it studied, breaking down family solidarity as a concept into generational solidarity——family cohesion has been treated as a global variable.

D: You are saying we have to take into account the cohesion of subgroups but there is some evidence that the cohesion of subgroups can detract or subtract from the cohesion of the group as a whole. I think one of the problems is that the rivalry between siblings sometimes depends upon or develops as Freud suggests, essentially as a modus vivendi. The introduction of the value of fairness arises out of the intolerable war that just about threatens to destroy siblings.

B: My impression is that solidarity increases over time. Their age differences have less and less meaning as differentiators over time and this leads to an increased desire for equity so that relations are immeasurably better.

D: Well, there are two things that have to be considered there. One is the dislocation and separation of children as they get older. The other is the far more subtle and sophisticated ways that they have of expressing hostilities in competitiveness. This takes on, in my mind, formidable proportions.

B: It may get displaced into pure competition rather than into sibling competition. The sibs may actually take some satisfaction in the achievements of their sibs at a later point in their life whereas it would have been a source of real conflict earlier when the only source of approval was maternal.

F: This discussion puts me in mind of a study of visiting patterns among families in Italy. In the lower class the parents tend to be relatively aggressive as they are elsewhere, it could be that the establishment of warm and lasting ties with the parents are not possible. Parents are seen too much as a punitive object to be escaped from as quickly as possible and the sibs, therefore, become a main source of support to each other.

This links up with the point about the atomization phenomena which carries this aggressivity one step further. That is, when an individual has the ability to manipulate the structure of rewards, he can keep everyone from being trustful of everyone else, so they can't or won't organize in common against the demands he makes on them.

G: Does the preferential treatment of children by parents fall into that more moderate category? Does the creation of a scapegoat have it's own consequences?

F: Well, I think that breeds a sense of injustice where it isn't destructive. But while it is unfortunate, it's possible for the child to handle it by saying, "Well, clearly there's injustice in the world and I've got to reckon with it, but at least it has a lot of regularity."

D: That, I think, is the point. If it is regular, it might then become perceived as rational, justified. It becomes intolerable if it gets capricious.

You know, there's also the problem we haven't touched on regarding the sources of competition in life and that leads right to the tremendous divorce phenomenon.

E: Do you think it's mainly competition that produces divorce?

D: I think it's a large part of the story, don't you?

E: I don't know. . . .

A: I don't think that, but there's an interesting inverse of sibling rivalry that arises whenever marital conflict starts to become important in the family. Very commonly, if there's a child, one way of fighting is to compete for the child's response to you and that must create a kind of vicious circle which becomes quite intolerable and probably also increases the feeling of separation of the parents.

HAMBLIN: I was talking to Murray Straus the other day and he said the general conclusion in the family literature is that you should give your love noncontingently to children. All I know is that the phenomenon that we are getting in our research indicates that nonconditional rewards lead to what looks like very disturbed behavior.

D: We've gotten exactly the same results. If you establish two levels of merit and then you distribute an initial reward equally to both they react like hell.

E: Now, what are you saying?

D: Well, you know, I'm saying exactly what he's saying but I wouldn't have thought it would be present at such an early age.

A: Well, in American culture, the theme of fairness is very strong.

B: We have an equivalent in the University with the shifting from a grading system to a system of Pass–No pass.

G: Well, on this grade business, these are things which have been defined as things to be obtained by performance. It would be, to say the least, inappropriate to generalize from this that the obtaining of affection on noncontingent bases would result in disturbance. Unless, in fact, the family is programmed to come to believe this. There's no need for affection to be defined as something that should be gained.

D: That's the problematic issue that is well worth investigating.

B: Well, it's a pretty poor system that can't differentiate, at least verbally, between love and approval.

A: But a lot of the literature seems to imply that there is no contingent reward whatsoever required or involved in the system. All of it ought to be noncontingent. That is what he is objecting to.

E: I'm not objecting to it, I'm . . .

B: That's an ideology that is tied in with the mental hygiene movement and so on, but I know of no families that even begin to buy it. Parents don't feel love of their children all the time and in any kind of equitable way. So, the ideology's very difficult to apply. . . .

C: I think the way you define it is "well, you've always got a home and I'll always try to help you out in your problems," and so forth. Now, that's love at one level, but it doesn't necessarily indicate how you feel about the person——can you tell a child that you're never going to be angry at them and you're never going to be hostile toward them?

B: I should think not. I can't see that it's even convincing.

A: It doesn't have any opposition to love. Families are beginning to reconceptualize the relationship of permissiveness and control to affection. Children apparently regard it as a sign of love and interest if you keep correcting them, if you exercise "firm control" over them——although it's a little hard for a middle class parent who was raised in the older tradition—permissive—to realize that children regard that as a sign that you don't care about them. So, what constitutes the evidence of love is, after all, a very difficult thing to identify.

G: We could throw away the word "love" altogether and distinguish between consistently responsible behavior—taking care of necessity, providing confidence in the environment—and approval or disapproval.

D: It seems to me we're right now at the heart of the problem of socialization. What is——to use that familiar analogy, what is the diet?

I: On this issue of conditional love, if I recall this literature correctly——the withdrawal of love technique leads to very strong consciences.

B: Yes, but what kind of evidence?

I: Oh, it's all that awful correlational stuff.

B: Exactly——and the intervening set of contingencies that have been operating over the period of time between measures makes the so called "causal jump" absolutely impossible.

A: Furthermore, those correlations might really be picking up punishment and not love.

C: Exactly——I would interpret "if you don't do this, I won't love you" as a punishment rather than a reward. It's using love as a punishment.

I: Well, that's what I meant when I brought it up.

PART II—PROBLEM SOLVING UNDER STRESS

STRAUS: In the remaining time there's one topic which we haven't really covered at all. It is of considerable interest to this symposium and that's the question of problem solving under the conditions of *stress* or *crisis*. I wonder if you would have any comments on this.

HILL: Well, let me define stress in such a way that it might lead us to pick up an agreement or a disagreement with one of Karl Weick's assertions. That is, families or groups who encounter a new problematic situation for which their past training and experience is inadequate tend to choose an earlier, more primitive, way of solving the problem than they use with the general run of problems that they encounter. Is that a fair interpretation?

WEICK: Yes——that would be an implication.

HILL: Now, that makes the stress an unusual stress that can't be handled in the routine manner—a new situation for which the private culture brings inadequate solutions. Now, what I don't understand is why the family group doesn't use the method which is the best that they've learned?

ZELDITCH: If their normal coping mechanisms worked, you wouldn't have a high level of stress. Stress is an interaction of the coping mechanisms and the conditions. So you may be locating stress in just those cases where, somehow, the best coping mechanisms are regarded by the family as just not working or, in fact, they may not work. Furthermore, they have to intuit, somehow, that they don't work.

HILL: Alright, but looking at the family over time, I am wondering whether they are not actually strengthened by a crisis. Whether they are not better prepared for the next one. The first one is a real rugged one to take, but are they better able to take disability of the breadwinner or disability of the mother in the family? Are they better able to take another institutionalization because they've had one before? Now, Cavan and Rank's research on the crisis of relief and Angel's on war separation would seem to indicate that the previous experience with crisis is the best predictor of successfully facing a new crisis.

INKELES: There's a very difficult problem here. The families which survived the first crisis are those with a crisis capacity. Therefore, the fact that they survived the crisis is a very good predictor. But if the other families either dissolved or were for some other reason lost from the population that you're studying, then you're starting your prediction of further crisis capacity with a big selection factor built into your sampling frame.

ZELDITCH: Do you know the types of families which survived as families but failed the first crisis? According to the theory you've enunciated here, they should be better off the next time.

HILL: Well, not exactly. We have some retrospective reports—and there may be plenty of embroidering of their successes. But there does appear to be this curious kind of contradiction where a certain proportion of the families have been strengthened by prior crisis.

WEICK: Just a couple of nuances about the stress and regression issue. First of all, I think we ought to be careful to divest the notion of regression of any kind of negative connotations; it wasn't intended in that way. I'm really talking about stylistic differences. Secondly I think my assumption is that the best family strategy for solving a problem probably is also the most vulnerable one. Vulnerable in the sense that it's used infrequently. It's less habituated than the others. It is, relative to the others, more complex and requires more coordination in order to pull it off——such that under stress, some of those elegant interlockings dissolve and more elementary kinds of styles—those requiring really much simpler kinds of interaction and exchange rules—are the ones more likely to appear.

Now, in terms of your pointing out that some families are strengthened by the first crisis, I think what I need to know in order to get going on that would be whether in meeting that they retreated to one of these earlier or more habituated levels——or, whether, in fact, they stuck with the highest level that they had come up with. My hunch would be that the family that might doggedly stick to what is really an elegant solution strategy might be the one that doesn't make it through that crisis because the interlocking system just doesn't come off quite that well and they can't get the problem handled, as opposed to those who kind of pull back to a strategy that at least they can handle and kind of handle almost automatically.

HILL: I think these studies are inexplicit about that.

WEICK: Yeah. I think if we had information to tease that out then we would really know, I think, more about what this meeting the first crisis does to them.

LEIK: I would still like to come back to a model which is more concerned with the accommodation of a number of individuals than with something called a family. If you have a behavioral system which is of this sort and something comes up which in any way interdicts either the accomplishment of things which they collectively agree upon, or which makes someone who is after his own ends less willing to go along with the others, then it seems to me that you're in an area of individual psychology if you ask whether it affects the abilities of any of these people. And, in effect, Karl was saying that it shouldn't necessarily affect the abilities of the individual to go after his goals. The remaining question, then, is the manner in which they accommodate to each other. It would seem reasonable to suggest that to the extent that they manage to get by——where they no longer have the feeling of the degree of stress and are still able to accommodate to each other——then that means that this stress at least has not caused them any particular problems, and certainly may have shown them that it is possible to retain trust in each other and in their relationship. But if, in fact, the stress situation intrudes upon their interpersonal relations, it intrudes upon their accommodation procedures and they can't get around this, then that's a self-defeating cycle. So in this sense, it seems to me, and in the sense of the interpersonal accommodations of these people, the effect is cyclic in either direction. You succeed to the extent that you succeed in getting by this problem, you increase the competence of the collective operation. To the extent that you do not succeed in this problem, you are that much more hesitant to trust these relationships the next time around.

HILL: That's Cavan's second proposition——that well-organized families have a net improvement. Poorly-organized families before the crisis have a negative decrement.

LEIK: That's not exactly what I'm saying. You're saying there's a property of organization and that affects the result. I'm saying that, regardless of what the state was at this time, should they somehow weather the circumstance, they will be more competent in whatever organization they had.

PART III—SOME MISCELLANEOUS RESEARCH SUGGESTIONS

LEIK: I just wanted to briefly describe a research project that I am involved in because I think it is pertinent to a number of the issues that we have been dealing with. We're working on some six-person exchanges. Each member has the prerogative of inviting others into an exchange. It's quite free in the sense that you can invite anyone—you don't have to accept. When two people agree, they go to the exchange booth and insert identifying cards. In turn, they receive some play money which can later be converted to real money. The amount they receive is an average of the values assigned to the two players. Only they don't know that. All they know is that they go through a series of inviting, accepting, receiving something, and trying to figure it all out. The game stratifies very rapidly with some very interesting consequences. Anyway this is by way of background. What I was wondering is what the effects would be if you had couples playing such a game.

We could arrange a double stratifying situation—partially incompatible— where the rewards go to the individuals, but where they, as a couple, have to select another couple—for example, where the husband would want to go with couple "X," because the guy in that couple is valuable to him, but the wife wants to go with couple "Y." You might need to introduce some separate training procedures to get this going.

Now this might bring in two or three different things that we have been talking about. It would require some decision on the part of each couple. They would have the necessity of making some sort of evaluation of the relative importance of each person's contribution. But, especially if you also involved kids instead of just the married couples, what might be possible is that you'd have a real vehicle for finding out what the symbolic, linguistic, gestural ways are for demanding control of the system or for asserting the priority of a status on an external criterion. Things which would get in the way of any kind of autotelic situations. You know, using O.K.'s approach trying to get the family to play games where they can see themselves as learners. But most important, this might be a way of getting reversals of dominant status patterns, or whatever else. The important variable that should appear would be the extent to which the external criteria are methodically brought into this situation that you are trying to make free of the preexisting patterns of the family.

We have found that it stratifies rather quickly. As a matter of fact, it stratifies from the top down. The guys who were good for each other or for everybody soon find this out. Everybody starts selecting high value people and selectively refusing to invite or accept from people that are of less interest. Now, if this were so structured on the sex dimension, then you have a situation in which an entire range of problems come into play. There is a specific problem to be solved, there are the implicit problems of status and power and so on in the family, and there are the extrinsic factors that are making these things necessary.

HILL: It sounds like "The company you keep."

LEIK: That's right—that's the whole system.

ZELDITCH: Aren't there ethical questions about doing such things?

LEIK: Yes. But what I'm suggesting, though——now, I don't care whether this is the game or not, it's just a way of getting the problems on the board——is whether it's possible to pose a game that involves an external system, that involves external role relationships, and that requires analysis of the symbolization of what's going to be pertinent. It's perfectly clear in the Stanford work that the external status factors are going to be dragged in if you don't have a way of purposely keeping them out. They're going to be dragged in by a lot of visual cues, verbal cues and so on.

*   *   *

HAMBLIN: One of the problems of designing exchange systems is their sheer manage-ment. So to help solve that and to develop helping patterns among students, we have been working on an experiment that I would like to briefly describe. It's sort of idiocy to have one teacher try to teach everybody. Brighter students can effectively help the less quick ones. So we have been dividing our fourth graders into five subgroups and running them through five different conditions of group incentives. One group gets paid off according to what the three slowest members do, another by what the average does, and another according to the three top members. A fourth group is based on individual performance, where the rewards go to the individual——and the fifth, or control, group is a non-contingent condition. They get paid regardless.

Well, one of the really interesting things is that in all of the contingent reward conditions the kids are working hard, they are making good progress and they are at ease——you know, they are disappointed once in a while, but by and large they are doing well and getting along well.

The other interesting thing is what's happening in the noncontingent group. What we get there is a lot of what looks like very disturbed behavior. It doesn't show up the first day. It usually happens toward the end of the first week. This has happened in each of the subgroups, since we cycle each group through each of the conditions. They complain that the system is unfair. They fight among themselves quite a bit, they have fights with the teacher and with the principal ——they cry or sit around a lot.

ZELDITCH: Is this noncontingent with respect to performance?

HAMBLIN: Right. It only depends upon attendance.

HILL: Sounds like a daily allowance.

HAMBLIN: Right. Anyway, I thought you would be interested in this finding especially with respect to the ideal of a democratic parent-child relation.

*   *   *

LEIK: Competition and responsibility in family problem solving is what we're con-cerned about and the implication is that we need the latter and we don't want the former. Furthermore, as far as competition is concerned, you could avoid it if you could avoid zero-sum type situations, that is, if you could avoid motivation for power, reward, or whatever else, and, if you could avoid estimates by a particular actor that the degree of conflicting interdependency is high or that others' motivation for power or rewards is high.

Now, assuming that you do wish to avoid competitiveness—I'm not sure you always do but assuming that you do—one of the problems may be that the supply is restricted by actual shortage. There's not too much you can do about that unless you can find some way of increasing supply. Something like affection should not be a problem. Something like money might be. On the other hand, the supply might be artificially reduced to maintain a high value on power or to maintain status by maintaining a relative monopoly on the supply. Do we have to worry about this in family problem solving? Well, as Karl suggested there may be "unequal access to data," which is relevant here.

In problem solving the prime resource is access to data if you are, in fact, going to go after problem solving in some kind of reasoned manner. Now, it seems to me we have frequent responses in families of something like "because I said so, I know." This is specifically a case of artificially created shortage which has something to do with the likely feeling of competition in the decision. Assumptions about age/sex role differentials might also create shortage, for example, the assumption that a male knows more about business or about politics and the female knows more about child rearing. These are tendencies to restrict flow of information, which is basic to the decisions which are made, for the sake of retaining a role distinction or a presumed superiority based on that distinction.

Now, to the extent that power is obtained here, it seems to me that power is obtained by virtue of intentional hoarding. Insofar as this is problematic, it would imply that you really have to work out some way to get the family to share information. On the other hand, it's possible that it's a consequence of the perceived press of business, not really enough time to go through all this information sharing——so that somehow we would have to find a way of knowing when it's sufficiently crucial to get people to share information to avoid crippling competitiveness and when it doesn't matter and they can go ahead and say "because I know."

Turning to the unintentional power monopoly, it seems to me we get into an interesting bind between these two terms. Many parents feel that it *is* responsible on their part to maintain a power monopoly. If there is a power monopoly, there is competition implied in the power sphere by virtue of trying to be responsible and this might lead to unintended circumstances. So it might be reasonable to consider something like a game context—autotelic—where we could have intentional redistributions of power allowing freedom of decision without typical monitoring, typical veto of the usual powerful person, perhaps reversing power providing for reversing monitoring, letting the kids say "you can't do it that way Mommy" or something like that. This would allow changes in perspective within the family in a learning context but not necessarily an authoritarian one. Yet it could be containable so that you don't foul up the entire family process and family structure as a consequence.

Now this leads me to a comment about the democratic family structure that is so glowingly talked about in much of the family literature. It seems to me that it is reasonable to suggest that a democratic structure, especially with small kids in the family, is inefficient for many decisions. It may, in fact, be irresponsible in many cases and may cause more frustration than it does reduction of competitiveness, which is presumably its intent. So I don't think that it's necessarily the case to say that we always want to reduce competitiveness by having no power differential. Rather, there ought to be ways of allowing a feeling of greater flux in the power differential, perhaps by programming occasions when power can shift without its having serious consequences.

Such occasions provide for shifts in perspective. One consequence of this might be to avoid motivation to compete. Some of our research is relevant to this. Barbara Meeker, at Washington, has been doing some work on strategies in games. One of the things she's done is to identify five strategies. The rational strategy is maximizing one's own payoff. "Equitable" strategy—I can't remember the exact name——minimizes the difference between contributions you make to yourself and someone else. A competitive strategy is one which maximizes the difference between your contribution to yourself and your contribution to others. An altruistic strategy maximizes your contribution to the other, regardless of what you get. And a group-game strategy maximizes the sum of payoffs to both. Now, you can show that strategies tend to reciprocate——you know, argumentative strategies tend to get argumentation in return, and so on, unless there is a relative certainty that the other person's always going to be a patsy. Then you're likely to get a pretty self-oriented kind of behavior and play a kind of cutthroat rationality. Other than that, this reciprocity seems to hold. I think you can demonstrate mathematically, logically, and particularly you can demonstrate in actual game situations that a "rational" orientation or a self-orientation is defeated by competitiveness compared to group gains in many circumstances. The fact that you compete gets him competing and the fact that the two of you are competing means you're concerned with maximizing differences, not with gains——meaning that you waste a lot of resources and you reduce possible gains for yourself.

So one question might be, could a game-learning situation, such as above, provide a greater recognition of the self-defeating strategies of competitiveness versus an optimizing kind of strategy? Various benefits for the family might be: more pleasant interaction, avoidance of loss of general resources such as time and energy. If such knowledge is shared then we could expect competitiveness to extinguish. Then if it does appear, it seems to me an obvious symbol that there's something other than just individual involved. There's some kind of interpersonal hangup, some sort of squabble with another individual for other reasons, and that really ought to be a red flag. Then we start looking at problems of interpersonal relationships, since you could assume with adequate training in this kind of thing that people wouldn't choose a self-competitive approach if they were convinced that it was a losing strategy.

A Look Back at the Thematic Structure of the Symposium Reflections on the System of Research

THOMAS F. CONDON

The backward look at the symposium which follows is intended as a playful respite from the characteristic seriousness, and deliberateness of a scholarly volume. In the pages which follow I attempt to provide for the reader a kind of impressionistic summary of what transpired. This comes in the form of a series of thematic "collages"—seven in all—which represent some of the unintentional, synergistic outputs of the exchange.

The length, pace and oral form of the symposium were such that no one perspective could possibly control or master what transpired. Furthermore, while the quality of expertise was superb, there was not a great deal of overlap in the approaches taken by the participants. Consequently, a reading, which is tuned to the gaps, might find shirttails aflap in the breeze of disagreement, oversight, divergence, self-contradiction, and an occasional connection. But it is not a critical bent which I wish to communicate. Rather it is a sense of the collective work done—sometimes inadvertently—that is in focus. There are some very provocative "gestalts" to be gathered from the transcript. These all have a common characteristic, that is, they generate some self-conscious reflections on the research enterprise.

To use an analogy, the trip ahead is like a family outing. Halfway to the picnic grounds someone discovers that *someone else* forgot to bring the can opener. Some families, feeling the trip an utter loss, might turn back leaving their members wrapped in private disenchantment. Other families might, upon discovering the omission, decide to view it as a minor inconvenience and continue blithely on their ways. The strategy that I pick is one somewhere in between. I would want to make the most of the oversight, figuring that blame shouldn't be retroactive, yet wonder how or why it happened, what other omissions like this one have or might occur, and how can they be avoided. In other words, the spirit of this strategy is to divest errors and omissions of any serious personal consequences, yet to take them as symptomatic of potential trouble. This spirit is consistent with the knowledge that "we are just barely conscious of how unconscious we really are."

This "autotelic" approach seems quite necessary for two reasons. First, because the participants might legitimately wish to disavow the linkage between what they said, what was intended, what was recorded, and what survives in the written record. Secondly, because the reader, like the editor, has a distinct advantage over the members of the symposium. We are trimmed for reception and have the advantage of replays. They were, on the other hand, rigged for productivity in a hot media, and had to contend with the impersonal pace, compete for the floor, and so forth—all factors which taxed their mastery of what was going on.

Incidentally, this way of looking at the symposium leads to a suggestion for future symposia. That is, were we to accept Weick's judgment that much more goes on in an "interlocking" event than we may think, and then link this up with some of Moore's principles for "clarifying an environment," we might employ audiovisual recorders in order to secure a better living record of what transpired. These could then serve a number of purposes. They might be used on the spot to allow participant monitoring, feedback, and clarification for further discussion. The tapes could be searched for meanings at metalevels and, of course, they could be edited, copied, and then used as the published record. Anyway this suggestion might lead to some interesting shifts in professional perspectives. The shift would definitely be on the "down" side—less caution in "how to say what I want to say," more attention to what a professional demeanor says and omits.

Each of the seven themes begins with a series of excerpts or paraphrasings from the transcription. These are, on intuitive grounds, related to the central idea, yet suggest some unique facet of it. The basic image of my approach is that the organizing idea is a hub and each statement is a kind of spoke. If, in reading through quickly, you keep this central image in mind, then each comment might help to spin off some new aspect—to put the central idea in variable relief.

Following each collage is a brief commentary on the theme, which is intended as a mere suggestion for how the effect might be read. Recall, now, that there are four levels to the symposium.

1. The prepared papers,
2. The recorded and edited discussions of the papers,

3. The editor's commentary—attempting to provide additional angles and sketches of what transpired. This was possible through the advantage of reruns.

4. The thematic collages as an impressionistic summary.

Each level has its own logic and its own shortcomings; and the purpose, therefore, of producing discrete levels is to provide multiple criteria for homing in on the message.

THEME ONE: THE FOCAL/TACIT DIMENSION: THE SILENT LANGUAGE OF RESEARCH

. . . if there is a conflicting message . . . if you say something that has favorable content but you do it in a whining voice, or other *negative paralinguistic cues*, you will flub your semantic intent. . . .

. . . isn't there a lot more absenteeism in underdeveloped countries? . . .

. . . well, there's a myth to that effect . . . but it's not true. It's because the *rest of the package* hasn't been provided. . . .

. . . and I guess the *attitude* you take toward that question (using families in the lab) has a lot to do with the way you *feel*. . . .

. . . these surplus kinds of problems enter much more thoroughly into families with adolescents. . . .

. . . these comments are rather extreme, but they suggest that . . . families will be segmented, withdrawn, ineffectual and fatalistic. . . . Surely this is in strong contrast to typical laboratory groups . . . OR IS IT? . . .

. . . most of the kind of sociolinguists that I have been talking about assume that it's rather useless to make a dichotomy between language and social system . . . the relation between these levels is most obvious when there is a discontinuity between them.

. . . How do you recognize a game as a game? For instance, you show me a game that reduced ill-mannered behavior, and I could show you a game with the same mathematical structure that wouldn't work. The kids wouldn't like it. . . .

. . . there are several kinds of problems that they face other than the PRESENTED problems which take time to work out so that they can get to the MANIFEST problem. . . .

. . . you could show them really that, in fact, they're not responding to each other. You could do this with a tape recording. Show her that he's *not responding to the content* of what she is saying. . . .

. . . Until I began to think about sociolinguistics, I never realized that the Rosenthal *effect* was communicated. . . .

. . . she spent half the summer trying to make them want to learn. Deciding on something that they really wanted to do was the *major task*. . . . The thing that got them was something very imaginative, but *not something we could have predicted*. . . .

. . . for example, *we are stuck* in the social sciences with fields in which just getting acquainted with what's there is a long process with minimal deductive consequences. . . .

. . . Latin peoples are able to produce more elaborate forms of expression than many of the verbally constipated Americans. But this kind of skill is *not terribly useful* in a culture which gives prime emphasis on precision of expression. . . .

. . . a teacher may be patient for ten days in a row . . . after a while she says 'now goddamn it I've been patient enough—I can't——I just can't stand it anymore' . . . or the very typical thing that happens to an anthropologist . . . experiencing a kind of *culture shock.* . . .

. . . in lab groups, problems *seem* to come in more discrete, specifiable fashion than may be true in families. . . .

. . . everytime our family starts to discuss a problem the LATENT content of the discussion is really "what are my rights". . . .

. . . compared to any natural social situation, what the laboratory reproduces is only selected aspects of the real world . . . what we will want to see, therefore, is just why laboratories are simplifications; and how . . . such simplifications can be made to say anything about more complicated natural settings. . . .

Of the seven themes, this one is the most central in importance. The main idea is that there is a vast, shadowy underworld of social meaning and significance. We tend to ignore this either because it is too familiar or habituated, or because its proportions exceed our sensible limits.

There are several ways in which this theme is important. First, at the present stage of social science development the percentage of relevant meanings and significances which we have been able to reconstruct into theoretical properties is minimal. So the symposium points us in the direction of discovering some new domains of variation—for example, surplus problems, background information, and so forth. Second, the tacit elements which are closest to our attention are the most likely candidates for reconstruction. So some attention to the ways in which this theme is developed might produce something more than the obvious in our research nets. Finally, the ways in which each participant gets at these underlying properties is tied up with his own brand of methodology. This suggests the need for a multimethod approach on the assumption that methods are complementary.

One way to portray this theme is to suggest an image like the following: (a) A multidimensional scale: ROCKS, ROSES, "RIGHTS"; (b) for which there are three key dimensions (1) the stability of the relation between the phenonenon and our representation of it, (2) the stability of generalizations from one representation to other members of the class, and (3) the social significance of the phenomenon. Our observations with respect to rocks are highly reproducible, general and trivial (except, say, in the case of a geologist). With respect to rights, the linkages between something observable and our representations of it is very complex, relies heavily on the observer's dispositions, and thus tends to be culturally or individually relative; these also tend to be of considerable consequence. The situation with respect to roses is somewhere in between. For while there is something clearly observable about a rose, the subjective significance attached to a rose is quite variable—"a rose is a rose is a rose . . .".

Several of the elements in the beginning of this collage suggest the kinds of things which might happen as we move down the scale toward *rights*. The suggestion that paralinguistic cues can enhance or contradict semantic intent indicates various levels of communication that differ in the degree of awareness on the part of the sender, and the degree of appreciation on the part of the receiver. Furthermore, there is the suggestion, particularly in Gumperz presentation, that the paralinguistic level is the more significant, but less attended, aspect.

Just why this may be so is hinted at in another element of the collage. Moore stated that in social science we are *stuck* with relatively *less productive* cultural contents. The connotation that "being stuck" carries is a kind of impatience with the significant but quagmirish contents of social science, and a sense of urgency to find the kinds of contents which our general scientific methods can handle. That is, there is a natural tendency to assimilate the representational tools which were developed for studying "rocks" and then to search the other end of the scale for contents which can be managed with those tools.

Robert Leik provides an example of this tendency when he questions, "Surely this is in strong contrast to typical laboratory groups . . . OR IS IT?" Leik was comparing the eleven properties that Weick had listed for family groups with his own experiences in the laboratory. His question indicates that the properties may have been operating in his lab groups but had been treated as noise.

Another aspect of this theme is that the tacit dimension may hold a lot more promise for eventual payoff than the focal dimension (although the reverse is true from the individual "career" angle) but will require some kind of reordering of scientific rules. Gumperz described a project by one of his students that produced a remarkable effect. But, while it was very imaginative, "it was not something we could have predicted." The scientific "superego" demands a mode of research which is precise, logical, and replicable. The sociological imagination, on the other hand, allows for a mode which is, in addition, creative, intuitive, and visceral.

As you think about this distinction, you begin to appreciate what Moore meant by "productive" cultural contents. They are the class whose members have been successfully represented, studied, used, mapped, and so forth and participate, therefore, in a well-established rhetoric. They are, in addition, that slice of social life which can be reproduced in the form of technology. The question naturally follows, "Just how much of the total pie of social life can be considered as productive?" The impression that one is left with, after evaluating the estimates contained in the symposium, is that the slice is very, very small.

This image of the focal-tacit theme, whereby we begin to self-consciously attend to some of these underlying dimensions and consequently shift the mode of doing science, suggests a different "hierarchy of knowledge" than the one offered by Weick in his paper. Briefly, there are two things wrong with Weick's borrowed hierarchy as it applies to social science: it is too *individual* and it is too much in the *head*. The first failing is relative to the phenomenon under study. Two questions point to the deficiency: What kind of *research system* is required to adequately represent some social system of interest? What kind of research system is needed to *generalize* across members of the same class as the social system of interest?

The second shortcoming occurs on the side of doing—that is the problem of internal-external validity. The question is, when dealing with social, as opposed to physical, processes, what are the risks involved in making generalizations. Zelditch, for instance, admires the power of experiments and their attendant assumptions, which can be used to be informative about one's theory. The theory in turn is informative about more general processes. Hamblin, on the other hand, feels that generalization is ill-advised, unless you *actually perform* the experiment on the new target population. In short, social science may be much more dependent on validity replications than sciences which lie toward the "rock" pole.

Gumperz illustrates this problem of generalization when he states that it's "rather useless to make a dichotomy between language and social system," at least if one is interested in the social uses of language. He argues that Chomsky approaches grammar from the biological side and arrives at a theory of *grammar* which is devoid of cultural content, and which is general. But a theory of usage, where all of the simplifying assumptions are unwarranted, depends on a careful analysis—a "doing" as opposed to "thinking"—of the social system boundaries of a class of users.

In a very real sense, social science is caught in a bind between the forces of legitimation, where methodology calls the tune, and the forces of relevance where experiences are absolutely essential. This dimension of tacit-focal languages of research, then, poses a whole series of problems or choices for a self-conscious social science:

1. To take on as scientific content problems which are culturally central (that is, are relatively discrete and specificable) or those which are in the background culturally (that is, opaque and quagmirish).

2. Treating, in Simon's terms, social science decisions as *design* problems and not merely as *choice* problems, creating routines which fit the demands of the environment.

3. Taking small theoretically manageable risks or relying on intuitive grounds as a basis for producing robust but relatively inexplicit effects.

4. Being comfortable in a culturally homogeneous workshop or allowing for degrees of "culture shock."

5. Restricting attention to strictly manifest or instrumental issues or of adjusting our constraints to occasionally allow expressive content to enter.

6. Representing the research process as serious and sacred or as playful, tolerant, and occasionally ludicrous.

7. Divesting our behavioral laboratories of contaminating social influences in order to be productive, or adjusting our scientific timetable, allowing it to reflect the kinds of processes we seek to understand.

8. Treating "surplus" or "presented" problems as the main text of inquiry.

9. Accepting existing attitudes or orientations or questioning their metaphoric roots. That is, without questioning the value of a general scientific method, what adjustments should be made in our expectations as we shift our focus from rocks to rights?

THEME TWO: RESEARCH AS A SOCIAL SYSTEM COORDINATED TO ITS RESEARCH ENVIRONMENT

. . . social scientists generally have taken one of several modes . . . detectives who go around solving puzzles, or inventors who provide expert solutions for people in trouble. . . .

. . . has written a nice critique of laboratory work saying that it's pretty "blah" because we have no powerful contingencies operating. . . .

. . . the modern small group researcher has set his intellectual sights pretty low. . . .

. . . the whole orientation, historically, of *behavioral* science has used (a mode) that is appropriate to the *natural* sciences which have passive subject matter that you can treat like a puzzle. . . .

. . . researchers tend to be a homogeneous lot and they tend to make (ethnocentric) assumptions. . . .

. . . What about somebody who has been slighted on games of strategy? Well, if he were a behavioral scientist . . . but his favorite models did not include *games of strategy*, he would have a hard time conceptualizing . . . understanding . . . the whole Meadian scheme of "significant other." He would tend to look at the world, say, as a detective. . . .

. . . it's a *strategic* question as to what kinds of definitions we should be giving our labs. . . .

. . . a group-game strategy maximizes the sum of payoffs to both (subject and researcher). And you can show that the *strategies tend to reciprocate.* . . .

. . . Games of strategy allow you to take the role of "reciprocal other." You can't play a game of strategy without putting yourself into the position of the other player . . . he is not a pattern of dead variables . . . you can't treat him as if he were a bug. . . .

. . . the capacity to experiment depends on a particular kind of social structure . . . always on some sort of authority structure in which the scientist has power over the subject. This social structure produces effects that are not found in natural settings. . . .

. . . this project is approximately ten years old and . . . this is a *team* effort . . . we think of ourselves as being about halfway through. . . .

. . . we pay a heavy price to not concentrate fully on the math or technology etc. . . . but the overall sense of BALANCE of a program is *terribly important.* . . .

. . . five years ago it finally got through to me that the middle class does not want change. . . .

. . . these more powerful designs allow you to both test your theory and at the same time provide *expert* solutions to the problems that ongoing groups have. . . .

. . . is it more important to know the *highest* template that (a research system) has evolved . . . or is it more important to know how many different kinds of templates are applied. . . .

. . . the Transfer Room is an area for group learning . . . where group structures form, which will eventually undertake *superordinate* tasks . . . without the Transfer Room the individual training in the booths *doesn't work.* . . .

. . . without these strategic definitions people get confused . . . hostile . . . possibly frightened . . . producing error variance all over the place. . . .

. . . with recurrent problems we tend to work out habit structures to provide standardized solutions . . . these become disrupted *only* when gross negative feedback occurs. . . .

This collage centers on the developmental question of the "efficacy" of the social system of social research. It's not too surprising that a symposium which began with a rather critical assessment of modern social research would take this theme up as one of major importance. But the manner in which it is treated is somewhat surprising. More often than not, a comment which addresses the theme was ignored altogether or quickly shunted aside. Perhaps as Zelditch argues in his paper, research is heavily dependent upon a social structure which is not itself questioned. There is not, therefore, a readily available vocabulary for discussing the properties of research systems.

By taking advantage of the opportunity for reruns, however, it is possible to identify a number of subthemes. These are:

1. The suggestion that the researcher-researched relation is subject to a developmental process: from a one-sided puzzle-solving perspective to a strategic transactional perspective.

2. A growing recognition of some of the threats to such development and, consequently, some sense of the importance of balance in the enterprise.

3. An increasing concern for the coordination of properties of the research system with the properties of the particular kind of subject matter.

4. The identification of competing modes for the conduct of social research.

5. The necessity of providing feedback mechanisms whereby productive research outputs become inputs to our working assumptions.

The overall image conveyed by these subthemes is like that of a long hazardous expedition with a potentially mutinous crew. Such a mission obviously requires individual discipline to the superordinate task, but this has a breaking point, where at least some of the members' wishes and needs require attention. There is a need to establish intermediate goals to sustain morale, but these carry the possibility of getting sidetracked, such as some alluring isle. Expeditions require some routinization, but this poses the danger of developing habit structures which may blind us to the recognition of our objective. Finally, there is always the risk that when we arrive at our destination the hosts may not be altogether friendly.

The question of relations between scientist and subject has a number of facets. First of all there is the problem of building some mutually acceptable definitions of social research. Without such definitions our research paraphernalia produce all sorts of error variance of unknown proportions. Furthermore, some attention should be given to the nature of the exchange involved. Secondly, as Moore pointed out, our subject matter has, in addition to the possibility of reactivity, an active side. Leik suggests how this might affect outcomes when he states that relational strategies tend to reciprocate. The implications are obvious. If we treat subjects as if they were bugs or dead variables, they might play dead, or refuse to participate, or produce some other distortion.

The problem of balance in a research program indicates that research is a complex of tasks or routines which require some overall coordination. These routines run from selection of a problem, securing of funds, and so forth to the selected type of analysis and presentation of results. Some choices within each routine are better established than others, but not necessarily more appropriate. So the problem is choosing, at the various choice points of an enterprise, routines which can fit together while still preserving the fidelity of the environment.

The concern for coordination between research-unit and study-unit hinges on the problem of adapting general scientific methods to particular kinds of subject matter. For example, there are two peculiarities of our study units which stand out; they are *collective* units which vary according to *sociocultural* patterns. The first peculiarity suggests the need for some kind of collective research unit hinted at in what Moore called a "team effort"— adequate to the mapping of the study unit. The second peculiarity, captured in the distinction between internal and external validity, also argues for some kind of collective research unit, extended, this time, in space. In other words, the issue of coordination raises the problem of some degree of proportionality between the system of inquiry and the target of study, considered both in terms of its structural complexity and its subjective significance.

Hamblin, for one, alerted us to the idea of different modes of doing social science. His remarks narrow down to a choice of assigning priority to "theory testing" or to "producing an effect." The suggestion is that if we choose the more traditional theory testing we are also choosing a one-sided puzzle-solving relation between researcher and researched. Such a choice would be developmentally regressive, on the assumption that we could take a "strategic" perspective. On the other hand, assigning priority to the ability to produce an effect implies an attempt to balance:

1. the scientist-subject relationship: equitable exchange.
2. intuition and the possibility of an adequate, reconstructed theory. One of the unfortunate properties of a formal theory is that it is insensitive to ethnocentric assumptions on both sides of the research relationship.

Some of the curious properties of social science are that acquired knowledge of human functioning accumulates from an *inferior* knowledge base, applies as much to the *inquirer* as to the subject, and can therefore be used to improve the knowledge base from which further inquiry is built. This evolutionary sense of science as a self-conscious process points to the need for providing feedback mechanisms whereby productive outputs become inputs to our working assumptions. This of course raises the problem of balance from a new angle. For example, the next collage suggests some of the limits on our perspective which would interfere with our ability to produce or handle feedback. But the central issue addressed here is how to plug new information—such as Piaget's genetic epistemology—into our basic working assumptions and still direct attention to our scientific routines.

THEME THREE: COGNITIVE LIMITS ON OUR PERSPECTIVE

. . . the problem that we faced from the outset had to do with realism . . . how much should the thing you do in the lab look like the thing you are trying to represent. . . .

. . . unfortunately one aspect of our project has overshadowed all others producing a severe distortion in the perception of what we're up to. . . .

. . . if attention span is heterogeneous among members, what might the effect be in terms of how long the problem solving discussion continues. . . .

. . . surely this is in strong contrast to typical laboratory groups . . . or is it?

. . . in general, we would claim that to omit a major class of folk models or perspectives would conceptually handicap the social scientist severely. . . .

. . . an autotelic environment is the best sort for learning complex material . . . where anxiety levels don't reach such a high level. . . .

. . . there is the notion of hierarchies of knowledge processes from more primitive to more complex, more complicated, and more vicarious forms. . . .

. . . the notion that it is independent (motoric) action which is crucial in learning is not so far fetched . . . Piaget emphasizes the crucial importance of the child's *action* in the development of cognition. . . .

. . . where problems are sufficiently recurrent that we can do so, we work out habit structures. . . .

. . . is it more important to know the *highest template* that a (research) group has evolved or *how many different kinds* of templates are applied to a problem. . . .

. . . the adequacy of a *simultaneous, that is a group, solution* depends on whether enough common terms appear . . . all those factors, like low energy level, etc., will tend to reduce the number of 'other' terms. . . .

. . . the paper is decidedly biased toward the role of retrospect in gathering meaning . . . often times you'll solve something before you——even realize that you had a problem. . . .

. . . I wonder if you don't see the possibility of maybe relaxing that assumption a little bit. . . .

. . . the real difficulty is, when you bring families into the lab, of starting to think concretely about them. . . .

. . . in the "solution-oriented" group, a proposed solution gets immediately evaluated, as opposed to *our wondering why* anybody brought it up in the first place. . . .

. . . the point being that if you look at some of these unique properties you find that certain variables *have not been looked at* thoroughly. . . .

. . . this factor of embedded problem solving alerts you to what happens to people who are trying to solve problems when they're working on other kinds of activities concurrently. . . .

. . . you bring them into the laboratory and there's a whole new set of cues . . . they look at the mike, they look at the mirror, they look at the experimentor . . . everything . . . and they construct *new* meanings around them. But this is not part of the decision making situation of the home. . . .

What is of general interest in this theme is the explicit attention given a number of factors which figure as limits, constraints or "blind spots" in human perspectives. Some of the comments were directed explicitly toward the researcher (realism) while others were aimed at the subjects (attention span). Regardless of the intended target, all of the observations carry implications for both sides of the relationship. Therefore they figure as factors of major uncertainty in the research process itself.

Looking at the issue from an interactive point of view—that is, some research process reciprocally linked to some subject process—it is apparent that the social sciences really have a badly confounded problem. Not only is there a problem of *reactivity* on both sides of the relationship, but our subjects are highly *active*. In the transcription this activity problem was described in the section on "place cues" or "private" culture—that is, the tendency to construct "new" meanings in our labs. In other words, social science has to cope with all the cognitive-affective hangups of science in general, plus it has to cope with a material which is ecologically highly variable, extremely subjective and particularized, and just barely perceptible.

Another slant to this problem of interaction is that these limits—on both sides—are a chronic threat to the emergence of viable group structures. While some scientific endeavors (such as comparative psychology) do not seem to imply much in the way of collective research structures, besides a common culture, it appears that social science does. Our natural cognitive limits are therefore impediments to be reckoned with in building appropriate structures.

There are several suggestions for tentatively "clarifying" some of these problems, in the interest of hastening the pace of development. If we use "habit structures" to refer to our current state, then two kinds of things can be done to overcome our present limits. The first allows for some new learning to occur. Since learning occurs under conditions where anxiety, for one thing, is at an optimal level (which means relatively free from evaluative monitoring), then it would seem necessary to provide for frequent "autotelic" opportunities in the paradigm. Second, since habit structures require feedback if they are to be responsive to external conditions, then we need to build in lots of provision for such exchanges—both on our side and between sides. In short, we need periodic exchanges among the diverse array of researcher perspectives (this symposium was such an instance) and occasional access to how research is going over with our subjects.

Developmentally, it was suggested that there are stages to this problem of our cognitive boundaries. Moore established contact with these in his discussion of the four folk models and their permutations. The sequence implied in that discussion indicates at least two stages: the twin-born stage of agent-patient perspectives, followed by the ability to sustain a self-other, strategic system. Another way to look at this is to consider the earlier stage as an "adversary" type of role relation—a pervasive type in our culture, such as legal, forensic, conjugal, and so forth. The adversary role assumes one member of a two party system is right (while the other is wrong) and that this can be demonstrated on the basis of some established standard or criteria. The more advanced stage, on the other hand, building upon and not necessarily replacing the earlier one, assumes less shortage of outcome (group gain) and a subjective, superordinate criteria (consensus, compromise).

In all, then, the collage of cognitive limits on research perspectives suggests five subthemes. These are:

1. There are natural cognitive limits, or limiting tendencies, shared by all individuals, whether researcher or researched, on perspective-taking ability—for example, shortness of attention span, "realism" or concreteness, puzzle solving one-sidedness.

2. The effect of these natural limits, on our ability to adequately represent stimuli, depends upon the nature of the external stimuli with which we interact, such as solution orientation, adequacy of habit structures, relation between doing and thinking.

3. These individual limits also have consequences for the amount of group work (on both sides) that can be accomplished—adequacy of simultaneous solutions, embedded problems, flexibility in the use of available templates.

4. There are several hints for coordinating situational properties with the type of work being performed. For example, learning new material, or creative exploration, is best done under autotelic conditions, where constraints are relaxed and evaluative anxiety is low.

5. Finally, a suggestion was made for a developmental sense of research perspectives, such as hierarchies of knowledge processes, strategic perspectives, experience with all the major classes of folk models.

THEME FOUR: THEORY AND THE SOCIAL SCIENCES

. . . What's important about the experimental process is not control . . . but the fact you are simplifying the processes that you are studying. . . .

. . . now language can be used to construct theories . . . this is what psycho-linguists have done . . . however, while they can tell us what *grammars* look like, they can't tell us what speech behavior looks like . . . we can study a system in this manner only so long as we make it *artificially simple*. . . .

. . . The purpose in part is to *simplify*, somehow, a theoretical process and abstract it from other processes, and produce that in the lab . . . then your problem is to apply (generalize) the theory to natural situations. . . .

. . . Now I believe that even if we were able to state any abstract principles of problem solving and applied them in any particular situation . . . *the part of the total variance* that we could explain would be very, very modest indeed because we would have *simplified* across a very large number of situations. . . .

*   *   *

. . . the implication being . . . if you accept one of these metaphors, then you're going to look at the family in a particular way . . . and one *ought to be alert* to that. . . .

*   *   *

. . . underlying the whole argument is the issue "what is the field of family sociology . . . what is the subject matter." . . .

. . . but there are problems that are peculiar to the family and these may or may not have a general solution. . . .

. . . the only thing really characteristic of the family is the peculiar combination of all these properties . . . actually I hadn't thought about it before, but one of the interesting properties is the *structural problem of families shifting through time* . . . I can't think of another system which has that property. . . .

*   *   *

. . . his basic image is the *communicating individual* operating under certain constraints, and, as I see it, sociolinguistics is a way of describing these communicative constraints. . . .

*   *   *

. . . we don't have anything that we're willing to call a theory, that meets the standards for theory construction . . . instead our efforts have been largely in the direction of coming up with *guiding principles* to help direct our efforts, and that's harder than you might think . . .

. . . he's not willing to call it a theory, but I would . . . he hasn't tested everything individually, what he's done is this engineering thing which produces *very robust effects.* . . .

*   *   *

. . . if a considerable amount of development changes are going on through certain periods in the family, essentially what you have are relative groups of strangers coming together in order to work on problems. . . .

*   *   *

. . . the goals of linguistic analysis deal with the strategies of behavior and not with the consequences . . . we're not *immediately* concerned with evaluating whether a certain kind of behavior is functional or not. . . .

. . . I've been beaten many, many times with the response well, it's a mistaken assumption . . . their language isn't more *impoverished*, it's just different . . . well, I don't *believe* that . . . I believe that on certain measures which are quite *standard.* . . .

. . . I think that we're beginning to know why these (intervention) programs don't work . . . this whole business of *enrichment* doesn't work because it's too grammatical . . . you see *they speak a language which we don't understand.* . . .

. . . now, on this issue of "deficit" or "different" . . . I would want to begin with the question of definition . . . what we need are whole families of meaning for things like performance. . . .

*   *   *

. . . merely to point to variations and suggest that these might make a difference, although it's a nice game for a critic to play doesn't advance science . . . one should make such observations only if he has a relatively specific theory which he feels would produce substantial differences. . . .

*   *   *

. . . there is no point in pretending that theories are always well formulated, definite and complete, or their variables always clearly general. . . .

. . . usually, at any particular time, it is only part of "T" (a theory), which is being investigated: one variable is being investigated while others are held constant. It, therefore, requires not one but a *whole program* of experiments to establish "T." . . .

This package of issues is concerned with the meaning and uses of "theory" in social sciences: its construction, its point of appearance in an investigation, and its relation to intuition on the one hand, and to logic on the other. Some of the synonyms and relatives employed in the text indicate the range of meanings associated with theory: metaphors, models, apperceptive mass, heuristic device, intuition, formal properties, basis of generalization, and "specific" theory. With this range of meaning, and the relevant contexts for each element in the range, it's fair to say that there is not a great deal of agreement among the participants as to the precise referent of theory. Nevertheless, each participant seems to have given it a central place in his definition of what the sociological enterprise ought to look like.

Zelditch's paper, for instance, rotates on the existence of a relatively precise theory which would specify relevant things to model, and then serve as the basis for generalization. He also states that "we don't have very many of these." Moore is critical of Hamblin's classroom games on the grounds that Hamblin doesn't have an adequate mathematical map to distinguish successful games from unsuccessful ones. Yet in describing his own project, Moore acknowledges a similar deficit when he states "we don't have anything that we're willing to call a theory." Robert Leik studiously attempts to avoid "conceptual quagmires." Still, he had recognized that this led him to treat a number of Weick's eleven properties as "noise" in his prior lab experiences.

One use for theory, which ordinarily does not come up, is suggested in one of Inkeles' remarks to Zelditch regarding the role of "critic." The use is, to put it crassly, "to beat up on someone," with the effect of leading to a kind of defensive paralysis. The remark seems to point to the need for appropriate delicacy in the handling of someone else's conceptual scheme. It's much easier to find flaws in a scheme than to build one, so unless one has a relatively specific theory, which would make a substantial difference, one ought not to play that role—at least not vigorously. On the other hand, Inkeles acknowledges the essential role of the critic in the advancement of science. So, the point that comes out of this seems to be twofold: the strength of counter-suggestions be scaled to the degree of fragility of the linkage between conceptual representations and the problematic character of the external system under study; even where it is appropriate, it probably should be divested of any long-term personal (such as career) consequences. This second point gets at one of the consequences of criticism: a reluctance to jeopardize one's career by taking risks—being vulnerable—even where there is a possibility of some scientific payoff.

To paraphrase Zelditch, if you assume that "how you *feel* has a lot to do with the *attitudes* you take," for example, toward the use of families in the lab, then a good deal more attention ought to be paid to the "tacit dimensions" of how we feel. These are, if you will, ascribed or inherited properties—Zelditch called them "particular kinds of social structure"—which determine, in large part, our attitudes. They are, furthermore, relatively unmonitored and inaccessible, so that the attitudes we take, are, at worst, highly ethnocentric and superficial.

Several comments serve to illustrate how several radically different "attitudes" might be applied to the same question. The question being addressed, by several discussants, was that of "simplification." The difference in attitudes can be attributed to the kinds of stresses one applies to various tasks within the total enterprise. Zelditch appears to stress the importance of theory construction—getting clear on what goes with what. But this attitude tends to suppress the problem of "applying the theory to natural situations."

Inkeles' comment illustrates the bind in this approach: an increase in clarity comes at the price of a decrease in explanatory power applied to the varieties of natural situations. The importance of this point cannot be over emphasized.

Gumperz' comment gives us a sense of the dimensions of the problem. He indicates that the grammarian's theory can be used as a model for developing a theory of speech behavior. The grammarian's theory assumes a universal, biologically programmed, linguistic capacity. Usage patterns, on the other hand, are particularized social conventions. Thus a theory of usage patterns is a more difficult undertaking, requiring some compromises between abstraction or simplification and attention to local detail. As Zelditch remarked in the context of the argument over natural versus artificial situations, we are always compromising between these two extremes and the hope is, through a whole series of researches, that we can get better and better at understanding what is going on.

To sum up:

1. Theory is an interaction between our powers of representation and the nature of the subject matter under investigation.

2. Given the intractable nature of our subject matter, and our meager powers of representation (cognitive limits), it seems unwise to allocate a large slice of our resources to the task of reconstructing our (surface) representations.

3. The alternatives, which tend to get surpressed when theory construction is stressed, include the following:

  a. To design systems which can produce robust, ameliorative, or other desirable effects, even in the absence of theory.

  b. To relax our constraints and give some play to hunches, intuition, and so forth, as guiding principles or metaphors.

  c. To invest more effort in field work, testing and adjusting working principles, and overcoming the ethnocentrism of our tacit assumptions.

  d. To attend to the structural requirements for a long range, programmatic approach to theory construction.

  e. To allocate some energy to the theoretical specification of those properties (across the basic data domains), which *others* could use, to produce desirable outcomes.

THEME FIVE: SAMPLING FROM THE BASIC DATA DOMAINS

. . . with respect to the type of tasks and the situation of administration, I would argue for a strategy where you vary them as systematically as you can. . . .

. . . it's a mistake to take a one-institutional approach. For instance, there's such an intimate relation between school and family processes that it's hard to consider the health of the child in one setting without considering the other. . . .

. . . I think you can get confused, when talking about the effects of rewards on behavior, between "performance" criteria and the notion of "competence." . . .

. . . now it seems to me that there is strictly too much assumption that you can *select samples* (of families) without knowing a great deal of *background information*. . . .

. . . he's not willing to call it a theory, but I would . . . it has a very formal quality that *social scientists are not accustomed to* . . . he's beginning to discover what the operating characteristics of the human organism are. . . .

. . . it's a situation which is very heavily dependent on the structure and effectiveness of a *larger system*. . . .

. . . the paper has raised a series of questions (interpersonal accommodation) which are *logically prior* to more typically studied questions of family problem solving. . . .

. . . have you reworked the correlations holding social class constant? . . . because these patterns may have become so widely diffused in the middle class . . . that what you seem to be *explaining* you are not in fact explaining. . . .

. . . it's really improper to generalize any experimental results without performing the same experiment in another situation, and demonstrating that it will hold the second time. . . .

. . . here the suggestion is made that a more appropriate laboratory technology is, for want of a better word, the generational kind of study. . . .

. . . there are two sources of irrelevant variability . . . you are always compromising between these two extremes (artificial-natural) . . . and you get better and better theoretical understanding of what is going on. . . .

. . . I don't think that any serious anthropologist would say that it's possible to describe a culture . . . we can describe *domains in cultures* . . . but only as long as we keep the boundaries flexible. . . .

. . . if, eventually, you want to make a statement of the *general principles* of problem solving, that should be a summation of what we have learned in a variety of different problem solving *situations*. . . .

. . . the idea that one experiment will produce for you all the results you want is one of those myths . . . that sociologists have. . . .

. . . the point isn't that they treated our *place cues* differently from theirs, but that they did so *predictably*. . . .

. . . I would still like to come back to a *model* which is more concerned with the *accommodation* of a bunch of individuals than with something called a family. . . .

. . . one of the main themes of my paper is that if we are going to understand what is going on . . . we should study *everyday behavior*. . . .

. . . the third principle of experimentation is varying the environment in such a way as to generate . . . not only different . . . but *predictably* different . . . forms of behavior. . . .

. . . researchers tend to be a homogeneous lot and they tend to make (ethnocentric) assumptions. . . .

The main effort in this collage is to identify a set of basic data domains,[1] from each of which any piece of research samples, and a set of issues which extend and amplify the notion of data domains. The six data domains can be described as follows:

Subjects (Referees). Members of this domain are the mediators between the inputs and the outputs of the research process. Nevertheless, as Moore argues, we tend to treat members of this class as if they were "patterns of dead variables." This attitude is conveyed by the connotation of the label which we apply to them (Cattell, for instance, chooses to call them "referees" rather than "subjects").

Gumperz maintained that we cannot meaningfully sample from this domain without first conducting a careful ethnographic study in order to identify population boundaries. The "place cues" controversy focused a considerable amount of attention on the referees, and was more or less resolved by Inkeles, who suggested that their reactivity or puzzlement would be manageable "if we knew the culture."

Researchers. Of all the domains, this one is, perhaps, the most understudied. Nevertheless, several commentaries pinpointed the types of questions which would be relevant here. Hamblin distinguished two competing role models for the conduct of social science: scientist and inventor. Moore stated that any social scientist who was not conversant with the strategic folk model would be unable to symbolically interact with his subjects. Weick identified several stylistic factors which would distinguish between members of this class: cognitive constraints, and factors affecting his selection of a metaphor.

Type of Research Setting. In the general discussion a number of comments touched on the contextual issue of the research setting. Hill, for example, wondered about the best possible setting for studying problem solving in the family. Responses to his query indicated a basic dilemma: assuring a meaningful setting for the subject comes at the cost of observer control. Leik indicated a related difficulty when he suggested that our training programs may be relevant but unacceptable to some classes of referees. Inkeles pushed this problem of setting—whether natural or simplified—even further along with several comments. When discussing absenteeism he remarked that the "total package" hadn't been provided. While discussing Helen Bee's paper he referred to "milieu effects." Both of these comments suggest that the meaning of a research environment requires some attention to a total web of meaning.

Moore provided several distinctions for identifying some immediate properties of the setting: test-like, anxiety producing, clarifying.

Theory (Metaphor). The data in this domain is a congerie of dimensions which can be subsumed under the question "what are the constraints on and

---

[1] The idea of data domains is indebted to Raymond B. Cattell, and the identification of some of the issues surrounding them is indebted to Donald T. Campbell.

the properties of the representations employed by participants in the research enterprise (such as observers and subjects)?" This domain has been treated separately in the preceding collage.

Stimulus-Response. The elements which are grouped in this domain are the focal behaviors of the observer and his subjects. They are what are typically called "variables". Moore attempted to distinguish several subclasses of this domain in his discussion of puzzles, games of chance and so forth. He also called attention to potential troubles when we make inferences from behavior to underlying structures (for instance his difference between competence and performance). Following a similar line of reasoning, Bee threw in a note of caution about the relation between language and thinking.

Zelditch invested a major part of his effort in the clarification of this domain. His insistence on "properties" as opposed to concrete entities touched not only members of this domain, but others as well.

Time. The dimension which defines this domain is that of time. This factor enters into the research puzzle in a variety of ways. Weick, for instance, in his discussion of a "developmental confound," used time as a process variable. Zelditch used time as a phenomenal constraint when he remarked about the myth that one-shot studies can get at all the answers. Inkeles used time as a way of partitioning rewards, for instance, immediate versus delayed, and as a way of classifying training procedures, for example, full time versus part time.

Crosscutting all of these data domains is a series of issues which can alert us to some of the problems of data sampling. The issues can be listed as follows:

1. the kind of inference structure relating observables to properties.

2. the relative importance allocated to "thinking" and "doing" in various methodological styles.

3. the influence of the social structure on research inputs and products.

4. the types of orientation taken to various levels of research units: for instance, is a group something more than its constituent parts.

5. the relational style (agent-patient) established in a research encounter.

6. the relation between stages of research, for instance, is the (scaling) order found in responses imposed by the method of collecting data.

7. the stability of any interesting research outcome when applied to different referee populations.

THEME SIX: EXPERTISE—POLICY IMPLICATIONS OF THE SYMPOSIUM

. . . the trouble is that we are too caught up in *the need* (or opportunity) *for action* . . . to take a careful look below the surface of language usage . . . people have set up so-called intervention programs with disastrous results. . . .

. . . we need to do something about the circumstances of these families . . . otherwise the training programs that we set up are going to be *acceptable but not relevant* to the people with sufficient leisure, and *unacceptable though relevant* to the people without. . . .

. . . I have a *sense of discouragement* about the possibilities of making significant changes by *direct* intervention in the family situations. . . .

. . . we are planning to do the *training* in the type of neighborhood houses that are fairly well integrated within the poverty community. . . .

. . . clearly there are a lot of other factors here which are not controlled . . . they are part of the working class *milieu* which you will not be able to directly transform by a retraining program. . . .

. . . our laboratories should be a kind of preserve where you are free from terribly serious consequences, but where you might emerge helped, and understand things a little bit better, and not be exploited. . . .

. . . the main line of her findings I think most of us are *probably prepared to accept.* They seem highly congruent with the great deal of information that we've been acquiring. . . .

. . . we're dealing with a wide variety of different systems, but since we are all middle class, we tend to make (profoundly ethnocentric) *assumptions.* . . .

. . . it seems to me that to some extent we're saying that we *ought* to be studying what the family *ought* to be solving. . . .

. . . my general strategy now is to find a natural group with a problem . . . take baseline measures . . . study what the problem is . . . and then run an experiment to try to modify the situation. . . .

. . . this approach allows you to *test* your causal assumptions . . . and at the same time to produce a substantial *effect.* . . .

. . . so the social policy implications might be, as terrible as it may sound, to *write off* the parental generation. . . .

. . . we're not interested in things which are *efficient,* but rather *efficacious* in changing the state of mind or attitude or position. . . .

. . . are there particular kinds of behavior which *interfere* with interpersonal *accommodation* . . . (if so) is it possible to find *powerful contingencies* to manipulate these interfering behaviors. . . .

. . . almost no *ethnographic work* worth the name has been done in American cities. . . . Now, if you want to induce language learning you have to change the *environment* rather than try to teach language. . . .

The issue of social science "expertise" appeared and reappeared quite often during the course of the conference. With each reappearance there was, however, a subtle shift in mood such that, by the end of the conference, this issue had a number of identifiable facets. A listing of some of these facets may produce some new impressions on the craft of sociology.

1. the urgent need for action competing with the pursuit of adequate information.

2. the greater ease of direct intervention coupled with a sense of discouragement as to its effectiveness.

3. the dilemma of relevant but unacceptable solutions, due to the differences in cultural assumptions between clients and professionals.

4. a reluctance to produce serious consequences, yet a recognition of the need for more powerful contingencies in the lab.

5. selecting among the competing modes for conducting social science: expertise versus scientific inquiry.

6. studying actual problems of the family or working on the problems which ought to be solved.

7. deciding to emphasize or not to emphasize technology: "coping with a dynamic society" rationale.

8. the dilemma of choosing between naturally occurring processes or following the simplification rationale.

9. choosing between such alternative conceptualizations as "different" or "deficient" when characterizing low status groups.

10. focusing attention primarily on human systems (personality, groups) or on the environment of these systems.

Inkeles introduced the distinction between "different" and "deficient," and, while his statement did not stir any immediate controversy, it does appear, after a rerun through the transcript, that his distinction is indeed controversial. The concept of deficiency has several related implications: first, that status is a simple dimension such that status groups can be unequivocally ordered; second, that underlying these ordered manifestations are genotypic properties of individuals or classes of individuals which can likewise be assembled in a simple order; third, that possession of inferior properties is, at least in part, a question of personal responsibility (but partially attributable to the milieu); fourth, that the condition of deficiency is at least to some extent a mutable one; and finally, that the social criteria for making these judgements are quite standard.

Using this set of issues as a kind of magnet, I went searching through the transcript in orded to find associated material. The data thus gathered suggests a number of competing perspectives. Gumperz, for example, argued that we don't really understand minority groups, and, that we substitute assumptions for data when dealing with them.

Several of Moore's statements suggest radically different perspectives. His contrast between "efficacy" and "efficiency" argues that current standards of performance are a throttle on human potential. Furthermore, he found a black ghetto more congenial than a white one for exploring linguistic po-potential. Moore's sense of "competence" captures this idea of human potential, and distinguishes it from the acquired contents of actual performance. Both Hamblin (operating characteristics) and Gumperz (Chomsky's notion of competence) reinforced this idea. What is of particular significance about this term is that it teases out a fundamental difference between biological potential and socialized abilities.

Hamblin provided us with a useful and "technical" definition of interaction. His definition can be taken as "performance is the developmental product of the interaction between "competency" and an actor's environment." What is of importance here is the distinction between an actor and his environment. The implication being that if there is a clear deficiency in performance it may well be attributable to the properties of the environment. The importance of these refinements (competence, performance and environment) is beautifully illustrated by the Moore project. His central purpose is to develop a clarifying environment wherein some of the gaps between performance and competence can be explored, and he has found it necessary to start with four-year olds.

Leik's discussion of artificial shortage poses some intriguing problems for a deficiency hypothesis. One question that could be raised (if there are such things as deficient environments for human development) is "is this deficiency due to the human exercise of power, controlling and allocating resources?"

Finally, Gumperz served us with a note of caution for deciding upon one or another of these competing perspectives. He argues for an issue orientation rather than a solution orientation. In his experience, an orientation, for instance, to the functional consequences of language usage has led to "disastrous results." As an alternative, he suggests a spirit of inquiry that is tuned to the underlying strategies employed, both as a means of identifying types of strategy, and as a means for classifying users.

THEME SEVEN: THE DILEMMA OF RISKTAKING AND PROFESSIONAL SANCTIONS

. . . when you bring the family into the lab there are things left behind. . . . There is a *private culture* of the family which exists not only in certain social situations, but is attributed to physical settings. . . .

. . . one thing that we've found about (natural) group discussion is . . . that *it's not true* that you can't tape record unobtrusively. . . .

. . . the second question concerns your use of the phrase "natural behavior." You said, "There's too much going on in families" to really get a handle on it. This is laid alongside the statement, "you simply can't reconstruct natural situations for the family in the lab." . . . Well, I don't think you can get *anything but natural behavior* in a lab. . . .

. . . the function of the critic . . . is a game, which if played too vigorously, can lead to paralysis . . . total discouragement. . . .

*   *   *

. . . we think there's something wrong with the historical folk models . . . they all presuppose a *static* frame of reference . . . *and so* we are trying to build dynamic models with *a heavy emphasis on technology.* . . .

. . . *it became apparent* to us ten years ago that modern technology had reached the point where it *would be possible* to create very subtle environments. . . .

. . . but do you think our models can be free of machine technology?
. . . No! Not if they are to be dynamic models. . . .

. . . You say it's a culture-free system . . . but it's a funny thing to say because it's a system so pegged to electronics that it's an enormously culture-bound system. . . .

. . . I'm wondering whether there are not negative consequences as the child leaves this constructive environment—such as peers or siblings who are outdistanced. . . .

. . . does this mean that in some way you're unable to deal with the cultural baggage that people acquire as they get socialized? . . .

. . . the kinds of problems that we were talking about yesterday are not . . . knowing an alphabet . . . things that are "machine type" or which occur at an early age . . . so it seems to me that the dynamic shifts in the games could simply have to do with interpersonal accommodation. . . .

*   *   *

. . . well, there does appear to be this curious kind of contradiction where a certain proportion of the families have been *strengthened by prior crisis.* . . .

. . . your prediction of further crisis capacity has a big selection factor built into your sampling frame. . . .

. . . do you know the types of families which survived as families but failed the first crisis? According to the theory that you have enunciated here, they should be better off the next time. . . .

. . . well, not exactly, we have some retrospective reports, and there may be plenty of embroidering. . . .

*   *   *

. . . we assumed that what the mother did in our situation would tell us something about her habitual patterns of interaction . . . I would think we're beginning to get some clues about why these kids have so much difficulty. . . .

. . . well, the instructions that you gave the mothers *may or may not* have played a *very substantial* role in the outcome. . . .

. . . have you attempted to rework these correlations with class controls, because . . . there are a lot of other factors here . . . they are part of the working class *milieu* which you will not be able to transform through retraining. . . .

. . . the main lines of her findings I think most of us are prepared to accept. They seem highly congruent with the great deal of information that we have been acquiring. . . .

. . . one of the things that differentiates your situation between the middle class and the working class mother is . . . the perception of it as a learning situation. . . .

... the findings universally are ... regarding mother's input to children ... that after the age of three the child in these families stops associating with the mother ... the major source of socialization, then, is the older sibling. ...

Of the seven themes, this one has the lowest degree of integrity and specificity. Yet, in a way, that is one of the reasons for leaving it in. The main problem addressed in this collage is illustrated by the popular characterization of some of our national policy makers: "he never makes little mistakes on his way to a grand fallacy." There are several interrelated points carried by this illustration which give the collage its loose fit.

First there is the quality of interaction between our scientific problem solving abilities and the external social systems which we attempt to register. At best our representations are crude, partial, short-sighted, and "solution-oriented."

Second, there is the bind between "personal experience" and the requirement of a scientific "universe of discourse." The effort required for articulating or calling up one's experiences works at cross purposes with the effort to make oneself understood.

Third, a lot of what is meant in a scientific exchange is assumed (that is, tacit) or reactive (contextual). Thus there is a tendency for the degree of shared meaning to imperceptibly drift in a more or less manner.

Lastly, these conditions make for a lot of vulnerability, both individual and professional, in one's representations. One consequence of this is a whole series of defensive measures such as reduced risk-taking, boundary maintenance, and restricted (professional) audiences.

Zelditch's stand on the "private culture" problem, for instance, rests on reasons that may have eluded his detractors' priorities: the importance of experimentation for casually testing a theory, which depends upon a process of simplification—for example, ruling out unwanted sources of variation. He thus prefers to work with groups which do not have a contaminating set of shared, but unknown, meanings.

Gumperz' comment on this problem, on the other hand, reflects an inclination to work with natural groups. In fact, his argument could be extended to mean that the more natural the group (and the research setting) the less obtrusive research paraphenalia would be, once the group was sustaining a focused encounter.

Weick's reply (the third quote in the first frame) to Zelditch is quite consistent with Zelditch's position. That is, Zelditch would agree that you get natural behavior when you bring the family into the lab, adjusted to the degree of familiarity between the family's natural setting and the lab. But admitting that behavior would be natural is quite a different thing from the ability to specify the natural properties. Furthermore, from Zelditch's point of view, unless the properties thus specified were crucial to the test of one's theory, one would want to rule them out.

Inkeles' comment about the "function of the critic" alerts us to a very interesting phenomenon: the reputational mass, or professional density, of a speaker. The comment suggests that there is a possibility that the persuasive power of one's argument may rely as much on the arguer's halo as on the content of his argument. In other words the description of one's position can get read as a set of prescriptions by others.

Moore appears to be somewhat contradictory in his treatment of the importance of technology. In describing the package of his project, he remarks that there is a tendency to perceive his project solely in terms of its technology—and that this is a distortion. A little later on he insists on the requirement for a heavy emphasis on technology, if we want to develop dynamic models. His insistence met with a good deal of resistance. In both kinds of statements, the culprit is the less tangible ingredient of his program. Distorted perception means that users of the project's products tend to ignore everything but the talking typewriter. Likewise, much of the resistance to the emphasis on technology is pegged to issues outside of the boundaries of Moore's program: different types of tasks; older, more encultured subjects; and larger systems such as the family or peer groups.

Where Moore was speaking from a strong position, one of Hill's controversial remarks was obviously much weaker. He suggested that some families appear to be strengthened by crisis. His detractors tended to attack the suggestion by shifting the context—making stronger demands on the suggestion than was originally intended: "prediction," "sampling," theoretic specificity, explanation.

The Bee presentation had a strong front—a lot of data—but proved to be vulnerable on the flanks. It is quite interesting to notice how her critics got at the flaws. For instance, Inkeles was quite supportive in his opening remarks, but then used his "milieu theory" as an artful coup de grace. One major difficulty with the milieu theory is that, while it may provide better explanation, it is much less specific with respect to the kinds of action that would remedy the situation.

Part Two

PRIOR VIEWS
AND APPLICATIONS

The family problem solving symposium was held to assist the five editors of this volume in their efforts to develop a five-year programmatic research project (National Institute of Mental Health Grant 15521). Some months previous to the symposium, three of the investigators presented their views on various aspects of problem solving at a session of the Society for the Study of Social Problems. Those papers and one by Robert Hamblin and his associates comprise this section. The papers, despite some modifications based on post-symposium thinking, therefore, largely represent the authors conceptualizations and research analyses before the symposium. They lack an appended discussion which would highlight critical issues or rechannel the focus with new ideas.

To some extent the authors themselves have served as their own discussants and attempted to "second guess" the critics. Thus Tallman, in linking family problem solving behaviors to the process whereby macro-issues become defined as social problems, answers the argument of an inverse relation between the two among individuals. Aldous carefully hedges with reservations her analysis based on a phase notion of problem solving to avoid the charge of an over-rational approach. And Straus, in the long tradition of research, tries to adduce evidence to support his explanation and eliminate alternatives.

The paper by R. Hamblin, G. Ferritor, and M. Kozloff was included as a consequence of the productive discussion Hamblin had with O. K. Moore concerning effective strategies of intervention research with children. Because Hamblin's concerns with disturbed children center on the socialization process as a problem families must somehow solve, this is a paper whose substantive content is of direct concern. The paper also serves as a welcome contrast to the other three which are more concerned with socialization for problem solving.

Two appendixes follow the Prior Views section. First, an annotated bibliography, following the lead of previous books of symposia we have found useful. It contains the limited amount of literature on family problem solving available. The second appendix contains a description of the research technique used in the investigation reported by Straus.

A Framework for the Analysis
of Family Problem Solving*

JOAN ALDOUS

The study of family problem solving behavior draws upon the concepts and research findings from a variety of disciplines. The absence of a cumulative research tradition in the area makes it difficult to integrate the various concepts into a unified framework of analysis. Many of the concepts are not the outcome of empirical investigations but are suggestive of possible research leads; and most have developed from investigations of individuals and ad hoc groups rather than of groups with a history. As a result, the several frameworks that are considered here are often speculative. In some cases, they are based on studies too recent to have given rise to follow-up research; in other cases, concepts about the family are suggested whose relevance to problem solving has not yet been tested. Thus the final framework delineated may be said to highlight one set of concepts that appears to be fruitful for analyzing family problem solving, but requires empirical testing to determine whether its promises are deceiving.

This paper is organized around the various phases in the problem solving process. The discussion begins with brief delineations of the relevant family

* This paper was prepared in conjunction with NIMH grant 1 RO1 MHi5521-01 for Research on Problem Solving Behavior of Family Groups and has benefited from the comments of my fellow problem investigators, Reuben Hill, Murray A. Straus, and Irving Tallman. I am indebted to Daniel A. Wackman for the chart. The paper is a revised version of one presented before the Annual Meeting of the Society for the Study of Social Problems, August 1969.

characteristics and the problem solving process followed by a definition of the central concept, problem. The main portion of the paper links family characteristics to the process of problem solution using various dimensions as an organizing device for classifying problems. Comparisons are made between the probable behavior of families and ad hoc groups. Several hypotheses that can serve as research guidelines are developed in the course of the discussion.

RELEVANT CHARACTERISTICS OF THE FAMILY

The family can be defined broadly as a small kinship group having the functions of socialization, sexual regulation, and reproduction. The positions included can and do vary within and across societies. One can usually distinguish, however, parent-child, sibling, and marital subunits. Though the discussion below focuses on the Euro-American nuclear family, much of it is applicable to extended family groups as well as to matricentric one-parent families.

The family like other primary groups with a history has system-like properties. It is composed of interdependent members who together share a group identity that sets them apart. It is, however, distinguished from other small groups by its age and sex structure. Because of the generational differences between parents and children as well as the sex differences in the marital dyad, the family develops an organization to compensate for its weaknesses in personnel. In this organization, to insure that tasks get allocated to those competent to perform them, power relations loom large. Communication networks become established to transmit required skills and social lore and to encourage learning through verbal reinforcements. The intimate and emotional quality of family life resulting from the family's functions is reflected in its affective structure. Many of the group's activities are devoted to maintaining these structures, which, along with the family's unique age and sex structure and its character as a group with a tradition, may be hypothesized to influence the family's problem solving processes. (See the paper by Karl Weik in this volume for family properties that derive from the group's composition and functions.)

PROBLEM SOLVING AS A LOGICAL PROCESS

From Dewey (1910) to the present (Brim, 1962), a number of philosophers, psychologists, and social psychologists have seen problem solving as a process involving a series of phases. There is general agreement as to these phases. The first is the identification and definition of the problem, followed by the collection of information relevant to the problem. Next comes an innovation stage aimed at producing action alternatives. The subsequent decision-making phase involves the choice of a course of action from among the alternatives generated in the preceding phase. After taking action, evaluation of the consequences of the action constitutes the final phase.

Rationality and Problem Solving

Although this sequence of phases was originally developed to illustrate problem solving by individuals, it can also serve as a useful organizing device for an analysis of family problem solving behavior. Some qualifications, however, are necessary. The posited process assumes more rationality in the problem solvers than may be warranted. Instead of the assumption that all outcomes of a specific problematical situation are known, or that each actor possesses an unchanging value hierarchy and knows the variables which control the various outcomes (Taylor, 1965), Simon's (1957) notion of bounded rationality seems more appropriate. To him, individuals and groups behave rationally but within a circumscribed range of alternatives and outcomes. They engage in seeking satisfying outcomes within the limited range of solutions they perceive as available. Groups, according to this view, do not necessarily attempt goal maximization in the initial phases of problem solving, but persist in their search for solutions only until they find a good enough alternative. If they fail, they tend to lower their standards.

Simon's conceptualization is useful to us in examining problem solving behavior in families. We would hypothesize that families seldom explicitly define a situation as a problem, plan an appropriate strategy for reaching the valued outcome, and then take action. Instead, because they are on-going groups concerned with group maintenance, they will handle the most recalcitrant features of the situation in which they find themselves through whatever available means previous experience has suggested may be effective.

In taking a given action, families become committed to certain lines of behaviors which entail outcomes previously perceived only dimly, if visualized at all. The outcomes take on positive valuation in the process of being attained. In case of failure of the expediently available measures, the family may consciously search for other means or revise its goals. If, on the other hand, some sort of positive outcome is reached, family members may be vague about the process by which the outcome was reached. The daily routines and the urgency of attention to newly critical situations press the family to dispose of problems and move on. Families are generally less problem oriented than solution oriented. The emphasis tends to be one of reducing the tension-laden situations to an innocuous level rather than submitting the problem to rigorous analysis and assessing the consequences of possible alternate strategies. One hypothesis reflecting this phenomenon would be that the pressure to work for a quality solution to a problem is generally less among families than among more self-conscious problem solving groups such as committees or task forces.

Exceptions to this hypothesis might be expected among families with adequate economic and educational resources to eliminate most of the every-day problems which burden families. These families can choose which situations to define as problematical as well as the sequence and time period in which they must be solved. They, thereby, achieve a certain measure of rationality and phasing of the problem solving process and, perhaps, an awareness of it. Families with the resources to undertake long-range problems also have the time to lengthen the stages of problem defining and information search necessary to produce solutions of high quality.

But the general failure of most families to prolong the initial phases of the problem solving process and to plan systematically an appropriate mode of attack can have some positive consequences. This general failure can lead to greater satisfaction with the solution at the evaluation stage than where problem solving has been a self-conscious process. The homely routine of family life that is one element contributing to the group's high consensus makes boredom an ever-present danger and puts a premium on novelty. Thus, one study (Hill, 1970) showed that families whose consumer purchases occurred because one action was contingent on another were more satisfied than families with carefully planned outcomes, perhaps because of the unexpected pleasures from the unplanned decision. And, as is true for other groups, the carefully planned outcome also must meet the higher quality standards of members. For that reason, it may prove deficient in the estimation of family members.

Problems Have Solutions

In addition to rationality, another assumption underlying the conceptualization of the problem solving sequence is that the elements in the situation can be manipulated and changed. This assumption that there is a solution open to all families for all problems certainly does not hold for such problems as unemployment, inflation, war service, and racial or sex discrimination. Aside from problems arising from social arrangements, and economic and political events which families can do little to control, many of the problems encountered concern interpersonal relations requiring personality changes in individual members which are unlikely to occur. Nor is it always clear just what changes in persons or resources would be necessary to solve the same problems. Because of the interdependence of family members, any behavioral change in one individual has repercussions for all the relationships that have developed up to this point in time. Benign changes in individuals may lead to malignant interpersonal conflict due to disruption of customary interaction patterns. Even when adult family members can exert some control, as in the expectable growth-related problems of child rearing, parents may have to await the passage of time to bring the level of cognitive development in children necessary for acquiring the beliefs, values, skills, and behaviors parents see as necessary socialization outcomes.

Thus, some of the most far-reaching problems families have are problems that they have little choice in making, facing, or solving. It may very well be that, as a result, the only problems families can be said to "solve" are relatively unimportant ones. Even here, it may only be families with enough economic security to insulate themselves from the impact of major societal upheavals that can afford the time and energy consciously to take on these problems. Consequently, it could turn out that *problem facing* rather than *problem defining* or *problem solving* will constitute the major part of a research effort devoted to investigating real families' reactions to real problems as opposed to the kind of laboratory-based family problem solving research described by Zelditch in the present volume.

Summary

The view of problem solving as a conscious, rational process with a positive solution that the individual or family clearly values and attempts to reach may be appropriate for ad hoc groups faced with solvable problems specified by the researchers. Families, on the other hand, are less apt to define their behaviors as problem solving than ad hoc groups and will, at the same time, experience more failures simply because their problems often lack immediate solutions.

THE DEFINITION OF THE CONCEPT OF FAMILY PROBLEM

A family problem is defined here to mean any situation or circumstance which threatens the family's values, or those of one of its members, requiring cognitive effort on the part of one or more of its members and interaction among family members to resolve the situation in a manner commensurate with their values. From the Gestalt tradition comes the notion that the problematic situation creates tension among family members to the point that one or more among them presses for change in the mode of dealing with the situation, or with the underlying values which entered into the original definition of the situation as problematical.

The above definition eliminates situations which, through familiarity or simplicity, permit the participants to take habitual action with a minimum of cognitive mediation (Osgood, 1953). It is broad enough to include situations requiring a choice among a number of action alternatives as well as situations where the production of original ideas is needed. Thus behaviors requiring creativity in decision-making come under this definition of problem solving.

The definitional requirement that more than one family member be involved in the problem solving process insures that it is family and not individual problem solving that is of concern. The definition of the situation as problematical, however, may stem from one individual, initially, whose demands make it a family matter. Conjunctive rather than disjunctive problems and problems involving more rather than less family personnel should supply a focus of investigation.

When one person alone can arrive at the single correct solution, the problem can be classified as the disjunctive, "eureka" type problem. At the other extreme of the coordination dimension are conjunctive problems (Weick, 1965). In *conjunctive* problems, all or most of the family members must make some response, as in problems arising from the addition or loss of family members. With problems requiring a cumulative effort, for example, one member's activities serve as the input for another and so may facilitate or disrupt the contribution of others. Such problems in the family often center on interpersonal relations having to do with child rearing or marital conflict.

FAMILY COORDINATION AND PROBLEM SOLVING BEHAVIORS

Problems can be classified according to the phases of the problem solving process in which their solution is undertaken and according to the behavioral demands they make of the family (Shaw, 1963). Such a latter dimension is the degree of coordination required of family members. The organization achieved by the family as an on-going group gives it an advantage over ad hoc groups in handling problems which require coordination of members' behaviors. Through coordination and summation of the actions of family members, the family can reach goals beyond the grasp of its members as individuals.

For short-run problems where the solutions are relatively apparent and of about equal quality, families are at an advantage over ad hoc groups. Their prior organization and experience with problem solving permits them to shorten the decision making and action implementation phases of problem solving. Family members do not have to waste time developing an organization and jockeying for position in a developing power structure. If ad hoc groups that have been able to maintain the same membership become more effective over time due to developing cooperative interaction patterns (Goldberg and Maccoby, 1965), how much more might this be expected with families? Relationships among members are already established, and if harmonious, a group consensus about ends and means from past successful role taking exists. In the optimum case, activities are synchronized, because there is mutual knowledge of expectations. Coordination, moreover, can serve to compensate for the deficits of junior family members. Authority figures already exist to set policy, integrate individual contributions, and keep the group's attention focused on the problem (Mulder, 1960).

The very elements that enable the family to coordinate its activities, however, handicap it in solving problems demanding a search for alternative solutions. The relevant problem characteristics here, of degree of familiarity with the problem and of the extent to which new solutions must be generated, crosscut the classification of problems according to the degree of coordination which their solution requires.

THE FAMILY AS AN ON-GOING PROBLEM SOLVING GROUP

The on-going nature of the family makes group maintenance an end in itself. As a consequence, there may be normative pressures against the verbalizing of disagreements which could threaten existing relations. The family's power, communication, and affective structure can be quickly activated to suppress conflict, which also cuts off the generation of innovative solutions. Indeed, for complex problems requiring assessment of a number of alternative solutions, the generation of a wide range of possible solutions is facilitated by competition and conflict among group members (Maier, 1963). The group is forced to search for better quality solutions when group members disagree as to the value of suggested alternatives. Beyond a certain point, of course, quality of solution fails to increase with conflict as the probability of reaching agreement among the group members falls (Bower, 1965). Though they may avoid the paralysis resulting from too much discord, families that minimize the expression of conflict fail to reap the benefits accruing from optimum discord.

It should be noted that the impacts of familial conflict differ between personality focused conflict and issue oriented conflict. Conflicts focusing on personalities, whether habitual or spasmodic, seldom have anything but negative effects on problem solving. Far from participating in the evaluation of suggested solutions in terms of the characteristics of the problem, the parties in conflict tend automatically to reject the solutions of their opponents in favor of their own.

Issue Focused Conflict

The situation differs when family conflicts center on issues and focus on the character of the problem to be solved. Individual members through positive past experience in problem solving and a strong supporting affective structure in the family possess the self-confidence to make additional suggestions and the self-worth not to feel threatened by the negative evaluations of others (Smith, 1968). Parents may actively implement the value that children as well as adults should express their ideas, subject only to the veto of superior logical or informational arguments. Such families, we would hypothesize, are disproportionately found among the highly educated and in ethnic groups with a strong intellectual heritage. These families also often have the economic resources to be able to choose the situations they define as problems and to program a time schedule for their solution.

For families with adequate economic and superior intellectual resources, problems can become opportunities for the exercise of pleasurable skills and take on a game-like character. A sort of playfulness may even develop in the solution process which is itself conducive to the generation of alternative solutions. The intellectual conflict which arises in arguing about means in such families can even contribute to their cohesiveness. The interpersonal hostility that sometimes accompanies the routine aspects of family living can be released productively in the problem solving process, thereby removing a threat to the affectional ties of family members. Power discrepancies based on age and sex differentials can be overridden in the intellectual arena to the exquisite pleasure of the weak and to the benefit of the family's problem solutions.

Families Are Conservative

Because of its socialization function, however, the family tends to be a conservative rather than an innovative group. The responsibility of parents to socialize their children into acceptable group ways can have a dampening effect on the search for solutions. Groups, more than individuals, seem to utilize socially defined evaluative criteria in making decisions. Thus, members in problem solving situations not involving factual questions tend to remind the individual of operative norms that he has not considered, thereby lessening his innovative attempts (March and Feigenbaum, 1960). The joint expectations that have developed over time would make this tendency even more pronounced among family groups. The common culture that family members share as a result of mutual socialization also limits the variation in individual perspectives that would lead to innovation.

The heterogeneity of attitudes present in cross-sex groups, another source of different ideas, may operate to a lesser extent in families. The same men and women who display differentiated role behavior when interacting with strangers show less variation in expressive-instrumental behavior and initiating interaction in the family (Leik, 1963). Persons who tend to be quiet in other groups are more active in the family and the active ones in outside groups are less so in the family setting. This muting of individual differences within the family also tends to inhibit the production of new ideas in a problem solving situation.

Risk Taking

The phenomenon of the "risky shift" which, one can speculate, might encourage "far-out" solutions is also probably less frequent in families. Individuals, it appears, are prepared to take higher risks in making decisions when participating in ad hoc groups in which they have little investment than they are willing to take when alone, thereby making a "risky shift." Kogan and Wallach (1967), in one interpretation, see the "risky shift" as a case of the individual's shifting the responsibility for possible failure to the group, but few families can afford the luxury of failure even when responsibility is diffused because problem solving failures can threaten their continuance.

Families would be prepared to take higher risks than individuals or ad hoc groups only when preserving the integrity of the family unit entails such risks. The value of group maintenance rather than diffusion of social responsibility would appear to dictate the risky decision. However, the freedom from anxiety due to diffusion of social responsibility, which might be conducive to departures from the obvious and the usual, would be absent from high-risk decisions within families. Under such conditions it would be difficult for the individual family members to avoid a sense of responsibility for the negative consequences of such decisions.

Given the family's age and sex structure, the norm of social responsibility (Berkowitz and Daniels, 1963) also acts to limit the sense of "diffusion of responsibility" that may be associated with participation in an ad hoc group. Moreover, the legal character of the family prevents adult members, and particularly the adult male, from divesting themselves of responsibility for family actions. Thus the lessened anxiety and increased spontaneity that comes with participation in groups where the individual can relinquish responsibility for the outcomes exists primarily among children who are the low power figures of the family.

In sum, families as on-going groups are concerned with issues of group maintenance. They tend to suppress conflict and to hold members to norms of responsibility in risk taking, both of which lower their propensity to generate a wide range of problem solutions. Families, as a result, should be more effective at solving problems demanding coordination of efforts than problems requiring a wide range of innovative solutions.

THE FAMILY'S AFFECTIVE STRUCTURE
AND PROBLEM SOLVING BEHAVIOR

Problems can be classified according to their difficulty and to their degree of similarity to other problems. The affective structure of the family is particularly relevant to these dimensions. This structure can encourage persistence of effort in the collection of information phase or even in the face of failure that may compensate for the family's weaknesses in innovation.

Normative approaches to problem solving have emphasized the tendency to focus on the solutions to problems rather than on the analysis of the problem itself (Maier, 1963). The Zeigarnik effect observed among individuals, for example, centers attention on unfinished problems and creates psychological tension within the individual that presses him to a quick solution. But the affective structure of the family, if supportive, can lessen pressure to come to a quick solution of the problem. The task payoff comes only after solving the problem, but social rewards from family members during the process can lead to persistence of effort and a more original solution.

Family members can give praise or other forms of emotional support immediately following behavior which not only supply cues to relevant behavior, but frees the family members to some extent from the capriciousness of a recalcitrant problem situation. Mutual emotional support can keep the group going because of the intrinsic pleasures of group interaction, even when the possibility of receiving extrinsic rewards from the problem's solution seems remote (Collins and Guetzkow, 1964). Thus the maintenance of family cohesion, while it may inhibit conflict and the search for alternate solutions, can contribute to persistence in the face of failure.

Increased effort in families, in fact, may be the link between emotional and instrumental behavior in family problem solving. Expressive behavior, positive and negative, appears to be related to family satisfaction in problem solving situations in the laboratory. Expressive behavior, however, is negatively related to the incidence of interpersonal agreement. However, the family's expression of positive affect leads to increased task effort. The latter, in turn, is related to coming to agreement on a decision (Leik, 1963). Thus expressive behaviors, we would hypothesize, are related to increased task performance and thus to successful problem solving by family members.

Problem Definition and Persistence

It is well to note, however, that the family's affective structure is only one factor in the sequence leading to persistence in problem solving. The family's persistance is also related to the degree to which the members are involved in defining and committing themselves to the problem. The research literature on effort enhancement is applicable here. If a person, through his own volition, has taken on a problem, he tends to respond with greater effort at task solution and with a heightened task evaluation to tedious, meaningless, and poorly rewarded tasks.

One explanation for the enhanced effort lies in dissonance reduction. The individuals must justify their efforts to themselves (Brehm and Cohen, 1959; Cohen, 1962). Since many family problems lack intrinsic interest, whether or not the family has defined the situation as a problem will influence the effort the members devote to the problem; and the amount of effort the family devotes to the problem, if it controls the requisite resources, will lessen the probability of failure. If outside agencies have forced the family to undertake the solution of a problem, the family will be less motivated to solve it. Even if some members become concerned about the problem, others in the family can discredit them by suggesting they are agents of outsiders.

THE FAMILY'S COMMUNICATION STRUCTURE AND PROBLEM SOLVING

The communication structure, particularly, ties problem solving to the family's function of socialization—in this case socialization for problem solving. Communication affects the skills children learn as well as their view of themselves as problem solvers. It is difficult to consider communication structure apart from family power structure, but we can begin with the content of communication, the problem solving concern of Helen Bee's paper in the present volume.

Parents vary in information, acquired through formal and informal education channels, that they can make available in the search for information phase of the family's current problem solving endeavors. However, they may communicate the information they do possess in a way that gives younger family members little sense of control over events affecting them. If parents give information primarily in the form of directions, children lack an overall picture of the problem and do not see how solution outcomes are contingent on their own actions. Under these learning conditions, children perceive reinforcement not as internally controlled through their own activities, but under the control of others (McGhee and Crandall, 1968), and so fail to develop a sense of being autonomous problem solvers.

The result is a lowering of achievement that appears in academic performance, and one can speculate, will also manifest itself in a lessened effort in all problem situations including those involving the family. Children who see solution payoffs as being controlled by others, may also be less persistent due to an inability to delay gratification. They will avoid solutions requiring action over a period of time and, depending upon the cooperation of others, in favor of an immediate solution over which they can exercise control (Mischel, 1961).

Family Codes

All families are constrained by their personal limitations in the range and reliability of available information sources, regardless of how active or skilled their children are in solving family problems. Each family, however, shares a common core of general information, which can prove an asset in problem solving since groups seem to utilize information better where there is some overlap of information among the members (Bower, 1967). Difficulty in reaching an agreement on what action to take occurs when individual group members have highly specialized information and little shared general knowledge with respect to a problem.

The communication structure, moreover, assists the family members to adjust their behavior one to another for the changes incumbent on problem solving and solution implementation. Existing networks contribute to successful role taking and to coordination of activities (Scheff, 1967). The communication codes that have developed through long familiarity enable family members to transmit information using a type of verbal or gestural shorthand. The decision making and action taking phases of problem solving are thereby expedited, unless the solutions required are too complex or innovative to be covered by the codes.

THE FAMILY'S POWER STRUCTURE AND PROBLEM SOLVING BEHAVIOR

The peculiar age and sex structure of the family gives rise to a power structure that conflicts with the communication demands for problem solving and socialization for problem solving. Exercise of power in the family has the double impact of "fate control" and "behavior control" (Thibaut and Kelly, 1959). Parents have "fate control" over younger children in the sense that they can mediate and even nullify the outcomes of children's actions. Older children and parents exercise "behavior control," in Thibaut and Kelly's terms, since through behavioral variations adolescents and parents can make other family members want to change their behavior.

Centralized Power

Particularly when younger children are present, the family power and communication structures necessarily are centralized in a form that limits the family to ideas from the parental power figures, and in very traditional families to the father. The original differences in ability between parents and children lower parental permissiveness for disagreement. As children mature unless the parents encourage the active participation of the maturing members, the latter may continue to limit their contributions. From the content of parental messages, children may fear the parental power to reward or punish and hesitate to participate in family decisions. Authority, initially based on age-linked ability can, as children grow up, come to rest primarily on ascriptive qualities of age. Family heads may be loath to utilize the information potential of weaker family members because to do so would threaten their self esteem. Their fear of competitors also may lead them to guard the information sources and problem solving skills jealously. Indeed, this fear of competition can grow out of the kind of inadequate socialization for problem solving the parents experienced as children that they in turn are passing on to their children.

In such cases of one-way communication, not only may the potential contributions of low status family members remain untapped, but the central power figure may be overloaded by coordination and innovative demands (Shaw, 1964). The low power figures will not bother those in authority with demands for explanation in these status-oriented families, to use Bernstein's (1964) terms, or volunteer information, thus foreshortening the search for alternatives phase. As a result, the family power structure developed initially from age, and to a lesser extent from sex differences, lowers the efficacy of the family's problem solving. Other things being equal, the typical family power structure operates counter to the predominance of volunteered rather than solicited information and minimizes the spread of participation and the coinciding of leadership and ability, all characteristics Lanzetta and Roby (1960) have found to be associated with group problem solving effectiveness in terms of number of errors made and speed of problem solutions.

Countervailing Tendencies

Although the power structure is most clearly revealed at the stage of choosing among alternative actions, such decisions in the family may be less arbitrary than would be expected, given its centralized tendencies. This is one of the reasons why the game models of decision making which have generated so many propositions about exchanges are less applicable to the family than to ad hoc or economic interest groups. Both game and exchange models assume that each of the actors will attempt to maximize the expected outcome of an interaction to his own advantage at the expense of others. Indeed, in the zero sum game, what one actor wins the other loses. In the family, however, the solution often involves one member willingly giving up something to another, such as the use of scarce resources, without expectation of reciprocity.

The duration of the family, its interdependence and its affective structure impose a common fate on the group with attendant greater cohesiveness and mutual influence that modifies the arbitrariness of fate control in conformity to the norm of social responsibility. The family power structure with the parents at the apex receives normative support from outside social agencies, and these norms are customarily internalized by younger family members through habituation. The family power structure, therefore, is customarily legitimated externally and internally. Because it is legitimized, role occupants in the resultant authority structure are limited in exercising power arbitrarily, first by the broad legal controls of the broader society and increasingly by the role expectations of the growing junior members as these latter develop in age and competencies. Coalition formations also strengthen the hands of children against domineering parents, and an alliance of mother and children may negotiate changes in the arbitrary edicts of an authoritarian father.

Certain strategies developed in mixed-motive game theory do have their place in family decision making analysis (Bernard, 1964). The strategic threat or strategic promise can serve to increase the power of lesser family members. In these forms of behavior control, by threatening to do something harmful to himself or to the family, the individual can forestall threatening family decisions. The force of threats and promises lies not only in the interdependence of family members but also in the emotional bonds that link them to one another.

Weakness and Power

The infant family member, because of his very weakness, retains a singular veto power. His inability to communicate clearly means that others must allow for and protect his interests. The same holds true for other family members who cannot be affected by communication due to intellectual incapacity or refusal to understand, and maximizing outcomes habitually at the expense of weaker family members can lead to family breakdown. Scapegoats rebel, as alternative situations appear, and refuse to implement decisions unfavorable to them. As a last resort, they may even leave home, thereby weakening the family's cohesion and its organization for task performance.

Thus, despite high fate control and the centralization of resources and expertise in the older members, as well as the assignment of formal authority to the parents, the family must take into account the stake and convictions of its weaker members to maintain its level of functioning. As children grow older there are tendencies toward decentralization of power in all families. Weik in his symposium paper is probably right in his reservations that customary power patterns and, we would add, their own extra-familial concerns lessen adolescents' participation. Even so, we would predict older children because of their own problems and self interest play more of a part in family problem solving with attendant advantages to the family as the choice-making among these alternatives. Finally, whether due to habituation or willing acceptance of the existing power structure, we would hypothesize that family members accept decisions on family problems more quickly than do members of other groups. Satisfaction with the decision should be greater and there should be more cooperation in its implementation.

CONCLUSION

By analyzing the interplay of family characteristics, types of problems, and phases of problem solving, often in comparison with ad hoc groups, it has been possible to highlight the problem solving strengths and weaknesses of families. (Figure 1 provides a schematic summary of the discussion.) The family's character as an on-going group with an age and sex structure that couples personnel shortages and personnel incapacities makes group maintenance a primary objective. In addition, the socialization function of the family makes it a conservative institution. Consequently, one hypothesis is that the family will be less successful than other small groups in coping with problems where previous experience is not applicable and innovative solutions are demanded.

The family will be more successful, however, in terms of time required to come to a decision and in implementing a decision, due to the consensus existing among family members reflected in the structuring of power, communication, and division of labor. Moreover, the affective structure can supply family members the emotional support that encourages persistence in the face of failure or premature problem solving. It can also serve to mitigate the tendencies toward authoritarianism present in centralized power structures characteristic of the heterogenous age and sex composition of most young families.

But because the family is an on-going group existing in an often recalcitrant environment and because it is composed of individuals in intimate contact, problems external to the family and exigencies growing out of interpersonal relations are ever-present. Families must incorporate problem solving into the routine of everyday life so that systematic planning to solve a problem occurs less often than with ad hoc groups. The conservative nature of the family gives a particular appeal to the unexpected rather than the expected outcome, so we can hypothesize that family members, despite the lack of planning and low innovativeness, are more satisfied with problem solutions than members of other groups.

Family characteristics	Identification and definition	Collection of information	Production of alternative solutions	Deciding among alternatives	Taking action	Evaluation of action
Age and sex structure	−	−	−			
On-going group maintenance			−	+	+	+
Communication structure				+	+	
Affective structure		+	(±)		+	
Power structure		−	−	+	+	+

Figure 1. Strengths and weaknesses of the family as a problem-solving group compared with ad hoc groups.
(Strengths = +; problematical = (±); weakness = −)

The group's continuance rests on the mutual trust and respect growing out of roughly equitable solutions to those problems endemic in group living, where everyone cannot have all his values fulfilled. Whether many families enjoy the luxury of having solved many problems or whether they have learned to live with them, have outgrown them, or have been subject to the intervention of outside agencies is an issue in problem solving that further systematic research will be needed to answer.

REFERENCES

Berkowitz, L. and Daniels, Louise R., "Responsibility and Dependency." *Journal of Abnormal and Social Psychology* 66: 429–436, 1963.

Bernstein, B., "Family Role Systems, Communication and Socialization." Unpublished paper prepared for the Cross-National Conference on Research on Children and Adolescence, University of Chicago, 1964.

Bower, J. L., "Group Decision Making: A Report of an Experimental Study." *Behavioral Science* 10: 277–289, 1965.

Brehm, J. W. and Cohen, A. R., "Reevaluation of Choice Alternatives as a Function of Their Number and Qualitative Similarity." *Journal of Abnormal and Social Psychology* 58: 373–378, 1959.

Brim, O. G., Jr., *Personality and Decision Processes: Studies in the Social Psychology of Thinking*. Stanford, California: Stanford University Press, 1962.

Cohen, A. R., "A 'Forced Compliance' Experiment in Repeated Dissonance." Pp. 97–104 in J. W. Brehm and A. R. Cohen (eds.) *Explorations in Cognitive Dissonance*. New York: John Wiley, 1962.

Collins, B. E. and Guetzkow, H., *A Social Psychology of Group Processes for Decision-Making*. New York: John Wiley, 1964.

Dewey, J., *How We Think*. New York: D. C. Heath, 1910.

Goldberg, M. H. and Maccoby, Eleanor E., "Children's Acquisition of Skill in Performing a Group Task Under Two Conditions of Group Formation." *Journal of Personality and Social Psychology* 2: 898–902, 1965.

Hess, R. D., "The Transmission of Cognitive Structures in Poor Families: The Socialization of Apathy and Underachievement." Unpublished paper, Psychological Factors in Poverty Conference, Madison, University of Wisconsin, 1967.

Hill, R., *Family Development in Three Generations: A Longitudinal Study of Changing Family Patterns of Planning and Achievement*. Boston: Shenkman and Co., 1970.

Hoffman, L. R., "Group Problem Solving." Pp. 99–132 in L. Berkowitz (ed.) *Advances in Experimental Social Psychology* 2. New York: Academic Press, 1965.

Kogan, N. and Wallach, M. A., "Risky-Shift Phenomenon in Small Decision-Making Groups: A Test of the Information Exchange Hypothesis." *Journal of Experimental Social Psychology* 3: 75–84, 1967.

Lanzetta, J. T. and Roby, T. B., "The Relationship Between Certain Group Process Variables and Group Problem-Solving Efficiency." *Journal of Social Psychology* 52: 135–148, 1960.

Leik, R. K., "Instrumentality and Emotionality in Family Interaction." *Sociometry* 26: 131–145, 1963.

Maier, N. R. F., *Problem-Solving Discussions and Conferences: Leadership, Methods and Skills.* New York: McGraw-Hill, 1963.

March, J. G. and Feigenbaum, E. A., "Latent Motives, Group Discussion and Quality of Group Decisions in Non-Objective Decision Problems." *Sociometry* 23: 50–56, 1960.

McGhee, R. E. and Crandall, Virginia C., "Beliefs in Internal-External Control of Reinforcement and Academic Performance." *Child Development* 39: 91–102, 1968.

Mischel, W., "Preference for Delayed Reinforcement and Social Reinforcement." *Journal of Abnormal and Social Psychology* 62: 1–7, 1961.

Mulder, M., "Common Structure, Decision Structure and Group Performance." *Sociometry* 23: 601–614, 1960.

Osgood, C. E., *Method and Theory in Experimental Psychology.* New York: Oxford University Press, 1953.

Scheff, T. H., "A Theory of Social Coordination Applicable to Mixed-Motive Games." *Sociometry* 20: 215–234, 1967.

Shaw, M. E., "Communication Networks." Pp. 111–147 in L. Berkowitz (ed.) *Advances in Experimental Social Psychology.* New York: Academic Press, 1964.

Shaw, M. E., "Scaling Group Tasks: A Method for Dimensional Analysis." T.R. No. 1, Department of Psychology, Gainesville, Florida: University of Florida, 1963, quoted in J. Richard Hackman, "Tests, Questionnaires and Tasks of the Group Effectiveness Research Laboratory, 1951–1964." T.R. No. 24, Department of Psychology, Urbana, Ill.: University of Illinois, 1965.

Simon, H. A., *Models of Man: Social and Rational.* New York: John Wiley, 1957.

Smith, M. Brewster, "Competence and Socialization." Pp. 272–320 in J. Clausen (ed.) *Socialization and Society.* Boston: Little, Brown, 1968.

Taylor, D. W., "Decision Making and Problem Solving." Pp. 48–86 in James G. March (ed.) *Handbook of Organization.* Chicago: Rand McNally, 1965.

Thibaut, J. W. and Kelley, H. H., *The Social Psychology of Groups.* New York. John Wiley, 1959.

Weik, K. E., "Laboratory Experimentation with Organizations." Pp. 194–260 in James G. March (ed.) *Handbook of Organization.* Chicago: Rand McNally, 1965.

Social Class and Sex Differences in Socialization for Problem Solving in Bombay, San Juan, and Minneapolis*

MURRAY A. STRAUS

A basic sociological proposition holds that differences in social position are associated with differences in behavior. Related to this principle is the question of identifying the factors which cause and maintain the differences in behavior between social groups. To attribute these differences to "culture" is not sufficient because such an explanation does not indicate the process which induces and maintains the difference in culture. In addition, not all such group differences are supported by a distinctive culture, unless one wishes to call any difference a cultural difference. Examples of the latter situation are differences between males and females sharing the same culture,

* This paper is a revision and combination of papers read at the 1968 meetings of the American Association for the Advancement of Science and the Society for the Study of Social Problems. I hope that the many generous people whose assistance made this long and complicated research possible will forgive the fact that space limitations preclude mentioning them here as I have done in an earlier report of this study (Straus, 1968). However, in relation to this paper, I am grateful to James Lally for statistical analysis and to Joan Aldous, Glen Elder, and Irving Tallman for comments and suggestions which aided in the revision of this paper.

Financial support of the field work was provided by the National Science Foundation, the United States Educational Foundation in India, and the Social Science Program of the Puerto Rico Department of Health. The analysis was supported by the Family Study Center and the Center for the Study of Technological and Social Change of the University of Minnesota and was completed with the aid of funds provided under Grant 15521 from the National Institute of Mental Health.

and probably also social class differences. For these theoretical reasons, and also because sex differences in behavior are probably universal, as are social status differences, this paper deals simultaneously with both of these major elements of position in the social structure. In addition, both social class and sex are known to be associated with differences in problem solving ability. Finally, at least some of the factors creating and maintaining social class differences in problem solving ability might also be applicable to the explanation of sex differences in problem solving ability, thus offering the possibility of an explanatory theory which would apply to both social class and sex differences in problem solving behavior.

The specific questions to be investigated are therefore: (1) To what extent are there social class and sex differences in problem solving ability among the samples of early adolescent children who participated in this research? (2) Are there social class and sex differences in certain aspects of parent-child interaction which, on theoretical grounds, should be associated with deficiencies in problem solving ability? (3) Are family-to-family differences in these aspects of parent-child interaction correlated with individual differences in problem solving ability? An affirmative answer to all three of the questions could be the basis for a theory which would provide at least a partial explanation for both sex related and social class related differences in problem solving ability.

The predominant theoretical position in social psychological studies of social class and sex differences in intellectual capacities, while not denying the possibility of genetic, nutritional, and other biological factors, has posited the major source of difference as outcomes of differential socialization and role ascription (Deutsch, Katz, and Jensen, 1968; Maccoby, 1966). The present study was undertaken within such a framework and specifically seeks to provide evidence bearing on what can be called a "socialization deficit" theory of social class and sex differences in problem solving ability. The results to be reported also offer a firmer basis for generalization than has typically been the case since they are based on a replicated study of the behavior of children and their parents in three very different societies.[1]

THE WORKING CLASS AND WOMEN AS DISADVANTAGED SOCIAL STRATA

Women have sometimes been referred to as society's largest disadvantaged minority group. To the extent that this is the case, women should share with other low status minorities such social deprivations as an ascribed position of inferiority, a stereotyped image of incompetence which serves to justify

---

[1] It is important to note that although this paper is couched in the rhetoric of socialization, thus implying a process extending over time, only cross sectional data have been presented. It is assumed that the parent child relationships analyzed in this paper were factors in the life of the children studied, but such an assumption must be checked by empirical data on developmental history. Research now in the planning stage will attempt to get such data by means of a longitudinal study.

their inferior placement in the social structure, and a socialization process which denies equal opportunity to acquire competence and which, to a certain extent, even teaches and enforces the inferior traits ascribed to women. It may not be stretching things too much to see an analogy between the socialization experience of lower class children and that of girls. Kirkpatrick (1963), for example, lists 36 analogies between the status of women and Negroes.

The extensive and readily available literature of social class differences in intellectual capacities (Deutsch, Katz, and Jensen, 1968; Glazer and Creedon, 1968) will not be reviewed at this point in order to allow room for a discussion of sex differences. The similarities, however, are many. For example, comparisons of lower class and middle class children have typically shown little or no difference in intelligence when tested in infancy and early childhood, followed by a progressively widening gap as the lower class children fall further and further behind their middle class age mates (Jones, 1954; Bayley, 1954; Hindley, 1962). Like slum children, girls start out with intellectual capacities equal to or greater than those of boys but as they mature the boys equal and excel the performance of girls until, in adulthood, men tend to have somewhat higher average intelligence test scores than women (summarized in Maccoby, 1966). Men are also known to excel over women in certain other traits indicative of social competency, for example, autonomy and resistance to group pressure (Allen and Crutchfield, 1963; Brim *et al,* 1962), freedom from anxiety (Bendig, 1960; Brim *et al,* 1962), and such creativity related cognitive styles as ability to break sets (Nakamura, 1958), and field independence (Witkin, 1950; Vaught, 1965). Although girls get higher grades in school, they have a lower level of aspiration (Walter and Marzolf, 1951), and women have lower achievement motivation scores than men, even when such motivation is measured in terms of achievement fantasy (McClelland, 1953). Perhaps the most striking evidence of the low achievement of women comes from the Stanford longitudinal study of gifted children (Terman and Oden, 1947). The subjects for this study were selected on the basis of their very high IQ, yet, even leaving aside those women who were housewives, the adult occupations of the women were undistinguished.

Although many more traits could be mentioned, space limitations require that this overly brief summary be concluded with mention of the sex differences in self-esteem and anxiety. These two aspects of personality have been singled out because, as the discussion to be presented later makes evident, they are related to competence in general, and probably to problem solving ability in particular. The available evidence suggests little or no overall difference in anxiety or neurotic symptoms at early ages, but in adolescence and adulthood numerous studies (summarized in Anastasi, 1958: 448-488) show girls to suffer from more psychological handicaps of this sort than boys. These results have also been found for a national sample of adults (Gurin, Veroff, and Feld, 1960).

On the basis of this brief review there seems to be sufficient evidence to warrant further investigation of the proposition that women share deficits in intellectual performance and achievement with those low in the socio-economic status hierachy. Thus, the first empirical question to be answered in this paper concerns the extent to which such differences are to be found among the children in Bombay, San Juan, and Minneapolis who were included in this research.

SAMPLE AND METHOD

A questionnaire was given to children in schools selected on the basis of their location in middle class or working class parts of Minneapolis, Minnesota, San Juan, Puerto Rico, and Bombay, India. This questionnaire permitted selection of families on the basis of social class. Approximately half of each sample was selected from the middle class areas and half from the working class areas. To be included in the working class, the child had to have a father engaged in manual work, the middle class group consists of children of white collar fathers. The sample sizes were 64 in Bombay, 45 in San Juan, and 64 in Minneapolis. In Minneapolis, 64 percent of the eligible families who were asked to participate did so. In San Juan, 88 percent coopera-tion was secured, and in Bombay the figure was 93 percent.[2] In Bombay and Minneapolis, the sample was further selected on the basis of the sex of the child but time and other limitations prevented this in San Juan. Thus, the sex difference data to be reported is limited to Bombay and Minneapolis.

The study was conducted in a university small-groups laboratory in Minneapolis, and in a room of the Puerto Rico Vocational Rehabilitation Center in San Juan. In Bombay rooms in the neighborhood school and in a municipal recreation center were used. Except for the light operator, all staff with whom the family interacted in San Juan and Bombay spoke the native language.

Task. The problem presented to the family was a puzzle in the form of a game played with pushers and balls. This task is a greatly simplified version of procedures first developed by Swanson (1953) and later modified by Hamblin (1958a, b). The choice of this task was part based on the assumption that the lower class persons "do not verbalize well in response to words alone" (Riessman, 1962) or, as Miller and Swanson (1961) put it, the lower class person tends to think and learn in a physical or motoric fashion. "Such people can think through a problem only if they can work on it with their hands. Unless they can manipulate objects physically they cannot perform adequately." It was hoped that a task which involved physical manipulation of objects would allow for such motoric thinking.

---

[2] Further details on the sample selection procedure are given in Straus (1969). The number of other children in the family was not used as a selection criterion, nor was the legal status of the union. It should be noted that the requirement of a natural child of at least twelve years of age undoubtedly produced an atypical working class sample. This is because of the instability characteristic of slum families everywhere.

It is difficult to describe adequately this task and the associated observational and scoring procedures within the space limitations of this article. Consequently, a methodological paper has been prepared for those needing such information (Straus and Tallman, 1966). However, it is hoped that the partial description which follows will be sufficient for purposes of understanding the findings.

The game was played on a court about 9 by 12 feet marked on the floor with two target boards at the front, as shown in Figure 1. Also at the front

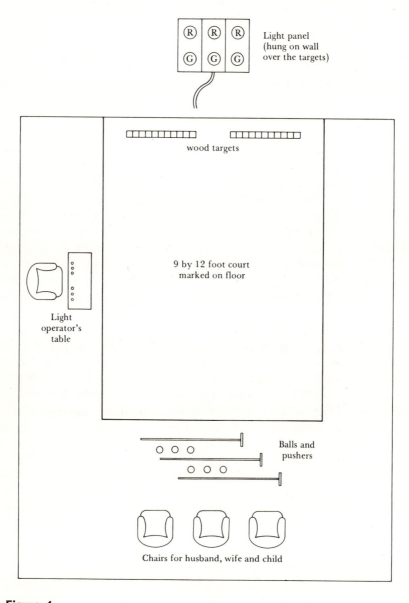

Figure 1.

of the room were three pairs of red and green lights, one pair of lights for each member of the family, and a blackboard to post scores after each period of play. Each family was told that the problem was to figure out how to play the game. The instructions given were ambiguous and designed to emphasize speed in performance and the need to play as a team. There were eight three-minute trials. The family's task was to infer the rules of the game with the aid of green lights flashed for correct moves and red lights for incorrect moves, and to use this information to exceed the average of "other families who have played this game."[3]

CLASS AND SEX DIFFERENCES
IN PROBLEM SOLVING PERFORMANCE

Problem solving ability is a polymorphous concept, requiring specification of the separate (though interrelated) components before either theoretical or empirical analysis can proceed. For purposes of this research, the problem solving process has been viewed as having the following components (after, among others, Brim, 1962; Dewey, 1933; Gagne, 1959): (1) problem recognition or identification, (2) information collection and idea generation, (3) decision, (4) implementation, and (5) evaluation. The measures of problem solving performance used in this study are confined to indexes of the idea generation and the implementation components. The former is a measure of ideational fluency, which will be called *creativity,* and the latter is a measure of number of correct moves in the experimental tasks, which will be called the *success ratio.*

Success Ratio. This score is based on the lights used to indicate correct and incorrect actions to the subjects. As previously noted, green lights were used to indicate a correct action and red lights indicated violation of some rule of the game. Electric counters wired to each signal light, therefore, recorded the number of successes and errors. The data reported here on the success ratio are the proportion that the green lights are of all lights flashed during each trial.

Measurement of Creativity. The data for scoring creativity in this study were from a verbatim listing of the suggestions for ways of playing the game offered by each family member, irrespective of either the practicality of the idea or whether it was actually tried out.[4] Some families were almost completely perseverative in their actions and never varied from the modes of play developed in the initial trials. The social interaction aspect of creativity was clearly observed in a few families in which one member suggested an

---

[3] In terms of the taxonomy of types of problems developed by Aldous (1968), this task would be considered a "conjunctive" problem.

[4] A verbal statement of the innovation was not necessary for it to be scored for creativity. A more complete description together with a manual for this technique of creativity scoring is given in Straus and Tallman (1966). I would like to express my appreciation to Fraine E. Whitney for development of the original version of the creativity scoring manual.

Table 1. Social Class Differences in Problem Solving and Parent-Child Interaction

Variable	Bombay			San Juan			Minneapolis		
	Middle (N = 32)	Working (N = 32)	t	Middle (N = 27)	Working (N = 18)	t	Middle (N = 38)	Working (N = 25)	t
A. Problem solving									
Success ratio	a	a	a	63.2	38.9	4.15**	55.6	51.4	1.72**
Creative responses	4.0	6.0	2.15**	4.0	1.8	2.98**	6.7	7.0	0.26
B. Parental control									
Father to child	56.3	28.3	3.97**	27.9	15.9	2.07**	38.2	20.1	3.65**
Mother to child	23.3	15.4	1.40	14.9	9.8	1.32	20.1	19.1	0.25
C. Child's control									
Child to father	6.4	6.9	0.20	10.7	3.1	3.65**	16.0	14.0	0.71
Child to mother	9.5	12.4	0.88	11.9	5.1	2.63**	19.7	15.5	1.33
D. Parental support									
Father to child	15.5	9.5	1.63	8.1	4.2	1.92*	16.5	6.9	3.80**
Mother to child	7.6	4.7	1.30	7.1	2.6	2.63**	7.8	5.4	1.67

a. No differences are reported because the working class families in Bombay experienced such difficulties with the task that a simpler version had to be used in order to be able to study variation in problem solving ability within the working class segment of the sample. See Straus, 1968, for further information.

  * $= p \leq .05$.
 ** $= p \leq .01$ (one tailed tests).

innovation in mode of play and was brought back into line by such comments as, "That's not the way this sort of game is played." At the other extreme were the uninhibited families who tried everything they thought of, for example, pushing the ball from between the legs while facing away from the target and using various alternations of colors and players.[5]

Findings. The mean scores shown in section A of Table 1 indicate that in all three societies the working class children performed more poorly in both aspects of problem solving ability than did the middle class. Moreover, as might be expected from the greater gap between social classes in Indian society, the deficit of the working class children is greatest in Bombay and least in Minneapolis.[6] The sex difference analysis shown in Table 2 is almost

---

[5] The validity of using innovations in game playing as a measure of creativity is, of course, not known. However, (1) the behaviors scored by this technique are congruent with the main conceptualizations of creativity (Anderson, 1959). (2) The behaviors used to index creativity in this study have the advantage of being based on a motor performance rather than a purely verbal performance and should, therefore, be more suited to tapping the creativity of children. (3) Although the creativity score is correlated with the "activity" score which indexes the amount of effort or engagement with the task (Straus, 1968), the low creativity scores of the working class children can not be attributed to differential engagement since there was essentially no social class difference in either the absolute level of activity (Straus, 1968: 423) or in the percentage that the child's actions formed of the total family activity in the task.

[6] See Straus (1968) for an explication of the lesser class differences in the more "modern" societies. A previous paper on sex differences in creativity (Straus and Straus, 1968) focused on a "conformity-inhibition" theory which, in the context of the present article, should be regarded as another of the many ways girls are denied as much opportunity as boys for exercising control over their lives.

Table 2.   Sex Differences in Problem Solving and Parent-Child Interaction

Variable	Bombay			Minneapolis		
	Boys (N = 32)	Girls (N = 32)	t	Boys (N = 32)	Girls (N = 31)	t
A. Problem solving						
Success ratio	59.6	41.9	3.53**	55.4	52.5	0.83
Creative						
responses	6.6	3.4	3.55**	8.1	5.4	2.71**
B. Parental control						
Father to child	40.2	44.3	0.53	33.3	28.7	0.87
Mother to child	18.1	20.6	0.43	19.3	20.1	0.20
C. Child's control						
Child to father	7.2	6.1	0.52	19.4	10.8	3.34**
Child to mother	11.9	10.0	0.57	22.5	13.4	3.24**
D. Parental support						
Father to child	15.8	9.2	1.84*	11.8	13.7	0.70
Mother to child	7.1	5.2	0.84	6.4	7.4	0.66

* $= p \leq .05$.
** $= p \leq .01$ (one tailed tests).

identical. The mean scores in Section A of Table 2 indicate that in both Bombay and Minneapolis girls tend to perform more poorly in both aspects of problem solving ability than do the boys. Again, as might be expected from the more inferior position of women in Indian society (Straus and Straus, 1968), the deficit of the girls is greater for the Bombay girls than for the Minneapolis girls.

PARENT-CHILD INTERACTION AND PROBLEM SOLVING ABILITY

The results just presented, although adding to descriptive knowledge of social class and sex differences, are primarily a prelude to the more important question of factors which might account for these differences. The data available from this study permit us to examine only one set of factors—the nature of the parent-child interaction; more specifically, the degree of control or power exercised by father, mother, and child over each other and the amount of support each provided the other. The choice of these two aspects of parent-child interaction was based on a theoretical analysis and integration of the literature which suggested that control and support are variables likely to be of crucial importance for almost all aspects of the socialization process (Straus, 1964), including development of the specific problem solving skills of this research. Moreover, by moving to the next higher level of abstraction and considering the creativity and success ratio scores of this research as components of a more general trait of *competence,* it is possible to draw on both the theoretical analyses of socialization for competence and the empirical studies of the familial antecedents of such components of competence as performance on tests of intelligence, self confidence, risk willingness, and achievement motivation. Probably the key point of theoretical linkage between conceptualizations of competence and the socialization variables examined in this research comes from the view that competency is established by a sequence of what Smith (1968: 312) has called "benign circles of productive engagement with the environment," which is to be contrasted with the antecedents of incompetence, "mired in vicious circles of self defeat."[7]

Space does not permit a review of the complex empirical studies on which this proposition is based. However, the processes which seem to be operating are illustrated by the longitudinal studies of the antecedents of rapid versus inhibited intellectual growth, achievement motivation, and creativity.

At the one extreme are the studies of institutionalized children whose constricted intellectual development has been well documented (Yarrow, 1964) and which seems to be a direct consequence of the lack of opportunity for "productive engagement with the environment" which is characteristic of many institutional settings. Among normally reared children, data from both

---

[7] The conceptualization of competence being used here is inherently evaluative in nature and is structured in terms of the demands and opportunities provided by a given society. It is based on the work of Inkeles (1966, 1968), Smith (1968), and White (1959, 1960, 1963), all of which view the competent person as an active, rather than a merely reactive, participant in the environment.

the Fels and the Berkeley longitudinal studies (Baldwin, Kalhorn, and Breese, 1945; Bayley and Schaefer, 1964) and a recent correlational study (Hurley, 1965) all show that intelligence is maximized by warm, supportive mothers. In a similar vein, studies of the antecedents of achievement motivation (summarized by Smith, 1968: 307) find "high need for achievement to be associated with achievement training by both parents and independence training by the father. Warm but dominating mothers who are much concerned with their son's performance contribute to high need for achievement in sons; dominating fathers to low achievement motivation."

The *processes* linking parental control and support with the development of competence are even less well researched than the gross relationships. One explanation argues that parental dominance prevents the child from achieving a sense of mastery. Thus, the child's point of view seldom makes a difference and this impotence is generalized from the area of parent-child (especially father-child) relations to the world at large, inhibiting attempts to manipulate the environment (Bee, 1969; Strodtbeck, 1958). Similarly, the lack of parental warmth and support are believed to be related to the development of low self-esteem, which in turn (possibly through building up a fear of failure) has a similar inhibiting effect on attempts to control the environment (Rosenberg, 1965).

On the basis of investigations such as those mentioned and the attempts to integrate them into a theory of socialization for competence, it is possible to formulate what might be called a "socialization deficit" theory to account, at least in part, for the inferior problem solving ability of girls and working class children. Such a theory holds that both girls and working class children are provided with less opportunity for productive engagement with the environment not only because of restrictions on activity imposed by social convention in the case of girls and by poverty in the case of the working class, but also because both girls and working class children receive less parental warmth and support while at the same time being subject to more arbitrary and authoritarian parental control. As a first step in testing this theory, data will be presented on social class differences in control and support. The hypotheses which follow from this theory predict that relative to boys and middle class children, girls and working class children are (1) more subject to parental dominance, but (2) receive less parental support.

The empirical evidence on sex differences in socialization practices shows no clear pattern. Several of the studies summarized by Maccoby (1966: 349-351) could be cited in support of these hypotheses and an equal number in the opposite direction. The literature on social class differences in parental power and support, although generally consistent with these hypotheses, poses certain problems of interpretation. On the one hand, the more authoritarian nature of parent-child relations in working class families have been well documented (Baumrind and Allen, 1967; Brody, 1968; McKinley, 1964). But simultaneously with this is the fact that working class families tend toward an "automatic" pattern of family organization with restricted amounts of joint activity of all types (Bott, 1957; Blood and Wolfe, 1960; Komarovsky,

1964; Nelson, 1966; Rainwater, 1966) and specifically, lesser involvement in what might be called "parenting" behavior (Bronfenbrenner, 1958; Kohn, 1963; Kohn and Carroll, 1960; Rosen, 1964; Straus, 1967). Moreover, the same deficits in "personal resources" (such as education, prestigeful occupational position, and money) which interfere with working class husbands playing the dominant role in relation to their wives, as prescribed by the values of working class society (Blood and Wolfe, 1960; Hoffman, 1960; Liebow, 1967; Komarovsky, 1965), may also operate to limit the actual amount of control exercised by working class parents over their children. Thus, although the values of working class parents may commit them to an authoritarian pattern of relationships with their children, the lack of personal resources for exercising power and the tendency toward a role segregated pattern of family organization are forces in the opposite direction. In the light of these conflicting factors, it was not possible to pose an a priori hypothesis concerning social class differences in degree of parental control. In summary, both on the basis of working class values and by deductive reasoning from the socialization deficit theory, the results of this study should show that parental control of working class children is greater than that of middle class children. But this expectation is countered by the lack of personal resources which would enable working class parents to act in terms of their child rearing values. What then do the data show?

CLASS AND SEX DIFFERENCES IN PARENT-CHILD INTERACTION

Control Scores. The procedure used in this research to measure parental control was the number of directive acts of each person which resulted in a change of behavior of the person to whom the act was directed. Scoring for this measure is quite simple. The observers recorded each act, using a key to show who originated the act, to whom it was directed, and if it was successful in controlling the behavior of the person to whom directed. For example, if the father tells the child to "shoot the ball now," this is scored as follows: HC+ if the child agrees verbally or by his action; HC— if the child explicitly refuses; and HC if the child simply ignores the power interaction which the father originated. It should be noted that although this system permits separate scores to be obtained for each actor's total control attempts, the present paper reports the "control +" or "effective power" scores.

The class differences in these control scores are reported in section B and C of Table 1. Looking first at the father-to-child and the mother-to-child control scores (section B) the results are consistently *opposite* to the hypothesis based on working class values. Although some differences are small, in every case it is the middle class children whose parents exercised greater control than was typical of the working class parents.

Turning now to section C of Table 1, which gives the child's ability to influence the behavior of the parents, the findings differ. For Bombay, the child control scores are consistent with the parental control scores since it is the working class children who were able to exercise greater power. But in San Juan and in Minneapolis, despite the greater power of the middle class parents, the *children* in these families were able to exercise more control than were the children in the working class families.

These results are obviously difficult to interpret. But it seems as though the situation is similar to that found by studies of spousal power; although working class parents may favor strict control of their children, they are not able to exercise even the degree of control characteristic of middle class parent-child relationships at this age level. As for the child's ability to control the behavior of the parents, the results for Bombay are the mirror image of the parental control scores. But for San Juan and Minneapolis, the middle class children, although more subject to parental control, simultaneously are more able to influence the behavior of the parents. At least for these latter two societies, the findings seem consistent with the picture which has emerged from much recent research which indicates that relative to middle class families, working class family organization is more role segregated and is characterized by a lower degree of involvement in almost all family roles. Thus, in the present study, the working class parents in both San Juan and in Minneapolis were found to exercise less control on the behavior of their children and working class children less control on the behavior of the parents.

The sex differences in these control scores are reported in sections B and C of Table 2. If we look only at the father-to-child and the mother-to-child control scores (section B), no support for the hypothesis of greater parental control of girls than of boys is found since the differences are all small and one difference is even in the opposite direction. However, when we turn to section C of Table 1, which gives the child's ability to influence the behavior of the parents, the differences are larger and are consistently in the direction of greater control for boys. From these results it would seem that although parents are about equal in controlling of boys and girls (at least in this laboratory situation), boys are allowed greater opportunity for control of this critical part of their environment.

Support Scores. Support was measured by means of a count of the number of supportive acts initiated by each person during the problem solving session. Each supportive act was classified as positive (+) or negative (—) on the basis of its assumed positive or negative contribution to group solidarity or integration. The support modalities used for this score and their classification as positive or negative are:

Positive	Negative
Praises	Blames, criticizes
Helps, cooperates	Hinders, refuses help of cooperation
Terms of endearment and liking	Terms of disparagement and dislike
Physical expression of affection (hugs, kisses)	Physical expression of dislike (pushes away, hits)
Encouragement, nurturance	Discourages, rejects

If, for example, a daughter received many red lights and the father consoled her by saying: "Don't worry, I'm getting red lights too," this would be scored HC+. But if the father said in disgust (or indicated nonverbally), "What's the matter with you? You're getting all red lights," this would be scored HC—. Similarly, if he gathers the daughter's balls for her this would be scored HC+, but if he pushed her balls out of the way making it more difficult for the child to get her balls, this would be HC—. However, for brevity, in this paper only the positive support scores are reported.

Inspection of the social class differences in support scores (section D of Table 1) shows that in every comparison the amount of support provided by the parents to the child is greater for middle class than for working class children.

Inspection of the sex-difference support scores (section D of Table 2) reveals that the amount of support provided by parents in Bombay is greater for boys than for girls. However, for the Minneapolis children, the results are reversed. That is, the girls received more support than the boys.

To the extent that supportive acts on the part of the parents are conducive to creating an image of self-esteem and self-worth in the child and to the extent that such a self conception is important for the development of competence (Rosenberg, 1965; Smith, 1968), the results of this research show that working class children are slighted as compared to middle class children. It therefore seems reasonable to conclude that the data presented on social class differences in both parental control and support are generally consistent with the socialization deficit theory and the specific hypotheses posed for testing on the basis of that theory. The sex difference results, although not as clear as the class differences, are also consistent with the theory. In both Bombay and San Juan, the girls, as hypothesized, received fewer supportive acts. Even the apparent inconsistency for the Minneapolis sample may not be an inconsistency. It will be remembered that the sex difference in *problem solving* ability was least for the Minneapolis sample. It is possible that the greater support received by the Minneapolis girls may be one of the factors which helped bring up the problem solving performance of this group of girls.

PARENT-CHILD INTERACTION AND PROBLEM SOLVING ABILITY

The evidence presented up to this point has shown social class and sex differences in problem solving ability and in two aspects of parent-child relationships which could, at least in part, account for the inferior performance of the girls and of working class children. If the data presented up to this point have been correctly interpreted, it follows that (1) parental control should be *negatively* related to the child's problems solving ability, but (2) parental support and the child's power should be *positively* related. To test these hypotheses, product-moment correlations were computed between each of the parent-child interaction variables and the problem solving performance variables, and are presented in Table 3.

Table 3. Correlation of Parent-Child Interaction Variables with Problem Solving Variables

Parent-child interaction variable	Correlation with problem solving variable*					
	Success ratio			Creative responses		
	Bombay	San Juan	Minne-apolis	Bombay	San Juan	Minne-apolis
A. Parental control						
Father to child	.11	.17	.04	−.27	−.04	−.16
Mother to child	−.10	.00	.16	−.10	−.04	−.06
B. Child's control						
Child to father	.01	.31	−.12	.26	.70	.61
Child to mother	.10	.32	−.01	.10	.69	.62
C. Parental support						
Father to child	.27	.14	.34	−.04	.08	−.21
Mother to child	.04	.17	.34	−.16	−.01	.04

* N = 64 for Bombay and Minneapolis so that $r \geq .20 = p \leq .05$ (one tailed test). For San Juan, N = 45, requiring an r of $\geq .24$ for the .05 level.

First let us consider the *parental* control variables (section A of Table 3). Only seven of the twelve correlations are in the predicted negative direction and only the correlation of father-to-child control for Bombay is significant. Turning to the *child's* ability to control his parents which, according to the argument just presented, is the more crucial aspect of the family power structure, the results given in section B of Table 3 at first seem contradictory. The correlations with the success ratio score for San Juan are significant; but no others are significant and two are even negative. However, the correlations with the creative responses score are, as predicted, all positive and five of the six are statistically significant.

Finally, section C of Table 3 gives the correlations of the problem solving performance scores with parental *support* and just the opposite pattern emerges. The correlations of parental support with creative responses are low and *negative,* whereas the correlations of support with the success ratio are all positive and three of the six are significant.

The pattern of correlations just described is not as confusing and contradictory as it may at first seem. In fact, despite irregularities and low correlations, the results shown in Table 2 can be summarized in propositional form. First, the greater the child's autonomy, as indicated by low parental control and especially by high child control, the greater his *creativity.* Second, the greater the parental support, the greater the child's *success ratio.* The meaning of these results comes into focus if we consider the success ratio as an indication of what Guilford (1967) has called "convergent thinking," and the creative responses score as indicative of his concept of "divergent thinking." This is because studies of the familial antecedents of these two aspects of intellectual performance suggest that pressures toward conformity tend to produce low creative children (Arasteh, 1968; Baldwin, 1948; Straus and Straus, 1968), whereas studies of the familial antecedents of high intelligence (a measure of convergent thinking in Guilford's taxonomy) suggest that lack of parental warmth and support tends to depress intelligence test performance (Hurley, 1965; Bayley and Schaefer, 1964).

SUMMARY AND CONCLUSIONS

Comparison of the performance of early adolescent girls and boys, and of middle class and working class children in Bombay, San Juan, and Minneapolis showed that the working class children in all three cities obtained lower scores than the middle class, and the girls in the two cities for which there was information scored lower than the boys, on measures of two aspects of problem solving ability: generation of creative solutions and implementation of correct solutions to the problem. Theoretical analysis of the socialization contexts which maximize competence in these two variables led to the formulation of a "socialization deficit" theory which holds that difference in problem solving performance should be associated with the extent to which parents provide warmth and support to the child and with the amount of control which they exercise over the behavior of the child. This theory led to the following hypotheses: (1) Parental control of girls and of working class children is *higher* than that of boys and of middle class children but parental support is *lower* for girls and for the working class; (2) the greater the parental control, the *lower* the problem solving ability; (3) the greater the parental support, the *higher* the problem solving ability.

The results showed that in respect to parental *support,* working class children and girls, as hypothesized, received less support than did boys and middle class children. However, in respect to *control,* contrary to the hypothesis, middle class parents exercised greater control than did working class parents. The lower degree of control exercised by working class parents in this sample was interpreted as reflecting a lack of the personal resources needed to exercise effective control. Thus, although working class parents may be more authoritarian, the extent to which they actually succeed in controlling the behavior of their adolescent children is relatively low. Moreover, the relatively high control scores of the middle class parents are probably more indicative of parental *involvement* than authority. This interpretation is enhanced by the finding that boys and middle class children in general, were simultaneously permitted to exercise greater control over the behavior of their parents than were girls or the working class children. The importance of these findings rests on the assumption that development of a feeling of mastery is important for socialization for problem solving. Children of middle class parents and boys tend to have greater opportunity to develop such a world view since, on the one hand, they can observe such behavior on the part of their parents (high parental control scores) and at the same time have the opportunity to themselves achieve control of an important part of their environment (high child-to-parent control scores).

The conclusions drawn from these correspondences between differences in problem solving ability and differences in parent-child interaction were further explored by directly correlating each of the measures of problem solving ability. These correlations seemed at first to provide little support for the socialization deficit theory. However, inspection of the pattern of correlations suggested that this is because the original hypotheses failed to differentiate between the two aspects of problem solving ability which were measured. When such a differentiation is made by taking the success ratio score as indicative of "convergent thinking" ability and the creative responses score indicative of "divergent thinking" ability, the results are consistent with both the theoretical and the empirical literature on the socialization contexts which maximize each of these abilities. Specifically, it was found that (1) the higher the control permitted the *child* and the lower the *parental* control of the child, the greater the child's creativity, and (2) the greater the parental support, the greater the child's success ratio.

There are some obvious limitations to these conclusions. For example, although this was a *laboratory* study, it was not an *experiment*, nor a longitudinal study. Consequently, causal inference from these findings carries with it the ambiguity inherent in all cross section research. In addition, the very fact that the findings are based on performance in a laboratory situation raises questions about their applicability outside the laboratory situation.[8] Finally, many of the correlations reported are low, so that aside from the question of statistical significance, they are primarily of importance as tests of a theory.[9] As Lippitt (1968) makes abundantly clear, even assuming valid findings, there is a long road between such findings and their application. Nevertheless, if the findings reported in this paper are taken as providing at least some support for what was called the socialization deficity theory, such a theory is a step in the process of reducing social inequality by assisting sectors of the society which are deficient in problem solving ability.

---

[8] See Straus (1969) and Straus and Tallman (1966) for a discussion of this problem in relation to the laboratory task used in this research and for references to other articles on the topic of the "external validity" of laboratory experimental data.

[9] It is also possible that the correlations presented in Table 3 are spurious in the sense that they result from confounding with social class. This could occur because there are social class differences in both parent-child interaction and in problem solving ability. To investigate this possibility, the correlations were recomputed separately for the middle class part and the working class part of the sample. Although some coefficients were reduced and some increased, none that were statistically significant dropped below this level, nor did any increase enough to meet the value needed for the .05 level with the total sample N. There was, however, one major reversal. For the Minneapolis sample, the lower class child's ability to control the behavior of the parents was found to be positively related to his success ratio ($r = .09$ for child-to-father control and .29 for child-to-mother control) whereas for the middle class children, the greater the child's power the less his success ratio score ($r = -.29$ for child-to-father control and $-.20$ for child-to-mother control). The positive coefficients for the working class are consistent with the theory presented in this paper. No satisfactory explanation has been developed for the negative coefficients of the middle class children. With the exception of this puzzling finding, the results of replicating the analysis within social class levels are consistent with the total sample findings presented in Table 3.

REFERENCES

Arastch, Josephine D., "Creativity and Related Processes in the Young Child: A Review of the Literature." *Journal of Genetic Psychology*, 112: 77–108, 1968.

Aldous, Joan, "A Framework for the Analysis of Family Problem Solving." Paper prepared for presentation at the Society for the Study of Social Problems Annual Meeting (mimeographed), 1968.

Allen, V. L. and Crutchfield, R. S., "Generalization of Experimentally Reinforced Conformity." *Journal of Abnormal and Social Psychology*, 67: 326–333, 1963.

Anastasi, Anne, *Differential Psychology: Individual and Group Differences in Behavior*. New York: The Macmillan Company, 1958.

Anderson, H. H., *Creativity and Its Cultivation*. New York: Harper and Row, 1959.

Baldwin, Alfred L., "Socialization and the Parent-Child Relationship." Child Development, 19: 127–136, 1948.

Baldwin, Alfred L. *et al*, "Patterns of Parent Behavior." *Psychological Monographs*, 58 (Number 3): 268, 1948.

Barry, Herbert III, Bacon, Margaret K., and Child, Irvin L., "A Cross-Cultural Survey of Some Sex Differences in Socialization." *Journal of Abnormal and Social Psychology*, 55 (November): 327–332, 1957.

Baughman, E. Earl and Dahlstrom, W. Grant, *Negro and White Children: A Psychological Study in the Rural South*. New York: Academic Press, 1968.

Baumrind, Diana and Black, Allen E., "Socialization Practices Associated With Dimensions of Competence in Preschool Boys and Girls." *Child Development*, 38 (June): 291–327, 1967.

Bayley, Nancy, "Some Increasing Parent-Child Similarities During the Growth of Children." *Journal of Educational Psychology*, 45: 1–21, 1954.

Bayley, Nancy and Schaefer, Earl S., "Correlations of Maternal and Child Behaviors with the Development of Mental Abilities: Data from the Berkeley Growth Study." *Monographs of the Society for Research in Child Development* 29, 1964.

Bee, Helen L., "Socialization for Problem Solving." Paper presented at the symposium on "The Family as a Problem Solving Group." Riverside, California, 1969.

Bendig, A. W., "Age-Related Changes in Covert and Overt Anxiety." *Journal of Genetic Psychology*, 62: 159–163, 1960.

Blood, Robert O. and Wolfe, Donald M., *Husbands and Wives: The Dynamics of Married Living*. New York: The Free Press, 1960.

Bott, Elizabeth, *Family and Social Network*. London: Tavistock Publications, 1957.

Brim, Orville G. *et al*, *Personality and Decision Processes*. Stanford: Stanford University Press, 1962.

Brody, Grace F., "Socioeconomic Differences in Stated Maternal Child-Rearing Practices and in Observed Maternal Behavior." *Journal of Marriage and the Family*, 30 (November): 656–660, 1968.

Bronfenbrenner, Urie, "Socialization and Social Class Through Time and Space." Pp. 400–424 in E. E. Maccoby, T. M. Newcomb, and E. L. Hartley, ed.,

Readings in Social Psychology. New York: Holt, Rinehart and Winston, Inc., 1958.

Deutsch, Martin, Katz, Irwin, and Jensen, Arthur R., ed. *Race, Social Class, and Psychological Development.* New York: Holt, Rinehart and Winston, Inc., 1968.

Elder, Glenn H., Jr. and Bowerman, Charles E., "Family Structure and Child-Rearing Patterns: The Effect of Family Size and Sex Composition." *American Sociological Review,* 28 (December): 891–905, 1963.

Dewey, John, *How We Think.* New York: Holt, Rinehart and Winston, Inc., 1933.

Gagne, R. M., "Problem-Solving and Thinking." Pp. 147–173 in P. R. Farnsworth and Q. McNemar, ed. *Annual Review of Psychology,* Palo Alto, California, 1959.

Glazer, Nona Y. and Creedom, Carol F., *Children and Poverty: Some Sociological and Psychological Perspectives.* Chicago: Rand McNally and Company, 1968.

Guilford, J. P., *The Nature of Human Intelligence.* New York: McGraw-Hill, Inc., 1967.

Gurin, Gerald, *et al, Americans View Their Mental Health: A Nationwide Interview Survey.* New York: Basic Books, Inc., 1960.

Hamblin, Robert L., "Group Integration During a Crisis." *Sociometry,* 11: 57–76, 1958.

——— "Leadership and Crisis." *Sociometry,* 21 (December): 322–335, 1958.

Hess, Robert D. and Shipman, Virginia C., "Early Experience and the Socialization of Cognitive Modes in Children." *Child Development,* 36 (December): 869–885, 1965.

Hindley, C. B., "Social Class Influences on the Development of Ability in the First Five Years." *Proceedings of the XIV International Congress of Applied Psychology,* 3: 29–41, 1962.

Hoffman, Lois W., "Effects of Employment of Mothers on Parental Power Relations and the Division of Household Tasks." *Marriage and Family Living,* 22 (February): 27–35, 1960.

Hunt, J. McV., *Intelligence and Experience.* New York: The Ronald Press Co., 1961.

Hurley, John R., "Parental Acceptance-Rejection and Children's Intelligence." *Merrill-Palmer Quarterly,* 11 (January): 19–31, 1965.

Inkeles, Alex, "Social Structure and the Socialization of Competence." *Harvard Educational Review,* 36: 265–283, 1966.

——— "Society, Social Structure, and Child Socialization." Pp. 73–129 in John A. Clausen, ed., *Socialization and Society.* Boston: Little, Brown and Company, 1968.

Jones, H. E., "The Environment and Mental Development." Pp. 631–696 in L. Carmichael, ed., *Manual of Child Psychology.* Second edition. New York: John Wiley & Sons, 1954.

Kent, Norma and Davis, D. R., "Discipline in the Home and Intellectual Development." *British Journal of Medical Psychology,* 30: 27–33, 1957.

Kirkpatrick, C., *The Family as Process and Institution.* New York: The Ronald Press Co., 1963. Pp. 163–165.

Kohn, Melvin L., "Social Class and Parent-Child Relationships: An Interpretation." *American Journal of Sociology,* 68 (January): 471–480, 1963.

———— and Carroll, Eleanor E., "Social Class and the Allocation of Parental Responsibilities." *Sociometry*, (December): 372–392, 1960.

Komarovsky, Mirra, *Blue-Collar Marriage*. New York: Random House, Inc., 1964.

Levinson, Daniel J. and Huffman, Phillis E., "Traditional Family Ideology and Its Relation to Personality." *Journal of Personality*, 23 (March): 251–273, 1955.

Liebow, Elliot, *Tally's Corner: A Study of Negro Streetcorner Men*. Boston: Little, Brown & Co., 1967.

Lippitt, Ronald, "Improving the Socialization Process." Pp. 321–374 in John A. Clausen, ed., *Socialization and Society*. Boston: Little, Brown and Co., 1968.

Maccoby, Eleanor E., "Sex Differences in Intellectual Functioning." Pp. 25–55 in Eleanor E. Maccoby, ed., *The Development of Sex Differences*. Stanford: Stanford University Press, 1966.

McClelland, David C. *et al, The Achievement Motive*. New York: Appleton-Century-Crofts, 1953.

McKinley, Donald G., *Social Class and Family Life*. New York: The Free Press, 1964.

Miller, Daniel R. and Swanson, Guy E., *Inner Conflict and Defense*. New York: Holt, Rinehart and Winston, Inc., 1960.

Nakamura, C. Y., "Conformity and Problem Solving." *Journal of Abnormal and Social Psychology*, 56: 315–320, 1958.

Nelson, Joel I., "Clique Contacts and Family Orientations." *American Sociological Review*, 31 (October): 663–672, 1958.

Rainwater, Lee, "Crucible of Identity: The Negro Lower-Class Family." *Daedalus, Journal of the American Academy of Arts and Sciences*, 95: 172–216, 1966.

Riessman, Frank, *The Culturally Deprived Child*. New York: Harper and Row, 1962.

Rosen, Bernard C., "Social Class and the Child's Perception of the Parent." *Child Development*, 35 (December): 1147–1154, 1964.

Rosenberg, M., *Society and the Adolescent Self-Image*. Princeton, New Jersey: Princeton University Press, 1965.

Smith, M. Brewster, "Competence and Socialization." Pp. 270–320 in John A. Clausen, ed., *Socialization and Society*. Boston: Little, Brown and Co., 1968.

Straus, Murray A., "Power and Support Structure of the Family in Relation to Socialization." *Journal of Marriage and the Family*, 26 (August): 318–326, 1964.

———— "The Influence of Sex of Child and Social Class on Instrumental and Expressive Family Roles in a Laboratory Setting." *Sociology and Social Research*, 52 (October): 7–21, 1967.

———— "Communication, Creativity, and Problem Solving Ability of Middle- and Working-Class Families in Three Societies." *American Journal of Sociology*, 73 (January): 417–430. Reprinted in Marvin B. Sussman, *Sourcebook in Marriage and the Family*, 3d Ed. Boston: Houghton, Mifflin, 1968.

———— "Methodology of a Laboratory Experimental Study of Families in Three Societies." In Reuben Hill and Rene Konig (eds.), *Families East and West*. Paris: Mouton, 1970.

———— and Straus, Jacqueline H., "Family Roles and Sex Differences in Creativity of Children in Bombay and Minneapolis." *Journal of Marriage and the Family*, 30 (February): 46–53, 1968.

——— and Tallman, Irving, "SIMFAM: A Technique for Observational Measurement and Experimental Study of Families." Mimeographed paper, 1966.

Strodtbeck, Fred L., "Family Interaction, Values, and Achievement." Pp. 135–194 in D. C. McClelland *et al, Talent and Society*. Princeton, New Jersey: Van Nostrand, 1958.

Swanson, Guy E., "A Preliminary Laboratory Study of the Acting Crowd." *American Sociological Review*, 18 (October): 522–533, 1953.

Tallman, Irving, "The Family as a Small Problem Solving Group." Paper presented at the Annual Meeting of the National Council of Family Relations (mimeographed), 1968.

Terman, Louis M. and Oden, Melita H., *The Gifted Child Grows Up*. Stanford: Stanford University Press, 1947.

Vaught, G. M., "The Relationship of Role Identification and Ego Strength to Sex Differences in the Rod and Frame Test." *Journal of Personality*, 33: 271–283, 1965.

Walter, L. M. and Marzolf, S. S., "The Relation of Sex, Age, and School Achievement to Levels of Aspiration." *Journal of Educational Psychology*, 42: 285–292, 1951.

White, R. W., "Motivation Reconsidered: The Concept of Competence." *Psychological Review*, 66: 297–333, 1959.

——— "Competence and the Psychosexual Stages of Development." Pp. 97–141 in M. Jones, ed. *Nebraska Symposium on Motivation* 1960. Lincoln: University of Nebraska Press, 1960.

——— "Ego and Reality in Psychoanalytic Theory. A Proposal for Independent Ego Energies." *Psychological Issues*, 3, 1963.

Witkin, H. A., "Individual Differences in Ease of Perception of Embedded Figures." *Journal of Personality*, 19: 1–15, 1950.

Yarrow, L. J., "Separation from Parents During Early Childhood." In M. L. Hoffman and Lois W. Hoffman, eds. *Review of Child Development Research*, Volume 1. New York: Russell Sage Foundation, 1964.

Socialization Disorders and Familial Exchanges

ROBERT L. HAMBLIN
DANIEL FERRITOR
and
MARTIN KOZLOFF

Many families experience serious problems with children who are slow in learning such patterns as talking, reading, arithmetic and/or who learn to behave in bizarre and disruptive ways. While such problems can be due to physiological damage or biochemical deficiencies (of either genetic or postnatal origin), in many instances they seem to be socialization disorders, that is, they are the natural result of inadequate or pathogenic learning environments either at home or at school. The remedy for such disorders involves the restructuring of social learning environments to accelerate the learning of certain behavior patterns and/or to reverse the learning of others.

During the past few years a number of us, at Central Midwestern Regional Education Laboratory and at Washington University, have been experimenting with learning environments for the remediation of these disorders, with several types of children. The purpose here is to review some of this research, specifically that with autistic children, since part of the remedial or therapeutic program for such children is conducted in the home by the parents. Hence, much of the paper deals with how we train parents to structure remedial learning environments.

Most, if not all, social learning environments involve exchanges which the children and others (parents and teachers) work over and over again on relatively fixed terms. Since learning theory is basic to an understanding of how working such exchanges produces long term behavioral effects, the paper begins with an introduction.

LEARNING THEORY

When most people think of learning they recall their own participation in formal educational systems which generally involved the acquisition of knowledge or understanding by listening to teachers, having discussions, reading books, working problems, taking notes, outlining, reviewing, taking tests, and so forth. This symbolic or verbal learning is essential in later stages of an individual's development; however, it is not the only kind of learning. Man has biological mechanisms which allow him to learn directly, via his own experience with his environment. It is through learning mediated by such mechanisms that human organisms develop habitual ways of working their environments to obtain sustenance or pleasure and to avoid destruction or pain.

When we began our investigations, we relied heavily on the learning theory that has emerged in psychology out of experiments with various types of animals. While the operating characteristics of the learning mechanisms of man and lower organisms are similar in many ways, our experiments with human subjects have led us to formulate our own theory of learning, one which is capable of describing the complexities of human learning data. In addition, we have been influenced heavily by the theories and by the brilliant experiments of B. F. Skinner, (1938, Holland and Skinner, 1961, Ferster and Skinner, 1957) and those who have subsequently worked in his tradition (Bijou and Baer, 1961, Ullman and Krasner, 1966, Reese, 1966). Also those who are familiar with O. K. Moore's work (Moore and Anderson, 1966) on human learning theory will notice the influence of his formulations.

An Overview

Though all learning environments, be they natural, mechanical, or social, differ in some ways, they are essentially similar in several others such as the following. (1) All such environments may be worked for reinforcers. Reinforcers may be defined as stimuli which induce changes in a person's feeling state. They are positive reinforcers if they induce a pleasant feeling state, negative reinforcers if they induce an aversive or painful feeling state. In general, people learn to work their environments to acquire positive reinforcers and to avoid or escape negative reinforcers. The learning occurs via the repetitive working of or interaction with the environment. In this way, the person directly experiences the consequences of his behavior and discovers the behavior which will or will not produce the reinforcers. Often, the strength of the reinforcers is gauged by the size of the change it produces in the person's feeling state, and *the stronger the reinforcers involved in the environmental response, the more quickly, the more easily the person will learn.* (2) The production and nonproduction of reinforcers, as mentioned, provides a person with a kind of feedback which allows him to learn how to work his environment. However, in addition to reinforcement, learning environments generally provide other forms of feedback, such as process cues which are predictive of reinforcement and may precede a response or occur among a sequence or chain of responses. The immediacy of feedback, whether it is reinforcement *per se* or process cues predictive of later reinforcement, is an important determinant of the rate of learning. Thus, learning can occur more easily, more rapidly, the more immediate the feedback.

(3) Learning environments also may vary in the consistency of their feedback; that is, in the degree to which the environmental response pattern to the person's behavior is invariant. In general, *the more consistent the feedback, the more quickly, the more easily the person will learn.* (4) Learning environments also may vary in the degree to which a person is allowed to set his own pace in working for reinforcers. In other words, some environments allow a person more freedom than others in that the response pattern neither rushes nor delays his work pattern. In general, *a person will learn more easily and more quickly the more freedom he has to set his own pace in working the environment for reinforcers.*

There have been some—Skinner (1968) and Moore for example—who, after considering similar lists, have concluded that machines provide the best learning environment for the human organism, that other human organisms are so unresponsive and so inconsistent that they generally hinder the learning process. This may be true in many situations, but not in all. Mankind, for example, generally provides almost all of his young with a near ideal environment in which to learn their first language. The results are indicative. Most children learn to talk fluently in sentences on their own, without formal instruction and with considerable pleasure. Even so, mankind has much to learn about being and providing an effective learning environment for others, particularly the young. It is not a simple matter for, as we have discovered, there are at least three types of learning—contingency, expertise, and habit learning—and each is promoted in a different way.

Contingency Learning

The first step in all learning is to gain insight into the contingencies which govern the environmental responses. The rate of contingency learning increases with the immediacy of environmental feedback, with its consistency, and with the strength of the reinforcers. Of these, the last is probably crucial because the degree to which a person attends to environmental features increases as the strength of related reinforcers increases. Attention, in turn, increases the rate of contingency learning.

For example, in learning a language, man's prime invention for manipulating his *social* environment, a child has to learn thousands of contingencies: associations between thousands of words and their referents; how to string or relate words together to convey messages (syntax); and how to emit the utterances appropriate for the production of reinforcement. This learning achievement is possible because in a verbal conversation the other person is generally responsive in that his feedback is usually immediate and relatively consistent, and thus early attempts at communication are generally reinforced strongly. In other words, verbal messages are usually the child's most efficient means of manipulating his social environment for reinforcers.

Expertise Learning

The manipulative actions required to produce environmental responses are often not easy, but require considerable expertise. Expertise develops as a function of reinforced practice. As a person repeatedly works his environment for reinforcers, the essential parts of the manipulative pattern (those which actually produce reinforcers) are gradually strengthened and the gross, superfluous parts weakened. The result of expertise learning, then, is an accelerating response rate which, when measured and plotted against time, depicts a typical learning curve.

The mathematical similarities between the expertise learning curves of different people, and, in fact, of different species suggest that expertise learning occurs automatically as a function of reinforced practice and that the operating characteristics of the biological learning mechanisms, as reflected in the laws of expertise learning, are not cultural artifacts but are culture free and genetically determined. (It is quite obvious, however, that the *content* of what one learns is largely determined by the cultural or social conditions in which he lives.)

Here again, the quality of the environment influences the rate of expertise learning because the rate of reinforced practice increases with pacing, with immediacy of feedback, and especially with the strength of the reinforcers.

In learning to talk, a child acquires a complex of behavior patterns, a hierarchy of abilities as it were, in which he demonstrates expertise—how to verbalize reliably and on call, the 41 basic sounds used in English, how to blend these sounds into words, how to string the words into sentences to *convey* messages, how to modulate the pitch and tone of the utterances, and so on. With the social environment structured as it is, the typical child starts practicing the verbalization of sounds when he is three to five months old and he usually develops his ability to converse fluently in sentences by the age of 42 months. Conversing also requires the more passive expertise involved in recognizing sounds and words and in grasping the meaning or the message which others convey with a string of words.

Habit Learning

The third type of learning occurs simultaneously with expertise learning, under the same basic conditions but perhaps at a much slower pace. A manipulative pattern which regularly produces reinforcement, by virtue of that fact, is gradually strengthened until it becomes habitual. The habitual nature of the pattern is manifest in reflexivity, perseveration, and generalization.

Reflexivity. Habitual behavior patterns are set off automatically by the stimuli which have repeatedly signaled reinforcement in the past. These activating stimuli sometimes include a specific hunger for the reinforcer which activates the pattern as well as any stimuli which may signal that the relevant contingencies are operative in the environment. One indication of increasing reflexivity is a decrease in the latency of the response in the presence of stimuli signaling that the reinforcement contingencies are operative.

Some people find it difficult to see the importance of reflexivity. However, it is one thing to think through a response pattern and another to do it naturally, spontaneously, without thinking. Certainly, it is possible to think oneself through many situations so as to produce few aversive consequences. However, in other situations the costs are substantial until the behavior pattern does in fact become reflexive. For example, as long as one has to think through the mechanics of verbalizing as well as one's message, his speech will remain painfully slow and effortful both for himself and others. To speak fluently, pronunciation, selection of suitable words, and the structuring of sentences has to be reflexive or nearly so.

Perseveration. When a manipulative pattern which has been strengthened by the repeated production of reinforcers in the past suddenly fails to produce reinforcers in the present, a person will not suddenly drop the pattern but will try it over and over again. It is as if he finds it impossible to believe that the manipulative pattern no longer produces reinforcers. However, just as habits are strengthened through repeated reinforcement, they can be weakened through repeated nonreinforcement. Hence, when contingencies are terminated, as they sometimes are in an experiment, the habitual manipulative pattern deteriorates as indicated by a deceleration of the response and, occasionally, an increase in superfluous (emotion) behavior. Usually referred to as *extinction*, this unlearning process is actually learning in reverse. It often takes as much cumulative nonreinforcement for a habit pattern to become extinguished as it took cumulative reinforcement to develop the habit in the first place.

The amount of perseveration, usually taken as the best single index of the strength of the habit pattern, is a function of a number of variables. The one worth mentioning here, in addition to the cumulative amount of previous reinforcement, is the schedule of previous reinforcement. (An intermittant schedule produces a stronger habit pattern than a continuous schedule).

Generalization. A manipulative pattern which has been strengthened by the repeated production of reinforcers in one environment will be tried by the person in similar environments to see if it works there, too. Through this process, termed generalization, the subject continues contingency learning; he discovers, through trial and error, the cues which allow him to recognize those environmental situations in which particular contingencies are operative and those in which they are not.

REINFORCERS AND CONDITIONING THEORY

Whenever an individual repeatedly manipulates his environment to produce reinforcement, not only does he learn as outlined above, but his feeling states are also subtly conditioned. The conditioning processes were first discovered by Pavlov (1960) in his famous experiments on the salivation reflex in dogs.

At first, many thought that Pavlovian conditioning processes did not occur in man. This was because conditioning involves reflexive patterns which many see as being almost irrelevant to human behavior. Human behavior is supposed to be predominantly voluntary rather than reflexive. Furthermore, when the appropriate experimentation was done, many of the known human reflexes turned out to be impervious to conditioning; for example, no one has ever been able to classically condition a stimulus to elicit a knee jerk.

However, what most of Pavlov's detractors failed to understand is that emotional responses are generally reflexive in nature and that they do condition easily. Hence, it is possible that all of man's socially determined hungers and aversive drives are *acquired and maintained* via the conditioning process.

Actually it was fortunate that Pavlov happened to choose salivation to work with in his experiments. Salivation reflects *anticipatory emotional responses* which in muted form are similar to the pleasures produced by eating food. Such, apparently, is the essence of all conditioned hungers; they are pleasant anticipatory emotional responses. As such they become conditioned whenever that which triggers them, like the bell, *repeatedly signals* something else which already produces a pleasant emotional response like that produced by the sight of meat powder or the actual eating of the meat powder.

As suggested earlier, conditioning occurs whenever direct learning occurs. Anything which repeatedly precedes or signals reinforcement—for example, the manipulative actions or the environmental feedback—will over a period of time become a conditioned reinforcer which produces pleasureful emotional responses similar to those produced by the original reinforcers. Thus, if conversing is repeatedly reinforced, conversing will eventually become a conditioned reinforcer.

Identifying That Which is Reinforcing

Ethologists, the expert observers of animal behavior, have recently shown that internal emotional states are generally reflected externally via reflexive responses, and the magnitude of the internal emotional response is generally mirrored by the magnitude of the external response which reflects it. Building upon such basic discoveries, Lorenz and his associates have done extremely clever motivational studies which have helped them determine the emotional responses involved in various ritualized behavior patterns for a number of species.

The ethologists' principles are of immediate use in identifying reinforcers. It appears, for example, that spontaneous smiling signals an influx in internal pleasure, particularly in children. Consequently, it is generally possible to infer accurately what gives children pleasure by observing that which produces smiling. Also, because children apparently look at or attend to reinforcers at least for a time, the intensity of their looking or their attention generally reflects the strength of the pleasure associated with the reinforcer. This is an extremely important point and it will be illustrated by an extended example.

Peter Wolff's (1961) experiments at Harvard show that most infants smile when they hear their mother's voice, starting at about six weeks. At this age, the response is only to the mother's voice; other voices and sounds even in the same octave range do not produce a smile. This suggests, then, that the mother's voice typically becomes a conditioned reinforcer during the first few weeks of the infant's life. Such conditioning would happen if, for example, the mother frequently talked to the child "to soothe" him over the frustration of waiting through preparation periods for his milk, talked to him while changing wet diapers, or while feeding him. Later, as he was "talked to" and cared for by other members of the family, the conditioning might generalize to those other voices and perhaps voices in general.

This early conditioning to voices is felt to be crucial in the infant's socialization. Approximately at four months the infant will begin to babble spontaneously. Theoretically, if the conditioning has occurred, it will remind him of others' voices and hence will produce a pleasurable sensation. In this event there will be an increase in the frequency of babbling and thus increase reinforced practice and with it the infant's expertise in producing sounds. The infant's increased practice and expertise will in turn increase the probability of direct reinforcement, such as pleasurable responses from others.

The importance of early conditioning to the voice in the socialization process is illustrated by the case of deaf children. Deaf children, who because of their anatomical deficits cannot be conditioned to the mother's voice, quickly pass through the reflexive babbling stage and henceforth will remain relatively mute. Later they are often taught to talk using rather special procedures (Bereiter and Engelmann, 1966).

As suggested earlier, social learning and conditioning occur when two or more persons repetitively work an exchange with one another for reinforcers. Our general finding has been that all socialization disorders among young children—the failure to learn the expected, conventional patterns and the learning of bizarre, disruptive patterns—exist because his adults fail to structure the environment with appropriate exchanges so the child is repeatedly reinforced for behaving in and hence learning the normal ways, and/or have, perhaps unwittingly, structured pathogenic exchanges in which the child is repeatedly reinforced for bizarre disruptive behaviors. In sum, our observations have shown that the environments of children with socialization disorders are either not responsive to pro-social patterns, or are responsive to nonsocial or even disruptive patterns, or both.

Our classroom experiments with nonverbal inner city children with hyper-aggressive boys, which generally support this thesis, have been reported elsewhere (Hamblin, et al, 1969). The thesis is also supported by the results, by research on the etiology and remediation of autism, and related childhood psychoses.[1]

INFANTILE AUTISM

There are several theories of the etiology of infantile autism. (See Rutter, 1968, for a discussion and evaluation of the supporting research.) While all of these theories have some evidence to support them, our investigations have lead us to a social theory of autism which has two parts: the first involves etiology or how autism may get started and the second, how autism is maintained.

Infantile autism may begin because, through some accident, the mother's voice fails to become a conditioned positive reinforcer to the infant during the first few months of his life. There are several ways that this accident might occur. The mother, for example, might never "talk" with the infant, particularly in a way that might signal sustenance by the mother and the emotional responses that sustenance produces. Alternatively, she might talk all of the time so that her voice does not become a consistent signal for reinforcement but only constant background noise. Also, as Bettelheim suggests, the mother might be mean to the child, her voice always signalling the onset of painful feeling states, in which case it would become a conditioned negative reinforcer. In any event, because the mother's voice is not a conditioned, positive reinforcer, the autistic infant, like the deaf infant, has a very short-lived reflexive babbling phase.

All of this is a grave tragedy for the child, for without verbal communication he is cut off from the normal processes of influencing others, of getting what he wants or needs. The autistic child, therefore, develops nonverbal

---

[1] We make the distinction here between early infantile autism and other forms of childhood psychoses such as childhood autism (Wing, 1966), a disorder which in its symptoms is nearly identical to infantile autism except it occurs later usually during the second and third year instead of during the first few months. These psychoses often appear to be the result of childhood training (for example, having the stomach pumped for aspirin or having an operation) which sends the child into a nonverbal shock. If prior to the trauma the child has been neglected and/or otherwise maltreated by his significant adults, and if after the trauma they become overly solicitous, pampering him at every turn, then the child will sometimes never start talking again but learns instead nonverbal means of communication, like the child with infantile autism.

means of communication even for getting and maintaining his mother's and/or other's attention.

Through simple trial and error procedures, such a child almost always learns that his mother will always respond if he acts violently or bizarrely enough. And she must, if only to placate or punish in vain efforts to stop his annoyances. He thus learns to play "get the mother's attention"; and this soon develops into "get mother exasperated, but stop just short of the point where she punishes and it really hurts." Here is an example of such a game observed in our laboratory school.

> Larry is allowed to pick out his favorite book. His mother then attempts to read it to him, but he keeps turning the pages so she cannot. The mother then gets up and goes to the shelf for four more books. Larry gets up and walks away from the table. The mother then *yells* at him to come back. He *smiles*!! Mother continues to talk to the child to try to get him back for the story. Finally, he comes over to the table and takes the book away from her. She lets him and goes back to the bookcase for another book. He then sits down and she begins to read. He tries to get up, but his mother pulls him back. Again. Again. She holds him there. He gets away and starts walking around the room. Goes to the toy cabinet. Mother gets up to go over and take a toy away from him. He sits on the floor. The mother comes over and sits down by him. He gets up and goes over by the door and opens it and tries to run out. In an angry voice she tells him he has to stay. He *smiles*!! She resumes reading. He gets up and starts walking around the table. She grabs him roughly as he comes by. He *smiles*!! He grabs the book away from her and she tries to get it back. She takes the book away from him and pulls him back to the table. Again he grabs the book away from her and she tries to get it back. Now, she takes the book away from him and pulls him back to the table. She is very upset. He grabs the book away from her and starts *laughing*. His mother takes the book back and tries to put him on a chair in the hall. Now she tries to come back into the room. Larry gets back ahead of her. The mother tries to close the door on him, but he is pushing to keep it open. She cannot or does not close it. Now she pushes him down on the ground and tries to close the door again. He gets his foot in the door and she can't close it again. She picks him up and carries him back to the chair in the hall. Smiling, he races back to the door as she tries to close it. The ten-minute period ends with the mother and child at the door. As the experimenter approached, the mother said, "He just does not like to be read to."

The above incident is typical of what happened when Larry's mother made demands upon him and it showed his behavior patterns at their worst. Of particular interest here, however, is the record of Larry's smiling. Since the observations were taken at a time when the authors were just becoming sensitive to behaviors which reflect emotional responses, they are probably not perfect. Undoubtedly, some of Larry's smiles were missed, as were some of his mother's behaviors which registered her inner turmoil.

Even so, it is rather evident that Larry was pleased, reinforced, every time he could see that he was succeeding in getting his mother angry. While the stream of interaction seems on the surface to be haphazard, the analysis suggests an underlying order which parallels the repetitive pecking and feeding observed in the usual animal learning experiment. It is as though Larry craved his mother's anger and repetitively "pressed a button" to earn more and more of it over and over again, never letting up. Ironically, in her efforts to teach Larry, his mother had unknowingly involved herself in a pathogenic exchange which was teaching Larry to become more and more psychotic. Such repetitive, if unwitting, reinforcement is always characteristic of the behavior of the autistic child's significant adult(s). Hence, it is our theory that autism, whatever its origins, is always maintained by a pathogenic exchange.

However, autistic teasing was not Larry's only problem. He had many behavior deficits, the most debilitating of which was his inability to talk functionally. Larry was echolalic. Like a parrot, he simply repeated in random fashion some of the words which he heard, perhaps because this was a way of getting attention.

We reasoned that if Larry initially failed to learn simply because certain reinforcers (primarily his mother's voice) which usually start infants on the road to talking were not conditioned and hence were ineffective, then he might learn to talk *even at age* 4½, if effective reinforcers were used in speech therapy. A number of reinforcers might have been used but we decided to use the strongest reinforcer of all, the one that requires the least prior conditioning—that is, food. Consequently, we had Larry take one to three of his meals each day in the laboratory, where he earned his food from the therapist bite by bite, first for phonemic imitation, then for saying the names of objects, then for asking for different types of food. Gradually, Larry learned to talk functionally. In fact, by the time the above incident occurred, the training had changed Larry to the point where he was beginning to converse in sentences, freely with the therapist. Although his sentences were still broken, he had a functional vocabulary of over 200 words.

Recall, however, that Larry, in the above episode, was completely involved in his teasing game; he talked very little, if at all. His new pattern of relating to the therapist in conversation had not yet generalized to replace his old ways of relating with his mother, perhaps because the mother continued to reward the old patterns. Repeated experiences like this have led us to the rather obvious conclusion that to break old habits and to effectively educate or re-educate a child, it is necessary to change the autistic child's familial environment.

How does one construct a relationship between mother and child which has the effect of acculturating the child, a relationship which will not deteriorate but will endure over time? The direct learning principles discussed so far do not give a ready-made answer. However, they do provide a basis for innovating a solution. The basic innovation used here is that of George Homans (1961) who has suggested that at least one type of equilibrium should obtain in an *exchange* situation where the responses of both parties to the exchange reinforce the other's behavior. Theoretically, as long as the reward each receives exceeds his incurred cost, to use Homan's terms, the relationship will maintain itself.

Looking at the relationship between Larry and the therapist who had succeeded in teaching him to talk, it was obvious that these simple conditions had obtained. Larry registered in many ways that he valued food and the attention he received when he talked for the therapist. In turn, the therapist was thrilled at Larry's developing speech patterns. Consequently, the responses of each to the other were keeping the other *behaving* and *learning*. Larry was learning how to talk and the therapist how to structure an acculturating exchange.

At this point we realized also that Larry's mother wanted him to learn to talk but was failing to help him to do so, primarily because she did not understand how to structure an exchange that would enable him to learn. So we analyzed further the exchange relationship between the therapist and Larry in order to be able to explain to the mother what to do and why.

In the analysis it became obvious that the therapist managed the exchange process deftly through the use of what will be called exchange and non-exchange signals. An exchange signal specified to Larry what he had to do to initiate the exchange, and when he did initiate an exchange, the therapist would then reciprocate with food. For example, the therapist might signal the exchange by asking a question: "What color is this?" Larry would then initiate the exchange by answering verbally with the word which described the color to which the therapist was pointing.

Whenever Larry tried to initiate a pathogenic exchange, nonexchange signals were used by the therapist to indicate simply that there would be no reciprocation. Thus, if Larry balked, if he walked away from the table, if he otherwise tried to tease, to upset the therapist, she would simply signal that there would be no such exchange by turning her head, by turning her back, by walking away, or by otherwise ignoring him. She would continue whatever nonexchange signal she chose until Larry, in turn, signalled that he was ready to resume the acculturating exchange by returning to his chair, by establishing eye contact, and so forth. In other words, the therapist structured the environment with exchanges that made the environment immediately, consistently, and powerfully responsive to Larry, thus making the environment an effective learning environment.

Following on this analysis, a ten-day program (Ferritor, 1960) was designed to teach Larry's mother to be an assistant therapist, to use the appropriate exchange and nonexchange signals and to reinforce meaningfully and effectively. After that training period, her acculturating exchanges with Larry were almost flawless and Larry's past learning with the therapist then generalized nicely to his interaction with his mother. The exchange analysis interspersed in parentheses at various points in the following episode gives a rather clear picture of a remarkable change—from pathogenic interchange to acculturating exchange in just ten days!

The mother begins by asking Larry questions (exchange signals). He responds to every question, giving a verbal answer (initiation). She gives approval for every correct response (reciprocation). Then she tries to get him to say, "This is a duck," by asking the appropriate question and pointing to the duck's picture (another exchange signal). He will not say it intelligibly but wants to turn the page (refuses to initiate the exchange; instead, he signals another exchange, that is, turning the page). The mother says, "As soon as you say 'duck,' you may turn the page" (a more powerful exchange signal). Larry responds, "duck" (correct initiation of the exchange) and the mother turns the page (valued reciprocation). He smiles. . . .

After seven minutes, Larry is still sitting down, they have finished one book, and are beginning a second. The mother turns the page and says, "What is he doing?" (exchange signal). Larry says "Flying a kite" (initiation). Mother says, "What color is the kite?" (exchange signal; she misses reciprocating). Larry replies, "orange" (an incorrect answer; an unsuccessful attempt to initiate this latest exchange). His mother's typical response once was "You know that is not orange," but now she just looks away (a nonexchange signal). "Blue," says Larry (an initiation of the exchange which his mother had signalled earlier). "That's right," says the mother and smiles at him (reciprocation). By now, ten minutes have passed and Larry is still sitting, responding to the story with his mother.

Note that the mother was able to run this exchange without reciprocating with food. From earlier episodes we had suspected that Larry would value his mother's attention and approval if he could earn them in a predictable exchange. This, as intimated earlier, is because the autistic teasing pattern seems to occur when the child craves a response from parents, but does not know how to get it the usual way, that is, by talking. However, now that the mother had learned to structure and work an acculturating exchange with Larry, he was able to earn her attention and approval quite regularly, as he wanted them simply by initiating the exchanges she structured.

For her part, the mother valued only the appropriate answers to her questions. Consequently, she would respond with her attention, the approval, and smiles when Larry initiated the exchange by answering the question correctly. When she failed to reciprocate (for example, when he said, "Flying a kite," and she responded not with approval but escalated with another question), Larry slipped back into a habit he had developed in his old echolalic days, that is, answering any question about color with the word "orange." Thus his mother made an error, not catastrophic, but serious enough to interrupt the smooth, typical sequence of exchange signal-initiation-reciprocation.

Larry's mother was trained as an assistant therapist in connection with Ferritor's dissertation project, which was an experiment with a before training–after training–follow-up design and which involved measuring various aspects of the child's conversation with his mother in the home during 60-minute periods when the mother and child were to behave as they usually did.

The data are summarized in Table 1. Note that Larry as well as the other three children did converse with mothers in the home situation. Even so, the amount and the quality of the conversation increased substantially after training and continued to increase (in all but Linda's case) through the three-month follow-up. The follow-up increase over baseline for total number of words was 239 percent, for number of different words, 232 percent, and for sentences, 183 percent. Hence, training the mothers to run normal language exchanges with their children produced substantial results.

Table 1.   Summary Results of Mothers' Training to Run Normal Language Exchanges with their Autistic Children

Child	Before training	After training	Follow-up
Measure: Total number of words used by child in half-hour period			
Mary	199	455	860
Larry	415	781	1331
Jerry	254	326	605
Linda	598	866	695
Average	366	612	873
Percent	100	167	239
Measure: Number of different words			
Mary	28	103	199
Larry	95	174	243
Jerry	47	65	96
Linda	124	170	151
Average	74	128	172
Percent	100	173	232
Measure: Number of complete sentences			
Mary	0	1	6
Larry	26	43	70
Jerry	11	33	54
Linda	84	114	89
Average	30	48	55
Percent	100	160	183

Since then, our training program has been elaborated (Kozloff, 1969) to train the mothers to remediate all of their child's socialization disorders. It now involves several well defined steps.

1. The first step is to have the mother keep the daily log describing fully her interchanges with her autistic child. This includes a description of what the child does during the day and what she does in response. She is asked particularly to note when she tries to get the child to do something, what the child does in response to her attempts, and then what she does in response to the child's response. What inevitably emerges from these logs is a description of a placation strategy. Mothers of autistic children typically tend not to ask their children to do anything; rather, they placate them by giving in to almost all of their demands. Also the log usually provides some material which ultimately can be used to sensitize the mother to the teasing pattern which usually typifies the relationships of the autistic child with members of the family.

2. After two or three weeks the mother is then asked to read several articles or short books on learning and exchange theory and on reinforcement and exchange therapy. To help prevent the mother from becoming discouraged, the material is selected to be interesting and is graded easy to hard. Furthermore, to reinforce her progress, the mother periodically meets with the therapist to discuss the material, particularly its relevance to child rearing practices. This is a crucial step in the training. Without a firm theoretical understanding, mothers find it impossible to be creative later on, and creativity is essential for success.

3. Once the mother progresses well into the reading, she is allowed to observe her child working exchanges with the therapist. This usually occurs after the child has become accustomed to imitating the therapist's motor responses, particularly after he has gained some skill in working puzzles. We have found it advisable to wait until the child has been socialized to this extent, if nothing else other than to continue to establish the therapist's expertise with the mother.

As the mother observes the child and the therapist working the exchanges, a second therapist begins to analyze the stream of behavior with the mother, illustrating the various concepts and processes learned about in the reading. This is continued until the mother is facile in analyzing the stream of behavior herself.

4. Then the mother is allowed to work with the child, taking the role of the therapist, running the imitation exchanges on motor tasks to which the child had become accustomed. The child that the mother works with in the laboratory is not necessarily her own. If, in the judgment of the therapist, the mother could encounter any problems with her own child, she is given a much easier child so that her initial experiences will be successful.

5. Also, to insure the success of these early exchanges, the mother is coached. The experimental rooms in the laboratory are fitted with a one-way wireless communication system. The mother wears a standard hearing aid, fitted with a telephone induction loop which can pick up and amplify any instructions by the therapist from behind a one-way mirror. Thus when the mother does not know what to do, or when she makes an error, the therapist suggests "You might . . ." or "Next time you might . . ." With this immediate help and feedback, the average mother is able to do about as well as the therapist from the very first day, with exchanges to which the child is accustomed.

At this time, the mother learns how to use exchange signals, how to use questions and direct instructions, and how to set up the various exchanges. She also learns how to use approval and food to reinforce appropriate responses from the child. She learns how to reinforce quickly, within one or two seconds of the appropriate response, and how to vary the reinforcement pattern sometimes using just approval and sometimes using approval as a signal for food reciprocation (this latter to strengthen approval as a conditioned reinforcer). The mother also learns how to move from continuous to variable reinforcement.

Also, as mentioned, the mother learns how to use nonexchange signals, that is, how to ignore irrelevant behavior, how to time out the child by dropping her head, looking away, or holding her head in her hands when the child is not cooperative or when he engages in moderately disruptive behavior. Also, she learns how to use a time-out room where she puts the child when she simply cannot ignore his behavior. It is always established ahead of time what precise behaviors are to result in a child's being placed in a time-out room and the mother is shown the most effective procedures (not talking while she takes the child by the hand to deposit him in the time-out room). She is instructed in the dangers of wearing out the time-out room, that it is effective only if used rarely and then only to the extent the therapeutic exchange is attractive.

6. Once she has mastered these basic skills, the mother is asked to coach one or two other mothers who are also in training. This gives her experience in handling problems which emerge suddenly. It gives her further experience in analyzing the flow of exchanges as they occur in the therapy room.

7. Next the mother is trained how to structure new exchanges with the child, how to use prompting procedures, how to use the child's ability to imitate to get new exchanges started. Also, she learns the shaping procedure, how to reciprocate for successively better approximations to the desired behavior pattern. She also has to learn how to move back and forth from the accustomed exchanges which are comfortable to the new exchanges which can be frustrating for the child. The goal is to teach her to press ahead until the child begins to evidence the slightest strain and then move back into more comfortable material, pressing ahead again, usually a little farther, until the child proceeds through the new material and becomes comfortable working the new exchange.

8. About this time the therapist spends several days in the home recording the flow of the child's behavior including the interaction between the mother and the child. Care is taken to observe the child at least twice during the various parts of his waking hours.

The therapist is equipped with a miniature tape recorder and a stop watch. He observes from an adjoining room and whispers into the recorder a flat description of events as they unfold in the household. The tape recorder is ordinarily turned up to the point where it picks up any talking which is part of the interaction between the mother and the child. The stop watch is used to get a measure of the duration of the various interchanges which are observed. From this flat description the therapist abstracts a description of the interchanges which characterize the interaction between the child and the other members of his family. This abstract, an example of which is given in Table 2, is then given to the mother to help her analyze the situation at home.

Table 2. Description of Home Interaction Patterns Given to the Mother During Parent-Training

Child's behavior	Parent's reaction
(1) Plays in bathroom or kitchen water.	(1) Chases after him, yells at him to stop: "Michael Hare, you get out of that water this very instant." (Usually he simply begins again.)
(2) Pulls and pushes for records.	(2) Gives him record—about 50 percent of time.
(3) Whines and cries if he is not given what he wants.	(3) Cuddles him and asks him what is wrong.
(4) Gets into food as it is prepared.	(4) Chases after him, yells at him to stop. (Usually he simply begins again.)
(5) Gets into pantry or lower cabinets.	(5) Yells at him to stop. (He usually continues.)
(6) Climbs on top of refrigerator.	(6) Yells at him to come down, or asks him to come down over and over again.
(7) Spins objects (plates, compacts, vases).	(7) Goes after him and takes object away (about 50 percent of time). Ignores him about 50 percent of time.
(8) Climbs onto kitchen counter, or pulls a chair up to the counter so as to climb up more easily.	(8) Usually tells him over and over to get down. And usually he does not. Eventually, she takes him down bodily.
(9) Plays with his food during a meal (slaps it with spoon, pours it back and forth with spoon).	(9) Repeatedly tells him to stop.
(10) Gets into records, pulls them out, creating a mess by record player.	(10) Goes after him and tells him to stop. Eventually ends up yelling at him as he continues to get into records.
(11) Stands up and rocks back and forth, often with thumb in mouth.	(11) Ignores.
(12) Sits idly fingering silky material.	(12) Ignores—unless it is something she is wearing.
(13) Stands outside and urinates (usually onto sidewalk).	(13) Gives him attention, as she usually says: "Why Michael Hare, I just don't understand you. . . !
(14) Pours, spills, and dumps things onto the floor, right in front of her (looks at her to see if she is getting upset).	(14) Usually gets upset after he makes a mess. She says: "Michael Hare, you're just doing that to tantalize me." Often yells at him to clean it up.

Then the mother is asked to suggest a program for herself and her family to follow in terminating the pathogenic interchanges and structure and replacing them with acculturating exchanges. The therapist coaches the mother through this plan by reinforcing what appear to him to be the good ideas with approval and by making suggestions when the mother appears uncertain as to what to do or when she suggests something that obviously will not work. To date, the experience has been that mothers typically do quite well at this stage. In fact, some become extremely creative, often suggesting approaches which turn out to be improvements over early staff procedures. We have the mothers work on just a few problems at a time, the more serious ones first. An example of a plan is given in Table 3.

Table 3.   Program Given to Parents to Restructure the Exchange Patterns in the Home

INSTRUCTIONS:

To ignore: Do not look at or talk to Michael while he is engaged in inappropriate behavior. Do not tell him to stop, or try to verbally divert his attention, or scold him, or threaten him with punishment.

To reward: For the present, give Michael approval (verbal, strokes, so forth). For certain things, food may be given (an afternoon snack for working puzzles for a while; a drink of juice for a household task). Make sure, of course, that the reward follows the behavior immediately—within a few seconds.

To time out: Without speaking, but with some vigor, take Michael to time-out room. Leave him in two minutes for first offense, four minutes for second offense, and so forth. Do not let him out if he is whining or tantruming.

Child's behavior	Your response
(1) Pulling and/or pushing a) For records	(1) a) Set aside several periods of the day during which Michael can work for a record (by picking up toys, clothes, working puzzles). Tell him, "As soon as you . . . , you can have a record." At any other time ignore him. To get it started, ignore him until he asks at an opportune time of the day. (Eventually, working for records was established 10 minutes after lunch. It was initiated with Mrs. H. saying, "It's time to work for a record." She would lead Michael to the table and prompt him to work puzzles.)
b) For bath	b) Ignore. Then, when it is proper time, tell him he may take a bath or whatever you usually say.
(2) Crying and/or whining	(2) Ignore. This will probably occur after he is ignored for pulling.

Child's behavior	Your response
(3) Playing with stove, getting into food in refrigerator or pantry, climbing on cupboards, getting into food being prepared (assuming that any of these things is disturbing to you).	(3) Time out from kitchen by removing Michael from kitchen and locking door from inside. Open in approximately three or four minutes and repeat each time he repeats inappropriate behavior. Don't let it escalate; don't wait and let him do it for a while. Remove him immediately. This will work if he likes being in the kitchen. If he does any of these things when you are not in the kitchen with him, remove him and lock the door.
(4) Climbing on refrigerator.	(4) Ignore.
(5) Playing with own food (spilling it, slapping it), or getting up from table *to mess around.*	(5) Take food away. No food until next meal. Ignore all appeals for food in between.
(6) Spinning objects.	(6) *Do not chase* him or have a tug of war. Take object away quickly and without speaking. Say "As soon as you . . . , you can spin this." (Have him perform a simple task.)
(7) Water play.	(7) Temporarily remove him from room and lock door. If he does this during a meal, remove him from the kitchen and lock him out, then take his plate away.
(8) All bizarre behavior.	(8) Ignore.
(9) Self-initiated working at puzzles, looking in magazines, picking up clothing, helping in kitchen, speech (any approximation).	(9) Reward verbally with strokes and, if convenient, with a bite of food. If he is engaged in such activity for more than a few minutes, reward him several times. Don't just wait until he stops. Reward him during activity if it is longer than 10 seconds or so. Be on the lookout for appropriate behavior and consistently reward it.

As may be noted in Table 4, the above procedures worked rather well in modifying the mothers' response patterns to their autistic children. It terminated their pathogenic exchanges, their reinforcement of bizarre-disruptive behaviors, and accelerated their reinforcement of the normal exchanges for constructive play activity, for appropriate speech, and for cooperation.

The data in Figure 1, which are typical, depict the time changes in behavior of a mother who received the above training and her six-year old autistic boy. The experimental data illustrate well the effects of our structuring

Table 4. Patterns of Exchange Reciprocation by Parents for Various Experimental Periods

Percentage of reinforcement

Response class	Hare Family			Nash Family			White Family		
	Prior to training	After training in the home	Follow up	Prior to training	After training in the home	Follow up	Prior to training	After training in the home	Follow up
Bizarre-disruptive	73	0	0	72	0	0	54	0	0
Episodes of constructive activity	54	100	100	0	100	100	50	None occurred	100
Appropriate speech	No speech present	100	100	No speech present	84	85	64	88	88
Cooperation	60	100	96	0	95	92	69	100	94

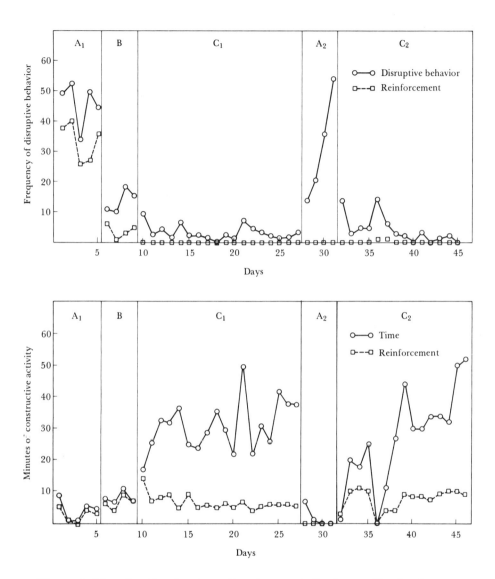

Figure 1. Changing the structure of exchanges in the home. The A_1 observations of the exchanges between the mother and child were made before the mother was trained. The B observations were made immediately after the mother was trained in the laboratory school. For the first seven days of the C_1 period the mother was coached in the home to change the pattern of exchanges observed in the A_1 period. In the A_2 condition the mother was asked to ignore the disruptive and the constructive exchanges. During the C_2 period she was instructed to again reciprocate constructive exchanges and ignore disruptive exchanges.

counter exchanges to decelerate one class of behavior—bizarre-disruptive behavior—and, simultaneously, in its place, to accelerate another class of behavior—constructive activity, such as chores and play.

CONCLUSION

As has been noted elsewhere (Hamblin et al, 1969), the above procedures work best when the children start therapy at age three, four, or five years. The sooner the better. Older children also respond but by age six the autistic pattern is so well developed, so well established, that reversing it is an extremely slow, extremely difficult process.

It turns out that many of the autistic children who responded to exchange therapy are relatively bright. One, in fact, was able to learn to read traditional orthography and i.t.a. simultaneously, faster than some of our normal five-year old preschoolers who topped out with a 149 IQ (Individual Stanford Binet). The laws of learning are apparently immutable. Without reinforcers even bright children do not learn. If these reinforcers happen to be the ones which are typically used in our culture in teaching a child how to talk, then he simply will not learn to talk, and in fact he will usually develop the other autistic symptoms. The autistic syndrome seems to be reversible by restructuring the child's social learning environment, particularly at an early age. It is not inevitable that autistic children end up vegetating in the back wards of mental hospitals.

The above illustrates how exchanges operate in parent-child relations to bring about their long-term learning effects. Let us suggest that all of the great interpersonal problems which families face involve the effective structuring of attractive acculturating exchanges and the avoidance of the various pathogenic interchanges, not just between parent and child but between family members generally. If the above theory and research sensitizes those interested in family problem solving to these problems, and to the possibilities of their solution, then this paper will have served its purpose.

REFERENCES

Bereiter, C. and Engelmann, S., *Teaching Disadvantaged Children in the Pre-school.* Englewood Cliffs: Prentice-Hall, Inc., 1966.

Bijou, S. W. and Baer, D. M., *Child Development: A Systematic and Empirical Theory.* New York: Appleton-Century-Crofts, 1961.

Ferritor, D. E., *Modifying Interactions Patterns: An Experimental Training Program for Parents of Autistic Children.* Unpublished doctoral dissertation, Washington University, 1969.

Ferster, C. B. and Skinner, B. F. *Schedules of Reinforcement.* New York: Appleton-Century-Crofts, 1957.

Hamblin, R. L., Buckholdt, D. R., Ferritor, D. E., Kozloff, M. A., and Blackwell, L. J., *The Humanization Processes.* New York: John Wiley & Sons, Inc., In Press.

Holland, J. G. and Skinner, B. F., *The Analysis of Behavior*. New York: McGraw-Hill, Inc., 1967.

Homans, G. C., *Social Behavior: Its Elementary Forms*. New York: Harcourt, Brace & World, Inc., 1961.

Kozloff, M. A., *Social and Behavioral Change in Families of Autistic Children*. Unpublished doctoral dissertation, Washington University, 1969.

Moore, O. K. and Anderson, A. R. "The Responsive Environments Project." In R. D. Hess and R. M. Baer, Ed., *Early Educator*. Chicago: Aldine Publishing Co., 1966.

Pavlov, I. P., *Conditioned Reflexes*. New York: Dover Publications, 1960.

Reese, E. P., *Analysis of Human Operant Behavior*. Dubuque: W. C. Brown, 1966.

Rutter, M., "Concepts of Autism: A Review of Research." *Journal of Child Psychology and Psychiatry*, 9, (1968), 1–25.

Skinner, B. F., *Behavior of Organisms*. New York: Appleton-Century-Crofts, 1938.

——— *The Technology of Teaching*. New York: Appleton-Century-Crofts, 1968.

Ullman, L. P. and Krasner, L., *Case Studies in Behavior Modification*. New York: Holt, Rinehart and Winston, 1966.

Wing, J. K. *Early Childhood Autism: Clinical, Educational and Social Aspects*. London: Pergamon Press, Inc., 1966.

Wolff, P. H., "Observations on the Early Development of Smiling." In B. Foss, Ed., *Determinants of Infant Behavior*. Vol. II. London: Methuen & Co., Ltd., 1961.

Family Problem Solving and Social Problems*

IRVING TALLMAN

INTRODUCTION

Man's concern with social problems, their causes and solutions, is as old as the history of human thought. It is this concern which, for many, represents the *raison d'etre* for the behavioral sciences. In fact, many scholars, despite differing philosophies and methodologies, agree that in the long run the measure of their efforts is the ability to find solutions to social problems (Lynd, 1945; Lundberg, 1947; see also Martindale's review, 1964).

Considering the centrality of social problems for students of human behavior and the acknowledged importance of the family as a socializing agent, we might expect the relationship between these two phenomena to be one of the better understood aspects of human behavior. Unfortunately, despite considerable research and scholarly activity devoted to this question, the cumulative effects have not resulted in significant theoretical advances. The principal reason for this lack of advancement lies in the difficulty in adequately defining the concept of social problems. The term too often has been used as an intellectual wastebasket and has depended less on careful definitions of the concept than it has on the ideology and values of the investigator. (See Martindale's 1964 and 1959 discussions of distinctions between normative and empirical theories.) It is not surprising, therefore, that efforts in this field have

* This is a revised version of a paper read at the annual meeting of the Society for the Study of Social Problems, August 20, 1968 in Boston, Massachusetts. Work on the paper was made possible by a grant from the National Institute on Mental Health #M.H. 15521-01 to the Minnesota Family Studies Center for the Study of Problem Solving Behavior in Family Groups.

I wish to express my appreciation to Joan Aldous, Glen Elder, Reuben Hill, Beverly Houghton, Don McTavish, Robert K. Merton, Ramona Morgner, Joel Nelson, Paul Reynolds and Murray Straus for their comments and criticisms of earlier drafts of this paper.

splintered in various directions and have failed to lead to a unifying set of generalizations.

On the assumption that an empirical theory concerned with social problems is possible, this paper will present a conceptual framework designed to link family behavior with the identification and politicization of social problems. Social problems will be considered in a generic sense rather than as an aggregate of disparate situations or inequitable social conditions. That is, an attempt will be made to define the social problem as an empirically verifiable phenomenon with characteristics which distinguish it from other related phenomena. In keeping with the central theme of this volume, social problems will be treated as a particular type of problem solving situation. From this perspective, we will examine the conditions under which situations are defined as social problems, the actions that are taken based upon such definitions, and the contribution families make to these processes.[1]

DEFINITION OF A SOCIAL PROBLEM

In an earlier paper Reece McGee and I attempted to define the concept social problem in such a way that it not only maintained its constitutive meaning but was conceptually and empirically distinguishable from such related concepts as social pathology, deviance, and social disorganization (Tallman and McGee, in press). What follows draws upon this earlier work.

A social problem may be defined as ". . . a situation which is perceived by some group as a source of dissatisfaction for its members and in which preferable alternatives are recognized so that the group, or individuals in the group, are motivated to effect some change" (Tallman and McGee, in press). Although this definition reflects a considerable degree of consensus in the field, it requires some specifications which establish the frame of reference under which a problem is considered relevant. For our purposes, a "sociologically relevant problem" occurs only when a social issue becomes politicized; that is, when attempts are made to change both public policy and public behavior with regard to a given social issue. Such attempts make the situation controversial, thereby bringing it to the awareness of increasing segments of the population. From this perspective neither social conditions nor aberrant behavior necessarily constitute social problems. It is not the amount of poverty which influences the transformation of impoverishment from a social condition to a social problem but rather the extent to which people become concerned

---

[1] It should be noted that viewing the social problem as a phenomenon in its own right represents a departure from previous research and theory in this area. Almost all of the previous research has focused on specific deviant acts or social conditions. Broadly speaking, the previous work can be summarized as following two distinct orientations: the first focuses on the pathological aspects of family life and therefore the contribution the family makes to such phenomena as mental illness (for example, Lidz, et al, 1965), crime (McCord and McCord, 1959), and alcoholism (McCord and McCord, 1960). The other approach tends to view family behavior as social problems *sui generis* as in the study of illegitimacy (Goode, 1960; Christensen, 1960; Davis, 1939), family disorganization (Goode, 1956, 1965; Bernard, 1956), fertility control (Davis and Blake, 1956; Hill, Stykos, and Back, 1959), and dependency (Geismar and La Sorte, 1964). In my opinion the specific focus of these studies has provided little insight into general processes linking the family and social problems.

about poverty and attempt to change that condition through social action. Similarly, it is not criminals that make crime a social problem (it is reasonable to assume that this group would like to keep their behavior from becoming a public issue) but those groups who may be aroused because crime continues or is rapidly increasing. The magnitude of a social problem can be defined, therefore, as the product of the number of people involved in a given social situation which has been defined as problematic and the passion aroused in these people about the situation. This definition provides the hallmarks, albeit crude, which enable us to consider social problems as empirical phenomena.

To politicize a situation, deliberate attempts must be made to increase its visibility to broader segments of the population. Visibility is vital because efforts to affect ameliorative changes generally require the mobilization of groups against sources of resistance to those changes. Attempts to change a situation will usually involve a confrontation with groups which either benefit from the status quo or, at the very least, are indifferent and, therefore, unwilling to implement change. In either case, the result is some form of conflict and exposure to risk. Risk may vary from endangering one's social prestige and position to placing one's freedom or life in jeopardy. Although there may be many motives for engaging in such risk taking behavior, the pervasive rationale accompanying such behavior in social problem situations is moral indignation which, according to Nisbet (1966), is a necessary component in any social problem. Moral indignation implies, first, a capacity on the part of the individual to hold a rather consistent set of beliefs concerning just and unjust conditions and, second, a faith in the mutability of unjust conditions, since one generally fails to be indignant about those things that cannot be changed.

In sum, three conditions are posited as requisites for transforming social situations into sociologically significant social problems; first, the situation must be perceived as problematic and amenable to change; second, it must arouse moral indignation; and third, there must be a willingness on the part of people to take the necessary risks to make the problem visible for a larger number of people.

It is a central thesis of this paper that the three conditions discussed above are not only requisites for the development of social problems, but that individuals vary in their capacity to affect these conditions. In this regard, an attempt will be made to show that individuals with the capacities to define situations in social problem terms, to experience moral indignation, and to engage in risk-taking behavior by and large come from families which have successfully solved their own internal problems and relations. If this is true, then we have the apparent paradoxical hypothesis that *significant social problems are rendered salient by the behavior of those persons whose families have been successful in their own problem solving endeavors and have trained their offsprings to be effective problem solvers.*

The remainder of this paper is devoted to presenting a set of propositions along with evidence supporting the plausibility and utility of the above hypothesis. Since there is little data available to directly test either the hypothesis or its underlying assumptions, I shall rely heavily on analogies drawn from small group research and theory.

CONCEPTUAL FRAMEWORK

Before considering the specific contributions of the family, it will be necessary to establish some general principles governing the processes by which people turn social situations into social problems. These principles will then provide the basis for determining which family experiences may be most important in influencing critical behavior patterns.

Of the three conditions posited for creating a social problem, perception and risk taking can be considered as behavioral processes energized by the third condition, moral indignation. In the discussion which follows we shall focus on factors contributing to each of these conditions but since moral indignation is viewed as a motivating force for both perception and action we shall consider it as it relates to each of these behavioral processes. We turn first to the issue of perception.

Conditions Leading to the Perception of a Social Situation as a Social Problem

Assuming that perception is selective (Bruner, 1951; Solley and Murphy, 1960; Segall, Campbell, and Herskovitz, 1966), we expect that people will differ both in the type of situations they perceive as problematic and in their general proclivity to define social situations as social problems. The former differences can be attributed to cultural and value orientations (Horton and Leslie, 1960); the latter imply a more general function pertaining to the individual's sensitivity to problematic elements in social situations. It is the latter issue which falls within the purview of the present volume and is of particular interest here.

The discussion which follows includes a fairly large number of inter-related variables. For that reason Figure 1 is presented to assist the reader in following the hypothesized relationships leading to the definition of a situation as a social problem. The arrows indicate causal relations and the $\oplus$ sign is used to represent the combining of variables in either an additive or multiplicative manner.

It can be seen from Figure 1 that environmental and experiential factors are viewed as independent variables, beliefs as mediating variables, and the content of percepts as well as perceptual thresholds as dependent variables.

Social problems can be subsumed under that category of universalistic rather than particularistic problems. Solutions to such problems have implications beyond the individual and his immediate friends or family in that they require long range planning and the mobilization of resources in excess of any

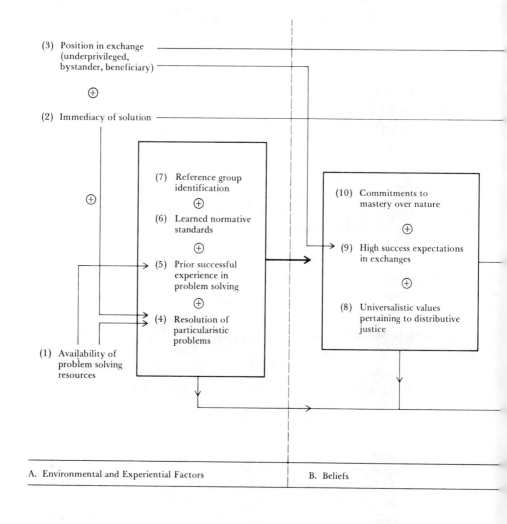

Figure 1. Model depicting the hypothesized relationship between variables influencing the perception of social situations as social problems.

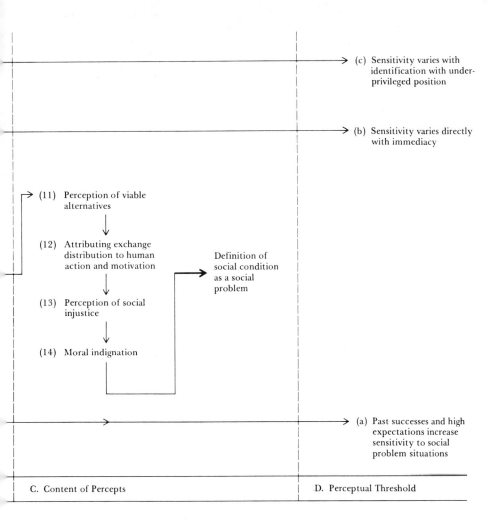

(c) Sensitivity varies with
   identification with underprivileged position

(b) Sensitivity varies directly
   with immediacy

(11) Perception of viable
   alternatives

(12) Attributing exchange
   distribution to human
   action and motivation

Definition of
social condition
as a social
problem

(13) Perception of social
   injustice

(14) Moral indignation

(a) Past successes and high
   expectations increase
   sensitivity to social
   problem situations

C. Content of Percepts

D. Perceptual Threshold

that could generally be provided by an individual or a small group. Our first task, then, is to establish conditions which lead to the perception of these types of long range, universalistic problems.

Three basic premises appear relevant in determining when people are able to involve themselves in universalistic problems. The first premise holds that any individual or group has a finite amount of resources to bring to bear in a given situation.[2] These include material and intellectual resources as well as energy, time, and affect. It follows that the commitment of resources to any given problem limits their availability for use in other situations. For example, there is evidence to suggest that during periods of severe deprivation, such as hunger or incarceration in a concentration camp, people lose all concern with external relations and devote their entire energies to personal survival. (See research summarized by Davies, 1962; Thibaut and Kelley, 1959, pp. 178–186.)

A second, and related, premise holds that people will give priority to those problems which are most immediate in their experience.[3] This suggests a priority of individualistic and particularistic problems over universalistic ones. It is also likely that persons deeply engaged in the resolution of immediate problems will be less ready to consider the long range or social implications of the problems with which they are confronted.

The third premise assumes that effective problem solving is usually a rewarding experience which pays off in group affection and increased self-esteem (Hoffman, 1965).[4] As a result, those people who have had positive problem solving experiences should be more oriented toward engaging in new problem solving activities (Berkowitz and Levy, 1956) and will therefore be prone to perceive situations as problematic.

On the basis of these premises we can infer that: *persons or groups who have successfully solved their immediate personal and particularistic problems will be more inclined to identify problems that have universalistic implications and long range solutions.*[5] The obverse of this proposition, is, of course, that persons who have *not* been able to solve their immediate or particularistic problems will avoid perceiving situations as social problems requiring social

---

[2] This is not meant to imply that individual and group differences in capacity do not affect the available resources but only that, for any group (or individual), there is a theoretical limit to these capacities.

[3] Indirect support for this premise comes from a number of diverse sources. See, for example, data on deprivation studies (Solley and Murphy, 1960), data relevant to pursuasion and attitude change (Miller and Campbell, 1959; Hovland et al, 1957), and research related to dissonance reduction (Rosenberg and Abelson, 1960).

[4] An assumption which seems to underline Moore's work; see also Smith, 1968.

[5] It should be noted that an alternative theory exists which is particularly popular among scholars who maintain a psychoanalytic perspective—that is, that involvement with abstract universalistic issues is a way of escaping from the anxiety of being unable to resolve immediate problems. Despite the popularity of this compensatory theory, my review of the literature has yielded virtually no empirical data to support it in the areas of either social action or interest in social issues. It should be noted, however, that the generalizations made in this paper are intended to be representative and do not refer to isolated or individual cases or, for that matter, relatively rare cases of psychopathology.

solutions. Support for this proposition comes from the research pertaining to deprivation referred to above (Davies, 1962; Thibaut and Kelley, 1959) as well as research on chronic conditions of poverty (Banfield, 1958). Davies (1962) summarizes this position by stating, "Far from making people into revolutionaries, enduring poverty makes for concern with one's solitary self or solitary family at best and resignation or mute despair at worst."

Not all universalistic problems involve social issues or can be interpreted as social problems, however. (See Klausner's 1968 discussion of stress seeking behavior, especially pp. 140–143.) Our question thus becomes one of determining the conditions under which people ready to engage in broad range problem solving behavior will orient themselves toward social issues as opposed to other areas of achievement or challenge. The obvious critical condition for such people is that a situation exists which the perceiver considers as unjust and responds to with feelings of moral indignation. We shall turn now to an examination of both situational and personal variables which contribute to establishing this condition.

Variables Influencing the Perception of Social Injustice. From the standpoint of the perceiver, a social problem can be considered within the framework of exchange theory in general, and the concept of distributive justice in particular (Homans, 1961; Adams, 1965). This framework suggests that people consider themselves as functioning within an exchange relationship with others in their environment. The exchange is governed, in part, by expectations as to what constitutes "just" returns based on the investments a person makes in a situation (Homans, 1961).[6] These expectations are based on previous experiences, normative standards, and reference group orientations. Thus, how an individual has been treated in the past, what he has learned about how he *ought* to be treated, and the people he compares himself with all should affect his expectations. (See Thibaut and Kelley's 1959 discussion of comparison levels and comparison level alternatives.) When these expectations are not met, that is, when there is a discrepancy between expected and actual rewards, the perceiver may interpret the situation as unjust. However, for such a situation to represent social injustice capable of arousing moral indignation, the cause of the injustice should be attributed to responsible persons who did little or nothing to prevent the perceived deprivations from occurring. In addition, the perceiver must assume that the persons responsible were aware that alternative modes of action were available. Only if alternatives exist and these alternatives are available to human actors can the situation be considered amenable to change. If change is not possible then feelings of social injustice and moral indignation are futile and, therefore, frustrating and likely to be avoided. Thus an earthquake may be disastrous to a com-

---

6 These investments correspond to the attributes an individual brings to a given situation and may vary from ascribed characteristics such as sex and ethnicity to factors such as special skills and available energy (Homans, 1961).

munity but people will not become morally indignant unless they feel that proper precautions were not taken by appropriate persons or that certain reactions to the crises resulted in inequitable suffering.

Since social problems are attributed to the actions of others, inferences can be drawn concerning their intentions and dispositions for future actions (Jones and Thibaut, 1958; Jones and Davis, 1965). Jones and Davis (1965) have shown that such inferences are initially made retrospectively from observing the effects of a given action; if these effects are seen as damaging to an individual or group, the inference of malevolence on the part of the actor can *only* be made if he is seen to have alternatives available to him. An act may be perceived as unjust without hostile or negative inferences made concerning the actor; this could occur if the perceiver considers that alternatives were available but the actor was either unaware of them or otherwise acted in response to legitimate norms. Thus, if the perceiver views the actors behavior as normative (from the actor's viewpoint, even if it is not from the perspective of the perceiver) it is less likely that negative inferences will be drawn. If the behavior is seen as normative, the intent of the actor is likely to be interpreted as conformity to social requisites and not personal or group volition (Jones and Davis, 1965). For example, the determination of police brutality hinges, in part, on whether the force brought to bear in a given situation is thought to be excessive, for only if the force is excessive can the police be considered as exercising choice—otherwise they are behaving normatively and if blame is to be leveled it must be at higher sources who are thought to have choices available.

The perceiver's reaction and the extent of his indignation should also depend on the perspective from which he views an unequal exchange. Three possibilities exist: he may view the situation as the deprived person in the exchange, as the beneficiary, or as a bystander observing the exchange. Qualitative differences should occur in reaction to each case. For example, deprived persons may be expected to respond with anger whereas beneficiaries are more likely to respond with feelings of guilt (Homans 1961; Adams, 1965). We can speculate that the reactions of bystanders will fall in either of the above categories depending on whether their fate is seen as interlocked with either the recipient or the beneficiary of the inequity. If he fails to identify with one or the other the situations will be less relevant to him and his emotional reaction will be correspondingly weak. Indirect support for this interpretation of the bystanders role comes from experiments conducted by Jones and de Charmes (1957). They report that subjects reacted less strongly to an accomplice's poor performance on a task when they thought the results did not affect them personally than when they believed their fate hinged on this performance. In the latter situation subjects were more likely to judge the actor in negative terms. It is not clear what actions persons experiencing these different emotional states may take. What is significant to note, for our purposes however, is that guilt may be as important a motivating force in identifying a social problem as anger. This will become an important consideration when we consider the family's role in the development of social problems.

Adams (1965), utilizing the principle that people in exchange situations will be motivated to maximize their gains and minimize their losses, suggests a differential threshold for perceiving injustice based on the extent to which one's outcomes suffer as a consequence of an exchange. On this basis we would predict, other things being equal, that deprived persons would be most likely to perceive the situation as unjust; second, would-be bystanders who interpret the deprived situation as relevant to their fate; third, would-be beneficiaries of the act; fourth, bystanders identified with the beneficiaries; and lastly, bystanders for whom the situation is irrelevant.

This order assumes, however, that the expected reward-cost ratios are constant for all groups—clearly this is not the case. As suggested earlier, there is evidence to indicate that these expectations vary with previous experience and reference group identification (Adams, 1965; Thibaut and Kelley, 1959). Such expectations are so closely tied with self image that they tend to be highly resistant to change. Although the evidence is not entirely consistent, it appears that people will lower their level of performance to keep it in line with their expected rewards rather than change their expectations (Aronson and Carlsmith, 1962). We might expect, therefore, that the same groups which have been traditionally deprived will have a higher threshold for perceiving a discrepent situation as unjust than a group which is the beneficiary of the exchange. This differential can be related, in part, to experience, normative standards, and comparisons with reference groups. In addition, it serves as a means of adapting to the frustration of repeated failures. By lowering expectations, the disappointment of low rewards will not be as great (Spector, 1956, reported in Adams, 1965). The converse of this principle is, of course, that the greater the successes the greater the expected outcomes (Thibaut and Kelley, 1959). It should follow that people with a history of past success and high levels of reward will have greater expectations of future rewards and, as a consequence, a lower threshold for perceiving injustice. Some support for this prediction comes from a classic study by Thibaut (1950). He divided subjects into two groups, giving one group an enjoyable task and the other a related but secondary and humiliating task. Those members of the underprivileged group whose situation was later changed by the experimenter to a more privileged status expressed greater hostility toward the original high status group than did those low status children whose situation did not change. The findings suggest that perception of injustice was greater among those whose expectations for improving their situation was met than among those whose situation remained unchanged.

It would appear, on the basis of available data, that expectations based on past experience have relatively more influence on the threshold for perceiving social injustice than either the desire to maximize rewards or position in the exchange situation. Assuming this differential weighting, the prediction can be made that those who are high in expectations and are deprived in an exchange will be most likely to perceive the situation as unjust and to react with strong feelings of indignation. We would expect the order of relations to the exchange situation to remain the same as that reported above for a *given level of expectation* and to be repeated for every lower level. Some support for this predicted order comes from evidence indicating that the more highly educated and successful Black Americans initiated and sustained the Black Freedom Movement (Pettigrew, 1964).

The reported association between rapid social change and the development of social problems (Davies, 1962; Kornhauser, 1959) may be accounted for at the social-psychological level by the relationship between social change and alterations in the established reward-cost expectations for particular groups; if these alterations result in increased upward expectations, sensitivity to injustice should also increase. The findings linking improvements in Black Americans' income, education, and living conditions with increasing demands for equality within the system (Pettigrew, 1964; also research reviewed in Tallman and McGee, in press) may be interpreted as partial evidence for such relationships.

Variables Affecting Actions Which Transform Social Situations Into Social Problems

Implicit in the definition of the situation as problematic is the demand for solutions. Since the types of problems we are discussing require the mobilization of resources usually greater than those available to single individuals or small groups the initial actions will be those intended to gain support from previously uncommitted persons. To accomplish this problems must be made visible to larger segments of the population and efforts made to ignite their moral indignation. (See Tallman and McGee, in press, for a more detailed delineation of this process.) This suggests the paradoxical situation in which the solution of a perceived problem requires increasing its magnitude as a social problem. Ideally those seeking to make a situation visible will wish to do it in a way that puts their cause in the best possible public light. This is not always possible, however, and since visibility is the paramount consideration, people may find themselves engaging in extreme and sometimes dangerous forms of nonconforming behavior in order to dramatize the situation. Thus suffragettes chained themselves to lampposts and young men burned draft cards and destroyed selective service records to dramatize opposition to the Vietnam war.

Since the resolution of social problems involves social change, attempts to make the situation visible will always involve some degree of nonconformity and therefore some risk. The two characteristics of risk taking and non-conformity, therefore, can be considered as common to all social problem activities; understanding the origins of these behaviors should provide some insight into conditions leading to the development of social problems. Unfortunately the research on risk taking and nonconforming behavior is minimal.[7] The available research does suggest, however, that there is some link between both of these aspects of behavior and effective problem solving. Klausner (1968), for example, summarizes his research as indicating that stress seekers are highly rational and tend to engage in carefully planned behavior. Torrance (1968), using a variety of psychometric measures, reports high associations between stress seeking behavior and high achievement. He also presents data linking autonomy, independent action, and nonconformity to creativity.

Self-esteem appears to be the critical personality variable associated with these kinds of behavior. There is considerable evidence indicating that people with high self-esteem are better able to withstand pressures toward conformity (see research reviewed in Smith, 1968; Hovland, Janis, and Kelley, 1953) and, as a consequence, are able to utilize a broader range of ideas in seeking problem solutions (Hoffman, 1965). Self-esteem also has been found to be associated with independence (Inkeles, 1968; Walster, 1965), high achievement, and general competence (Smith, 1968). Implicit in the work of Klausner and Torrance is an association between high self-esteem and risk taking behavior. Since we know that previous success and self-esteem are linked (Smith, 1968), we can infer that people who have been successful in the past will be more likely to risk new challenges. Such people will also tend to believe that man, not fate, determines destiny (Rotter, 1966). It is not surprising, therefore, that people with high self-esteem appear more likely to display an interest in public affairs (Rosenberg, 1965; pp. 318–323). In fact, there are data which suggest that persons with a history of past success, positive self-evaluations, and moral commitments (sense of civic duty) are more likely to be political activists (Milbraith, 1965: 48–89).

Considering the affinity between political activism and the behaviors which make social problems visible, we might reasonably expect the same behavioral attributes to be associated with both forms of activity. One qualification to this hypothesis seems necessary however; that is, persons active in defining social problems should more often be identified with groups who have been blocked from access to legitimate political routes. There are two principal reasons for this qualification. The first is that a social problem of any magnitude involves nonconformity behavior which implies actions taken out of the legitimate arena for resolving political issues.[8] The principal function of such extra-legitimate action is to generate sources of power not available to the group within ordinary political routes.

The reason for predicting greater activity to those denied access to

---

[7] Nonconformity is used here in the sense that Merton (1957, 1966) uses the term; that is, as opposed to aberrant forms of deviant behavior and indicating a willingness to openly advocate a non-normative position.

[8] This is so even if the problem is eventually resolved through ordinary political channels. Examples of problems which require extra-political activity and were resolved within the legitimate channels are myriad. Two such examples are women's suffrage rights and labor struggles of the early part of this century.

legitimate political routes derives from the exchange model discussed above. From this model we would expect persons most responsive to injustice to be members of deprived groups with high expectations. There is good evidence to indicate that underprivileged groups have relatively poor access to channels of political influence (Milbraith, 1965). Members of underprivileged groups, seeking to change the situation, are, therefore, more likely to use extra-legitimate channels to achieve their goals.

This suggests the hypothesis that those persons identified with groups in a relatively weak political position but with personal or group success in relevant areas of achievement will be most likely to engage in the kinds of activities that turns a situation into a social problem. Recent research on farm protests, student revolts, and racial conflict can be used in support of the hypothesis. Morrison and Steeves (1967), in a review of research on the relatively militant National Farm Organization, report that in comparison to nonmembers, N.F.O. farmers have more productive farms, more education, and a higher level of living. They also indicate a higher level of technological adoption and innovation. Flacks (1967) presents evidence indicating that student activists, as compared to nonactivists, were more likely to come from high status families and to share the value orientations of their fathers. Pettigrew (1964) presents similar findings for Negro activists.

In summary, it is posited that persons likely to perceive situations as social problems and to take the types of action which increase the visibility of these problems will be those who are capable of *perceiving alternative solutions* to problems, have *high expectations of success*, and maintain an *internally consistent set of moral values*, thereby increasing the propensity for moral indignation. In addition, they will have sufficient *self-esteem* to enable them to *believe in man's mastery of his environment, withstanding pressures toward conformity*, and to engage in *risk-taking behavior*. Each of these attributes has been suggested here either as a factor in contributing to effective problem solving behavior or a consequence of experiences in effective problem solving. (See also Brim, et al, 1962, and Hoffman, 1965.)

Figure 2 provides a graphic depiction of the hypothetical relationships.

THE FAMILY AND SOCIAL PROBLEMS

If the above formulation is valid the family's influence on the development of social problems will lay in large part in the problem solving experiences it provides for its members. These influences should be twofold. First, it should influence expectations, establish normative standards, and provide the necessary experience for validating aspects of the individual's self-concept. Second, the family in its role as chief socializing agent forges the orientations which sensitize individuals toward problem solving situations and train offspring in the skills necessary to deal adequately with such situations. Our analysis of the family's contribution, therefore, will focus on these two aspects of family group experiences and socialization.

The following propositions pertaining to each of these aspects of family influence can be derived from the discussion presented in the previous section of this paper.

The first proposition states: *Individuals whose families have been successful in solving their internal problems will be more likely to engage in the transformation of social situations into social problems.* This is based on the assumption that members of successful problem solving families will have the available resources, sufficiently high expectations, and the interest to tackle social problems from a long range, universalistic perspective. It is possible that members of families that have not resolved internal problems may be swept into collective action around a given issue once it is visible; but if, as suggested, their orientations are particularistic, this action should be related only to the alleviation of their immediate problem and not the resolution of a social issue.

The second proposition states: *Families that provide the type of socialization experiences which foster autonomy, participation in the family decision*

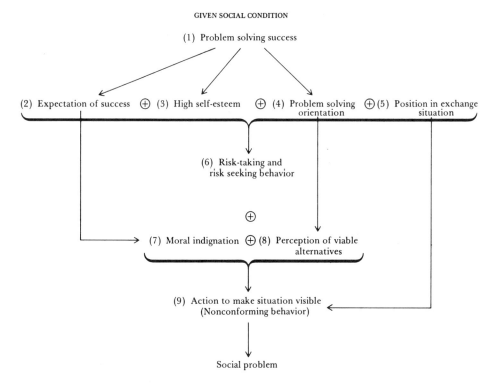

Figure 2. Variables Affecting Actions Which Transform Social Situations into Social Problems.

making process, and high self-esteem will produce members more likely to engage in the identification and development of social problems. This proposition is based on the assumption that increasing the visibility of a social problem is an essential phase in efforts to resolve the problem; therefore, people with the attributes of good problem solvers should be more inclined to engage in behaviors which increase the salience of the problem for larger numbers of people. Engaging in such behaviors requires the internal resources necessary to withstand pressures toward conformity as well as to engage in risk-taking activities.

The propositions focus on two distinct aspects of family life: (1) the consequences of resolving or failing to resolve pressing problems and, (2) the relationship between experiences in problem solving, and the development of attributes associated with social activism. We turn now to the first of these aspects.

Consequences of Effectiveness in Family Problem Solving

In order to examine the possible effects of family problem solving for its members, a series of fundamental problems which most families must face will be posed, and the consequences of successfully or unsuccessfully dealing with these problems will be explored.

Family Commitment. A major decision any group must make is whether it wishes to survive as an entity. This will vary with the degree of dependency of the group members on the group. This dependency varies, in turn, with the attractiveness of the group to its members, as compared to available alternatives (Thibaut and Kelley, 1959). Since the family is uniquely suited to provide its members with nurturance and affection, it seems reasonable to infer that these services represent the basis of its attractiveness. Whatever the problems impinging upon the family from external sources, its primary task is to maintain adequate internal functioning in order to meet the expressive needs of its members (Parsons, 1968; Burgess and Locke, 1945). Internal problems, from this viewpoint, are paramount and the imposition of the external world on the family is, in the first instance, interpreted in terms of its effect upon the family's interior operations.

There are, of course, persons for whom the family is not an attractive alternative, and yet, for a variety of reasons, may not be willing to dissolve their affiliation. Some of these people may seek outlets in social action groups. However, to the extent that such people are seeking to solve expressive problems, their energies are less likely to be expended in actions relating to the purported social purposes of the organization. As a consequence, they may constitute a rearguard element, but are unlikely to directly contribute to the formulation of a social problem. It is also possible that some people may forego a commitment to family life because of their devotion to a given cause. However, when such people are effective, it is probable that their behavior is not compensating for inadequacies within their families but rather, to the contrary, is a consequence of relatively successful family experiences. This is because, as I shall attempt to demonstrate in the next section of this paper, the attributes necessary to mobilize oneself and others for purposeful action are generally forged within an atmosphere of positive family relationships.

Physical Maintenance. Assuming some commitment to the family, a fundamental problem that must be faced is feeding, sheltering, and clothing its members. Research on family behavior typically tends to ignore this fact, probably because it is taken for granted and also because it has infrequently been a critical issue in the samples studied.[9] The physical maintenance issue, however, cannot be ignored. Since the survival of the family as a group is directly involved, all other issues are secondary if this one is not at least minimally resolved. This suggests, for example, that those people who are first to articulate poverty as a social problem will not be directly involved in the experience, since their energies are not dissipated by the daily concerns of food and lodging. As reported earlier, a number of studies indicate that people whose income level is low are not active agents in effecting social change.[10]

Group Consensus. Given some resolution of the problems of physical maintenance, the family will be confronted with problems inherent in all groups—that of developing minimal consensus concerning the allocation of responsibilities and the nature of family goals.

Research in small ad hoc groups suggests that effective problem solving in terms of adequate task oriented behavior requires group consensus and control of interpersonal conflict (Bower, 1965, pp. 277–289). If this is true for task oriented groups, it should be especially true for families which serve as the prime agency for meeting the expressive needs of its members. Students of the family have increasingly stressed the critical role played by the resolution of expressive problems (Parsons and Fox, 1952, pp. 31–44; Farber, 1959). Geismar, La Sorte, and Ayres (1962, pp. 51–56) report that family malfunctioning appears more serious when there is a breakdown in expressive roles as compared to instrumental roles. It is not unreasonable to infer, on the basis of these data and the small group research, that the resolution of expressive problems requires initially some system of communication which can lead to the accurate articulation and understanding of meanings of given acts and, secondly, some consensus as to role expectations for various family members

---

[9] I am not referring here to other aspects of research on low income families, but only to the issue of the salience of physical maintenance in the lives of these people. One possible exception is the research reported by Geisman and La Sorte, 1964, especially Chapter 3.

[10] It is possible that education operates as a confounding variable and the results might be different if the effects of education were controlled. Levens (1968) in her study of welfare recipients reports some tendency, though not statistically significant, for recipients with higher education to be more active in an organization designed to improve their conditions. However, education was not as critical in determining activism as other variables such as feelings of personal efficacy.

(McCall and Simmons, 1966, especially Chapter 8). Failure to develop consensus, if it does not result in the dissolution of the family system, may well result in weakening the boundaries of the nuclear family and may be associated with an extension into sex-linked, close-knit networks of relatives and premarital peer group relationships (Bott, 1957). Nelson (1967) in a study of working class women found that individuals with such close-knit networks are characterized by rather inconsistent value orientations with great dependency on peer group opinions. On the other hand, individuals with loose-knit networks which are associated with companionship-type marriages tend to develop internally consistent value orientations (Nelson, 1967). Elsewhere Nelson (1966) reports that women in the close-knit networks are generally more insulated from their environment. These data suggest that members of families which have not achieved minimal consensus will be less concerned with issues external to their primary groups. At the same time, their dependency on peer group values makes it difficult for them to hold internally consistent views, perhaps making them more vulnerable to group contagion and, therefore, to mobilization for short term collective action.

Boundary Maintenance. The next issue with which most families must contend is maintaining their security and integrity in relation to pressures from the outside world. This corresponds with Hess and Handel's (1959) notion that all families must face the problem of defining their own boundaries and the areas of interconnectedness operating both within these boundaries and with the external society. There are two critical issues here. One is the degree to which the family is integrated into the larger society, and the other is the family's ability to protect itself from penetration by the representatives of society. Generally those families which are least integrated into the society are also least able to insulate themselves from intervention by outside agents. These agents may be beneficent in intent, such as welfare workers, or punitive, such as law enforcement representatives—in either case they are able to intrude on some families with or without their consent. As a consequence, such families are apt to give up decision making power to these external sources, thereby jeopardizing their autonomy and status position. In addition, as Blau (1955) and Homans (1961) illustrate, the abrogation of decision making responsibility to others in nonreciprocal situations results in resentment toward the decision makers on the part of the dependents. This suggests some qualification of the notion that low income families are more insulated and have less interchange with the larger society. What seems probable is that the interchanges at a formal level with society's social control agents are more frequent than in other social strata and represent a superordinate-subordinate relationship in which the family is deprived of decision making alternatives and, hence, further restricted in its opportunities for developing problem solving skills. Some of the recent work by Rainwater and his colleagues (1966) suggest that attempts to maintain the family's boundaries and identity against intrusions from the larger society is a central issue for low income black families. If, as suggested, families that are successfully integrated in the larger society are also safer from intrusion by outside forces, their members should be less dependent upon each other for support against a hostile world and more willing to engage in activities involving larger social issues. Conversely, the activities of members of those families which cannot protect their boundaries should be more circumscribed and less venturesome since, in a very concrete sense, they are on the defensive against forces which threaten their sense of identity and integrity. Again, it seems clear that such persons are in no position to define situations as social problems although they may well welcome support in their struggle from outside sources and willingly align themselves with groups who promise them help.

It should be noted that these problematical situations are not uniformly critical for all families. For example, most families in the United States do not have to solve problems of physical survival and biological maintenance and so may be able immediately to move on to problems of internal cohesion. For those whose lives are deeply rooted in family traditions, problems of consensus may be inconsequential. Similarly, where the family's integration into the community is established and status firmly ascribed, problems of boundary maintenance may not be relevant. In any case, we would predict that members of families who have not solved these generic problems are least likely to develop a sense of social morality or engage in forms of social action.

Intra-Family Experiences and the Development of Critical Attributes

We turn now to an examination of intra-family experiences in problem solving. Since the family functions both as a problem solving unit and as a training group for developing individual problem skills and abilities, both of these functions are relevant for our purposes.

Two general sets of variables appear significant in this context; they are: (1) the types of controls or power exercised over family members, and (2) the distribution of support and affection within the family group. (See, for example, Straus, 1964, pp. 318–326; Becker, 1964; Schaefer, 1959.) These variables operate to coordinate the family's activities and to encourage or discourage the contributions of individual members to the resolution of problems. Although affectional relationships may operate independently of the norms relating to the family power structure, there should be greater family cohesiveness if the affectional structure supports (or at least does not interfere with) the power structure. If these two structures are not compatible the likelihood is that divisive coalitions and cliques will develop (Strodtbeck, 1957). Since cohesive groups are likely to be more accepting of individual members than noncohesive groups, the members of cohesive groups should be freer to make contributions without fear of loss of favor, thereby increasing the effectiveness of the group's problem solving activities (Hoffman, 1965, pp. 99–132). Such cohesion provides an atmosphere for the expression of conflicting viewpoints,[11] an important element in problem solving behavior (Hoffman, 1965). Further, there are data to suggest that group cohesiveness enables individuals and groups to engage in greater risk taking than is the case when such support is lacking (Wallach, Kogan, Bem, 1964, pp. 263–274). The family, by providing approval, praise, and affection, is also critical in effecting the self-esteem of the family group members. There is considerable evidence indicating that people with high self-esteem are better able to withstand pressures toward conformity (Smith, 1968, pp. 270–320; Hovland, Janis, and Kelley, 1953), and, as a consequence, are able to utilize a broader range of ideas in seeking problem solutions (Hoffman, 1965). As noted earlier, high self-esteem has also been found to be associated with risk taking and an interest in public affairs.

To summarize briefly, intra-family experiences and relationships should play a prime role in developing the capacity of family members to withstand group pressures toward conformity and to provide the support necessary for engaging in controversy and risk-taking behavior. These attributes have been shown to be critical for effective group problem solving; they also are important elements in expanding the visibility of social problems. In addition, the family is a principal agent for developing self-esteem among its members. Self-esteem, in turn, is correlated with a number of key attributes necessary for engaging in problem solving behavior. Again these attributes appear to be virtually identical to those with which I have characterized persons capable of engaging in the formation of a social problem; that is, they are individuals willing to seek out stressful situations, capable of independent interpretations, and concerned with social issues. There is, then, some basis for inferring a connection between effective family problem solving behavior and behavior which can transform social situations into social problems.

We have assumed that these behaviors are learned in the process of engaging in family problem solving activities. I shall attempt to illustrate how this learning may take place by focusing on one example of a critical family role, that of the father, and examining how it affects and is affected by the problem solving process.

Paternal Roles and Problem Solving: An Illustration

From the point of view of problem solving behavior, the father appears to hold the key position in the family. This is because his roles give him both an unique perspective for exercising leadership and, at the same time, place him in the most vulnerable position. The pervasive expectation in this society, as in most, is that the father's role is one of family provider (Zelditch,

---

[11] Aldous makes the point that because of the importance of solidarity, families rather than encouraging the expression of opposing viewpoints may tend to restrict such expressions. This may be true in the overall sense in which families are compared with other groups. However, within families as a group type, and assuming the priority of group consensus, it seems reasonable to infer that cohesive families will encourage greater discussion for arriving at agreed upon ends than noncohesive families.

1955; Barry, Bacon, and Child, 1957). This puts his position in jeopardy when forces outside of the family make it difficult to carry out this role according to his and his family's expectations. Although the extra-family pressures on the father are probably greater than they are for the mother, he has, at the same time, more contacts with the outside world, thereby increasing his opportunities for alternative group alliances. This greater number of alternatives both increases his power within the family and makes him the most likely persons to dissolve the family unit (Thibaut and Kelley, 1959).

We can assume that the more adequately the father functions in his various roles the more he will be rewarded within the family (Blood and Wolfe, 1960, pp. 187–188) and, perhaps as a result, the greater his commitment to the family (Aldous, 1966). The approval and support received from family members should contribute to his self-esteem, enabling him to exercise leadership with sufficient security to allow for open channels of communication and conflicting ideas. What is suggested here, then, is that the father's self-esteem will vary with the degree to which he has had previous success in problem solving endeavors. Since self-esteem is associated with problem solving and problem seeking behavior (Smith, 1968; Torrance, 1968), this creates a spiraling pattern of success (Smith, 1968).[12] What signifies success is, of course, related to the types of problems a family is faced with and their normative expectations. Thus, it is likely that the low income black father with a steady job experiences as much approval from his family and friends as a white collar professional who is particularly successful at his endeavors. This positive reinforcement makes problem solving an attractive form of activity and orients successful groups to seek out additional problems (Berkowitz and Levy, 1956; Hoffman, Burke, and Meier, 1963). Effective problem solving within the family should, therefore, influence the propensity of offspring to develop a problem solving orientation. The father who considers himself a successful problem solver is likely to prove a more effective model for the child, not only because of his competence, but also because his success provides him with sufficient self-confidence to allow the child to make contributions while at the same time holding the child responsible for adequate performance in goal-directed activities. It is this combination of providing the child with support while allowing him the freedom to contribute to problem solutions and objectively evaluating the results, which appear to me to underly some of Moore's success with underprivileged children and characterizes the behavior of mothers of successful problem solving children described by Bee.

I have not intended in the above discussion to argue that the family is the only group through which an individual may learn to be an adequate problem solver. There are certainly other primary groups that may fulfill the necessary conditions. What seems likely, however, due to the ubiquitous

---

[12] It is, of course, difficult to isolate the independent variable in this spiraling process—certainly the social structure plays either a facilitative or inhibiting role. Similarly, the various family goals as determined by differing value orientations affect the difficulty of the tasks undertaken and the types of problems faced.

influence of the family, is that such fortuitous, extra-family influences are relatively rare.

Family Problem Solving and Social Problems

A fundamental assumption in this paper is that significant social problems do not merely exist in the environment but are defined by persons who become morally indignant about a situation and attempt to make visible to sizable segments of the population both the situation and the perceived moral injustice. This requires individuals who are oriented toward seeing situations in problematic terms and are willing to act on that perception at some risk to themselves. Such persons may, in fact, seek out stressful situations. On the basis of the formulation presented in this paper, therefore, we would expect that people whose actions initially increase the magnitude of a social problem are more likely to come from families which have had a history of problem solving success and have allowed open discussion and controversy to take place within the home. We also hypothesize that those families struggling to solve internal problems of maintenance, cohesion, security, and status will be less likely to participate, or to have offsprings that participate, in the development of social problems of any magnitude. This is because such families have neither the available resources nor the backlog of problem solving successes which create an affinity for problem solving behavior. Conversely, families which have solved their internal problems should be more likely to seek out problems in the environment. Whether this kind of problem seeking behavior results in defining a situation as a social problem depends on the particular value and moral commitments individuals hold. However, the self-assurance characteristic of effective problem solvers makes it possible to maintain a firm set of moral expectations since they have confidence, based on previous experience, that situations are rectifiable and goals are attainable.

The importance of structural variables cannot be underestimated. It seems apparent that low income families and families from minority groups subject to discrimination will find it much more difficult to solve their internal problems and to provide successful problem solving models for their children. We expect, therefore, that persons active in defining social problems come from higher social strata, have been relatively successful in dealing with their environmental problems, and have positive identifications with their families.

It is, of course, possible that the relationship suggested between family problem solving behavior and social problems is spurious, merely reflecting commonly acknowledged social class differences. A critical test of this hypothesis, then, would require assessing the relationship between problem solving skills and activism within a given social stratum and opportunity structure. The research on student activists provides one such test. Although activist students tend to be centered in the most prestigious and academically oriented institutions (Peterson, 1966), there are fundamental differences between activists and nonactivists on these campuses. Trent and Craise (1967) report that activists had ". . . far more interest in intellectual inquiry, tolerance for ambiguity, objectivity and independence of thought" than nonactivist or moderate groups. We can interpret these results as indicating a greater problem solving orientation among activists. Similarly, Keniston (1967, pp. 108–137), in his comparison of what he termed "alienated" and protesting students, reports that alienated students, although they come from the same social strata as the protesters, are less committed to academic values and intellectual achievement than the protesting student. They are also less likely to take part in organized group activities. When they do become involved in demonstrations, unlike the activists, they usually prefer peripheral roles and avoid responsibilities. Finally Keniston notes, "Whereas the protesting student is likely to accept the basic political and social values of his parents, the alienated student almost always rejects his parents' values." These findings offer some support for the hypothesis that activists as compared to nonactivists come from homes which allow open discussion while maintaining consensus on basic values.

A social problem of some magnitude cannot develop entirely from the behavior of activists, however. As noted earlier, activists must be able to mobilize larger numbers of people to their cause. One way of achieving this is to offer solutions to immediate and pressing problems, thereby proffering hope that a remedy is possible. Thus, the effective rallying cry for the poverty stricken is food, shelter, and clothing; for the Black American, it is sufficient power to withstand the encroachment of the dominant society. It is in keeping with the sequential notion of family problems that the very poor seem to have little concern with the race issue, and attempts to mobilize black communities against the Vietnam war have generally been ineffective. Further, the activities of these mobilized groups are not always clearly directed toward the moral grievances which their leaders want rectified—although their actions may still be consonant with attempts to resolve their immediate problems. Thus the stealing, bickering, and distrust which reportedly characterizes the behavior of many of the poor people who marched on Washington may have embarrassed their leaders, but seems appropriate from the perspective of their unresolved problems.

In summary, the conceptual framework presented here suggests the following sets of hypotheses. First, with regard to activists in social problem areas, they should be more likely than nonactivists to (1) come from intact families, (2) have positive identifications with their parents, (3) have a personal and family history of problem solving success, (4) give evidence of greater creativity and indicate a tendency to seek out stressful situations, (5) have a strong commitment to abstract or generalized moral issues as opposed to considerations of personal aggrandizement, (6) have relatively high self-esteem and a sense of personal efficacy, and (7) tend to be less concerned with immediate family issues. The second set of hypotheses relate to those people who come from families with unresolved internal problems. These people should (1) be less likely to be activists, (2) become involved in social issues only under circumstances which promise resolution for their immediate problems, and (3) be guided in their problem solving behavior less by strategic considerations and more by attempts to seek gratification of their immediate needs.[13]

This paper has attempted to account for one possible source of influence on the development of social problems. What the extent of this influence is we cannot say—certainly what happens within the family does not determine social problems irrespective of social conditions. On the other hand, social conditions do not, by themselves, create social problems. Linking family problem solving with the development of social problems does, however, offer a possible means for explaining such important and unanswered questions as (1) who are the people who identify and make social problems visible, and (2) how can we account for the family role in the development of social problems in other than passive or reactive terms? Asserting that it is competent and successful families which provide the individuals who create conditions of visible social strife seems less paradoxical when we consider their behavior as an extension of problem solving activity. In fact, we might expect that as the society more adequately meets the needs of larger segments of the population, these segments will also engage in the identification and, therefore, in the solution of social problems.

REFERENCES

Adams, J. Stacey, "Inequity in Social Exchange." In L. Berkowitz, ed. *Advances in Experimental Social Psychology*, Vol. 2. New York: Academic Press, 1965.

Aldous, Joan, "Lower-Class Males: Integration into Community and Family." Paper presented at Sixth World Congress of Sociology, Evian, France, 1966.

Aronson, Elliot and Carlsmith, J. Merrill, "Performance Expectancy as a Determinant of Actual Performance." *Journal of Abnormal Social Psychology*, 65:178–183, 1962.

Banfield, Edward C., *The Moral Basis of a Backward Society*. New York: The Free Press, 1958.

Barry III, Herbert, Bacon, Margaret K., and Child, Irwin L., "A Cross-Cultural Survey of Some Sex Differences in Socialization." *Journal of Abnormal and Social Psychology*, 55:327–306, 1957.

Becker, Howard S., *Outsiders*. New York: The Free Press, 1963.

Becker, W. C., "Consequences of Different Kinds of Parental Discipline." In J. L. Hoffman and L. W. Hoffman, ed. *Review of Child Development Research*. New York: Russell Sage Foundation, 1964.

Berkowitz, Leonard and Levy, B. I., "Pride in Group Performance and Group Task Motivation." *Journal of Abnormal and Social Psychology*, 53:300–306, 1956.

Bernard, Jesse, *Remarriage*. New York: Dryden Press, 1956.

Blau, Peter M., *The Dynamics of Bureaucracy*. Chicago: University of Chicago Press, 1955.

---

[13] We have research underway to test these hypotheses with a national sample of war resistors and a comparable sample of men classified 1A in the draft. This is, of course, only a beginning effort. What is necessary is a sampling of a wide range of social problems.

Blood, Robert O. and Wolfe, Donald M., *Husbands and Wives: The Dynamics of Married Living*. New York: The Free Press, 1960.

Bott, Elizabeth, *Family and Social Networks*. London: Tavistock, 1957.

Bower, Joseph L., "Group Decision Making: A Report of an Experimental Study." *Behavioral Science*, 10:277–289, 1965.

Brim, Orville, Glass, David, Lavin, David, and Goodman, Norman, *Personality and Decision Processes: Studies in the Social Psychology of Thinking*. Stanford, California: Stanford University Press, 1962.

Bruner, Jerome S., "Personality Dynamics and the Process of Perceiving." In R. R. Blake and G. V. Ramsey, ed. *Perception: An Approach to Personality*. New York: The Ronald Press Co., 1951.

Burgess, Ernest W. and Locke, Harvey J., *The Family*. New York: American Book Co., 1945.

Christensen, Harold T., "Cultural Relativism and Pre-Marital Sex Norms." *American Sociological Review*, 25:31–39, 1960.

Davies, James C., "Toward a Theory of Revolution." *American Sociological Review*, 27:5–19, 1962.

Davis, Kingsley, "Illegitimacy and the Social Structure." *American Journal of Sociology*, 45, 1939.

Davis, Kingsley and Blake, Judith, "Social Structure and Fertility." *Economic Development and Social Change*, 1956. Pp. 211–235.

Farber, Bernard, *Effects of a Severely Mentally Retarded Child on Family Integration*, monograph. Social Research on Child Development, 1959.

Flacks, Richard W., "The Liberated Generation: An Exploration of the Roots of Student Protest." *Journal of Social Issues*, 23:53–75, 1967.

Geismar, L. L., La Sorte, M. A., and Ayres, B., "Measuring Family Disorganization." *Marriage and Family Living*, 24:51–56, 1962.

Geismar, L. L. and La Sorte, M. A., *Understanding the Multi-Problem Family*. New York: Associated Press, 1964.

Goode, William J., *After Divorce*. New York: The Free Press, 1956.

———— "Illegitimacy in the Caribbean Social Structure." *American Sociological Review*, 25:21–30, 1960.

———— *Women in Divorce*. New York: The Free Press, 1965.

Hess, Robert D. and Handel, Gerald, *Family Worlds*. Chicago: University of Chicago Press, 1959.

Hill, Ruben, Stycos, Joseph M., and Back, Kurt, *The Family and Population Control: A Puerto Rican Experiment in Social Change*. Chapel Hill, North Carolina: University of North Carolina Press, 1959.

Hoffman, L. Richard, "Group Problem Solving." Pp. 99–132 in L. Berkowitz, ed. *Advances in Experimental Psychology*. New York: Academic Press, 1965.

Hoffman, L. Richard, Burke, R. J., and Meier, N. R. F., "Does Training with Differential Reinforcement on Similar Problems Help in Solving a New Problem?" *Psychological Report*, 13:147–154, 1963.

Homans, George, *Social Behavior: Its Elementary Forms*. New York: Harcourt, Brace and World, 1961.

Horton, Paul B. and Leslie, Gerald R., *The Sociology of Social Problems*, 2nd ed. New York: Appleton-Century-Crofts, Inc., 1960.

Hovland, Carl I., Janis, Irving L., and Kelly, Harold H., *Communication and Persuasion*. New Haven: Yale University Press, 1953.

Hovland, Carl I. et al, *The Order of Presentation in Persuasion*. New Haven: Yale University Press, 1959.

Inkeles, Alex, "Society, Social Structure and Child Socialization." Pp. 73–129 in J. A. Clausen, ed. *Socialization and Society*. Boston: Little, Brown and Co., 1968.

Jones, Edward E. and Davis, Keith E., "From Acts to Disposition." In L. Berkowitz, ed. *Advances in Experimental Social Psychology*, Vol. 2. New York: Academic Press, 1965.

Jones, Edward E. and de Charms, Richard, "Changes in Social Perception as a Function of the Personal Relevance of Behavior." *Sociometry*, 20:25–85, 1957.

Jones, Edward E. and Thibaut, John W., "Interaction Goals as Bases of Inference in Interpersonal Perception." In R. Tagiuri and L. Petrullo, ed. *Person Perception and Interpersonal Behavior*. Stanford: Stanford University Press, 1958.

Keniston, Kenneth, "The Sources of Student Dissent." *Journal of Social Forces*, 23:108–137, 1967.

Klausner, Samuel Z., "The Intermingling of Pain and Pleasure." Pp. 135–168 in S. Klausner, ed. *Why Man Takes Chances*. Garden City: Anchor Books, 1968.

Kornhauser, William, *The Politics of Mass Society*. New York: The Free Press, 1959.

Levens, Helene, "Organizational Affiliation and Powerlessness: A Case Study of the Welfare Poor." *Social Problems*, 16:18–32, 1968.

Lidz, Theodore, Fleck, Stephen, and Cornelision, Alice R., *Schizophrenia and The Family*. New York: International Universities Press Inc., 1965.

Lundberg, George A., *Can Science Save Us?* New York: Longmans Green, 1947.

Lynd, Robert S., *Knowledge For What?* Princeton: Princeton University Press, 1945.

Martindale, Don, "Social Disorganization: The Conflict of Normative and Empirical Approaches." In H. Becker and A. Boskoff, ed. *Modern Sociology Theory*. New York: The Dryden Press, 1957.

———— "Evolution of Sociology." In G. K. Zollschan and W. Hirsch, ed. *Exploration in Social Change*. Boston: Houghton Mifflin Company, 1964.

McCall, George and Simmons, J. L., *Identities and Interactions*. (Especially chapter 8.) New York: The Free Press, 1966.

McCord, William and McCord, Joan, *Origins of Alcoholism*. Stanford: Stanford University Press, 1960.

Merton, Robert K., *Social Theory and Social Structure*. New York: The Free Press, 1957.

———— "Social Problems and Sociological Theory." Pp. 775–823 in R. K. Merton and R. A. Nisbet, ed. *Contemporary Social Problems*. New York: Harcourt, Brace and World, Inc., 1966.

Milbrath, Lester W., *Political Participation*. Skokie, Ill.: Rand-McNally Company, 1965.

Miller, Norman and Campbell, Donald T., "Recency and Primacy in Persuasion as a Function of the Timing of Speeches and Measurement." *Journal of Abnormal and Social Psychology*, 59:1–9, 1959.

Miller, Daniel R. and Swanson, Guy E., *Inner Conflict and Defense*. New York: Harper and Row, 1960.

Morrison, Denton E. and Steeves, Allen D., "Deprivation, Discontent, and Social Movement Participation: Evidence on a Contemporary Farmers' Movement, the N.F.O.," *Rural Sociology*, 32:421–422, 1967.

Nelson, Joel, "Clique Contacts and Family Orientations." *American Sociological Review*, 31, 1966.

—— "Marital Norms and Individualistic Values." *Journal of Marriage and the Family*, 29:475–484, 1967.

Nisbet, Robert A., "The Study of Social Problems." In R. K. Merton and R. Nisbet, ed. *Contemporary Social Problems*. New York: Harcourt, Brace, and World, Inc., 1966.

Parsons, Talcott and Fox, Renee, "Illness Therapy and the Modern Urban American Family." *Journal of Social Issues*, 8:31–44, 1958.

Parsons, Talcott, "The Normal American Family." In M. Sussman, ed. *Sourcebook of Marriage and the Family*, 3rd ed. Boston: Houghton, Mifflin Company, 1968.

Peterson, Richard E., *The Scope of Organized Student Protest in 1964–65*. Princeton: Educational Testing Service, 1966.

Pettigrew, Thomas F., *A Profile of the Negro American*. Princeton: D. Van Nostrand Company, 1964.

Rainwater, Lee, "The Crucible of Identity." *Daedalus*, 95:172–216, 1966.

Rosenberg, Milton J. and Abelson, Robert P., "An Analysis of Cognitive Balancing." Pp. 112–163 in M. J. Rosenberg et al, ed. *Attitude, Organization, and Change*. New Haven: Yale University, 1960.

Rosenberg, Morris, *Society and the Adolescent Self-Image*. Princeton: Princeton University Press, 1965.

Rotter, Julian B., "Generalized Expectancies of Internal vs. External Control of Reinforcement." *Psychological Monographs*, 80, 1966.

Schaefer, E. S., "A Circumplex Model of Maternal Behavior." *Journal of Abnormal and Social Psychology*, 59:226–235, 1959.

Segall, Marshall H., Campbell, Donald T., and Herskovits, Melville J., *The Influence of Culture on Visual Perception*. Indianapolis: Bobbs-Merrill Co., Inc., 1966.

Smith, M. Brewster, "Competence and Socialization." Pp. 270–320 in J. A. Clausen, ed. *Socialization and Society*. Boston: Little, Brown, and Co., 1968.

Solley, Charles M. and Murphy, Gardner, *Development of the Perceptual World*. New York: Basic Books, Inc., 1960.

Spector, A. J., "Expectations, Fulfillment, and Morale." *Journal of Abnormal and Social Psychology*, 52:51–56, 1956.

Straus, Murray, "Power and Support Structure of the Family in Relation to Socialization." *Journal of Marriage and the Family*, 26:318–326, 1964.

Strodtbeck, Fred L., "Family Interaction, Values, and Achievement." In D. C. McClelland et al, ed. *Talent and Society*. Princeton: D. Van Nostrand Co., 1957.

Tallman, Irving and McGee, Reece, "What is a Social Problem?" In E. Smigel, ed. *Handbook of Social Problems*. Skokie, Ill.: Rand McNally. (In press.)

Thibaut, John W., "An Experimental Study of Cohesiveness of Underprivileged Groups." *Human Relations*, 3:251–278, 1950.

Thibaut, John W. and Kelley, Howard H., *The Social Psychology of Groups*. New York: John Wiley & Sons, 1959.

Torrance, E. Paul, "Comparative Studies in Stress Seeking in the Imaginative

Stories of Pre-Adolescents in 12 Different Subcultures." In S. Klausner, ed. *Why Man Takes Chances*. Garden City: Anchor Books, 1968.

Trent, James W. and Craise, Judith L., "Commitment and Conformity in the American College." *Journal of Social Issues*, 23:34–51, 1967.

Wallach, Michael A., Kogan, Nathan, and Bean, Daryll, "Diffusion of Responsibility and Level of Risk Taking in Groups." *Journal of Abnormal and Social Psychology*, 68:263–274, 1964.

Zelditch, Morris, "Role Differentiation in the Nuclear Family: A Comparative Study." Pp. 307–351 in T. Parsons and R. F. Bales, ed. *Family Socialization and Interaction Process*. New York: The Free Press, 1955.

Appendix I

ABSTRACTS

ABSTRACTS serve the purpose of providing a concise overview of literature. They are not intended to replace the original research, but rather provide access to the research. An abstract makes its reader aware of the range and scope of the literature available. As always, abstract sources are selective, this one is no exception. It is the intention of the following abstracts to provide an overview of the literature on problem solving. As many of the research articles on the specific topic of family problem solving were abstracted as could be located. No doubt there are some which were inadvertently missed, but the goal of this project was to get all of the family problem solving research abstracted. Then in addition, other small group problem solving research was added. These did not nearly cover all the literature available, but should give the reader a taste of the other literature. Articles selected deal with variables applicable to families such as size of group studied and kind of problem solved. The bibliographies which the symposium participants included provided some citations to additional literature which has been abstracted. It would be advantageous for the interested reader to examine *Psychological Abstracts* and *Sociological Abstracts* for further literature on problem solving, since this compilation is not complete.

The articles abstracted have been selected from literature published between 1950 to 1970 with the bulk of them from the 1960's. Most of the articles are from journals which can be found easily in any large university collection. Generally speaking, it should be no problem for an interested reader to locate the original article. Please observe that almost all of the research is from English language periodicals.

Nancy Dahl
Director
Inventory of Published Research
in Marriage and Family Behavior

Annotated Bibliography

Bateson, N., "Familiarization, Group Discussion and Risk Taking." *Journal of Experimental Social Psychology*, 1966, 2, 119–129.

Research Problem: To test the hypothesis that the risky-shift phenomenon in group decision-making is due to increased familiarity with the problems. *Methodology:* The sample consisted of 109 subjects from three different collegiate sources, 90 men and 19 women. All responded to five items from the Choice Dilemmas test. Subjects were then placed in one of three experimental conditions control; subjects individually prepared written arguments on controversial issues not related to the choice dilemmas; alone, subjects prepared written arguments on the choice dilemma problems; group, subjects discussed choice dilemma items in three-person groups and attempted to reach a unanimous decision. All subjects then individually retook the initial test. Four to eight days later a recollection test of the fill-in-the-missing-word type was given to test recall of choice dilemma items. *Findings:* Recall was essentially equal in group and alone conditions, less in control condition. Group and alone subjects showed a risky shift of about the same magnitude, while controls showed no significant shift. Results support the hypothesis.

Blood, R. O., Jr. and Hamblin, R. L., "The Effect of Wife's Employment on the Family Power Structure." *Social Forces*, 1958, 36, 347–352.

Research Problem: Effects of wife's employment on power relationships between husband and wife by testing two hypotheses: (1) Working wives shift toward equalitarian authority expectations more than do housewives; and (2) Husbands of working wives change toward equalitarian authority expectations. *Methodology:* 160 couples, half with working wives and half with nonworking wives from home towns of upper division students at the University were given questionnaires. The couples were matched for employment of wife, number of years married, wife employed for at least a year. Eight additional demographic variables were controlled. *Findings:* Husbands of working wives do a greater proportion of housework than do husbands of housewives. On the average, working wives have a larger percentage of adopted suggestions than do housewives. Working wives more often change toward equalitarian authority expectations and housewives change towards traditional authority expectations. This is true for husbands of those wives also.

Blood, R. O., Jr. and Wolfe, D. M., "The Power to Make Decisions." *Husbands and Wives*, New York: The Free Press, 1960, 11–46.

Research Problem: To measure the power of husbands and wives to make decisions in their marriage. Power can be defined as the ability of one partner to influence the other's behavior. *Methodology:* The sample consisted of 909 married women living in the Detroit area and Southeastern Michigan. The sampling design consisted of a multi-stage probability sampling. All the women were interviewed in their homes for about an hour. The eight questions used to measure power were included in a larger study of 110 questions on how American marriages operate. *Findings:* The balance of power falls slightly in the husbands' direction although Detroit families as a whole are relatively equalitarian. The more resources a partner has the higher the power. Education, social status, income, occupational status, all were related to increased power in decision making. Life cycle changes made a difference in power with middle age wives having the highest power. In the Negro family, the wife's power was higher relatively with 44% of the Negro families ranking as wife dominant and only 20% of the white families.

Bower, J. L., "Group Decision Making: A Report of an Experimental Study." *Behavioral Science*, 1965, 10, 277–289.

Research Problem: To determine how cooperative (team) versus competitive (foundation) goals and rewards, information, and decision groups affect efficiency of group decision making. Hypotheses are: (1) Teams will do as well or better than foundations; (2) groups with good information will do better than those with poorer information; (3) groups operating under a rule of unanimity will make better decisions than those operating under majority rule, but will have a more difficult time making any decision at all. *Methodology:* 62 three-man groups were given a problem in which they were to act as a financial committee making investment decisions. Payoffs were manipulated to encourage either cooperation or competition, groups were given varying amounts of information about the proposed investments, and either a majority rule or a unanimity was required. Groups communicated only in writing. *Findings:* Hypothesis (2) is supported. As for hypothesis (1), teams made better decisions than foundations when unanimity was required, but under majority rule the reverse is true. Hypothesis (3) is not supported, since the favorable affect of majority rule on foundations was reflected in the aggregate.

Brown, L. B., "The 'Day at Home' in Wellington, New Zealand." *Journal of Social Psychology*, 1959, 50, 189–206.

Research Problem: Examination of husband's, wife's, and children's roles in the household in terms of who decides what is to be done and who acts. Comparison with Australian findings. *Methodology:* This research consisted of a questionnaire survey of 138 children who were 12 or 13 years old from a typical sample of Wellington. A statistical comparison with the results of a study of Melbourne and Perth was done. *Findings:* There is in Wellington more joint decision making and more flexibility of functioning together with a definite separation of areas of authority and action of husband and wife than there is in Australia. Wellington families are nearer the optimum pattern of Ocser and Hammond which lies between the syncratic and automatic family structures, with social and economic activities largely cooperative with a proportion of separate work activities.

Burchinal, L. G. and Bauder, W. W., "Decision-Making and Role Patterns Among Iowa Farm Families." *Marriage and Family Living*, 1965, 27, 525–532.

Research Problem: Relation of geographical residence to spousal decision making and task performance. *Methodology:* Questionnaire administered to husbands and wives from an area probability sample were used to select families from three studies. Residence in farm, small city, open-country non-farm, village, large city from two Iowa counties, to assess differences in residence and decision making, residence and wives' task performance. *Findings:* There were no significant differences in decision-making patterns for the various residential types. There were no significant differences in husband-wife roles for the various residential areas. Wives had a significant difference for handling of family finances but no consistent relationship was found with place of residence.

Dyer, W. G. and Urban, D., "Institutionalization of Equalitarian Norms." *Marriage and Family Living*, 1958, 20, 53–53.

Research Problem: Analysis of attitudes concerning family decision making in a nonmarried group and a married group. *Methodology:* A question was given to two groups at Brigham Young University, unmarried male and female students, and married students. 300 students comprised the sample, equally divided among the sexes, randomly selected from all upper and lower division courses offered in one school quarter. *Findings:* All groups agreed on equalitarian norms for child-rearing responsibilities. All groups felt that decision making should be equal in all areas except "who should be the head of the family." Married women saw this as the husband's role, single women saw this as equal. The sample did not agree as to norms for management of the family finances. Attitudes for sharing of household tasks remain traditionally divided between husband's and wife's tasks. Author concludes that equality of norms have been institutionalized.

Empey, L. T., "An Instrument for the Measurement of Family Authority Patterns." *Rural Sociology*, 1957, 22, 73–75.

Research Problem: To test the usefulness of Stone and Landis' scale for measuring family authority patterns. *Methodology:* Probability sample of 1,981 Washington State high school seniors taken in 1954 was given the Stone-Landis family authority patterns scale. *Findings:* The Stone-Landis scale may or may not represent the whole universe of adolescent attitudes indicating perceptions of family authority patterns. The items are scalable for a sample different from the one on which the scale was developed. The scale can be made more efficient by using intensity analysis as an empirical means of distinguishing among homes perceived as authoritarian, intermediate, and democratic.

Ferreira, A. J. and Winter, W. D., "Family Interaction and Decision-Making." *Archives of General Psychiatry*, 1965, 13, 214–223.

Research Problem: Inquiry into the conjoint behavior of the family triad (father, mother, child) while making a family decision which stems from joint efforts of, and has impact upon, all three. *Methodology:* 125 families were tested, divided into four groups: 50 normal, 15 schizophrenic-producing, 16 delinquent-producing, and 44 maladjusted families. The questionnaire was administered individually, and then to the family as a unit. There were seven situations; this study compares three questions filled out individually and then as a family. *Findings:* It was concluded that normal families differ in demonstrable ways from abnormal families. Normal families have a much greater agreement in what their members liked or disliked prior to exchange of information, spent less time in reaching a family decision, and arrived at more appropriate decisions in terms of a better fulfillment of family members' individual choices. This appears to be experimental corroboration for what is becoming a common clinical impression—that where the child is the identified patient, the father-mother-child triad is malfunctioning.

Geiken, K. F., "Expectations Concerning Husband-Wife Responsibilities in the Home." *Marriage and Family Living*, 1964, 26, 349–352.

Research Problem: Analysis of family household task division among married couples and expectations of this among adolescents. *Methodology:* A questionnaire was given to 190 married couples living in a University of Wisconsin graduate student community and 36 junior and senior high school students, composed of an equal number of males and females from a rural community in Wisconsin. High school students were enrolled in a marriage education course. Analysis was done on three areas of responsibility in housekeeping activities, authority patterns, and child care. *Findings:* Among married couples, the area of responsibility most frequently shared was authority patterns, child care next, and housekeeping least. Couples without children or with employed wives shared housekeeping tasks. The older the children, the more couples shared in their discipline. Sharing in family finances occurred to a greater extent during the first year of marriage and when wife was unemployed. Expectations of high school sample were similar to behavior found in married couples.

Goldman, M., "A Comparison of Group and Individual Performance Where Subjects Have Varying Tendencies to Solve Problems." *Journal of Personality and Social Psychology*, 1966, 3, 604–607.

Research Problem: To investigate relationships between performance of two individuals on a problem solving task and their performance as a team on the same tasks. *Methodology:* 66 undergraduates took the Wonderlic Intelligence Test (form D). Of these subjects, 36 were paired so that there were three items which: (1) both initially answered correctly; (2) both subjects gave different wrong answers; (3) both subjects gave the same wrong answer; (4) one gave the correct answer while the other answered incorrectly. Each pair then took the test as a group with free discussion. Results on the items on which pairings were based were tabulated for each of the four conditions. *Findings:* The groups did as well or better than the individuals. The best performances were when both had initially given the correct answer. The groups performed poorly only when both members had initially given the same incorrect answer.

Grove, G., "Attitude Convergence in Small Groups." *Journal of Communication*, 1966, 3, 214–222.

Research Problem: To investigate social influence in small groups. Hypotheses are that (1) group members, (2) majority members, and (3) deviate members of groups with discussion opportunity will converge more in their attitudes than deviates limited to traditional social influence. *Methodology:* 381 undergraduate students were administered Likert-type Attitude Scales; the 40 low scorers and 40 high scorers on "capital punishment" and "grading system" were divided into four-man groups with either 3 pro and 1 con or 3 con and 1 pro member. Each group was subjected to one of five treatments: (1) Control—individual retaking of questionnaires; (2) Asch type—each member asked for numerical evaluation, which is publicly posted with the deviate last, followed by a post-test; (3) 15 minute discussion, Asch-type treatment, and post-test; (4) 15 minute discussion plus post-test; (5) 25 minute discussion plus post-test. *Findings:* All three hypotheses were supported, although trends were not always statistically significant. Convergence effects were particularly noted in the long-discussion and discussion-plus-Asch-treatment conditions.

Hall, J. and Williams, M. S., "A Comparison of Decision-Making Performance in Established and Ad Hoc Groups." *Journal of Personality and Social Psychology*, 1966, 3, 214–222.

Research Problem: To compare the decision-making performances of established and ad hoc groups under conditions of high and low substantive conflict. *Methodology:* 285 individuals from the ranks of management were divided into 40 groups of six to nine members. Twenty had shared 50 hours or more of in-group activity. The remaining 20 were ad hoc groups. The problem involved determining in what order 11 jurors would change their votes from "guilty" to "not guilty." (Characters were from the film "Twelve Angry Men.") *Findings:* The established groups did significantly better than ad hoc groups. Ad hoc groups tended to respond to conflict with compromise, established groups with increased creativity. Ad hoc groups were limited by members prediscussion resources, while established groups were not.

Heer, D. M., "Dominance and the Working Wife." *Social Forces*, 1958, 36, 341–347.

Research Problem: Effect of shift in wife's role on the decision-making process. *Methodology:* 138 interviews divided into four equal groups: working-class, working wife; working-class, nonworking wife; middle-class, working wife; and middle-class, nonworking wife. In each family there was a minimum of one child. The husband was between 26 and 46 years old. The sample includes only Irish Roman Catholics from Boston, sample selected from a list of parochial school children. *Findings:* Both wife's work and social class are significantly related to family decision making. The working-class, working wife is more influential than the middle-class, working wife. There are no large differences between the working wife and the housewife in personality of dominance to explain greater decision making. Positive association between number of children and husband's influence. Speculate: Roman Catholic wives practicing rhythm but having fewer children were able to exert influence over husband for required abstinence. This also true in decision-making and freedom to work.

Heer, D. M., "Husband and Wife Perceptions of Family Power Structure." *Marriage and Family Living,* 1962, 24, 65–67.

Research Problem: Extent of husband-wife agreement on relative dominance in decision making. *Methodology:* Interviews with 38 couples living in the Boston Standard Metropolitan Statistical Area. Approximately one quarter were working-class, working-wife families; one quarter working-class, housewife families; one quarter middle-class, working-wife families; and one quarter middle-class, housewife families. All had at least one child of elementary school age and a father in the age range 26 to 46 years, and all were Roman Catholic families of Irish descent. *Findings:* In all groups there was substantial agreement; 84% of all husbands and wives concur. There is a tendency in all groups for each spouse to minimize his own influence in decision making. This is most pronounced in the working-class, working-wife group and least pronounced in the working-class, housewife group.

Heer, D. M., "The Measurement and Bases of Family Power: An Overview." *Marriage and Family Living,* 1963, 25, 133–139.

Research Problem: To build a revised theory for analyzing family power. *Methodology:* Secondary research on Willard Waller's and Blood and Wolfe's theories on family power. *Findings:* The revised theory proposes that the greater the difference between the wife's value of the resources her husband contributes to the marriage and the resources that she might earn outside the marriage the greater the power of the husband. The partner with the least interest is more likely to exploit the other. The wife with small children has less power than she did before the children were born, and than she may have after they are in school. Heer hypothesizes that the family member with the greatest interest in a certain decision will exert the greater influence on that final decision.

Hoffman, L., Burke, J. R., and Maier, N. R. F., "Does Training with Differential Reinforcement on Similar Problems Help in Solving a New Problem?" *Psychological Reports,* 1963, 13, 147–154.

Research Problem: Investigation of the questions whether the prior experience in solving a simpler but related problem helps to solve a more difficult problem, and whether the positive or negative evaluations of simpler problem solutions affect the later success of the test problem. *Methodology:* Maier's hatrack problem gives the task to build a stable rack from two boards and a clamp. The test problem was to build this structure toward the center of the room; the simpler problem was to build a structure any place in the room. Ninety male students were involved in the attempts. Thirty students were given the test problem directly; the remaining 60 students got the test problem after solving the simpler problem. They formed the Prior Experienced Condition. *Findings:* The results of the attempt showed that the experience with the simpler problem has exercised an inhibitory rather than a facilitating effect on the ability to solve the test problem. 50% of the 30 students with no experience solved the problem, but only 25% of the 60 students with prior experience solved the problem. Positive and negative reinforcement showed no differential effects.

Hoffman, L. R. and Maier, N. R. F., "Valence in the Adoption of Solutions by Problem-Solving Groups: Quality and Acceptance as Goals of Leaders and Members." *Journal of Personality and Social Psychology,* 1957, 6, 175–182.

Research Problem: To determine how manipulation of "quality" and "acceptance" goals affects the valence (algebraic sum of positive and negative comments) in problem solving groups, and whether assigning an acceptance goal to the leader reduces his tendency to dominate. *Methodology:* 268 male subjects from the introductory psychology course were assigned to three- and four-man groups; one member of each group was randomly designated as the leader. The problem was the Parasol Assembly Problem involving efficiency in industrial production. Leaders and members were separately given instructions to seek either the highest quality group decision or satisfaction of the leader (for members) or members (for leaders). All four possible combinations of quality-acceptance were used. Remarks during discussion were recorded and analyzed, and at the end each participant rated his satisfaction-dissatisfaction on a six-point scale. *Findings:* As previously found for leaderless groups, the solution adopted tended to be the first one which passed a certain threshold of support and the one with the highest valence (preponderance of positive over negative remarks). Members' valence for the solution and satisfaction with it are positively correlated. The leaders in all cases had higher valences than the members indicating preponderant influence. This was most marked in the condition where leaders sought quality and members sought acceptance, and lowest where both leaders and members had a quality goal. Assigning an acceptance goal to leaders did not reduce their tendency to dominate.

Hoffman, L. W., "Effects of the Employment of Mothers on Parental Power Relations and the Division of Household Tasks. *Marriage and Family Living,* 1960, 22, 27–35.

Research Problem: To determine whether mothers' employment outside the home affects parental power relations and division of household tasks by testing these hypotheses: (1) The employment of the mother outside the home will function to decrease her participation in household tasks and to increase that of her husband; (2) the employment of the mother outside the home will function to decrease her decision-making in household tasks (activity control) and to increase that of her husband; (3) the employment of the mother outside the home will function to increase her power viz-a-viz her husband. *Methodology:* Paper and pencil interviews with the children and mailed questionnaires answered by the mother given to a total sample of 324 intact families with at least one child in the third through sixth grades of three elementary schools in Detroit. The schools were selected so that the sample represented Detroit socio-economically but was relatively homogeneous ethnically. Within this group were 89 families with working mothers and 89 families with nonworking mothers who were closely matched with respect to traditional sex role ideology, male dominance ideology, husband's occupation, number of children under 13 years of age, and age of oldest child. *Findings:* For the matched sample, hypothesis (1) was supported, with employed mothers participating less and their husbands participating more in all areas. This pattern remains unchanged when fulltime workers are differentiated from parttime workers. Hypothesis (2) is supported; working mothers have significantly less activity control than nonworking mothers and their husbands have significantly more. No difference in power scores was found between working and nonworking mothers in the matched sample. For the total sample, however, working mothers had significantly more power than nonworking mothers. For the total sample, endorsement of traditional sex role ideology is associated with low father participation in Mothers-Household Area and in Total Activities, nonworking women are more likely to endorse it than working women. Endorsement of male dominance ideology did not relate to power scores or to mother's working status. Women who endorsed male dominance, as well as those who completely rejected it, showed the originally hypothesized positive relationship between the mother's working status and power. However, women who indicated reserved rejection of male dominance showed an inverse relationship. The matched sample showed a similar pattern.

Hoyt, C. and Stoner, J. A. F., "Leadership and Group Decisions Involving Risk." *Journal of Experimental Social Psychology*, 1968, 4, 275–284.

Research Problem: To determine whether the risky-shift phenomenon in group decision making is due to a high risk member's taking leadership of the group. Hypotheses are: (1) Individuals who tend to be risky on some items will tend to be risky on others, thus there are risky individuals and cautious individuals; (2) the risky individuals are more capable of influencing others, thus risk-takers are leaders and cautious persons are followers. *Methodology:* The sample included 57 men and 2 women enrolled in two graduate-level business administration courses and 69 men and one woman participating in management-training seminars for military and civilian personnel of the U.S. Department of Defense. A choice-dilemma test was administered individually, then subjects were assigned to one four-member and 25 five-member groups on the basis of similarity of scores. Groups were to discuss and reach a consensus on each item. *Findings:* The hypotheses were not supported. In these homogeneous groups the tendency to choose riskier alternatives than in individual decisions was not eliminated or appreciably reduced.

Johannis, T. B., Jr. and Rollins, J. M., "Teenager Perceptions of Family Decision Making." *Family Life Coordinator*, 1959, 7, 70–74.

Research Problem: Extent to which decision-making in a sample of families reflects the joint or family centered pattern in general and for each of three areas of family activity: income production and use, household tasks, and the control and care of children. *Methodology:* Questionnaire given to 1,072 respondents who were enrolled in the tenth grade in the eight public and private high schools in Tampa, Florida during April 1953. They were from intact white families. This was part of a larger sample of 1,584 representing 91% of Tampa's tenth grade population. *Findings:* In 63% of the cases, joint decision making by father was reported, and an additional 11% saw the children as also taking part. Significantly, more families were matricentric and less equalitarian when father and mother had completed different amounts of education and when the mother worked. Significantly more male respondents than female respondents saw their families as patricentric and more females than males as either equalitarian or democratic in the sense of using a family council. Decision making was found to be shared in one half or more of the families for only seven of the forty-three activities selected for study. Decision making was more frequently shared in activities which traditionally have been participated in by both fathers and mothers. The teenage respondents, both males and females, saw themselves as playing little part in decision making about the 43 activities studied.

Johannis, T. B. and Rollins, J. M., "Teenager Perception of Family Decision Making About Social Activities. *Family Life Coordinator*, 1960, 8, 59–60.

Research Problem: Patterns of decision making and extent of shared decision making about social activities. *Methodology:* Interviews with 1,073 families with one or more children attending eight public and private high schools in Tampa during April 1953. Median age of fathers was 44 years, of mothers, 40 years, and of respondents, 15 years. Over one half of the fathers and one half of the mothers who worked were employed in blue-collar and service occupations. *Findings:* The proportions of families in which decision making was reported as shared varied from 72% in deciding who is to go together on outings to 44% on who is to visit the children's friends. Who is to use the family car and belong to clubs were the two other decisions which were not shared in at least three fifths of the families. Teenagers saw themselves as participating in decision making concerned with social activity far less frequently than did their parents. Fathers (84%) and teenage sons (24%) more frequently participated in deciding who was to use the family car than did mothers (52%) and teenage daughters (13%). Decisions regarding entertaining in the home are more frequently made by mothers (85%) and teenage daughters (37%) than by fathers (66%) and teenage sons (26%).

Kenkel, W. F., "Dominance, Persistence, Self-Confidence, and Spousal Roles in Decision-Making." *Journal of Social Psychology*, 1961, 54, 349–358.

Research Problem: Relationships between personality characteristics of spouses and the way in which they divide task-oriented and social-emotional actions in decision making. *Methodology:* The sample consisted of 25 married student couples who had at least one child, in which the husband was providing the major support for the family and in which the wife was not in the labor force. Each couple was asked to decide, within about a half hour, how to spend a hypothetical gift of $300 which could be neither saved nor used for an item which they had already decided to purchase. *Findings:* Persistence among both males and females had a definite negative effect on influence. Men high in dominance had more influence, but among women, dominance and influence were negatively related. Among both males and females, those high in self-confidence made more problem solving attempts. Self-confident women had greater influence. Self-confident men were less likely to have more influence than their wives and about as likely as other males to have equal influence.

Kenkel, W. F., "Husband-Wife Interaction in Decision-Making and Decision Choices." *Journal of Social Psychology,* 1961, 54, 255–262.

Research Problem: Relationships between the behavior of spouses in a decision-making session and decision outcome. *Methodology:* Fifty married couples in which the husband was a college student were asked to decide, within about a half hour, how they would spend a hypothetical gift of $300 which could not be saved or spent for anything they had previously decided to buy. The session was tape recorded. *Findings:* In 40% of the cases, husband and wife did an equal amount of talking, items chosen were more likely to be wife-household items. In the bulk of the remaining cases (42%), the husband talked more and items chosen were more for children and husband and fewer household items. In 60% of the cases, the husband contributed more ideas and suggestions than his wife. Among these couples more wife-household and joint family items were chosen. When husband and wife contributed ideas equally (20% of the cases), they were more likely than any other type to choose joint-family and household items. When the wife contributed more ideas (18%), more items for the children were chosen. In couples where the wife specialized in the social-emotional role (72%), items were less frequently for her personal use and more for children, joint family, and household use. When the husband is the social-emotional leader, the proportion of personal items for the wife goes up and household items decrease.

Kenkel, W. F., "Influence Differentiation in Family Decision-Making. *Sociology and Social Research,* 1957, 42, 18–25.

Research Problem: A test of the traditional spousal role conception of male dominance using interaction process analysis of husband-wife economic decision-making session as the criterion. *Methodology:* Both tape recording and observer's behavioral ratings, using Bales' Interaction Process Analysis protocol, of actual session plus presession measure of "expected influence" were given to a random sample of 25 couples drawn from a list of 750 married undergraduates living on-campus at Iowa State University. Couples' discussion focused on disposing of $300 gift. Measures included amount of action, ideas, amount of influence, and positive affect. Influence equaled individual's ability to have his wishes reflected in group decision. *Findings:* Of all spouses, 48% expected husband to be dominant while only 10% favored the wife; 42% expected about equal influence.

However, based on objective coding, author reports that a majority of the participants (56% of both husbands and wives) had only medium degree of influence. Furthermore, only 28% of husbands had a high degree of influence.

Kenkel, W. F., "Sex of Observer and Spousal Roles in Decision-Making." *Marriage and Family Living*, 1961, 73, 185–186.

Research Problem: To test these hypotheses: (1) Wives would talk more when the observer was female, would contribute more of the problem-solving attempts, and would have more influence on the decision outcome than when the observer was male; (2) wives observed by a woman would be less likely to restrict themselves to the role of social-emotional leader. *Methodology:* Fifty couples with a child or children in which the husband was a college student and the wife was not employed outside the home. Half were contacted and observed by a male researcher and the remainder saw only a female worker. Each couple was asked to decide how they would spend a hypothetical gift of $300 that could neither be saved nor used for something they had already decided to purchase. They were observed during the interaction that followed. *Findings:* 64% of the wives in the female-observed group talked as much or more than their husbands, as opposed to 52% of the other wives. The wives gave more suggestions, ideas, and evaluations when observed by a woman. While not great, the difference is in the hypothesized direction. For the sample as a whole, women tended to specialize in social-emotional or expressive behavior. However, 36% of the husbands performed an equal number or more expressive actions than their wives when observed by a woman as opposed to 20% of the other husbands. Of the wives 92% in the female-observed sample had high or medium influence, as compared with 72% of the other wives. High influence among the wives was over twice as likely to occur in the group observed by the woman researcher.

Kenkel, W. F., "Traditional Family Ideology and Spousal Roles in Decision-Making." *Marriage and Family Living*, 1959, 21(4), 334–339

Research Problem: A pilot study on the relationship of "traditional family ideology" and roles played in decision-making. *Methodology:* A sample of 25 married student couples (not more than one child, wife not working) were given a test of traditional family ideology, with subscales of conservatism, exaggerated masculinity, and authoritarian submission. Results compared with roles in observed decision-making session, measured by Bales' Interaction Process Analysis. *Findings:* It was expected that those who scored high in traditional family ideology would act in traditional roles in decision-making, that is, husband would more highly influence decision-making and talk more, and wife would play "emotional" role. This was not supported by findings. There was no clear relationship between attitudes and actions in decision-making. This could be because of small size of sample, methodological weakness, application of theory to study, or in central theory itself.

Kogan, N. and Wallach, M., "Effect of Physical Separation of Group Members Upon Group Risk-Taking." *Human Relations*, 1967, 20, 41–48.

Research Problem: To determine whether the increased risk-taking tendency in group, as opposed to individual, decisions is observed when group members are physically separated. *Methodology:* A sample of 96 undergraduates was divided into five-person groups on the basis of age similarity and probable lack of prior acquaintance, and each group was randomly assigned to the discussion with consensus or discussion-without-consensus categories. In each case subjects were placed in booths where they could communicate with but not see other group members and asked for individual decisions on twelve choice-dilemma situations. In the consensus groups, members were asked to discuss the situations and arrive at a group consensus, then again indicate individual decisions. In the no-consensus groups there was five minutes of discussion on each item, followed by a second individual decision. *Findings:* In all cases the risky-shift phenomenon was observed at statistically significant levels. Individual decisions after discussion were riskier than those before discussion, as was the group consensus.

Kogan, N. and Wallach, M. A., "Risky-Shift Phenomenon in Small Decision-Making Groups: A Test of the Information-Exchange Hypothesis." *Journal of Experimental Social Psychology*, 1967, 3, 75–84.

Research Problem: To test the hypothesis that exchange of information among group members is the factor responsible for the risky-shift phenomenon in groups as opposed to individual decision-making. *Methodology:* 117 female volunteers from the senior class of Douglass College were assigned to 24 five-person groups, or 12 pairs of groups, of which one pair was excluded from analysis since one of its groups did not manifest a risky shift. In all groups, initial individual decisions on the choice-dilemmas tasks were made. In the first group of each pair, the problems were then discussed and new individual decisions called for. The second group listened to a recording of the first group's discussion then made new individual decisions. *Findings:* A significant risky shift was observed in all groups, but that of the discussing groups was greater than that of the listening group. This indicates that another factor besides information exchange contributes to the phenomenon.

Leik, R. H., "Instrumentality and Emotionality in Family Interaction." *Sociometry*, 1963, 26, 131–145.

Research Problem: Two aspects of family interaction, instrumentality, and emotionality are studied in two respects: the differentiation of sex roles and the effects upon consensus and satisfaction. *Methodology:* Nine three-person families participated in 27 experimental triadic discussions. One third of the discussion groups were homogeneous with respect to age and sex, one third had the age-sex structure of a family but consisted of strangers, and one third were actual families. All groups were given the problem of reaching consensus on issues of some relevance to family values or goals. *Findings:* The traditional male role, instrumental, nonemotional behavior, as well as the traditional female role, emotional, nontask behavior, appear when interaction takes place among strangers. These emphases tend to disappear when subjects interact with their families. The satisfaction of family members is positively related to emotionality and negatively related to instrumentality, but agreement in families is negatively related to emotionality and positively related to instrumentality.

Madaras, G. R. and Bem, D. J., "Risk and Conservatism in Group Decision-Making." *Journal of Experimental Social Psychology*, 1968, 4, 350–365.

Research Problem: To test the hypothesis that in a group risk-takers are more highly regarded than risk-rejectors and therefore an individual tends to be more risky in a group. This is an attempt to explain the previously reported risky-shift phenomenon in group decision-making. *Methodology:* Sample consisted of fifty male undergraduates from the Carnegie Institute of Technology. Subjects were presented with 10 choice-dilemma situations and told that the central figure had accepted or rejected the risk at a certain level. They were asked to evaluate each central figure on several Semantic Differential scales. In a second experiment, five of the items were altered to introduce "moral" values which had been shown to produce a conservative shift. Ten subjects rated the five conservative items where the central figure accepted the risk and five risky items where he rejected the risk. Another group of 10 subjects rated "conservative-rejected" and "risky-accepted" central figures. Two other experiments were designed to test (1) shifts in discussed versus nondiscussed items and (2) tendency of groups to judge probability of success while at the same time to be more willing to accept risk. *Findings:* The main hypothesis was supported by experiment; risk-takers were more favorably rated. Introduction of the "moral" elements reversed this situation. In the third experiment there was a significantly greater risky-shift on the discussed items, and in experiment four there was a group shift toward pessimism in evaluating chances of success, but the risky-shift phenomenon was still observed.

March, J. G. and Feigenbaum, E. A., "Latent Motives, Group Discussion and the Quality of Group Decisions in a Non-Objective Decision Problem. *Sociometry*, 1960, 23, 50–56.

Research Problem: Investigation of the hypothesis that the group decision on problems involving unconscious motives is more consistent with generally accepted social norms than the individual opinions. *Methodology:* The test was made with 71 students who were divided into five- and three-man groups. The task was to rank five female photographs according to each ones individual criterion of beauty, and then to reach group decision. Additionally, a post-interaction judgment of the same individuals was recorded. *Findings:* In a study of group decision-making it was proven that pre-interaction individual judgments are less consistent with generally shared social norms than would be either group decisions or post-interaction judgments by the same individuals.

Marquis, D. G. and Reitz, H. J., "Effect of Uncertainty on Risk Taking in Individual and Group Decisions." *Behavioral Science*, 1969, 4, 281–288.

Research Problem: To determine the effects of varying degrees of uncertainty on risk taking in individual and group decision-making. *Methodology:* Three different samples of 34, 29, and 38 persons, respectively, participated in an experimental gambling situation where chances of winning and prizes were systematically varied so that the greater the uncertainty, the greater the potential reward. An additional 40 persons in nine groups participated in a comparable experiment as groups. *Findings:* Uncertainty reduces the willingness of individuals to take risks. This effect increases as uncertainty increases. Group discussion does not result in risk bias in the absence of uncertainty. Group discussion enhances prior expected values.

Marin, M., "Father's Role in Child Rearing." *Sosiologia*, 1966, 3(2), 68–76. (Finnish)

Research Problem: To determine the role of the father in the socialization of the child. *Methodology:* A sample of 44 communes in Finland was first drawn. In these communes 1,817 randomly selected families, having at least one child under three years, were interviewed in 1959. The mother was the respondent. *Findings:* About one half of the fathers take part in some form of child care. Of the background variables, only the mother's employment outside the home affects this participation. There seems to be a tendency for the father's participation in child rearing to cumulate; when the father takes part in one form of child rearing, he is apt to take part in other forms, too. Decisions concerning child rearing are mostly made by both parents; if not, they are usually made by the mother. The role of the punisher is usually taken by one of the parents, usually the one who is more aggressive. The background factors influence more on the amount of interaction between the father and the child than on the father's attendance to punishment or child care.

McConville, C. B. and Hemphill, J. K., "Some Effects of Communication Restraints on Problem-Solving Behavior." *Journal of Social Psychology*, 1966, 69, 265–276.

Research Problem: To test the hypothesis that the greater the restriction on freedom of communication the less efficiently the groups would perform on a problem-solving task. *Methodology:* 120 members of local women's organizations were divided into 30 four-man groups. Their task involved a puzzle that had to be mutually solved. In ten groups, no communication was allowed but each individual submitted her solution in writing to the experimenter. In ten other groups, members could send solutions to other members. In the remaining groups messages of any kind may be sent to other members. *Findings:* The hypothesis was not supported. The no-communication groups performed best, followed by free-communication, and limited-communication groups.

Middleton, R. and Putney, S., "Dominance in Decisions in the Family Race and Class Differences." *American Journal of Sociology*, 1960, 65, 605–609.

Research Problem: Relation of race and class differences to dominance in family decisions. *Methodology:* Four groups of ten couples each; white and Negro college professors and white and Negro skilled workers were matched for length of marriage and age. Two hypotheses were tested using a questionnaire. The hypotheses stated that middle class socioeconomic status is positively related to equalitarian decision-making irrespective of race and that working class status is related to traditional patterns of decision-making. *Findings:* There were no differences between racial and occupational groups in dominance as indicated by the hypothesis; all groups appeared equalitarian. Families where wife is employed are more patriarchal than when wife is not employed. Working wives are less dominant in child-rearing, recreation, and role attitudes. No difference in dominance between the two groups in purchase, living standard areas.

Millican, R. D., "A Factor Analysis of Canadian Urban Family Expenditures." *Canadian Journal of Economic and Political Science*, 1964, 30, 241–243.

Research Problem: Family consumer behavior. *Methodology:* Questionnaire survey of urban families instituted by the Dominion Bureau of Statistics, Prices Division, completed in 1959. Sample was drawn from all cities with 15,000 plus population. Multistage probability sample of 3,031 households, drawn from self-representing areas of Canadian Labour Force Survey. N = 1,900 or 63% of estimated spending units of the original sample. Factors analyzed were income, expenditures, rental of dwelling, age. *Findings:* Choice of goods and services are not simply function of income but are based on the presence of four factors: income, age, family size, age composition of family. Consumption requires a complex-function explanation rather than a simple income-expenditure one.

Mills, T. M., "Power Relations in Three-Person Groups." *American Sociological Review*, 1953, 18, 351–357.

Research Problem: To test George Simmel's idea that a three-person group breaks into a "pair" and an "other." *Methodology:* 48 three-person groups were asked to create a single dramatic story from T. A. T. cards. Groups were assembled in a room with an adjacent observation room. Each act was rated as to who initiated the act and to whom it was directed. *Findings:* The three-person group was found to be unstable. The solidarity of the "pair" appeared to be strengthened by the opposition of the "other." Likewise, the most threatening effect on any member of the threesome was the solidarity of the other two.

Moore, O. K. and Anderson, S. B., "Modern Logic and Tasks for Experiments on Problem Solving Behavior." *The Journal of Psychology*, 1954, 38, 151–160.

Research Problem: To determine if there was a source of tasks rich enough to yield a multitude of problems of varying levels of complexity, solvable through the use of one basic set of instructions and readily adaptable for many experimental purposes, and if such a source of tasks was available, to effect an adaptation for use in studying human problem solving behavior. *Methodology:* The calculus of propositions, also called "Sentenial Calculus" was taught to 50 subjects. They were Naval enlisted men with GCT scores of 2.4 (range 1–4) and mean educational level of 11.5 years (range 8–16 years). Following the instruction period, all subjects were given test sets of problems. *Findings:* Forty of the fifty subjects were able to work the problems with sufficient proficiency that they would be able to participate in problem solving experiments using calculus problems. The calculus tasks possess the characteristics which make them efficacious for experiments in higher order problem solving.

Moore, O. K. and Anderson, S. B., "Search Behavior in Individual and Group Problem Solving." *American Sociological Review*, 1954, 19, 702–714.

Research Problem: To discover if individuals and groups differ in their approach towards complex rational problems and to discover if groups are more efficient than individuals in problem solving. *Methodology:* The subjects were 24 Naval enlisted men. All subjects were approximately the same age, equally intelligent, and had similar educational backgrounds. The subjects were given training in 12 laws of calculus. They were then matched on the results of a test of knowledge of these laws so that six individuals' scores approximated the mean scores of six groups of three men. Ten 30-minute sessions of problem solving using the laws were held. *Findings:* Neither in terms of correct responses or in terms of incorrect responses do groups differ from individuals as a whole. Groups and individuals solved virtually the same number of problems. There was a slight tendency for individuals to solve problems earlier than groups, but the difference in time for groups and individuals was not statistically significant.

Mulder, M., "Communication Structure, Decision Structure and Group Performance." *Sociometry*, 1960, 23, 1–14.

Research Problem: To test two hypotheses: That groups with more centralized decision structures will be capable of better group performance; and more centralized structures are characterized by vulnerability. *Methodology:* Investigation and comparison of the performance of more centralized so-called wheel groups and less centralized circle groups. 104 college students divided into four-person groups were tested. Results were determined by measurements from questionnaires, by direct observation during the session, and by analysis of the material. *Findings:* The results of the experiment support the hypothesis. The more centralized the decision structure of groups, the better the group performance is in regard to speed, quality (fewer errors), and efficiency. It is, however, characterized by a smaller communication output or input. The most centralized interaction structures demonstrate a greater vulnerability at the beginning of the work, which leads to negative performance results, as long as centralized decision structures have not developed.

Myerhoff, B. G. and Larson, W. R., "Primary and Formal Aspects of Family Organization; Group Consensus, Problem Perception, and Adolescent School Success." *Journal of Marriage and the Family*, 1965, 27, 213–217.

Research Problem: Relationship of intra-family consensus and problem perception to school success of adolescent boys. *Methodology:* The sample consisted of 73 adolescent boys and their parents. The boys were selected from a Southern

California urban high school and represented a known and controlled range of racial, ethnic, religious, IQ and socioeconomic groups. They were classified as aggressives (N = 16), underachievers (N = 14) and well-adjusted (N = 44). Interviews with boys and parents to indicate importance of specific items to respondent and extent to which he felt the item constituted a problem. *Findings:* The higher the family consensus, the greater the likelihood that the adolescent son was well adjusted in school. High problem perception was positively related to poor performance and adjustment at school. There is no correlation between family consensus and perception of problems.

Nakamura, C. Y., "Conformity and Problem Solving." *Journal of Abnormal and Social Psychology*, 1958, 56, 315–320.

Research Problem: To test three hypotheses: The major hypothesis posits a negative correlation between tendency to conform and achievement in problem solving when the influence of intelligence is statistically removed. The second hypothesis states that the negative partial correlation is higher for problems that require restructuring than for straightforward problems. The sex differences in certain types of problem solving are associated with sex differences in conformity. *Methodology:* The subjects were drawn from an introductory psychology course at the University of California, Berkeley. There were 77 women and 64 men. They were given tests of problem solving, conformity, and intelligence. The problem solving test consisted of 10 restructuring and 10 straightforward problems. *Findings:* The results supported the first hypothesis but failed to confirm the second and third hypotheses.

Olsen, M. E., "Distribution of Family Responsibilities and Social Stratification." *Marriage and Family Living*, 1960, 22, 60–65.

Research Problem: Relation of family role position and responsibility for household tasks in three social status groups. *Methodology:* 391 wives were interviewed from three social status areas to test the hypothesis that the distribution of responsibility within a family has a positive, differential relationship to socioeconomic class. *Findings:* Hypothesis was supported; assumption of responsibility by wife is least in the high socioeconomic status area and highest in the low socioeconomic status area. Husbands in the middle status area take on more responsibility than those in the high or low areas. The least responsibility is given to children in middle status homes. Only high status families make use of outside help.

O'Rourke, J. F., "Field and Laboratory: The Decision Making Behavior of Family Groups in Two Experimental Conditions." *Sociometry*, 1963, 26, 4, 422–435.

Research Problem: To confirm the hypothesis that the quality of the interactive behavior of small family groups as well as individuals within the group is contingent on the environmental situation (home or laboratory) and on the structure of the group (father-mother-daughter or father-mother-son). *Methodol-*

ogy: 24 groups of three persons—parents and one child—were tested. (The sex and age of participating children were controlled.) The test consisted of three phases: Two pictures about decision problems were shown by a projector (after 25 minutes of preparation) and a written summary requested. Discussion of two decision problems. Collecting data on group consensus and the ranking of the alternatives. Measurements on the decision-making behavior were made at home and in a laboratory setting using the short form of the Bales Interaction Process Analysis. *Findings:* The results of the experiment support the hypothesis. The group's interactive behavior changed as the subjects moved from home to laboratory. The positivity of fathers and children decreased, while that of mothers increased. Female child families exhibited higher total volumes of acts (were more active) but male child families had higher levels of positivity. The positivity of fathers of female children was higher than that of fathers of male children. The outcome for mothers was the opposite. Among the children the females had higher levels of positivity than the males. Positivity can be defined as the net total proportion of positive social-emotional response of individuals and/or groups.

Putney, S. and Middleton, R., "Effect of Husband-Wife Interaction on the Strictness of Attitude Toward Child-Rearing." *Marriage and Family Living,* 1960, 22, 171–173.

Research Problem: Investigation of the processes by which couples set policy with regard to their children. *Methodology:* Ten couples from each of four groups: middle-class white, middle-class Negro, working-class white, and working-class Negro. All were American born, had at least one child, had been married at least two years, were between the ages of twenty-five and forty-nine if male, twenty and forty-four if female, and were residents of the same small southern city. The four groups were matched on years of marriage and age. The groups were given a questionnaire on child-rearing problems which was answered first individually, then jointly by each couple. *Findings:* A strong general tendency to take the strict position was noted, with no significant differences between males or females or the racial or class groups. The joint questionnaires tended to be even stricter than those completed individually. Differences of opinion tended to be resolved in favor of the stricter position among all four subgroups.

Rabow, J., Fowler, F. J., Bradford, D. L., Hofeller, M. A., and Shibuya, Y., "The Role of Social Norms and Leadership in Risk-Taking." *Sociometry,* 1966, 29, 16–27.

Research Problem: To test the hypothesis that norms relevant to group decisions favor the risky shift, and manipulation of the normative situation can produce a conservative shift. *Methodology:* 128 college students were divided into eleven six-person and seven five-person groups, plus four residual groups. Three items from the Wallach and Kogan Choice Dilemmas task, two items altered to involved persons to whom the subject is committed and two items presenting a norm conflict comprised the instrument. Procedure included individual decision, group discussion and unanimous decision, and individual post-test. *Findings:* The hypothesis was supported. The first three items showed a risky shift, the remaining five did not. There was no difference between groups whose members were strangers and those who were well acquainted. The leaders tended to have more extreme positions, either risky or conservative, than other group members.

Rettig, S., "Group Discussion and Predicted Ethical Risk Taking." *Journal of Personality and Social Psychology*, 1965, 2, 629–633.

Research Problem: To test the hypothesis that the prediction of unethical behavior would occur more frequently under conditions of group discussion, privacy (individual's decision not made public), and impersonality (subject hypothetical). *Methodology:* Subjects were 160 undergraduates equally divided by sex and within the various judgment conditions. In the group conditions, the problems were discussed in self-selected three- and four-person groups. The problems involved predicting whether a hypothetical subject (impersonal form) under various conditions. *Findings:* The hypothesis was supported. Results indicated that interpretation of censure and rewards, rather than responsibility diffusion, was responsible for the increased ethical risk taking in the group discussion condition.

Shomaker, P. K. and Thorpe, A. C., "Financial Decision-Making as Reported by Farm Families in Michigan." *Michigan Agricultural Experimental Station Quarterly, Bulletin*, 1963, 46(2), 335–352.

Research Problem: Relation of husband's age, educational level of spouses, family size, net worth, and organizational participation of the family to financial decision-making. *Methodology:* 100 interviews with husbands and wives from two central Michigan counties serving as the population universe. The sample was selected for stage in life cycle when family is well-established with highest income and expenses, one child present at home between age 12–18 years, a middle-income group with half of income derived from farming, husband under 54 years of age, farm operated independently, spouses native-born, and no long illnesses present in family's history. *Findings:* 56% of families consulted sources other than people to make financial decisions. Reading materials and the radio appeared most influential; references to these sources increased with educational level and decreased with size of families. Husband's age and level of education influenced attitudes about adequacy of information available, whereas, wives with a high school education felt that they had adequate information. Of the sample, 88% discussed the problem with salesmen, neighbors, relatives, specialists, leaders in the community for the highest income group. Younger, small-size families, with high net worth reported discussing the problem a great deal (69%). Of the sample, 59% said husband made the decision and 34% said the decision was made jointly. When husband or wife had college training the husband was the sole decision-maker. This was true also when spouses had grade-school education. High school educated group had joint decision-making. An increase in income had a corresponding increase in joint decision-making. (Data was not always consistent here.)

Stone, C. and Landis, P. N., "An Approach to Authority Patterns in Parent-Teenage Relationships." *Rural Sociology*, 1953, 18, 233–242.

Research Problem: Relationship of authoritarianism to teenage adjustment problems in three kinds of residential groups and various occupational groups. *Methodology:* 4,310 high school seniors, representative of all high school seniors in the state of Washington, were given a questionnaire which was analyzed using the Guttman scale to assess democratic or authoritarianism of the family. *Findings:* Over 40% of boys classified families as democratic, only 22% of the girls. 21% of boys and 22% of girls classified families as authoritarian. Over 50% of girls classified families in the intermediate range and only 38.7% of boys did. Farm and city boys saw parents as almost equally authoritarian, but town boys saw parents as more democratic. Comparison of occupational groups found the farm family was the most authoritarian and the middle-class nonfarm family the most democratic for treatment of teenage boys. Chi-square tests were significant for more harmonious relations with democratic perceived parent than authoritarian. Children from democratic families liked their home and level of living irrespective of income.

Straus, M. A. and Cytrynbaum, S., "Support and Power Structure in Sinhalese, Tamil, and Burgher Student Families." *International Journal of Comparative Sociology*, 1962, 3, 138–153.

Research Problem: Comparison of power and patterns of support in three ethnic, linguistic, and religious groups with a TAT projective test. *Methodology:* 103 Sinhalese-Buddhist, 36 Tamil-Hindu, and 12 Burgher-Protestant students who entered the University of Ceylon in 1950. Cases were selected to construct three ethnic, linguistic, and religious groups. These subjects were administered TAT projective tests as part of physical upon college entrance. *Findings:* TAT score cards elicited sufficient descriptions of interactions to warrant continued application as a measure (average number of interactions per card was 12.2). Wife-mother followed father as the most frequent originators for power (as perceived by child). Burgher father was the less frequent originator of power than the other two but more frequently originated support interactions. Power is most salient for Sinhalese, then Burghers, and least for the Tamils. Behavior of parents was consistent with Tamils, most rigidly patriarchal of all three, Burghers equalitarian, and Sinhalese least patriarchal of all. Among all three groups, one member will seek to provide support for another without any solicitation. Support relationships were not as consistent with participant observations and known attitudes of the three groups.

Straus, M. A., "Communication, Creativity, and Problem Solving Ability of Middle and Working Class Families in Three Societies." *American Journal of Sociology*, 1968, 73, 417–430.

Research Problem: To test the assumption that there are large social class differences in the ability of family groups to deal with novel problem solution. Four hypotheses were tested: (1) Working class families have a lower ability to solve a laboratory problem; (2) one of the factors accounting for social class differences in family problem solving ability is to be found in patterns of communication; (3) lower creativity scores would be found in the working class sample; (4) despite differences due to unique features in each culture, the structural pressures on the working class (such as lack of privacy and insufficient resources to make planning a meaningful act) result in a similar set of social class differences in all urban-industrial societies. *Methodology:* 64 Bombay families, 64 Minneapolis families, and 45 San Juan families participated in the sample. The working class families were defined as those having a father engaged in manual work. The families were asked to play a game and to discover the rules of the game. The Bombay working class sample were given a slightly easier task which was assumed to be psychologically equivalent to the task assigned to the other groups. *Findings:* In all three cultures it was found that considerable concordance was found in the way middle-class families are differentiated from working class families. In all three societies the middle class families were more effective problem solvers, the middle class demonstrated more fluency and flexibility, plus much higher volume of communication. The differences between the working and middle class families showed that the more urbanized and industrialized the society, the *smaller* the social class differences in these behaviors.

Strodtbeck, F. L., "Husband-Wife Interaction Over Revealed Differences." *American Sociological Review,* 1951, 16, 468–473.

Research Problem: To test the hypotheses: that the partner given the most power in the larger cultural and social situation will win the most decisions in the small group situation; and that the partner who is most active in interactions (talks most) will win the most decisions. *Methodology:* 10 couples from each of three different cultures with different views on the power relationship between husband and wife. The cultures were: (1) Navaho—wife deemed more powerful; (2) Mormon—husband deemed more powerful; and (3) Texan—held to fall between the two extremes above, though not very explicit as to the actual power relationship prevailing. *Findings:* Navaho wives won more decisions and Mormon husbands won more decisions; Texans gave slight favor to husbands in number of decisions won. Spouse who talked most won most. (Note: 10 couples from a previous pilot study were included in this section of the analysis.) Overall conclusion: "It has been shown that the disposition of these reconciled decisions is related both to power elements in the larger social and cultural organization and amount of participation in the small group situation." Hypothesis was supported.

Strodtbeck, F. L., "The Family as a Three-Person Group." *American Sociological Review,* 19, 23–29.

Research Problem: Analysis of techniques used by families in resolving disagreement and comparison with findings for other three-person groups. *Methodology:* The sample consisted of 48 groups of father, mother, and adolescent son. Three criteria were considered: ethnicity, the families were predominantly second generation (the son, third) divided equally between Jews and Italians;

socioeconomic status, equal numbers of high, medium, and low; and the son's achievement, half of the boys were underachieving in school and half were over-achieving. Reveal difference technique was used. From individual responses on a 47-item questionnaire, three items were selected where mother and father have taken one alternative and the son the other, three with father and son against mother, and three with mother and son against father. The families were asked to reach agreement on these items, and the discussions were tape-recorded. *Findings:* Mills found the highest rate of support was between the two most active members. No such relationship is found in the family groups. There is a significantly lower mean index of support in the family groups than in Mills' ad hoc groups. In a "solidary" family, with high indices of support between the members of the major coalition, the position of the third person was not as weak as in the same situation in the ad hoc group. Participation ranks are most stable in the solidary situation for both types of three-person groups.

Summers, D. A., "Conflict, Compromise and Belief Change in a Decision-Making Task." *Journal of Conflict Resolution*, 1968, 12, 215–221.

Research Problem: To determine how manipulation of instructions and payoff affects tendencies to compromise and change beliefs in a dyad with conflicting beliefs. *Methodology:* 40 University of Colorado undergraduate men were assigned to pairs on the basis of conflicting beliefs about determinants of minority status and given a decision-making task involving these beliefs, after initial individual decision differences were discussed. In the persuasive condition, subjects were told they would be evaluated on their skill at convincing the partner of their convictions, and in the compromise condition, they were instructed to seek a mutually acceptable solution. Some pairs were paid off in accordance with their instructions, while in remaining pairs, payoff was absent. *Findings:* The subject with the more extreme initial position is more apt to compromise, and compromise by one subject is not necessarily associated with compromise by the partner. In fact, the opposite is true in this situation. Compromise tends to be inversely proportional to initial differences between partner's judgments. Compromise and subsequent belief change are positively correlated. Presence or absence of payoff did not affect subjects' behavior.

Tallman, I., "The Family As a Small Problem Solving Group." *Journal of Marriage and the Family*, 1970, 32, 94–104.

Research Problem: To develop a model for family problem solving behavior. *Methodology:* The author attempts to hypothesize the variables critical for effective family problem solving and place them within an ideal typology. *Findings:* Effective family problem solving requires open channels of communication for all family members competent to contribute to a problem situation. Effective family problem solving requires that the group remain sufficiently flexible so as to admit additional members into critical communication networks at such stages in the family life cycle when they are able to make appropriate contributions. Effective family problem solving requires some centralization of authority which serves to coordinate the problem solving efforts of the various family members.

This implies a necessary division of labor within the family and the legitimation of the authority of a central leader. Effective problem solving requires the ability of families to communicate and evaluate conflicting ideas without regard to the status of the persons initiating the communication. Effective family problem solving requires consensus among the family members as to family goals and the roles played by the various family members in arriving at problem solutions.

Teger, I. and Pruitt, D. G., "Components of Group Risk Taking." *Journal of Experimental Social Psychology*, 1957, 3, 189–205.

Research Problem: To investigate effects of group size, initial level of risk and discussion versus information exchange as factors producing the risky shift phenomenon in group decision making. *Methodology:* A total of 165 volunteer subjects, male undergraduates of the University of Delaware were assigned at random to various conditions and participated in groups of three to five. All made initial individual decisions on the choice dilemma task. The conditions were: (1) group discussion and consensus in groups of four and five; (2) same as (1) with groups of three; (3) participants could "exchange notes" in three rounds of public balloting. There was no attempt to reach consensus and new individual decisions followed; (4) (control) second individual decision only. *Findings:* Degree of risky shift in discussion conditions was positively correlated with group size. Risky shift was greater under discussion conditions than under the information-exchange condition. The extent of risky shift on a given problem was positively related to the initial level of risk on that problem.

Tuckman, B. W., "Personality Structure, Group Composition, and Group Functioning." *Sociometry*, 1964, 27, 469–487.

Research Problem: To test the hypothesis that more abstract individuals (such as individuals who perceive a more multi-faceted world and who think in terms of alternative interpretations and approaches) would adopt a group structure which was more flexible and open than homogeneous groups of concrete individuals. It was further hypothesized that the abstract groups would display more environmental sensibility, a more informational orientation, greater differentiation, and a more integrated strategy in dealing with the task than would concrete groups. *Methodology:* 36 subjects were selected from 64 who had been given the seven personality tests. The selected subjects were those who best fit the four personality characteristics. The task they performed was the SOBIG stock market game. The task represents a simulation of the stock exchange. *Findings:* Homogeneous teams did react as their personality tests predicted. The groups behaved in a way that the individual members would have been expected to behave.

Weinstein, E. A. and Geisel, P., "Family Decision-Making Over Desegregation." *Sociometry*, 1962, 25, 21–29.

Research Problem: Relation of demographic factors, characteristics of decision-making process, and general attitudes to participation in school desegregation by Negro families. *Methodology:* Mothers from 88 Negro families with children who are eligible to attend a desegregated school by selection from a survey for eligibility in affected school districts (families were not randomly selected) were interviewed by trained, Negro, female interviewer. *Findings:* Segregated families are lower in SES, slightly more of them come from rural areas, and express concern over separating children in different schools, are more alienated, do not have pioneer attitudes although they had favorable attitudes toward education. Decision-making process is the same in both social groups (parents who participated in desegregation and those who did not). Authors feel that alienation is the most important underlying variable.

Wilkening, E. A. and Bharadwaj, L. K., "Dimensions of Aspirations, Work Roles and Decision-Making of Farm Husbands and Wives in Wisconsin." *Journal of Marriage and the Family*, 1967, 29, 703–711.

Research Problem: To test the assumption that the instrumental role structure of the farm family is composed of many separate dimensions, and also to determine the differential involvement of husbands and wives in these dimensions by interrelating the measures separately for both husbands and wives. *Methodology:* Interview schedule and questionnaire was given to a sample of 500 Wisconsin farm families selected by a multistage area probability sample design by the Wisconsin Survey Research Laboratory. Both husbands and wives met the following criteria: married before Jan. 1, 1961, husband less than 65 years old and farming in 1961, income from farming between $1000–2500. Other characteristics: native-born, average age of wife, 42, average number of children, 3, similar religious backgrounds. *Findings:* The value placed upon specific goals by one spouse is different from that placed by the other spouse. In other words, the level of goal-striving for the family in specified areas, as indicated by the respective spouses, reflects their own interest and involvement in those areas as well as their agreed upon family goals. The instrumental task and decision-making structure of the contemporary farm family is multidimensional in that one spouse is more involved in some areas and the other is involved in other areas. There is a specialization of decision making as well as in the performance of tasks, with joint involvement in certain areas.

Winter, W. D. and Ferriera, A. J., "Interaction Process Analysis of Family Decision-Making." *Family Process*, 1967, 67, 155–172.

Research Problem: To test the ability of the Interaction Process Analysis system to differentiate among families with schizophrenic, maladjusted, delinquent, and normal children. *Methodology:* The sample consisted of 90 triads of father, mother, and child, divided into four groups: 35 with normal children, 33 with emotionally maladjusted children, 10 with schizophrenic children, and 12 with delinquent children. The children were at least 9½ years old, and the family members were white, literate, native-born Americans in good health who had been living together as a family for more than two years. Each family was given a set of three TAT cards and asked to make up a story connecting them in the order given. At the end of five minutes, a spokesman was to report the story to the experimenter. The procedure was repeated three times, with different cards and spokesman each time, for each family. Discussions were tape-recorded. *Findings:* Scoring reliability tests with 300 statements from five stories independently scored by two raters revealed 33% disagreement. Normal and maladjusted families have the highest total interaction scores, schizophrenics the lowest, and delinquents in between. Schizophrenic families show the greatest deviation from equal participation, mainly due to withdrawal of the child. They also tended more than the others to ask for suggestions, opinions, and help rather than giving them. Schizophrenic and delinquent families asked a greater percentage of questions than normals and maladjusted. The Interaction Process Analysis method is more clearly related to the behavior of the child than to the behavior of his parents. This method does not differentiate between families having normal and maladjusted children. The clearest differentiation is between normals and schizophrenics, with delinquents less clearly differentiated.

Wolgast, E. H., "Do Husbands or Wives Make the Purchasing Decisions?" *Journal of Marketing*, 1958, 23, 151–158.

Research Problem: Determination of which spouse makes the decisions about purchases and/or economic affairs for the family. *Methodology:* Interviews with a national cross-section sample was drawn for a panel study. Multistage sampling was conducted with five successive interviews over a period of 2½ years. Respondent in the family was selected by a random method and subjects consisted of a representative group of husbands or wives, in the aggregate not couple pairs. The sample was urban. *Findings:* Both spouses agree that handling of economic affairs is a joint endeavor. If not joint, then wife assumes decision-making role. Husband and wife reports of decision-making patterns for four kinds of items: car—both equal, husband responded 31%, wife 23%; for savings—both equal, husband responded 47%, wife 49%; for money and bills—both equal, husband responded 31%, wife 26%; wife only—husband responded 39%, wife 43%; for household good—both equal, husband responded 53%, wife 51%. Division of responsibility increases with age and length of marriage. Plans and wishes of spouse are generally known. The wife's plans are more thought out but less sure of fulfillment.

Appendix II

SIMFAM

Financial support for this research was provided by the National Science Foundation, the National Institute of Health, the University of Minnesota Graduate School, and the United States Educational Foundation in India.

Among the many individuals and organizations to whom the authors are indebted are Mrs. Cecelia E. Sudia, who was co-investigator during the development of the research procedures and during the testing of the Minneapolis sample; Howard R. Stanton and Carlos Albizu-Miranda of the Social Science Program, Puerto Rico Department of Health, under whose auspices the San Juan sample was studied; and Prof. K. M. Kapadia and the faculty of the Department of Sociology, University of Bombay, under whose auspices the Bombay sample was studied. We are indebted to the teachers and principals whose cooperation in administering the sample selection questionnaire was crucial, but whom we cannot identify since to do so would endanger the anonymity of our respondents.

We also wish to express appreciation to the able group of research assistants who staffed the various studies: The head research assistants, who played a very large role in the success of the Bombay and San Juan studies and who also recorded the creativity protocols, were Sitaram P. Punalekar and Eudaldo Baez-Galib. Fraine E. Whitney developed the original version of the creativity scoring manual. In Minneapolis, Sheldon Schneider served as experimenter and recorded the creativity protocols. The signal lights were operated by Jacqueline H. Straus (Bombay and San Juan), Elba Rivera (San Juan), and Anne-Marie Hare (Minneapolis). The power and support score observers were Achala H. Karnik and Sharayu Mhatre (Bombay), Bruce Lerner and William Makela (Minneapolis), and H. Scott Cook, and Maressa and Roberto Rodriquez (San Juan). Data processing was carried out with the aid of Monte R. Blair, Wessley Burr, Fraine E. Whitney, Larry Kaplan, Ray Oldenburg, and Jacqueline H. Straus.

Finally, we wish to express appreciation to those whose comments and suggestions aided in the development of this research and in the revision of various papers reporting on it, particularly: Dana H. Bramel, Reuben L. Hill, George Levinger, Fred L. Strodtbeck, Guy E. Swanson, and Ben Willerman.

SIMFAM: A Technique for Observational Measurement and Experimental Study of Families

MURRAY A. STRAUS
and
IRVING TALLMAN

I. PURPOSE AND DEVELOPMENT

The use of laboratory and direct observational techniques in research with families is a relatively new development. Such techniques offer considerable advantages over the usual cross-sectional studies in allowing for the assessment of behavioral processes and avoiding some of the difficulties resulting from the use of self-report data. In this report we will describe a particular technique used in laboratory and home situations. The technique is capable of providing information on a wide range of behaviors not easily tapped by other methods. Its principal advantages are threefold: First, it allows us to manipulate variables experimentally and, therefore, more directly assess cause and effect relations between variables. In this sense it provides the opportunity for testing theoretically propositions in a relatively unambiguous manner. Secondly, the technique allows us to simulate critical elements of important family situations such as problem solving behavior reactions to crises, conflict behavior, and so forth. Finally, it provides a means for measuring aspects of the interaction of family units under conditions which tend to absorb the family members' attention in certain tasks so that they are relatively less conscious of being observed by outsiders. The technique has been used in both cross-class and cross-cultural research with some success. In addition, it is highly flexible and amenable to modification and variation to suit specific

381

research needs. It is also a promising diagnostic tool for family and marriage counseling (Olson and Straus, 1968). Some of these as yet untried applications and modifications are also explored in this paper.

Initially the technique was designed to provide measures of five aspects of family behavior and interactional structure: (1) Power, which serves as an index of the leadership structure of the family; (2) Support, which indexes the social solidarity of the family; (3) Communication, including measures of channels or structure, volume, and linguistic skills; (4) Problem solving ability of the family group; and (5) Creativity, or ideational fluency and flexibility. In addition, the technique provides a setting for measurement of several other family characteristics. Each new usage of the technique has produced measures of other variables and the limit has not yet been reached.

We call the technique the "Simulated Family Activity Measurement," (abbreviated in this paper as SIMFAM). The term "simulated" is included in the name because, the technique provides a framework within which experimental analogs or simulations of naturally occurring conditions can be introduced for purposes of experimental study.[1] A variety of such experimental simulations are possible. However, this paper will describe only those experimental variations which we have so far used.

SIMFAM makes use of direct observation of family interaction under standardized conditions. The standardized conditions are in the form of games which most families find enjoyable. The technique does not depend on the willingness or ability of the subjects to respond to questionnaire or interview items.[2] In addition, the motor performance basis of the SIMFAM is intended to make the technique suited to investigations of lower class families who might have difficulty with purely verbal tasks such as most of these just cited.

Development

The techniques described in this paper were originally intended to measure only the effects of stress or crisis on the leadership and social solidarity of the family. The remaining measures were developed when it became apparent during the pretesting that the technique might also be used to elicit and measure problem solving ability, communication, and creativity. This aspect of the development of SIMFAM is mentioned because it explains why only the first two of the five variables are the same level or type of phenomena.

It may also be helpful in understanding the objectives and the characteristics of this technique to be aware of the fact that two somewhat conflicting traditions in social psychology have influenced the development of the SIMFAM

---

[1] This use of the term simulation represents only one of the many procedures falling under that general heading. See the selections in Guetzkow, 1962.

[2] Discussions of the advantages and limitations of "situational performance," or "direct observation" tests applied to family behavior may be found in Straus, 1964a; Yarrow and Raush, 1963; and Garmezy, Farina and Rodnick, 1960. For examples of specific attempts at direct observational measurement see Drechsler and Shapiro, 1961; Garmezy, Farina, and Rodnick, 1960; Goodrich and Boomer, 1963; Haley, 1962; Mishler and Waxler, 1966; Smith, 1958; Schulman, Shoemaker, and Moelis, 1962; and Strodtbeck, 1958.

technique: the psychometric tradition and the laboratory experimental tradition. From the psychometric tradition has come an awareness of the limitations of self-report measures and a desire to explore the potential advantages of observed performance measures of family behavior. From the experimental tradition has come an awareness of the limitations of field studies for testing theoretical hypotheses of a causal explanatory nature and a desire to explore the potential advantages of the laboratory experiment for testing theoretical explanations of family behavior.

The psychometric tradition emphasizes the degree to which behavior in the standardized performance situation is a miniature replica of behavior in the natural setting; that is, validity in the sense of "content validity," "concurrent validity," or "a theoretical validity" (APA, 1954; Brunswick, 1954). The experimental tradition, on the other hand, is primarily concerned with control of the innumerable factors with which the theoretical variable under study is typically confounded in the natural setting. As Zelditch and Hopkins succinctly put it, the manipulations and behaviors in laboratory experiments ". . . are never descriptive of the real world, but they are not intended to be. Their purpose is to construct and test theory, not to match reality as commonly experienced" (Zelditch and Hopkins, 1961; Zelditch and Evan, 1962). The experimentalist is not worried if the behavior he observes in the laboratory is "phenomenally different" from that in the natural setting, as long as it is "conceptually parallel," (Reicken, 1954) and as long as the experiment has "internal validity" in the sense that the experimental stimulus makes a significant difference (Campbell, 1957). Thus, Campbell notes that the emphasis of the psychometric and the experimental tradition are ". . . to some extent incompatible, in that the controls required for internal validity often tend to jeopardize representativeness."[3]

Results reported in the papers describing the two substantive analyses so far carried out with this technique (Straus, 1964 c, d) suggest that it can meet the criterion of producing significant differences (see the section on Construct Validity for references). In addition, the present paper describes some of the formal properties of SIMFAM which should, if our reasoning is correct, also make for external validity in the sense of phenomenal correspondence between the behavior observed in the laboratory and the natural setting.

II. VARIABLES MEASURED

The following discussion provides an indication of some of the important variables that are amenable to measurement. With increasing use, we find the

---

[3] The prototype of the pure experimental situation involves subjects being randomly assigned to different experimental conditions. This clearly is not feasible when we use natural families. To the extent that families represent a group with an established history and patterns of relationships we do in fact introduce a systematic bias into the procedure. However, if the elements which constitute bias are amenable to measurement and can prove a base for sampling, we can to some extent combine the goals of representation with the advantages of experimentation.

technique allows us to introduce and test a continuingly large number of family related variables.

Power is defined for purposes of this paper as social interaction which controls the behavior of others. It is a central attribute of the family as well as all other social groups (Parsons and Bales, 1955; Cartwright, 1959). The power structure or leadership pattern of the family affects almost all other aspects of family behavior, and is particularly important in the study of socialization (Straus, 1964). Research on the power structure of the family is of long standing, but has been hampered by cultural bias and the use of value laden and prescriptive terminology such as "family democracy" and "authoritarian."[4]

It is important to distinguish between *power* (or influence or control), as measured by the SIMFAM technique, and *authority*, the right to exercise power. Self-report measures of power, even when phrased in terms of actual past events, tend to elicit normative statements of appropriate authority and, hence, tend to be uncorrelated with patterns of interpersonal control which are measured by SIMFAM (Olson, 1969; Rollins, 1969).

Support is social interaction which establishes and maintains a positive affective relationship among members of the family group. Like power, support has long been recognized as central to the maintenance of group life. In much recent sociological literature, it is termed "social-emotional" behavior, and defined as "activity which maintains the relations between members," (Levinger, 1964) or "the expression of affection . . . and a symbolization of common membership through supportive, accepting behavior (Zelditch, 1955).

Like the power variable, support has had a checkered research history due, in part, to the influence of a similar value laden prescriptive approach. The term support has the merit of covering a broader range of modalities for expressing positive affect and, since it is newer, also has the advantage of a break with the prescriptive connotations of terms such as affection and love.

Communication is the exchange of shared meanings among people (Kretch, Crutchfield, and Bollachey, 1962). This variable represents a different level of phenomena than power and support since communication is the medium or process which makes all social interaction possible. There can be no human social structure (for example, no leadership pattern) without communication. Thus, aside from the inherent scientific interest in this basic social process, an understanding of the communication processes is important for the study of almost all aspects of the family, including socialization, problem solving ability, marital happiness, the family determinants of schizophrenia, and contraceptive usage (see, for example, Epstein and Westeley, 1959; Karlsson, 1951; Roby and Lanzetta, 1956; Weblin, 1962; Hill, Stycos and Back, 1959). This variable, both conceptually and from a measurement perspective, involves a number of related factors. For example, we have been able to assess frequency of messages sent, channels of communication, coalitions within the family, language codes, and language styles.

---

[4] See Straus, 1964a, for a discussion of prescriptive measures and terminology.

Problem Solving Ability

Problem solving is the process of developing a new response to situations for which no existing behavioral pattern is available to achieve a goal. It is a complex process which involves a number of separate though interwoven elements (Kelley and Thibaut, 1954). It involves previous learning but is also a learning experience itself. Like learning it cannot be directly observed but must be inferred from an observable performance. In the experiments described below, several observable performances are used to index problem solving ability: the ratio of correct to incorrect moves in the experimental games, the speed with which correct moves become predominant, the number of different problems solved, and the ability to verbalize the correct solution. It is believed that this score reflects the ability of the family to infer general features from specific events and to apply that knowledge to achieving a goal.

It should be clear from the above description that even the specific aspect of problem solving ability measured by the SIMFAM technique is a polymorphous variable, and that the concept of "problem solving ability" is somewhat teleological because it is an outcome which can occur as a result of a number of processes, including trial and error and "insight." Caution is therefore needed to avoid the tendency to use such teleological concepts as explanations of behavior. However, when used as a dependent variable it does provide us with a means for distinguishing the relative abilities of different groups. It also allows us to assess the effect of certain variables on this ability. Specifically, the use of experimentally varied indepedent variables, and the ability of such a research design to control for extraneous variables, enables the researcher to conclude with some confidence whether or not such variables contribute to problem solving ability.

Creativity is also a polymorphus teleological concept and must be treated with the same caution as "problem solving ability." However, in the case of creativity, the factor analytic studies of Guilford, et al provide a basis for specifying certain aspects of creativity which are measured by SIMFAM. Specifically of the five "thinking factors" important for creativity, SIMFAM is concerned only with the two which Guilford (1959) calls "production factors" and "divergent thinking factors."[5]

The *production* factors refer to the ability to produce a large volume of ideas, expressions, arrangements, and so forth. This aspect of creativity is represented in the SIMFAM battery by a measure of ideational frequency or "fluency." The *divergent thinking* factor refers to the extent to which the subject goes off in different directions. It is represented in the SIMFAM battery by a measure of ideational uniqueness or "flexibility." Operational

[5] See also Mooney's grouping (1957) of the different aspects of creativity into four aspects: (a) the environmental milieu giving rise to creativity, (b) the personal characteristics of the creative person, (c) the creative process, and (d) the creative product, 1958, pp. 170–180.

definitions of the SIMFAM "fluency" and "flexibility" measures are given in a later section.

It is almost universally recognized that creativity has meaning only in a social context. Yet most of the existing measures of creativity are individual measures and do not take into account the social context of the creative process. The SIMFAM creativity measures have the advantage of being based on behavior occurring in the context of one of the most important of all human groups, and also a group which is particularly important in the development or inhibition of creativity (Getzels and Jackson, 1961). The SIMFAM creativity measure therefore may be useful in studying this important aspect of the socialization process.

Operational Limitations

Although it is believed that measures of power, support, communication, creativity, and problem solving ability will be useful in many investigations, the conceptual boundaries and limitations of each of the variables measured must be borne in mind.

The names given to the variables and the descriptions of these variables are intended to convey the nature of the *concepts* which the SIMFAM technique is designed to measure. It should be noted, however, that when specific *operations* are applied only limited aspects of each concept are measured.

One example is the power source. It is indexed by the number of directive acts initiated and the effectiveness of these acts in modifying the behavior of the actor to whom they are directed, or in terms of the "ultimate" or "final say" type of power.[6] The concept of power, of course, is far more complex than the distinction between immediate and ultimate power indicates (Heer, 1963). For example, both immediate power and ultimate power may be expressed through a variety of modalities, each of which may have different consequences for other aspects of intra-family roles.[7] Thus, although a measure based on the frequency and effectiveness of directive acts in response to an immediate problematic situation clearly fits the conceptual definition of power given above, it is only part of that concept. The same thing holds for the other four measures. Like almost all measures in the social sciences, they do not encompass all of the implicit meanings attributed to their concepts.

III. THE TASKS

Although a number of different tasks have been developed which are appropriate for the SIMFAM technique, the discussion will focus on two

---

6 But see the discussion of this distinction in Section VII. The technique for measuring intrafamilial power developed by Herbst (1954) may also be classified as indexing immediate power, whereas that used by Blood and Wolfe (1960) is intended to index ultimate power.

7 A classification of some of these modalities may be found in Straus and Cytrynbaum, 1962.

tasks which we have used most frequently and from which most of our data have been gathered. It is important to note, however, that the tasks referred to below are not the only ones applicable. Moreover, as will be noted in more detail later, even these two tasks can be modified and altered to meet different experimental requirements.

The primary criteria used in the development of the tasks to be described are: (1) The task must be sufficiently ambiguous and novel so that previous experience with similar activities does not influence participants' expecta-

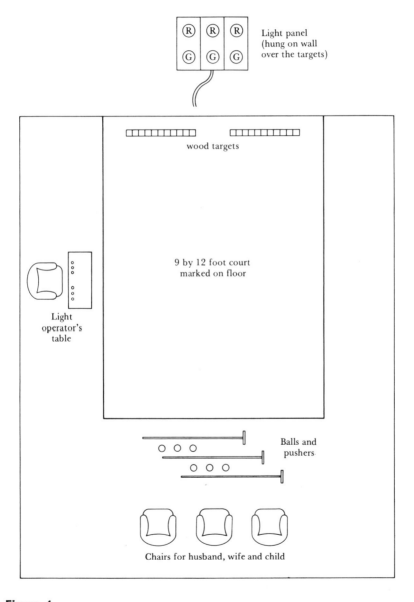

Figure 1

tions of success or failure or predetermine their participation patterns. (2) The task should be challenging and engrossing so that participants' absorption in the activity diminishes the impact of the observation techniques. In our experience games involving physical activity appear to be the most effective means of bringing about the total involvement of family members. Also the use of physical activity is thought to be a more appropriate type of experience for lower income families than tasks involving abstract symbols or mental manipulations. This factor is particularly important in cross-class comparisons of problem solving. (3) The task should provide feedback concerning the family's performance in order to maintain interest and motivation.

The Ball and Pusher Task

This task has been used most extensively in the research up to this time. It is a greatly simplified version of procedures first developed by Swanson and later modified by Hamblin (1958a, 1958b). The game is played on a court about 9 by 12 feet marked on the floor, with two wooden targets at the front of the court, as shown in Figure 1. Also at the front of the room are three pairs of red and green lights mounted on a single board. One pair of lights is for the husband, one for the wife, and one for the child. The family plays this game for eight three-minute innings or trials. The first four trials are designed to simulate a normal problem solving situation. The last four trials are intended to simulate problem solving under a simulated "crisis" or stress condition.[8]

Instructions to Family. The explanation given to the family in first inviting their cooperation is that they will be participating in a study to find out what families do when they have to solve a problem. In addition, they are told that the problem is in the form of a game or puzzle.

On arrival the family is shown both the experimental room and the observation booth. The observers in the booth are introduced as "the people who will watch you play and record the scores. They are in this room so that they will not get in your way or distract you."

After being seated, a white band is tied to the husband's wrist, a yellow band to the wife's wrist, and a blue band to the child's. The family is then told that "the problem to be solved is to figure out how to play this game." Each person is handed a typed set of instructions and these are also read aloud by the experimenter. These instructions are given in Appendix A. The instructions are ambiguous and are designed to emphasize speed in performance, the importance of playing the game as a team, and communicating with each other.

In essence the instructions simply say that the way to solve the problem is

---

[8] Bahr (1969) reports that six trials (three precrisis and three post-crisis) period provide adequate data if the subjects are informed that there will be a seventh trial. This avoids the tendency to a last trial let-down.

to start playing in any way they wish. If what they do is correct, a green light will be flashed. If what they do is wrong, a red light will be flashed. By noting which color light flashed, the family can figure out the rules of the game and use this information to get as high a score as possible.

Scores. The average score supposedly made by other families is given on a blackboard next to the place where the score of the family playing is posted. The scores are posted as follows:

Game number	1	2	3	4	5	6	7	8
Average family's score	21	40	55	90	122	156	191	218
Your score	——	——	——	——	——	——	——	——

For each family the following scores are posted after each trial: 17, 35, 54, 94, 120, 138, 190, and 222. The use of these artificial scores is designed to motivate the family to further effort since they receive scores which fluctuate around those of the average family.

Light Operation. In contrast to the predetermined scores posted on the blackboard, the red and green lights correspond to the actual use of correct or incorrect modes of play and serve as immediate reinforcements.

It is not possible for the subjects to know if the lights and the posted scores agree because the game is played rapidly and the rules given to the subjects are so ambiguous that any set of numerical scores is plausible. For example, the instructions state that some kinds of correct moves get more points than others and some kinds of errors will cost more points than others.

Detailed instructions for the light operator are given in Appendix B. These require that a green light be flashed whenever a participant shoots a ball of the color of his wristband against a target using a pusher of the same color. A red light is flashed for any of the following errors: not using a pusher and ball of the same color as the wristband, shooting from any position other than from behind the baseline, retrieving a ball by pushing it out of the court with the pusher (balls are brought back to the baseline by simply picking them up), or pushing a ball in such a way that it rolls out of the court. This last rule was added to slow down the action for greater accuracy in scoring.

The Bean Bag Task

Although the ball and pusher task has been used successfully with both middle-class and lower-class families in Minneapolis, San Juan, and Bombay, it was felt desirable to have a task which could be used in the homes of the families being studied. The need for such a task arose from the concern that a university laboratory setting (or even a local school setting) may influence the mode of interaction among family members as shown by O'Rourke (1963). Moreover, a university or school setting is more familiar to middle-class families than working-class families who may feel relatively more comfortable in such surroundings. Consequently, for research aimed at studying social class differences in family interaction and problem solving behavior, it was felt that equally optimal conditions for both classes could best be effected by conducting the experiment in families' homes, thereby holding environmental pressures relatively constant. This requires a portable game which demands little space. Accordingly a bean bag game was developed which, like the ball and pusher game, calls for a nonskilled type of physical activity. Subjects throw the bean bags at a multicolored chart which is placed on the floor (Figure 2). As in the ball and pusher game, each family member is given a different colored wristband. There are three bean bags corresponding in

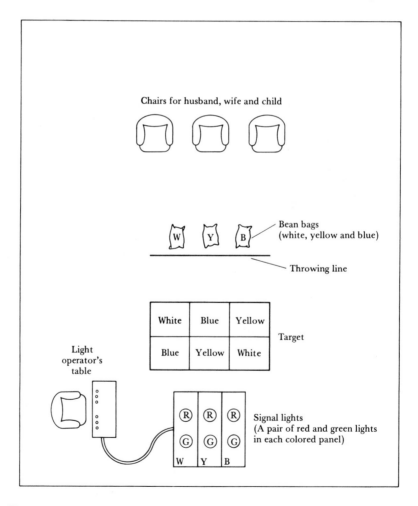

Figure 2.

color to the wristband. Family members infer the game rules from flashes of red and green lights as described in our earlier discussion of light operation.

The home administration of the bean bag task makes observational techniques somewhat more difficult because it eliminates the use of a separate observation booth. However, the game has proved so absorbing that the presence of observers has no obvious inhibitory effect. All sessions were tape recorded to provide data for analysis of verbal communications. The bean bag task has been used successfully in a study of 115 families (Tallman and Miller, 1970) so that it seems clear that the SIMFAM technique is useful in a home situation. The fact that the SIMFAM procedure need not be limited to the laboratory adds greatly to its flexibility and utility.

Protocol Excerpt

It may be helpful in understanding these procedures if a specific example is given. The scoring procedures used for this example will be explained in a subsequent section.

Let us imagine that Mr. and Mrs. X and their daughter are seated in their chairs after having the ball and pusher task explained to them. A bell rings followed by the instructions, "You may begin now":

		Scoring			
Actor	Action	Problem Solving	Power	Support	Creativity
HUSBAND	(gets up) "I have a white scarf so this must be my pusher. Use the same color pusher."	—	HW+ HC+	—	Color use (pusher)
WIFE	"OK. Then this yellow one is for me, and I bet those balls go with it."	—	—	—	Color use (balls)
HUSBAND	(shoots white ball into space between targets) "I got a red light."	1 Red	—	—	—
DAUGHTER	(shoots blue ball, hits target)	1 Green	—	—	—
HUSBAND	"Good shot! "Looks like you have to hit that thing rather than get it inside."	—	—	HC+	Target
HUSBAND	(to wife) "Hit that board."	—	HW+	—	—
WIFE	(pushes ball and hits target)	1 Green	—	—	—
DAUGHTER	"That's great."	—	—	CW+	—

The above sequence would typically take less than one minute. Note that the task has been taken seriously and not relegated to a child's sphere of activity. In fact the latter reaction has never occurred in the almost 300 families so far tested. Families which proceed in this way—trying things out one by one, paying attention to the lights, and informing each other of their observations—typically learn all the remaining rules within the first 3-month trial or by early in the second trial. They then get green lights almost all the time and derive much enjoyment and satisfaction from their performance.

IV. MEASUREMENT TECHNIQUES

A minimum of two persons is necessary to observe and record the SIMFAM variables. One of these persons records the power, support, and communication scores. The problem solving ability score is recorded in several ways. One method is to use a stop watch to record the time the entire family takes to find a solution. Problem solving is also recorded automatically by electric counters connected to the red and green signal lights which are operated by a light operator sitting in the experimental room with the family. Finally, in some of our research, families have been asked to verbalize the problem solution.

The data needed for the creativity score is recorded by the experimenter who explains the task to the family and who posts the scores on the blackboard. In addition, in the work done up to this point, the entire session has been tape recorded. This was done in part as insurance against inadequacies in the directly recorded scores, but especially to provide a means of obtaining other scores and ratings should the needs of the research later require other variables. It is also used to analyze the language skills of participants. A description of specific procedures for observing, recording, and scoring each of these variables follows.

Power. As mentioned above SIMFAM can measure two different aspects of power. One is the estimate of who in the family is best able to induce other members to act on his suggestion; the other is the determination as to which family member is most likely to make the final decision. For convenience we shall refer to the first form of power as "influence" and the second as "decision power." Influence is defined as "any direction, instruction, suggestion, or request intended to control or modify the behavior of another member of the family. A three element code is used. The first element specifies the *originating actor* and is abbreviated H, W, or C for Husband, Wife, or Child. The second specifies the *recipient actor* using the same abbreviations. The third element specifies the *effectiveness* of the power assertion by the use of a plus sign (+) for a directive act with which the recipient complies, a zero (0) for a power assertion which is ignored, and a minus (−) sign for those which are explicity rejected. For example, if the husband tells the child to "Shoot the ball now," this is scored as follows: HC+, if the child agrees verbally or by his action; HC−, if the child explicity refuses, and HC if the child simply ignores the power interaction which the father originated.

It should be noted that this system permits separate scores to be obtained for each actor's "effective power." The latter is the percentage of power acts initiated which are scored as "+". Observers independently record power using one of the techniques described in Appendix C. The sum of the two observers' entries are used as the influence scores, although the average of the two could also be used.

Support. The same two observers who record power also record supportive interactions, specifying in a similar manner the initiating and recipient actor. However, in the case of support, acceptance or rejection of the act by the recipient is ignored. Each supportive act is classified as positive (+) or negative (−) on the basis of its assumed positive or negative contribution to group solidarity or integration. The support modalities used for this score and their classification as positive or negative are:

+	−
Praises	Blames, criticizes
Helps, cooperates	Hinders, refuses help or cooperation
Terms of endearment and liking	Terms of disparagement and dislike
Physical expression of affection (hugs, kisses, etc.)	Physical expression of dislike (pushes away, hits)
Encouragement, nurturance	Discourages, rejects

If, for example, the wife is receiving many red lights and the husband says to her "Don't worry, I'm getting red lights too," this would be scored HW+. But if the husband said in disgust (or indicated nonverbally) "What's the matter with you? You're getting all red lights," it would be scored HW−. Similarly, if he gathers the wife's balls for her, this would be scored HW+, but if he pushes her's out of the way making it more difficult for the wife to get her balls, this would be HW−.

The same type of recording techniques and score sheet used for power is also used for support and the two observer's scores are also pooled in the same way. (See Appendix C.)

Communication Frequency. The communication score is a measure of frequency with which each member of the family interacts with each other. It is obtained by combining the power scores with the support scores, disregarding the sign of the score.

Since the power and support scores include gestural as well as verbal communication, the communication score derived from them also has this quality. Nevertheless, some communications are not included because the power and communication scores are not intended to be exhaustive. That is, some acts (such as general explicatives) are not included under either power or support. In practice, however, most interactions tend to be coded under either power or support. The communication score therefore appears to be a reasonable index of the frequency of interaction within the family.

Communication Flow. The flow or channels of communication are charted by analyzing the direction of the messages. Using techniques similar to those developed by Bales (1950) it is possible to determine how many messages each member of the family initiated, to whom these messages were sent, and whether the reaction was direct, absent, or indirect (that is, mediated through another family member). By computing the basic initiating rate of each family member and the reaction patterns of the family members, it is possible to chart the flow patterns of communication within families. These data in combination with power and support scores should enable us to determine the types of coalitions which develop in different family structures. We suspect that this type of analysis may prove of value in understanding family problem solving processes.

Charting the flow of communication also makes it possible to determine the extent to which all family members are integrated or conversely the kinds of coalitions that can exist within family settings.

Linguistic Ability. Skill in the use of language may be measured from tape recordings of family interaction during the sessions. The criteria presently used for measuring this ability derive from the work of Basil Bernstein (1960, 1961, 1962, 1964). These measures include the articulation of vowels, median and final consonants, length of remarks, complexity of verbalization, length of sentences and the use of subordinate clauses. These measures are designed to help distinguish between what Bernstein (1960, 1964) terms public or restrictive and formal or elaborative language.

Problem Solving Ability. Electric counters connected to each of the red and green lights are located in the pushbutton console used by the light operator. At the end of each 3-minute trial the light operator records on the form shown in Appendix A the number of red and green lights flashed for each member of the family.

A score representing the degree to which the family (and each member separately) has learned and utilized the rules of the game is obtained from either the ratio of green (or success) lights to red (or error) lights, or the ratio of green to red plus green lights, or by subtracting the number of red lights from the number of green lights. Since this score is available for each 3-minute trial, a learning curve may be plotted for each family or each sample or subsample of families. Similar computations can be made using the time taken to solve problems.

Activity Level. Since each use of the ball or the bean bag is given either a red or green light, the combination of the frequencies recorded for correct and incorrect moves (red and green lights) provides an indication of each person's level of overt activity in response to the task.

Creativity. The experimenter who guides the family through the problem also records for each member of the family a verbatim list of each idea put forward concerning how to play the game, or each new mode of play which is tried. Actual use or practicality of the idea is ignored in recording the creativity protocol and in scoring.

The resulting protocols are scored for two variables. These are patterned after the scoring systems developed by Guilford (1956), Wilson and Guilford (1953), and Torrance (1962). One score is comparable to Guilford's "fluency" factor score. It is the number of different ways of playing the game originated by each person, for example "Shoot from the left corner." The second score is comparable to Guilford's "flexibility" factor and is the number of different principles or approaches used in responding to the task. For example, "Shoot from the left corner," and "Shoot from the center," would contribute two points to a family's fluency score, but only one point to their flexibility score since the same principle (angle of shot) is involved in both. But if someone suggests "bounce the ball," this would fall into another of the twelve categories used to score flexibility and hence would be scored for flexibility as well as fluency. Appendix D lists the categories used to score flexibility and the specific responses classified under each category.[9]

Derived Scores

The set of observational categories described in the previous sections provides the basis for a number of scores and classifications. Since a large number of such scores are possible and since their utility depends on the study in which they are to be used, the following examples can only be considered as illustrative of the potentialities of this method.

Problem Solving Contribution. The red and green light scores can be used to obtain a measure of the relative importance or contribution of the husband, wife, and child to the solution of the problem. For this purpose we have used the percentage of each person's green light score to the total number of green lights obtained by the family.

Leadership Typology. The power scores previously described are group properties in the sense that they are measures of interaction. However, each score is focused on the interaction of a single actor, for example, the power score for the husband. But such scores do not take into account the fact that the meaning of the power acts is partly dependent on the frequency of power acts by other members of the group.

One method of taking this fact into account is by using a two-dimensional property-space position measure. This is done by dividing the power scores of the husbands and the wives at the mean or median of their respective distributions. Four types are then formed: (1) *Husband-led* families are those in which the husband is high in power and the wife low. Operationally this is determined from the SIMFAM power scores by classifying as husband-led those families in which the husband's score is above the median for husbands and the wife's is below the median for wives. (2) *Wife-led* families are

---

[9] One analysis using the fluency and the flexibility scores yielded essentially comparable results, suggesting that the two scores may be combined to give a more reliable total creativity score.

those in which the wife's score is above the median and the husband's below. (3) *Autonomic* families are those in which neither husband nor wife attempts to direct the activities of the other. The husband and the wife are below the median in power acts. (4) *Syncratic* families are those in which both husband and wife are high in directive interaction. Operationally, those are the families in which the power scores of both the husband and the wife are above the median.

Expressive Leadership. The many studies of leadership conducted in the past few years have produced a welter of conflicting findings. However, one fact which is clear from these studies is the need to abandon the single trait theory of leadership. One approach is to view leadership as a product of the interaction between the characteristics of the potential leader and the characteristics of the group. In addition, there is often a functional differentiation with one person fulfilling one type of leadership role and another fulfilling another type. A common type of differentiated leadership is between "instrumental" leadership and "expressive" leadership (Parsons and Bales, 1955; Homans, 1950; Slater, 1961; Straus, 1960; Thibaut and Kelley, 1959). The power typology described above may be considered a measure of instrumental leadership. The same techniques of classification described for the power scores may be applied to the support scores to derive a typology of expressive leadership. In addition, comparing the power and support for the different family members provides a measure of role differentiation within the family.

Circumplex Typology

Research on the factor analytic structure of small groups (including families) has suggested that power and support are central and universal reference axes around which other aspects of group behavior may be arrayed.[10] Such an arrangement has been called a "circumplex" ordering of factors (Guttman, 1954). Furthermore, the location of a group in this two-dimensional coordinate system (that is, the relative strength of power and support acts) has important consequences for many aspects of family behavior, and especially for the socialization function.

The SIMFAM power scores may be used in conjunction with the support scores to classify families on the power and support circumplex. The simplest procedure for doing this is to divide the population of families at the median in respect to their power scores and their support scores, and then classify each family as either: (1) low power and low support (these may be considered as "ignoring" type families), (2) low power and high support, or "indulgent" families, (3) high power and low support, or "demanding" type families, and (4) high power and high support, or "protective" type families. The extent to which families falling into each of the four quadrants formed

---

[10] A summary of these studies with application to the family is given in Straus (1964b).

by the SIMFAM power and support scores actually fit these hypothetical descriptive terms is one of the many areas of empirical study possible with this technique.[11]

Additional Measures

Although we believe that the measures so far described are of considerable theoretical importance for research on families, they by no means exhaust the possible modes of behavior which can be categorized from the sample of family interaction elicited by SIMFAM. Most of the available observational category systems, such as the Bales "Interaction Process Analysis" (1950) or others described in standard works on observational procedures (Hynes and Lippitt, 1954; Weick, 1967), are applicable with this procedure. In addition, tape recordings can be used as the basis for scoring variables which may not be envisioned in the original design but which subsequently become necessary. Strodtbeck has developed a technique (described in a personal communication) which avoids the high cost of preparing a typed transcript. Two or more raters listen to the tape (or time samples of it) and then classify the family on graphic or other rating scales for the variables desired.

Post-Experimental Interview Variables

Upon the completion of the last trial, the family may be interviewed or asked to complete a questionnaire. In one instance in our own research (Straus, 1967) we interviewed the families on their subjective definition of the experimental situation in order to obtain data on the "demand characteristics" (Orne, 1962) of the experiment. For other samples we employed a one page questionnaire which yielded scores designed to indicate: (a) the amount of effort put into the task, (b) enjoyment of the game during each set of trials, (c) evaluation of adequacy of performance of each member of the family, and (d) rating of the extent to which the subject enjoyed playing with each member of the family. The combination of the last two scores produce a solidarity score. Post-experimental data has also been used to determine whether the experimental manipulations were effective as well as the salience of experimentally induced situations.

V. EXPERIMENTAL VARIATIONS

The SIMFAM procedures described up to this point can best be categorized as a *structured performance* set of measurement techniques (Straus, 1964, pp. 370–372), rather than an *experimental* technique. However, SIM-

---

[11] The names given to these four types are based on purely theoretical considerations as outlined in Straus (1964b). However, data now being analyzed suggest that these terms are appropriate descriptions of the families falling in each of the quadrants, and especially those in the "ignoring" and "demanding" quadrants.

FAM provides a framework within which other factors may be introduced and varied, thus making possible experimentation with families in the exact sense of experimentation.

By "exact sense of experimetation" we mean research in which the investigator applies or varies the independent variables, as contrasted to non-experimental studies in which families differing in pre-existing characteristics are studied. The size of the family group is a simple but theoretically important element of family organization which can be studied experimentally. The research conducted to date has been confined to three-person groups of husband, wife, and a teenage child, ignoring any other children in the family. However, much could probably be learned by comparing two random samples from a universe of multiple child families. The first sample would participate in the experiment as three-person groups, and the second sample would include two children. Similarly, the technique can be used to compare the behavior of nuclear families with experimentally assembled family groups which include a grandparent.

The use of the SIMFAM to study the consequences of varying the number of children, or the consequences of extended generational links, is only partially experimental since such persons must exist in the natural state in order to be available for experimental inclusion. However, experimental studies with the SIMFAM need not be confined to variables of this type. In fact, in this section we describe procedures for the experimental study of certain variables which are more difficult to experimentally manipulate. These are: (a) stress or frustration, (b) communication patterns, and (c) differential knowledge of family members. These experimental treatments have been developed for our own research, and should be regarded as only suggestive of the variables which can be experimentally varied within the SIMFAM framework.

Crisis Simulation

The SIMFAM technique provides an opportunity to observe family behavior under a standardized frustration condition. For reasons to be explained below, this condition is assumed to be isomorphic with certain aspects of naturally occurring family crises. However, the utility of the technique does not depend on the correctness of this assumption, but only on the more readily accepted assumption that the procedures used create some kind of stress or frustration for the family.

The main feature of the crisis manipulation consists of changing the rules of the game for the fifth through eighth trial. No matter what the family does, they receive only red penalty lights, except for one green light given in the sixth trial and two given in the seventh trial. In addition, the scores posted on the blackboard remain at 94 for periods five through eight. The unchanging score of 94 is in sharp contrast with the scores posted for the family after games one through four, which were intended to motivate the family and to provide a feeling of increasing achievement. The failure of the family to add to the 94 points it has accumulated by the end of trial four is intended to have the opposite effect. In conjunction with the use of only red lights, the intent is to create a sense of lack of accomplishment and frustration which, for reasons to be explained below, is considered to be a mild stress or crisis type of experience.[12]

The intent of these procedures, like the intent of all laboratory simulation, is to produce a situation which is isomorphic with a naturally occurring event in only a limited number of theoretically relevant characteristics (Zelditch and Hopkins, 1961). In the present case the key elements of a crisis which these procedures are designed to simulate are the suddenness of the change, the apparent irrationality of the change, and the ineffectiveness of previously successful modes of adaptation. In addition, the use of an occasional green light during the crisis trials is intended to simulate the fleeting or illusory solution which so often happens in natural crisis, for example, when a man is told that jobs are available at a certain place, applies, and is rejected.

These are key elements of naturally occurring crises.[13] In the laboratory it is neither possible nor desirable to produce these elements with anything approaching the intensity with which they occur in such naturally occurring crises as disabling illness or unemployment, or even minor crises such as difficulty in finding suitable housing in a new city, or receiving rejections from the colleges to which a child had applied. On the other hand, informal observation of the families so far studied and data presented in a paper dealing with family leadership and solidarity in the crisis situation (Straus, 1964d) show that observable and statistically significant differences are produced by these procedures, and suggest that Swanson and Hamblin who first developed this technique of crisis simulation were correct in asserting its isomorphism with a natural crisis. However, in the light of the theoretical assumption that a person tends to respond to the world as he anticipates the "significant other" in that situation would respond or expect him to respond (Mead, 1934) and the recent demostrations of how this important aspect of social interaction can affect the behavior of experimental subjects (Orne, 1962; Mills, 1962; McGuigan, 1963; Rosenthal, 1963, 1964), there is clearly a need for empirical research to specify the *subjects* definition of the SIMFAM experimental situation.

Experimental Variation of Communication and Knowledge

The bean bag task version of SIMFAM is currently being applied to a study of the effect of flow of communication, power structure, language ability, and the use of expert knowledge on family problem solving (Tallman, 1966). . The experimental technique allows us to manipulate each of the

---

[12] The extent to which the scores and other procedures actually succeed in first motivating the family, then in providing a feeling of satisfaction and accomplishment, and finally in creating a situation isomorphic with a crisis, is discussed later in the paper.

[13] See the theoretical analysis and summary of research in Hansen and Hill, 1964.

variables so that their independent, cumulative, and interaction effects on family problem solving can be determined in a relatively clear cut fashion. This is done by having the families participate in five trials in which the experimental conditions vary. In each of these trials the game rules are changed, thereby establishing different problems for the family to solve. The procedures used in the study are described briefly below.

Preliminary Instructions. After meeting the family the experimenter gives a general explanation. He states that our interest is in learning how families go about solving problems. Subjects are told that we want them to try hard on all of the problems and, in order to encourage them to do so, each family will be paid according to the number of points scored in each trial. This is in addition to the ten dollars promised them for participating in the study. This technique is designed to maintain a continuing high level of motivation for all families. It is expected that even families for whom the additional money may not seem important will have their interest piqued by this device. One assistant is assigned to entertain all children in the family who are not participating in the study. Friends or relatives who are present are asked to leave the room in which the experiment is being conducted.

The equipment and the use of the light panel and the need to infer game rules from the green and red lights are explained to the families. Each of the five trials contains two playing periods of two minutes with a half minute break between the periods. In each trial the family is required to solve for new rules under different conditions of communication and access to knowledge.

Trial X. This initial trial is designed to familiarize families with the game procedures and provide them with a positive set about their own performance level and potential. This is done by having the family participate in a game whose rule is very simple so that virtually every participant solves the problem.

Trials 1 and 2. During these trials family members are told that they can talk both during the play periods and during the break. The communications are recorded on a tape recorder and by an observer. These trials provide base measures of the flow of communication, power, and language skill. Problem solving ability is measured by the time it takes the family to reach a solution. A solution is defined as the ability of all family members to receive green lights three times in a row. The light board is designed to automatically flash a blue light when this occurs so that both the family and the experimenter are alerted when the problem is solved.

Two trials are used because two different types of problems are involved —one, requiring cooperation between the family members and the other capable of being solved by the activities of individual members. The research was designed, in part, to assess how the various independent variables influence the solution of each of these problems.

Trial 3. The purpose of this trial is to enable us to determine whether certain patterns of communication and power restrict the opportunity of "experts" to apply their knowledge in the resolution of the problem. In this trial each family member is given a different set of written instructions (Appendix B). Two of these instruction sets contain ambiguous statements; the third set contains principles directly related to solving the problem. The useful instructions are distributed to different family members in each cell of the research design. Thus, one third of the fathers, mothers, and sons are made knowledgeable, and an equal number of fathers, mothers, and sons in each of the power conditions (husband decides, wife decides, and equalitarian) are given meaningful information. The trial is conducted (in all other ways) in the same way as trials 1 and 2.

Trial 4. In this trial family members are not allowed to talk or gesture during the play periods. At the break, however, each member may transmit one message. The purpose of the trial is to control flow of communication and allow language skill to vary.

Trial 5. In this trial members may not talk or gesture either during the play periods or the break. This provides a control on both flow of communication and language style. If these two variables are critical in contributing to social class differences in problem solving then the differences should be greatly diminished when the variables are controlled.

Ethics of Experimental Variations

Placing families in a situation which is intended to induce changes in family power structure and patterns of mutual support raises important ethical questions.[14] The problem faced by the experimenter is to keep the manipulation from being traumatic to the individual and sufficiently circumscribed so that the eventual explanation to subjects does not embitter them or make them resentful. This is especially important in working with natural groups like the family where the manipulation may affect future relationships. These necessary etchical limits on the experimental manipulations may restrict the strength of an experimentally induced variable to the extent that it is too weak to produce observable differences, even if the theory being tested is correct.

Experience with the frustration condition in the ball and pusher task suggests that this treatment avoids either of these extremes. On the one hand, the

---

[14] These ethical considerations are by no means unique to experimentation with families. Almost all experimental manipulations involve some degree of deception. Moreover, some degree of deception occurs in most survey research. Rarely are participants told the real intent of the questions asked. To do so would usually create a bias in responses which could affect the validity of the results. Despite this, two recent analysts of the problem (Ruebhausen and Brim, 1965) maintain that respondents must be informed in specific detail of all the purposes of the research before they can ethically be interviewed. Other analyses of this difficult and important problem may be found in Beecher, 1959; Berg, 1954; Gross, 1956; Ivy, 1948; and Shimkin, 1953.

informal observations of family reactions to the simulated crisis reported later in this paper, and the changes in power and support scores reported in another paper (Straus, 1964d) both show that observable effects are produced by the crisis simulation. On the other hand, these effects, while sufficient to produce the small changes necessary to test theoretical propositions, occur in the context of a game situation in which the focus is on a type of puzzle to be solved. The subjects are not informed that power and mutual support are being observed and it is hoped that they do not perceive changes as having taken place in respect to these two variables.

To aid in this process of focusing attention on the task rather than on interpersonal relations and to provide an opportunity for tension release and satisfaction of curiosity, a post-experimental session is held. The family is told that, as they probably suspected, the rules of the game were deliberately changed, making is impossible to solve the puzzle. They are also told that the purpose is to find out how many different things and what kinds of things people try out when faced with an insolvable problem. Each family is assured that they performed well, and in turn almost always expressed relief on learning that the problem was not really solvable.

Despite the focus on learning and playing the game, some families do perceive changes in power and support (Straus, 1967). But even when this is the case, it is believed that the game context in which such changes take place enable the effects to be dismissed as unimportant because games and puzzles constitute what Anderson and Moore call an *autotelic* activity (Anderson and Moore, 1960). That is, they contain their own goals and sources of motivation, and at the same time the rewards and punishments connected with failure to play the game correctly are normatively confined to the intrinsic features of the game and do not generally carry over to other aspects of life. Thus, a businessman may be known as a miserable golf player without damaging his general self-esteem or his reputation as a businessman.

We believe that the norms restricting the consequences of autotelic activities to the activity itself applies sufficiently to the games used for the SIMFAM technique to insulate the subjects from changes in self-esteem or in family structure brought about by the crisis treatment.

VI. NORMS AND RELIABILITY

Norms

The families so far studied by means of the SIMFAM technique represent special populations and the number of cases is small. However, some information about their performance may be of value to those using the technique. Consequently, Tables 1 and 2 present means and standard deviations for performance in the ball and pusher task of 64 families in Minneapolis, Minnesota. Half of these families are middle class in occupation and area of residence and half are working class. The sample was selected from families with a ninth grade child in two junior high schools and is part of a

Table 1. Means and Standard Deviations of Activity Level and Problem Solving Ability Scores for 64 Minneapolis Families

| Variable* | Actor | Trial Number | | | | | | | | Total | |
| | | 1 | | 2 | | 3 | | 4 | | | |
		Mean	SD	Mean	SD	Mean	SD	Mean	SD	Mean	SD
Activity	H	13.5	8.6	14.5	10.2	15.4	11.8	18.2	12.4	62.0	38.4
(Number of moves)	W	12.4	5.9	12.8	6.4	13.1	7.0	14.7	6.8	53.2	21.7
	C	14.1	7.8	14.2	8.2	14.4	7.5	16.1	9.8	58.7	25.7
	F	39.8	17.6	41.5	20.9	42.8	21.4	48.4	23.8	173.9	76.2
Problem solving ratio	H	41.9	19.0	54.0	21.9	61.9	24.7	68.9	17.8	56.7	16.1
(per cent that green	W	38.4	20.4	48.1	21.4	58.5	22.4	62.9	20.0	52.5	15.8
lights are of all lights)	C	45.7	21.2	49.8	23.9	60.4	19.7	63.1	19.0	54.1	14.0
	F	40.4	15.8	50.5	18.3	60.1	18.1	65.1	15.3	53.9	14.1

* See sections II and IV for descriptions of these variables.

three society comparative study. The data for the similar samples in Bombay, India, and San Juan, Puerto Rico, are presented elsewhere (Straus, 1967) and are not repeated here for lack of space.

Table 2. Means and Standard Deviations of Selected Creativity, Power and Support Scores for 64 Minneapolis Families

Variable*	Actor	Mean for Trials 1-4	SD
Creativity, combined	H	11.5	5.5
(Responses plus categories)	W	8.2	4.6
	C	7.0	4.6
	F	22.8	6.7
Power +	H	37.5	22.8
(Directive acts complied with)	W	20.2	14.8
	C	17.9	7.0
	F	75.6	35.5
Power −	H	3.7	3.7
(Rejected directive acts)	W	4.4	7.0
	C	3.3	3.7
	F	10.4	8.1
Support +	H	13.7	10.9
(Positive intent)	W	7.7	5.3
	C	12.3	8.2
	F	33.6	17.4
Support −	H	4.8	5.1
(Negative intent)	W	4.0	4.2
	C	3.5	4.1
	F	12.3	9.4

* See sections II and IV for descriptions of these variables.

Table 3. Observer Consistency Reliability Coefficients

		r		
Variable		Bombay (N = 64)	Mpls. (N = 66)	San Juan (N = 45)
Power vs Support		.85	.86	.75
Power	+	.98	.91	.78
	0	.43	.59	.55
	−	.55	.85	.71
Support	+	.96	.90	.68
	−	.68	.70	.80

The limited nature of the samples for which data is available also did not make it worthwhile to present more detailed normative data such as frequency or percentile distributions. It should be noted that the distributions were often skewed towards the zero end, and this is reflected in the frequent high standard deviations. Use of such frequency and per cent data for analyses of variance correlations may cause difficulties. It is possible, however, to deal with some of these difficulties by using a square root transformation for the frequency data and an arc-sine transformation for the percent data (see Walker and Levy, 1953).

Reliability

There are two aspects of reliability applicable to instruments of this type, *temporal consistency* and *scorer consistency*. No information on the former is available. In respect to scorer consistency, data is available on the consistency between the two observers who record the power and support scores, and on consistency in scoring (but not in recording) creativity.

Table 3 presents the coefficients of correlation between scores recorded by independent observers, for samples of families in Bombay, Minneapolis, and San Juan. These correlations show that the judgments concerning whether to classify an act as power or support, and whether to classify that act as "+" or "−" are made with a fair degree of consistency. However, agreement on the ignored power category ("0") is low. This occurs, in part, because some of the acts falling under this heading result from observers occasionally forgetting to add the sign to their score entries. Similar reliability coefficients were obtained by Bahr (1969) who reported r's of .76 to .98 (mean of .92).

VII. VALIDITY

A definitive assessment of the validity of the SIMFAM technique is not possible with the data now available, and considerable research will be required to produce the evidence needed for such an assessment. However, a preliminary assessment of certain aspects of validity is possible and is presented in this section.

Content Validity

Content validity is ". . . evaluated by showing how well the content of the test samples the class of situations or subject matter about which conclusions are to be drawn. Content validity is especially important in the case of achievement and proficiency measures.

"In most classes of situations measured by tests, quantitative evidence of content validity is not feasible. However, the test producer should indicate the basis for claiming adequacy of sampling or representativeness of the test content in relation to the universe of items adopted for reference." (APA, 1954, p. 13).

Content Validity of Power, Support, and Communication Measures. The content validity of these SIMFAM scores depends on the extent to which the sample of interaction observed as the family attempts to solve the problem is characteristic of the way in which family members would interact with each other in at least some natural settings. The use of game-tasks should contribute to content validity for two reasons. First, the involvement and the excitement of playing the game lessens the family's awareness of being observed and therefore allows them to interact less self-consciously. Second, the task and the instructions are designed to channel efforts at demonstrating good performance into the objective endeavor of solving a specific problem, rather than into efforts to demonstrate "good" family interaction.

On the basis of experience with samples of lower-class and middle-class families in Bombay, Minneapolis, and San Juan, it is believed that these expectations have been borne out. We feel that the game was typically found to be interesting and engrossing by the families studied, and that most families enjoyed the game at least during the four precrisis trials. Further, we found that without exception, families at all social levels took the task seriously. In fact, among the families which served as controls (and therefore played the game for eight trials without the crisis), a number became so engrossed that they did not want to stop playing after the eighth period.

Finally, an indirect but objective indicator of involvement in the game is the fact that our early fears of the parents regarding it as a child's activity were not borne out. With rare exceptions the parents become highly involved in the task and typically have the highest power and support scores (see Table 2).

Stress Situation. The procedures used to create a stress or crisis situation also seemed to be effective. Behavior which we feel indicated a sense of sudden loss of a valued achievement occurring was usually observable in the statements and actions of the subjects. There were frequent statements of perplexity and disappointment and intense efforts were made to try out new modes of play to overcome the inability to acquire a high score. The statistical evidence is clear: After the introduction of the crisis treatment, both the number of power assertions and the number of creative responses go up sharply (Rollins, 1969), especially for those not previously active (Straus, unpublished; Bahr, 1969).

These reactions are in marked contrast to our early fear that simply changing the rules of the game, and giving all red lights and no increment in score, would prove to be too transparent a manipulation. It is true that perhaps a third of the families made a statement such as "Oh, they changed the rules on us." However, this was almost invariably followed by a statement such as "Well those other families figured out the new rules and we have to do it too." Thus, observable behaviors suggest that the techniques used in the first four trials produce a high level of involvement and a feeling of accomplishment so that the contrasting last four trials were perceived as a deprivation of a goal (high score) which the family's experience in the first four trials taught them to value.

Content Validity of Problem Solving Ability and Creativity Scores. The experimental problem requires the subjects to infer general features from specific events, and to apply that knowledge to achieve a specific goal. This crucial ability is important for adequately coping with the demands of a rapidly changing urban industrial society.

An attempt has been made to provide the opportunity for lower-class families to exhibit their ability along those lines through modalities which are allied to their usual pattern of behavior. Specifically, the lower-class person is widely believed to ". . . not verbalize well in response to words alone" (Riesman, 1962); or, as Miller and Swanson put it, the lower-class person tends to think and learn in a ". . . physical or motoric fashion. Such people can think through a problem only if they can work on it with their hands. Unless they can manipulate objects they cannot perform adequately" (Miller and Swanson, 1960). It was for this reason that Moore and Anderson's assertion of the superiority for laboratory experimentation of purely symbolic tasks (Moore and Anderson, 1954a, 1954b) was rejected in favor of game tasks which involves physical manipulation of objects in response to nonverbal symbols (red and green lights). It is believed that this feature of the tasks makes them more suited to working class and other low literacy populations, while at the same time meeting the criteria outlined by Moore and Anderson for tasks to be used in research on problem solving.

Contextual Sources of Invalidity

The information and judgments presented in this section suggest that the SIMFAM technique samples behaviors comprising the traits which the technique purports to measure. However, no human interaction goes on in a social vacuum.

Bringing lower-class families into a university laboratory setting is sometimes a threatening experience for them. This may affect the resulting measures in a number of ways. First, in relation to the power, support, and communication measures, it may serve to attenuate the interaction, or worse, to alter the relative frequency of different kinds of acts (O'Rourke, 1963; Kenkel, 1961). Second, in relation to the problem solving ability and creativity scores, such as "official" setting may lead to a "negative expectancy," especially among lower-class families with a history of inadequate performance in schools and "middle-class organizations" of all types. If this is the case, there is evidence to show that such expectancies will influence performance and therefore impair content validity.[15]

---

[15] See Orne, 1962, and for the other side of the coin, that is, *experimenter* expectancies unconsciously influencing the performance of subjects, see Mills, 1962; McGuigan, 1963; and Rosenthal, 1963, 1964.

Although the possibility of such contextual sources of invalidity is a real one, it is felt that certain other features of the task and the setting reduce the chances that such effects actually have an important influence on the results. First, it will be recalled that the task is exciting and engrossing for the subjects. Thus, even those who showed initial signs of anxiety soon became absorbed in the game and appeared at ease. Second, to reduce the initial anxiety (and in the case of the lower-class subjects, the social distance between them and the experimenter), the family was met at the building door, informal clothes were worn, and a "warm-up" conversation was held in which the family was served a soft drink. Finally, in one of the studies we attempted to further minimize the context problem by use of a temporary laboratory in a local school, that is, by locating the work in a familiar territory or setting. Although these features of the task and these steps to reduce the strangeness of the situation seem to be effective, there is no firm evidence of the extent to which this is the case. Research using this technique in the subject's home is now beginning and this will provide some evidence on the possible confounding effect of the laboratory setting.

Concurrent Validity

Concurrent validity is evaluated by showing how well scores on the test being validated correspond to other known measures of the variable. The difficulty with many concurrent validity analyses is that the instrument with which the test being evaluated is compared may also be of unknown validity. This is clearly the case in respect to most of the SIMFAM variables. We might, for example, correlate the SIMFAM power score with the widely used self-report measure of intra-family power used by Blood and Wolfe. However, Olson (1969) has evidence which suggests that the Blood and Wolfe measure primarily indexes normative *authority* rather than interpersonal control. Similarly, in respect to creativity, the "independent" measure of creativity which we have available to correlate with the SIMFAM measure may index a different aspect of this complex variable or it may be less valid measure than our own. With these cautions in mind, we can consider Table 4, which presents the correlation of the SIMFAM creativity scores with Form A of the Minnesota Tests of Creativity (Torrence, 1962) for 48 of the children in the Minneapolis sample.

Table 4. Correlation of SIMFAM Creativity Score With Minnesota Test of Creative Thinking for 48 Minneapolis Children

Sample	N	Correlation (r)
Total	48	.17
Social Class: Working	25	.19
Middle	23	.33
Sex of child: Male	25	.17
Female	23	.27

Examination of Table 4 shows that the largest correlation is for the working class part of the sample, and this is only 33. For the total sample, the correlation is only 17. Although all of these correlations are positive, they offer only minimal evidence of concurrent validity. At the same time, these correlations must be judged in the light of the fact that they are about the same magnitude as the validity coefficients available for the Torrence test.

Construct Validity

The studies so far completed using the SIMFAM technique suggest that the SIMFAM measures index theoretically meaningful patterns of family behavior. For example, the studies conducted by Straus reveal social class and sex differences in power and support which are consistent with many empirical studies and certain theoretical formulations (Straus, 1967). Analyses of the relationship between intra-family power and communication patterns and the problem solving ability of family groups have been fruitful (Straus, 1968; Tallman and Miller, 1970). In an analysis of data for a sample of Bombay families, Straus (in press) has also shown that the power exercised by husbands in joint households is greater than by husbands who are not resident in such a traditional pattern. Even stronger results were shown for the wives; those who were free from the traditional joint household arrangement exercised far more power during the SIMFAM game than did the wives in joint households.

Finally, the reader has available for inspection in this volume the results of a three society comparative study of family-interactional patterns measured by SIMFAM and their relationship to the problem solving ability of the child. This study provides cross-culturally replicated evidence that parental power and support and the child's power are related to the child's creativity and his success in obtaining correct problem solutions (see also Straus and Straus, 1968).

Internal and External Validity

The preceding discussion of validity was based on the assumption that behavior in the experiment must be a replica of behavior under natural circumstances. Such an assumption is necessary if SIMFAM is to be used as a diagnostic tool or to describe the family's behavior in other circumstances. However, for purposes of testing explanatory hypotheses, such an assumption is unnecessary; it is only necessary for the experimental procedures and behavior to correspond to the real world in respect to the theoretically specified aspects or variables. Moreover, the theoretically specified variables need not be present with the full intensity found in the natural setting, nor even be manifest in the same form as in nature. According to Zelditch and Hopkins (1961):

> The relevance of a theoretical concern is crucial to cutting through a good deal of the dispute over the "artificiality" of laboratory experimentation. Events in the laboratory often bear little or no resemblance to events normally occurring in

the real world, and for this reason may appear to many "unnatural" and to some trivial. But the theoretical importance of events is not determined by their frequency in nature. It is determined by their relevance to theoretical concepts. And theories often contain concepts that refer to events occurring only rarely, if at all, in the real world. Such concepts are simpler, more general, and, in a sense that is more accurate than usual, less "superficial" than more graphic concepts. Though the events to which they refer seldom occur, then, those concepts prove more capable of interpreting the real world. But to examine the types of events to which they refer often requires the construction of "artificial" systems. Such systems are never descriptive of the real world, but they are not intended to be. Their purpose is to construct and test theory, not to match reality as commonly experienced."

The distinction made by Campbell between "internal" and "external" validity of social experiments corresponds in certain ways with Zelditch and Hopkin's view:

> First, and as a basic minimum is what can be called *internal validity*: did in fact the experimental stimulus make some significant difference in this specific instance; the second criterion is that of *external validity, representativeness, or generalizability*: to what populations, settings, and variables can this effect be generalized? Both criteria are obviously important, although it turns out that they are to some extent incompatible, in that the controls required for internal validity often tend to jeopardize representativeness.
>
> If one is in a situation where either internal or external validity . . . must be sacrificed, which should it be? The answer is clear. Internal validity is the prior and indispensable consideration. The optimum design is, of course, one having both internal and external validity (Campbell, 1957).

In the case of the SIMFAM technique, the section on content validity was intended to show the basis for claiming external validity, at least in respect to those aspects of each variable which it is intended to measure. However, along with Zelditch and Hopkins and Campbell, we believe that the question of internal validity is of greater importance. The results reported in Straus (1964c, 1964d, 1967) show that the experimental treatment ". . . did in fact . . . make some significant difference . . . ," thus providing some evidence of internal validity. Moreover, besides the difference due to the stress or crisis treatment, many other important relationships among SIMFAM variables and between social class and SIMFAM variables have been found (Straus, 1964c, 1964d). Thus, irrespective of the extent to which the SIMFAM laboratory task is "artificial" or "trival," the results so far obtained suggest that the technique has internal validity in the Campbell sense, and is fruitful for testing theoretical explanatory hypotheses in the Zelditch and Hopkins sense.

Cross-Cultural Validity

The use of a standardized task to generate a sample of family behavior does not guarantee that the subjective definition of that task is the same for all families. As long as the SIMFAM technique forms part of an experiment within a single culture group, this problem may be met by the usual technique of random assignment. However, in nonexperimental designs, differences in performance of cultural groups such as social classes or ethnic groups, may represent differences in their subjective definition of the situation and of what is expected of them in that situation, rather than representing differences in the family's usual mode of behavior in respect to the variables measured.

This is, of course, the classic criticism raised in connection with all standardized cross-cultural research, whether conducted in the laboratory or by questionnaire or interview.[16] The implication of this criticism, if taken literally, is that any cross-cultural research, other than informal holistic studies, is not possible. This may be true, but rather than accept such a constricting preconception, it seems wiser to proceed empirically, while at the same time making use of techniques such as those outlined by Orne (1962) to determine the way different groups perceive the experiment and what is expected of them as subjects.

This type of analysis has been undertaken to examine social class differences in perception of the purpose of the experiment and the behavior expected of participants by utilizing data from post-experimental interviews. These data are reported in another paper (Straus, 1967). They show that 78 percent of the lower-class and 84 percent of the middle-class subjects perceived the purpose of the experiment as an investigation of "intelligence," or "problem solving." However, about half of the subjects also mentioned as one of the purposes such goals as "to see who runs things," "if we help each other;" which were clearly classifiable under the headings of power and support. Thus, a substantial proportion of the sample perceived the interpersonal relationship objective of the study—probably because the instructions for the task laid emphasis on "working together," "talking things over," and so forth. Although it would have been preferable for a smaller proportion to have perceived these latter objectives, the critical point for evaluating the utility of the technique in cross-class and other cross-cultural studies is the fact that there were only small percentage differences between social classes in the perception of each type of objective.

Similar results were obtained when the post-experimental inquiry was focused on subjective definitions of behavior which would be appropriate for families in this situation (rather than the aims of the researcher described above). To secure data on this point we asked the following question: "Everyone who cooperates in something like this starts out by wondering what they are *really* supposed to do, and if they will do it correctly. Now, try to think back to before the game started and tell me what your idea was at that time

---

[16] See the articles in two recent issues of the *International Social Science Journal:* "Data in Comparative Research," 16 (1964), No. 1; and "Opinion Surveys in Developing Countries," 15 (1963), No. 1; and also Hudson, Barakat, and LaForge, 1959; Jacobson, Kumata, and Takeshita, 1964; and Blood and Takeshita, 1964.

about how to do a good job. That is, I would like you to tell me all the things you thought we wanted to see you do."

As in the case of the question on the aims of the research, almost everyone in both social class groups (91 and 94 percent) mentioned solving the puzzle or playing the game correctly. In the lower-class sample, 44 percent also mentioned that they should carry out some kind of supportive act such as helping each other, praising, showing warmth or friendliness, and so forth. The percentage of middle-class families who perceived this as expected of them in the experiment was larger, but only by 11 percent. A difference of this size is well within the likelihood of chance occurrence. So also is the eight percent difference between the 38 percent of the lower-class sample and the 45 percent of the middle-class sample who perceived that some kind of power structure, such as "the husband should take leadership" or "everyone's views must be considered," was what was expected of them.

These "definition of the situation" data, together with the use of direct observation of behavior and the ambiguity of the experimental tasks, all suggest that the SIMFAM technique may prove helpful in securing comparable data not only in cross-class research but also in cross-cultural studies. The ambiguity of the tasks is particularly important. If, as in the present case, the task is unique to the experience of the participants in the sense that they have never had to solve a similiar type of puzzle, the possibility of bringing biasing or confounding expectations to the experiment are restricted. Further, if the family members cannot approach the experiment with a task-specific frame of reference, they will be more likely to accept the "definition of the situation" provided by the experimenter. This could conceivably eliminate one of the major problems in cross-cultural research. We are not claiming that SIMFAM is a culture free test, nor do we maintain that experimental research can conquer the interminable problems which exist in conducting crosscultural research. Rather, we wish to suggest that the SIMFAM technique and experimental research in general may in fact be more suited for cross-cultural research than some of the methods generally used.

None of this may be effective in eliciting cross-culturally comparable material, just as some have despaired of being able to formulate cross-culturally comparable interview questions. However, some grounds for optimism about the utility of observed performance measures for cross-cultural research comes from the apparent success of several studies using this technique (Milgram, 1961; McClelland, 1961; Rosen and D'Andrade, 1959; Schachter et al, 1954; Stanton and Litwak, 1955; and Strodtbeck, 1951, 1958). In any case the issue requires empirical resolution rather than *a priori* pronouncements.

VIII. SUMMARY AND EVALUATION

A technique for measuring the power, support, and communication structure of families, and their creativity and problem solving ability, has been described. The measurement of these variables is based on direct observation of family interaction during performance of a standard task. The set of tasks, observational categories, and quantitative scores, are together called the "Simulated Family Activity Measurement" (SIMFAM) technique.

It is believed that SIMFAM will be found useful in research, and possibly also as a technique for clinical assessment of families because of the following characteristics:

1. It is based on direct observation rather than "self-report" data. It therefore provides a method for obtaining data on variables which are difficult or impossible for many subjects to directly verbalize.

2. It is a motor task in the form of a game. This should make it a more appealing task to lower-class families, and also one which permits them to make use of the "motoric" thinking claimed to be characteristic of lower-class individuals.

3. The speed with which the game is played and the enjoyment of the game, which is typical of the experience of families so far tested, may minimize the confounding effects of self consciousness and attempts to present one's self in the best light.[17]

4. The focus of the problem presented to the family is on the objective task of determining the rules of the game. Thus, the motivation to present one's self in a favorable light is channeled into task performance rather than family interaction, thereby allowing for a more natural sample of family interaction.

5. All members of the family have an approximately equal opportunity to play the game and contribute to the solution of the task. This is because the games are purely artificial, thereby eliminating the effects of previous experience. In addition, no physical skill is necessary.

6. The tasks provide an opportunity to compare a normal situation presenting few difficulties in the task performance with behavior in a stress situation in which environmental adaptation is blocked.

7. The technique provides scores for each actor and each possible "role system" such as "husband to wife" and "husband to child," as well as total family scores.

8. The technique has considerable flexibility due to the many ways in which the basic procedures outlined in this paper may be systematically varied, and due to the wide variety of ratings and scores which can be obtained from the protocol of the family's performance.

APPENDIX A: INSTRUCTIONS FOR BALL AND PUSHER TASK

Instructions For Subjects

As you may know, there is a lot of interest these days in how groups solve problems. But we really know very little about what happens when families and other groups try to solve problems. That is why we have asked the three

---

[17] For an example of such a social desirability set in direct observation studies without an engrossing task, see Vidich, 1959. On the other hand the "revealed difference" technique developed by Strodtbeck (1951, 1958) structures the interaction in a way which is believed to avoid this phenomena.

of you in to play this game. We want to see how you work together to solve a problem or figure out a puzzle.

The problem is to figure out how to play this game, and then to get as high a score as you can using this information. We can tell you only a few things about the way to get a high score. You will have to figure out the rest. Here are the rules and hints which we can give you:

1. Points are gained by shooting these balls. Everytime you make a point or points, a green light over there will flash.

2. You must figure out the rules of the game by noting what you did when a green or red light is flashed.

3. Penalties will be given each time you break a rule. Everytime you lose a point or points, a red light over there will flash.

4. When shooting you must stand back of this line or your shot will not count.

5. Everytime a light flashes, it should be a problem for you. You should work together to figure out what you did that gained or lost points. You must gamble a lot and try a lot of things to find out what these other rules are. This problem requires that you hit a happy medium between playing and talking if you are to get as good a score as you can.

6. You will have a limited amount of time in which to play. The plan is that you will have a total of 34½ minutes to solve the problem. You will play for 3 minutes, take a 1½ minute rest, play for another 3 minutes, take a second 1½ minute rest, and so on for 8 periods of play. During these rest periods you must return to your present seat.

7. This is a kind of emergency situation. You have to work fast. You have to keep planning and thinking together while you work and during the rest periods. Since you are working on this problem as a team, you may talk to one another at all times during the play periods and the rest periods.

8. After each playing period, your score will be put on the blackboard. Here are some things you should know about these scores:

    a. The scores are total family scores. They are not individual scores. Your job is to get the highest possible score for your team. This will take everyone's work and enthusiasm.

    b. As in many games, the points you gain in each period are added to those you made before that. Thus, if you gain 4 points the first period and 10 points during the second period, your score at the end of the two periods is 14 points gained.

    c. The scores recorded on the board are the remainder left over after subtracting the number of penalties you receive from the points you gain. Penalties are *not* carried over from period to period.

    d. The different ways of getting points and penalties have different scores. An example of this is the set-up in football of giving 6 points for a touchdown, 1 point for making the kick after the touchdown, and giving different numbers of yards in penalties for breaking different rules. At the beginning of the play, you will get an immediate credit bonus of points. In other words, you start with some points "in the bank." You will not be able to keep your own scores. Our score keeper here will watch closely and be responsible for that. He will record your score after each period of play.

9. Now for special notes:

a. Please don't throw the equipment. It breaks!

b. Please speak up so the observers can hear you, and keep the equipment as quiet as you can.

c. Once we get under way, we cannot answer any questions. You will get your instructions from this recorder. This is so that everything can be properly timed. However, you may ask the light operator for the color of the light that was just flashed, or who did the thing that caused her to flash the light.

10. Notice that here on the blackboard is a set of scores. These are the average scores of a group of families who worked with us while we pretested this problem. We put these scores on the board to give you an idea of how you are doing as the game progresses. I might say that the ability to figure out a rather complex situation is what is important in this game. We have seen many families work hard to make many successful shots only to lose most of the points gained through penalties because they failed to learn these other rules. We think you should be able to do as well or better than these pretest families did, but to do so you have to work hard too.

11. This is a complete set of instructions. You may look at them at any time. ANY QUESTIONS?

Light Operation Instructions

A. Rules of the Game

A *green light* is signaled every time a player pushes a ball of the same color as his wristband, using a stick of the same color, in such a way that it hits one of the wood barriers. The players may shoot in any order and at any time.

A *red light* is signaled if the player violates any of the following rules:

1. The color of the ball and pusher used by each player must correspond to the color of his wristband.

2. The player must stand behind the line when he pushes the ball. Standing on the sides of the court to push the ball, even though outside the line, is not correct.

3. The player's pusher must not cross the line.

4. The ball must hit one of the two targets at the end of the court.

5. The ball may be retrieved in only two ways, (a) the player may pick up the ball with his hand, either inside or outside of the court; (b) the ball may roll back across the base line.

6. The ball must stay inside the court after it has hit the target unless it rolls back to a player across the base line.

B. Additional Instructions

1. *Duration of Lights.* Although the term "flashed" is used in these instructions, the light operator must actually keep the light on for more than a brief flash so that the player has a chance to see what was signaled. This is especially important in the early stages of the game.

2. *Both Green and Red Lights may be Signaled.* Both a green and a red light may be flashed for a single play of the ball in order to facilitate learning the rules of the game. This often occurs in connection with the rule that the ball must not roll out of the court; if the ball is correctly shot against the target a green light is first flashed as the ball hits the target. If the ball then rolls out a red light is subsequently flashed. Both a green and a red light may be flashed simultaneously to indicate that a correct and an incorrect move have been made simultaneously.

3. *Failure to Shoot from Behind Base Line.* The instructions read to all families clearly state this rule. It is not left to the players to discover themselves because failure to play from behind the base line leads to a number of other erroneous interpretations of the rules, such as playing the game like pool, or hitting the ball to one another. Also when the game is played from the sides the balls roll out of the court more easily. The effect of not enforcing this rule from the beginning is that the light operator's job becomes almost impossible and the players become confused.

There are two ways in which this rule is violated: (a) The player stands in approximately the correct location but tends to step over the line as he shoots; (b) the player shoots from the side of the court or from the inside. If the players shoot from the sides of the court or from well inside the court it is sometimes possible to guide them back to where they belong by flashing green lights to the player who accidently shoots from the right location. However, if this does not work and the base line rule is not being observed by the end of the first trial the family should be told the rule again as they start the second trial. Such a reminder should not be given to families who are playing from the correct location but who, through carelessness, tend to cross the line as they shoot, or who stand only slightly inside the line as they shoot.

4. *Incorrect Color Use.* Second in importance among the rules is the one requiring use of the same color stick and armband. In fact, unless at least one player is using the correct color stick there is no point in flashing red lights for other infractions of the rules. The reasons for giving priority to this rule are:

a. It is extremely difficult for the light operator to flash green lights accurately if the players are not using the correct color balls and pushers.

b. Many other things are tried out (some of them correct) for which the subject thinks he is getting red lights. Consequently, when the right color pusher is finally used it is very difficult for the family to learn the other rules.

c. The subjects become discouraged by the continuous red lights so that by the time they begin using the right color pusher the game is too far gone to really give the feeling of success with which the family is supposed to enter the crisis period.

5. *Procedures to Correct for Incorrect Color Use.* During the *first two* trials:

a. Give a red light as the player hits the balls and keep it on until just before the ball hits the target or stops rolling.

b. Give a green light for the first few times the correct colors are used, even if the subject steps across the line as he shoots the ball and even if the ball is not likely to hit the target.

c. Once the family has learned the color rule, resume enforcing the other rules by giving a red light for errors but, only *after* a green light is flashed for correct color use until they are sure of the color rule.

If the subjects do not use the correct color pusher until the beginning of the *third* trial, observe the same procedures as above except to be slower to enforce the other rules.

6. *Notes on Color Use.*

a. If even one subject picks up the correct color pusher before the end of the third trial there is a reasonable chance of the problem being solved.

b. Families using the wrong color pusher can sometimes be led to use the right color pusher if, during the rest periods, the experimenter takes the pushers from each player and places them back on the floor as they were at the beginning of the game.

c. As long as a subject uses the correct color pusher there is no need to be concerned if he is still using the wrong color ball. It is very rare for a player to not think of matching the ball to his pusher fairly soon after making the first change. Therefore give only red lights until the ball color matches the pusher *if* the correct color pusher is being used.

7. *Other Situations Requiring Intervention.* A family which has misinterpreted the rules in such a way as to make it impossible for the light operator to flash green lights should be corrected. This should be done at once in the case of players whose actions are dangerous such as those who throw or bat the balls; or at the beginning of the next trial in the case of players who shoots from the sides of the court or from the inside. These corrections, however, should be avoided if possible.

APPENDIX B: INSTRUCTIONS FOR BEAN BAG TASK

Instructions for Subjects

We want to thank you for participating in this study. Our main interest is to find out how families go about making decisions. We want to see how you work to solve a problem under different conditions. There is no right or wrong way to do this; we want to watch you and see if we can learn which ways work better. All that we want you to do is try your best to solve the problems. In order to encourage you to do your best we will pay you a dollar after each game if your family score is high enough.

I'm sure all of you have played many games. Most games come with a set of rules, but this one is different. The problem for you is to figure out how to play this game and then to get as high a score as you can using this information. We can tell you only a few things about how to get a high score. Your job is to figure out the rest.

Here are the rules we can give you:

1. As you can see, the game equipment consists of three different colored bean bags, arm bands, and a colored target.

2. Points are gained by tossing the bags. Every time you make a point or points, a green light will flash in the panel which has the same color as your arm band. (This is illustrated by the operator flashing green lights.) Penalties will be given each time you break a rule. The red light will flash when a rule is broken. (This is illustrated by the operator flashing red lights.)

3. In each game there is only one rule. You can tell when you have learned the rule if *ALL 3 of you get green lights 3 TIMES IN A ROW.* (Operator flashes green lights for each color in order 3 times.) This is very important, REMEMBER ALL THREE OF YOU MUST GET GREEN LIGHTS 3 TIMES IN A ROW.

4. Please speak up so that your voice will come through on the tape recorder.

5. You will play the bean bag game six times, each with different rules. Each game will consist of two playing periods. You will play for 2 minutes, have a 1 minute rest period, and then play for 2 more minutes. This will be repeated five more times. The first game will be to help you get familiar with the procedure and will not count on your final score.

6. Only one person can throw a bean bag at a time. That means that you can't all throw at once.

Trial X

EXPERIMENTER: This playing period will be two minutes long. There will be a 1-minute break and another 2-minute playing period. You may talk over what you are doing. Remember to watch the red and green lights and remember all three of you must get green lights three times in a row for you to have solved the problem. YOU MAY BEGIN NOW. (2 minutes)

EXPERIMENTER: Your time is up. Now you may have a 1-minute rest period. During the rest period you may talk over what you did that resulted in a red or green light. (1 minute) Now we will begin the second playing period. During this second 2-minute playing period the rule will be the same as it was last time. You may talk over what you are doing. Remember to watch the red and green lights and remember all three of you must get green lights three times in a row for you to have solved the problem. YOU MAY BEGIN NOW. (2 minutes)

EXPERIMENTER: Your time is up. During the rest period between games, I will give you 1 minute to talk over what you think the rule was in the game you just played. Then I will ask you to tell me what you think it is. (1 minute) What do you think the rule is? (Experimenter may nod, say "fine, all right, and so forth.)

Trial I

EXPERIMENTER: Now that you have the idea, the rule will be different this time. You may again talk as much as you wish. Remember to watch the red and green lights. And remember you must all get green lights three times in a row. YOU MAY BEGIN NOW. (2 minutes) Your time is up. During the rest period discuss what resulted in green lights. (1 minute) The second playing period will be 2 minutes long. During this second 2-minute playing period the rule will be the same as it was last time. You may talk over what you are doing. Remember to watch the red and green lights and remember all three of you must get green lights three times in a row for you to have solved the problem. YOU MAY BEGIN NOW. (2 minutes) Your time is up. I will give you 1 minute to talk over what you think the rule was in the game you just played. (1 minute) What do you think the rule is?

Trial II

EXPERIMENTER: This third game will be the same length as the last, but the rule will be different. You will be given 2 minutes in the first playing period and then a 1-minute rest period. You may talk over what you are doing during the game. Remember to watch the red and green lights and remember that all three of you must get green lights three times in a row for you to have solved the problem. YOU MAY BEGIN NOW. (2 minutes) Your time is up; I will give you a 1-minute rest period to talk over what you think will help you in the second playing period. (1 minute) In this second playing period remember you are looking for the same rule you were in the first period. You may talk over what you are doing. Remember to watch the red and green lights and remember that all three of you must get green lights three times in a row for you to have solved the problem. YOU MAY BEGIN NOW. (2 minutes) You may now discuss what you as a family think was the rule in this last game, and then I will ask you to tell me what you think it was. (1 minute) What do you think the rule was?

Trial III

EXPERIMENTER: You've done very well so far. This game will be the same length as the last, but the rule will be different. During this playing period you may again talk as much as you wish. Remember to watch the red and green lights and remember that all three of you must get green lights three times in a row for you to have solved the problem. This time, however, I will give you a few written hints that may help you to figure out the rule. (E hands out cards and picks them up immediately. As soon as E collects the cards E says:) YOU MAY BEGIN PLAYING. (2 minutes)

EXPERIMENTER: Your time is up. During the rest period you may discuss what you have been doing so you can improve on it for the next playing period. (1 minute) During the second 2-minute playing period the rule will be the same as it was the last time. You may talk over what you are doing. Remember to watch the red and green lights and remember that all three of you must get green lights three times in a row for you to have solved the problem. YOU MAY BEGIN NOW. (2 minutes)

EXPERIMENTER: Your time is up. During the rest period I will give you 1 minute to talk over what you think the rule is. Then I'll ask you to tell me what you think it is. (1 minute) What do you think the rule is?

Trial IV

EXPERIMENTER: This game will be the same length but the rule will be different again. This time you may not talk or gesture to each other while you are playing. This playing period will be 2 minutes long. After 2 minutes you will be given a 1-minute rest period when each of you may give one hint that you think will help solve the problem. You should keep planning and thinking while you work and also during the rest period. Remember all three of you must get green lights three times in a row for you to have solved the problem. YOU MAY BEGIN NOW. (2 minutes)

EXPERIMENTER: Your time is up. Each of you may give one hint that you think will help find out the rule. Let's begin with you _____ and next _____ and last _____. Now see if you can use these hints to help figure out the rule in the next playing period. During this second 2-minute playing period the rule will be the same as it was last time. Remember that all three of you must get green lights three times as it was last time. Remember all three of you must get green lights three times in a row. Please do not talk or gesture to each other while you are playing. YOU MAY BEGIN NOW. (2 minutes)

EXPERIMENTER: Now I will give you 1 minute to talk over what you think was the rule in this last game. (1 minute) Can you tell me what you think it was?

Trial V

EXPERIMENTER: You have been doing very well. During this playing period you may not gesture at all to your family. Try as hard as you can to determine the rule yourself. This time during the rest period you will not be allowed to give any hints to your partners. Remember, the rule you are trying to find in this game is different from the ones in the other five games. Remember to watch the red and green lights and remember all three of you must get green lights three times in a row for you to have solved the problem. YOU MAY BEGIN NOW. (2 minutes)

EXPERIMENTER: The first playing period is up. During the rest period this time you may not talk to your partners. Think about what you did that received a green light in the last period. (1 minute)

EXPERIMENTER: During the second 2-minute playing period the rule will be the same as it was the last time. Remember all three of you must get green lights three times in a row for you to have solved the problem. Please do not gesture or talk to your partners. YOU MAY BEGIN NOW. (2 minutes)

EXPERIMENTER: Your time is up. Again I will give you 1 minute to talk over what you think the rule was in the game. (1 minute) What do you think the rule was? You have all done very well in working on this problem. Most families have much more trouble than you had. Thank you for your help. Before you leave would you fill out this questionnaire to help us evaluate the game.

Game Rules

Set X (Always used in Trial X). All must throw to same color squares as the color of armband and bean bag.

Set A. All must throw bag to form triangle on the target.

Set B. All must throw in the following order: yellow, blue, red.

Set C. All must throw bag somewhere off target.

Set D. All must exchange bean bags and use exchanged bag.

Set E. All must throw to a different corner square.
In Trial III, two family members are given ambiguous hints and one member is provided with a hint designed to provide him with special knowledge enabling him to solve the problem.

For all problems, the ambiguous hints are as follows: (1) The lights are very important, keep your eye on your lights and the others in your groups; (2) think about the tosses that result in green lights.

The special hints were: For Set A: Remember it is possible to form designs like a triangle, using all the bean bags on the target. For Set B: Think about the order in which you throw the bean bags. For Set C: Do you think you always need to throw on the target? For Set D: Do you think you always need to use the same bean bag? And for Set E: The bean bags shouldn't all be on the same square or in the middle of the target.

APPENDIX C: RECORDING TECHNIQUES FOR POWER AND SUPPORT

A variety of methods can be used to record power and support, ranging from a simple listing on a sheet of paper to a multiple-pen electric recorder such as those manufactured by Esterline-Angus. The method of listing on a sheet of paper has the advantage of simplicity and low cost, but the disadvantage of requiring the observer to take his eyes off the subjects when recording the scores. The multiple-pen recorder is expensive but has the advantage of giving the exact timing of each power act. In addition, checking reliability is greatly facilitated since the scores of the two observers are recorded in parallel lines and any discrepancy can be easily observed.

Still another method of recording, and the one used foremost of the families so far tested, makes use of a Stenotype machine. Observers can learn to operate these by touch alone with a half hour of practice, and the Stenotype machine is completely silent. In addition, used machines can be purchased for between five and fifteen dollars each.

Only eight of the stenotype keys are used: those in the second bank of keys from the bottom. The four keys on the right are used to indicate the actors: Husband, Wife, Child and Experimenter or experiment, and the four at the left side are used to indicate whether the act is support +, support −, power +, or power −.

The protocols obtained by any of these systems of recording are summarized on scoring forms such as the one in Figure 3. Many different forms are possible. The one suggested has the advantage of permitting a wide variety

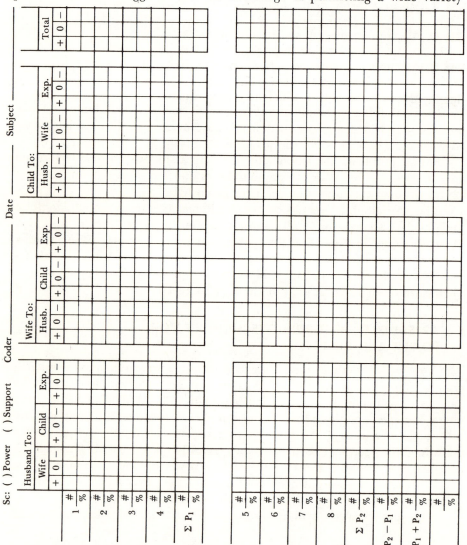

Figure 3. Scoring Summary for Power or Support.

of second level scores to be computed from it without having to go back to the original protocols. Next the scores of the two observers are added together (or averaged) and entered on a third copy of the scoring form. Finally, this third or combined score sheet is used to compute summary scores for the four "normal" trials, the four "crisis" trials, and for the total period of observation.

APPENDIX D: CREATIVITY SCORING MANUAL
(Ball and Pusher Task)

A sample protocol is included as Part IV of this study. This may be used to practice scoring and may then be checked against the scoring shown for this protocol on the page which follows it.

I. Fluency

Fluency is measured by the frequency of "relevant" responses to the task. A relevant response is defined as: (a) A positive or negative action, direction, suggestion, or question directed toward the ultimate solution of the problem, such as "Change ball color," "Try crossing," "Use same color balls," "Don't cross line"; (b) A statement which clearly implies a mode of play, such as "I walked in too soon," "Play it like marbles," and so forth.

Scoring

Mark *every* entry on the protocol with one of the following symbols:

R = Relevant response: See definition above.

I = Irrelevant response: In theory the observer should not have recorded any irrelevant responses. However, in practice, to avoid omitting possibly relevant behaviors, it is better for the observer to err on the side of recording everything which might conceivably be scored for creativity, leaving it to the scorer to make the final decision on relevancy. Irrelevant responses are primarily expressions of affect or general exhortations, such as: "Relax," "Quit that," "The rules have changed," "Work together as a family," "I can't help anybody," "Keep track of your own balls," "What now?" "Try harder," "Someone goofed."

D = Duplication: Items which have previously been entered *anywhere* on the protocol.

II. Flexibility

Flexibility is the number of different principles or modes of playing the game utilized or suggested by the subjects. The flexibility score will almost always be lower than the fluency score because several different ideas may fall under the same general principle of play, that is, "Shoot from the right side," and "Shoot from the left side" are both classified under a single principle (angle of shot) even though each contributes a point to the fluency score. The categories used for classifying responses for flexibility are:

1. Boundary Maintenance
2. Angle of shot
3. Speed, strength, bounce, etc. of shot
4. Color
5. Equipment use or combination (except color)
6. Target
7. Playing sequence
8. Ball retrieval
9. Speed of game, starting time
10. Number of balls used
11. Posture and physical position
12. Other

Scoring

1. After each item on the protocol marked "R" put the appropriate category number. For example, "R 1" means a response classified as falling into the Boundary Maintenance category. In practice this is done at the same time that each item on the protocol is classified R, I, or D.

2. Tabulate the frequency of each category on the scoring sheet, separately for trials 1 through 4 and 5 through 8, as shown in the sample score sheet.

3. Note that the "Total Categories" score for the family (the 4th, 8th and 12th boxes in the last line of the scoring form) is obtained by counting the number of categories used by the husband, wife, and child combined. In the example shown the husband used categories 1, 6, and 7 during trials 1 through 4; the wife used categories 1, 7, 9, 11, and 12; and the child numbers 7 and 10. This gives a Total Categories (flexibility) score of 3 for the husband, 5 for the wife, and 2 for the child. But since some of the same categories were used, the family "Total Categories" score is 7 rather than 10.

III. Flexibility Scoring Guides

1. Boundary Maintenance

Look for:

1. Reference or concern for *line, square,* or *court,* or actions which show such a concern.

2. Consequences of concern for boundary, such as "From outside the court," "Try crossing over," "Steps back from line," or "It's ok to walk down the side."

Examples:

May cross line	Not supposed to step on the line
You can walk down side	From the outside
Touch the line (or don't)	What about stepping over the line
Not beyond yellow (line)	Stay in and play
You shoot out here	If you push stick across line . . .

Let it roll out (or don't)
Pusher behind line
Try stopping them from rolling out
Leave them outside if they roll out
Keep balls well back of line
Try crossing
Behind line
Keep with yellow lines
Stand far enough back
Get way up close to the barrier
Can walk down side
Don't put pusher in square
Shoot in square so it doesn't go out of bounds
Can stop them from rolling out
Walk out the side rather than the back
One at a time start behind the line (also scored 7)
Can't move pusher past the line

You can come in from the back
Shoot from way back here
Line up the balls right on the yellow line before pushing
Can shoot from as far behind the line as you want to
Keep all the balls in
Don't put the stick over the line
Maybe you're supposed to come out now
Leave the stick behind
Don't go in with the stick in your hand
Shoot from inside
Don't put pusher inside to get the ball
Get inside
Should we go in the court at all?
Get a red light whenever you go over the line (out of the square)

2. Angle of Shot

Look For: Actions as well as statements which indicate that the subject is trying out a different angle, shooting from the side instead of the center, or the reverse.

Examples:

Shoot from corner (or don't)
Shoot at an angle
From side

Shoot straight
Change angle when the bell rings

3. Speed, Strength, Bounce of Shot

Look For: The way the ball is sent toward the target; that is, hard, soft, slow, fast, bounced.

Examples:

Push or roll softly, easy
Don't hit so hard
Don't make them bounce
Shuffle easy
Follow the ball right up
Be gentle with the balls
Shoot hard to return (also gets an 8)
Hit the board easily (also gets a 6)
Shoot and try and rebound and hit another ball (also gets a 5)
Bounce it
Balls must stop rolling

Roll easy slow, like marbles
Throw the ball
Hit the ball
Roll it nice and easy so it doesn't go out (also gets a 1)
Throw the ball
Do it with an even stroke so it doesn't bounce
Take it easy and shoot carefully
Put english on the ball
Push it all the way to the target

4. Color

Look For: Changes in use of equipment which are carried out for purposes of color change even if the term color or specific colors are not mentioned, especially: "Change (or exchange)," "Sticks," "Change balls," "Use your own balls."

Examples:

May change blue

Colors have different weights

Before colors have something to do with it

Use your own stick, balls

Change sticks

Don't hit any others

Change colors

Change balls

Use different color balls

The goal keeper is to keep the ball from touching

Don't hit the blackboard

Get in between the boards

Try not hitting the target

Shoot for center

Behind the target

Make the ball stay there (by target)

One in the middle and hit with the other ball

Hit into some chairs

Go down middle

Hit the other board

Aim for the center

Throw balls behind the bumper

Have to hit the end of the box

Use ball and stick of the same color

See if use the same ball

Try to shoot one of yours

Shoot with your own pusher

Two balls of different colors

Don't hit her ball with your ball

Try other person's ball

Shoot someone else's ball, you get a penalty

Take turns according to color

Change wrist-bands

You start first and try the center (also number 7)

Try to put it in the box

Change boxes . . . switch over to the other target

Alternate from one board to the other

Just hit the bumper

Maybe get more points if you get it in the box

Rotate bumpers

Don't hit the boxes

Maybe you can put the ball behind the bumper

Change positions to match the boards (also number 11)

Hit alternate sides

5. Equipment Use or Combination
(except Color and Number of Balls Used)

Look For:

1. Comparison with a sport: "like pool," "like shuffleboard."

2. Ways to use or handle the equipment which are *not based on the color* of the equipment: "Hold pusher with both hands."

3. Score under 4 if the purpose of the equipment use is to secure a same color combination, or under 10 if the reference is to the number of balls to use.

Examples:

Hit one ball with another (or don't)

Don't lift the pusher

Like in shuffleboard, marbles, pool

Change pushers around (reverse ends not exchange between player)

Just one hand

Hold pusher down more, down more

Turn target around

Hit it with the side of the pusher

Shoot first and let it return

With bevel edge of pusher

Don't hold the ball with your hand

Use left hand

Use other ball to knock out this ball (also 8)

Push the balls back and forth to each other

Bang the pusher down as you shoot

Line them up first

Use pushers upside down

Use only one pusher

Don't hit another ball

What happens when you hit some-one's ball?

Try spreading the balls out before shooting

Can't (or must) hit another ball when shooting (but see category 6)

Follow through like golf

Try rolling by hand

Set own ball in and hit it with another ball

Change blackboards around

Put the mallet down

Play it like hockey

Put the ball down with the holes down

Put the pusher down when you get to a ball

6. Target

Look For:

1. Destination of the ball: "In the center," "To the (or hit the) boards (or barriers)."

2. Hitting one ball with another *if* this act in itself is seen as getting a point.

3. Any designation of a target, whether or not in agreement with the rules to the game.

Examples:

Have to get in the middle of the barrier

Shoot more towards the . . .

Must hit board, middle, side of board

You do one target and you the other

Shoot one then the next one into it

Try to knock other person's ball

Middle again

Get in a circle but do not hit targets

In the center

Switch shooting at different targets

Hit your own ball, other's ball, other balls (see 2. above)

Can hit either board

All hit center

7. Playing Sequence

Examples:

Wait for the ball

Don't go get yours till I have shot

Can't leave before balls stop

Switch 3 times

Wait for ball to stop rolling (of retrieve to shooting)
Me first
Play in order
In order, W H C
All shoot together
Shoot one at a time
Distance from the barrier counts differently and determines shooting order
Take turns
Wife should shoot first
In order Yellow, Blue, White
Keep shooting while I retrieve
Just one shot at a time
Shoot in same order as chairs
Each one shoot twice
Sequence is the main thing
All try at once
Take turns
Whoevers' ball comes back first should shoot first
I walked in too soon
Let . . . go by himself
Switch balls, sticks, pushers, so forth
It doesn't matter if you hit another ball
Maybe one color scores higher than another

Work separately
Don't shoot till Daddy's out
One at a time
Start before you
Change order
In order
One person set up the balls
Do it in routine
Let . . . shoot first
Shot too close together
No rule against shooting when someone else is
Can shoot anytime
Wait until the ball stops rolling
Two at a time
Shouldn't both shoot at the same time
Colors take turns
Change turns
We're out of order
Rotate (places)
Penalties for shooting two in a row
Keep shooting until I miss
Use same color balls and sticks
Exchange colors
Try another (color) ball

8. Ball Retrieval

Look For: Ways of getting the ball after it has been shot toward the target.
Examples:

Slide them out with the pusher
Catch it before it rolls out
Run and get the ball before it bounces out
Cross and catch it before it goes out
Walk in after the balls
Hit ball *out* (with other ball)
Push ball *out*
Pick up balls
Just pick up the ball to get it back
Straight back and out

When outside of square pick up the inside and pull out
Step in and pick up the balls
Wait until the ball stops rolling before picking it up
You get the balls while we are still playing
Do not get the balls while others are playing
The ball has to stop rolling
Got to come right back

Someone picked up the wrong ball
One person get all balls
Let's all go in and get the balls
Get the ball after each shot
This time don't go after them
Push the ball out
Take turns picking balls up while others are shooting
You try to get yours
Try to shoot it out of the court now
Don't put the pusher inside to get the ball (also No. 1)
Go after each ball
Each must get his own balls

Hit the ball and bounce it back to you
Maybe you should pick it up before it goes out
Walk around to get the balls out
Can't touch my ball
Hit hard enough so the balls come back
Leave the stick behind
Take turns picking up the balls
Can pick up each others ball (also No. 4)
Grab the balls before you cross the line (also No. 1)
We'll throw the balls back
Use other mallet to knock out the ball

9. Speed of Play

Look For: Speed with which the players are to act, as opposed to how hard or fast the ball is shot, which is scored under 3.

Examples:

Work fast
Go faster, play faster

Play real fast
Keep an even pace

10. Number of Balls Used

Examples:

Throw with *one* ball (also coded 3)
Depends on number of balls
One ball for each side
Two balls at once

2 at a time
Try 2 balls
Maybe two at once
Both balls

11. Posture and Physical Position

Look For: Statements or acts which specify:

1. The subject's position in relation to *each other*, rather than to the court or the barriers, in which case it would be scored as 1.

2. Posture while playing (but ways of holding the equipment are scored as 5).

Examples:

Let's switch places
Try it sitting down
Stand straight
Too far back (if in relation to other players)
Change places, positions

When only one person in at a time, don't get a penalty
You shoot at one end and I'll shoot at the other
All shoot from the same place
Stand in a different place

Walk down so you'll be ready to pick up (also No. 8)

Shoot from down here

Keep on your side when it comes back

Switch sides . . . wrong side

Get your balls on the floor so you are ready

Can't be in the court when someone else is shooting

Stand in the same order as the light

Bend over to hit the ball
    panel colors

Cross over to the other bumper

Get as close to the board as you can get

Move over inside to correspond with color (also No. 4)

Maybe stand back until all are done

It's the way we stand when we shoot

Kneel when you shoot

Change places according to color (also scores 4)

Hold your left hand up when you shoot

12. Other

Look For: Any response which does not fit into one of the previous eleven categories, and which is not irrelevant or a duplication.

Examples:

We are supposed to be doing something different

Past the ½ way (on the court)

Must get more than one point per hit

Makes no difference how you shoot

Can shoot while balls are rolling

Blow at them

Shoot ball from where it is

Put the (target) boards together

Accuracy is most important

Shoot the ball from where it is

Maybe we should change rules with different periods

Must change at half time

Leave balls on floor

IV. SAMPLE PROTOCOL – UNSCORED

Trial No.	H	W	C
1.	In order Me first Not beyond the yellow line In order Must hit board Hit the ball out In order	Start before you	
2.	Change order Balls at once	One at a time Change places	2 balls at once

3.		Makes no difference
		  how you shoot
		
		Faster
		
		Can shoot while balls
		  are rolling	

4.		Can walk down side Play faster	Can't leave before balls stop
5.			Work separately

6.	Shoot more toward the
	  center
		Don't shoot till
		  Daddy's out
		
		Have it get in middle
		  of barrier
			Must get more than one
			point per hit

7.	You shoot out there	Let's switch places Switch 3 times	
8.			Catch it before it rolls out

IV. SAMPLE PROTOCOL—SCORED

Trial No.	H	W	C
1.	In order *R7* Me first *R7* Not beyond the yellow line *R1* In order *D* Must hit board *R6* Hit the ball out *R6* In order *D*	Start before you *R7*	
2.	Change order *R7* Balls at once *D*	One at a time *R7* Change places *R11*	2 balls at once *R10*
3.		Makes no difference how you shoot *I* Faster *R9* Can shoot while balls are rolling *R12*	
4.		Can walk down side *R1* Play faster *D*	Can't leave before balls stop *R7*
5.			Work separately *R7*
6.	Shoot more towards the center *R6*	Don't shoot till Daddy's out *R7* Have it get in middle of barrier *R6*	Must get more than one point per hit *I*
7.	You shoot out there *R1*	Let's switch places *R11* Switch 3 times *R11*	
8.			Catch it before it rolls out *R8*

SIMFAM CREATIVITY SCORING FORM
(For use with Ball and Pusher Task)

Subject **SCF** Coder **B.L.**

Subject # **62**

Category	Periods 1–4 H	W	C	Periods 5–8 H	W	C	Total H	W	C
1. Boundary maintenance	/	/		/			2	/	
2. Angle of shot									
3. Speed, strength, bounce, etc. of shot									
4. Color									
5. Equipment use or combination									
6. Target	//			/	/		3	/	
7. Playing sequence	///	//	/		/	/	3	3	2
8. Ball retrieval						/			/
9. Speed of play		/						/	
10. Number of balls used			/						/
11. Posture and physical position		/			//			3	
12. Other		/						/	
				Σ			Σ		

	Periods 1–4 H	W	C		Periods 5–8 H	W	C		Total H	W	C	
Total responses	6	6	2	14	2	4	2	8	8	10	4	22
Total categories	3	5	2	7	2	3	2	5	3	6	3	8

REFERENCES

American Psychological Association, American Educational Research Association, and National Council on Measurements Used in Education, Joint Committee. *Technical Recommendations for Psychological Tests and Diagnostic Techniques.* Washington, D.C.: American Psychological Association, 1954, 13.

Anderson, A. R. and Moore, O. K., "Autotelic Folk-Models." *Sociol. Q.,* 1960, 1, 203–216.

Bahr, Stephen J., "Simfam As a Measure of Conjugal Power." Paper presented at the meeting of the National Council on Family Relations, 1969.

Bales, R. F., *Interaction Process Analysis.* Reading, Mass.: Addison-Wesley, 1950.

Beecher, H. K., *Experimentation in Man.* Springfield, Illinois: C. C. Thomas, 1959.

Berg, I. A., "The Use of Human Subjects in Psychological Research." *Amer. Psychologist,* 1954, 9, 108–111.

Bernstein, B., "Language and Social Class." *Brit. J. Sociol.,* 1960, 2, 271–276.

Bernstein, B., "Social Class and Linguistic Development: A Theory of Social Learning," J. Floud and C. A. Anderson, Ed. *Education, Economy and Society.* New York: Free Press, 1961.

Bernstein, B., "Linguistic Codes, Hesitation Phenomena and Intelligence." *Language and Speech,* 1962, 5, 31–46.

Bernstein, B., "Social Class, Linguistic Codes and Grammatical Elements." *Language and Speech,* 1962, 5, 221–240.

Bernstein, B., "Family Role Systems, Communication and Socialization." Unpublished paper prepared for the Conference on Development of Cross-National Research on the Education of Children and Adolescents, University of Chicago, 1964.

Blood, R. O., Jr. and Takeshita, J., "Development of Cross-Cultural Equivalence of Measures of Marital Interaction for U. S. A. and Japan. *Transactions of the 5th World Congress of Sociology,* 1964, IV, 333–344.

Brunswik, E., *Systematic and Representative Design of Psychological Experiments.* Berkeley: University of California Press, 1947.

Burwen, L. S. and Campbell, D. T., "The Generality of Attitudes Toward Authority and Non-Authority Figures." *J. Abnorm. Soc. Psychol.,* 1957, 54, 24–31.

Campbell, D. T., "Factors Relevant to the Validity of Experiments in Social Settings." *Psychol. Bull.,* 1957, 54, 297–312.

Campbell, D. T. and Fiske, D. W., "Convergent and Discriminant Validation by the Multitrait-Multimethod Matrix." *Psychol. Bull.,* 1959, 56, 81–105.

Campbell, D. T. and Tyler, Bonnie B., "The Construct Validity of Work-Group Morale Measures." *J. Appl. Psychol.,* 1937, 41, 91–92.

Drechsler, R. J. and Shapiro, M. I., "A Procedure for Direct Observation of Family Interaction in a Child Guidance Clinic." *Psychiat.,* 1961, 24, 163–170.

Epstein, N. B. and Westely, W. A., "Patterns of Intrafamilial Communication." *Psychiatric Res. Reports,* 1959, 11, 1–8.

Garmezy, N., Farina, A., and Rodnick, E., "The Structured Situational Test: A

Method for Studying Family Interaction in Schizophrenia." *Amer. J. Orthopsychiat.*, 1960, 30, 445–452.

Getzels, J. W. and Jackson, P. W., "Family Environment and Cognitive Style: A Study of the Sources of Highly Intelligent and of Highly Creative Adolescents." *Amer. Sociol. Rev.*, 1961, 26, 351–359.

Goodrich, D. W. and Boomer, D. S., "Experimental Assessment of Modes of Conflict Resolution." *Fam. Process*, 1963, 2, 15–24.

Gross, E., "Social Science Techniques: A Problem of Power and Responsibility." *The Scientific Monthly*, 1956, 83, 242.

Guetzkow, H., Ed. *Simulation in Social Science*. Englewood Cliffs, New Jersey: Prentice-Hall, Inc., 1962.

Guilford, J. P., "Structure of Intellect." *Psychol. Bull.*, 1956, 53, 267–293.

Guilford, J. P., "Traits of Creativity," H. H. Anderson, Ed. *Creativity and Its Cultivation*. New York: Harper and Row, 1959, 142–61.

Guttman, L., "A New Approach to Factor Analysis: The Radex," P. Lazarfeld, Ed. *Mathematical Thinking in the Social Sciences*. New York: Free Press, 1954.

Haley, J., Family Experiments: A New Type of Experimentation." *Fam. Process*, 1962, 1, 265–293.

Hamblin, R. L., "Group Integration During a Crisis." *Human Relat.*, 1958, 11, 67–76.

Hamblin, R. L., "Leadership and Crises." *Sociometry*, 1958, 21, 322–335.

Hansen, D. A. and Hill, R., "Families Under Stress," H. T. Christensen, Ed. *Handbook of Marriage and the Family*. Skokie, Ill.: Rand-McNally, 1964, Chapter 19.

Heer, D. M., "The Measurement and Bases of Family Power: An Overview." *Marriage Fam. Liv.*, 1963, 25, 133–139.

Herbst, P. G., "Family Relationships Questionnaire," O. A. Oeser and S. B. Hammond, Ed. *Social Structure and Personality in a City*. London: Routledge and Kagan Paul, 1954.

Hill, R., Sytros, J. M., and Back, K. W., *The Family and Population Control*. Chapel Hill: University of North Carolina Press, 1959.

Homans, G. C., *The Human Group*. New York: Harcourt, Brace & World, 1950.

Hudson, B. B., Barakat, M. K., and LaForge, R., "Introduction: Problem and Methods of Cross-Cultural Research." *J. Soc. Issues*, 1959, 15, 5–19.

Int. Soc. Sci. J. "Data in Comparative Research," 1964, 16, No. 1; and "Opinion Surveys in Developing Countries," 1963, 15, No. 1.

Ivy, A. C., "The History and Ethics of Use of Human Subjects in Medical Experiments." *Science*, 1948, 108, 1–5.

Jacobson, E., Kumata, H., and Gullahorn, Jeanne E., "Introduction: Problems and Methods of Cross-Cultural Research." *Publ. Opin. Q.*, 1960, 24, 205–223.

Karlsson, G., *Adaptability and Communication in Marriage: A Swedish Prediction Study of Marital Satisfaction*. Uppsala: Almqvist and Wiksells, 1951.

Kelley, H. H. and Thibaut, J. W., "Experimental Studies of Group Problem Solving and Process," G. Lindzey, Ed. *Handbook of Social Psychology*. Reading, Mass.: Addison-Wesley, 1954, 735–785.

Kenkel, W. F., "Sex of Observer and Spousal Roles in Decision Making." *Marriage Fam. Liv.*, 1961, 23, 185–186.

Kretch, D., Crutchfield, R. S., and Ballachey, E. L., *Individual in Society*. New York: McGraw-Hill, 1962, 273–307.

Levinger, G., "Task and Social Emotional Behavior in Marriage." *Sociometry*, 1964, 27, 443–448.

McClelland, D. C., *The Achieving Society*. Princeton, N.J.: Van Nostrand, 1961.

McGuigan, F. J., "The Experimenter: A Neglected Stimulus Object. *Psychol. Bull.*, 1963, 60, 421–428.

Mead, G. H., *Mind, Self, and Society*. Chicago: University of Chicago Press, 1934.

Mead, M., "The Human Study of Human Beings." *Science*, 1961, 133, 163.

Messick, S., "Personality Measurement and the Ethics of Assessment." *Amer. Psychologist*, 1965, 20, 136–140.

Milgram, S., "Nationality and Conformity." *Scientific Amer.*, 1961, 205, 422–435.

Miller, D. R. and Swanson, G. E., *Inner Conflict and Defense*. New York: Holt, Rinehart and Winston, 1960.

Mills, T. M., "A Sleeper Variable in Small Groups Research: The Experimenter." *Pacific Sociol. Rev.*, 1962, 5, 21–28.

Mishler, E. G. and Waxler, Nancy E., "An Approach to the Experimental Study of Family Interaction and Schizophrenia." *Archives of Gen. Psychiat.*, 1966, 15, 64–74.

Mooney, R. L., "A Conceptual Model for Integrating Four Approaches to the Identification of Creative Talent," C. W. Taylor, Ed. *The Second (1957) Conference on the Identification of Creative Scientific Talent*. Salt Lake City: University of Utah Press, 1958, 170–180.

Moore, O. K. and Anderson, Scarvia B., "Modern Logic and Tasks for Experiments on Individual Problem Solving Behavior." *J. Psychol.*, 1954, 38, 151–160.

Moore, O. K. and Anderson, Scarvia B., "Search Behavior in Individual and Group Problem Solving." *Amer. Sociol. Rev.*, 1954, 19, 702–714.

Olson, David H., "The Measurement of Power Using Self-Report and Behavioral Methods," *Journal of Marriage and the Family*, 1969, 31, 545–550.

Olson, David H. and Straus, Murray A., "Direct Observation of Family Roles as a Diagnostic Tool in Marriage and Family Therapy," Paper read at the meeting of the American Psychiatr. Assoc., 1968.

Orne, M. T., "On the Social Psychology of the Psychological Experiment: With Particular Reference to Demand Characteristics and Their Implications." *Amer. Psychologist*, 1962, 17, 776–783.

O'Rourke, J. F., "Field and Laboratory: The Decision-Making Behavior of Family Groups in Two Experimental Conditions." *Sociometry*, 1965, 26, 422–435.

Parsons, T. and Bales, R. F., *Family, Socialization and Interaction Process*. New York: Free Press, 1955.

Riecken, H. W., Ed. "Narrowing the Gap Between Field Studies and Laboratory Experiments in Social Psychology," Interuniversity summer research seminar on field and laboratory studies, *Soc. Sci. Res. Council Items*, 1954, 8, 37–42.

Riesman, F., *The Culturally Deprived Child*. New York: Harper & Row, 1962, 77.

Roby, T. B. and Lanzetta, J. T., "Work Group Structure, Communication and Group Performance." *Sociometry*, 1956, 19, 105–113.

Rollins, Boyd C., "The Integration of Laboratory and Field Methods in the Study of Marital Interaction," Paper read at the meeting of the National Council on Family Relations, 1969.

Rosen, B. C. and D'Andrade, R., "The Psychosocial Origins of Achievement Motivation." *Sociometry*, 1959, 22, 185–218.

Rosenthal, R., "Experimenter Outcome-Orientation and the Results of the Psychological Experiment." *Psychol. Bull.*, 1964, 61, 405–412.

Rosenthal, R., "On the Social Psychology of the Psychological Experiment: The Experimenter's Hypothesis as Unintended Determinant of Experimental Results." *Amer. Scientist*, 1963, 51, 268–283.

Ruebhausen, O. M. and Brim, O. G., Jr., "Privacy and Behavioral Research." *Columbia Law Rev.*, 1965, 65, 1184–1211.

Schachter, S. et al, "Cross-Cultural Experiments on Threat and Rejection." *Human Relat.*, 1954, 7, 403–439.

Schulman, R. E., Shoemaker, D. J., and Moelis, I., "Laboratory Measurement of Parental Behavior." *J. Consult. Psychol.*, 1962, 26, 109–114.

Shimkin, M. D., "The Problem of Experimentation on Human Beings." *Science*, 1953, 117, 205–207.

Slater, P. E., "Parental Role Differentiation." *Amer. J. Sociol.*, 1961, 67, 296–311.

Smith, Henrietta T., "A Comparison of Interview and Observation Measures of Mother Behavior." *J. Abnorm. Soc. Psychol.*, 1958, 57, 278–282.

Stanton, H. R. and Litwak, E., "Toward the Development of a Short Form Test of Interpersonal Competence." *Amer. Sociol. Rev.*, 1955, 29, 668–674.

Straus, M. A., "Family Role Differentiation and Technological Change in Farming." *Rural Social.*, 1960, 25, 219–228.

Straus, M. A. and Cytrynbaum, S., "Support and Power Structure in Sinhalese, Tamil, and Burgher Student Families." *Int. J. Comp. Soc.*, 1962, 3, 140–153.

Straus, M. A., "Measuring Families," H. Christensen, Ed. *Handbook of Marriage and the Family*. Skokie, Ill.: Rand-McNally, 1964a, Chapter 10.

Straus, M. A., "Power and Support Structure of the Family in Relation to Socialization." *J. Marriage Fam.*, 1964b, 26, 318–326.

Straus, M. A., "Family Leadership and Integration in an Experimentally Simulated Crisis in Relation to Social Class." Unpublished paper, 1964d.

Straus, Murray A., "The Influence of Social Class and Sex of Child on Instrumental and Expressive Family Roles in a Laboratory Setting." *Sociology and Social Research*, 1967, 52 (October); 7–21.

Straus, M. A., "Communication, Creativity, and Problem Solving Ability of Middle and Working-Class Families in Three Societies." *American Journal of Sociology*, 1968, 73 (January): 417–430.

Straus, M. A., "Methodology of a Laboratory Experimental Study of Families in Three Societies," R. Hill and R. Konig, Ed. Paris: Mouton, 1970.

Straus, Murray A., "Husband-Wife Interaction in Middle and Working Class Nuclear and Joint Households in Bombay," *Studies in Honor of K. M. Kapadia*. Bombay: Univ. of Bombay, in press.

Straus, Jacqueline H. and Straus, Murray A., "Family Roles and Sex Differences in Creativity of Children in Bombay and Minneapolis." *Journal of Marriage and the Family*, 1968, 30 (February), 46–53.

Strodtbeck, F. L., "Family Interaction, Values and Achievement," D. C. McClelland et al, ed. *Talent and Society*. Princeton, N.J.: Van Nostrand, 1958, 135–194.

Strodtbeck, F. L., "Husband-Wife Interaction Over Revealed Differences." *Amer. Soc. Rev.*, 1951, 16, 468–473.

Swanson, G. E., "A Preliminary Laboratory Study of the Acting Crowd." *Amer. Soc. Rev.*, 1953, 18, 522–533.

Tallman, Irving and Miller, Gary, "Class Differences in Family Problem Solving: The Impact of Hierarchical Structure and Language Skills," Paper read at the meeting of the American Sociological Association, 1970.

Thibaut, J. W. and Kelley, H. H., *The Social Psychology of Groups*. New York: John Wiley and Sons, 1959.

Torrance, E. P., *Guiding Creative Talent*. Englewood Cliffs, N.J.: Prentice-Hall, 1962.

Vidich, A. J., "Methodological Problem in the Observation of Husband-Wife Interaction." *Marriage Fam. Liv.*, 1956, 18, 234–239.

Weblin, J., "Communication and Schizophrenic Behavior." *Fam. Process.*, 1962, 1, 5–14.

Weick, K. E., "Systematic Observational Methods," G. Lindzey and E. Aronson, Ed. *Handbook of Social Psychology*, rev. ed. Reading, Mass.: Addison-Wesley, 1967.

Wilson, R. C., Guilford, J. P., and Christensen, P. R., "The Measurement of Individual Differences in Originality." *Psychol. Bull.*, 1953, 50, 362–370.

Wolfe, D. M., "Power and Authority in the Family," D. Cartwright, Ed. *Studies in Social Power*. Ann Arbor: University of Michigan, 1959, Chapter 7, 99–117.

Yarrow, Marian R. and Raush, H. L., Ed. "Observational Methods in Research on Socialization Processes: A Report of a Conference." Sponsored by the Committee on Socialization and Social Structure of the Social Science Research Council, n.d.

Zelditch, M., Jr. and Evan, W. M., "Simulated Bureaucracies: A Methodological Analysis," H. Guetzkow, Ed. *Simulation in Social Science: Readings*. Englewood Cliffs, N.J.: Prentice-Hall, 1962, 48–60.

Zelditch, M., Jr. and Hopkins, T. K., "Laboratory Experiments with Organizations," A. Etzioni, Ed. *Complex Organizations: A Sociological Reader*. New York: Holt, Rinehart and Winston, 1961, 464–478.

Indexes

Author Index

441

Subject Index